Robert Titter
s/v Wanderer

# Atlantic Islands

*Bermuda, Azores, Madeira Group,*
*Canary Islands and Cape Verdes*

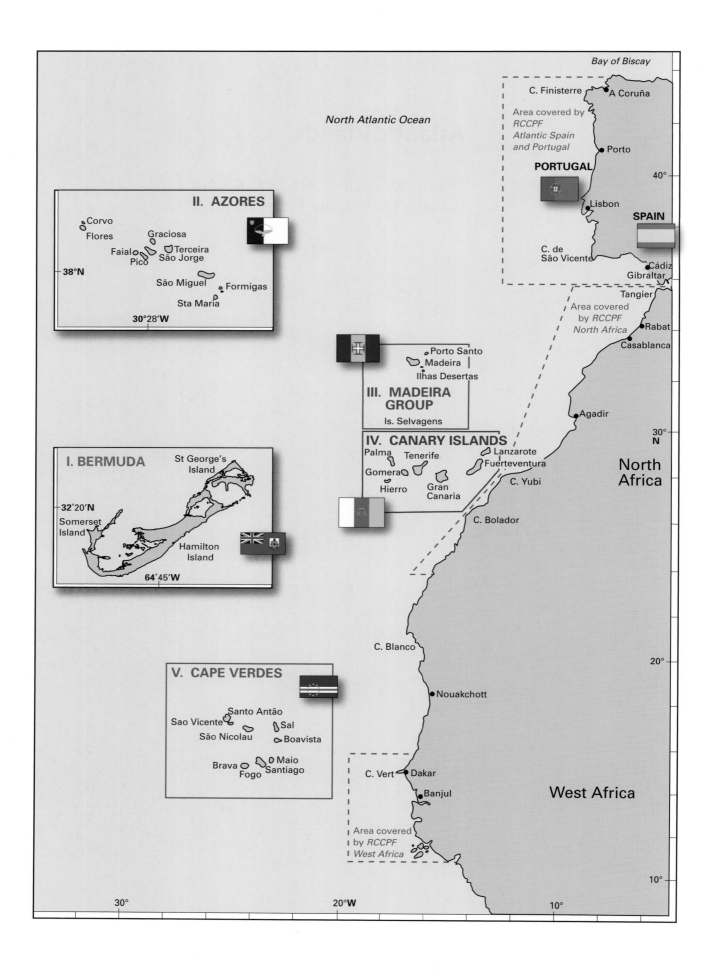

North Atlantic Ocean

Bay of Biscay

C. Finisterre • A Coruña

Area covered by
*RCCPF
Atlantic Spain
and Portugal*

• Porto

**PORTUGAL**

40°

Lisbon

**SPAIN**

C. de
São Vicente

Cádiz
Gibraltar
Tangier

Area covered
by *RCCPF
North Africa*

Rabat

Casablanca

## II. AZORES

Corvo
Flores          Graciosa
          Faial    Terceira
          Pico   São Jorge
38°N
São Miguel      Formigas
          Sta Maria
30°28′W

Agadir

30°
N

**North
Africa**

## III. MADEIRA GROUP

Porto Santo
Madeira
Ilhas Desertas

Is. Selvagens

## IV. CANARY ISLANDS

Palma      Tenerife     Lanzarote
Gomera               Fuerteventura
     Hierro    Gran
              Canaria           C. Yubi

## I. BERMUDA

St George's
Island

32°20′N

Somerset
Island

Hamilton
Island

64°45′W

C. Bolador

C. Blanco

20°

• Nouakchott

## V. CAPE VERDES

Santo Antão
Sao Vicente          Sal
     São Nicolau      Boavista

Brava      Maio
     Fogo   Santiago

C. Vert • Dakar

• Banjul

**West Africa**

Area covered
by *RCCPF
West Africa*

10°

30°                    20°W                    10°

# Atlantic Islands

*Bermuda, Azores, Madeira Group,
Canary Islands and Cape Verdes*

 RCC PILOTAGE FOUNDATION

Anne Hammick FRIN & Hilary Keatinge

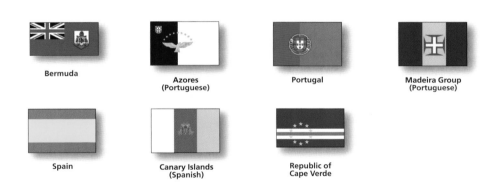

Bermuda

Azores
(Portuguese)

Portugal

Madeira Group
(Portuguese)

Spain

Canary Islands
(Spanish)

Republic of
Cape Verde

Imray Laurie Norie & Wilson

Published by
**Imray Laurie Norie & Wilson Ltd**
Wych House The Broadway St Ives Cambridgeshire PE27 5BT
England
✆ +44 (0)1480 462114 *Fax* +44 (0) 1480 496109
*Email* ilnw@imray.com
www.imray.com
2016

First edition 1989
Second edition 1994
Third edition 1999
Fourth edition 2004
Fifth edition 2011
Sixth edition 2016

© Text: RCC Pilotage Foundation 1989, 1994, 1999, 2004,
    2011, 2016
© Plans: Imray, Laurie, Norie & Wilson Ltd 1989, 1994, 1999,
    2004, 2011, 2016
© Photographs: Individually credited

ISBN 978 184623 649 5

British Library Cataloguing in Publication Data. A catalogue
record for this book is available from the British Library.

This work, based on surveys over a period of nearly 25 years, has
been corrected to March 2016 from sea and land-based visits to
the ports and harbours described, from contributions by visiting
yachtsmen and from official notices.

This product has been derived in part from material obtained
from the UK Hydrographic Office with the permission of the
UK Hydrographic Office, Her Majesty's Stationery Office,
Licence No. GB AA - 005 - Imray
© British Crown Copyright, Atlantic Islands 2016
All rights reserved.

British Library Cataloguing in Publication Data.
A catalogue record for this title is available from the British
Library.

Printed in Croatia by Zrinski

**Updates and supplements**

Any mid-season updates or annual supplements are
published as free downloads available from
www.imray.com. Printed copies are also available on
request from the publishers.

**Find out more**

For a wealth of further information, including passage
planning guides and cruising logs for this area visit the
RCC Pilotage Foundation website at www.rccpf.org.uk

**Feedback**

The RCC Pilotage Foundation is a voluntary, charitable
organisation. We welcome all feedback for updates and
new information. If you notice any errors or omissions,
please let us know at info@rccpf.org.uk

# Contents

**THE RCC PILOTAGE FOUNDATION**

The RCC Pilotage Foundation was formed as an independent charity in 1976 supported by a gift and permanent endowment made to the Royal Cruising Club by Dr Fred Ellis. The Foundation's charitable objective is "to advance the education of the public in the science and practice of navigation".

The Foundation is privileged to have been given the copyrights to books written by a number of distinguished authors and yachtsmen. These are kept as up to date as possible. New publications are also produced by the Foundation to cover a range of cruising areas. This is only made possible through the dedicated work of our authors and editors, all of whom are experienced sailors, who depend on a valuable supply of information from generous-minded yachtsmen and women from around the world.

Most of the management of the Foundation is done on a voluntary basis. In line with its charitable status, the Foundation distributes no profits. Any surpluses are used to finance new publications and to subsidise publications which cover some of the more remote areas of the world.

The Foundation works in close collaboration with three publishers – Imray Laurie Norie & Wilson, Bloomsbury (Adlard Coles Nautical) and On Board Publications. The Foundation also itself publishes guides and pilots, including web downloads, for areas where limited demand does not justify large print runs. Several books have been translated into French, Spanish, Italian and German and some books are now available in e-versions.

For further details about the RCC Pilotage Foundation and its publications visit www.rccpf.org.uk

## PUBLICATIONS OF THE RCC PILOTAGE FOUNDATION

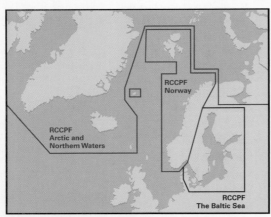

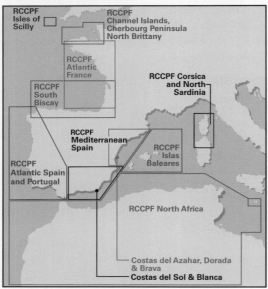

*Imray*
Arctic and Northern Waters
Norway
The Baltic Sea
Channel Islands, Cherbourg Peninsula & North Brittany
Isles of Scilly
Atlantic France
South Biscay
Atlantic Islands
Atlantic Spain & Portugal
Mediterranean Spain
   Costas del Sol and Blanca
   Costas del Azahar, Dorada & Brava
   Islas Baleares
Corsica and North Sardinia
North Africa
Chile
Black Sea

*Imray Nautical app for iPad*
Chile North
Chile South
Isles of Scilly

*Adlard Coles Nautical*
Atlantic Crossing Guide
Pacific Crossing Guide

*On Board Publications*
South Atlantic Circuit
Havens and Anchorages for the South American Coast

*The RCC Pilotage Foundation*
Supplement to Falkland Island Shores
Cruising Guide to West Africa
Argentina
Brazil

*RCCPF Website www.rccpf.org.uk*
Supplements
Support files for books
Passage Planning Guides
ePilots - from the Arctic to the Antarctic Peninsula

# Foreword

RCC Pilotage Foundation *Atlantic Islands* will reach its 30th year during this 6th edition. Unique amongst the RCCPF publications it has remained under the same authorship for all of this time. The Pilotage Foundation remains deeply indebted to Anne Hammick for creating and nurturing *Atlantic Islands* so painstakingly and for so long. Anne has kept watch over many changes in the islands through the years, frequently visiting in person and developing a broad network of contributors, most of whom are visiting yachtsmen and women but several of whom are native or adopted islanders. They have helped to ensure that *Atlantic Islands* remains the essential reference for any yacht visiting the islands and the Pilotage Foundation is grateful to all of them for the continuing updates.

The coverage of *Atlantic Islands* has evolved and grown to the point where it was becoming an overly burdensome task for just one person. The Pilotage Foundation is profoundly grateful to Hilary Keatinge who has taken on the task of bringing the Canary Islands section up to date. Hilary has also created a completely new section covering Bermuda. Low lying and coral reef strewn, Bermuda is very different to the island groups in the eastern Atlantic, but it continues to be an important staging post for many yachts heading east to the Azores, as well as being a sailing destination in its own right. We hope that its inclusion in this edition will be helpful to yachts on an Atlantic circuit or heading to Europe from North America. Like Anne, Hilary has spent time in the islands researching for this edition and building her own network of helpers. The Pilotage Foundation is grateful to them all.

Five disparate island groups within one volume, covered by two authors, make for a complicated publication. Thanks to Lucy Wilson and her team at Imray who have done a wonderful job in bringing it all together and presenting the information so clearly and attractively.

Do visit our website at www.rccpf.org.uk for a range of further information including useful links, logs and blogs. If you are cruising the islands we would love to hear from you; contact us via the feedback page on the website or email us at info@rccpf.org.uk

Jane Russell
*Editor in Chief*
*RCC Pilotage Foundation*
*March 2016*

## Acknowledgements

### Bermuda and the Canary Islands

There are many to thank for advice and friendship during my reconnaissance of these Atlantic islands. To Anne Hammick who has done such an enormous amount of work over the years to develop and keep up to date the content of the Canary chapter, and my thanks to her for her seamless handover of years of research. On the home front a big "thank you" to Gunner and Christy who read every word, to Chris Hawkesford, Michael Derrick, Colin Rowley, and to my bilingual sister Valerie. In the Canaries so many helped with my task but especially Mel Symes, Keith & Stephanie Charleton, Alex & Clive Moreham, Juan Pereira, Oliver Solonas, Richard French. Alan Spriggs, Angela & Keith Riley, Jim Grey, Ian Bevis, Juan Dominguez, Johnny Dale, Agustín Martin, Shane Gray, Richard Sanderson, Javier Vinagre of Puertos Canarios.

And for the new Bermuda chapter my thanks to Bermudian Ralph Richardson, who knows everything there is to know about the waters around Bermuda, to Grahame Rendell, Mark Soares & Sandra, Paul Doughty, Robin Judah and from my home base Nick Riley and Martin Walker. Finally, my grateful thanks to the Imray team and to our editor Jane Russell for always being at the end of the line.

Hilary Keatinge
*March 2016*

### The Azores, Madeira and the Cape Verdes

I long ago lost count of how many fellow yachtsmen have assisted me with feedback, photos, encouragement and comments during the 30 years since I started work on the first edition of *Atlantic Islands*. It must run into many hundreds if not thousands, however, and each edition would have been the poorer without them. Many have sent feedback for successive editions over the years, often for more than one island group.

Those who particularly stand out this time around for their assistance, advice and photographs are (in alphabetical order): Paul and Rachel Chandler of *Lynn Rival*, Ed and Megan Clay of *Flycatcher of Yar*, Mike and Liz Downing of *Aurora B*, Ilona Kooistra and Frans Veldman of *Omweg*, Myra ter Meulen and Margreet Parlevliet of *Menina*, Kath McNulty of *Caramor*, Sean Milligan of *Escapade of*

For centuries Punta Orchilla, El Hierro, Canary Islands formed the western limit of the known world, also serving as a prime meridian prior to 1884
*Anne Hammick*

## Key to symbols used on the plans

| | English | Portuguese | Spanish |
|---|---|---|---|
| ⚓ | harbourmaster/ port office | *diretor do porto/ capitania* | *capitán de puerto/ capitania* |
| ⊖ | customs | *alfândega* | *aduana* |
| ⛽ | fuel (diesel, petrol) | *gasoleo, gasolina* | *gasoil, gasolina* |
| ▭ | travel-lift | *e pórtico* | *grua giratoria* |
| ▶ | yacht club | *clube náutico, clube naval* | *club náutico* |
| 🚿 | showers | *duches* | *duchas* |
| *i* | information | *informações* | *información* |
| ✉ | post office | *agência do correio* | *oficina de correos* |
| ⚓ | anchorage | *fundeadouro* | *fondeadero* |
| Ⓐ | chandlery | *fornecedore de barcos* | *efectos navales* |

See Appendix IV, page 440, for further Portuguese and Spanish terms commonly used in a marine context.

*Kirkwall*, Mungo Morris and Rosie Spooner of *Morvargh*, Harald Sammer of *Taniwani* and Linda and Andy Thornton of *Coromandel*. I would also like to thank Henry Adams, Therese and Howard Beswick, Steve Burrows, David Caukill, Mike Eastman, Mike Gill, John Head, Uwe Sander, Andy Scott, Chris Smith and Sue Thatcher for the use of their photographs.

Equally essential is the help of many local people, most but not all involved with marinas or marine businesses, who greet me as an old friend when I do my rounds in the run-up to a new edition. My research would be infinitely less enjoyable and certainly less successful without their assistance.

Taking the latter first, for the Azores – in the same order as the islands appear in the text – I would particularly like to thank Tiago Pimentel, manager of Lajes das Flores Marina; Duncan Sweet of Mid Atlantic Yacht Services, Horta; José Dias, manager of Velas Marina; Thomas and Any Dargel of Boat & Sail Service, Ponta Delgada; and Anabela Costa of SailAzores Yacht Charter. José Toste and Eduardo Elias of the Azores Promotion Board also went out of their way to assist, as did Luis Filipe Cabral and Carina Franco of SATA, the *Sociedade Açôreana da Transportes Aérios*, who very kindly helped defray the cost of my extensive travels around their beautiful archipelago.

In Madeira, Cátia Carvalho Esteves was helpful as always, despite having moved on from Quinta do Lorde Marina, and it was a privilege to spend an evening learning more about the Ilhas Selvagens from Dr Frank Zino and his wife Buffy, together with Dr Manuel José Biscoito of the University of Madeira. Further south, my only reliable contact in the Cape Verde islands continues to be Kai Brossmann of Mindelo Marina and boatCV, a fount of information on all aspects of the islands way beyond Mindelo or São Vicente.

Coming closer to home, Jane Russell of the RCC Pilotage Foundation and Lucy Wilson of Imray, Laurie, Norie and Wilson have both been endlessly patient and cheerful, and it was reassuring to know that the Canaries section was safe in Hilary Keatinge's very capable hands. My final thanks must go to my sister, however, who helped me research the first edition back in 1987 and continues to offer encouragement, advice and a listening ear, and who produced some champagne to celebrate when this edition was finally finished.

Anne Hammick
*March 2016*

# Passages to and from the Islands

## Passage planning

Whilst point of departure and arrival, timing and route are often dictated by outside factors, some basic rules should be observed when planning an ocean passage; most importantly that there are places and times which do not mix well, such as the western Atlantic during the tropical hurricane season and the northern Atlantic in autumn and winter when gales come with increasing frequency.

Other considerations to be taken into account, particularly for the longer passages, are the size and type of yacht, crew strength and experience, and range under power. Neither, at least with private yachts, should the important matter of crew happiness be neglected – for instance, most could easily make the passage from Bermuda to the European mainland without calling at the Azores, but only if the skipper wishes to risk a mutiny.

Charter yachts, or others with paid crews, timetables and deadlines, clearly have other priorities.

## Wind and current circulation

Weather systems revolve around the North Atlantic in a generally clockwise direction, powered by the permanent high pressure in mid-ocean and the relatively low pressures surrounding it. Though local winds can and do run counter to this general rule – the Azores in July, for example, frequently experience winds out of the eastern quadrant – the prevailing direction becomes more dominant as one heads south, until in November westerlies seldom occur in the Canaries on more than two or three days in the month while in the Cape Verde islands they are virtually unknown. Further information on the weather conditions likely to be encountered in

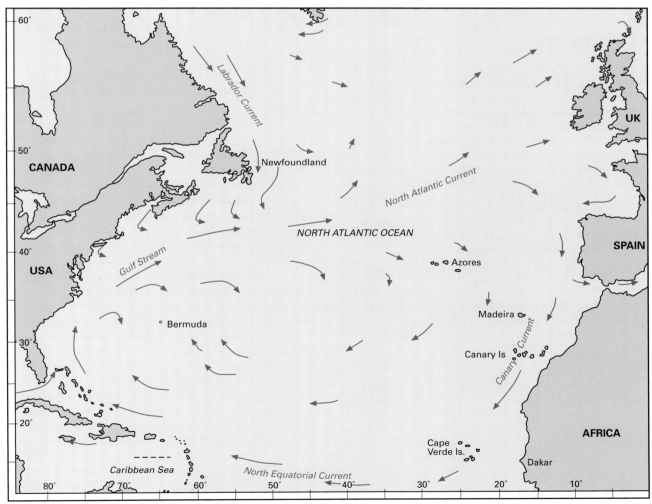

**CURRENT CIRCULATION IN THE NORTH ATLANTIC**

each of the five island groups will be found in their respective sections, on pages 16, 53, 172 and 367.

Being largely wind-driven, current circulation around the North Atlantic is also clockwise. Bermuda lies within a few hundred miles of the eastern wall of the Gulf Stream and is subject to the large and variable eddies generated off its edge. The Azores are also affected by a branch of the North Atlantic Current (Gulf Stream) setting generally southeast or south, while the Madeira archipelago, the Canaries and the Cape Verde islands lie in the path of the southwest-going Canaries Current. Around the Azores currents seldom exceed 0·5 knots, but speeds tend to increase further south to one or 1·5 knots through the Cape Verde islands. Current flow in all areas may be increased following long periods of strong winds or where the general flow is obstructed, such as between, or around the ends of, islands. Equally it may be cancelled out or even reversed by strong, sustained opposing winds, but this is only temporary.

## Passage charts

See Appendix I, page 430, for full details of large-scale charts

### British Admiralty

| Chart | Title | Scale |
| --- | --- | --- |
| 3133 | Casablanca to Islas Canarias (including Arquipelago da Madeira) | 1,250,000 |
| 3134 | Islas Canarias to Nouakchott | 1,250,000 |
| 3135 | Nouakchott to Bissau and Arquipelago de Cabo Verde | 1,250,000 |
| 4011 | North Atlantic Ocean – Northern Part | 10,000,000 |
| 4012 | North Atlantic Ocean – Southern Part | 10,000,000 |
| 4014 | North Atlantic Ocean – Eastern Part | 10,000,000 |
| 4103 | English Channel to the Strait of Gibraltar and the Arquipélago dos Açores | 3,500,000 |
| 4104 | Lisbon to Freetown | 3,500,000 |
| 4114 | Arquipélago dos Açores to Flemish Cap | 3,500,000 |
| 4115 | Arquipélago dos Açores to the Arquipélago de Cabo Verde | 3,500,000 |

### US National Geospatial-Intelligence Agency

| Chart | Title | Scale |
| --- | --- | --- |
| 121 | North Atlantic Ocean (Northern Sheet) | 5,870,000 |
| 125 | North Atlantic Ocean (Southeastern Sheet) | 5,281,950 |
| 126 | North Atlantic Ocean (Northeastern Part) | 3,619,020 |
| 103 | English Channel to the Strait of Gibraltar including the Azores | 3,500,000 |
| 104 | Lisbon to Freetown | 3,500,000 |

## Sources of further information

In addition to the vast and ever-growing resources to be found on the internet (see Appendix II, Websites, page 434-437) a great deal of useful information is given on both the British Admiralty *Routeing Chart (North Atlantic Ocean)* (*NP 5124*) for the relevant month and in the US National Geospacial-Intelligence Agency's *Atlas of Pilot Charts, North Atlantic Ocean* (*Pub 106*), the latter containing individual charts for all 12 months and measuring 52cm x 71cm (20½in x 28in). The same information, if slightly less detailed, is to be found in smaller format – 43cm x 30cm (17in x 12in) – in both James Clarke's *Atlantic Pilot Atlas*, now in its 5th edition, and the somewhat similar *Cornell's Ocean Atlas* by Jimmy and Ivan Cornell, and also on Imray-Iolaire *Chart 100, North Atlantic Ocean Passage Chart*, which concentrates mainly on the yacht-friendly months of April to July and October to December inclusive.

All the above give averages and extremes of wind strength and direction, current flow, wave and swell heights, visibility, temperature, barometric pressure, iceberg limits etc., and are based on data collected during many thousands of observations over the past 200 years. While the averages remain broadly correct, however, few would dispute that recent years have produced some major climatic anomalies with exceptional weather becoming more frequent, more extreme and often more unseasonable, and none of the above have yet had time to reflect this.

The 6th edition of RCC Pilotage Foundation' *Atlantic Crossing Guide*, and the 7th edition of Jimmy Cornell's *World Cruising Routes*, are valuable at the planning stage and go into considerably more detail about many of the possible routes than can be included here. Finally, the British Admiralty Hydrographic Department's *Ocean Passages for the World* (*NP 136*), first published in 1895, remains a classic in its 6th edition, though slanted more towards the needs of merchant shipping than towards yachts.

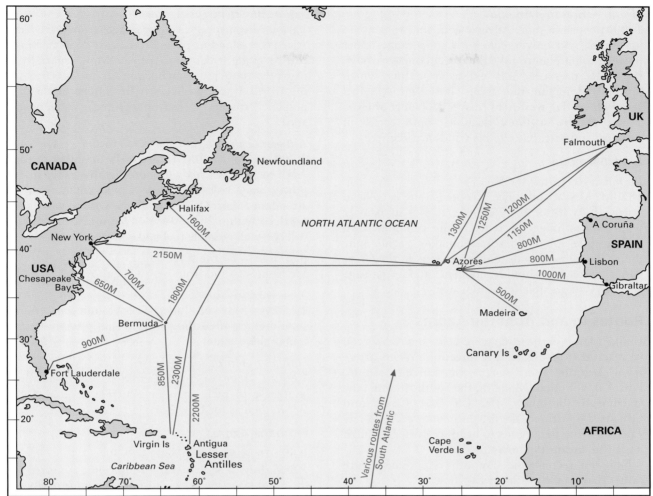

**ROUTES TO AND FROM BERMUDA AND THE AZORES**

## Routes to and from Bermuda

Yachts visiting Bermuda broadly split into two groups. Many European based yachts, on the homeward ocean passage of an Atlantic circuit, head north from the Caribbean in late April/May, call at Bermuda, and then head northeast to pick up favourable wind and current for their passage to the Azores or beyond. North American yachtsmen also find Bermuda a convenient port of call when heading to or from the Caribbean. In addition there are several regular and long-established yacht races from the American East Coast to Bermuda, most of which take place in June. Crews' major concern will be crossing the Gulf Stream, but the hurricane season is from 1 June to 30 November, with the greatest risk between mid August and mid October.

Note that recommended months refer to departure rather than to the passage as a whole.

## Possible routes with distances to nearest 50M
### *To Bermuda*

*The Lesser Antilles to Bermuda*
850M or more. April to June. Southeasterly winds should aid the early stages of the passage, later decreasing to light variables or calms. A northwest-going current of about 0·5 knots can be expected until within 100 miles of Bermuda. Plenty of fuel should be carried, some kept in reserve for the final approach.

*The USA to Bermuda*
Distance according to departure point. May or June. In May, light southwesterlies alternate with stronger north or northeasterlies, creating unpleasant seas in the Gulf Stream. By June the chance of northerlies has decreased, balanced by the possibility of an early season hurricane. The further north the departure point, the more windward work will be likely, and it may be worth diverging from the direct course in order to cross the Gulf Stream as quickly as possible, having made additional westing while still in the Labrador Current.

*Horta, Azores to Bermuda*
1800M. April to June. Adverse wind and current are inevitable, and only yachts with good range under power should plan to take the direct course through the high pressure and extensive calms which normally dominate this area. Those with less fuel should head due west to at least 50W before altering course southwest, only ducking south earlier if forecasts indicate that reliable winds are likely.

### From Bermuda

*Bermuda to Horta, Azores*
1820M. May to July. The accepted route is to head northeast to 38° or 40°N in order to pick up heavier winds and stronger currents before running down the latitude for the Azores. Smaller yachts may prefer the lighter winds and flatter seas of the Great Circle route, but should anticipate a slow passage and carry all possible fuel and water.

## Routes to and from the Azores

Unlike islands in the trade wind belts, the Azores can be reached from almost any direction. Yachts arrive from Britain and Northwest Europe, Spain, Portugal, Gibraltar, Madeira, the South Atlantic, the Caribbean, Bermuda, the US East Coast and Canada. Departure is slightly more limited, with few yachts leaving the islands to head westwards though it is by no means unknown.

Note that recommended months refer to departure rather than to the passage as a whole.

### Possible routes with distances to nearest 50M

### To the Azores

*Falmouth to Ponta Delgada or Horta*
1,150M and 1,200M respectively. May to August. Keep as near the rhumb-line as conditions permit. The current sets southeast and prevailing winds are between southwest and northwest. If faced with a limited weather window or prolonged, fresh southwesterly airstream consider sailing to southwest Ireland, possibly Crookhaven. When the wind veers the boat will be significantly up to windward, and the crew 'shaken down' and ready for the longer passage.

*Bayona or Lisbon to Ponta Delgada*
800M. May to August. A rhumb-line course, allowing for south-going current and the likelihood of northerly winds, particularly in midsummer. If sailing the reverse leg it is vital to avoid making landfall south of the intended destination, or the last part of the passage may degenerate into a tedious beat against both wind and current.

*Gibraltar to Ponta Delgada*
1,000M. May to August. Coastal or direct route to Cabo São Vicente, then as for Lisbon. Reverse leg similar.

*South Atlantic to the Azores*
Various distances. Pleasant passages from St Helena, Ascension Island or ports on the east coast of Brazil can be made leaving in April or May, especially if using the route recommended in *Ocean Passages for the World*. If followed closely this offers the shortest possible crossing of the inter-tropical convergence zone.

*Antigua or the Virgin Islands to Horta*
2,200M and 2,300M respectively (if sailed direct). April to June. Yachts with considerable range under power may risk the Great Circle route with its attendant calms. Others would be wise to work well north to within 200–300M of Bermuda, but should still carry all possible fuel and water.

*Bermuda to Horta & reverse*
See Routes to and from Bermuda, above.

*New York to Horta*
2,150M. May or June. The rhumb-line course should enjoy prevailing southwesterly winds and a favourable current.

*Halifax to Horta*
1,600M. June or July. Definitely worth heading southeast to pick up a fair current around 40°N 57°W, then as for New York.

### From the Azores

*Ponta Delgada to Madeira*
500M. July to September. A rhumb-line course, with the current setting between southeast and southwest and winds likely to be northwest to northeast – probably a very pleasant passage. The reverse leg is possible but likely to be hard on the wind throughout.

*Ponta Delgada or Horta to Falmouth*
1,250M and 1,300M respectively. May to August. Work north or north-northeast until approximately 47°N to make the best use of east-going currents and avoid Biscay. Prevailing winds are southwest through northwest. An alternative strategy is to break the passage in northwest Spain and pick one's weather for crossing the Bay.

## Routes to and from the Madeira Group

Most yachts arriving in the Madeira group do so from the northeast, having come direct from mainland Europe, and continue south or southwest towards the Canaries or directly across the Atlantic. However, the passage from the Azores to Madeira has much to recommend it and occasionally a few yachts returning northwards from the Canaries also call in.

Note that recommended months refer to departure rather than to the passage as a whole.

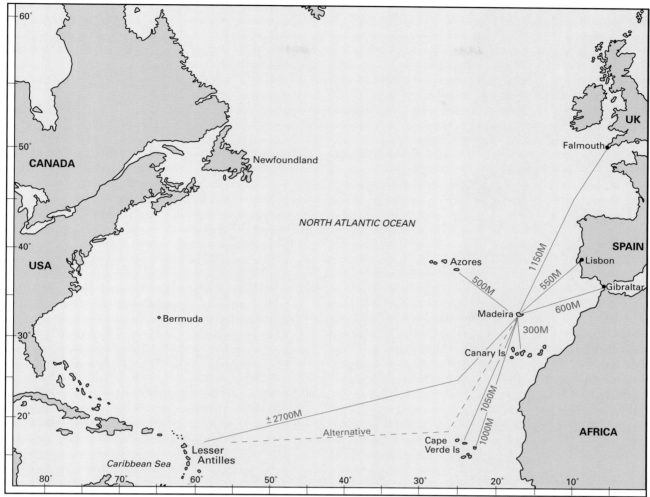

**ROUTES TO AND FROM THE MADEIRA GROUP**

## Possible routes with distances to nearest 50M

### To Madeira

*Falmouth to Madeira*
1,150M. May to August. Basically a rhumb-line course with some extra westing early on to clear Ushant and Finisterre, but not keeping so far off the Iberian coast as to lose the Portuguese trades. There is an excellent chance of favourable winds and current once past the latitude of Finisterre.

*Lisbon to Madeira*
550M. May to October. A direct course, allowing for the south-going current. Winds are generally northwest to northeast with occasional calm periods.

*Gibraltar to Madeira*
600M. May to October. A rhumb-line course, allowing generously for the south-going current once outside the Strait. It is usually possible to lay the course without problem, though westerly or northwesterly winds sometimes blow later in the year.

*Ponta Delgada to Madeira*
See Routes to and from the Azores, opposite.

*Gran Canaria to Madeira*
300M. All year. A rhumb-line course, but into the southwest-going current and prevailing northeasterlies.

*Ilha do Sal or São Vicente, Cape Verdes, to Madeira*
1,000 and 1,050M respectively. As for Gran Canaria to Madeira – only more so, being more than three times the distance.

### From Madeira

*Madeira to Gran Canaria*
300M. All year. Another direct course with favourable wind and current. The reverse leg would almost certainly be to windward.

*Madeira to Falmouth*
1,150M. May to August. The early part of the rhumb-line course would be into the current and probably the wind, though there is a good chance of this freeing in the later stages. Most will opt either to swing west via the Azores, or to close the Iberian coast south of Lisbon and coast-hop north to A Coruña prior to crossing Biscay.

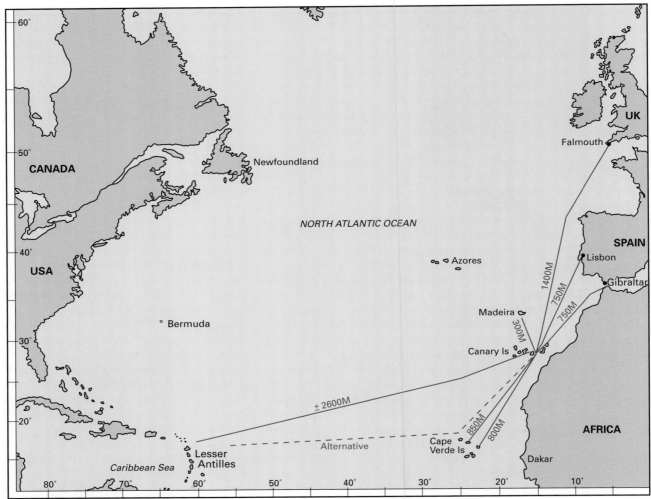

**ROUTES TO AND FROM THE CANARY ISLANDS**

*Madeira to Lisbon*

550M. May to October. A direct course, most probably to windward and allowing for the south-going current.

*Madeira to Ilha do Sal or São Vicente, Cape Verdes*

1,000 and 1,050M respectively. Most likely to be sailed in October to March or April, though feasible at almost any season. A rhumb-line course, aided by the southwest-going current and prevailing winds between north and east.

*Madeira to the Lesser Antilles*

±2,700M. November to April. It is always necessary to head well southwest before altering course for the Caribbean, but the best latitude at which to turn varies with the position of the trade wind belt. The 'classic' turning point of 25°N 25°W is often successful, but some seasons it is much too far north and yachts may have to continue down to 20° or 18°N before finding good winds. A rhumb-line should then be possible, with favourable current and following winds.

## Routes to and from the Canary Islands

Many yachts arrive in the Canaries from Madeira, others from mainland Europe or occasionally the Azores. The vast majority depart west or southwestwards across the Atlantic.

Note that recommended months refer to departure rather than to the passage as a whole.

### Possible routes with distances to nearest 50M

### *To the Canary Islands*

*Falmouth to Gran Canaria*

1,400M. May to August. Basically a rhumb-line course with some extra westing early on to clear Ushant and Finisterre, but not keeping so far off the Iberian coast as to lose the Portuguese trades. There is an excellent chance of favourable winds and current once past the latitude of northwest Spain.

*Lisbon to Gran Canaria*

750M. May to October. A direct course, allowing for the south-going current. Winds are generally northwest to northeast with occasional calm periods.

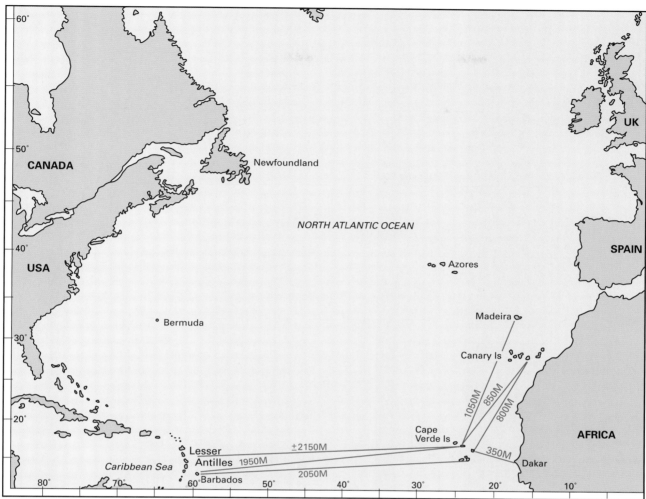

**ROUTES TO AND FROM THE CAPE VERDE ISLANDS**

*Gibraltar to Gran Canaria*
750M. May to October. A rhumb-line course, allowing generously for the south-going current once outside the Strait. It is usually possible to lay the course without problem, though westerly or northwesterly winds can blow later in the year.

*Madeira to Gran Canaria*
See Routes to and from Madeira, above.

### From the Canary Islands

*Gran Canaria to Falmouth*
1,400M. May to August. As for *Madeira to Falmouth*, page 5.

*Gran Canaria to Lisbon*
750M. May to October. As for *Madeira to Lisbon*, opposite.

*Gran Canaria to Ilha do Sal or São Vicente, Cape Verdes*
800M and 850M respectively. Most likely to be sailed in October to March or April, though feasible at almost any season. A rhumb-line course, aided by the southwest-going current and prevailing winds between north and east.

*Gran Canaria to the Lesser Antilles*
±2,600M. November to April. As for Funchal to Antigua, though in some years it will not be necessary to sail very far southwest before picking up the trade winds.

## Routes to and from the Cape Verdes

Lying squarely in the path of the northeast trades, the vast majority of yachts arriving in the archipelago do so from Madeira or the Canaries, with the occasional one from Gibraltar via West Africa. Equally, a very high proportion depart for the Caribbean or South America, though a few head south or southeast towards Africa.

Note that recommended months refer to departure rather than to the passage as a whole.

### Possible routes with distances to nearest 50M
#### To Cape Verdes
*Madeira to Ilha do Sal or São Vicente*
1,000 and 1,050M respectively. Most likely to be sailed in October to March or April, though feasible at almost any season. A rhumb-line course, aided by

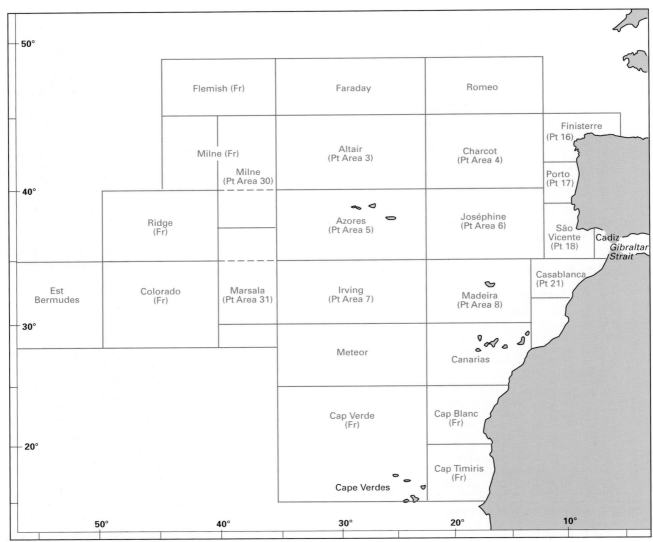

**INTERNATIONAL WEATHER FORECAST AREAS**

the southwest-going current and prevailing winds between north and east.

*Gran Canaria to Ilha do Sal or São Vicente*
See Routes to and from the Canary Islands, above.

*Dakar to Ilha do Sal*
350M. October to April. Northerly winds near the African coast may free to give northeasterlies nearer the islands, but as allowance must be made for the south-going current it would be wise to keep well to windward.

### From Cape Verdes

*Ilha do Sal to Dakar*
350M. October to April. Similar to the reciprocal, but with a good chance that the wind will free on closing the African coast.

*São Vicente or Santiago to the Lesser Antilles*
1,950 – 2,150M. November to April. Without the need to search southwards for the trade winds, a rhumb-line is generally the best course. With favourable winds and current this should be a fast and enjoyable passage.

## Weather forecasts

Extremely comprehensive details of all official weather forecasts worldwide will be found in the *Admiralty List of Radio Signals, Volumes 3(1)* and *3(2)*, the former covering Europe, Africa and Asia and the latter the rest of the world including the Americas. Thus the eastern Atlantic Islands are covered by *Volume 3(1)* and Bermuda by *Volume 3(2)*. Reprinted annually, they can be updated via the weekly *Notices to Mariners*, available online at www.ukho.gov.uk. The US equivalent is *Worldwide Marine Weather Broadcasts*, published online by the National Oceanic and Atmospheric Administration (NOAA) at www.noaa.gov. Yachts equipped with Weatherfax or HF receivers are advised to carry the relevant volume(s). It should be noted that times quoted for weather messages, navigational warnings

# Meteorology on the internet

An ever-increasing amount of weather-related information can be found on the internet. As of August 2015 the following were all up and running, though much information is duplicated over several sites.

**www.aemet.es** – website of the Instituto Nacional de Meteorología Marítima (the Spanish Met Office), in seven languages including English (click on 'Welcome' at top right), though translations of forecasts themselves may need to be done via one of the online translation programs. Surprisingly user-friendly

**www.ecmwf.int** – the European Centre for Medium-Range Weather Forecasts, featuring pressure charts 10/15 days ahead, plus dozens of useful links

**www.magicseaweed.com** – good swell forecasts

**www.mailasail.com** – MailASail data optimisation service for accessing weather and emails via satellite phone

**marine.meteofrance.com/** – the marine section of the Meteo France site. Reasonably easy to follow even for non-French speakers

**www.meteo.pt** – website of the Instituto de Meteorologia (the Portuguese Met Office), in Portuguese and English. 'Sea' and 'Marine forecast' bring up a Navtex-style synopsis and forecast in English for the selected area, with ten-day general forecasts and weather warnings also available

**www.metoffice.com** – website of the UK Met Office, with marine (and aviation) forecasts for the UK and near Atlantic waters, though not nearly as user-friendly as it used to be

**www.passageweather.com** – described as 'Weather forecasts for Sailors and Adventurers', this well-designed site features animated wind and pressure charts and tropical storm warnings amongst much else. Complete with low-bandwidth and mobile web versions

**www.predictwind.com** – a relatively high-tech site offering specialised forecasts and weather routing for everything from ocean racing to kite surfing. Only the basics are free, however, with a sliding scale of charges according to the package purchased. Worth investigating

**www.sailmail.com** – SailMail allows access to weather data and emails via HF radio and includes data compression and firewall protection

**www.sat.dundee.ac.uk** – the website of the Dundee Satellite Receiving Station at Dundee University, offering images from orbiting and geostationary satellites, plus some useful links. (Free) registration is necessary for full access

**www.weatherbase.com** – a source of weather records and monthly statistics (not forecasts) for more than 16,000 cities worldwide. Fascinating!

**www.weather.bm** – from the Bermuda Weather Service and including smallcraft warnings, long-term climate data, tropical storm warnings plus five-day general and marine forecasts

**http://weather.gmdss.org** – JCOMM Oceanography and Marine Meteorology, giving access to current Navtex weather forecasts (but not navigational warnings) worldwide

**www.weather.mailasail.com/Franks-Weather/Home** – headed 'Frank Singleton's Weather and Sailing Pages', long-established and incredibly comprehensive. Believed to be the only meteorological website constructed by a yachtsman (and retired senior forecaster with the UK Met Office) for other yachtsmen. Contains links to many useful sites plus, crucially, advice on how to get the best out of them. The explanation of GRIB files and their use is particularly recommended

**http://weather.noaa.gov/fax/otherfax.shtml** – website of the US National Weather Service, and offering a wide range of surface analysis and forecast charts, though not all of them clear to the amateur at first glance

**www.weatheronline.co.uk** – detailed six-day synoptic charts for most parts of the world leading, via maps and clicking, to forecasts (1-day to 14-day) for individual areas and islands, in 16 languages. Somewhat intrusive advertising

**www.windfinder.com** – an intuitive and user-friendly site offering 'Wind, waves and weather for kitesurfers, windsurfers, surfers and sailors'. And it does, with seven-day forecasts for thousands of locations with particular emphasis on wave height and direction, including ocean swell. Recommended

**www.windguru.cz** – originally intended mainly for windsurfers and kitesurfers, though a favourite with many cruising yachtsmen. Registration is required, initially free but with a subscription-based 'PRO' alternative

**www.winlink.org** – a similar service to Sailmail (see opposite) but via the (free) amateur radio network using airmail software (www.siriuscyber.net/ham/)

**www.wmo.ch** – website of the World Meteorological Organization, the branch of the United Nations tasked with promoting co-operation between national meteorological offices and hydrological services. No forecasts as such, but reams of interesting reading in various languages.

**www.worldclimate.com** – WorldClimate offers a fascinating archive of past weather data (no current or forecast information), though not specifically maritime

**www.wunderground.com** – Weather Underground was one of the first sites providing weather information online and still carries a vast range of marine and land-based weather information including interactive maps, local barometric readings and severe weather warnings

These three sites give straightforward on board access to basic GRIB based forecasts:
**www.grib.us**
**www.zygrib.org**
**www.pocketgrib.com**

and traffic lists are normally given in Universal Time (UT or, previously, GMT). This contrasts with harbour and marina radio schedules, which are generally governed by office hours and are therefore quoted in Local Time (LT).

Most yachtsmen now receive the bulk of their weather information from the internet. Sites vary in their coverage and presentation and are very much a matter of personal choice, but those sites listed on page 9 are among the most used.

### Swell

Atlantic swell is always a factor to consider around the shores of the islands as well as on passage. The swell is often generated by distant weather systems and may run completely contrary to local wind conditions. Monitor swell forecasts, particularly if you plan to anchor overnight, are leaving the boat for any length of time or are planning an entry into one of the harbours that is susceptible to swell. Many of the internet weather sites show predicted swell direction and height for several days in advance. In order to gain a more complete picture of what the local sea state is likely to be you will need to factor in any more local, wind generated waves as well as any current or tidal effects.

### GRIB and internet weather forecasts

GRIB files are available as free downloads from the internet and have become a very popular source of weather data worldwide. GRIB (GRidded Information in Binary) is the format used by international meteorological institutes to transfer large, computer modelled, three dimensional data sets and has become the foundation of most modern weather forecasts. GRIB files can be accessed ashore or on a limited bandwidth connection on board, either by HF radio or satellite telephone and by a variety of routes. The files can be downloaded via compression software which reduces the file sizes and minimises the time to download. It is possible to select and save settings, which helps to speed up the downloads of data for your area and altitude.

Although the graphical presentation varies considerably, many of internet weather sites are GRIB based and the forecasts are purely computer generated. However, some internet weather forecasts incorporate an interpretation of the data by meteorological specialists who take into account local factors within their predictions. It is not always easy to know which forecasts are interpreted and which are not. Computer generated predictions are useful and may include data for swell height and direction as well as information about wind speed and direction, but they may not reflect localised conditions, particularly in the vicinity of weather fronts, tropical depressions or other rapidly

changing conditions. Nor is it likely that they take account of acceleration zones or land and sea breezes. Hence it is wise to monitor a variety of weather information on a day-to-day basis, including synoptic charts if you have access to them. This enables you to build up a more complete picture of the weather patterns unfolding across the North Atlantic and will allow you to better interpret the weather information you receive.

### Navtex

Five Navtex stations currently operate within the area covered by this book, with another three stations on the European mainland also covering Atlantic waters. Much of the information is available online through either http://marine.meteofrancecom or http://weather.gmdss.org – see Meteorology on the Internet, page 9.

*Bermuda* transmits weather bulletins and navigational warnings in English (B) on 518kHz four-hourly from 0010.

*La Coruña* (Spain) transmits in English (D) on 518kHz with weather bulletins at 0830 and 2030 and navigational warnings at 0030, 0430, 1230 and 1630. Equivalent transmissions in Spanish (W) on 490kHz are broadcast four-hourly from 0340, and at 1140 and 1940.

*Monsanto* (Portugal) transmits weather bulletins and navigational warnings in English (R) on 518kHz four-hourly from 0250 and Portuguese (G) on 490kHz four-hourly from 0100.

*Ponta Delgada* (formerly Horta) transmits weather bulletins and navigational warnings in English (F) on 518kHz four-hourly from 0050, and in Portuguese (J) on 490kHz four-hourly from 0130.

*Tarifa* (Spain) transmits in English (G) on 518kHz with weather bulletins at 0900 and 2100 and navigational warnings at 0100, 0500, 1300 and 1700. Equivalent transmissions in Spanish (T) on 490kHz are broadcast at 0710 and 1910, and at 0310, 1110, 1510 and 2310.

*Porto Santo* transmits weather bulletins and navigational warnings in English (P) on 518kHz four-hourly from 0230, and in Portuguese (M) on 490kHz four-hourly from 0200.

*Las Palmas* transmits navigational warnings in English (I) on 518kHz four-hourly from 0120, with weather bulletins at 0920, 1320 and 1720. Equivalent transmissions in Spanish (A) on 490kHz are broadcast four-hourly from 0000, with weather bulletins at 0000,1200,1600

*Ribeira de Vinha* (São Vicente, Cape Verdes) transmits weather bulletins and navigational warnings in English (U) four-hourly from 0320, and in Portuguese (P) on 490kHz four-hourly from 0230. (This station is reported to be unreliable).

**SafetyNET**

The GMDSS Inmarsat EGC SafetyNET service provides weather and navigational safety information by satellite, and thus coverage extends beyond that of Navtex. Of the transceivers available Inmarsat C, capable of handling data only, is the simplest.

The eastern Atlantic islands fall within NAVAREA/METAREA II, administered by France, with weather information transmitted at 0900 and 2100 and navigational information at 0430 and 1630, while Bermuda is in NAVAREA/METAREA IV, administered by the United States, with weather information transmitted at 0430, 1030, 1630 and 2230, and navigational information at 1000 and 2200.

All messages are in English. Further information, including the downloadable *SafetyNET Users Handbook*, will be found at www.inmarsat.com.

## Horizontal chart datum and waypoints

Positions given by modern satellite navigation systems are normally expressed in terms of World Geodetic System 1984 (WGS84) Datum – in practice identical to the previously used WGS72, but sometimes differing by more than 500m from the datum of charts based on older surveys. New editions of British Admiralty charts are either based on WGS84 Datum or carry a note giving the correction necessary to comply with it, but charts published by other nations' hydrographic offices may use different datums when covering the same area.

Every effort has been made to relate the plans throughout this guide to WGS84 Datum, and all the island and harbour plans use it.

## Caution and request

Although considerably improved over the past decade, maintenance of lights and other navigational aids throughout the Atlantic Islands can still be poor and even major lights may occasionally be out of service for long periods. This is particularly true of remote areas such as the Ilhas Selvagens, where maintenance can be rendered difficult if not impossible by bad weather, and of the Cape Verde islands, where many lights simply do not work – ever.

The northern groups are for the most part accurately charted, though the rapid development of both tourist complexes and new harbours can prove confusing. The larger Cape Verdean harbours have also been surveyed relatively recently, but in other parts of the archipelago charts may be dangerously inaccurate.

In all the islands corrections may take many months to filter through the system before they appear in the weekly *Admiralty Notices to Mariners*,

and in the case of the Cape Verdes a few of the changes described in the second (1994) edition of this book have yet to be officially recognised. For all these reasons, even a brand new chart, fully corrected, should not be assumed to be fully up-to-date in all respects.

Where changes come to the notice of the author and/or publisher they will be incorporated in the ongoing supplement to this book carried on Imray's website at www.imray.com. Feedback is very welcome, and should be sent by email to info@rccpf.org.uk . Alternatively, the feedback form available on www.rccpf.org.uk may be used. Thank you.

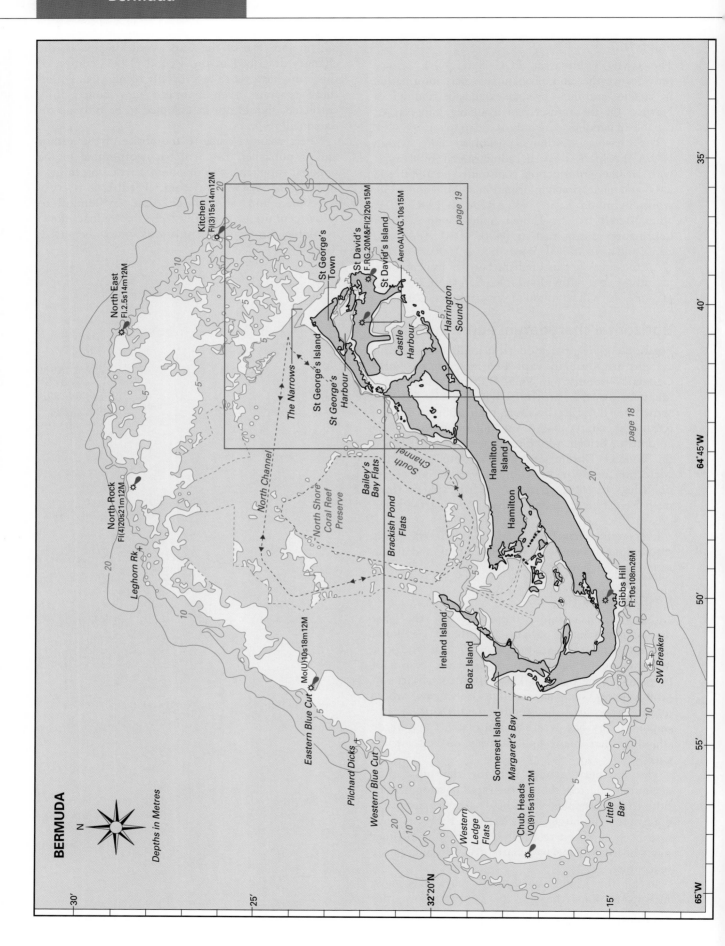

BERMUDA

N

Depths in Metres

Kitchen
Fl(3)15s14m12M

North East
Fl.2.5s14m12M

North Rock
Fl(4)20s21m12M

Leghorn Rk

St George's Town

St George's Island

St George's Harbour

The Narrows

North Channel

North Shore Coral Reef Preserve

Bailey's Bay Flats

Brackish Pond Flats

South Channel

St David's
F.RG.20M&Fl(2)20s15M

St David's Island

Aero Al.WG.10s15M

Castle Harbour

Harrington Sound

Hamilton Island

Hamilton

Gibbs Hill
Fl.10s108m26M

SW Breaker

Ireland Island

Boaz Island

Somerset Island

Margaret's Bay

Chub Heads
VQ(9)15s18m12M

Western Ledge Flats

Little Bar

Eastern Blue Cut
Mo(U)10s18m12M

Pilchard Dicks

Western Blue Cut

page 19

page 18

35'

64°45'W

50'

55'

65°W

30'

25'

32°20'N

15'

20

10

5

5

20

10

5

20

10

20

5

# 1. Bermuda

## Historic port of call

Bermuda is a regular port of call for those returning to Europe from the Caribbean, usually in May or June before the hurricane season. North American boats also call in en route to Europe in the early summer or going south to the Bahamas and to the Caribbean or beyond in the autumn. Bermuda is the destination of several races starting, among other places, in Newport, Marion and Annapolis. And the biggest race of them all, The America's Cup, will be sailed for the first time on Great Sound, in June 2017. Increasingly Bermuda plays host to international fishing tournaments. This island has more to offer than just being an in-and-out staging post; it has weather and anchorages to beguile the adventurous cruiser for a week or two or three… and with a good rib or tender the crew can really explore the *Bermudas*, or Somers Isles as they are sometimes called.

## Geology

There is not much evidence on show of Bermuda's volcanic origins, most has eroded away or is deep underwater while the highest point on the island is Town Hill at just 79m. Fringing the north and west of the island there is an extensive protective coral reef, unique in that it is so far north of the equator but sustained by the warm waters of the Gulf Stream. In the beginning there were twelve larger islands and over a hundred smaller ones. Today six are linked with bridges and causeways, about 22 miles from one end to the other, and it is just the names that give a clues to their separate origins: Ireland, Boaz, Somerset, Main, St David's and St George's.

Gibb's Hill Lighthouse is conspicuous on the southwestern corner of the islands *Hilary Keatinge*

## Courses and distances within Bermuda (approximate)

| Harbour | Distance |
| --- | --- |
| St George's to Dockyard entrance via the South Channel | 14M |
| St George's to Dockyard entrance via the North Channel | 17M |
| St George's to Hamilton Harbour via the South Channel | 17·5M |
| Dockyard to Hamilton Harbour | 3·5M |

The Heydon Trust chapel, the smallest church on the island, as built in the early 1600s *Hilary Keatinge*

## History

It was a Spanish explorer, Juan de Bermúdez, who in the early 16th century gave his name to the islands, but they did not attract settlers at that time. Maybe it was the eerie nocturnal cry of the Bermuda petrel, commonly known in Bermuda as the Cahow, still in residence on Nonsuch Island, or the tales of shipwrecks, or even the loud howls of wild hogs, for it became known as the 'Isle of Devils'. Then, in 1612, the first purpose-built British emigrant ship Sea Venture, heading for the southern states of America, was wrecked off Castle Harbour; this event would lead to the colonization of the island. Over the years, and right up to the end of the 20th century, Bermuda was a pivotal maritime station for fleets from both sides of the Atlantic and the local shipwrights were highly regarded both for their design and workmanship; the configuration of sail and stays known as the Bermuda Rig is common to the majority of yachts to this day. Perhaps less well-known, the ingenious clinker-roofs on nearly every

The clinker roofs are designed to catch every drop of rainfall *Hilary Keatinge*

house on the island, designed to save every drop of rainwater, are testament to the boat building skills of the islanders. Today Bermuda is self-governing as a British Overseas Territory, and the economy is based on its financial sector and on tourism.

## General information

### Time

AST (Atlantic Standard Time) UTC / GMT –4 hr. Daylight saving time +1 hr, early March – early November.

### Nationality and language

This small island is a great melting pot of nationalities – from the Americas north and south, the Caribbean, from Europe the English, the Irish, and many with a Portuguese background from the Azores. Most people speak English, though there are some areas where Portuguese is spoken.

### Currency

The currency is the Bermudian dollar (BMD), it is on a par with the US$ and on the island they are used interchangeably. Bermudian dollars cannot be bought or sold off the island (note: there is no foreign exchange office at the airport).

### Shopping

Hamilton has a wide selection of shops, including a very good bookshop on Queen Street. The best-tailored Bermuda shorts are to be found in The English Sports Shop on Front Street. St George's and Dockyard are mainly geared to the tourist. Food shopping and chandlery are mentioned under individual marinas.

### Medical

Bermuda has good modern medical facilities. Make sure to have adequate travel health insurance, as treatment can be expensive.

*Emergency*

If an emergency at sea contact Bermuda Radio on Ch 16. Emergency number for an ambulance by phone is 911.

King Edward VII Memorial Hospital in Paget East has an emergency department ☎ +441 298 7700. For dental problems seek advice at the hospital.

*Pharmacies*

In Somerset Village (10 minutes from Dockyard) in St George's, and two in Hamilton.

### Getting around on Bermuda

There are no hire cars on Bermuda. And although the visitor may not notice it, no household may own a second car without a special reason; the island is just too small.

*Taxis*

There are lots of taxis, around 600 on the island; the drivers are self-employed. Taxis are metered, but note there is a surcharge after midnight. A four-passenger taxi for a sightseeing tour is $50 per hour. From St George's to Hamilton with 4 passengers would be $31. The full tariff of rates is clearly set out on the website www.Bermuda-attractions.com or www.bermuda4u.com

*Scooters or mopeds*

For many visitors this is the best way to get about. There are several rental companies; the charge for a day is about $50 plus fuel. Photo ID is required. A helmet is included with the rental.

*Buses*

Bermuda's friendly pink buses cover the island from east to west. To check the schedules go to www.bermudabuses.bm. Be aware that the services are reduced at weekends. Dockyard to Hamilton takes just over an hour, St George's to Hamilton 58 minutes on average.

*Ferries*

Ferries run from Hamilton, Dockyard, St George's, Rockaway, and from Hamilton to the south shore. For schedules go to www.seaexpress.bm Reduced schedules at weekends.

*Tickets for buses and ferries*

There are Transportation Passes for 1,2,3,4 days or more, these are good if using the services several times a day. For the visitor it is likely to be better to buy a booklet of 15 tickets, or just a one trip token. These can be bought at Tourist Offices, post offices and bus/ferry terminals. Cost is $5 a single ticket, less for the multiples. Enquire at a tourist office for a booklet explaining the routes, zones and fares, or go to www.bermuda-attractions.com. If paying by cash on the bus or ferry it is necessary to have the correct fare in coins, no change is given, notes are not accepted.

## Essential reading

A must for any crew planning on visiting Bermuda is The Bermudian Tourist Board publication, available online, this sets this out very clearly all the rules and regulations for cruisers, and an enormous amount of useful information: www.gotobermuda.com

## Public holidays in Bermuda

| | |
|---|---|
| 1 January | New Year's Day |
| Friday before Easter | Good Friday |
| May (around 24) | Bermuda Day |
| June (third Monday) | National Heroes Day |
| August (Thursday closest to 1 August) | Emancipation Day |
| August (Friday closest to 1 August) | Somer's Day |
| September (first Monday) | Labour Day |
| 11 November (or nearest Monday) | Remembrance |
| 25 December | Christmas Day |
| 26 December | Boxing Day |

## Personal documentation

A valid passport is required. No visa is required for British, EU, US, Canadian, or Australian passport holders. For other nationalities check with a British embassy or www.gov.bm. Bona fide visitors are allowed to remain in Bermuda for up to 90 days. If wishing to extend make an appointment to visit, in person, the Immigration Headquarters in Hamilton, ☎ +441 295 5151. To leave a boat in Bermuda for any period of time application in writing must be made to the Collector of Customs well before the effective date. During the hurricane season permission may be given for an extended stay of boat and/or crew.

See under *Entry Procedure* below.

**I. BERMUDA**

Looking northeast from Long Bay on the north shore of Somerset island  *Hilary Keatinge*

# Sailing and navigation

### Communications

Bermuda Radio monitors all shipping round the island. They keep continuous watch on 2182 kHz and 4125 kHz, VHF Ch 16 and DCS 2187.5 kHz, VHF Ch 70 (MMSI number 0031000001) and VHF Ch 16 and 27 .

Bermuda Radio is located at Fort St George, St George's ℡ +441 297 1010 operations@rccbermuda.bm (Duty Officer 24hrs)

Note that VHF channels 10, 12 ,22, 70 are not to be used for intership traffic.

### Navigational warnings and weather information

Initial announcements are made on 2182 kHz and VHF Ch 16. Full information follows on 2582 kHz and VHF Ch 27. Broadcast four-hourly from GMT 0035, (0435, 0835, 1235, 1635, 2035)

Detailed marine forecast on www.weather.bm

Continuous local weather on:
Weather Channel VHF Ch 2 (WX02), 162.4 MHz.

### Navtex

NAVAREA IV (North), Station 'B', Call sign ZBR, Frequency 518 kHz

Four-hourly from GMT 0010 (0410, 0810, 1210, 1610, 2010), giving Notices to Mariners, weather for Western North Atlantic, South West North Atlantic, and local forecasts.

### Climate and weather

The climate is sub-tropical, the average high is 29°C/85°F and it is not likely to fall below 16°C/62°F, with high humidity from July to October. Any winter weather from the north is mitigated by the influence of the Gulf Stream. The Bermuda-Azores High Pressure, predominant in the summer, with its associated southerly winds, can make it hot and humid. There is rainfall throughout the year and the island landscape is lush and verdant.

### *Winds*

Bermuda is not in the Trade Wind Belt. Its winds are mostly influenced by the position of the Bermuda-

## Hurricanes

Bermuda lies in the Hurricane Belt and the locals will be on the alert from August through October. These tropical revolving storms form over the warm waters near the equator and in certain conditions they will intensify as they move west into the Caribbean or northwest towards the eastern seaboard of the US. The track of hurricanes can be highly unpredictable but the ones that curve northwards are those that pose the most danger for Bermuda.

The island was hit by two in quick succession in October 2014. Hurricane Joaquin passed just to the west of Bermuda in October 2015.

An owner leaving their boat in Bermuda over the hurricane season (June through to early November) should check their insurance policy for the small print concerning cover for damage caused by a 'named storm'.

Azores High. The prevailing wind is southwesterly with an average wind strength round the island of 12 knots (15-20 knots in June). However, the island is influenced by the weather systems coming off the eastern seaboard of the United States; the passage of a front can bring gale force winds.

The best source of Bermudian weather information comes from Bermuda Radio with coverage up to 25 miles offshore. Call them up on Ch 16, whether coming or going, and they will be happy to pass on their latest report.

### *Currents*

Currents in the vicinity of Bermuda are unpredictable, though a northerly set is the most common. The islands lie within a few hundred miles of the eastern wall of the Gulf Stream, which frequently sets up large eddies, and though currents seldom exceed 0·5 knots, they may reverse direction within a matter of days.

### Tidal range

The average rise and fall varies between 3–4 feet (1·25m). The largest known range at Bermuda Esso Pier in St George's is 4'6" (1.41m). Tide table is downloadable from www.weather.bm

Bermuda Radio, on the hill above St George's, overlooks all the action afloat around Bermuda  *Hilary Keatinge*

## Entry procedure

There are now two main options:

*St George's Yacht Reporting Centre*
3 Ordinance Island, St George's ① +441 297 1247

*Hamilton Yacht Reporting Centre*
Fairmont Hamilton Princess Marina, 76 Pitt's Bay Road, Pembroke, Hamilton.

Other reporting centres may be set up for special rallies and races.

Department of Immigration, Hamilton
① +441 295 5151

HM Customs Bermuda, Hamilton
① +441 295 5392

All boats must check in on St George's Island unless prior arrangements have been made to check in at the Fairmont Hamilton Princess Marina in Hamilton.

Pre-arrival check-in forms can be prepared and emailed; for a copy of the form go to: www.marops.bm

This form is short and simple to fill in.

Bermuda is now part of the SailClear service and, if registered, details of the boat will be passed on in advance, when requested, to local authorities.

When 30 miles off yachts must call up Bermuda Radio on Ch 16, from where you are likely to be asked to transfer to Ch 27, giving ETA and details of any special requirements. Bermuda Radio will ask for details of the vessel, crew and the safety equipment on board. A boat that does not make contact is likely to be called up by Bermuda Radio. Bermuda Radio centre will monitor the boat through their arrival and will give any assistance required, including details of any shipping movements on the approach. Boats should remain in

The Customs dock at Ordnance Island, St George's first port of call for most  *Hilary Keatinge*

Customs dock

radio contact with Bermuda Radio at least until they have completed arrival formalities.

Code flag 'Q' must be flown until clearance is granted. On arrival in St George's boats should immediately head for the customs quay on the north side of Ordnance Island. An officer may come to the boat or the owner should report to the office to obtain clearance from Customs, Immigration and Health. The office is open 0800–2400. An arrival tax of $35 is payable by each crew member.

If arriving out of hours, between 2400–0800, a boat may anchor off in Powder Hole (approx. 800m due south of Ordnance Island), all crew must stay on board. The boat should head in to Ordnance Wharf as soon as the office opens at 0800.

### Crew joining in Bermuda

All visitors to the island arriving by air must show a return air ticket. Arriving crew members flying in on one-way tickets will require a letter from the captain/owner of the boat they are joining. The letter must give the name and details of the boat they will be joining/departing on, plus the name, date of birth, address, passport details and nationality of each crew member. The arriving crew must present this letter to the Immigration Officer at the airport and must pay the Landing Permit fee ($35US or BMD). If the arriving crew do not have such a document they will be required to buy a return ticket and claim the refund later.

### Crew leaving from Bermuda

Responsibility for the departure of crew either by yacht or by air lies with the captain/owner of the boat concerned. Any crew member flying out from Bermuda must have *in writing*, and signed by the owner/skipper, full details of the boat and all the crew on board with arrival dates as well as the flight details and personal details (name, date of birth, nationality, passport number) of each crew member leaving by air.

### Pets

If travelling with a pet on board a special import permit is required. Check on www.animals.gov.bm

### Customs

Customs will require a list of fresh food on board, wines and spirits and any prescription drugs or medication.

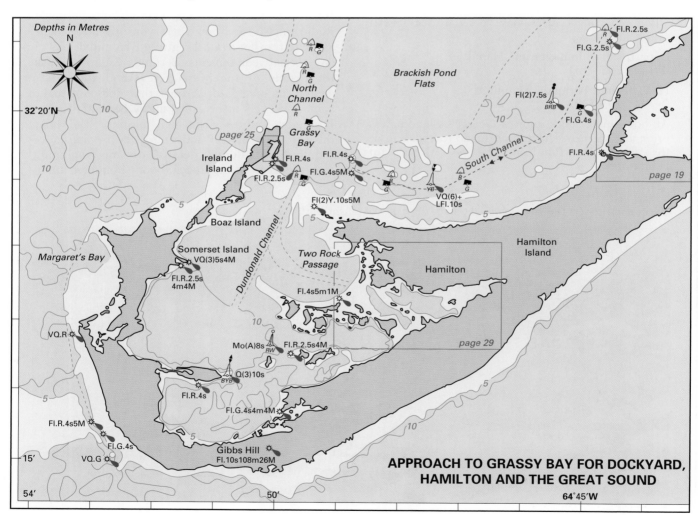

**APPROACH TO GRASSY BAY FOR DOCKYARD, HAMILTON AND THE GREAT SOUND**

### Firearms

If carrying a flare pistol, or any other firearm including a spear gun, this must be declared and it is likely it will be put in bond for the period of stay.

### Procedure on departure

On departure all boats must check out with the Customs Office on St George's Island (or at Fairmont Hamilton Princess Marina if that was where the boat was checked in) and boats should also contact Bermuda Radio, who will advise on weather conditions and traffic.

## Approach to Bermuda

### Buoyage IALA region B

(Green buoys, numbered evenly, are Port hand buoys, Red buoys are Starboard hand buoys).

If approaching from the north or the west keep ten miles off to avoid the extensive reefs that wrap around the north and west of the island. As well as SW Breaker off the southwestern corner 32°13'N 64°51'W and the NE Breakers 32°29'N 64°42'W, there are several buoys off the reefs, but it is not always easy to pick them up, so the whole area needs to be given a wide berth including the Kitchen Shoal well to the northeast at 32°26'N 64°83'·7W.

If coming from the south or southeast there are no dangers until the well marked and well lit approach channel at the extreme east of the island is identified. The first landmark is likely to be St David's Lighthouse (R and G sectors 20m plus Fl(2)20s15M) on the southeast corner of the island. It is very deep until within a mile off this end of the island. A red and white pillar buoy [Mo(A) 6s] 2·3 miles east of the island marks the entrance to the channel. The entrance channel splits into two arms: one leading through Town Cut to St George's and one leading north through The Narrows to the main channel around to Dockyard and Hamilton.

Unless you have arranged to clear in at Hamilton you should head straight to St George's. *See Entry Procedure above.*

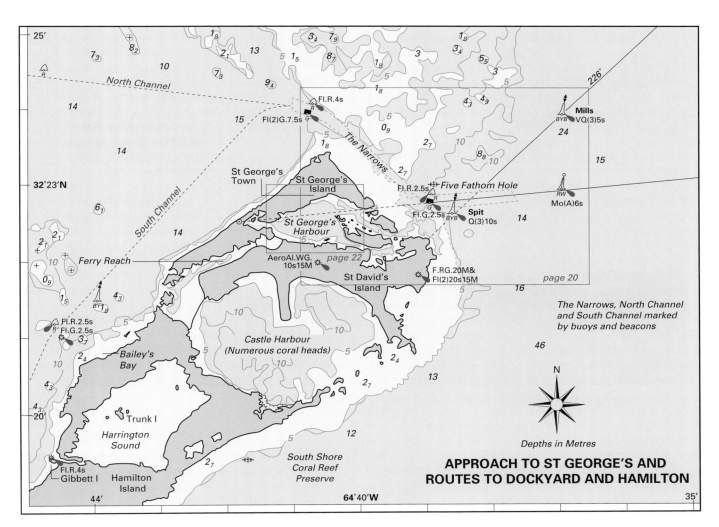

APPROACH TO ST GEORGE'S AND
ROUTES TO DOCKYARD AND HAMILTON

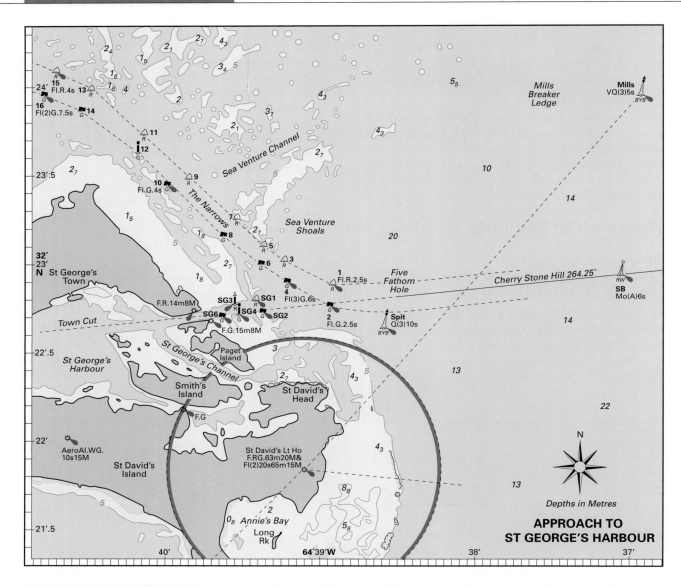

**APPROACH TO
ST GEORGE'S HARBOUR**

Depths in Metres

Looking northeast to St David's Lighthouse across Annie's Bay  *Hilary Keatinge*

# St George's

**32°22'N  64°40'W**

## The first settlement

This is where it all began for Bermuda as we know it today. St George's was founded in the early 17th century as result of the well-documented shipwreck of Admiral Sir George Somers. It was a key naval and military base right up to the last century and much of the town reflects that past, with most of the buildings constructed before 1800.

The town has had its ups and downs and the last down has to have been when in 2011 the cruise ships no longer came through the narrow channel into the harbour; they have just got too vast and the price for enlarging the Town Cut Channel to accommodate these monsters of the oceans was just too great in terms of cost and land.

Today the town is mainly a tourist day-out for the cruise ship passengers that are based at Dockyard, but it has a growing importance as a yacht and superyacht base. Once into the harbour it is relatively safe and boat crews have good transport links with the rest of the island.

## Approach

St George's harbour is approached via the Town Cut Channel which is well-buoyed and lit. Keep a good lookout for any vessels departing through the Town Cut which is narrow, but Bermuda Radio will advise on this. Take care not to confuse the Town Cut Channel into St George's with the entry to The Narrows. The Narrows leads north to the marked channel round to Dockyard and Hamilton.

Once through the Cut follow the buoyed channel (three red starboard buoys) into the harbour. Head for Ordnance Island which is to the north of the third buoy.

For a yacht there is a second possible entry, southeast of the Town Cut but it should only be attempted with local knowledge.

## Arrival procedure

Tie alongside the Customs dock on the NE corner of Ordnance Island in about 3m. Bermuda Radio will direct deeper draught boats. See Entry Procedure page 17 for important details on completing the formalities.

## Harbours and anchorages

## Bermuda Yacht Services (BYS)

32°22'·79N  64°40'·57W

### Harbour Communications

VHF Ch 14 (Emergency Services 24hrs) through contact first with Bermuda Radio Ch 16 or Ch 27
☏ +441 297 2798
0800–1600 weekdays, 0800–1200 Saturdays during peak season, 0800-1200 weekdays only, off season
9 Ordnance Island, St George's, Bermuda
PO Box GE21, St George's GE05
info@bdayacht.com
www.bdayyacht.com

The Bermuda Yacht Services (BYS) Dock Master's Office is on the southern side of Ordnance Island in what was previously the attractive terminal building for the cruise ships.

The team at BYS has a very impressive range of services on offer. The company is run by Mark Soares. Mark is a true professional, he has had years of experience on boats of all sizes and he knows the marine industry in Bermuda intimately. Shore-side he is more than ably assisted by his mother Sandra (until she retires!).

BYS is a lead provider for a number of vital services at sea so if a boat is in trouble when within range they will come out to assist in their 'Line One rescue boat'. In port they offer services as agent or guardian; they will find berths, moorings, specialist shipwrights or dockyard lift out and provide an endless source of local knowledge both ashore and afloat.

In conjunction with the Corporation of St George's, BYS can dock a superyacht or a visiting 30-footer, alongside or med-style off the docks. They also manage the berthing of yachts at St George's Dinghy & Sports Club. To date there is no marina in St George's, but there are definitely plans, and under the leadership of BYS it is hoped to build a floating 38-berth marina with all the facilities lacking at present.

### Berths

It is not essential to enquire about a berth or mooring in advance, though larger boats would be well advised to do so during the peak months: April-June, October-November. On confirmation give an approximate ETA and then call up on VHF Ch 16 or

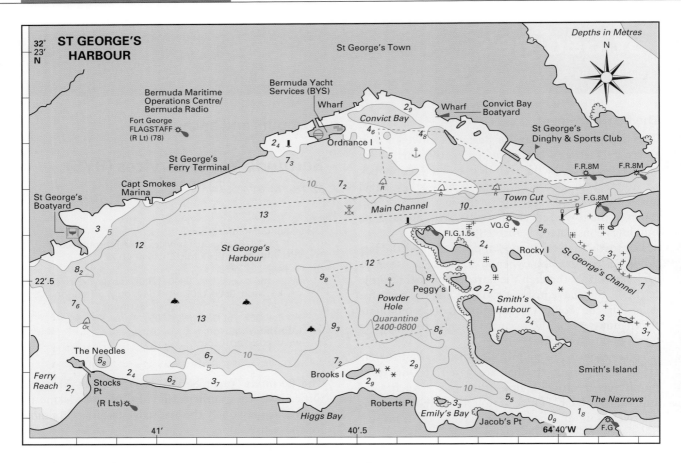

St George's Town

### ST GEORGE'S HARBOUR

Depths in Metres

Bermuda Maritime Operations Centre/ Bermuda Radio

Fort George FLAGSTAFF (R Lt) (78)

Bermuda Yacht Services (BYS)

Wharf

Convict Bay

Wharf

Convict Bay Boatyard

St George's Dinghy & Sports Club

Ordnance I

St George's Ferry Terminal

Capt Smokes Marina

St George's Boatyard

St George's Harbour

Main Channel

Town Cut

F.R.8M  F.R.8M

F.G.8M

Fl.G.1.5s

VQ.G

Rocky I

St George's Channel

Powder Hole

Peggy's I

Smith's Harbour

Quarantine 2400-0800

The Needles

Brooks I

Smith's Island

Ferry Reach

Stocks Pt

(R Lts)

Roberts Pt

Emily's Bay

Jacob's Pt

Higgs Bay

The Narrows

F.G

27 when within range. Once Customs, Immigration and Health formalities have been cleared (see above) BYS can be reached on VHF Ch 14 and staff will help with mooring or tying up alongside during working hours, 0800–1600. Boats may be berthed alongside one of the many wharfs, or stern to on the south side of Ordnance Island, but only with a reservation. It is not possible to have water or electricity connected to a boat in St George's at present. Toilets are in the office building, during office hours. For all other services ask Sandra in the Dock Master's Office.

### Charges

These are per metre, per night (2015):

$3.50 up to 24m at the town docks alongside
$7.00 over 24m at the town docks alongside
$7.00 over 24m alongside, S side of Ordnance Island
$5.75 over 24m med-style S side of Ordnance Island
Transient mooring $125.00 per week

Bermuda Yacht Services are well placed on the waterfront at St George's  *Hilary Keatinge*

Looking out from Captain Smokes' Marina   *Oatley family*

# Captain Smokes' Marina

32°22'·68N 64°40'·95W

### Harbour Communications
VHF Ch 73
☎ +441 297 1940,
0745-1700 Monday – Saturday
McCallan's Wharf, 13 Wellington Street,
St George's Town
info@csmokesmarina.com
www.smokesmarina.com

## A small marina but the oldest on the island

Run by the Oatley family since 1986, they moved to the present site in the mid 90s. It is just a five-minute walk away from St George's. Captain Smokes' has space for half a dozen boats, moored med-style off the wharf. Having given your ETA there will be someone on hand to assist with berthing. It is essential to pre-book. There is water and electricity (110 or 24 volts) from the wharf. Free WiFi, and showers with access by key. Good security with the gates locked at night. Fuel or other supplies can be delivered to the boat. For any other advice on services or supplies seek advice in the office.

## Charges

$2 per ft per night, including water and electricity.

# St George's Dinghy & Sports Club

32°22'·74N 64°40·'07W

### Harbour Communications
☎ +441 297 1612
*Club hours*  From 0600 (closing time depends on clients / season)
24 Cut Road, St George's GE03
info@stgdsc.bm

### Berth Enquiries
VHF CH 14 Bermuda Yacht Services working channel
☎ +441 297 2798
info@bdayacht.com
www.bdayacht.com

## A sports club with a view

This lively club was founded in 1946 to bring together sports enthusiasts of many disciplines; the idea was to pool resources for a clubhouse for social and sport related gatherings. Visitors do not need a letter of introduction from a home club and may use the Club facilities including 'a balcony with the best views of St George's Harbour, especially at sunset'.

## Berths

Visiting boats are generally berthed stern to the breakwater, (depth 15ft at the southern end, 4ft northern end). In the event of a strong southwesterly boats will be advised to anchor off. Berths are managed by the Bermuda Yacht Services (BYS) Dock Master and should be booked well in advance. Dock staff from BYS will be on hand when a boat arrives, between 0800 and 1400, info@bdayacht.com, and they handle paperwork and payment.

Facilities include water and electricity, for which an extra charge is made, free WiFi, showers ($3 token for 5 minutes, available from the bar), launderette (BM$ only) and barbeques.

St George's Dinghy and Sports Club  *Hilary Keatinge*

Light airs for a fleet leaving St. George's through the Town Cut *Hilary Keatinge*

## Charges

$2 per ft per night, electricity $15.00 per night (single 30amp connection), water is metered at $0.15 per gallon.

## Anchorage in St George's Harbour

Keeping well clear of the entry channel there are two recognized anchorages, Powder Hole, where yachts that arrive between 2400–0800 *must* anchor, or Convict Bay in the northeast of the harbour (see plan page 22). There is no charge for anchoring.

## Facilities in St George's

*Medical Services* Lamb Foggo Urgent Care Centre in St David's, approx 15 minutes in taxi; open 1600–2400 Monday–Friday, 1200–2400 weekends. ✆ +441 298 7700

*Banks/ATMs* Butterfield Bank, with an ATM. King's Square, open 0900–4000 Monday–Friday

*Shops/provisioning* Somers Supermart 0700–2100 Monday–Saturday, 0800–1900 Sunday, they will deliver to a boat. Discount for boat crews.
Robertson's Drug Store 0800–1730 Monday–Saturday, 1600–1800 Sundays.
Churchill's, for wines and spirits 0800–2100 daily, 27 York Street.

*Buses* Regular services to Hamilton. Schedules for buses and ferries from the Tourist Office or www.bermuda-attractions.com, or www.bermuda4u.com

*Ferry to Dockyard from Penno Wharf* Trip takes about 50 minutes, frequent services during a weekday, but check the schedules for evenings and weekends.

*Airport* 10–15 minutes by taxi

*Boatyard* St George's Boatyard with a 35-tonne travel lift. 19/25 Wellington Slip Road, St George's ✆ +441 297 0877, sgby@ibl.bm 0730–1600 Monday–Friday

*Sail Makers & Sail repairs* Ocean Sails/Doyle. This company can handle sails of any size or weight. Their loft is at 60 Water Street, St George's. ✆ +441 297 1008, info@oceansails.com

*Chandlery/Hardware* Godet & Young Hardware, 27 Wellington Street, St George's (just up from Smokes' Marina). ✆ 1-441 297 1940, gy@northrock.bm

# Dockyard, Ireland Island

**32°19′N 64°50′W**

Come the end of the 18th century the British Royal Navy was in need of a base to maintain its maritime supremacy on the western side of the Atlantic, not just to supply and repair their battleships, but to augment their fleet. To counter the threats to their supply routes by enemy privateers the British Navy

needed ever lighter and faster boats. On the islands that made up the western edge of Bermuda were highly skilled craftsmen who were developing a more efficient design for sailing boats, one that today is the base of most sail configuration, the Bermuda Rig. The Bermudian sloop became the

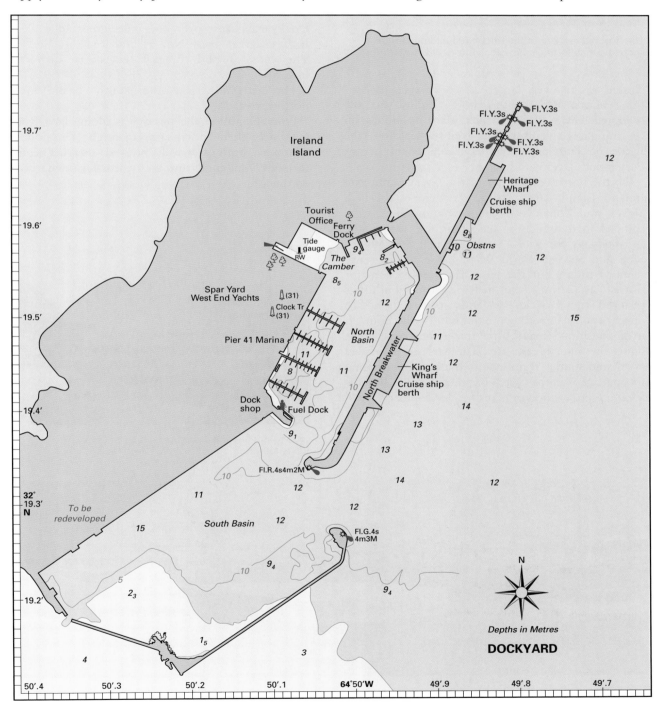

**I. BERMUDA**

The restored exterior of the Dockyard buildings, inside a shopping mall for the cruise ship visitors  *Hilary Keatinge*

chosen design, with larger vessels carrying two or three masts. Perhaps the most famous was the schooner HMS *Pickle*, which made headlines on returning to England with news of the victory of the Battle of Trafalgar (there is a replica of her at Portsmouth Dockyard UK).

On the northwest corner of the Great Sound, on Ireland Island, large dockyards were established. Slaves and convicts of many nationalities were shipped in to build the base that was key to the British Navy for over 150 years, right through the First and Second World Wars. No naval presence remains today, but the base has become a major tourist attraction, the historic stone buildings restored, the area cleverly landscaped so as not to appear too swamped by the thousands who pour off in a constant stream from the giant cruise ships lining the outer breakwater. The harbour is divided north and south. At present all the action, including the marina, is in the North Basin. The South Basin is awaiting finalization of plans for development.

## Harbours and anchorages

## Dockyard

32°19'·34N  64°50'·05W North breakwater

### Approach

The only safe approach to Dockyard from anywhere other than Hamilton is from the northeast, along the rather confusingly named South Channel which runs close along the north shore of Bermuda. The channel is well marked with a least depth of 8.1m. After the final pair of channel buoys (29 and 30) you come to Grassy Bay. The entrance to the North Basin at Dockyard is just over one mile almost due west, between green buoy No. 34 and Red (lit) No. 33. The ends of both breakwaters curve distinctly inwards.

The entrance, via the south basin faces northeastwards.

From Hamilton the passage is along Two Rock Channel then northeast through Dundonald Channel; both are well buoyed. Having come through Dundonald turn westwards for the harbour entrance.

Cruise ships line the outer breakwater at Dockyard
*Hilary Keatinge*

The entrance to Dockyard  *Hilary Keatinge*

# Pier 41 Marina

32°19'·40N 64°50'·08W

**Harbour Communications**
VHF  16 (Ch 14)
☎ +441 238 4141
*mobile* +441 705 4141 (Willie Freeman)
0800–1800 winter, 0700–1900 summer, 7 days a week
Pier 41 Marina, 22 Freeport Drive, Dockyard, Sandys
MA 01 Bermuda
dockmaster@pier41.bm
www.pier41.bm

### A friendly marina with a full range of facilities

Originally built over 100 years ago, this marina was an Atlantic staging post for vessels heading for the Americas, the Caribbean and Europe. Today it is not such a transit post as many are permanent berth holders. There are usually some vacancies for visiting yachts but it is advisable to phone or email in advance to confirm there will be a berth available. The Dock Shop by the fuel berth is the main hub of the marina.

### Approach

Pier 41 is immediately to port on entering the North Basin. Contact the Marina Manager before arrival with an ETA and then call up on Ch 16 (possibly going over to Ch 14) on final approach. It is advisable to arrive in daylight. There is no surge problem in the marina but strong winds may raise a chop. Do not attempt it if winds are blowing over 40 knots.

Someone, most likely the Marina Manager, will be on hand to help with lines. There are five pontoons with 140 berths alongside finger pontoons for boats of up to 50ft, and berthing alongside for those of up to 100ft.

### Formalities

The Marina Manager will arrange to see the paperwork. It is essential to have completed Bermudian entry and customs formalities at St George's.

### Charges

$3.50 per ft per day, including water. Electricity is metered. Discounts for a stay of over a month.

### Facilities

*Water and Electricity* On the pontoons. The water source, which also supplies the cruise ships is of good quality.
*Showers* Access with the security key.
*WiFi* Provided by TBI, payable by credit card.
*Laundrette* Access with security key. Takes 25c coins.
*Pumpout* Can be arranged with local contractor
*Security* The marina is gated, keys from the Dock Shop, no deposit, security is said to be good.
*Fuel* During office/shop hours as above. Fuel dock in front of the Dock Shop.
*Bottled Gas* Propane refills only. Bermuda Gas and Utility, Serpentine Road, Pembroke ☎ +441 295 3111. 0800-1700 weekdays.
*Medical Services* Ask at the Dock Shop.
*Banks/ATM* No banks but ATMs close by.
*Shop/provisioning* Dock Shop has daily supplies. There is a supermarket two miles away, on a regular bus route, or taxi.
*Cafés & restaurants* Many in the complex.
*Taxis* Near the cruise ship passenger exit.
*Buses* The schedule can be downloaded, or get a copy from the tourist office near the ferry terminal (See Introduction).
*Airport* A one-hour taxi ride.
*Ferry* Regular to Hamilton, also a service to St George's.
*Dive Services* Ask the Marina Manager who can arrange.

### Anchorage

In most conditions it is possible to anchor south of Lodge Point in 4-5m, reasonable holding.

### Boatyard

See West End Yachts below.

The Dock Shop is key to Pier 41 Marina   *Hilary Keatinge*

**I. BERMUDA**

# Spar Yard Marine Solutions Ltd and West End Yachts Ltd

**Harbour Communications**
☎ +441 234 2234
0800–1600
10 Smithery Land, Ireland Island
*Mail* PO Box MA251, Mangrove Bay MA BX Bermuda
office@sparyard.bm
www.sparyard.bm

### Full service boatyard in the heart of Dockyard

Spar Yard Marine Solutions Ltd and West End Yachts have pooled their resources (2015) and the present yard (address above) will be renovated and expanded in the coming years. Already with the largest travel-lift on the island it is nevertheless planned to install a much larger one capable of accommodating wider multihulls. Long term hard standing is possible; enquire in advance. Boats are stored in specially designed hurricane cradles. The yard is as protected from weather as it can be. Boats must have full insurance cover; note that some contracts do not include damage done by a 'named' storm. If you are planning on having a boat lifted out for repair, or for any other reason, you must fill out a form for Customs; this can be done when checking in to Bermuda, or the boatyard office can arrange it. Living aboard is only allowed while work is in progress. DIY is allowed but if using outside contractors prior permission is necessary; ask in the office.

## Facilities

*Travel-lift* 70-tonne, maximum beam that can be accommodated is 19ft.

*Engineers, riggers, shipwrights* All on site

*Liferaft servicing* This cannot be done on the island, liferafts have to be sent to the USA.

*Chandlery* Dealers for Volvo, Vetus, Styre, Dometic, Northern Lights, Kohler, Luger, Master Volt, Selden. The yard stocks a wide array of marine supplies should you require them.

In Hamilton the chandlery PWs has a very wide range of goods. Situated at 37 Serpentine Road. ☎ +441 295 3232 enquiries@pwmarine.bm Open 0800–1700 Monday – Saturday.

*Importing parts* Parts can be flown in from the US in a matter of days. FedEx have a limit of 8ft on the size of parcels. British Airways can take on larger consignments. It is important to note that imports are taxed at 33.5%, however consignments for a *boat in transit* are duty free but MUST be marked 'For boat in transit'.

*Sail repairs* Ocean Sails/Doyle This company can handle sails of any size or weight. Their loft is at 60 Water Street, St George's. ☎ +441 297 1008 info@oceansails.com
Dockyard Canvas, canvas repair and replacement. 23 Freeport Road, Sandys, MA 04 ☎ +441 234 2678, dccl@cwdba.bm

*Water and electricity* Available in the yard.

*Showers and washroom* On site, always open.

*Security* Main gates are closed out of hours, a pedestrian gate is left unlocked. CCTV cameras are monitored by the police station.

Dockyard slipways are in constant use  *Hilary Keatinge*

# Hamilton

32°17'N  64°46'W

## The vibrant hub

The capital city Hamilton is the centre of the island in every way, situated on the northern shore of the harbour and almost exactly halfway between Dockyard in the west and St. George's to the east - all interlinked by bus and ferry. It is a hub of international financial businesses that have changed the landscape in the last twenty years with their rising glass and chrome offices. But the colonial past is there too in the row of colourful waterside stores, and with the Cathedral behind, still conspicuous, just! There are several marinas, including two very new ones, a beautiful Yacht Club and some anchorages to explore.

## Harbours and anchorages

## Hamilton Harbour

### Approach and entry

The only approach is from the west, from the Great Sound through the buoyed Two Rock Passage. Watch out for the ferries, particularly those going WNW to Dockyard as they have right of way, as do all outbound craft in this channel. There are no hidden dangers in the marked channel and once through the channel there is mostly good depth.

Two Rock Passage, looking southeast into Hamilton Harbour  *Hilary Keatinge*

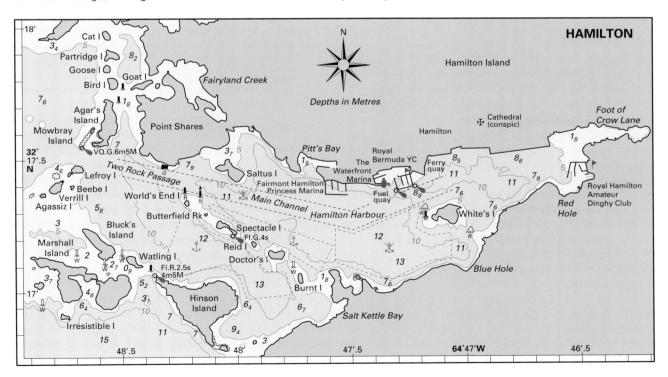

Looking across the harbour over the Fairmont Hamilton Princess Marina  *Fairmont Hotels*

In Hamilton Harbour there are two big anchorages (see plan), moorings to hire and four possible berthing options. Three marinas are adjacent to each other on the north side of the harbour; the Fairmont Hamilton to the west, The Waterside, then The Royal Bermuda Yacht Club. In the southeastern corner of the harbour is the Royal Hamilton Amateur Dinghy Club.

### Boatyard and repairs for all boats in Hamilton

Marina Offices will advise, most haul-outs can be arranged at West End, in Dockyard (see page 28)

*Bermuda Marine Services*  Tim Patton, 3 Windy Ridge Road, Warwick, PG 01 Bermuda
☎ +441 236 4059  *Mobile* +441 734 8824

### Chandleries in Hamilton

*PWs* Stock a wide range of chandlery, clothing and charts, they also have an onsite service team.
☎ +441 295 3232. Open 0800–1700 Monday–Saturday
37 Serpentine Road, Hamilton
*The Marina Locker* A wide range of electronics, fishing gear and foul weather gear. Not far from the centre of Hamilton at 15 Gorham Road.
☎ +441 295 9950, marloc@ibl.bm

# Fairmont Hamilton Princess Marina

32°17'·21N  64°47'·31W

**Harbour Communications**
VHF  Ch 16, Ch 75
*Dock Master* ☎ +441 705 7431 always contactable
**Marina Office**
☎ +441 295 3000 (this is the hotel switchboard)
0730–1700 weekdays
Princess Marina, 76 Pitts Bay Road, Hamilton HM08
*Mail* PO Box 837, Hamilton, HMCX, Bermuda
david.carey@fairmont.com
www.fairmont.com/hamilton-bermuda

### A well appointed marina

This marina, very close to the heart of Hamilton, a ten-minute walk to the centre, was opened in 2014 as part of a luxury hotel complex. The marina has all the very latest facilities, with berths for 60 boats inside, plus the possibility of berthing up to 30 more outside either lying off, med-style or alongside the 510ft breakwater. Advance booking is preferred and long-stay is possible.

### Bermuda Customs and Immigration check-in

If arranged beforehand, and permission is granted to bypass St. George's, boats may formally check-in to Bermuda at this marina. But the paperwork *must* be arranged in advance with the harbour master, David Carey.

## Approach and Berthing

Having come through Two Rock Passage the large pink hotel complex which backs the marina will be seen on the northern shore. There are no hidden dangers on approach, but entry can be difficult in a strong southeasterly. Boats must contact the marina office on VHF or by mobile before arriving. Berthing is alongside on substantial finger pontoons. Visitors in the marina may use the hotel facilities (pools, beach club) with discretion.

## Formalities

If this is the boat's port of entry to Bermuda the harbour master will advise on the timing and procedure of checking-in with Immigration and Customs who have a small office in the marina, but personnel are only in attendance when required.

## Charges (2016)

*Low season*
January 1 – June 22, August 9 – December 31, $3 per ft

*High season*
June 23 – August 8, $5 per ft.

Not including water and electricity, which are metered.

## Facilities

*Water and electricity* On all pontoons and on the breakwater.
*WiFi* Free, check with the office.
*Showers* Ask at the office for a card.
*Pump-out facility* Two in the marina. Use of holding tanks not yet compulsory, but regulations being planned.
*Security* 24/7 Personnel and CCTV round the marina.
*Fuel* For boats leaving within 24hrs duty free fuel can be arranged by the Dock Master.
*Ice* On the premises.
*Bottled gas* Propane only. Bermuda Gas and Utility, Serpentine Road, Pembroke. ☎ +441 295 3111 refills only. Open 0800–1700 weekdays.
*Medical services* Ask in the Marina Office or in the hotel.
*Banks/ATM* ATM in the hotel. Banks in the city.
*Shops/provisioning* A good supermarket less than 5 minutes from marina and they will deliver.
*Taxis* At the hotel entrance.
*Buses* In the city.
*Airport* About 40/45 minutes by taxi.
*Ferry* 10-minute walk to terminal, ferries to St George's and Dockyard.

# The Waterfront Marina

32°17'·23N 64°47'·20W (breakwater end)

**Harbour Communications**
VHF Ch 72 not 24 hr
☎ +441 295 1233
Summer (April–October) 0800–1800 Monday–Saturday, 0800–1700 Sundays and Holidays.
Winter (November–April) 0800–1700 Monday–Saturday. Closed Sundays and Holidays
Waterfront Marine Sales and Service Ltd.
90 Pitts Bay Road,
*Mail* PO Box HM840, Hamilton HM CX
dockmaster@thewaterfront.bm
www.thewaterfront.bm

## Small marina at the edge of Hamilton

The Waterfront Marina is part of a prestigious modern complex with offices and some retail, including an excellent supermarket. The marina has 50 berths, takes boats up to 60ft, with infrastructure rated to Class III hurricane conditions. Though usually full booked, there is some possibility of a visitor being able to book in for a short stay.

## Approach and entry

Come through the Two Rock Channel and the marina is at the western end of Barr's Bay, past the Hamilton Princess Marina and next door to the Royal Bermuda Yacht Club. There are no hidden dangers on approach. The fuel dock at the entrance, with the harbour office above, is a pretty two-story building with a distinctive Bermudian (clinker) roof. 8ft depth inside the marina but beware of shallower patch (6ft) at the fuel station end of the outer breakwater. There is a line of red buoys used to hold boats off the breakwater. The white buoys are mooring buoys belonging to the Yacht Club.

## Berthing

Contact the marina before arrival giving your ETA and someone will be on hand to help with lines.

## Formalities

Visit the Marina Office with the usual papers. This is not a Port of entry and entry to Bermuda formalities must have been completed on arrival on the island.

## Charges

$5 per ft per night, inside the marina, $4 if outside on the breakwater, includes water and WiFi. Electricity is metered. Longer term rates on application.

## Facilities

*Water and electricity* On all pontoons
*WiFi* Ask for code at the marina office.
*Showers* Under the marina office, always open.
*Launderette* Quick & Lickie Laundry will collect and return ☎ +441 295 6097

*Pump-out* This can be arranged by the office.
*Weather forecast* Ask in the office.
*Security* 24hrs, patrols and CCTV.
*Fuel* Attended 0800-1800 Monday–Saturday, 0800–1700 Sunday. Self-service out of hours, will accept most credit cards. The fuel station is run by PWs not the marina.
*Bottled gas* Propane refills only. Bermuda Gas and Utility, Serpentine Road, Pembroke. ☏ +441 295 3111 Open 0800-1700 weekdays.
*Medical services* Can be arranged through the Office.
*Banks/ATM* An ATM and bank in the complex.
*Shops/provisioning* Miles Market in the complex.
*Cafés, restaurants, hotels* Many, with Harry's Restaurant and Bar at the marina exit, open 1200–2200 Monday–Saturday, not open on Sundays.
*Taxis, buses & ferries* All a short walk away in Hamilton.
*Airport* A 30-minute taxi ride.

The stylish foyer of the RBYC  *Hilary Keatinge*

# Royal Bermuda Yacht Club
32°17'·22N 64°47'·18W (breakwater at SW angled point)

**Harbour Communications**
  VHF  Ch 74
  ☏ + 441 295 2214
  0900–1700
  15 Point Pleasant Road, Hamilton HNM 11
  *Mail* PO Box HM 894, Hamilton HM DX, Bermuda
  www.rbyc.bm
**Marina Manager**  Reggie Horseman
  ☏ +441 704 5290
  marina@rbyc.bm
**Assistant Secretary Overseas Guests**  Donny Heslop
  ☏ +441 294 6706
  secretary@rbyc.bm

## A club with a long history

Founded in 1844 under a calabash tree by a group of gentlemen, mostly officers in the British army, the Royal Bermuda is the third oldest club with a Royal Warrant, received in 1846. It is a club that prides itself on its contribution to sailing at all levels, from boat design and match racing to its well respected sailing academy. The Club is host to the biennial Newport Bermuda Race and other international events, and members revel in the fiercely competed Fitted Dinghy racing. The Club boat *Contest III* is pictured on page 33 with the past Commodore, Somers Kemp, at the tiller.

The marina, with 122 berths, is fully reserved for members, with a waiting list. But there are occasions when a berth may be vacant, or more likely there is space alongside, or moored off the breakwater med-style. Contact the Marina Manager in advance giving some idea of date of arrival and length of

The Royal Bermuda Yacht Club surrounded by the shiny financial sector offices  *Hilary Keatinge*

A tall visitor leaves the downtown waterfront, Hamilton  *Hilary Keatinge*

possible stay. He is not available at the Club on weekends, unless there is a regatta. However if you have pre-arranged to arrive at a weekend someone will be at the marina to assist. Be aware that Bermuda is in the hurricane zone and if leaving a boat for any time during the season it is essential to discuss the possibilities with the Marina Manager who may suggest alternative berthing, possibly on a swinging mooring. Visitors may use the very splendid Club facilities.

### Charges

Alongside one night during peak season (April 1–Nov 30) is $4 per ft alongside, and med-style $3 per ft.

Off season is $3 and $2 per ft respectively.

### Facilities

*Water and electricity* Available on the breakwater.
*WiFi* Available free, get the code from the Marina Manger.
*Showers* To the left of the main building.
*Launderette* To the left of the main building, $3 a load, Bermudian coins only (ask for change at the accounts office).
*Weather forecasts* Available on request.
*Security* 24/7. Obtain an access card (for small deposit) as gates are closed after 2000.
*Fuel* 0800–1700 from PWs, see above. Can be paid for with credit card out of hours.
*Gas bottles* Propane refills only. Bermuda Gas and Utility, Serpentine Road, Pembroke. ① +441 295 3111 0800–1700 weekdays. 15-minute walk.
*Shops/provisioning* 5-minute walk from the marina.
*Banks* Close by in the city.
*Taxis, scooter hire, buses, ferries* Close by in the city.
*Airport* A 20 minute taxi ride, approximately $30.

An extreme version of the Bermuda rig is sailed very competitively in Bermuda today (the Fitted Dinghy)  *Tom Clarke*

# Royal Hamilton Amateur Dinghy Club

32°17'·25N  64°46'·33W

**Harbour Communications**
VHF  Ch 73 (not always monitored)
☎ +441 236 2250,
0900–1700 weekdays
*Dock Master* dockmaster@rhadc.bm
RHADC, 25 Pomander Road, Hamilton, PG05
secretary@rhadc.bm

### An active club with a wide range of facilities

The Club has been in existence since 1882 and today it has a busy racing schedule for dinghies and keelboats, and sailing courses for all ages. The Club is also co-sponsor of the biennial Marion Cruising Yacht Race, first run in 1977 when navigation was celestial; if using a sextant in the race today a boat is given a time bonus. The Club lies at the east end of Hamilton Harbour and has 100 berths. If space allows, visitors are welcome, pre-booking is essential, contact the Club Secretary.

### Approach and entrance

From the eastern end of the Two Rock Passage, the Club is about 2M east across Hamilton Harbour. There is good depth up to the marina entrance. Visitors are normally berthed on the breakwater that runs north-south with a minimum depth of 2.4m. The breakwater is not lit. Call ahead of time with ETA. Do not enter the marina unless advised to do so by the Dock Master who will be on hand to help with lines.

### Berthing

Charge for berthing, including water and WiFi and the use of the Club's facilities, is $4.00 per metre, per day. A deposit of $250.00 is required at the time of reservation.

### Facilities

*Water* Available from pedestals, 25 feet hoses are supplied. Additional hoses can be arranged by contacting the Dockmaster. No charge.
*Electricity* 110v/220v Available. $25 per day. Have long shore power leads of 50ft – 100ft, and split-tails if possible.
*WiFi* Ask for code at the office. No charge.
*Showers* Ask for code at the office.
*Launderette*  Approximately 1·5 miles away.
*Pump-out facility*  None
*Weather forecast* Available from the office.
*Security* The area is fenced, with a swipe card used for access. CCTV around the premises.
*Fuel* Fuel dock at PW's at the Waterfront Marina
*Bottled gas* Propane refills only. Bermuda Gas and Utility, Serpentine Road, Pembroke. ☎ +441 295 3111 Open 0800–1700 weekdays.

*Medical services* Hospital is approximately 5 minutes away.
*Banks/ATM* about 1 mile away.
*Shops/provisioning* 15 minutes walk into Hamilton.
*Taxis* Need to order.
*Buses* Bus stop on the High Road.
*Airport* 20 minutes by taxi.
*Ferry* In Hamilton.

# Mills Creek Marine Ltd

32°18'·02N  64°48'·06W

**Harbour Communications**
☎ + 441 292 6094
0900–1700, weekdays only
17 Mills Creek Road, Pembroke HM 05
millscreek@ibl.bm
www.millscreekmarine.bm

### Approach from Great Sound

A small boatyard northwest of Hamilton. The yard has a 30-tonne capacity travel lift. They will lift boats of up to 50ft. There are no berthing facilities other than prior to liftout. The minimum depth in the slipway is 3m and approach to the boatyard is through crowded moorings. No capacity for long term storage but the yard can undertake a wide range of repairs and maintenance tasks. DIY is allowed and there are the usual facilities. The yard is not gated and security is the responsibility of the boat owner.

It is a 20-minute walk into Hamilton, a 45-minute taxi drive to the airport.

# Anchorages around Bermuda

**Positions given are purely for identification purposes and NOT for navigation**

Special thanks go to the local yachtsmen who advised on these anchorages: Ralph Richardson, Paul Doughty and Grahame Rendell.

## ⚓ 1 Granaway Deep
32°16'41N  64°48'35W

Fringed with islands that divide it from Hamilton Harbour, there is a passage through at Timlin's Narrows, marked by a lighthouse (32°17'·03N 64°48'·22W) and a beacon, or from Great Sound.

There are several possibilities in this area including:

## ⚓ 2 Paradise Lake
32°17'05N 64°49'59W

An attractive bay, which is surrounded by islands Hawkins, Long, Nelly, with Beta Island, Gamma and Delta to the south. Anchor in 6m good holding. Considered a Hurricane Hole. There are a lot of private mooring buoys. Note of caution: Do not enter in poor visibility at night or in strong southerlies.

I. BERMUDA

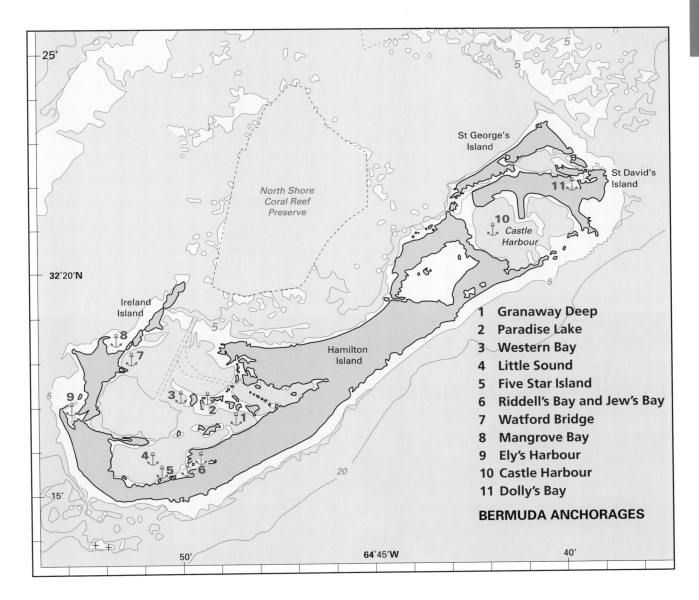

1  Granaway Deep
2  Paradise Lake
3  Western Bay
4  Little Sound
5  Five Star Island
6  Riddell's Bay and Jew's Bay
7  Watford Bridge
8  Mangrove Bay
9  Ely's Harbour
10 Castle Harbour
11 Dolly's Bay

**BERMUDA ANCHORAGES**

Looking northwest across Jews Bay with Riddell's Bay far right  *Hilary Keatinge*

## ⚓ 3 Western Bay
32°17'·09N  64°49'·54W

Off Hawkins Island, Great Sound. Good in a strong easterly.

## ⚓ 4 Little Sound
32°15'·49N  64°50'·47N

Good shelter except in easterlies. Best anchorages will be found on the south side of the bay. Use of a trip line is advised; this was a US Navy anchorage and there are remnants of heavy ground chain. The bay is surrounded by private properties and moorings.

## ⚓ 5 Five Star Island
32°15'·21N  64°50'·37W

There is more depth round to the west, in many conditions a calm anchoring spot.

## ⚓ 6 Riddell's Bay and Jew's Bay
32°15'·41N  64°49'·54W

On the east side of Little Sound are worth exploring in a dinghy as they are shallow.

## ⚓ 7 Watford Bridge
32°18'17N  64°51'·29W

On the eastern side of the causeway linking Somerset and Current Island, and to the south, anchor in 6–8ft, sand and clay, but turtle grass. Holding reasonable. Good protection in winds from SSW to NW. It is on a ferry route.

## ⚓ 8 Mangrove Bay
32°18'28N  64°51'·55W

Leaving Dockyard head north, do not cut the corner, to pick up the small boat passage marked by posts southwards to Mangrove Bay. This is off the

Making entry into Ely's Harbour through the shallow draught entrance  *Hilary Keatinge*

Eyeball navigation off the west coast of Bermuda *Hilary Keatinge*

northeastern side of Somerset Island. It is an attractive bay, close to Cambridge Beaches. There is excellent snorkelling in this area. It would be worth seeking local knowledge on the best sites.

## ⚓ 9 Ely's Harbour
32°17'·01N  64°52'·48W

Off the other end of Somerset Island is Ely's Harbour, one of the most beautiful anchorages in Bermuda. Deep draught boats should wait for High Water. Keep close to the buoyed channel and no not be tempted to enter via the NW gap. It is buoyed to clear the off shore reefs, turn in at the R/G buoy. There are lots of private moorings, but usually room to anchor in 6–15ft, sand and mud, good holding.

## ⚓ 10 Castle Harbour

South of St George's is Castle Harbour. The entrance is west of Gurnet Rock (32°20'·18N 64°39'·46W) and east of Castle Island. A good chart and eyeball navigation will be required but apart from the end of the runway that juts into the harbour, it is very beautiful. A tour of the Nature Reserve on Nonsuch Island can be arranged with a prior booking: ☎ +441 293 2727.

## ⚓ 11 Dolly's Bay
32°21'·99N  64°39'·89W

Off St George's Harbour, with a shallow draft boat Dolly's Bay is said to be a sheltered spot. Seek local knowledge before attempting.

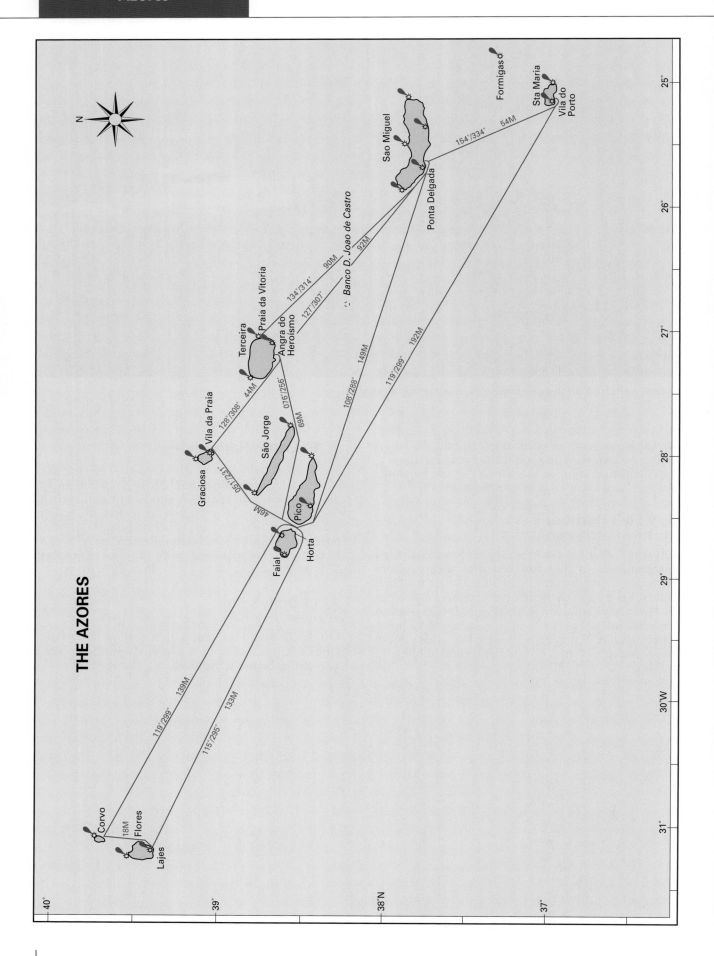

THE AZORES

# II. The Azores

## The archipelago

The nine islands which form the Azores archipelago seem to have a uniqueness and appeal out of all proportion to their size – tiny, irregular pieces of land only 2,335km² in total, scattered over some 58,000km² of ocean and hardly more than dots on the North Atlantic chart. Perhaps this explains why many yachtsmen pass through the islands with only a brief stop at Horta for sleep, water and fresh food. Others may assume that there is only the one safe harbour in the archipelago, or that the islands must be so similar that there is little point in visiting more than one. Both those ideas could hardly be further from the truth. The islands form a varied, unspoilt and relatively uncrowded cruising ground waiting for any yacht – and crew – capable of the ocean passage.

The Azores lie about 750M west of mainland Portugal, somewhat to the east of the Mid-Atlantic Ridge and along the margins of the Eurasian and African Plates. Over millions of years these weaknesses in the earth's crust have allowed molten lava to seep through to the surface and form volcanoes, whilst at the same time new rock forming along the Mid-Atlantic Ridge pushed the older rock outwards – a process which is still continuing and causing the Atlantic Ocean floor to widen by 0·5cm each year. This accounts for the fact that the oldest lava in the Azores is a mere four million years old, whilst that in the Cape Verde islands, much nearer the African coast, is as much as 120 million years old. As the volcanoes grew, with later eruptions having to work upwards through ever greater thicknesses of older lava, the volcanic activity grew fiercer and more explosive, in many cases eventually disintegrating the entire cone to form a vast crater or *caldeira*. Only the massive Pico still retains most of its original height in one classic cone, but though apparently dormant it is now ringed with monitoring devices ready to detect the least hint of a build-up of pressure within.

Elsewhere in the Azores one finds vast lava fields – several formed within recorded history – sulphur caves, lava tunnels, boiling geysers and hot or cold mineral springs. Sterile pumice and ash still cover the western end of Faial, where a major eruption occurred off the Capelinhos peninsula in 1957, and all the islands have areas of dark, basaltic lava,

## Courses and distances within the Azores

| Harbour | Course / Reciprocal | Distance |
|---|---|---|
| Lajes, Flores – Vila Nova, Corvo | 002° / 182° & by eye | 18M |
| Lajes, Flores – Horta, Faial | 115° / 295° | 133M |
| Vila Nova, Corvo – Horta, Faial | 119° / 299° | 139M |
| Horta, Faial – Madalena, Pico | 089° / 269° | 4·5M |
| Horta, Faial – Velas, São Jorge | 067° / 247° | 22M |
| Horta, Faial – Vila da Praia, Graciosa | 051° / 231° | 46M |
| Horta, Faial – Angra do Heroísmo, Terceira | 076° / 256° & by eye | 69M |
| Horta, Faial – Praia da Vitória, Terceira | 080° / 260° & by eye | 80M |
| Horta, Faial – Ponta Delgada, São Miguel | 108° / 288° | 149M |
| Horta, Faial – Vila do Porto, Santa Maria | 119° / 299° | 192M |
| Vila da Praia, Graciosa – Angra do Heroísmo, Terceira | 128° / 308° | 44M |
| Vila da Praia, Graciosa – Praia da Vitória, Terceira | 112° / 292° | 48M |
| Angra do Heroísmo, Terceira – Ponta Delgada, São Miguel | 127° / 307° | 92M |
| Praia da Vitória, Terceira – Ponta Delgada, São Miguel | 134° / 314° | 90M |
| Ponta Delgada, São Miguel – Vila do Porto, Santa Maria | 154° / 334° | 54M |

Organpipe rocks, Flores, witness to volcanic activity long ago  *Anne Hammick*

though few are as spectacular as the imposing 'Organpipe Rocks' in Flores. With the high sea-cliffs laying much of the volcanic structure open to view, as well as the opportunity to study small-scale volcanic activity at first hand, it is hardly surprising that the islands have long been considered a geologists' paradise.

Volcanic soils become very rich and fertile after a period of weathering, particularly in warm, moist climates, allowing the Azores a vegetation which combines the best of temperate and tropical. Some areas of the original thick forest still survive, mostly as protected national parks, but the native plants such as myrtle, juniper, heather, holly and yew are now heavily outnumbered by naturalised newcomers including conifers, laurel, cedar, chestnut and eucalyptus. Bamboo and ferns thrive in the undergrowth and two unique species of orchid have evolved, found nowhere else in the world. The excellent *Açores Flores* (*Azores Flowers*) by Erik Sjögren details nearly 100 native and introduced plants and flowers and where they may be found, in four languages. Though currently out-of-print, used copies are sometimes available online in the UK, and it may sometimes be found in tourist offices and bookshops in the islands – if a copy is encountered it should be snapped up without hesitation.

The fauna side was originally less varied, with only seabirds, a few land birds and, surprisingly enough, bats – *Nyctalus azoreum*, which is unusual in that it flies in daylight. Quite small at around 10–12cm and dark brown in colour, it exists in all the islands with a total population estimated at between 2,000 and 5,000. All the land mammals were brought by man, doubtless some unintentionally, whilst several of the introduced birds have gradually evolved into distinct subspecies over the centuries. *Birds of the Atlantic Islands* by Tony Clarke (Helm Field Guides) is a useful handbook.

The iconic cone of Pico, seen from Faial  *Anne Hammick*

A sperm whale decorates a weathervane in Folga, Graciosa
*Anne Hammick*

The Azorean economy has changed little over the last 500 years. There is almost no industry – agriculture is still the mainstay, the most important crops being grains, fruit and vines. Stock-raising of cattle, sheep and pigs is important on all the islands, with butter and cheese exported in quantity. Fishing, particularly of tuna for canning or freezing, is a fairly recent industry, though fishing for food must always have taken place. Big game fishing is an even more recent innovation and several world records for tuna, swordfish, ocean bonito and shark are held from Horta and Ponta Delgada.

The whaling industry, once the islands' second money-earner, is now a part of history and facilities to process the carcasses no longer exist. Whales have not entirely disappeared from the economy, however, with whale and dolphin-watching enterprises based in several of the islands. Having spent many years quietly rotting away on old slipways, a good number of the elegant double-ended whaleboats have been carefully restored for use in inter-island regattas, while new ones are once again being built. Santa Cruz das Ribeiras, west of Lajes do Pico, is particularly famous in this regard.

Tourism as a source of employment and income is on the increase in all the islands, particularly São Miguel, Terceira and Faial. A fair proportion of those visiting turn out to be Azorean expatriates and their children who, having emigrated during the 19th and 20th centuries, are now returning in increasing numbers to meet relatives and re-establish family roots. Most of the restaurants appear to cater largely for local people, with prices to match, other than in Terceira where personnel from the American air base provide a reliable source of custom. The lease on the base is also reputed to bring in sizeable funds, most of which stay in the islands.

The Azores remain amongst the decreasing number of places in the world where as many foreign visitors arrive by yacht as by air. A single yacht passing through Horta in 1930 had increased to 59 in 1970, around 200 in 1978, over 800 in 1988, and 1,200 or so by 2015. In the nearly 30 years since Horta Marina welcomed its first yacht, it is thought that some 32,000 boats and around 120,000 yachtsmen and women have passed through the harbour. Even so, relatively few cruise the islands in detail and it would be rare to talk to a skipper who had visited all nine islands, or even the eight larger ones, in a single season. It is worth making the effort – despite ever-increasing numbers of yachts the friendliness of the islanders towards their crews remains unchanged, not only in Horta but throughout the Azores as a whole. Unless bound by a very tight schedule it is well worth taking the time to experience a cruising area with a fine climate, delightful people, stunning scenery, welcoming marinas and surprisingly empty anchorages.

**III. THE AZORES**

A Santa Maria windmill – each island has its own characteristic style
*Anne Hammick*

Corn is ground for local farmers by a watermill outside Fajã Grande in Flores *Anne Hammick*

Fishermen bait hooks at Porto da Caloura, São Miguel *Anne Hammick*

## History

When the Portuguese claimed and colonised the Azores in the early 15th century they were uninhabited, with no human traces of any kind. However, it seems almost certain that although the Portuguese were the first to settle the islands, others had been aware of their existence centuries before. Various sources credit their discovery to the Phoenicians in the 6th century BC, the Carthaginians a few hundred years later, the Norsemen – though if they had known of the Azores why should they have chosen instead to settle in Iceland? – and even the Chinese. The earliest reliable reference to the islands dates back to 1154AD when Sherif Mohammed al Edrisi, an Arab explorer and geographer at the court of King Roger II of Sicily, compiled a globe and descriptive manuscript entitled *El Rojari* which mentions nine islands lying to the northwest of the Canaries. They were next described by a Spanish friar writing in the early 14th century, and appear clearly on a Genoese chart of 1351, now kept in Florence.

History is less specific about the Portuguese connection, with some sources stating that Diogo de Silves, a pilot in the service of King João I of Portugal, rediscovered the islands in 1427 while others suggest that a copy of the Genoese chart was taken to Portugal in 1428 and given to King João's son, Prince Henry the Navigator. Either is possible – hemmed in by its powerful Spanish neighbour, Portugal was forced to look overseas to expand and colonise, with seaworthy caravels exploring the African coast and far out into the Atlantic. Prince Henry the Navigator (who rarely went to sea himself) spent much of his life at Sagres collecting and studying accounts of early voyages and such charts and maps as could be obtained, and would doubtless have paid well for such a valuable addition. Whatever his source, by 1431 Prince Henry was confident enough to send a small fleet

You can take a horse to water ... and if it's on the tiny island of Corvo you won't have to go far! *Anne Hammick*

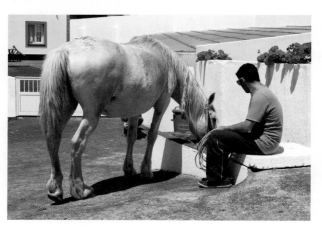

Manueline-style carving around the church door at Santo Espírito in Santa Maria  *Anne Hammick*

commanded by Gonçalvo Velho Cabral in search of the elusive islands. With incredible bad luck, after crossing more than 700 miles of ocean Cabral and his men found only an isolated group of rocks, and one can imagine the disgust with which they named them the Formigas (the Ants) before turning for home. They must also have been dogged with exceptionally bad visibility not to have seen the 590m peak of Santa Maria just 20M to the southwest. Presumably Prince Henry was less than pleased with their lack of success, since Cabral was sent westwards again the following summer and on 15 August 1432 finally landed on Santa Maria.

Unlike many men of vision, Prince Henry was also practical and concerned with the settlement of his newly acquired islands. A Royal Edict dated 2 July 1439 is the oldest existing document regarding colonisation, at which time only Santa Maria and São Miguel were definitely known. The central group – Terceira, Graciosa, São Jorge, Pico and Faial – were added to the list around 1450, with Flores and Corvo far to the west not discovered until 1452. Cabral became the first governor or *capitão donatório*, based at Vila Franca do Campo in São Miguel, and work began on clearing the land for cultivation. Large areas of the dense natural forest were burned, volcanic boulders heaped into walls and windbreaks, and wheat, oranges, sugar cane and

The restored *Misericordia* church, which overlooks the marina at Angra do Heroísmo, Terceira *Anne Hammick*

vines brought from the mainland. However, Portugal was unable to provide enough potential colonists, a difficulty partially solved by the intervention of Prince Henry's sister, the Infanta Isabella, Duchess of Burgundy and Countess of Flanders. Thousands of Flemings from her husband's estates were eager to escape the wars and persecution of the low countries (now Belgium and Holland) by emigrating to the Azores, as were Bretons from France and a scattering of Scots, Italians and Irish, all hoping for better lives. One of the early governors of São Miguel was Rui Gonçalves de Câmara, son of João Gonçalves Zarco who discovered Madeira. Why he left his father's island is not clear, but he almost certainly brought some Madeiran families with him, and very possibly Moorish and African slaves.

As the land was gradually cleared and cultivated, the small groups of thatched wooden huts built by the first settlers began to be replaced by stone cottages, usually built in the traditional style of the area from which each family had come. Even now this gives a valuable clue as to their origins – while low, whitewashed buildings with doors and windows outlined by broad stripes of colour are typical throughout all the islands, their chimneys vary dramatically, from the circular detached towers of Santa Maria to the sharp-edged wedges of Terceira. Many of the leading families of the 15th

century still have descendants in the islands, and even more of the farmers and country dwellers are likely to have lived in the same cottages for generations, until recently most never leaving their own island throughout their entire lives.

In contrast to this, as settlement and agriculture spread through the islands they gained importance as a port of call for ships exploring ever westwards. Columbus stopped briefly at Santa Maria in 1493 on his return from the 'new world', in 1498 João Fernandes Labrador left Terceira with the fleet of John Cabot to explore the land which still bears his name, the following year Vasco de Gama anchored briefly at Angra on his way back from India, and in the early years of the new century the Corte Real brothers, also from Terceira, led expeditions to Newfoundland and Canada. Its superior natural harbour soon led to Angra becoming the leading town in the Azores, particularly after the destruction of Vila Franca do Campo on São Miguel in 1522 by an earthquake and landslide. When, in 1534, Angra was granted a bishopric its dominant position was assured, even though each island still retained its own *capitão donatório* appointed by the King of Portugal.

Later in the 16th century Angra played an important part in Portuguese history when, in 1580, King Phillip II of Spain invaded mainland Portugal claiming the throne, the country and all its overseas territories, following the death of King Sebastão II. Dom António, Prior of Crato and claimant to the Portuguese throne, fled to Terceira to organise his opposition with the help of the English and French, but after two years of resistance the island finally fell to the Spanish, the last Portuguese territory to do so.

The Spanish were quick to realise the value of the islands for their treasure galleons returning from the Americas, and within a few years the harbours at Angra and, to a lesser extent, at Horta had become magnets for pirates and privateers of all nationalities, including English, French and Venetian, traditional enemies of Spain who had supported the Prior of Crato. Castles were built to protect the two anchorages and provide secure storage for valuables (the Spaniards must have built well, as both have survived for more than four centuries), but even so Horta was attacked repeatedly by English fleets in the 1580s and 1590s, whilst raids by Moorish and North African pirates continued as they had done almost since the islands' discovery. Under Spanish rule Angra became capital of the archipelago, and although on the restoration of Portuguese independence in 1640 under the house of Bragança the system of independent governors was reintroduced, it never lost its position as the economic and commercial centre of the islands. Eventually, after a long period in the 17th and 18th

Whaleboats in the *Casa dos Botes* at São Mateus da Calheta, Terceira (see page 127) *Anne Hammick*

centuries during which the islands largely went their individual ways, remote from mainland Portugal, a central government under a single Captain General was again set up in Terceira in 1766 by the Marquês de Pombal, powerful adviser to King José I.

True to form, Terceira was also the island to become most heavily involved in Portugal's constitutional struggles between 1829 and 1832, when it supported the Liberals under Dom Pedro against the Absolutists led by his brother Dom Miguel. Dom Pedro established his Regency in Terceira and used the island as a base from which to plan his invasion of the mainland. After the successful Liberal revolution in 1832 the Azores became a province, with the islands grouped into three administrative districts based on the three main ports of Horta, Angra and Ponta Delgada, a situation which in modified form still exists today.

It was logical that the harbours should give their names to the administrative areas. Even with the improvements in farming and stock-rearing introduced in the 19th century, the sailing ships which filled the ports, always in need of provisions, labour and often crew, were a constant source of revenue and employment. Chief among these were the American whaling ships, about which Herman Melville wrote in *Moby Dick* in 1851:

'Not a few whalers come from the Azores, where the Nantucket ships often cast anchor to make up their crews with the solid peasants of these rocky islands... It is not known why, but the best whalers come from among these islanders.'

It is likely that the local whaling industry, which until thirty years ago hunted sperm whales with hand harpoons from lightweight open boats propelled only by oars, originated with seamen who had returned home after crewing on American whaling ships. Many, however, chose not to return, and from the early 19th century the Azores had very high emigration, with many islanders tempted to leave for New England, Bermuda, California or Brazil.

In 1855 the islands lost some of their remoteness when the first transatlantic cable was laid via Horta, soon to become a base for several big cable companies, and as the number of steamships increased the British-run Fayal Coal Company set up a bunkering station in the harbour. This would have been the scene which greeted Joshua Slocum when he arrived in May 1895, 21 days out of Boston, quite possibly the first singlehanded sailor ever to visit Horta. In *Sailing Alone Around the World* he recounted his impressions:

'Early on the morning of July 20 I saw Pico looming above the clouds on the starboard bow. Lower lands burst forth as the sun burned away the morning fog, and island after island came into view. As I approached nearer, cultivated fields appeared. Only those who have seen the Azores from the deck of a vessel realize the beauty of the mid-ocean picture... At 4.30pm I cast anchor at Fayal... It was the season for fruit when I arrived at the Azores, and there was soon more of all kinds of it put on board than I knew what to do with. Islanders are always the kindest people in the world, and I met none anywhere kinder than the good hearts of this place... I remained four days at Fayal, and that was two days more than I had intended to stay.'

In the same year that Slocum visited Faial the islands were granted limited autonomy, though no real economic independence – Slocum remarks how all mail had to go via Lisbon, even if the vessel carrying it put in at the Azores. By 1900 the population was reckoned to stand at just over a quarter of a million, the vast majority of whom were poor and uneducated, much as in Portugal itself. When the monarchy was overthrown in 1910 and the country became a republic little changed in the Azores throughout the long period of political instability before Dr Salazar took over, establishing a virtual dictatorship in 1932 with himself as head of a one-party state. During the First World War Portugal had remained neutral until 1916, when it joined the Allies and US naval bases were established in the islands.

A hint of the 20th century finally arrived in the Azores in the 1930s when American flying boats began to visit Horta en route for Europe. However, this can hardly have prepared the islanders for World War Two when, although Portugal again remained neutral, the strategic importance of the

**II. THE AZORES**

Paved pedestrian streets add to the relaxed atmosphere in Velas, São Jorge *Anne Hammick*

began to be sent abroad in increasing numbers. However, it has ruefully been said that the Azores' greatest export has long been people – more than 100,000 emigrated to the US alone in the first half of the 20th century, leaving approximately 320,000 islanders by 1950, nearly half of them in São Miguel. Of these another 74,000 left for the US and Canada during the 1960s and '70s, though many sent money back to relatives and an increasing number – or their children – have returned to settle, often using skills learned abroad and giving a much-needed boost to the local economy.

Portugal's right-wing dictatorship was finally overthrown in the 'Carnation Revolution' of 25 April 1974, which led to the Socialists gaining power. In reaction to this, and possibly encouraged by the independence granted to Portugal's colonies, in 1975 demands were made for total independence, mainly by the São Miguel-based *Frente de Libertação dos Açôres*. These received little local support throughout the archipelago as a whole, however, particularly after the group stated that it was prepared to use violence if necessary to achieve its aims, and were largely defused when, under the Constitution of April 1976 the Azores became an autonomous region with its own assembly and regional government, at the same time sending five members to the Portuguese parliament in Lisbon. An attractive flag was designed – which most visiting yachts fly together with their Portuguese courtesy ensign – and since 1980 the islands have issued their own stamps.

Perhaps the most obvious physical changes apparent to visiting yachtsmen are the many new or extended breakwaters which have turned dubious inlets into viable anchorages or fully-fledged marinas, not that all yachtsmen would consider the latter a change for the better. Also, after an apparently slow realisation of the economic benefits conferred by visiting yachts – not just in terms of marina fees, but in increased business to local shops, restaurants, taxi firms and even the local airline – by 2015 there was no doubt the message had been fully understood, and local entrepreneurs were looking to meet the needs of both local and visiting boat owners.

It is difficult to believe that it is little more than 30 years since the islands' very first marina opened in Horta, but with most of the islands and nearly all of the marinas some distance apart, and with each offering different attractions to visitors, there seems little doubt that the Azores will retain their position as one of those magical destinations remembered with nostalgia and affection wherever ocean-going sailors gather.

Azores was felt to be such that both Britain and the United States considered annexing them. Finally Portugal broke off diplomatic relations with Germany and allowed the Allies to build air bases in Santa Maria and Terceira, while British naval units fighting the Battle of the Atlantic used Horta as a base from 1943 until 1945. After the War Portugal became a founder member of NATO, enabling the US Air Force to retain their air base in Terceira, sharing runway facilities with the Portuguese Air Force and civilian airlines. The airport at Santa Maria was handed over to the Azores shortly after hostilities ended. Hopes that the airports might lead to increased agricultural exports proved optimistic, with air freight too expensive for bulk crops although such exotic items as São Miguel pineapples

# General information

## Nationality and language

The Azores are an autonomous region of Portugal and as such are part of the European Union. Portuguese is spoken with an accent which varies from island to island, with many Azoreans speaking French or English as a second language. Spanish is generally understood, though sometimes on sufferance (it is only 500 years since Spain invaded their country, and Portuguese memories are long).

Certain place names, including Praia (beach), Santa Cruz (Holy Cross) and Lajes (literally a paving stone, but in this case a flat lava shelf running out into the sea), are common throughout the Azores and can give rise to confusion if the island is not specified.

## Portuguese representation abroad

*Portuguese embassies*
   *London*: 11 Belgrave Square, London SW1X 8PP
   ☏+44 20 7235 5331, londres@mne.pt
   *Washington DC*: 2012 Massachusetts Ave, Washington DC 20036
   ☏+1 202 350 5400, mail@scwas.dgaccp.pt

*Portuguese national tourist offices*
   *London*: 11 Belgrave Square, London SW1X 8PP
   ☏+44 20 7201 6666,
   tourism.london@portugalglobal.pt
   www.visitportugal.com
   *New York*: 590 Fifth Avenue, 4th Floor, New York, NY 10036
   ☏+1 646 7230200, tourism@portugal.org,
   www.portugal.org

## Diplomatic representation in the Azores

The following are consulates (embassies are to be found in Lisbon):
   *UK*: British Honorary Consulate, Rua Domingos Rebelo 43A, 9500-234 Ponta Delgada, São Miguel ☏ +351 296 628175, amgm@net.sapo.pt
   *USA*: Consulate of the United States, Avenida Principe do Monaco, 6-2F, 9500-237 Ponta Delgada, São Miguel ☏ +351 296 308330, ConsPontaDelgada@state.gov

## Personal documentation

With the Azores the westernmost European Union border there is strong enforcement concerning visas and passports. Currently most EU nationals (including UK citizens) and those from the USA and Canada can visit for up to 90 days in a six-month period on a valid passport, no visa being required. Extensions are issued by the *Serviço de Estrangeiros* (Foreigner's Registration Service) which has a branch in most larger towns, or failing that by the local police.

Citizens of other countries should inquire at a Portuguese embassy or consulate before departure.

## Temporary residency

It is said to be relatively easy, though time-consuming, for an EU citizen to obtain temporary Azorean Residency, valid for between three and twelve months. It is issued by the *Serviço de Estrangeiros e Fronteiras* (Immigration and Border Control Department) in Ponta Delgada, open 0900-1500 weekdays at Rua Marquês da Praia e Monforte 10, Apartado 259, 9500-089 Ponda Delgada, ☏296 302230, dir.acores@sef.pt, www.sef.pt/. Establishing temporary residency is reported to cost around €200 per person, but offers substantial savings on SATA flights within the islands and to/from continental Portugal, as well as possible discounts on long-term berthing.

## Time

The Azores use UT −1, with local daylight saving (+1 hour) from late March until late October when the islands effectively revert to UT.

## Money

Portugal, including the Azores, is part of the Eurozone. Most visitors rely on credit/debit cards, both for purchases and to withdraw cash – ATMs, often referred to as *multibancos* – are widespread and accept all major cards. Most offer instructions in a choice of languages, including English.

Sterling, US dollars and other major currencies are readily exchangeable in banks, as are travellers cheques, but are less likely to be accepted by shops, hotels or restaurants. Banks normally open 0830–1500 weekdays only, though *Bureau de Change* offices may be open considerably longer hours, including all day Saturday.

Most restaurants, shops, car rental companies and other concerns welcome payment by credit card – principally Visa and MasterCard, with American Express less widely accepted – but it is as well to confirm this in advance, particularly where fuel (for both yachts and vehicles) is concerned.

## Shopping

Facilities for storing up have improved beyond all recognition since the first edition of this book was researched in the late 1980s, and it is difficult to think of any standard item which would not be available in the large hypermarkets serving Horta, Angra do Heroísmo, Praia da Vitória and Ponta Delgada at prices comparable to those of mainland Europe. Shopping in other towns is necessarily more limited, and some indication will be found in the text for each harbour.

Regional specialities in the Azores include excellent cheese – traditionally from São Jorge and Pico though other islands, including Flores and Corvo have now set up cheese factories – wine from Pico, Graciosa and Terceira, and pineapples from São Miguel. Superb plums, apricots, grapes and figs grow in nearly all the islands. Almost every town, together with many of the smaller villages, has a produce market selling fruit and vegetables which vary according to season.

Some notes regarding ships' stores – principally fuel, bottled gas and chandlery – will be found on page 56.

## The whaling heritage and scrimshaw

Whatever one's feelings about whaling, there is no denying that it had a profound influence on all the Azorean islands. Those interested in the 'industrial heritage' aspect will appreciate the five sheets in the *Cultural Routes of the Azores: Whaling Heritage* series, available in Portuguese and (first-rate) English from larger tourist offices at no charge. Split into Flores & Corvo, Faial, Pico, Terceira, Graciosa & São Jorge and São Miguel & Santa Maria, each sheet gives location details plus a photo and short history of all the lookouts, beaching ramps and processing works in its area, as well as a brief chronology of local whaling form the early days in the 1870s to the last whales killed off Pico in 1987.

On a related topic, a stay in Horta would not be complete without a visit to the Scrimshaw Museum above the Café Sport, and many cruisers will be tempted to buy a piece from one of the scrimshanders still working, mainly in Faial or Pico. However, before choosing a souvenir note that many countries have legislation controlling the import of whale-derived products. Both producer and vendor should display certificates permitting them to deal in such goods, and if this is done it is then legal for an EU citizen to buy and own scrimshaw or whalebone items and to transport them between EU countries. Non-EU citizens would be wise to check the situation regarding their home country. Note also that with the growing scarcity of teeth some scrimshanders are now engraving on hard plastic as an alternative to tooth or bone, while mass-produced pieces may occasionally be moulded rather than engraved. While there is clearly much to be said

for the former, which may exhibit just as much skill as 'traditional' scrimshaw, most people would rather avoid the latter. It should be easy enough to tell the difference on close inspection.

## Communications

### Mail

In theory all *Portos dos Açores SA* marinas are happy to hold mail for visiting yachts, though in practice it would be unwise to have anything important sent to either Lajes das Flores or Lajes do Pico as poor weather might well mean the yacht diverting elsewhere. So also are the Marina da Praia da Vitória, Terceira and, in Horta, both the Café Sport and Mid Atlantic Yacht Services. Incoming mail can be slow – up to a fortnight from the UK to the three islands with international airports, even longer to the more remote islands – though outgoing mail is usually much quicker. Finally, it is worth stressing that the word 'Portugal' should always be included on the envelope.

Post office opening hours vary, but stamps (*selos*) can also be bought at newsagents and souvenir shops where the green *correio* sign is seen, or from vending machines, which list current rates but do not give change. There are two classes of mail, *correio azul* and *correio normal* – effectively express and fairly slow – with the former also noticeably more reliable.

### Incoming packages

Import problems may be encountered if ordering parts from outside the EU as dutiable goods usually require Customs intervention. If possible avoid using a courier service such as DHL, UPS, FedEx, TNT or the like – Customs are likely to confiscate the goods at Lisbon airport, and getting duty and fees paid is costly and time consuming. The addressee will also be expected to pay the forwarding costs to the Azores even though, as the original destination listed on the shipper's airway bill, this has already been paid for.

Many beautiful pieces of scrimshaw are on display at the Scrimshaw Museum above Horta's famous Café Sport. Here José Henrique Azevedo, son of the legendary 'Peter', welcomes some unusual customers to the café *Anne Hammick*

Importing goods from the USA to the Azores is best accomplished using the US Post Office and any of their overseas services – see www.usps.com/ for details. Packages sent this way normally transit Lisbon without hassle and clear through Azorean Customs in a day or two.

If in Horta and arranging the import of an essential item it would almost certainly be worth consulting Mid Atlantic Yacht Services – see page 82 – for advice.

### Telephones

As in many countries, public telephones are seen as a lower priority with the widespread use of mobile (cell) phones, but are still to be found in most towns. Not all, however, take coins, some requiring cards purchased from post offices, supermarkets and bars. Mobile coverage throughout the islands is generally excellent, with only a few 'holes' in the narrower mountain valleys.

Calls to the United Kingdom begin with the prefix 0044, followed by the area code (without the initial zero) and number. Calls to the United States and Canada begin with the prefix 001 and the area code plus number. The US access code for AT&T, www.att.com, is 800 800 128.

The international dialling code for Portugal, including the Azores, is +351. The islands share three area codes – +351 292 for Flores, Corvo and Faial, +351 295 for São Jorge, Graciosa and Terceira, and +351 296 for São Miguel and Santa Maria – and the relevant code needs to be included when dialling any landline number, even when calling from within the same island. Any telephone number not starting with one of these sequence can be assumed to be a mobile.

The costs incurred by using a mobile phone abroad are beyond the scope of this book, and individual phones may need 'unblocking' before they will work at all. If planning to spend some time in one country (remembering that the Azores and Madeira comprise a single entity in this context) it may be cheaper to buy a new phone or at least a new SIM card. The Portuguese have one of the highest rates of mobile phone – or *telemóvel* – ownership in Europe and most shops will have at least one salesman with fluent English.

### Internet access

With email the communication method of choice for nearly all cruising sailors, free WiFi is now available in or near all the archipelago's marinas, as well as in many town squares, libraries, etc – see individual harbours for details.

## Electricity

Mains electricity is 220v 50Hz, as is standard throughout mainland Europe, and yachts from elsewhere should beware a probable difference in both volts and cycles. Mains power is provided in all the archipelago's marinas but is unlikely to be available elsewhere. 380v 3-phase current is available to yachts in some areas of both Horta Marina and the west marina at Ponta Delgada.

## Transportation

### International flights

Although all the islands have commercial airports, only Faial (Horta), Terceira (Lajes) and São Miguel (Ponta Delgada) handle regular international flights. After many years during which TAP (*Transportes Aéreos Portugueses*) www.flytap.com, and *SATA (Sociedade Açôreana da Transportes Aérios)* www.sata.pt had an effective monopoly, in early 2015 access was opened up to other carriers including Ryanair, with a weekly flight from London Stansted, and easyJet, from Lisbon only. If booking connections with inter-island flights it is important to remember that Azores time (UT −1) is one hour behind both UK and mainland Portuguese time (UT), irrespective of local summer time.

The airports at Horta and Ponta Delgada are both a short taxi ride from the harbour, whilst Lajes on Terceira is some 24km from Angra do Heroísmo but only 8km from Praia da Vitória. In July and August, when many expatriate Azoreans return to visit their relations, flights fill up early and it may be necessary to book well in advance.

### Inter-island flights

SATA runs an excellent and very reliable inter-island service, with offices at all the airports and in the larger towns. While it may be possible to get on a flight at short notice throughout most of the year, advance booking is generally necessary during the summer – and if a reserved ticket is being held until a stated time, be certain to redeem it by then or it is likely to be sold elsewhere. Timetables and fares will be found at www.sata.pt. If booking connections with international flights it is important to remember that Azores time (UT −1) is one hour behind both UK and mainland Portuguese time (UT), irrespective of local summer time.

### Ferries

Until recently the Azores were served by two ferry companies, Atlânticoline and the much smaller Transmaçor, though it appears they may now have amalgamated. Previously Atlânticoline linked all nine islands by means of three ferries, ranging from the tiny *Arial* which carries a dozen foot passengers between Flores and Corvo, to the 650 or so people and cars carried by *Santorini* and *Hellenic Wind*. Transmaçor served the three central islands, running a frequent service between Faial, Pico and São Jorge for foot passengers, cars and bicycles, which need to be checked in well before departure time. See www.atlanticoline.pt, in Portuguese and English, for timetables and fares.

*Road transport*

Cars can be hired on all the islands other than Corvo, though some of the roads may give pause for thought. The standard of driving in mainland Portugal leaves a great deal to be desired, and though driving on Azorean roads is generally much less fraught a good watch needs to be kept for suicidal quad-bikers who sometimes appear to forget the difference between roads and open fields. Many Azoreans also follow the mainland tradition of 'free range' parking and view blind bends, the brows of hills and even roundabouts as acceptable places to leave a car.

All car hire firms accept major credit cards and will require a credit (not debit) card number to be left as 'deposit'. Most will encourage the hirer to take out further insurance beyond the CDW (collision damage waiver) which is normally included. Minor – but expensive – scrapes are relatively commonplace so this may be wise, though if hiring frequently it may prove more economic to buy annual car hire insurance. Either national or international drivers' licences are accepted, provided the former has been held for at least one year, and it is a legal requirement to carry one's passport and driving licence at all times when at the wheel. The majority of filling stations have attendant service, but even in the 21st century some still do not accept credit cards.

There are bus services on all the islands other than Corvo – where most things are within walking distance – and fares are generally cheap. However, being intended primarily for local people, they tend to run into town in the morning and back in the afternoon, the opposite of what the visitor wants, but it is generally possible to see something of the countryside if not around the whole island. Both tourist and marina offices should have bus timetables, which are seldom on display at bus stops (marked *Paragem* or *Paragem de Autocarro*).

Taxis are available almost everywhere. A taxi tour is an excellent way to see any of the islands, and there are many knowledgeable, English-speaking drivers whose commentary will add much to the interest. There are set tariffs for frequently-used routes, but as many taxis do not have automatic tariff counters the fare for a longer trip should be agreed in advance.

*Walking and hitchhiking*

There are many superb walks in the Azores along both footpaths and made-up roads, enabling the visitor to see a degree of detail missed by faster forms of transport. However, some of the most spectacular viewpoints are at the top of long, steep hills, when a taxi up and a downhill stroll may combine the best of both worlds. An alternative is to hitchhike – local people are generous in offering rides, though larger groups may present more of a problem. A copy of *Azores: Car Tours and Walks* by Andreas Stieglitz in the *Sunflower Landscapes* series (www.sunflowerbooks.co.uk) will add to the enjoyment, as will any in the *Azores Walking Trails* series, http://trails.visitazores.com/en, available from tourist offices and consisting of a leaflet containing brief details of each walk, in Portuguese and English, plus with a section of large-scale map.

## Medical

The emergency number throughout the EU, including Portugal and its islands, is 112. It is claimed that calls are answered within six seconds and an English-speaker is always on hand if required.

The only immunisation required is against yellow fever if coming from certain Central American and African countries, though many yachtsmen will also choose to keep vaccinations against tetanus and polio up to date. Medical facilities in the Azores are good, with at least one hospital on every island other than Corvo and no shortage of doctors and dentists (and veterinary surgeons) in all the larger towns. Many of those with medical training speak English, often fluently. Pharmacies abound, and usually appear to have good stocks of both non-prescription medicines and general items such as suntan creams and shampoo, often under familiar brand names. There are opticians in the larger towns, and wearers of glasses would be wise to carry a copy of their prescription (in addition to at least one reserve pair).

Consider taking out medical insurance, and if an EU citizen apply for a free EHIC (European Health Insurance Card) via www.ehic.org.uk. This covers the costs of medical treatment needed following illness or accident, though it may not be as comprehensive as would be the case in the UK and some contribution may be necessary. Neither does it cover the cost of repatriation, should that become necessary.

Needless to say, anyone with a chronic or recurring condition should take a good supply of medication with them even though, unlike its precursor the E111, the EHIC does cover the cost of treatment for a pre-existing condition. Every cruising yacht should, of course, carry a comprehensive first aid kit with instructions for its use.

**II. THE AZORES**

*Rosquilhas* – circular breads eaten only at the festival of *Espírito Santo* – are baked in their hundreds for distribution to local people  *Anne Hammick*

## National holidays

Much the same as in mainland Portugal. The four holidays marked with asterisks were officially suspended in 2012 due to the economic crisis, with re-evaluation scheduled for 2018, but the Azoreans enjoy their public holidays as much as anyone so it is likely that most will still be observed.

In addition each island, town or area celebrates its own municipal holiday, and dates of these are given in the text. Almost everything except cafés and restaurants is likely to be shut, but there may be the bonus of a festa (festival) with processions, street food, and noisy fireworks late into the night.

Local celebrations, such as the *Sanjoaninas* festivities at Angra de Heroísmo, Terceira, during the third week of June, can lead to serious congestion in marinas and anchorages. If planning to attend it is wise to arrive several days in advance.

| 1 January | New Year's Day *(Solenidade de Santa Maria, Mãe de Deus)* |
|---|---|
| moveable | Good Friday *(Sexta-feira Santa)* |
| moveable | Easter *(Páscoa)* |
| 25 April | Freedom Day *(Dia da Liberdade)* |
| 1 May | Labour Day *(Dia do Trabalhador)* |
| moveable | *Corpus Christi *(Corpo de Deus)* (60 days after Easter Sunday) |
| 1 June | Azores Day *(Dia dos Açores)* |
| 10 June | Portugal or Camões Day *(Dia de Portugal, Dia de Camões)* |
| 15 August | Feast of the Assumption *(Assunção de Nossa Senhora)* |
| 5 October | *Republic Day *(Implantação da República)* |
| 1 November | *All Saints' Day *(Dia de Todos-os-Santos)* |
| 1 December | *Restoration of Independence Day *(Restauração da Independência)* |
| 8 December | Feast of the Immaculate Conception *(Imaculada Conceição)* |
| 25 December | Christmas Day *(Natal do Senhor)* |

## Useful websites

A list of websites offering practical information about the Azores archipelago will be found in Appendix II. Websites – see page 434.

# Regulations and taxes

### Entry and regulations

The Q flag should be flown on arrival from outside the European Union, together with a Portuguese courtesy flag and, preferably, the archipelago's own flag – see page 39.

Despite Portugal having been a member of the EU since 1986, and the total lack of any overland border controls on the mainland, this flexibility has yet to reach the Azores, certainly where those travelling by yacht are concerned. In addition to visiting the marina office with the usual ship's papers, passports and evidence of insurance, it is also necessary to clear into and out of each individual island with some or all of a bewildering array of officials – the *Serviço de Estrangeiros e Fronteiras* or *SEF* (Immigration), the *Alfândega* (Customs), the *Polícia Marítima* (the maritime police, who also have some coastguard duties), and *the Guarda Nacional Republicana* or *GNR* (effectively the local police). In most marinas the job is simplified by the necessary paperwork being copied to whichever officials wish to see it, who may then choose to visit a yacht or to call the skipper to their office. In other harbours it is still necessary to visit multiple offices, particularly in the case of a non-EU registered yacht. Procedures differ from island to island, and though an effort has been made to describe these in the text, the best recourse must always be to ask the marina officials about local requirements.

In harbours with no marina the *Polícia Marítima* and/or *Guarda Nacional Republicana* are still likely to have a presence, though little English may be spoken. It may be helpful in this situation if a copy of the computer printout from one of the *Portos dos*

*Açores SA* marinas is retained, as it carries answers to the standard questions and so pre-empts potential language difficulties. Alternatively, the *Yachtsman's Ten Language Dictionary* – see page 438 – devotes several pages to Formalities.

Outward clearance – usually required between islands, and occasionally between harbours – generally involves revisiting the same officials. Not all work at weekends, and it may be possible to arrange inward and outward clearance in a single visit. If outward clearance, valid for 24 hours, has been obtained and then the passage is aborted after departure and the yacht returns to harbour even for a few hours, it will technically be necessary to re-obtain clearance – even when the second departure falls within the original 24 hours.

### Pets

All pets carried aboard should be vaccinated against rabies, micro-chipped, and have up-to-date paperwork to prove it. Their presence aboard must be declared on arrival at each harbour, and their 'passports' presented along with those of the human crew – it would be wise to keep the animal confined below until this has been done. Provided all is in order and the boat has come directly from an European country (including those outside the EU) or elsewhere in the Azores nothing more is likely to be required, although the final decision rests with the local *Guarda Nacional Republicana (GNR)*.

If the yacht has arrived from outside Europe owners are advised to consult the detailed regulations to be found at http://ec.europa.eu/food/animal/liveanimals/pets/nocomm_third_en.htm before departure. In theory animals should only enter the EU through a designated 'travellers' point of entry', in the Azores only Terceira and São Miguel, but in practice – providing the paperwork is in order – some flexibility is normally exercised, though again this is up to the local GNR, who may require the pet to be kept below until given the all clear by a local vet.

Those making a round tour should be aware that, although correctly chipped and inoculated animals may enter Great Britain, Ireland or the Channel Islands through official entry channels, cruising pets are NOT admitted aboard yachts. For current regulations see the Pet Travel Scheme section at www.defra.gov.uk, the website of the UK's Department for Environment, Food and Rural Affairs.

Finally – and more likely to apply to Fido than to Tiddles – many Azorean marinas have resident wildlife including ducks and geese. Woe betide the cruising pet who celebrates freedom ashore by killing one of these!

### The Schengen area

Confusion frequently arises between the EU and the Schengen area, which are not the same – the former is effectively a customs union, whereas the Schengen area is concerned with immigration and was created as a means to avoid the need for passport control when moving between member states. Similarly, a Schengen visa, if required, is valid for all member states. Despite being members of the EU, the UK and Ireland have never signed the Schengen Agreement, whereas a few countries, including Norway and Iceland, which are not EU members, are signatories (the same is true of Switzerland, but it is difficult to sail directly to Lake Geneva).

In the Azores, only Faial, Terceira and São Miguel (effectively the islands with international airports) are official Schengen border posts under the Schengen Agreement. The smaller islands – Flores, Corvo, Pico, São Jorge, Graciosa and Santa Maria – are not, despite being favourite landfalls and departure points for yachts. Fortunately, reasonable flexibility is nearly always extended to arriving yachts, who are normally allowed a limited but undefined period before clearing in fully at one of the 'big three'. This latter requires no extra paperwork as it is handled concurrently with clearance into the relevant island.

The same is true on departure from the larger islands, though either way it is unlikely to pose a problem. Most yachts departing from Santa Maria are heading either for the Portuguese mainland or for Madeira, while those shaping a course northwards for the UK or Ireland may need to go through national passport and customs controls on arrival, when Schengen status becomes irrelevant.

### International Certificate of Competence

Portugal – and by extension the Azores – is among the European countries which in theory requires that visiting skippers carry 'evidence of competence' – for UK citizens, effectively either the RYA Yachtmaster or Yachtmaster Ocean certificate, or the International Certificate of Competence. Though seldom inspected, lack of one of these could be a problem in the event of an accident or insurance claim. In the UK the ICC is administered by the Royal Yachting Association, www.rya.org.uk, at a cost of £43 (free to RYA members). An examination may have to be taken if an equivalent certificate is not already held.

### Port limits

Formal port limits have been set up around many harbours in the Azores, inside which various local bye-laws may apply. Scuba diving is forbidden within these areas on security grounds, although swimming and snorkelling is generally permitted. If wishing to scuba dive – perhaps to check the yacht's hull or propeller – it is essential to seek permission from the authorities first. Limits for individual harbours are given in the text where known.

## Value Added Tax (*Imposto sobre o Valor Acrescentado, or IVA*)

Value Added Tax, commonly referred to as VAT, is known in Portuguese as *Imposto sobre o Valor Acrescentado* (IVA). The Azores enjoy a reduced rate, currently 18% on most items, as against 23% in mainland Portugal and 20% in the UK. Various purchases including water, fuel, food and pharmacy items pay lower rates. A boat registered in the EU and on which VAT has been paid, or which was launched before 1 January 1985 and is therefore exempt on grounds of age, can stay indefinitely in any EU country without further VAT liability.

Non-EU owned and registered yachts visiting the EU are allowed a period of 'Relief from Customs Duty and VAT' of 18 months (though see below), while the length of time for which the yacht has to remain outside the EU before beginning a new 18 month period is not specified. If VAT has not been paid the vessel may only be used by her owner and may not be chartered or even lent to anyone else. Note also that EU citizens do not benefit from this relief period, and are required by law to pay the tax in the first EU country visited.

Under EU law the 18 month VAT exemption period may be extended by a further six months – or rather the 'clock can be stopped' for up to six months – provided the yacht is ashore or otherwise immobilised. This extension is at the discretion of the local *Alfandega* (Customs), however, and as of 2015 the officials in Terceira (based at Angra do Heroísmo, but also responsible for Praia da Vitória) differed from their counterparts in the other Azorean islands in choosing not to make it available. In theory it would be possible to appeal this decision to higher authority in São Miguel, but this would inevitably be time-consuming and possibly expensive.

If wishing to import a yacht permanently into the EU, the Azores are a favourable venue in which to do so due to their lower VAT rate. It would, in theory, be possible to carry out the procedure oneself, but considerable time and a good knowledge of Portuguese would be required. Several companies, including Mid Atlantic Yacht Services in Horta – see page 82 – will assist with the formalities. Contacting them at least six weeks before the expected arrival date will help streamline the process, which may then be achievable within five working days after reaching Horta, particularly if email is checked regularly whilst at sea. Alternatively Bensaude Shipping Agents Lda, ☎292 293031/33, www.shipping.bensaude.pt, although primarily concerned with larger vessels, also handles VAT and importation through their offices in Horta, Praia da Vitória, Ponta Delgada and Vila do Porto.

## Lighthouse tax (*Taxa de Farolagem e Balizagem*)

All yachts sailing in Portuguese waters are liable to pay lighthouse tax, which is collected by the *Polícia Marítima*, usually from an office within the *Capitania*. The usual passport and ship's papers will be required. (This may be news to many, as in surprisingly few harbours is *Taxa de Farolagem e Balizagem* even mentioned).

In 2015 visiting yachts paid a modest €2 for the first six months, irrespective of the cruising area or size of yacht, but if remaining in Portuguese waters beyond that time it became payable annually at the 'local' rate. This was calculated on a sliding scale – €6 if remaining within a radius of 6 miles, €8.50 if sailing only in the local island group (western, central or eastern), €11.50 if sailing throughout the Azores but not beyond, or €56 to cover all Portuguese waters.

## 'Long-stay' tax (*Imposto Unico de Circulação*)

Yachts which remain in Portuguese waters for a total of more than 183 days in any 365 day period, whether local or foreign-registered and afloat or ashore, may be liable to pay a tax known as *Imposto Unico de Circulação* (not dissimilar to the road tax familiar to UK motorists). It is calculated according to engine capacity, with full exemption for vessels with engines of less than 20kw (26·8hp) and those registered before 1986.

Payment used to be something of a nightmare, as until recently payment of any tax in Portugal required a *Número de Contribuinte* (*Número Fiscal*), which in turn could not be obtained without either a permanent address in the country or a 'fiscal representative'. Fortunately the law has been relaxed and a *Número de Contribuinte* can now carry a non-Portuguese address, though a letter from the marina in which a yacht spends the majority of the year may also be accepted and the *Número de Contribuinte* waived entirely.

Payment is made at the local *Finanças* office (where the usual passport and ship's papers will be required, and some English is likely to be spoken), and in 2015 was set at €2.59 / kw or €1.93 / hp), a rise of slightly under 5% per year since 2011. The minimum rate, for a yacht with a 20kw engine, will therefore be €51.80. Reminders are not sent out when renewal is due – it is the owner's responsibility to keep payment up-to-date.

# Cruising

The Azores have been a favourite port of call for cruising yachtsmen since Joshua Slocum visited in 1895, but only in the past few decades have they become a cruising ground in their own right. The busiest time for transients is May, June and early July, when both Horta and Ponta Delgada marinas are likely to be busy. In July the crowds begin to thin out, and this is an ideal time for yachts based in northern Europe to cruise the islands, making their passage home across Biscay in early to mid August ahead of the autumn gales.

Summer temperatures are very pleasant – hot but seldom excessively hot – averaging 19°C in June rising to 23°C in August, though daily temperatures can occasionally reach 30°C for weeks at a time. Rainfall varies from island to island, much more falling in high areas than on the lower islands or at sea, but showers have a habit of appearing without warning when least appreciated. However, whole days of rain are rare in midsummer, the 'rainy season' occurring in September and October.

The nine islands are spread over a distance of almost 300M in longitude and 170M in latitude. Other than the passage from Flores or Corvo towards Faial or others of the central group and, for all but the fastest yachts, Faial to Terceira and Terceira to São Miguel, it is generally possible to leave and arrive in daylight. In fact, with the sole exception of Lajes do Pico, all the marinas can safely be approached in darkness provided conditions are benign, the latter being less important with Horta, Praia da Vitória and Ponta Delgada where long breakwaters give protection well before the marina itself is reached. See individual harbour details regarding the need to make prior contact, which may not be possible outside office hours.

## Barometric pressure and winds

The sailing season in the Azores is at its best from June to the middle of September, by which time all but the largest yachts should have left to head east or southeast. Yachts leaving for the UK or northern Europe would be well advised to leave by mid August at the latest. Those intending to remain in the Azores outside these months must be prepared for sudden and drastic changes in weather conditions as the path of the North Atlantic depressions moves south during late autumn and winter.

During the summer the climate is governed to a great extent by the activity and strength of the Azores High. When this is strong and well established – with the barometer reading 1030mb or more – there may be days or even weeks of almost flat calm relieved by gentle land and sea breezes around the coasts. Equally, in years when the high never forms or remains weak, changeable weather of the British summer variety is the rule, and damp, misty weather may persist until well into June.

A sudden drop in barometric pressure accompanied by a south or southeast wind foretells the approach of a depression, which on arrival may produce gusts and squally conditions up to 30 knots (but seldom gale force) as the wind veers through southwest into the northwest or north as the depression passes. The most important, and least predictable, variant is probably the speed with which the low will approach and pass, sending southeast winds and swells into the many Azorean harbours open to that direction.

Prevailing winds in the early summer (May and June) are generally westerly, sometime veering northwest in the eastern part of the archipelago. Though winds average 11–16 knots and include a 4% incidence of calms, there is also a 1% chance of gales (30+ knots), at least until the end of May. During July and August southwest winds are most common in the western islands, while further east there is more chance of northwest or northerlies. Winds typically blow at 10 knots or less, with a 6% chance of calms and, according to published data, no gales at all (though some might dispute that). Prevailing wind direction stays much the same throughout September, though picking back up to 11–16 knots and again including a chance of gales, though also a 3% incidence of calms.

Island topography can greatly affect the strength and direction of winds in certain areas so that the true wind may not be found until up to 15M offshore. Katabatic squalls have been reported close to several of the higher islands, most notably along the north coast of Pico and west coast of Flores.

## Visibility

Fog is uncommon in the Azores, particularly in summer, though low cloud can sometimes obscure the higher parts of the islands. Haze can sometimes reduce visibility to less than 5M although the horizon appears to be sharp, a phenomenon more common around Flores and Corvo than further east, and generally limited to southerly winds. More often visibility is near perfect, the higher islands occasionally being spotted at 50M or more and routinely at 30M. Heavy rain squalls, which may reduce visibility to 0·5M or less with very little warning, seldom last for long and if making an approach when overtaken by one it may be wise to stand off until it passes.

## Currents

The islands lie in the path of the Azores Current, an offshoot of the North Atlantic Current (Gulf Stream) which sets south or southeast at no more than 0·5 knots.

## Tides and tidal streams

Admiralty Tide Tables, Volume 2: *The Atlantic and Indian Oceans including tidal stream predictions* (*NP 202*), published annually, covers the Azores with Ponta Delgada as standard port. However, many more yachtsmen will turn to the internet and the UK Hydrographic Office's excellent *EasyTide* program at www.ukho.gov.uk/easytide, which gives daily tidal data for at least one harbour on every island other than Pico and São Jorge. Following a suggestion from this author, the island name is now included in cases where the harbour name alone (Lajes, Santa Cruz) is insufficient.

Maximum mean spring range varies from 1·2m in Flores and Corvo to 1·4m in São Miguel and Santa Maria, with mean neap range increasing from 0·5m to 0·7m over the same area.

Tidal streams run north, northeast or east on the flood and reverse direction on the ebb, and are strongest in the Canal do Faial where 2 knots may be reached at springs.

## Magnetic variation

Variation throughout the Azores ranges from 10°50'W in Flores to 8°18'W in Santa Maria, in 2016 averaging 9°32' and decreasing by 9'E annually. Exact figures will be found together with the other Navigation data for each island.

## Weather forecasts

The Azores are covered by Navtex transmissions from Ponta Delgada (formerly from Horta) in English as well as Portuguese (see page 137). In addition, weather bulletins and navigational warnings for the entire Azores are broadcast twice daily from the *Centro de Comunicações dos Açores* in São Miguel on MF and VHF frequencies (see page 137), though one might question the logic of the latter, with the archipelago spanning some 200 miles while VHF seldom exceeds 25 miles. Various websites carrying worldwide weather information are listed on page 9.

## Radio communications

Since the withdrawal of the very useful *NP289 – Maritime Communications, United Kingdom and the Mediterranean*, those wishing to carry details of all official radio communications in the Azores archipelago now need to invest in three UKHO volumes – *NP281(1) – Maritime Radio Stations*; *NP283(1) Maritime Safety Information Services* and *NP 286(1) Pilot Services, Vessel Traffic Services and Port Operations*.

## Buoys and lights

The few buoys and many lights in the Azores adhere to the IALA A system, based on the direction of the main flood tide, as used throughout mainland Europe. If arriving after a transatlantic passage one should bear in mind that this is opposite to the IALA B system to be found throughout North America, Bermuda and much of the Caribbean.

Note that not every light listed in the text can be shown on the plans, in particular on the small-scale 'island' plans. Refer instead to the relevant – and preferably corrected – chart.

## Charts

The most detailed charts of the Azores archipelago are those published by the Portuguese *Instituto Hidrográfico*, www.hidrografico.pt, which covers the islands on 13 sheets – six of them new editions since September 2012. The 13 comprise a small-scale chart of the entire archipelago, three medium-scale charts covering the western, central and eastern groups, and nine showing either an island plus several inset harbour plans or harbour plans alone. A *Catálogo de Cartas Náuticas* listing both paper and electronic charts can be downloaded from the Portuguese version of the *Instituto*'s website by clicking, *Produtos, Cartografia Náutica* and *Catálogo de Cartas Náuticas*, but unfortunately they cannot be bought online. It is a legal requirement for Portuguese-owned boats to carry relevant charts, but even so it is difficult to source them once in the islands – ParreiraAzor near Angra do Heroísmo and MAP in Ponta Delgada sell Portuguese charts of local waters, but there is currently no stockist in Horta.

British Admiralty charts, www.ukho.gov.uk, cover the archipelago on five sheets, with five small-scale plans and 10 approach and harbour plans. They are stocked by Mid Atlantic Yacht Services in Horta and MAP in Ponta Delgada, but it would make sense in economic as well as safety terms for a British yacht to buy before departure, as prices are approximately double those in the UK. Alternatively, Imray Laurie Norie & Wilson Ltd, www.imray.com, are official agents and will mail corrected Admiralty charts worldwide.

Finally, Imray's *Imray-Iolaire* series covers the archipelago on a single sheet, *E1*, at scale of 1:750,000, with 10 inset approach and harbour plans, and is stocked by Mid Atlantic Yacht Services in Horta and Boat & Sail Service in Ponta Delgada. (The five sheets formerly produced by the US National Geospatial-Intelligence Agency were withdrawn in October 2014 in compliance with international agreements between NGA and other chart producing nations.)

See Appendix I, page 430, for chart lists.

## Chart datum and satellite derived positions

All current editions of British Admiralty charts of the Azores are based on WGS84 Datum, allowing satellite-derived positions to be plotted directly onto them without further correction. For a fuller explanation see Horizontal chart datum on page 11 of the Passages section.

### Guides, pilots, etc.

The archipelago is covered in the British Admiralty's *West Coasts of Spain and Portugal Pilot (NP 67)* which is of course written with very much larger vessels in mind. In addition, the 6th edition of *The Atlantic Crossing Guide* includes brief passage planning notes, with additional harbour details for Lajes das Flores, Horta and Ponta Delgada and other information. They are also mentioned – even more briefly – in Rod Heikell and Andy O'Grady's *Ocean Passages and Landfalls*, and in *World Cruising Routes* and *World Cruising Destinations* by Jimmy Cornell.

Once in the islands, the *Azores Marinas Guide* published annually by Publiçor contains basic information on all the islands other than Corvo and Graciosa, plus photographs, plans (the latter not all north up) and contact details of all nine Azorean marinas. The advertisements might also be of use. It is not always easy to find – ask in tourist, marina and harbour offices – and be sure to check the year (most carry either calendars or notice of forthcoming events) as this is not displayed on the cover and older editions are misleading.

### Berthing fees at Portos dos Açores SA marinas

All Azorean marinas other than those at Praia da Vitória (Terceira) and Vila Franca do Campo (São Miguel) are the responsibility of *Portos dos Açores SA*, as are all commercial and fishing harbours. The marinas at Praia da Vitória and Vila Franca do Campo each belong to their local *Câmara Municipal* (town or city council), as will the marina planned for Cais da Barra in Graciosa.

Overnight berthing fees for visiting yachts are standard across all seven marinas administered by *Portos dos Açores* SA, irrespective of facilities – or lack of them. By 2016 prices had remained static for more than six years so an increase is clearly overdue, but it was not expected until 2017 at the earliest. Neither is the usual mantra of 'check the website' much help, as the group's website at www.marinasazores.com was unavailable in early 2016, though expected to be reinstated in a much-improved format (and at the same address) towards the end of the year.

In 2016 overnight berthing fees stood at €8.44 for yachts of 8–10m, €10.18 for 10–12m, at €8.44 for yachts of 8–10m, €10.18 for 10–12m, €15.42 for 12–15m, €21.34 for 15–18m and €32.71 for 18-25m, which included water and electricity but not showers. Both IVA (VAT) at 18% and a 4% 'residue' charge (basically to pay for garbage disposal) were levied on the basic fees, bringing them up to €10.30, €12.42, €18.81, €26.03 and €39.91 respectively. Multihulls pay a 50% surcharge and discounts are available for longer stays. All *Portos dos Açores SA* marinas accept payment by major credit/debit cards other than American Express. Showers are either charged shower or per crewmember/day, which may include a towel.

For information about fees at Praia da Vitória and Vila Franca do Campo see pages 132 and 147 respectively.

Portugal is famous for its *azulejos* (blue and white ceramic tiles), used here to commemorate the rebuilding of the tiny quay at Baía de São Lourenço, Santa Maria, in 2011. Sadly, Atlantic waves have done their worst since then *Anne Hammick*

II. THE AZORES

Waves break inside 'whale rock', near Punta da Barca on Graciosa's north coast *Anne Hammick*

## Hauling out and laying up

A growing number of harbours in the Azores have facilities to haul a yacht, though few have sufficient hardstanding for yachts to be stored ashore long-term. As of 2015 there were travel-lifts intended primarily for yachts at Horta (20-tonne capacity, though currently limited to 15 tonnes), Angra do Heroísmo (50-tonne), Praia da Vitória (35-tonne), Ponta Delgada (25-tonne) and Vila do Porto (75-tonne). In addition – and an emergency – Lajes das Flores had a 22-tonne capacity harbour crane, Vila Nova do Corvo a 40-tonne capacity crane, Velas similar but only 12-tonne, and the fishing harbours at Vila da Praia and Vila Franca do Campo 80-tonne and 75-tonne travel-lifts respectively.

Only Terceira has generous space ashore for laying up, at both Angra do Heroísmo and Praia da Vitória, with Vila do Porto at Santa Maria a recent addition to the list, but in all cases it would be wise to book well in advance. Further information on all three will be found under their respective harbour details. Both Horta and Ponta Delgada, despite having the largest marinas in the archipelago and being possible venues to haul out for a short period to carry out maintenance, have barely enough space to accommodate local boats long-term, let alone visitors.

The prospects for laying up afloat are much better, with yachts regularly wintering in Horta and Praia da Vitória, with smaller numbers at Angra do Heroísmo, while Vila do Porto also has great appeal combined with excellent shelter, though slightly more remote in terms of international travel. Unfortunately the west section of Ponta Delgada Marina is totally unsuited to winter usage, at least until the swell problem is addressed, while neither the east basin, nor Vila Franca do Campo further down the coast, are likely to have space for visitors.

The Azores can and do suffer severe winter gales and if leaving a yacht unattended it would be wise to organise *guardinage* (regular checking of lines, fenders and possibly battery state), but beyond that a well-secured yacht should encounter no more problems than if wintering in a British marina.

## Ships' stores

### Water and electricity

In marinas, both of these are assumed to be available at all berths – where this is not the case it is stated in the text. If a public tap exists conveniently near an anchorage this will normally be mentioned, but the absence of available fresh water may not be.

### Fuel

As of 2015 the marinas at Horta, Velas, Angra do Heroísmo, Ponta Delgada, Vila Franca do Campo and Vila do Porto all had fuelling berths where diesel (*gasóleo*, pronounced *gas-OH-leo*) and petrol (*gasolina*, pronounced *gas-ol-EE-na*) could be pumped directly into a yacht's tank. In both Horta and Ponta Delgada megayachts could also be fuelled by road tanker, a method also available in some harbours where pumps were not installed such as Lajes do Pico and Praia da Vitória, though this could take several days to arrange and in most cases a minimum quantity (possibly shared between several yachts) was stipulated. Elsewhere it was a case of either carrying cans from the nearest filling station or arranging with them to deliver, or preferably delaying refuelling for a more convenient harbour.

If buying fuel at a filling station it is worth paying particular attention to pronunciation, as if the stress falls on the final vowels of *gasóleo* a Portuguese-speaker may well hear it as *gasolina*, with disastrous consequences. Confusion can also arise with paraffin or kerosene (*petróleo*, pronounced *petr-OH-leo*, though both *parafina* and *querosene* are likely to be understood) though less potentially dangerous than if the situation were reversed. Paraffin is available in two grades – poor quality from some filling stations (suitable for cleaning machinery but not for lamps or stoves) and a more expensive grade from chemists which burns well. Methylated spirits is *álcool metílico* (*AL-cool met-IL-ico*) and surgical spirits *álcool etílico* (*AL-cool et-IL-ico*).

### Bottled gas

The only cylinders which can now be exchanged in the Azores are those produced by GALP. All others, including Camping Gaz, must be sent for refilling – though see page 84 – a service only available in Faial, Terceira and São Miguel and which normally takes at least two working days. Take care not to run out on Flores, Corvo, Pico, São Jorge, Graciosa or Santa Maria! Only butane is available, but refilling a bottle designed for propane with butane incurs no safety risk as it is stored at a much lower pressure. Ideally the yacht's regulator should be changed to suit the gas in use, but this is largely to maximise efficiency. Very old, rusty or damaged bottles may occasionally be refused.

*Chandlery*

Yacht chandlery is generally in short supply other than in Horta and Ponta Delgada, though resources on both Terceira and Santa Maria are fast improving – see under individual harbours. Due to transportation costs, prices tend to be high. Elsewhere, basic items such as rope, paint and sometimes fenders may be found in hardware stores. Good English is spoken in all the chandleries, where catalogues facilitate ordering specific items from suppliers in Europe or further afield. No duty is payable on spares or equipment ordered from within the EU, but importing parts from elsewhere (including the US) can be a lengthy process involving a variable import duty (usually 6–12%) plus administrative and handling charges – see Incoming packages, page 47.

## Introduced hazards

### Undersea cables

Every island has at least one set of fibre-optic cables connecting it to the outside world, and several have two or three. With the sole exception of those running out from close north of the ferry and cruise ship terminal in Horta – see page 79 – all are lit, the details for each appearing in the Lights information for either the island, the nearest harbour or both, and where possible the position being marked on the relevant plan. Each light covers a 'protected sector' inside which anchoring is prohibited, for obvious reasons. Fines have been mentioned (though not specified) for those infringing these areas, and were damage to be caused there is no doubt the penalty would be severe.

### Marine reserves

Twenty-seven marine reserves now exist throughout the Azores, many created in the past few years. Locations are included in the approach notes for each island, and where possible their bounds are shown on either island or larger-scale plans. More exact perimeters will be found on current Portuguese and Admiralty charts.

Details of exactly what is – and what is not – permitted within their limits are given the *Grupo Anual de de Avisos aos Navegantes* published online by the Portuguese *Instituto Hidrográfico*, www.hidrografico.pt, and summed up in the British Admiralty's *West Coasts of Spain and Portugal Pilot* (*NP 67*). Many prohibitions – such as dredging, 'exploitation of the seabed', removal of archaeological material, the introduction or removal of marine animals or plant species, and the introduction, capture or killing birds – are unlikely to be relevant to yachts, but others are. These include simply passing through the reserve, anchoring in it, diving, and any type of fishing.

Responsibility for marine reserves lies with the local *Polícia Marítima*, whose permission should be sought before heading for one of the inviting anchorages – such as Baía de São Lourenço on the east coast of Santa Maria – which lie within them. In some harbours, including Vila do Porto at Santa Maria, the *Polícia Marítima* have an office in the marina building, otherwise they are normally to be found at the *Capitania*.

## Caution

Although growth in harbour and marina developments throughout the Azores has slowed in the past six years, doubtless due in large part to the recession, changes are still taking place and are certain to continue. Works in progress frequently remain unlit, posing a hazard to those approaching after dark, while new features are often slow to be reported through the official channels. Thus even a brand new chart, fully corrected, should not be assumed to be fully up-to-date in all respects.

# Flores

## Introduction

Many yachtsmen remember their visit to Flores as the highlight of their time in the Azores. Only 17km long by up to 14km wide, it has a land area of some 143km², almost all of it magnificent scenery. The second memory of Flores will be of the people. Even amongst the friendly Azoreans they stand out in their readiness to help others which, until Porto das Lajes took over from Santa Cruz as the main harbour in 1994, was essential to a safe landfall. The sight of a yacht approaching the narrow rocky entrance to Santa Cruz would immediately bring the ferryman or his son, or perhaps a local fisherman, rowing out in a heavy dinghy to escort the newcomer in – and all with no thought of payment. As one 1998 visitor put it: 'the friendliness of the people of Flores outweighs any possible shortfall in facilities'.

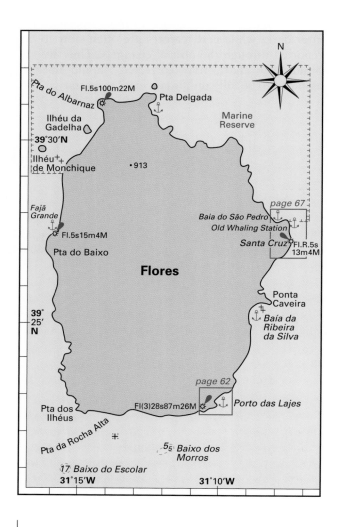

Flores and Corvo, separated by less than 10M of Atlantic Ocean, lie 120M west-northwest of Faial and were the last of the Azores to be discovered by the Portuguese, who arrived in 1452. However, several atlases and charts of the previous century had identified the 'islas de corvos marinis' – the islands of the sea crows – or in one case 'de raca' – of eagles. Amongst the early colonists were the three brothers of Jobst van Huerta who settled Faial, attracted by rumours of silver and tin, and one Wilhelm van der Haegen, also a Fleming, who in 1470 lived at Ribeira da Cruz, before leaving Flores in favour of São Jorge. Settlement began in earnest in 1504 under Captain João da Fonseca, with immigrants from Madeira and Terceira as well as mainland Portugal, its success being attested in the town charters granted to Santa Cruz and Lajes soon after. Later in the 16th century Flores became a base for resistance to the Spanish domination of Portugal – aided, amongst others, by Sir Walter Raleigh – but after the Spanish victory of 1580 it became a favourite target for pirates and privateers of all nations attracted by the rich treasure galleons returning from the New World. In 1587 Santa Cruz was attacked by the English fleet, at war with Spain, whilst Tennyson's stirring lines beginning 'At Flores in the Azores Sir Richard Grenville lay', and recounting the battle in 1591 between the *Revenge* and a large Spanish squadron, will constitute many yachtsmen's sole previous knowledge of the island.

Until comparatively recently the inhabitants lived a very isolated existence, exporting some whale oil, honey and cedar wood to Faial and Terceira via the occasional sailing ship and, during the 18th and 19th centuries, often supplying crew for the American whalers, who prized Azoreans as amongst the finest seamen and harpooners. The 20th century brought better communications with the outside world, including telephones, television and, of course, most recently the internet. The French meteorological observatory set up in the 1960s became a satellite tracking station before its closure in July 1993 – the buildings have now been converted into a hotel – and the much-enlarged airport handles several dozen civilian flights each week, many passengers being emigrants to the USA and Canada returning to visit relatives, and vice versa. The already good road system is expanding, and the breakwater at Lajes, completed in 1994, not only allows cargo to be unload alongside instead of via lighters, but also shelters the small marina which opened in July 2011.

## Navigation

**Magnetic variation**
10°50'W (2016) decreasing by 9'E annually

**Tidal Streams**
Tidal streams set north or east on the flood and south or west on the ebb at up to 1·5 knots. At springs the tidal current between Flores and Corvo can run strongly enough to give rise to noticeable wind over tide conditions.

**Lights**
**Ponta do Albarnaz** Fl.5s100m22M
035°-vis-204°, 214°-vis-258°
Grey tower and buildings, red lantern 15m
**Santa Cruz (Pedra Açucareiro)**
Fl.R.5s13m4M 156°-vis-308°
White column, red bands 6m
**Ponta das Lajes**
Fl(3)28s87m26M 263°-vis-054°
Square white tower and building, red lantern, 16m
**Fajã Grande** Fl.5s15m4M
White post, red bands on white base 6m

**Coast Radio Station**
**Flores** 39°28'N 31°13'W, remotely controlled from Lisbon
**VHF** Ch 16, 23 (24 hours)

Even so, life for many of the 4,000 or so islanders appears to be changing relatively slowly. Many still make a living from farming and stock-raising – Flores gives the impression of being able to grow almost anything in its rich volcanic soil, a reddish tan where recently disturbed, weathering to a gritty grey or black. It must be amongst the loveliest places in the world, the scenery a succession of stunning panoramas, albeit often shrouded in mist. Rolling hillsides end in vertical cliffs, with silver ribbons of water cascading hundreds of feet into valleys where whitewashed cottages cluster amongst meadows full of piebald cows and waving sweetcorn. Narrow roads lead up to the 914m mass of Morro Alto and overlook deep green lakes – seven in all – lying in the craters of extinct volcanoes, their sides thick with blue hydrangea, pine, cedar and eucalyptus.

Corn cobs drying outside a house in Fajã Grande
*Anne Hammick*

A waterfall cascades down the cliffs behind Fajã Grande, on Flores's wet west coast *Anne Hammick*

Smooth grassy hills reminiscent of England's West Country sport granite ridges like spines along their crests and bare volcanic plugs on their summits, whilst dwarfing the village of Mosteiro are the *Rochas dos Bordoes* – Organpipe Rocks – a black basalt crag formed of vertical columns full of angles and facets, a mosaic of sunlight and shadow.

The lasting memory, though, is of lush vegetation – in the deep valleys, edging the tiny fields, and stretching up the sides of the hills. Thousands of flowers line the roadsides – red and yellow canna lilies, blue agapanthus, orange montbretia, pink climbing roses, and thick banks of deep green fern. It's easy to see why, after a short time as Ilha de São Tomás, the early settlers renamed their new home 'the Isle of Flowers'.

### Holidays and festivals

In addition to the national holidays listed on page 26, Lajes celebrates its official holiday on 17 June, with that of Santa Cruz following a week later. The Festival of *Espírito Santo* is celebrated about six weeks after Easter, with the Feast of St John on 24 June. An Emigrants' Festival, to which islanders return from all over the world, takes places in Lajes on the third weekend in July.

Flores received its name for a reason, even though many of the flowers which now grow wild – including these canna lilies – are not endemic *Anne Hammick*

## Approach

Situated almost exactly halfway between mainland Portugal and Newfoundland, Flores is the most westerly of the Azores, whilst at 31°16'·5W the off-lying Ilhéu de Monchique qualifies as the westernmost land in Europe. Thus for yachts arriving from Bermuda, the USA and Canada, Flores is likely to be the first island sighted and in clear weather may be spotted from at least 40M off. However, clouds blanket the higher areas for much of the time and the whole island may be completely hidden by mist at 5M although the yacht is in bright sunshine.

If approaching around the south of the island, allow an offing of at least a mile even in light weather to be sure of clearing the breaking rocks just over 0·5M south of Ponta da Rocha Alta – 39°21'·3N 31°13'·9W is a suggested 'turning mark'. In heavier weather it would be prudent to remain south of Baixo do Escolar, as although it carries a reported 17m the water shoals very sharply from around the 80m mark and confused seas are likely to result. 39°19'·3N 31°15'W, 3M south of Pta dos Ilhéus, gives generous clearance to both Baixo do Escolar and the 5·5m Baixo dos Morros.

Possible hazards on approaching from the west or northwest are the small island and rocks off Ponta Delgada at the northern tip of the island and Ilhéu de Monchique, just under a mile west-northwest of Ponta dos Fenais. There are no off-lying hazards on approach from the east, but it would be unwise to close the island in darkness from any direction without local knowledge. Much of the coast consists of high volcanic cliffs and headlands with vicious fringing rocks, and even in daylight an offing of at least 0·5M should be maintained.

A marine reserve covers the coastline from Ilhéu de Monchique in the northwest to Baia do São Pedro, just north of Santa Cruz on the east coast – see plan – extending some distance offshore. See page 57 for details of restrictions, etc.

Sun breaking through the mist which surrounds Caldeira Funda – a very typical combination on Flores's damp moors *Anne Hammick*

## Harbours and anchorages

# Porto das Lajes

39°22'·74N 31°09'·94W (breakwater head)

### Tides
Predictions for Porto das Lajes are available via
Admiralty *EasyTide* – see page 54
Time difference on Ponta Delgada: –0006
*Mean spring range* 1·2m
*Mean neap range* 0·5m

### Lights
**Ponta das Lajes** Fl(3)28s87m26M 263°-vis-054°
   Square white tower and building, red lantern, 16m
**Breakwater** Fl(2)R.12s14m9M
   White column, red bands 5m
**Praia** DirIso.WRG.6s9m9/6/6/M
   265·5°-G-268·5°-W-271·5°-R-274·5°
   White column, red bands, red ♦ topmark 6m
**Marina, east mole** Fl.R.5s9m2M
   White column, red bands 5m
**Marina, west (inner) mole** Fl.G.5s6m2M
   White column, green bands 3m
*Note* Almost completely masked by the east mole
   A mobile phone mast marked by red lights stands on
   the cliffs close north of the harbour

### Harbour communications
**Lajes das Flores Marina**
   VHF Ch 16, moving to 10 as the working channel, but
   the signal is weak and it may not be possible to
   establish contact until after rounding the breakwater.
   ✆+351 292 593148, *mobile* +351 910 001889
   *Note* The mobile number is marina manager Tiago
   Pimentel's own, so should be used sparingly outside
   office hours.
   0800–1200 & 1300–1700 weekdays only
   marinaflores@portosdosacores.pt or
   tpimentel@portosdosacores.pt
**Harbour Authority**
   There is currently no permanent VHF watch, though
   Ch 16 may be monitored at times and the English-
   speaking ships' pilot uses Ch 14 to communicate with
   incoming ships
   ✆+351 292 593148
   0900–1700

### Harbour anchorage with small marina

Formerly an open bay with a small stone quay, a substantial breakwater some 450m in length was completed in 1994. Whilst its primary purpose was to provide an alongside berth for the supply ship and large fishing vessels, it greatly improved shelter in the bay which now offers protection from all quarters other than east and northeast. After many years of discussion, in early 2009 work finally began on a small marina, the seventh in the *Portos dos Açores SA* chain, which was formally opened in July 2011. Between 20 and 30 yachts are normally to be seen in the harbour during the summer, and several hundred pass through Lajes each year, some of them staying a considerable time. On one occasion in 2014 nearly 50 boats managed to squeeze in, 15 at anchor and the rest (some of them residents) in the marina.

The sudden elevation of the small town of Lajes to the position of premier port of the island is reflected in much improved facilities and communications, though Santa Cruz remains the island's principal town with airport, hospital and government buildings and no visit to Flores is complete without some time spent there – but arriving by land, not water.

Lajes is also attractive, though other than the church it has relatively few old buildings. The town has expanded considerably over the past few decades, both around the well-kept central gardens and along the main road to the west, but one does not need to go far out of town to find a countryside little changed for many years. An excellent view over the harbour can be enjoyed by crossing the bridge on the road out of town to the north and taking the second cobbled track leading off to the right. At the end of the track is a small public garden complete with stone benches and a barbecue – not a bad place for a sundowner or even supper on a calm evening.

### Harbour approach and entry
If approaching Lajes other than from elsewhere on the east coast of Flores, see the island Approach opposite.

The final approach to the outer harbour is straightforward and there are good depths off the breakwater, but its end is buttressed by a protective cone of large boulders and should be given at least 50m clearance.

### Caution
In winds from east or northeast – particularly those which have blown long enough to produce noticeable swell – the anchorage and particularly the marina become first uncomfortable, then untenable and finally downright dangerous. This is partly due to a 'washing machine action' right through the marina, which causes damage to boats, broken mooring lines and burst fenders, and partly due to the overcrowding which such conditions quickly produce due to the reluctance of skippers to leave for the passage east. The very experienced yachtsman referred to overleaf sums it up well: 'if you can safely but uncomfortably anchor in the bay, the marina is a better choice. If you feel that anchoring would not be safe, don't go into the marina'.

Official figures state that on average both wind and swell come from the west or southwest for 328 days each year, as compared to around 63 days when it blows from the east or northeast (though the latter appear to be becoming more common in summer). On only three or four days each year does the swell exceed 4m, but one only has to study the main breakwater light – see photograph on page 64 – to get an idea of the forces involved. Be warned!

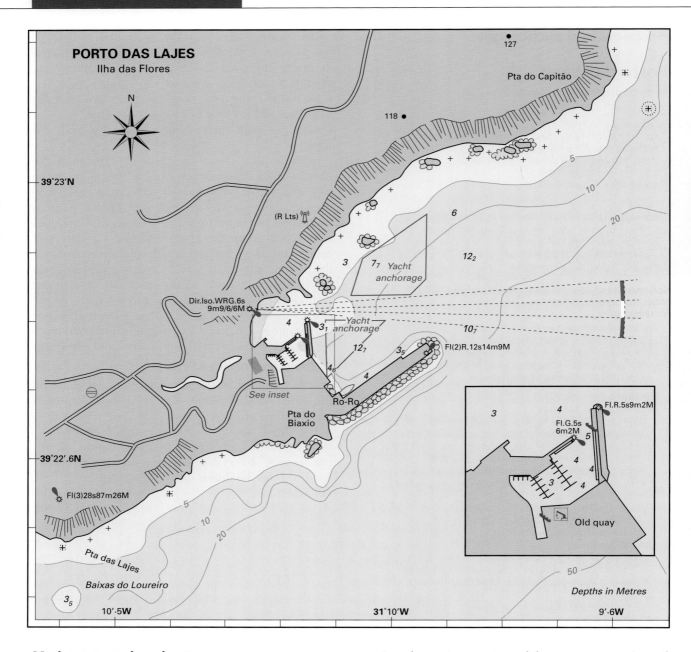

PORTO DAS LAJES
Ilha das Flores

## Marina approach and entry

The marina's east mole comes into view on rounding the main breakwater, with a number of masts beyond. Take a moment to study these and assess whether or not the marina is likely to have space available. It has an entrance width of 20m and a 30m diameter turning area, so skippers of larger and less manoeuvrable yachts may be wise to anchor on arrival and investigate by dinghy. If entry looks viable, continue past the east mole, allowing generous clearance as rubble extends for some distance beyond its end – though not too generous, as two rocks lie off the shore right opposite. Once past the east mole there is plenty of room off the beach in which to turn.

An alternative, suggested by a very experienced yachtsman who has visited the marina a number of times in his 49-footer, is to take an initial swing towards the beach to look into the marina, before turning to starboard away from the entrance and back out towards the harbour. This confirms (or not) the initial assessment regarding space and, if the decision is made to enter – and the yacht has suitable handling characteristics – puts her in a good position to begin the approach going *astern*. If taking a swing past the entrance does not appear safe due to waves breaking beyond, entering the marina would be equally unwise. For a yacht which handles well astern, with or without a bow-thruster, entering stern-first allows for a rapid and controlled exit if there is no berth available or the movement appears too great.

Northeast winds discourage long stays in the small marina at Porto das Lajes, seen here from slightly north of west ... *Anne Hammick*

... but it is often packed to capacity when conditions are benign  *Tiago Pimentel*

### Berthing

The marina manager's office is in the commercial harbour and he works somewhat limited hours (see Harbour Communications, page 61) so it is unlikely that a yacht will be met on arrival. There is no reception pontoon, and unless communication has already been established on VHF or mobile phone it is up to the skipper to choose a suitable berth (though he may later be asked to move).

All berths are alongside pontoons or fingers, with visitors most likely to be placed on the 60m pontoon inside the east mole (where it is normally possible to raft two or three abreast), on the 30m pontoon inside the northwest mole (said to be the quietest spot as regards surge), or alongside one of the fingers on either side of the northeast pontoon (limited to 12/13m LOA). In settled conditions yachts can also secure to the outside of the marina's northwest mole, a particularly good spot for multihulls. Depth is not a problem, with 5m along the east mole, 4m between it and the northeast pontoon, and 3·5m between the pontoons, but there is nearly always some surge, making long nylon warps and/or steel springs or 'rubber-snubbers' advisable.

No one denies that the marina is small – most would say too small – and visitor numbers look set to continue rising. In 2012 just 200 yachts visited during the entire season, in 2013 that number grew to nearly 300, and only bad weather in early 2014 which saw many yachts continue straight to Horta caused a dip in that year's figures. The typical size of yachts making the Atlantic crossing was also underestimated at the planning stage. Four boats in the 13/14m range take up the entire east pontoon, and beam is also critical – some of the narrower slots will only take two boats if their combined beam is less than 7m. The overcrowding problem is also compounded by the understandable reluctance of many new arrivals to move on.

## II. THE AZORES

Lajes village, harbour and the surrounding coastline, seen from high ground to the west  *Anne Hammick*

The lighthouse on Lajes breakwater – flattened one side, bulging the other, and held in place by wire stays. Its predecessors seldom survived to see a second winter
*Anne Hammick*

Larger yachts may be permitted to berth alongside the outer part of the main breakwater in 5m or more, if it is not required for commercial vessels, or bow- or stern-to at the old quay, northwest of the RoRo berth, in 3·5m or more. Permission must first be obtained from the marina office, however, implying anchoring on first arrival.

## Anchorage

There are two designated anchorage areas – see plan – straddling the 10m line over sand, gravel and rock. A RoRo berth has been created in the angle formed by the outer breakwater and the old quay, and the approach and turning area of the ships which use it must not be impeded.

Considerable swell works into the harbour during winds from the east or southeast and, whilst protected by the cliffs from northerly winds, a northerly or even northwesterly groundswell may work around the island to make the anchorage uncomfortably rolly. This is aggravated by the surrounding topography which conspires to send a light southwesterly across the anchorage, thus encouraging yachts to take the swell beam-on. Good anti-chafing gear will be needed if relying on a rope anchor rode.

Dinghies can be left at the steps inside the old quay, or at the small northwest pontoon (see plan).

## Formalities

The marina office is housed in the large new *Delegação Marítima* building on the root of the outer breakwater, out of sight of the marina, and must be visited on arrival with the usual passports (including those for any four-legged crew), ship's papers and evidence of insurance. Hours are officially 0800–1200, 1300–1700 weekdays only, and though marina manager Tiago Pimentel sometimes comes in at the weekend to check a yacht out it would be considerate to pay the marina bill on Friday – there are no other departure formalities. Tiago speaks excellent English despite never having lived outside the Azores, and is unfailingly friendly and helpful.

The *Alfândega* (Customs) also have an office in the *Delegação Marítima* building, but there is normally no need to visit as the necessary data is forwarded by the marina office. The *Polícia Marítima* (maritime police), and *Guarda Nacional Republicana* (GNR) prefer to remain mobile and generally visit new arrivals in situ. The *Serviço de Estrangeiros e Fronteiras* (Immigration) do not appear to take an active interest in yachts.

Clearance is treated in a rational manner as befits an island people accustomed to the dictates of the weather, and should a yacht arrive at the weekend and be unable to remain until Monday there will be no repercussions if formal clearance is delayed until its next port of arrival, most often Horta. Clearance into the Schengen area is treated with similar flexibility. Like all the smaller islands, Flores is not a 'border post' under the Schengen Agreement – see page 51 – but the paperwork can be deferred for a reasonable period until the yacht reaches Faial, Terceira or São Miguel.

## Charges

Lajes das Flores Marina is part of the *Portos dos Açores SA* chain, and shares their basic price structure – see page 55 – despite having few facilities. Payment can be made using most major credit/debit cards other than American Express.

Lighthouse tax – *Taxa de Farolagem e Balizagem* – is sometimes collected by the *Polícia Marítima*. At just €2 for six months visitors have little to complain of, but it is worth keeping the receipt. See also page 52.

## Facilities

*Boatyard* None as such, but welding is available, as are repairs to GRP and timber. Enquire at marina office.
*Travel-lift* None, and no place for one, though the mobile crane in the commercial harbour is capable of lifting up to 22 tonnes in an emergency.
*Diving services* Nothing official, though several people in the town have diving equipment – ask at the marina office. Permission to dive (though not to snorkel) within the port must also be obtained in advance.

*Engineers & electrical repairs* Skilled mechanics and electricians are available, together with a number of well-equipped workshops, but spares of any kind would be a problem – and a visitor cannot expect to jump any local queue in busy periods.

*Chandlery* None as such, though João António Vieira Lourenço Lda, ☎+351 292 593154, on Rua do Espirito Santo about 1·5km from the harbour just off the road towards Fajã Grande, stocks tools, paint, s/s fastenings and yacht rope amongst the general hardware. Open 0900–1200, 1300–1730 weekdays, and either 0900–1130 or 1030–1300 Saturday. More limited hardware is also sold by both João Germano de Deus & Filho Lda and Luis Gregório de Freitas Lda – see *Shops/provisioning* below.

*Showers* Cold water showers available free in the white and blue block overlooking the quay. It appears most unlikely that a proper services block will be built in the foreseeable future.

*Launderette* None in the town. Mrs Pimentel (mother of marina manager Tiago) provides a laundry service, normally with a 24 hour turnaround.

*Fuel* There is no fuel pump in the harbour, though yachts can normally take on limited amounts by can – a stop-gap before reaching Horta. Arrange via the marina office or direct with the João Germano de Deus & Filho Lda filling station, ☎+351 292 593606, near the supermarket of the same name. Open 0830–1230, 1330–1730 weekdays, 0830–1300 Saturday, closed Sunday, with some English spoken. Payment must be made at the filling station, by cash and in advance, after which delivery normally takes place within an hour or two (and at no extra cost). The filling station has a few containers but it is preferable to use the yacht's own.

*Bottled gas* The Germano filling station exchanges GALP cylinders, but there is no chance of getting other bottles filled.

*Banks* Two, both with ATMs, plus several more in Santa Cruz.

*Shops/provisioning* A choice of three: The largest is Armazém Hélio's (aka Florcash Lda) down a well-signed lane to the left just beyond the sports hall on the road towards Fajã Grande(open 0900–1800 weekdays and 0900–1900 Saturday – unusually for Flores, it does not close at lunchtime).

The other two are close to each other near the top of a steepish hill (go straight over the little roundabout beyond the church and keep on until you reach a T-junction). Germano de Deus & Filho Lda (open 0900–1230, 1330–1830 Monday, 0900–1230, 1400–1830 Tuesday–Friday, and 0830–1600 Saturday) lies to the left, and is the larger of the two with a particularly good wine section. Larger orders can be delivered to the harbour.

The third, and smallest, of the three – Luis Gregório de Freitas Lda – lies a short distance down the road to the right, and is open 0900–1800 Monday–Saturday inclusive. Owner Luis Marcelino speaks excellent English and is not only happy to deliver to the harbour but will also open his shop on Sunday if requested. He can be contacted on ☎+351 292 593038, but note that this is his home telephone number so should not be used without forethought. Alternatively, if unwilling to disturb Sr Marcelino, Freitas Braga & Braga Lda in Fazenda, about 2km up the road towards Santa Cruz, is open is open 1400–1800 on Sunday.

A final note: in Flores eggs are often sold in plastic bags – unless you fancy a rather gritty omelette take your own box!

*Cafés, restaurants & hotels* The long-established Beira Mar snack bar/restaurant will be found just up the road from the harbour, with others in the town, but for an outstanding evening meal go to Sylke and Uwe Steiner's Restaurante Casa do Rei, ☎+351 292 593262, *mobile* +351 922 259289, www.restaurantcasadorei.com, about 1·5 km out of Lajes on the road towards Fajã Grande. Much of the food comes from their own farm and the rest nearly all from Flores. Sylke, who is German but speaks fluent English and Portuguese, will phone for a taxi to take you back to the harbour.

Lajes also has a small hotel, open high season only, plus self-catering cottages run under licence from the *Câmara Municipal*.

*Medical services* Health centre, ☎+351 292 593662, just beyond the *Câmara Municipal* (town hall), with pharmacy in the same building, both open weekdays only. For serious medical attention it is necessary to go to the hospital in Santa Cruz.

## Communications

*Mailing address* Marina das Lajes, Rua da Autonomia, 9960–439, Lajes das Flores, Flores, Açores, Portugal. (As a visit to Flores by yacht remains weather dependent, however, it might be wiser to have mail sent direct to Horta for collection.)

*WiFi* Free WiFi in the harbour area, covering the marina and adjacent anchorage, but of variable speed and reliability. If it is having a bad day walk up the slope to the Beira Mar (see above) where the WiFi is said to be excellent.

*Car hire* Only one car hire firm in Lajes willing to deliver to the marina, though several more in Santa Cruz. Ask at the marina office.

*Taxis* Several based locally – ask at the marina office.

*Buses* Regular service to Santa Cruz and Fajã Grande – ask at the marina office for a current timetable.

*Ferries* The Atlântico Line, www.atlanticoline.pt, runs services between all the Azorean islands. Of most interest to visiting yachtsmen will be the ferry to Corvo, which runs three times a week in the early part of the summer, doubling to six times a week in July and August. In contrast to her larger sisters the tiny *Ariel* carries only 12 foot passengers, so may be sold out well in advance. Book online, or at the RIAC offices in Lajes and Santa Cruz, but note that the ferry departs from the latter, not the former.

*Air services* Inter-island airport at Santa Cruz, with regular flights to Faial, Terceira and São Miguel.

## Baía da Ribeira da Silva

39°25'·38N 31°08'·7W (anchorage)

### Anchorage protected from northerly swell

In the light northerlies which follow a frontal passage the anchorage at Lajes becomes rolly, and much better shelter is reported to be found in the Baía da Ribeira da Silva (Baía da Preguica on some charts), about 3M north of Lajes and 2M south of Santa Cruz. The bay lies north of Ponta da Fora – a spectacular volcanic headland, riven with bright red strata and vented by lava tubes – and immediately south of Ponta Caveira. The Baixa do Bezerro shoal lies in the northern part of the bay but is said to be visible nearly all the time and the bottom, of sand with very large boulders, is clearly visible at depths of 5–10m. Avoid anchoring off the waterfall in the middle of the bay, as the holding is generally poor.

The bay is surrounded by a boulder beach, the Fajã de Pedro Viera, across which flows the Ribeira da Silva, from which ships filled their water tanks in the early 19th century. It is possible to wade up the river through a beautiful gorge to a waterfall in a cylindrical chamber. Paths can be followed through the undergrowth and trees to the village of Caveira, but the bay itself remains totally unspoilt.

Looking south across Baía da Ribeira da Silva on the east coast of Flores *Steve Burrows*

## Santa Cruz (Porto das Pocas)

39°27'·08N 31°07'·54W (quay)

**Lights**
**Santa Cruz (Pedra Açucaeiro)** Fl.R.5s13m4M
156°-vis-308° White column, red bands 6m
*Note* Two pairs of leading lights guide local smallcraft into Porta das Poças and the nearby Porto Velho, but neither should be entered by yachts, **day or night**. FR on airport control tower 570m NW

**Harbour communications**
**Harbour Authority**
VHF Ch 11, 16
☎+351 292 592224
0900–1230, 1400–1730

### A harbour best visited by land

One of the smallest and most nerve-racking of harbours, prior to the construction of Lajes breakwater in 1994 yachts wishing to visit Flores had little choice other than Santa Cruz. Once inside protection is good, but both entry and exit are hazardous in the extreme and more than one yacht has been lost in the attempt. For many years the standard practice was to wait outside until a local man came out in an open boat to guide one in, the same process happening in reverse on departure. However, yachts are no longer welcome at Santa Cruz and entry should not even be considered in anything larger than a RIB, perhaps on a visit from Lajes some 5·5M down the coast.

If entering by RIB or dinghy take it very slowly and stick carefully to the leading line on 285°, marked by two red and white poles, one halfway up the cliff and one on the cliff top. Watch out for buoys and floating lines, and take care to avoid the shoal in the centre of the harbour, particularly at low tide or if surge is affecting water levels. Although a RIB would probably be permitted to lie alongside for an hour or two – the quay has been enlarged at the expense of the old slipway – take care not to impede local craft, including the Corvo ferry, needing access to the crane or steps.

Even if all formalities have been completed at Lajes, it would be wise to carry passports and copies of other documentation, if only to confirm ownership of one's arrival vessel.

The town of Santa Cruz is pleasant but not outstandingly attractive and the older part can be circumnavigated in ten minutes. The baroque parish church of São Pedro is worth a visit, as are both the town museum and the whaling museum at São Pedro (see below).

Facilities include water from a tap on the quay and fuel by can from a filling station a short walk away. There are several banks and three or four supermarkets, no shortage of hotels, cafés and

Looking across the runway to the tiny (and dangerous) harbour at Santa Cruz
*Anne Hammick*

restaurants, plus a small hospital, ☏ +351 292 590273, with pharmacy next door. There is a post office, open 0900–1230, 1400–1730 weekdays only, and free WiFi available in the airport foyer and elsewhere. A bus service links Santa Cruz to all parts of the island, including Lajes, Ponta Delgada and Fajã Grande, with taxis also readily available and several car rental companies. Nearly all the latter are based at the airport, which handles inter-island flights, mostly via Faial.

## Anchorages on the northeast coast of Flores

# Old Whaling Station (Boqueirão)
39°27'·79N 31°07'·69W (quay)

**Lights**
**Boqueirão cables** Fl(2)R.8s15m4M 052°-vis-102°
White column, red bands 3m. Marks submarine cables

### Narrow inlet open to the east

This deep narrow inlet approximately 0·75M north of Santa Cruz was once popular with yachts too large or deep to enter the tiny harbour further south, and vessels of more than 25m are reported to have used the cove. However, it is several years since a yacht last visited, nearly all preferring the marina or anchorage at Lajes – and with good reason.

Rocks lie up to 200m off the headland north of the inlet, but the entrance is reasonably wide and may be taken on a bearing of 235°. With no room for proper

The narrow cleft where whales were once landed and hauled up to the processing factory is still visited by the occasional yacht – but not in these conditions
*Anne Hammick*

**ANCHORAGES AROUND SANTA CRUZ**
Ilha das Flores

39°28'N

Baía de São Pedro

Chimney (conspic)

Old Whaling Station

Fl(2)R.8s4M (cables)

Santa Cruz

N

Runway

Fl.R.5s13m4M

Old Harbour

Depths in Metres

Porto das Pocas

285°

39°27'N

Pta Espigão

31°08'W        31°07'·5W

II. THE AZORES

scope in the 15m depths, normal practice was to secure 'all-fours' between the steps and rings on the rocks opposite, about one-third of the way across. The cables which run out from the small quay would also make conventional anchoring a non-starter. Protection is good from all winds other than east, when the cove quickly becomes untenable, and visitors were always advised to warp their boat around and lie facing outwards so as to facilitate hasty departure if necessary. The old steps and ramp – up which whale carcasses were dragged for processing – provide a convenient landing, with a 15 minute walk into the centre of Santa Cruz.

A four-star hotel has recently opened at the top of the steep hill leading up from the cove, with the *Fábrica da Baleia do Boqueirão* museum in the disused whale processing factory opposite. The museum, open 0900–1230, 1400–1730 weekdays, closed weekends and holidays, covers the entire process from spotting the whale and alerting the whaleboats (of which there are two in the museum), to catching and processing, and incorporates much of the original machinery still in situ.

## Baía do São Pedro

39°27'·74N 31°08'W (steps)

### Anchorage open to the north and east

The Baía do São Pedro is perhaps the safest anchorage in the area in winds from southeast through southwest to northwest, being easy to enter and equally easy to leave if necessary, though at spring tides the current sweeps quite strongly into the bay. It falls just within the marine reserve mentioned on page 60 – see page 57 regarding restrictions, etc – and permission should, in theory, be sought from the harbour authority in Santa Cruz before using the anchorage.

Approach on a course of between 170° and 220°, giving reasonable clearance to Baixa Vermelha to the north and the rocks lying up to 200m off Ponta São Pedro to the east. Although very clear, the water is deep and the bottom largely rock, making a tripline advisable. Depths of around 10m may be found well in, though some may prefer to stay further out in 15m or more and it is clearly essential not to impede the line of the runway.

Steps and a ramp provide convenient landing, but due to almost constant swell the dinghy should be carried well back. It takes about 15 minutes to walk into Santa Cruz.

## Porto do Ponta Delgada

39°31'·17N 31°12'·42W (quay)

### Interesting but exposed anchorage

Tucked under high cliffs near the northern tip of Flores, Porto do Ponta Delgada (see island plan page 58) – a tiny corner of a larger bay – has a small quay and a crane used by local fishing craft. The bay, which is open from northeast to southeast, appears deep and there are no known hazards in the approach, though large rubble blocks extend well beyond the end of the mole (which is unlit). The bottom is of rock and large stones, making a tripline advisable. There is nothing at the landing, but by following the steep road inland first a public tap and then a village (with basic facilities including a small supermarket and several bars) will be found.

Like the Baía do São Pedro, Porto do Ponta Delgada is covered by the marine reserve mentioned on page 60.

Baía de São Pedro, north of Santa Cruz, looking southeast. The end of the runway can just be seen on the right
*Anne Hammick*

'Porto' do Ponta Delgada in the extreme north of Flores – not to be confused with the true port of that name on São Miguel *Anne Hammick*

## Anchorages on the west coast of Flores

# Fajã Grande
39°27'·58N 31°15'·72W (quay)

**Lights**
**Fajã Grande** Fl.5s13m4M
    White post, red bands beside small white building 6m
**Ldg Lts on 156°** Oc.G.6s10/18M
    Green lanterns on telegraph poles 28m apart

### The most westerly anchorage in Europe

This wide bay, sheltered by towering cliffs from the northeast through east to south, (see island plan page 58) provides an attractive and viable anchorage in settled easterly weather. (In August 2000 one yachtsman praised it as: 'a paradise off a weather shore when the wind was howling from the east-southeast'). However, it is prone to swell running down the coast from the north, as well as Atlantic swells rolling in from the western quadrant. Powerful katabatic squalls have been reported in strong easterlies, but these are more likely at some distance from the shore. It is the most westerly village, and the most westerly anchorage, in Europe.

If approaching other than from directly offshore give a generous berth to the rocks which run out from both ends of the bay, and do not venture much beyond the line of the inner quay face without careful eyeball navigation as there are several awash rocks off the beach. Fortunately the water is very clear. Anchor in 7–8m over boulders, with a tripline advisable. Dinghies can be landed at the small quay (with steps) or at the wide slipway/sunbathing area. Although lit, Fajã Grande is suitable for daylight approach only – in fact the entire west coast of Flores should be given a wide berth in darkness or poor visibility.

There is a café/restaurant immediately behind the slipway where swimmers' (ie. cold) showers are available and water cans may be filled. The village boasts several small supermarkets, the one next to the church being surprisingly well-stocked, with a range of fruit and vegetables and large freezers. It is open exceptionally long hours – 0630–1415, 1515–2100 daily, 0700 Sundays and holidays – and the helpful owner speaks good English. Most credit/debit cards are accepted – potentially very useful, as there is no bank or ATM in the village. A bus service links Fajã Grande to Lajes and other parts of the island. Excellent walking can be enjoyed in almost any direction, with surf, waterfalls and birdsong the only sounds.

The wide bay at Fajã Grande seen from the south  *Anne Hammick*

# Corvo

**Between 39°40′N–39°44′N and 31°05′W–31°07′W**

## Introduction

Corvo is the most northerly and by far the smallest of the Azorean islands with an area of only 17·5km², being 7km long by up to 4·5km wide. It consists of a single oval volcanic cone, Monte Gordo, which reaches 770m and contains a crater 1·5km in diameter and over 300m deep. Two small lakes and seven tiny islands lie inside the caldeira.

Corvo was discovered together with Flores in 1452, although their existence as the *'ilhas dos corvos marinis'* was almost certainly known prior to that date (see the Introduction to Flores). Due to its remoteness colonisation did not take place until 1548 when a small settlement was established at Vila Nova do Corvo, the only landing place amongst the island's high cliffs and rocks. A self-sufficient pastoral community developed, living by stock-raising, limited arable farming and fishing, a pattern which still continues. Bonfires were used to communicate with passing ships and with Flores, using a code to indicate particular needs such as a priest or doctor, and limited only by the haze which often surrounds both islands cutting Corvo off for weeks at a time.

Emigration has been high since the 18th and 19th centuries when American whaling ships called in search of crew, and the current population of around 430 is only half that of 60 years ago. Vila Nova do Corvo – sometimes referred to as Vila do Corvo or simply Vila – has remained the island's only settlement. Created a borough in 1832, it is proud of its status as the smallest town in Portugal. The old quarter is now a conservation area where ancient cottages fringe narrow streets and steep pathways, many of the tiny front yards also housing two or

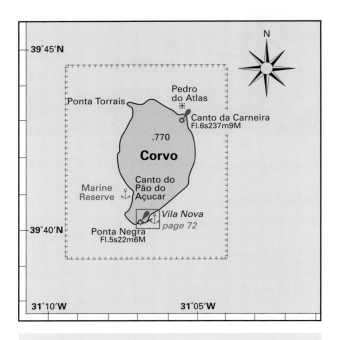

## Navigation

**Magnetic variation**
10°40′W (2016) decreasing by 9′E annually

**Tidal Streams**
Tidal streams set north on the flood and south on the ebb at up to 1·5 knots.

**Lights**
**Ponta Negra** Fl.5s22m6M
    Hexagonal white tower near white windmill 3m
**Canto da Carneira** Fl.6s237m9M
    White column, red bands 4m

Corvo's peaceful *caldeira* on a misty day. The seven islands within the two small lakes are claimed to resemble those of the Azores archipelago in miniature *Anne Hammick*

Beware of the dog! *Anne Hammick*

three pigs. There are few locks to be seen, no jail, and crime is almost unknown. Be wary, though, of straying off the beaten track and onto private property – for its size, Corvo has a disproportionate population of large dogs. Though most are chained up, a few are not and all take their guard duties seriously – and very loudly.

While wandering around the 'old' town, even the non-religious should pause to admire the *Matriz* (parish church), built in 1795 – plain outside and strikingly beautiful within. Like most churches in the Azores, the door is seldom locked. In contrast, the modern *Casa do Bote* housing the tourist office, near the south end of the runway, appears only to open in the high season (July and August).

Over recent decades communication with the outside world has improved markedly, first with a meteorological and radio station, then a telephone system (and more recently fast internet), and finally via a passenger airport with regular flights to Flores, Faial and Terceira, opened in 2005. Weather permitting, a 12-seater passenger ferry runs a service between Corvo and Santa Cruz das Flores, six days a week in the high season and two or three at other times. Many local people have spent some time abroad, usually in America or Canada, and thus speak English, but a smile and a wave means the same in any language and visitors are made to feel particularly welcome.

### Holidays and festivals

In addition to the national holidays listed on page 50, Corvo celebrates the Festival of *Espírito Santo* about six weeks after Easter and holds its official holiday on 20 June. However, the greatest celebrations are reserved for the Feast of *Nossa Senhora dos Milagres* on 5 August.

### Approach

With a maximum height of 770m Corvo may be visible from 30M or more in clear weather, appearing from all directions as a single flat-topped mass, largely edged by steep cliffs. However clouds frequently cover the island, and sea mist may obscure it (and its light) until little more than 5M off in apparently good visibility.

Although most of the coast consists of sheer cliffs, with close off-lying rocks and no hazards extending more than 500m from the shore, depths generally shoal steeply and the echo sounder gives little advance warning. If approaching from the north, beware the submerged rock known as Pedra do Atlas, which lies about 450m off the northeast coast at 39°43'·4N 31°05'·3W, with a reported 2·2m clearance. In 2012 the Portuguese *Avisos aos Navegantes* (*Notices to Mariners*) reported seismic activity on the northwest coast of Corvo, centred on 39°42'·6N 31°07'·6W, but it has not been mentioned since.

A marine reserve covers the entire coastline and the surrounding seas for several miles offshore – see page 57 regarding restrictions, etc.

## Harbours and anchorages

## Vila Nova do Corvo (Porto da Casa)

39°40'·31N 31°06'·58W (molehead)

**Tides**
Predictions for Vila Nova do Corvo are available via Admiralty *EasyTide* – see page 54
Time difference on Ponta Delgada: –0010
*Mean spring range* 1·2m
*Mean neap range* 0·5m

**Lights**
**Ponta Negra** Fl.5s22m6M
    Hexagonal white tower near white windmill 3m
**Boqueirão cables** Fl(2)R.8s11m3M 127°-vis-202°
    White column, red bands 3m. Marks submarine cables
**Molehead** Fl.R.4s7m3M
    White column, red bands 4m

**Harbour communications**
**Polícia Marítima**
    VHF 16
    ☎ 292 596146
    weekdays only

### Anchorage off Portugal's smallest town

An open bay, sheltered by Corvo itself from the west and north, Porto da Casa at Vila Nova do Corvo is the only possible landing on the island. A concrete mole about 90m in length faces a boulder beach, providing some additional shelter plus convenient dinghy landing. It may be possibly to lie alongside in calm conditions if the mole is not required for unloading cargo or by the Flores ferry. Even so, Porto da Casa remains very definitely a fair weather port-of-call which usually experiences some swell, and is untenable in any easterly wind or swell, even if very light. Relatively few yachts visit Corvo so the reception is welcoming. The more usual way to visit is via the ferry from Flores – much better than nothing, but necessarily more limited regarding time.

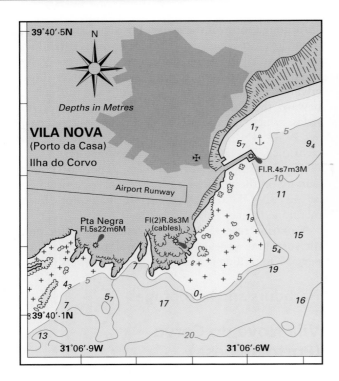

VILA NOVA
(Porto da Casa)
Ilha do Corvo

Depths in Metres

The old houses of Vila Nova ('new town') peer out from their cradle in the hills  *Anne Hammick*

In 2015 mention was made of plans to extend the mole, but this was not imminent and no further details were available.

### Approach and anchorage

Give the southeast tip of the island at least 500m clearance – thus remaining well outside the 10m contour – and do not close the end of the mole until it bears around 300°. Cables run out from an inlet on the south coast, but can safely be ignored by yachts. If approaching Porto da Casa from the south or east the white-painted wall sloping down to the harbour is prominent. There are no hazards in the final approach, but it would be wise to proceed slowly in order to assess the situation at the mole – ie. whether it will be possible to lie alongside or not. Although the mole is now lit, night approach is not advised.

The best spot for anchoring is a matter of debate. One skipper found excellent holding in 18m over sand at 39°40'·27N 31°06'·37W, where the boat was very comfortable in shelter from west through to northeast. Another went into 10m, just outside the line of the mole, and also found good holding. If anchoring close in, a tripline is essential as a chain (to which a mooring may be attached) lies on the seabed near the end of the mole. Holding is patchy amid the same ostrich-egg sized boulders which line the beach, though a weight slung from the chain or

A narrow cobbled street in the old part of Vila Nova  *Anne Hammick*

The short stone mole at Porto da Casa, looking almost due east  *Anne Hammick*

rode will encourage the anchor to work in. The water is crystal clear, making it easy to see what the anchor is up to many metres below.

If remaining overnight a conventional anchor light in the forward rigging is essential, as fishing boats come and go at all hours. A second light suspended from the boom may be unofficial but will provide additional peace of mind. Dinghies can be landed on the (very rough) slipway or at the steps by the crane, though should not be left afloat at the latter.

### Berthing

Yachts are permitted to berth alongside the mole if it is not required for unloading cargo or by the Flores ferry (most of the small fishing boats live ashore, craned in and out as needed). The mole's outer third (ie. about 30m) carries at least 4m, but long lines will be needed as the massive bollards are some 25m apart. Shore access may also be difficult at times, as there are no ladders and the mole stands nearly 3m above the water at low tide. There is generally some surge even in offshore winds, so good fendering will be required together with anti-chafe protection where warps come in contact with the concrete mole.

### Formalities

Officials from both the *Guarda Nacional Republicana* (GNR) and the *Polícia Marítima* are likely to come down to the mole when a yacht arrives (though the latter is not on duty at weekends). If, as is usual, the yacht has arrived from Flores or Faial there are few formalities, but if it has arrived from outside the Azores some paperwork will be necessary pending full clearance on reaching one of the larger islands. In common with all the smaller islands, Corvo is not a 'border post' under the Schengen Agreement – see page 51.

### Facilities

*Boatyard & travel-lift* None, though in an emergency the mobile crane on the quay can lift up to 40 tonnes.
*Engineering* No specialist marine engineer, but local experience with diesels of all sizes is necessary to keep both the fishing boats and the Flores ferry in commission. No chance of sourcing spare parts, of course.
*Water* Fresh water from a tap at the root of the mole.
*Toilets* Good public toilets on the slope up from the quay.
*Showers* Swimmers' (ie. cold) showers near the island's only beach, at the west end of the very short runway.
*Fuel* By can from the filling station beyond the roundabout at the root of the mole.
*Banks* Two, both with ATMs.
*Shops/provisioning* Several small supermarkets. The largest, Loja do Cabral (open 0900–1200, 1330–1800 weekdays, 1000–1300, 1400–1730 Saturdays), is about 500m from the harbour on the junction of Estrada para O Caldeirão and Caminho da Horta Funda. Though not somewhere to store up for a long passage, it has all the basics.

*Cafés, restaurants & hotels* Restaurante Traineira at the top of the slope up from the quay serves tasty local dishes at very reasonable prices, and Restaurante O Caldeirão, south of the runway opposite the two white windmills, has also been recommended. The relatively new Hotel Comodoro already boasts 13 rooms with more being built – Corvo's first 'real' hotel!
*Medical services* Pharmacy and small health centre, ☏+351 292 596153, though serious cases are sent to the hospital in Flores.

### Communications

*WiFi* Free WiFi is available in several locations, including at the airport and in the town's tiny main square.
*Car hire & taxis* No car hire, but several taxis and at least one minibus offering trips up the to caldeira. The walk back down is enjoyable, even for boat-softened feet.
*Ferries* Atlânticoline (see page 48) runs a service between Corvo and Flores for foot passengers only, six days a week in the high season and two or three at other times.
*Air services* Frequent, but not daily, flights to/from Flores, Faial and Terceira.

## Canto do Pão do Açúcar

39°40'·83N 31°07'·15W (anchorage)

### Dramatic anchorage for calm conditions only

A viable day stop and, in very settled conditions, a night one as well, has been reported in the small bay at Canto do Pão do Açúcar (literally, the 'corner of the sugar loaf') on the west coast of Corvo, most easily identified by the tall rocks which fringe the bay to the north. About 8m will be found over a bottom consisting of enormous boulders with only the occasional free area of sand, and an anchor tripline is recommended. Landing beyond the narrow beach is not possible in the immediate vicinity, though a dinghy with a reliable outboard could go to the bathing area at the west end of the runway.

Scenic anchorage at Canto do Pão do Açúcar on the west coast of Corvo *Mike Gill*

# Faial

Between 38°31'N–38°39'N and 28°36'W–28°50'W

## Introduction

Faial is the most westerly of the central group and, though the competition is growing, still has the best facilities for yachts to be found in the Azores. It has always been the most popular landfall for yachtsmen arriving after an Atlantic crossing, many of whom stay so long that no time is left for exploring the other islands. In fact a surprising number of visitors never venture outside Horta, a great pity on an island with so much to offer.

Faial is one of the smaller islands, with maximum dimensions of around 22km by 15km giving it a land area of 173km². Its highest point is Cabeco Gordo on the rim of the *caldeira*, at 1,043m. Many of the 16,000 or so inhabitants still live by farming, though fishing and trade at all levels are also important and the service industries, particularly cafés and restaurants, provide seasonal employment in Horta itself.

Approaching by yacht, Faial appears an island of contrasts. Few landscapes could look more barren and uninviting than the sterile volcanic cliffs of Ponta dos Capelinhos in the extreme west, but further east the island is green and lush, its roads lined with flowers and the cottages white or pastel with square sash windows and doors heavily outlined, usually in blue. Blue also are the massed hydrangeas which earned Faial its nickname of *Ilha Azul* – 'Blue Island'. Introduced from China in the 18th century, they have since become naturalised and are perhaps one of the best known features of the Azores as a whole.

The Latin name of the plant, *Hydrangea hortensia*, often causes understandable confusion. Horta actually owes its name to an early settler, one Joste van Huerter (or Josse van Hurtere), a Fleming who became the first '*donee*' of the island under the patronage of Isabella, Duchess of Burgundy and sister of Prince Henry the Navigator. By 1468 when the Flemings arrived the island had already been inhabited by Portuguese immigrants for nearly ten years, but:

> 'In those days Flanders was visited with great wars and dire distress and the Duchess sent men and women of all sorts and conditions, eke (also) men of religion and ships loaded with furniture and tools for husbandry and building homes ... the which folk were two thousand in number ... in company with the noble Knight Josse Van Hurtere, Lord of the Manor at Moerkirchen in Flanders.'

In fact van Huerter and his three brothers seem to have had other reasons for coming to Faial, after hearing rumours of rich silver and tin deposits. These turned out to be no more than travellers' tales, but silver or no silver van Huerter and his Portuguese wife, previously a lady-in-waiting to the Infante, did well in their new home. Corn, sugar, grapes and woad grew readily in the fertile soil and soon the van Huerter family were wealthy enough to build a fine house at Porto Pim, near the bay which constituted Faial's main harbour. There their daughter married Martin Behaim, traveller and creator of the Nuremberg Globe, who undoubtedly used his sojourn in Faial in the late 1480s to collect information from passing seamen.

In common with the rest of the Azores and mainland Portugal, Faial was occupied by Spanish forces from 1580 until 1640, during which time the island saw both prosperity and bloodshed. Although the fort of Santa Cruz had been established in 1565 it was unable to withstand the invaders, and defences were strengthened under Spanish rule – the fort of São Sebastião and the Spanish Gate, both at Porto Pim, date from that period – but even so the busy harbour was a tempting target for privateers, particularly the English who regarded Spain as their enemy. In 1589 the Earl of Cumberland attacked and burnt the town, and in September 1597 Sir Walter Raleigh landed with 500 men and again burnt Horta to the ground.

The 17th and 18th centuries appear to have been fairly peaceful, other than a serious earthquake in

1672, one of at least seven since the island has been inhabited. Faial was already becoming known as 'the garden of the Azores' and when Captain Cook, no stranger to lush and exotic landscapes, visited in 1775 he noticed the 'hills studded with handsome abodes, gardens and coppices'.

The island supported the Liberals in the political struggles of the early 19th century and was visited by King Pedro IV in 1832. Horta was granted city status the following year, and in 1876 the building of the 750m breakwater began. Although the harbour had declined with the coming of steam, it saw renewed prosperity as a base for American whaling ships, as many as 400 being anchored in the harbour at once, as witnessed by old photographs. Many carried local men among their crews, leading indirectly to growing emigration to the United States and Canada. The little raised turrets on the roofs of many of Horta's older homes, built to watch for approaching ships, probably date from this time.

The Azores have long been established as an important source of meteorological data, the first observatory being built on the hill of Monte das Mocas overlooking Horta. The need to transmit meteorological information to the mainland led in 1885 to the laying of the first of many cables, the Azores' first direct link with Lisbon and the outside world. By the early years of the 20th century transatlantic cables were being laid via Horta, with British, American, German and Italian companies involved. The buildings they commissioned to house their offices and equipment still line the road behind the town, looking more like country houses than one-time offices, and within a few years more than 300 foreigners were employed by the cable companies. Further links were laid in the 1920s, and even thirty years later cable was still considered more reliable than radio. However, greater automation had cut the numbers needed for maintenance and operation, and even before the advent of satellite communications the era of bridge evenings, garden parties and dances amongst the expatriate community was on the wane, with the last cable company leaving the island in 1969.

Of equal importance in the early 20th century were the beginnings of air travel, heralded in 1919 when the American Navy pilot Albert C Read landed his tiny NC4 seaplane in Horta harbour at the end of the first transatlantic flight ever made. Others followed his lead – in 1929 the massive 12-engined Dornier DOX visited, as did Charles Lindbergh in 1933 on behalf of Pan Am, who used the harbour for their Pan Am Clippers between 1939 and 1945. The first foreign airline to establish a base was Lufthansa, with Imperial Airways (later to become British Airways) and Air France following between 1937 and 1939. The island's first airfield was not opened until 1971, but has been enlarged several times since.

Horta harbour was used by Allied fleets during both world wars, but perhaps of even greater danger to the islanders than war was the first major volcanic eruption for nearly three centuries. It began in mid-September 1957 with a series of earthquakes which themselves caused damage, and week or two later submarine eruptions were noticed about 1km off Ponta dos Capelinhos at the western tip of the island, growing until steam, ash and pumice fragments were being hurled hundreds of metres into the air. By mid-October an island nearly 100m high had been formed and layers of ash and pumice covered much of western Faial. A quiet spell at the end of the month proved brief, and by mid-November the former island was attached to Faial by a narrow isthmus. The cycle of alternating active and quiet periods continued into 1958, the loose ash being reinforced at intervals by lava flows until by August the cone had grown to 144m. At least 300 houses were destroyed by the associated earthquakes or buried by ash, and the noise of the eruption could often be heard in Flores 130M away. The island's cattle had long since been moved to mainland Portugal and many children were temporarily evacuated to the relative safety of Pico. Some 15,000 people – nearly half the island's population – took the decision to emigrate, many to the United States.

Volcanic activity had largely ceased by the end of October 1958, leaving a new headland 160m in height and Faial 2·5km² larger than a year earlier. It was calculated that at least 140 million cubic metres of material had been ejected, and on one occasion nearly 2m of ash fell in a single night. Steam rose at intervals for several years, but none has been seen since 1979 and the volcano is thought to be extinct. The newly formed cliffs, mostly of loose ash and pumice, have been eroded by winter storms and less than 1km² of the extra area remains. Thirty years ago the old Capelinhos lighthouse, now almost invisible from seaward and with its roofless buildings half covered, appeared to be standing on the edge of a desert, and even 50 years after the last eruptions much of the area is still barren, with clumps of bamboo, tamarisk and tough grasses still fighting to colonise the loose sand and ash. The whole complex, including the excellent underground Interpretation Centre, demands a minimum of two hours' exploration which may include the chance to climb to the top of the old lighthouse. Summer opening hours (1 June to 30 September) are 1000–1900 Tuesday – Friday, 1100–1800 weekends, closed Monday, with shorter hours in winter. However, for all the interest of the Centre's photographic displays and films of historic volcanic activity, not to mention captioning in English as well as Portuguese, returning visitors may regret the loss of the surrounding area's unique, somewhat eerie, atmosphere.

Volcanic activity may have ceased, at least for the time being, but seismic shifts continue and in the early hours of 9 July 1998 Faial suffered a major earthquake which left at least five people dead, three villages almost completely demolished and nearly 3,000 homeless. Although the epicentre, measuring 5·8 on the Richter scale, is estimated to have been under the sea some 9M northwest of Faial, villages near the fault line which dissects the island (said to be where the Eurasion and North African plates abut) were particularly badly hit. Yachtsmen asleep in Horta marina were awakened by violent shaking, as though a sail was flogging in the wind, but the town suffered relatively little damage. Relief operations began almost immediately, though hampered by the aftershocks which continued for several months.

For a short while after both the Capelinhos eruption and the 1998 earthquake the central *caldeira*, which dominates the island, was declared a possible danger area – at the time of the Capelinhos eruption fumaroles in the interior began to steam and the lake partially drained away. The crater is nearly 2km in diameter and 400m deep, with a short tunnel at the end of the road giving access to the steep interior. A path runs around the rim, providing magnificent views over the island and towards Pico and Faial, and normally the area is a favourite picnic spot for locals and visitors alike – it should certainly be high on the list of places to visit. The exterior slopes are almost bare except for short grass on which sheep and cattle graze, whilst the crater, which is partly covered with natural forest, has been declared a nature reserve.

A second reserve has been set aside nearer Horta, on the slopes of Monte da Guia and Monte Queimado just south of the town. Both hills are protected areas where the indigenous vegetation including Azores heath, Azores candleberry myrtle and Azores cedar still flourish. It was the candleberry myrtle, which can reach 6m, that gave the island its name when the early settlers mistook it for beech – *faya* – indicating how prevalent it must once have been. Monte da Guia, ascended by a winding road, is a miniature horseshoe crater enclosing the tiny Caldeira do Inferno, which although open to the sea is also part of the nature

The disused Capelinhos lighthouse near the western end of Faial *Anne Hammick*

## Navigation

**Magnetic variation**
9°43′W (2016) decreasing by 9′E annually

**Tidal Streams**
Tidal streams can run strongly in the Canal do Faial, the flood setting northwards at up to 1·5 knots and the ebb setting southwards, with an eddy on the ebb setting strongly into the Baía da Horta. The Canal do Faial (which is relatively shallow) can become extremely rough at times, with tidal races off all headlands and in particular off Ponta da Baía do Cavalo just north of Horta itself.

**Lights**
**Vale Formoso** LFl(2)10s111m13M
　White tower, small red lantern 14m
*Note* Repeatedly observed to have considerably less than the stated range
**Gaivota** Fl.3s12m5M
　Yellow column on rocky island
**Horta breakwater** Fl.R.3s19m11M
　Red lantern on white framework tower 15m
**Ponta da Ribeirinha** Fl(3)20s135m12M
　133°-vis-001° White column 6m
**Ponta dos Cedros**
　Fl.7s148m12M White tower 4m

**Coast Radio Station**
**Faial** 38°35′N 28°45′W, remotely controlled from Lisbon
**VHF** Ch 16, 25, 26, 28 (24 hours)

reserve and forbidden to all power-driven boats. The lower Monte Queimado ('burnt hill'), its summit crowded with tiny fields unsuspected from below, is worth climbing simply for the view it affords over Horta – though the bottom of the path, hidden behind some cottages, can be difficult for the visitor to find.

No one island can be said to typify the Azores but, if time is limited and only one harbour and island can be visited, a few days in Horta and a taxi-tour around Faial will probably create an ambition to return with a more leisurely schedule.

### Holidays and festivals

In addition to the national holidays listed on page 26, Faial holds its official holiday on 24 June. The Festival of *Espírito Santo* and Feast of *Nossa Senhora das Angústias* are celebrated about six weeks after Easter, and the Feast of St John on 24 June. Sea Week – *Semana do Mar*, see page 81 – starts on the first Saturday in August.

## Approach

Approached from west or northwest Faial appears relatively low and rounded, and although visible at up to 30M in clear weather will often not be seen until after the summit of Pico, some 15M beyond, has been identified.

Prominent headlands at Ponta dos Capelinhos and Ponta do Castelo Branco make a landfall on the southwest coast reassuringly simple after a long passage, though care must be taken not to confuse the two lighthouse towers. The old lighthouse, close northeast of Ponta Comprida, is of grey stone and can be seen on the skyline when southwest of Faial. The replacement lighthouse at Vale Formoso is seen against the hillside, and is thus considerably less conspicuous in daylight.

There are few off-lying dangers and clearance of 0·5M is plenty, though much of the coast may be approached closer in safety. Rocks in the bay north of Ponta do Castelo Branco and around Ponta do Forte should be given a wide berth. The approach from north and northeast is clear, other than rocks close inshore around the headlands where tide rips can also build up. If approaching from southeast the Baixa do Sul (also known as Chapman's Rocks) with 7m depths should be avoided if any sea is running. A conspicuous white conical building with a circular dish stands on Monte da Guia, south of Horta and a windfarm (six towers) on hills to the north.

In May 2010 underwater seismological activity was detected about 8·5M northwest of Faial – close to the probable epicentre of the 1998 earthquake described opposite – and although no further activity has been reported it could recurr at any time and some may prefer to avoid the area around 38°43′N 28°57′N.

In the past few years much of the southeast coast of Faial has been designated a marine reserve, vastly expanding that around Monte da Guia and Monte Queimado mentioned above, with others east of Ponta dos Cedros on the north coast, and around the western headland of Ponta dos Capelinhos and Ponta do Castelo Branco in the southeast – see plan page 74. Details of restrictions, etc. will be found on page 57.

**II. THE AZORES**

## Harbours and anchorages

# Horta

38°32'·03N 28°37'·28W (breakwater head)

**Tides**
Predictions for Horta are available via Admiralty
*EasyTide* – see page 54
Time difference on Ponta Delgada: –0002
*Mean spring range* 1·2m
*Mean neap range* 0·5m

**Lights**
**South (main) breakwater** Fl.R.3s19m11M
    Red lantern on white framework tower 15m
**Boa Viagem on 285°** DirIso.WRG.6s12m9/6/6M
    276°-G-282°-W-288°-R-294°
    White column, red bands with red ♦ topmark 6m
**North (cruise & ferry terminal) breakwater**
    Fl.G.3s12m9M White post, green bands 4m
**Marina mole**
    Fl(2)G.5s6m2M Post 3m
**Ldg Lts on 195°** Iso.G.2s13/15m2M
    White posts, red bands and x topmarks 8/9m, 12m
    apart

**Harbour communications**
**Horta Marina**
    VHF Ch 10, 16
    ✆+351 292 391693
    0800–1200, 1300–2000 daily from 1 May to 15 August,
    otherwise 0800–1200, 1300–2000
    marinahorta@portosdosacores.pt
**Mid Atlantic Yacht Services**
    VHF Ch 77
    ✆+351 292 391616
    1000–1300, 1400–1700 weekdays, 1000–1300 Saturday
    mays@mail.telepac.pt
    www.midatlanticyachtservices.com
**Port Authority**
    VHF Ch 11, 16
    ✆+351 292 208300,
    0800–1200, 1300–1700
    geral@portosdosacores.pt
    www.portosdosacores.pt
**Capitania**
    VHF 11, 16
    ✆+351 292 208010,
    0900–1230, 1400–1700
    capitania.horta@amn.pt
    www.amn.pt

**Navigational security information**
VHF 13 (24 hours) Shipping movements in both harbours

**Port limits**
A circle, radius 4M, centred on Horta breakwater light –
see Port limits, page 51.

### The crossroads of the Atlantic

The marina at Horta first opened in 1986, to the
general approbation of visiting yachtsmen, and has
been followed up by an ongoing programme of
harbour and marina improvements. First the main
breakwater, built in 1876, was reinforced with steel
and concrete and a container area created at its root
to ease cargo handling, soon followed by a short
mole in the southeast corner – apparently built

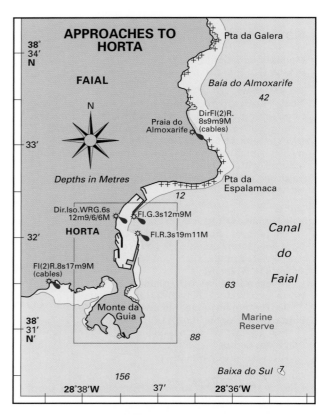

partly of masonry rubble from the 1998 earthquake
– to create a fishing and smallcraft area. Then, after
several years in the planning and building stages, the
marina's new 'south basin' was officially opened in
2002, increasing berthing to a maximum of 300
yachts, though up to 350 can be squeezed into the
harbour in busy periods, including many at anchor
and much rafting up. The north basin, with its
narrow entrance, remains probably the safest place
in the archipelago to ride out storm or hurricane
force winds. Both the reception quay and the
building overlooking it – which houses all the
relevant authorities – have been enlarged, and the
entire facility is run with efficiency and friendliness.

Horta's most recent project has been the
construction of an entirely new north harbour,
intended for cruise ships and inter-island ferries
though megayachts may also be berthed there if the
south harbour is full. It was formally opened in July
2012, doubtless to the relief of those who favour
anchoring in the south harbour and were regularly
disturbed by ferries passing at speed. The only
downside is a rather longer walk to the ferry
terminal – about 1·2km – for those catching an early
ferry to Pico.

Major developments are also planned for the
southern part of the south harbour, including more
berthing and a new boatyard/layup area, but work is
unlikely to start before 2018. The approach to the
reception quay will not be affected, but take care if
continuing further into the harbour in darkness after
that date.

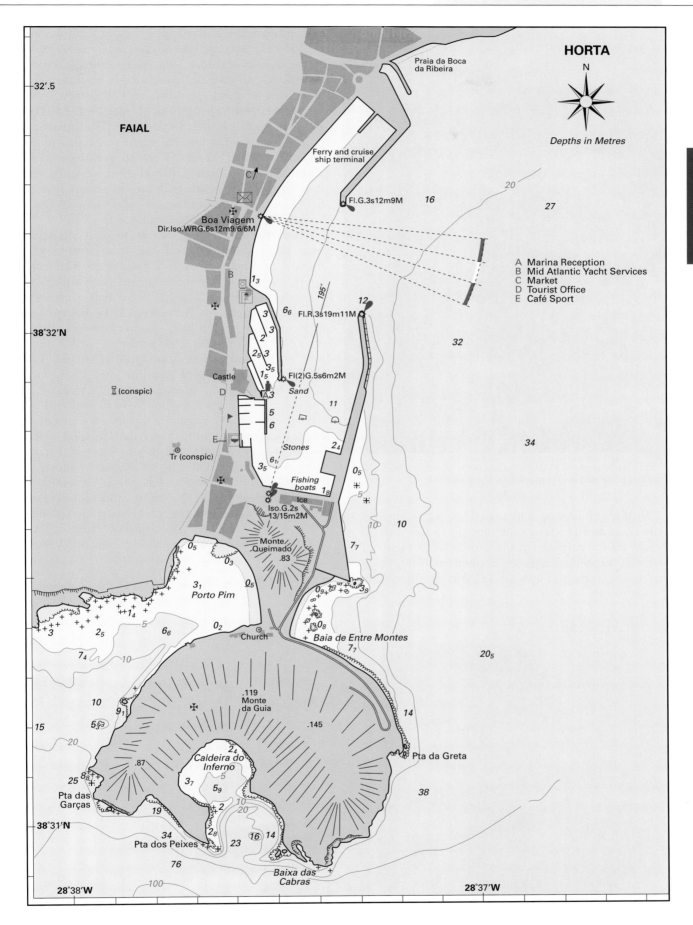

HORTA

N

*Depths in Metres*

FAIAL

Praia da Boca
da Ribeira

Ferry and cruise
ship terminal

Fl.G.3s12m9M

16

20

27

Boa Viagem
Dir.Iso.WRG.6s12m9/6/6M

A Marina Reception
B Mid Atlantic Yacht Services
C Market
D Tourist Office
E Café Sport

32°.5

38°32'N

C

B

1₃

6₆

195°

Fl.R.3s19m11M

12

3
3
2  3
2₅  3
3₅
1₅

Fl(2)G.5s6m2M

Castle

*Sand*

32

Ĭ (conspic)

D

A 3

5

6

11

E

Tr (conspic)

*Stones*

2₄

34

3₅  6₁

*Fishing
boats*

1₈

0₅

Ice
Iso.G.2s
13/15m2M

Monte
Queimado
.83

7₇

10

10

0₅

0₃

0₅

3₁
*Porto Pim*

0₅

Monte
da Guia
.119

0₉

3₈

0₈

Church

0₂

*Baia de Entre Montes*

7₇

20₅

1₄

2₅

5

6₆

7₄

10

14

38°32'N

10

9₁

15

5₉

20

.145

Pta da Greta

Caldeira do
Inferno

2₄

5

38

.87

3₇

5₉

25

8₈

Pta das
Garças

19

2

38°31'N

34

2₈

16  14

Pta dos Peixes

23

76

*Baixa das
Cabras*

100

28°38'W

28°37'W

and although this had dropped back to 1,260 yachts by 2014 the average size of boat was considerably bigger. Yachts of under 10m are becoming a rarity, and though no statistics are available it is estimated that average cruising yacht size had grown from around 11m (36ft) in 1990 to at least 14m (46ft) by 2015 – with beam to match. The growing proportion of large cruising catamarans also poses problems when space is at a premium. The authorities are rightly proud that, despite the enormous rise in numbers, Horta has never lost its EU 'Blue Flag', indicating an outstandingly clean harbour, since this was first awarded in 1987.

Once ashore, the long narrow town is attractive with good shopping, and the local people still friendly and helpful towards yachtsmen. The Café Sport, overlooking the harbour, has been a meeting place for yachtsmen for well over half a century. Founded by Henrique Azevedo in 1918 and run for many years by his son José – always known as Peter, who died in November 2005 at the age of 80 – it is now in the care of Peter's son José Henrique. The single café has expanded since the late 1990s, with associated shops in Horta, Ponta Delgada and elsewhere, and other Café Sports in Lisbon and on the Algarve. Local recognition includes the renaming of the western part of Rua Vasco da Gama, on which the original café stands, as Rua José Azevedo (Peter). In the rooms above the café an impressive museum of Azorean scrimshaw has been assembled, comprising nearly 1,000 exhibits and representing the work of some 20 different scrimshanders. Open 1000–1800 Monday to Saturday, 1000–1200, 1500–1800 Sunday, and highly recommended. Visit

Horta harbour from a little west of south, photographed from a commercial aeroplane ... *Anne Hammick*

Visitor numbers have increased fairly steadily over the years and Horta is now one of the four busiest yacht transit harbours in the world. 1,135 yachts of over 30 nationalities passed through in 2000, rising to 1,300 boats and around 5,000 people by 2009,

... and the reciprocal, but from the ridge running out to Ponta de Espalamaca  *Anne Hammick*

www.petercafesport.com to learn about the famous Café, the Scrimshaw Museum, the Azevedo family and a good deal else besides, in Portuguese and English.

Back downstairs, the walls of the world-famous café are hung two and three deep with burgees bearing the names of some of the best known yachts in the annals of ocean cruising. The same names once appeared on the famous breakwater wall, where the crews of visiting ships and yachts have been painting their names and insignia for many decades, and such was the pressure on space that old paintings were often obliterated to make way for new. The marina's concrete walls offered a new and much more convenient venue, but within two seasons they were completely covered, with boats, birds, whales, charts, burgees, cartoons and abstract designs providing an outdoor art gallery. When wall space ran out crews began painting on the marina mole itself, so that from any vantage point the entire area resembles a brightly coloured patchwork – generally including several figures absorbed with brush and paint pot. The tradition has grown up that it is unlucky to leave Horta without making one's mark, and it would seem that cruising yachtsmen are a superstitious breed.

Horta's third claim to fame amongst cruising yachts is its annual Sea Week, *Semana do Mar*, www.semanadomar.net, which starts on the first weekend in August. Long a local festival with music, dancing and craft displays ashore, dinghy and swimming races in the harbour, and culminating in the 'Canal Race' for visiting yachts on the final Sunday, the *Clube Naval de Horta* has gradually added a number of other races to its programme. Handicapping is necessarily something of a lottery, protests are firmly discouraged, and yachts of all types and nationalities take part in a spirit of competitive *entente*. The week finishes with a prizegiving and party to which all competitors are invited. Unfortunately it sometimes falls a little late in the season for yachts returning to northern Europe, but is very definitely worth staying for if the schedule permits.

## Approach and entrance

*By day* quite straightforward, though the harbour cannot be seen until the last headland is cleared and a course can be steered for the end of the south breakwater. There are good depths directly off it, though it should not be rounded too closely in case of a fishing boat leaving at speed. On rounding the south breakwater the marina mole and reception berth will be seen dead ahead. The gap between south and north breakwaters is more than 400m wide, so unless a large vessel is entering or leaving the north harbour it should not affect a yacht further

south. Neither harbour has a buoyed entry channel, and both have 5 knot speed limits.

*By night* the town lights of Horta are very bright and, if approaching along the south coast of Faial, will be seen over the Baía do Porto Pim before Monte da Guia is rounded. The south breakwater light will probably be identified first, and many yachts will not enter even the red sector of Boa Viagem, which is intended for those entering the north harbour. During Sea Week in early August thousands of coloured lights illuminate the town and harbour, and make picking out the navigation lights more difficult than usual.

The south end of the marina wall carries a large angular sculpture lit by white floods to which, after many years, a starboard hand light has at last been added. Two ship's mooring buoys are laid in the harbour, together with a few local moorings, and during the busy summer season there are likely to be a number of yachts lying at anchor, possibly unlit.

## Berthing

On arrival, yachts of up to 15m or so should go alongside the reception quay (least depth 3·5m) to be allocated a berth. If the quay is full, however, and there is any swell running, rafting up is not recommended due to surge and anchoring will be found preferable while awaiting one's turn.

It is helpful if yachts of more than 15m LOA call on VHF or satellite phone during their approach, while the very large indeed should notify the marina of their ETA on departing their previous harbour. In both cases they are likely to be directed straight to a berth in the south basin. This can take five yachts of 30–35m LOA and 5–6m draught on the southernmost fingers, with another seven of 18m LOA and 4–5m draught inside (see plan). The very largest generally berth on the outside of the 120m south mole in 5–6m, and only when this is already occupied are the main breakwaters, both south and north, pressed into service.

Visitors of more modest size are usually allocated a berth in the older north basin, either alongside a finger or rafted up against the wall. If directed to the shoreward side of C pontoon (the northernmost), note that the wall slopes down steeply to the waters edge. Beneath this lies a band of loose black lava rocks which extend outwards about 2m from the wall and are barely awash at low tide. Further out there are a few larger rocks or piles of rocks, some as much as one-third of the way across the channel, which could pose a particular hazard to the rudder if going astern. The very clear water does help in locating them, however.

Yachts taking part in a rally will normally be grouped together if the marina office is notified in advance by the organisers.

Looking south-southwest into the 'old' harbour, with the marina on the right  *Anne Hammick*

## Anchorage

After many years during which anchoring was discouraged, it is now accepted as necessary during the busier parts of the year, in particular for multihulls. Holding is generally poor over large stones, though there are some sand patches. The daily charge (see below) includes unlimited water, either from the reception quay or by can from elsewhere in the marina, and those at anchor are welcome to leave dinghies at any convenient point in the marina and to use the toilets, showers and launderette on payment of the usual fees.

Various large chains lie across the harbour, possibly dating back to seaplane days, joined more recently by abandoned ground tackle from smaller vessels as well as other detritus such as car tyres. Even a trip-line may not dislodge an anchor fouled by the former, while the latter can give a false impression that the anchor has bitten when it has not. Be warned!

## Formalities

Marina manager Armando Castro has an office on the upper floor of the marina administration building overlooking the reception quay. Formalities are generally completed on the ground floor, however, often by José Lobão who joined the staff when the marina opened and, in June 2016, will have manned the front office for an impressive 30 years. Both men speak excellent English and know their marina inside out. Office hours are 0800–1200 and 1300–2000 daily from 1 May to 15 August, otherwise 0800–1200 and 1300–2000.

The *Serviço de Estrangeiros e Fronteiras* or *SEF* (Immigration), *Alfândega* (Customs) and *Polícia Marítima* all have offices in the marina reception building, and must be visited even if clearance has already been obtained elsewhere in the Azores. The *SEF* keep the same hours as the marina office; the Alfândega and Polícia Marítima are both open 0900–1200 and 1300–1700 daily. In Horta the *Guarda Nacional Republicana* (*GNR*) are not directly involved, although copies of paperwork are forwarded to them. Together with Terceira and São Miguel, Faial is a 'border post' under the Schengen

Agreement – see page 51. Fortunately this does not entail extra paperwork, as clearance into Portuguese waters and the Schengen area are handled concurrently.

On departure the marina office must be visited first to settle the bill, and copies of the receipt presented at all three offices. There is no requirement to move the yacht herself back to the reception quay. If any of the crew are leaving by air it is necessary to advise the *Alfândega* a day or two in advance in case they should wish to come and inspect the yacht.

## Charges

Horta Marina is part of the *Portos dos Açores SA* chain, and shares their basic price structure – see page 55. Payment can be made using most major credit/debit cards other than American Express.

There is a flat rate for anchoring, applicable to all monohulls and multihulls irrespective of length. As of 2015 this stood at €6.08 per day – as it had for at least six years – and included unlimited water and other use of other marina facilities – see Anchorage, above.

## Facilities

Horta undoubtedly has the best facilities for yachts in the Azores, and in particular the continuing success of Mid Atlantic Yacht Services (see under Harbour Communications for contact details), vastly eases the situation for visiting yachtsmen needing to get work done. In addition to English, owners Duncan and Ruth Sweet speak French, German and Portuguese and have good contacts in mainland Portugal. MAYS, which is to be found opposite the root of the marina mole, is Azorean agent for over a dozen international manufacturers (including Raymarine – for which it is a licensed Service Centre – Volvo Penta, Yanmar, Vetus, Garmin, Jabsco and Frigoboat) and can organise importation and fitting of most items. The company specialises in engineering, electronics, rigging and deck hardware, but amongst its other services will assist with EU yacht importation (see page 52). They also run a free book-swap and display a four-day weather forecast updated daily. Office hours are 1000–1300, 1400–1700 weekdays, 1000–1300 Saturday.

*Boatyard* There is a small, open lay-up area in the southwest corner of the harbour where, in theory, DIY repairs and other work can be carried out. Unfortunately much of the very limited space is occupied either by long-term lay-ups or by abandoned and semi-derelict yachts, and though the marina office handle bookings and charges, a long wait is likely. Water and electricity are laid on, and workmen can be employed if required. Horta Yacht Center (see Chandlery, below) offer repair, maintenance and antifouling amongst their services.

*Travel-lift* A 20-tonne capacity hoist – though currently limited to 15 tonnes, 15m and 2·9m draught – stands in the southwest corner of the harbour. Book via the marina office, whose personnel operate the hoist and where suitable supports can be organised. Proof of insurance will be required.

*Diving services* Norberto, ☏+351 292 293891, *mobile* 962 824028, norbertodiver@mail.telepac.pt, with premises near the *clube naval*, primarily offers sport diving and whale-watching but can also handle underwater repairs or assessments. Nearby Central Sub ☏+351 292 249870, centralsub@sapo.pt, www.centralsub.com, also offer tuition, sport diving and whale watching, in addition to underwater inspection, hull cleaning and other work. Official permission should first be sought – see Port limits, page 51.

*Engineers* MAYS is agent for various international manufacturers (see head of this section) and has a long-established reputation. Engineering is also among the services offered by Horta Yacht Center (see Chandlery, below).

*Electrical & electronic repairs* Once again MAYS heads the field, with competition from Horta Yacht Center and João Neves, *mobile* +351 918 063427.

*Sail repairs & canvaswork* Ralf Holzerland ☏+351 292 293149, *mobile* 914 922111, whose work has been highly praised by visiting skippers over many years, will collect, repair and return sails, but does not make them from scratch. Sail repairs are also among the services advertised by Horta Yacht Center.

*Rigging* MAYS stocks 1x19 wire plus a broad range of swageless fittings up to 12mm and some rigging components for larger dimensions. Also among the services offered by Horta Yacht Center (see Engineers, above).

*Liferaft servicing* A technician/inspector from mainland Portugal visits Pico annually, usually in March or April, to service liferafts for local commercial craft. Over-wintering yachts may wish to have theirs serviced at the same time – consult MAYS regarding timing and transport. Most major brands can be handled.

*Chandlery* By far the widest range is available at MAYS, who manage to pack an impressive variety into their small premises and will order parts and equipment not in stock. The focus tends towards the practical rather than the showy – epitomised by their decision to limit clothing to foul weather gear, boots, gloves and hand-knitted caps.

Other sailing clothing as well as a more limited range of general chandlery will be found at Horta Yacht Center, *mobile* +351 926 890202, maresemarinheiros@hotmail.com, www.hortayachtcenter.pt, on Rua Vasco da Gama (opposite the Forte de Santa Cruz), open 0900–1200, 1230–1900 weekdays, 0900–1300 Saturday).

Finally Horta Sub, also on Rua Vasco da Gama, has limited chandlery, clothes and outboard motors amongst its large choice of fishing equipment. Hardware stores throughout the town sell reinforced hose, electrical fittings, etc. in addition to hand and power tools of all kinds.

*Charts* MAYS carry a good range of Imray books and charts, plus a selection of Admiralty charts and publications, independently printed almanacs, etc. and will order items not in stock. Not a cheap option for a boat sailing from the UK, however – an Admiralty chart will cost about twice as much as it would have if bought before departure.

The João Luis Copy Centre on Praça da República offers large-sized photocopying in addition to computer printing, etc. Note, however, that most charts and all pilot books – including this one – are subject to copyright.

*Showers* In the semi-circular building in the northwest corner of the marina area, open 0800–1145, 1300–1900, 2100–0700, 1 May – 15 August, otherwise 0800–1145, 1300–1630.

*Laundry* There is a large laundry room in the shower and services block of the marina. Normally attendant service by machine or DIY at large sinks, though it may

Yachts moored three or four abreast against the quay which runs south from the white marina reception building. The wall of the northern marina basin runs in from the right of the picture and the Observatório Principe Alberto de Mónaco (see page 75) is prominent on the skyline *Anne Hammick*

**II. THE AZORES**

Just a few of the many hundreds of paintings which adorn the marina walls at Horta *Anne Hammick*

sometimes be necessary to return to move one's load from washing machine to dryer. Open 0800–1145, 1300–1900 1 May – 15 August, otherwise 0800–1145, 1300–1630, but go early as there are only five washers and two dryers to serve the entire marina and a queue often builds by mid-morning.

Alternatively call either the Lavandaria Rosa ✆+351 292 391557, *mobile* +351 962 821723, which will collect and return laundry to the marina seven days a week, or visit the Horta Laundry, ✆+351 292 391911, on Rua Conselheiro Medeiros (the road leading towards the market), which also offers dry cleaning.

*Electricity* At all berths and on the marina wall. Yachts must provide their own cable and standard European plug, plus adaptor if needed (all components are available from MAYS, assembled or separately). 220v 50Hz is available in both basins, with 380v 3-phase in the south basin and on parts of the north wall.

*Fuel* Both diesel and petrol are available at the marina reception quay, and yachts are encouraged to fill up on arrival to avoid a return visit. The concession is run by the Clube Naval de Horta, and from mid-April to mid-August operates the same hours as the marina office (0800–1200 and 1300–2000 daily). Payment can normally be made by credit/debit card.

If more than 5,000 litres (about 1,130 UK gallons / 1,400 US gallons) are required, arrange bunkering via MAYS (see above) or Bensaude Shipping Agents Lda, ✆+351 292 293031/33, who have an office at Rua Vasco da Gama 42. Delivery is by truck to the south breakwater.

*Bottled gas* Exchanges of any cylinders other than GALP's own have been discontinued throughout the Azores, and though MAYS normally have a few filled Camping Gaz bottles available for exchange they will only accept empties in good condition. Otherwise most cylinders can be refilled (with butane only), via either the attendant at the marina fuel pumps, MAYS or Horta Yacht Center. Allow at least two working days, though if bottles are taken to MAYS by 1100 they will normally be ready for collection before the office closes at 1700.

*Banks* Numerous, all with ATMs. There is also an ATM in the marina reception building.

*Shops/provisioning* Several reasonably well-stocked supermarkets in the town centre, plus a vast Continente hypermarket on Rua Princípe Alberto do Mónaco (which leads uphill from opposite the old church at the south end of the harbour), open 0830–2100 daily. A branch of Worten (a Portuguese-wide retailer of electrical and electronic goods) shares the same entrance on the right.

Closer to home, the Spar 'Yachts Pantry' conveniently located opposite the Forte de Santa Cruz is open 0900–1830 weekdays, and 0900–1300 Saturday, closed Sunday. Alternatively Loja do Triangulo, a locally-owned shop selling fresh goods (grown and baked) as well as wine and handicrafts, sourced entirely from Faial, Pico and São Jorge operates from premises on Rua Serpa Pinto in the northern part of the town.

A good selection of souvenir, clothing, chemists and other shops will be found in the older part of the town, though see the note on page 47 if considering a piece of scrimshaw. Books on Azorean subjects in a number of languages can be purchased at Base Peter Zee and elsewhere, while the MAYS office houses an extensive book-swap, again in several languages.

*Produce market* A small fruit and vegetable market, with a fish market behind, lies towards the northern end of town. The best variety is generally to be found on Friday, but it is always necessary to go early for a good selection, particularly of fish.

*Hotels, restaurants & cafés* A wide variety of restaurants, snack bars and cafés, plus hotels and other accommodation ranging from four-star downwards.

*Medical services* Hospital, ✆+351 292 200200, outside the town – many of the staff speak some English – plus dentists and opticians.

## Communications

*Mailing addresses* C/o Horta Marina, Cais de Santa Cruz, 9900-017 Horta, Faial, Açores, Portugal; and Café Sport, Rua José Azevedo (Peter) 9, 9900-027 Horta, Faial, Açores, Portugal. Mid Atlantic Yacht Services, Rua Cons. M. da Silveira, 3, PT9900–144 Horta, Faial, Azores, Portugal.

*WiFi* Available in both parts of the marina and the nearer anchorage – ask for the password when checking in. Additionally, the Câmera Municipal provide fast free WiFi in the public gardens overlooking the north marina, complete with electrical sockets (look on the trees...). The Café Internacional, on the corner opposite, offers patrons free WiFi and mains power (a four-way adaptor is provided), as well as having its own computer/printer combination available to rent by the hour.

*Car hire* at least four companies, three of them on the Rua Conselheiro Medeiros, just inland from the marina.

*Taxis* Taxi ranks outside the Estalagem de Santa Cruz and near the market.

*Buses* Circular route around the island – timetable from the tourist office.

*Ferries* Regular departures to Madalena (Pico) and Velas (São Jorge), with less frequent services to Angra do Heroísmo (Terceira). See Transportation, page 48.

*Air services* The airport is about 10km from Horta, with services to the UK via Lisbon as well as well as inter-island flights. See Transportation, page 48.

# Praia do Almoxarife

38°33'·4N 28°36'·55W (quay)

**Lights**
**Almoxarife cables** Dir.Fl(2)R.8s9m9M
(daylight range 5M) Directional on 224·5°
White column, red bands 4m. Marks submarine cables

## Beach anchorage open to the east

An open bay 1·5M north of Horta, which can also be reached by bus, Praia do Almoxarife has a pleasant dark sand beach with clear water for swimming and a short mole at its north end with steps suitable for dinghy landing. It is protected from south through to northwest, but is recommended only as a daytime anchorage, and only after the completion of formalities at Horta. Care must be taken to avoid anchoring near the cables detailed above, but the red and white light strucure is easy to pick out somewhat south of the church.

Approaching from the south, Ponta da Espalamaca (Ponta da Baía do Cavalo on some charts) is fringed by off-lying rocks to a distance of about 200m, but the prominent church almost on the beach can safely be approached bearing between 256° and 296°. Good anchorage in 7–8m over sand and rock is to be found both south of the small quay, which has a water tap and a café at its root, and in a small bay about 500m further north, beyond Pta do Areal and the Baixa do Feno. Public gardens (including a children's play area), a campsite and the impressive grey and white church lie behind the beach to the south of the quay, with a few shops a short walk inland.

# Baía do Porto Pim

38°31'·48N 28°37'·67W (centre of bay)

**Lights**
**Porto Pim cables** Fl(2)R.8s17m9M
(daylight range 1·7M) 345°-vis-013°
White column, red bands 4m. Marks submarine cables

## Enclosed bay where anchoring is forbidden

Anchoring in the Baía do Porto Pim is forbidden, for fear of damaging the cables marked by the above light. It is mentioned here largely to emphasise that point, though there is nothing to prevent the crews of yachts berthed in Horta visiting by a dinghy which can be hauled up on the sand.

The northern edge of the Baía do Porto Pim is fringed with volcanic rocks, but in the centre the fine sandy bottom shoals evenly towards the beach, a popular spot with local people and visitors alike where a bar and (cold) swimmers' showers are to be found. Alternatively, if berthed in Horta the beach at Porto Pim is only 10 minutes away on foot. While in the area don't miss the *Fábrica da Baleia* (the old whale processing factory, now a museum) on the south side of the bay. From 15 June to 15 September opening hours are 1000–1800 daily, with shorter hours at other times.

Contrasting views north-northwest into Baía do Almoxarife, courtesy the Pico ferry and a commercial aeroplane. The dark sand beach (*praia*) can be seen in both *Anne Hammick*

An unusual view north over Horta, with Monte da Guia and Baía do Porto Pim in the foreground, taken from a commercial aeroplane *Anne Hammick*

II. THE AZORES

# Pico

Between 38°23'N–38°34'N and 28°02'W–28°33'W

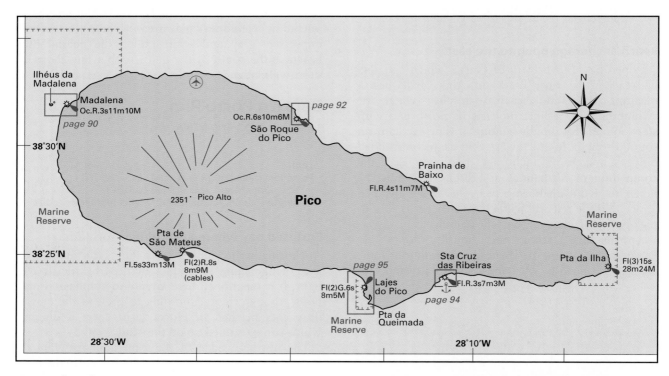

## Introduction

Pico is dominated by the 2,351m volcanic peak after which it is named and which lies approximately one-third of the way along its west to east axis, and for most visitors the sight of this perfect volcanic cone reaching into the clouds will be one of the most enduring images of the entire Azores. However, the mountain – often referred to as Pico Alto – comprises only part of the island, which is approximately 48km long by up to 15km wide, its area of about 445km² making it the second largest in

Pico wine was famous in the 18th century and is gradually making a comeback  *Anne Hammick*

the group after São Miguel. Neither is it the only volcano on the island. Small, isolated cones and craters dot the uplands, particularly in the western part, while eight small lakes lie further east towards Pico Topo, at 1,633m the second highest peak. Other evidence of volcanic activity are the lava beds known as *mistérios* (mysteries), legacies of eruptions in the 16th and 18th centuries and only now beginning to support vegetation. There are long galleries and caves in the slopes above Madalena and Lajes, caused by escaping gas bubbles as the lava cooled. The *Gruta das Torres* (Cave of the Towers), discovered in 1990 and just a few kilometres from Madalena, is the largest of these – in fact the largest lava tunnel in the entire archipelago – and has been open to visitors since 2005. Hard hats and lamps are provided, after which small groups are taken on guided tours (in several languages, including English) through the first 450m of the cave. Check opening times at the tourist office in Horta, then ask directions or get a taxi from Madalena.

A guide is no longer mandatory if wishing to climb Pico, though most who have done so recommend it as adding to the interest even if not required for safety. It is possible to book an entire 'package' including transport to and from Madalena ferry terminal – look for leaflets in the tourist office or the Café Sport. If intending to make the ascent

## Navigation

**Magnetic variation**
9°36′W (2016) decreasing by 9′E annually

**Tidal Streams**
The flood tide sets north in the Horta channel at up to 1·5 knots, and east in the Pico-São Jorge channel, maximum 1 knot. The ebb sets west and south at similar rates. Quite severe tide rips can build up around headlands in wind against tide conditions.

**Lights**
**Madalena north breakwater** Oc.R.3s11m10M
    White tower, three red bands 7·5m
**São Roque do Pico (Cais do Pico)** Oc.R.6s10m6M
    White structure containing red lantern, on wall, 5m
**Prainha de Baixo** Fl.R.4s11m7M
    White tower, red bands 3m
**Ponta da Ilha** Fl(3)15s28m24M 166°-vis-070°
    Square white tower and building, red lantern 19m
**Lajes do Pico** Fl(2)G.6s8m5M
    Green and white banded column 3·5m
**Ponta de São Mateus** Fl.5s33m13M 284°-vis-118°
    Lantern on white tower 13m
**Galeão cables**
    Fl(2)R.8s8m9M (daylight range 1·7M) 315°-vis-010°
    White post, red bands 4m. Marks submarine cables
*Note* The leading lights of five small harbours – Manhenha, Porto do Calhau, Areia Larga, Santo Amaro and Calheta da Nesquim – are not included here as being suitable only for local fishing craft.

**Coast Radio Station**
**Pico** 38°24′N 28°14′W, remotely controlled from Lisbon VHF Ch 16, 24, 26, 27 (24 hours)

independently, check in at the interpretation centre at the top of the single road (passports are required) to be given an electronic tracker to return on the way down. A charge of €10 per person is made – or up to €400 should you need to be rescued! Guide posts mark the way, with the next one or two generally in view.

The mountain's lower slopes are forested up to about 1,500m with shrubs reaching a further 500m, but the final 300m or so is bare lava, snow-covered in winter, rendered even more difficult by the 40° ascents and loose footing of ash and pumice. Pico Alto is crowned by a crater some 300m in diameter and 30m deep. Within lie steaming fumaroles – it

The 'path' up Pico, with one of the many white marker poles on the skyline *Mike Downing*

must be remembered that whilst semi-dormant the volcano is by no means extinct – and the 70m cone of Pico Pequeno (Little Pico), the highest point not only in the Azores but in all of Portugal. As might be expected, on a clear day the views from the summit are superb, though often the peak is blanketed by cloud. Certainly the ascent is only for the fit and energetic, with some parties opting to spend the night in the crater itself in order to watch both sunset and sunrise. The mountaintop gets extremely cold at night, even in summer, and warm clothes and sleeping bags are essential.

It would be a mistake to assume that Pico Alto is the island's only attraction and, other than perhaps São Miguel, it is probably the most popular of all the islands for touring by hire car or taxi. The scenery is surprisingly varied. As the road along the south coast leaves Madalena and winds through the heart of the wine area it seems to run between a maze of black lava walls, built with vast toil over the centuries to protect the vines from the Atlantic winds. Until recently many of the tiny vineyards which they enclose lay deserted and derelict, but now areas which have plainly been untended for decades are being brought back into use, such is the resurgence in popularity of Pico wine. In the 18th century *Vinho do Pico* was exported to America, England and even the imperial court of the Russian Tsars, but the vines were attacked by disease in the late 19th century and although replaced by more resistant plants from California have never recovered their international fame. While in the Azores be sure to sample the full range – a rich, pale gold wine slightly reminiscent of Madeira, light reds and *verdes* – all serving admirably to wash down a picnic lunch of the fruit and cheese for which Pico is also renowned.

Sometimes called 'the orchard of the Azores' – though this seems not entirely fair to its neighbours – Pico supplies much of the produce in Horta's market, including apples, pears, apricots, peaches, plums, oranges and, for those able to stay until late August or September, almost more figs than anyone can eat. Where the land is too rugged for vines or fruit trees cattle are pastured, particularly toward the eastern end of the island on the lush slopes of Pico Topo and its fellows. The result is several varieties of cheese – one dry, white and somewhat crumbly, one yellow, harder and reminiscent of a mature Cheddar, and finally what appears to be the only soft, French-style cheese produced in the entire Azores.

Pico was the centre of Azorean whaling until the practice was forbidden in 1984, with at least 300 carcasses a year processed at the factory near São Roque which subsequently reopened as a museum. The last whale hunt actually took place in 1987, as an 'act of protest' while the cameras rolled, though by then little of the animal was of commercial value other than the teeth. There was also a processing factory near Lajes, the chief harbour for the open whaleboats, where a whalers' museum has been created in the *Casa dos Botes* and the Whalers' Festival is celebrated each year on the last Sunday in August. Finally, in June 2014, a small museum opened in Madalena which concentrates not on killing or processing whales, but on the creatures

A freshly-painted whaleboat on the slipway at Santa Crus das Ribeiras *Anne Hammick*

A worn stone bollard on the hauling ramp at São Caetano on Pico's south coast – mute testimony to the hundreds of sperm whales dragged ashore for dismemberment *Anne Hammick*

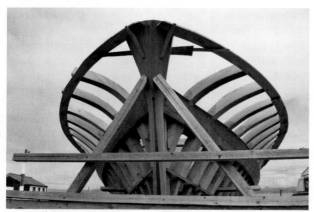

Traditional wooden fishing boats have long been built at Santo Amaro on Pico's northeast coast ... but are likely to go to sea with the latest in electronic charting and fishfinders *Anne Hammick*

themselves. Further details of all three will be found under the relevant harbours.

Both north and south coasts are punctuated by small harbours, or more accurately 'rampas', built mainly for recovering whale carcases and with launching boats a very secondary consideration. This explains their rough surfaces dotted with worn stone bollards – cranes are normally used to launch and recover modern smallcraft.

At Santa Cruz das Ribeiras a few miles east of Lajes, the building of whaleboats has taken on a new lease of life, something undreamed of a few decades ago, with several boats commissioned for export to New Bedford in the US. Not surprisingly most of the best scrimshanders in the Azores now work from Pico, producing intricate designs and carvings on whalebone or teeth, though the latter are becoming scarce and expensive (see also page 47). Lajes was the first town on the island and once its capital, receiving its town charter in 1502 more than 200 years before Madalena, and is now home to the island's only – if fairly diminutive – marina.

The north coast of Pico is generally more spectacular than the south, from the lava arches, stacks and sea caves at Cachorra near Madalena in the west to the almost sheer 415m cliffs at Terra Alta in the east. At Santo Amaro, a few miles down the road from Terra Alta – a road banked with hydrangeas, wild roses and yellow ginger lilies (known locally as *conteira*) – heavy wooden fishing boats are built and repaired. Massive timber frames are left to season, and then planked up as they have been for centuries, but there tradition ends. By the time launching day arrives the larger vessels will be fully equipped with the latest in GPS, radar, fishfinders and all kinds of radio.

More evidence of the 21st century lies near Madalena in the guise of Pico's airport, built more than 20 years ago but still able to take only small, inter-island planes. The vast majority of visitors arrive via the ferry from Horta, past the Ilhéus da Madalena, otherwise Ilhéu Deitado and Ilhéu em Pé (Lying Isle and Standing Isle), and into the sheltered waters behind the tall breakwater. Until this was completed in the late 1980s disembarking from the ferry could be hazardous, and in bad weather the island was occasionally cut off for days or even weeks at a time. If the silhouette of Pico has been likened to something out of a Japanese painting, perhaps Hokusai's famous picture of the white-crested, curling wave might sum up the islanders' relationship with the sea.

### Holidays and festivals

In addition to the national holidays listed on page 50, Lajes celebrates its official holiday on 29 June, Madalena on 22 July (when the Horta–Madalena ferry may run until 0130 or 0220), and São Roque on 16 August. The Festival of *Espírito Santo* is celebrated about six weeks after Easter, with the Feast of Saint Mary Magdalen on 20–23 July, Whalers' Week on 20–26 August and a Harvest Festival in September.

## Approach

The 2,351m volcanic peak after which the island is named lies approximately one-third of the way along its west/east axis. Lower peaks and craters form a secondary area of high ground (over 1,000m) further east. In good visibility Pico can be visible from well over 50M and forms a spectacular backdrop on approach to Faial – once seen it is quite unmistakable. However, the topmost part is frequently lost in cloud even when the sky is otherwise clear.

Other than the Ilhéus da Madalena and associated rocks almost 1M offshore due west of Madalena harbour there are no serious off-lying dangers, and 0·5M clearance when coastal sailing is a safe margin.

Three marine reserves have been created in recent years – a large one around the west end of the island, and much smaller ones around Lajes do Pico on the south coast and Ponta da Ilha in the extreme east, as shown on the plans on pages 86 and 95. See page 57 for details of restrictions, etc.

## Harbours and anchorages

## Madalena

38°32'·18N 28°31'·98W (breakwater head)

### Tides
Time difference on Ponta Delgada: +0003
*Mean spring range* 1·2m
*Mean neap range* 0·5m

### Lights
**North breakwater** Oc.R.3s11m10M
  White tower, three red bands 7·5m
**West breakwater** Fl(3)G.8s5M
  White column, green bands 4m
**Ldg Lts on 139°** Fl.G.6s16/20m5M
  White posts, red bands 8m, 128m apart
  (expected to be replaced by a sectored light in the near future)

### Harbour communications
**Harbour Authority**
  VHF Ch 16, 11
  ☎+351 292 642466, +351 292 623303
  0900–1200, 1400–1700, weekdays only

### Port limits
A circle, radius 1M, centred on Madalena molehead light – see Port limits, page 51.

## Small ferry and fishing harbour

Originally little more than an open bay, the construction in 1987 of a long north breakwater, and the more recent addition of a shorter one to the west, have much improved the protection in Madalena. Even so, some swell is likely to work in with winds from the western quadrant. Most yachtsmen still prefer to leave their boats in Horta and visit Pico by ferry, touring the island by taxi or hire car or – for the more energetic – scaling the heights of Pico itself.

The new west mole runs out from Ponta do Arieiro, incorporating a natural reef. The mole's inside face is sloping rather than sheer, and it is unusual in that there is a lower – almost awash – section near its root, apparently intentional and not the result of storm damage. In its protection lie two swimming pools, one natural and one not. Jutting out into the eastern part of the harbour is the new ferry terminal, comprising a short and partially covered pier on a northwest/southeast axis. Two long pontoons line the 'old' inner harbour, plainly intended for official and whale-watching craft but also ideal for dinghy landing.

The small town is a hotch-potch of attractive old buildings – notably the imposing church – and smart 'new builds', with only a few remaining semi-derelict ruins. It is worth a few minutes' wander, even if intent on going further afield, and time should certainly be earmarked to visit the small new museum mentioned in the island introduction. Unlike the various whaling museums, which either concentrate on the men and their fragile craft or the means by which the carcases were processed, the *Museu de Cachalotes e Lulas* (situated near the renovated windmill) is devoted to sperm whales and the giant squid on which they feed. Originally the collection of Dr Malcolm Clarke, it explains and

Madalena from the southwest, photographed from a commercial aeroplane *Anne Hammick*

II. THE AZORES

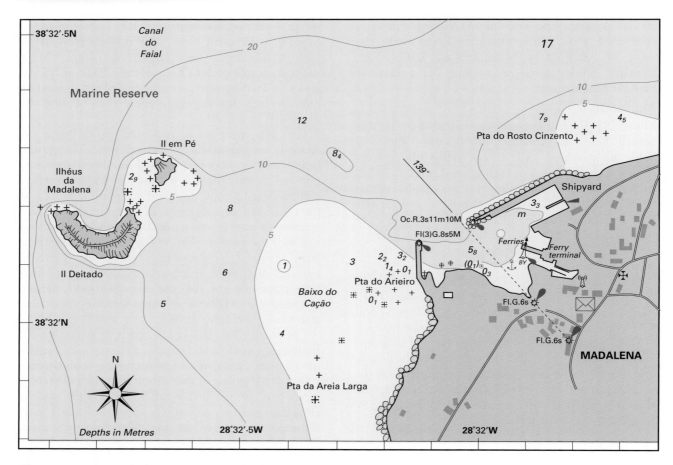

illustrates the whale's anatomy, biology and physiology in layman's terms – fascinating for those of us lucky enough to have observed these ocean giants from the deck of a yacht. Open 0930–1730 weekdays, 1330–1700 weekends.

### Approach and entrance

Approach is best made leaving the Ilhéus da Madalena to starboard, in order to avoid Baixo do Cação west of Ponta do Arieiro. The approach from north or northwest is straightforward, and although the leading line on 139° passes close to the end of the

north breakwater – which was extended at the same time that its opposing arm was built – it should still be followed. (Observation of the Horta-Madalena ferry confirms that it also favours the east side of the entrance). The ferry tends to depart at speed, as do some fishing boats, in which case hasty evasive action may be necessary.

### Berthing and anchorage

The additional protection offered by the new west mole has made securing to the north breakwater a more appealing prospect. 3m or more will be found

Approaching Madalena from the northwest, with the old north breakwater on the left and the recently-completed west breakwater on the right  *Anne Hammick*

almost to its root, the best option for yachts as the outer portion is often occupied by fishing boats. Some surge is likely even in light conditions, but it is perfectly tenable given good warps and fenders. Large bollards stand near the edge about 15m apart, with two or three iron rings set into the face of the wall between them – good anti-chaffing gear will be needed, particularly if using the former. There are no steps or ladders. The old ferry quay opposite has similar bollards, plus three sets of steps and several giant (and doubtless very black) fenders. Apparently it is still used from time to time, particularly in conditions of heavy swell, but that is no time for a yacht to be in Madalena anyway. Like most commercial areas, both spots can be noisy and gritty.

Prior to the construction of the west breakwater it was possible to anchor in the southern part of the harbour in 6–8m over sand, and there seems no obvious reason why this should not still be permitted, provided the new ferry quay is not impeded. (The new RoRo ferries turn close to the quay, driven by powerful bow and stern-thrusters and almost rotating in their own length.) An (unlit) north cardinal buoy lies southeast of the quay's end, and a spot southwest of this buoy in about 5–6m appears the most promising. Several rocks lie close inside the 5m line, making it necessary to eyeball in carefully in good daylight. Fortunately the water is exceptionally clear.

### Formalities

Unusually for the Azores formalities are very relaxed, probably because the harbour makes no official provision for visiting yachts. In practice, provided space is available and the boat has already cleared in at Horta, a short (two or three day) visit is normally permitted. The skipper should visit harbourmaster Sr Norberto Cardoso in his office at the south end of the new ferry terminal, but as he does not work at weekends and has no cover for illness or holidays this may prove difficult. There is no fee for berthing or anchoring.

Neither the *Guarda Nacional Republicana* (GNR) nor the *Polícia Marítima* maintain a permanent presence in town – both are based along the coast in São Roque – though the *Polícia Marítima* may call at the ferry terminal around departure time and combine this with a visit to any foreign yachts.

### Facilities

*Boatyard* Situated near the root of the breakwater, with two marine railways mainly used by inter-island ferries and small commercial craft, and acres of concrete hardstanding. A keel yacht could certainly be brought ashore in an emergency, but the area appears more suited to DIY maintenance of multihulls – rare in the Azores.

*Water* By can from taps at the small fish market overlooking the inner harbour (closed for renovation in 2015) and elsewhere.

*Showers* Swimmers' (ie. cold) showers beside the pool at Ponta do Arieiro.

*Fuel* By can from a filling station a few hundred metres along the road leading south out of the town. (There is a pump for fishing boats on the breakwater, but the fuel is untaxed and not available to yachts.)

*Banks* Several, all with ATMs.

*Shops/provisioning* Well-stocked supermarket directly behind the filling station mentioned above, plus other shops.

*Cafés, restaurants & hotels* A growing number of all three.

*Medical services* Small hospital, ☎+351 292 622241, just south of the town.

### Communications

*WiFi* At the café /restaurant opposite the new ferry terminal, and elsewhere.

*Car hire & taxis* No shortage, clustered around the new ferry terminal.

*Buses* Daily services along the north and south coasts of the island.

*Ferries* Regular service to/from Horta, São Roque etc – see Transportation, page 48.

*Air services* Inter-island airport on the road to São Roque.

Yachts alongside Madalena's north breakwater
*Anne Hammick*

Looking out of the harbour over the flat roof of the ferry terminal. The Ilhéus da Madalena are on the right, with the rounded hump of Faial's Monte de Guia in the centre
*Anne Hammick*

**II. THE AZORES**

# São Roque do Pico (Cais do Pico)

38°31'·85N 28°19'·14W (breakwater head)

**Lights**
**São Roque do Pico (Cais do Pico)** Oc.R.6s10m6M
    White structure containing red lantern on wall 5m
**Breakwater** Fl.G.3s11m2M 120°-vis-030°
    White tower, green bands 4m

**Harbour communications**
**Port Authority**
    ☎+351 292 642466
    0800–1200, 1300–1700
**Harbourmaster**
    VHF Ch 11, 16
    ☎+351 292 642326
    0900–1230, 1400–1630
    delegmar.sroque@amn.pt

**Port limits**
A circle, radius 1·5M, centred on São Roque do Pico
breakwater light – see Port limits, page 51.

## Harbour anchorage open to the east

Until the 1984 the site of Pico's largest whale-processing factory, normally accounting for at least a sixth of the archipelago's annual catch, a 200m breakwater was built a few years later to provide the island with a deep-water harbour and container port. Shelter is good from south through west to northwest, though the harbour is fully open to the east. Strong katabatic gusts can pour down off the slopes of Pico, almost doubling the mean windspeed.

The view of the mountain is superb, making the volcano appear almost symmetrical, and there are attractive walks in the hills behind the village. The

whaling factory, which closed in 1984, reopened ten years later as the *Museu da Indústria Baleeira*, with much of the original machinery still in place. Open 0900–1230, 1400–1730 Tuesday to Friday, 0900–1230 weekends, closed Monday.

In 2015 the finishing touches were being put to a small, L-shaped basin near the root of the breakwater intended for small fishing boats (no yachts!). This was probably the origin of persistent rumours that *Portos dos Acores SA* were planning to build Pico's second marina at São Roque in the near future, a rumour firmly denied by top officials in Horta.

### Approach

*By day* Straightforward. If coming from the northwest the green and white banded column on the breakwater end is visible from a distance against the town; from the east the dark chimney of the old whale processing factory is distinctive. There are no hazards if approaching from offshore, but if approaching from the east or southeast the Baixo do Cais and off-lying rocks must be given at least 200m clearance.

*By night* The breakwater light can be approached bearing between 130° and 295° and rounded at least 50m off.

### Anchorage and moorings

It is possible to anchor anywhere in the centre of the harbour, avoiding moored fishing boats and traffic to and from the breakwater wall. However, depths are great – 15m or more – and the bottom rocky, so a tripline is strongly advised. The water is usually very clear.

There are a number of moorings in the harbour, none occupied in May 2015, but few would care to leave their yacht on an unknown mooring even to visit the whaling museum.

Dinghies can be left at one of the small inner quays or adjoining slipways where whales were once hauled ashore.

### Formalities

Visit the *Polícia Marítima* in the *Delegação Marítima* (harbour office) at the west end of the seafront and the *Guarda Nacional Republicana* who occupy a building marked *Poste de Despacho* at the other end of the town, with solid arched doorways and a single turret topped by a handsome whale weathervane. It may well ease clearance if the computer printout which one is given in Horta or Ponta Delgada is available.

### Facilities

*Boatyard/engineers* Nothing specifically for yachts, though local skills clearly exist – witness the beautifully renovated and maintained whaling boats (now used for racing) and their original tow-boats.

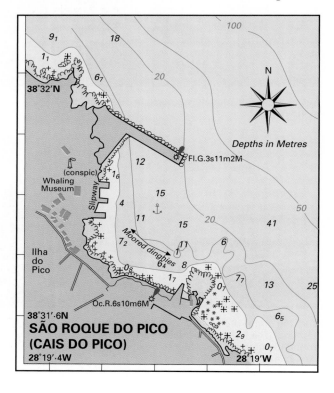

Looking northeast over the harbour at São Roque do Pico, with the old whale-processing factory on the left and São Jorge in the far background  *Anne Hammick*

**Water** By can from a tap at the rear of the *clube naval* boat store (it would be courteous to ask before helping oneself). Alternatively there is a tap let into the wall near the São Roque light structure.

**Showers** At the *clube naval*. Generally kept locked, but available for a small fee on request.

**Fuel** By can from a filling station on the road leading inland from near the São Roque light structure, or another about 500m along the coast road leading southeast.

**Clube naval** The *Clube Naval de São Roque* have premises near the whaling museum, with a large store full of sailing dinghies in addition to a busy waterfront restaurant.

**Banks** Several, all with ATMs.

**Shops/provisioning** Several small supermarkets at the southeastern end of the town.

**Cafés & restaurants** Along the seafront.

**Medical services** Small hospital, ☏+351 292 642328, outside the town.

### Communications

**WiFi** Free WiFi and computers in the tourist office / information centre overlooking the harbour.

**Car hire & taxis** Available, though not a place to leave a yacht unattended whilst exploring the island.

**Buses** To Madalena and elsewhere.

**Ferries** The regular service to Madelena, Horta and Velas (São Jorge) was suspended during 2015 while work was in progress at the root of the breakwater, but is likely to be resumed.

**Air services** Inter-island airport on the road to Madalena.

Pico's *Museu da Indústria Baleeira* should not be missed if visiting São Roque do Pico
*Anne Hammick*

The small harbour at Santa Crus das Ribeiras seen from hills to the northeast
*Anne Hammick*

# Santa Cruz das Ribeiras

38°24'·34N 28°11'·15W (molehead)

### Lights
**Santa Cruz das Ribeiras** Fl.R.3s7m3M
Red lantern on red and white post (the latter almost totally masked by the breakwater) 3m

### Small, attractive harbour anchorage

One of the oldest settlements on Pico, Santa Cruz das Ribeiras has a small fishing harbour protected from the southwest by a short breakwater and from west through to northeast by steep terraced and wooded slopes. In addition to being one of the main centres of whaleboat building in the Azores, several restored craft are kept, fully-equipped, in a boathouse at the head of the harbour. Their elderly guardians appear happy for visitors to look around, while a stroll along the road to the west may be rewarded by the chance to examine new hulls under construction by Sr João Tavares, who has built boats not only for use throughout the Azores but also for the New Bedford Whaling Museum in Massachusetts.

**II. THE AZORES**

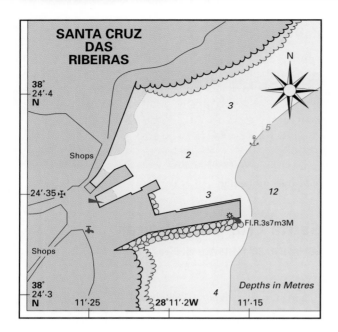

SANTA CRUZ
DAS
RIBEIRAS

Depths in Metres

## Approach

No problems from either direction, though if coming from the southwest the dark grey concrete breakwater may be difficult to identify against the rocks behind until bearing at least 010°.

## Anchorage and berthing

Anchor in line with the end of the breakwater in about 5m over sand, rock and stones. A tripline is advisable. There are several sets of steps at which a dinghy could be landed.

Rocks circle the end of the 130m breakwater – if intending to lie alongside do not close the face until at least 20m in. At least 2·5m should be found from there to its mid point, but it is important to confirm that no large fishing vessels are expected. There is nearly always some surge.

Few yachts visit Santa Cruz das Ribeiras, but *Menina* has been there several times
*Myra ter Meulen and Margreet Parlevliet*

## Facilities

*Water* Tap near the small crane on the inner quay.
*Bank* Not as such, but an ATM right behind the slipway.
*Shops/provisioning* Small general store in the village.
*Cafés & restaurants* Two cafés near the harbour, and a restaurant about 10 minutes' walk westward.

## Communications

*Taxis* Available, though it would probably be necessary to order by telephone Lajes or Madalena.
*Buses* Services to Madalena and elsewhere along the main road, a steep walk up from the harbour and village.

# Lajes do Pico

38°23'·94N 28°15'·47W (breakwater head)

**Lights**
**Breakwater** Fl(2)G.6s8m5M
 Green and white banded column 3·5m
**Port hand buoy** No.2 Fl(2)R.5s3M
 Red buoy, ■ topmark
**Port hand buoy** No.6 Fl.R.3s2M
 Red pillar buoy, ■ topmark
**Starboard hand buoy No.3** Fl.G.3s2M
 Green pillar buoy, ■ topmark
**Inner quay** Fl.G.5s6m3M
 White post, green bands 4m
*Note* For information only – do not even *think* about entering at night....

**Harbour communications**
**Lajes do Pico Marina**
 VHF 16
 ☎+351 292 672121, *mobile* +351 916 373052
 0800-1200, 1300-2000 weekdays from 1 June to 15 August, otherwise 0800-1200, 1300-1700, with flexible hours at weekends throughout the year
 marinalajes@portosdosacores.pt
**Harbourmaster**
 VHF Ch 11, 16
 ☎+351 292 672389
 0900–1230, 1400–1630

## The Azores' smallest marina

Lajes was the earliest settlement on Pico and its first capital. Hints of its past importance can be detected in some of the older buildings, including the two churches, and particularly in the engineering of the impressive hillside road running southwards out of the town. It was also the centre of Pico's whaling fleet, which operated out of the small inner harbour (the factory buildings are about 1km further north) now occupied by the archipelago's smallest marina. It is also home to the island's oldest whaling museum, the *Museu da Indústria Baleeiras*, appropriately situated on Rua dos Baleeiras almost opposite the harbour, open 0915–1230, 1400–1730 Tuesday to Friday, 1400–1730 weekends, closed Monday. In addition to the *Santa Terezinha*, a 10·75m whaleboat built in 1928 and on display complete with harpoons, lances and other whaling

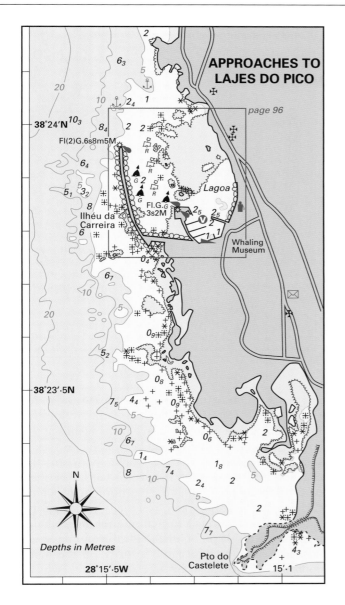

implements, the museum has a valuable collection of scrimshaw and whalebone items and a growing library on the subject, and is worth a visit whatever one's feelings are regarding whaling. Many of the best scrimshanders still working in the Azores live on Pico, several running small workshops in Lajes where scrimshaw and whalebone items can be bought (but see the note on page 47). Several nearby concerns offer whale and dolphin-watching excursions.

### Approach and entrance

The approach from the west is clear, but if coming from the south the banks between Ponta do Castelete and the breakwater are best given clearance of at least 600m (outside the 20m contour), until the breakwater head bears due east. Look for a red and white radio mast on a small hill, bracketed by a blue building with a grey roof to the left and a low white building with a brown roof to the right – the breakwater will come into view in front.

The breakwater and its inconspicuous light structure should not be rounded too closely (rubble lies off it following repeated winter storm damage), after which one turns south to follow the buoyed entrance channel. In all but the lowest of tides – best avoided, in any case – at least 3m should be found as far as the reception quay, but it is essential to stay well within the channel, particularly at the final turn to port – swing wide and on no account cut the corner. It goes without saying that first-time entry should be made at very slow speed, with a crewmember on the bow if possible. The water is extremely clear.

Approach at night, other than possibly to anchor off, is not feasible.

II. THE AZORES

Looking south-southeast into Lajes do Pico, with the six buoys lined up almost perfectly *Anne Hammick*

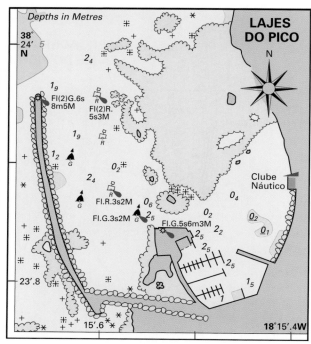

The quay at Lajes do Pico, with the white 'Whalers Monument'. Arriving yachts should secure to the pontoon at centre left  *Anne Hammick*

## Anchorage

The seabed north of the outer breakwater head is relatively clear of dangers outside the 5m contour. About 6m will be found over sand and rock some 200m north of its head, and there are other viable spots further northwest. A tripline is advisable.

## Berthing

Lajes do Pico Marina opened in June 2008 and, like most in the Azores, is owned and run by *Portos dos Açores SA*. As mentioned above it is very limited in size, and although there are nominally about four dozen berths most are only suitable for very small, shallow runabouts. The north side of the northernmost pontoon provides berthing for five vessels of up to 14m LOA, all alongside finger

pontoons in 3m or more, but as of 2015 the outer four of these were occupied long-term by locally-owned boats (one of which also had an anchor at the bow). In good weather it may be possible to tuck a small and narrow visiting yacht between the residents, but more often the visitor will be berthed on the floating pontoon at the reception quay, which currently lacks fresh water, electricity and security. (The latter not entirely a formality, after three whale-watching RIBs kept on the central pontoon were slashed a year or two ago). Security on the main pontoons is provided by electronic gates which, unusually, need a card to exit as well as enter.

The single yacht pontoon at Lajes do Pico, full to capacity in early July 2015  *Harald Sammer*

In light of the restricted size it is essential to make phone contact before arrival – preferably before leaving one's previous harbour – and to call up on VHF or mobile phone on approach. Failing this, secure to the pontoon alongside the reception quay in about 2·5m, which has a generous number of cleats. Having secured, spare a glance for the 'Whaler's Monument' erected in 2001 and the much older 'try works' and 'flensing platform' which form part of the quay itself (see also page 47).

Protection in the inner harbour is excellent, but surge may affect the reception pontoon around high water, and strong winds and swell from the west or southwest could make leaving a very dicey prospect indeed.

### Formalities

Visit the marina office with the usual ship's papers, passports, etc. Turn left on leaving the quay and walk a short distance up Rua do Baleiros. The well-marked *Polícia Marítima* is on the left, with the marina office almost opposite, on the upper floor. Manuel Hélder Silveira and his deputy José de Sousa Tomé both speak some English, José's being particularly good.

The *Polícia Marítima*, *GNR* and *Serviço de Estrangeiros e Fronteiras* (Immigration) will be informed of a foreign yacht's arrival by the marina authorities and may visit the yacht. Pico is not a 'border post' under the Schengen Agreement – see page 51 – and if arriving from outside the Schengen area clearance should first be obtained at Faial, Terceira or São Miguel.

### Charges

Lajes do Pico Marina is part of the *Portos dos Açores SA* chain, and shares their basic price structure – see page 55 – despite having almost no facilities. Payment can be made using most major credit/debit cards other than American Express.

In 2015 a 25% discount was offered to those berthed at the reception quay, but this will be discontinued when (if?) fresh water and electricity are laid on.

### Facilities

*Boatyard, travel-lift, etc.* Nothing at all, and nothing planned – another reason for being extremely careful on entry and departure…

*Toilets* Returning cruisers will be glad to know that the (underground) public toilets in the grassy area opposite the marina office are now cleaned regularly and are very much improved.

*Showers* The service block planned for the quay has been put on indefinite hold. In the meantime it is possible to use the free (cold) showers at the *Clube Náutico*.

*Fuel* A small fuel trailer is brought down to the reception quay most evenings to refuel fishing and whale-watching boats, and marina officials can arrange for yachts to refuel at the same time (at a somewhat higher price than the commercial vessels). There is a filling station at the far end of the road past the marina office, looked after by the shop next door.

*Bottled gas* Nothing available other than GALP's own cylinders.

*Banks* Several in the town, with ATMs.

*Shops/provisioning* Most daily needs can be met in the town, otherwise visit the large new shopping centre on the road north out of town.

*Cafés, restaurants & hotels* A growing number of all three.

*Medical services* Small hospital, ☎+351 292 672123, just beyond the *Polícia Marítima* building, with a pharmacy in the southern part of the town.

### Communications

*WiFi* Free service in the harbour area, including the marina.

*Car hire* Whale rent-a-car, ☎+351 292 627009, mobile +351 911 589905, info@whalerentacar.com, is an offshoot of one of the many whale-watching concerns and claimed in 2015 to have nearly 20 cars.

*Taxis* Taxi rank on the road north out of town.

*Buses* To Madalena and elsewhere – timetable from the marina office.

The 'flensing platform' and 'try works' on Lajes quay. Whales were 'flensed' to remove the blubber, which was stacked in circular depressions before being boiled up in the 'try pots' (small furnaces) *Anne Hammick*

The *Clube Náutico* at Lajes occupies three old whaleboat houses, but these days the boats are used for sport, not hunting *Anne Hammick*

# São Jorge

Between 38°32′N–38°45′N and 27°45′W–28°19′W

## Introduction

Variously said to resemble a sword blade, a cigar and a sleeping animal, São Jorge is a long, narrow island and literally the central island of the central group. It suffers the physical misfortune of being eclipsed by its neighbour Pico, even though it is itself something of a geological oddity. Nearly 54km long by only 7·5km wide, almost all the coast consists of steep volcanic cliffs, with low tongues of lava (*fãjas*) extending out to sea in a few places, and a high percentage of its 246km² lies above the 300m contour. Unlike Pico, São Jorge consists of a whole string of volcanic peaks, lower to the northwest, reaching their greatest height of 1,053m at Pico do Esperança roughly halfway down the chain, and then gradually losing height to the southeast so that the 942m Pico dos Frades stands well above its neighbours.

From a distance São Jorge reminds one of the serrated backbone of a sleeping brontosaurus, but this impression of a mountainous island is not entirely correct. The high land above the steep and rugged coast forms a rolling plateau, dotted with small white villages set amongst rounded hills, though from deck level this can be hard to believe. Sections across ancient volcanoes stand like plates from a geology textbook, with dipping and swooping strata of brick red, yellow, tan, olive green and grey, each with its range of tones and shadows. Bright green bushes of Azores heather (*Erica azorica*) cling dangerously to every niche, and narrow waterfalls tumble into the sea below. São

## Navigation

**Magnetic variation**
9°32′W (2016) decreasing by 9′E annually

**Tidal streams**
Tidal streams generally set east on the flood and west on the ebb at up to 1 knot, though countercurrents may sometimes run close inshore south of São Jorge. Tide rips can build up around Ponta de Rosais and Ponta do Topo in wind against tide conditions.

**Lights**
**Ponta de Rosais** Fl(2)10s282m8M 320°-vis-283°
    Futuristic concrete tower with vertical ribs 27m
**Ponta do Norte Grande** Fl.6s34m12M
    White tower, red bands 5m
**Ponta do Topo** Fl(3)20s60m20M 133°-vis-033°
    White tower, red lantern and buildings 16m
**Ponta Forcada (Ribeira Seca)** Fl.3s64m6M
    Red column, white bands 4·5m
**Ponta da Queimada** Fl.5s37m10M
    White column, red bands 6m

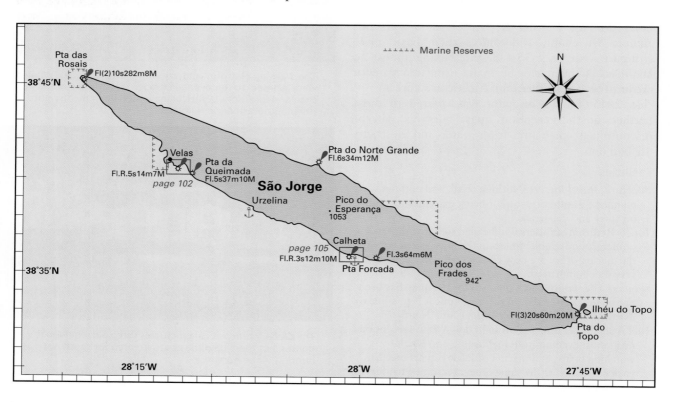

Jorge is seldom without its long, narrow cloud, whose dampness keeps the island moist without great rainfall. Vines grow on some of the gentler southern slopes, oranges, bananas and plums thrive, and the thousands of fig trees produce more fruit than can be harvested.

However, the real wealth of São Jorge lies in its fertile upland plateau where animals have grazed for well over 500 years. Although the early villages were built on the low-lying *fãjas* along the south coast, the clifftop land was slowly cleared, its timber valuable in itself. A small part of that native forest still survives as the Forest Reserve of Sete Fontes (Seven Fountains) near Rosais, one of three protected areas on the island. (The other, contrasting, areas are the tiny lagoon of Caldeira de Santo Cristo in the Ribeira Grande region, and the low-lying Ilhéu do Topo off the southeast tip of São Jorge, used as summer pasture for sheep as well as being a nature reserve and seabird nesting sanctuary.)

For decades the dairy and stock-rearing industries have been run according to modern co-operative farming methods, with carefully bred Holstein, Shorthorn and Friesian herds. With the whole economy relying on cattle, the flowery meadows of the upland serra form one vast pasture, the large fields divided by low stone walls or the familiar hydrangea hedges, served by modern dairies where milk from the entire district can be collected and processed. Perhaps it was the many Flemish immigrants who first began making the delicious cheese for which São Jorge is famous. Large flattened footballs weighing up to 5kg (11lb), a sizeable wedge makes an excellent edible souvenir which will keep without chilling for as long as it remains uneaten.

It may also have been the Flemish who introduced the island's characteristic thick coverlets and rugs, woven out of unbleached wool on hand looms and distinguished by their raised and textured patterns, second cousin to the Aran sweater. Another way in

Stress-free milking on a small farm in northern São Jorge
*Anne Hammick*

which the islanders employ their artistic talents is by decorating the island's quiet roads for the many religious festivals. A wooden pattern is placed on the road, leaves and different coloured petals carefully placed inside it, the pattern removed, and water used to keep the design fresh and in place. Hundreds of squares and oblongs may snake down the centre of the road for several kilometres before one encounters a busy knot of islanders slowly working their way forward – and woe betide any driver who runs his or her wheels over their handiwork!

A good deal of effort has been put into São Jorge's growing tourist industry and there is a small airport for inter-island flights, but most visitors still take the ferry from Faial to Vila das Velas, the imaginatively named 'Town of the Candles' or possibly 'of Sails' – either would be appropriate. Many arrivals are returning emigrants – the population dropped by a third during the latter part of the 20th century, but is now starting to recover – perhaps inspired by the story of the barefoot local boy who became an American ranching millionaire and returned to his native island as a major benefactor. His statue still stands in the main square at Velas.

Ilhéu do Topo off the south east tip of São Jorge, with Ponta do Topo lighthouse on the right  *Anne Hammick*

The bell-tower of the old church at Urzelina, all that remained following a volcanic eruption in 1808 (see page 104)
*Anne Hammick*

Like all the islands São Jorge offers many lovely walks, but it is necessary to work the buses (timetables from the marina office or the tourist office near the root of the breakwater) to access them. The downside (literally!) to most routes is that you start at about 400m above sea level, go down to the sea, and then have to make your way up again, but the scenery is stunning.

### Holidays and festivals

In addition to the national holidays listed on page 50, Velas celebrates its official holiday on 23 April with that of Calheta following unusually late in the year on 25 November. As elsewhere, the Festival of *Espírito Santo* is celebrated about six weeks after Easter. Velas Cultural Week takes place early in July, with a 'July Festival' following during the second fortnight of the month.

### Approach

Viewed from north or south São Jorge appears as a regular if rather serrated plateau almost entirely fringed by steep cliffs. However, if approaching 'end on' from east or west the island appears much smaller, with little of the plateau to be seen. The heights of Pico can often be seen over São Jorge if coming from the direction of Graciosa.

There are few off-lying hazards, and depths shelve steeply except around the fãjas (the lava flows running out into the sea) and at either end of the island, where at least 0·5M clearance should be allowed.

Four marine reserves exist around São Jorge – covering Ponta dos Rosais and Ponta da Ilha at each end of the island, a 3·2M stretch on the northeast coast, and the two bays west of Velas in the southwest, as shown on the plan on page 98. See page 57 for details of restrictions, etc.

One by-product of this returning wealth has been a building boom, with many new houses on the outskirts of the town positioned on the slopes to enjoy the imposing views of Pico, while from seaward the modern Estalagem das Velas hotel looks oddly out of place, as though intended for a Mediterranean resort complete with amplified music and crowded beaches. Another sign of increasing local wealth is the number of runabouts and sportsboats kept in Velas Marina. Local people have always owned small fishing craft, but boats kept purely for recreation are a luxury which is still fairly new.

Windows with triple-sashes are common on São Jorge, particularly near the north coast, but almost unknown elsewhere in the Azores  *Anne Hammick*

A lizard suns himself on a lichen-covered wall. A few damp crumbs or a splash of water are often appreciated!
*Anne Hammick*

## Harbours and anchorages

# Vila das Velas

38°40'·68N 28°12'·17W (breakwater head)

### Tides
Time difference on Ponta Delgada: –0003
*Mean spring range* 1·3m
*Mean neap range* 0·5m

### Lights
**Breakwater** Fl.R.5s14m7M
   White tower, three red bands 7m
**Velas cables**
   Fl(2)R.8s12m9M (daylight range 1·7M) 033°-vis-061°
   White post, red bands on breakwater 5m. Marks
   submarine cables
**Ship anchorage Lts in line on 304·3°**
   *Front* Iso.R.5s12m6M Red post, white band 9m
   *Rear*, **Ermida do Livramento**, 803m from front,
   Oc.R.6s54m7M Red lantern on small grey chapel 8m
   *Important* These lights indicate the offshore ship
   anchorage and are NOT leading lights
**Marina southeast mole** Fl(3)G.9s8m3M
   White column, green bands 4m
**Marina west mole** Fl(3)R.9s4m3M
   White post, red bands 2·8m

### Harbour communications
**Velas Marina**
   VHF Ch 10, 16
   ☎+351 295 432118, *mobile* +351 963 698900
   0800–1200, 1300–2000 daily, 15 May –15 August,
   otherwise 0800–1200, 1300–1700
   marinavelas@portosdosacores.pt
**Port Authority**
   ☎+351 295 412047
   0800–1200, 1300–1700
**Harbourmaster**
   VHF Ch 11, 16
   ☎+351 295 412336,
   0900–1230, 1400–1730
   delmar.velas@mail.pt

### Small marina in attactive bay
Velas has long been a favourite spot with visiting yachtsmen, though prior to the opening of the marina in 2008 visits ashore always required a weather eye open for southerly windshifts. With one's boat safe in the marina it is now possible to spend days exploring this beautiful island – and very well worth it. Dramatic 200m cliffs encircle the harbour from northwest through to southeast, with the breakwater – which is becoming ever busier with container ships and ferries – providing protection from the west and southwest. Having already been extended at intervals over the years, the breakwater will almost double in length when a 150m extension is completed – see plan overleaf. After several years of delay, work finally started in December 2015 with a planned finish date of late 2017 or 2018. Providing ample clearance is given while work is in progress this should not affect visiting yachts, other than improving protection to both marina and anchorage.

As with any commercial breakwater it should not be rounded too closely, even when complete.

The vast amount of new building in and around the town of Velas threatens to swamp the old town, though the superb view of Pico forms an understandable attraction. A high stone wall dating from the days of the pirate threat surrounds the harbour, its 18th-century baroque gateway unique in the Azores. Also of interest are the 17th-century parish church, where the usual black on white stonework is surmounted by an almost oriental dome, and the solid 18th-century town hall with its twisting basalt columns facing the well-kept public gardens. Much of the town centre is pedestrianised, and in an archipelago noted for its intricate stone pavement designs Vila das Velas has some of the most impressive.

An inexpensive taxi ride takes one to the *miradouro* (viewpoint) on the cliffs above the harbour, from which it is worth strolling down the old road, now a footpath, to appreciate fully the ever-changing scenery. If there is a swell running it is also worth walking along the seafront west of the *Estalagem das Velas* hotel to watch the lava arch blow-hole in action. About an hour after sunset the hundreds of Cory's shearwaters which nest on the cliffs above the harbour exchange their usual brief call for a peculiar 'ah-kee-kee-kee' at considerable volume whilst circling the anchorage. This tails off after a few hours, but may be heard at intervals all night and again at dawn.

A yacht race from Horta to Velas and back is organised annually for a weekend in early July. The racing itself is informal but the hospitality memorable, and the entertainment laid on – all part

Looking down on the harbour at Vila das Velas from cliffs to the northeast before work on the extension began
*Anne Hammick*

II. THE AZORES

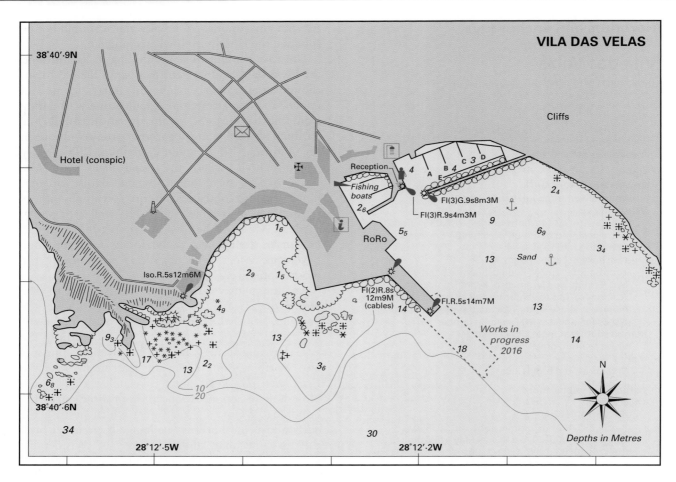

**VILA DAS VELAS**

of Velas's annual 'cultural week' – has included bull running on the quay (no injury to the bull), regional meals, coach tours of the island, displays of Azorean dancing and singing, and impressive fireworks. If in the area round this time the Horta–Velas race should not be missed.

Looking northwest into Velas Marina from the deck of a manoeuvring ferry, with the white-roofed reception building on the left  *Anne Hammick*

## Approach and entrance

*By day* If approaching from westwards, 400m offing should be maintained until the end of the breakwater bears at least 025°. There are no dangers from eastwards other than rocks close inshore around Ponta Queimada. The marina is hidden from the south until the breakwater has been rounded, when its narrow entrance comes into view straight ahead. Even with a ship alongside the breakwater, there is ample space to circle in the harbour if necessary.

When viewed from well above a pale area becomes visible in the marina approach. The photographer later checked it with a handheld echo sounder and found 7m, and a few days later marina manager José Dias dived on it and confirmed this depth. It is understood to be a patch of very bright weed which becomes almost luminous in strong sunlight.

*By night* Approach may be made with the breakwater light bearing between 333° and 025° – allow generous clearance as rocks extend some distance beyond its base. The marina is lit on either side and, with the considerable ambient light from town and harbour, night entry should not pose problems in normal conditions.

## Berthing

Velas Marina has been highly praised ever since it opened early in 2008. It is, however, quite small – only a dozen or so of its 79 berths can take visiting yachts in the 12–15m range – making it wise to phone from one's previous harbour to check that space will be available. Depth is not likely to be a problem, with at least 3–4m throughout. It is advisable, though not essential, to call on VHF or mobile phone before arrival to ensure there will be space and to allow staff to direct you straight to your berth, particularly during the mid-June to mid-August 'busy season'. Otherwise secure at the reception/fuel quay (see plan), though this position experiences the worst of any swell and is generally too uncomfortable for a long stay. The owner of a lightly-crewed 49-footer equipped with a bow-thruster states that he normally backs into the marina, as 'it makes it easier to pick a berth, or to exit again if there is nothing suitable' – a strategy not viable for all hull designs, however!

Visiting yachts are normally berthed on 'A' pontoon (see plan), which has four 10m fingers on its west side, shorter fingers to the east, plus a hammerhead. The fingers are substantial with pillars at their ends allowing them to berth longer and heavier boats, though beam may become a limitation, and two or even three yachts – the largest around the 17m mark – may be rafted against the hammerhead in light conditions. If larger yachts have to use the berths on the east side of the pontoon a very tight turn becomes necessary, in which case willing helpers and old-fashioned warping seem to be the rule. The hammerhead of 'B' pontoon can take another yacht of 15m or more.

Visitors may also be placed on 'E' pontoon, which parallels the southeast wall. The outer part carries around 4m, and though this decreases along its length all berths have at least 3m. It experiences least

surge, offset by a longer walk to get ashore. The inner parts of 'A' pontoon plus all of 'B', 'C' and 'D' are apparently reserved for local boats, many quite small, though a visitor of 10m or less might well be tucked into a vacant 'local' berth.

On the face of it the marina appears vulnerable to strong southeasterlies, in terms of both wind and swell, but it seems that conditions are at their worst when a southeasterly wind combines with swell from the west or southwest, as the swell rebounds from the cliffs which run southeast towards Ponta da Queimada. Fortunately such a combination is very rare in summer, but sadly it rules out Velas as a possible over-wintering venue.

Security is excellent, with the pontoon gate and the services block both accessed by magnetic card, even though the crime rate in Velas is very low.

## Anchorage

Anchor north of a line from the marina west mole to Ponta Queimada to the southeast in order to give the RoRo ferry room to turn – large ships normally back into the harbour. The bottom is a mixture of rock and sand, with a reasonably wide shelf within the 10m line. Although a few mooring buoys remain, these are very old and should not be used even in light conditions.

Even with the extended breakwater the anchorage will remain highly weather-dependent, with the ever-present possibility of having to leave at short notice. An anchor light should be displayed if remaining overnight and a tripline would be a wise precaution.

Dinghies can be left inside the marina provided they do not impede other users, and those at anchor are welcome to use the toilets, showers and launderette.

## Formalities

Visit the marina office on the west mole with the usual ship's papers, passports and insurance documents, though it is likely that marina master José Dias will already have come by to introduce himself. In common with all his colleagues throughout the Azores he speaks very good English (as well as French and some German), and is unfailingly helpful and polite. Checking in will be particularly speedy if the yacht has already visited Horta, as José should be able to access details on the *Portos dos Acores SA* computer system. As of 2015 José had no deputy, so on his (rare) days off, port captain Filipe Silveira (who also speaks excellent English) may stand in.

The offices in the administration block intended for the *Polícia Marítima*, *Guarda Nacional Republicana* (GNR) and *Alfândega* (Customs) remain unused as all prefer their old premises around the root of the breakwater. None need to be visited, though one or more may call by a visiting

Velas Marina on a busy day in July *José Dias*

**II. THE AZORES**

yacht, particularly one flying a non-EU flag. São Jorge is not a 'border post' under the Schengen Agreement – see page 51. If arriving from outside the Schengen area clearance should, in theory, first be obtained at Faial, Terceira or São Miguel, though flexibility is nearly always exercised in the case of a short visit.

### Charges

Velas Marina is part of the *Portos dos Açores SA* chain, and shares their basic price structure – see page 55. Payment can be made using most major credit/debit cards other than American Express. There is no charge for anchoring.

### Facilities

*Boatyard* Nothing suitable for yachts, although work is carried out on local smallcraft. In all but the direst emergency it would be far preferable to limp over to Horta.

*Travel-lift* No travel-lift or bay for one, though in an emergency yachts of up to 12m / 12 tonnes can be lifted by the harbour crane, which has a spreader and suitable slings. The yachts seen ashore in some photographs are all owned by local people, as are the props they rest on.

*Mechanical and electrical repairs* José Dias has excellent contacts, as well as being an engineer himself, and can arrange mechanical and electrical repairs, serving as interpreter if necessary.

*Chandlery* Very limited stock at Ciclo Agro Pecuario on Avenida do Livramento in the far west of the town, with a slightly wider choice at JRS & Irmão Lda, ☎+351 295 414263, *mobile* +351 912 259538 on the road to Urzelina (just past the windmill, before the town proper). Anything beyond the very basics would need to be ordered from MAYS in Horta (see page 82).

*Showers* Excellent showers in a block on the north side of the marina. Access is by card, but even so the building is locked from 2000 until 0700.

*Launderette* In the same block as the showers, with two washing machines and one dryer. Hours as above.

*Fuel* A pump (diesel and petrol) on the marina reception quay, which also serves the fishing boats.

*Bottled gas* Nothing available on the island other than GALP's own cylinders.

*Banks* Numerous banks in the town, all with ATMs.

*Shops/provisioning* Several supermarkets, the largest (open 0830–2000 Monday – Saturday, 0900–1800 Sunday), on Avenida do Livramento slightly west of the town centre.

*Cafés, restaurants & hotels* Many throughout the town.

*Medical services* Small hospital, ☎+351 295 412122, in the southwestern part of the town, with adjoining pharmacy.

### Communications

*WiFi* Good WiFi throughout the marina, also accessible from the nearer anchorage. There is no password.

*Car hire* Several companies in the town – a day spent exploring the island is particularly recommended.

*Taxis* Taxi rank on the square close west of the harbour. Some arrive on spec to meet ferries and other ships.

*Buses* Routes along the south coast and elsewhere, but not all return to Velas the same day.

*Ferries* Regular service to/from Faial and Pico, with less frequent links to Terceira.

*Air services* Inter-island flights from the small airport east of the town.

## Urzelina

38°38'·63N 28°07'·72W (quay)

**Lights**
**Urzelina** Fl.R.6s9m6M
Red lantern on white and yellow banded wall 4m

### Fair-weather anchorage

A small bay lying between Velas and Calheta, protected from northwest through north to southeast but heavily fringed with rocks, Urzelina offers an attractive daytime anchorage with very clear water but would quickly become untenable in onshore winds.

Several small wooden windmills stand on the low promontory to the west amongst overgrown vineyards, and there is a large sea cave a short distance east to explore by dinghy. Inland, the old church tower is the only survivor of the 1808 eruption of Pico da Esperança, when the rest of the village was buried beneath lava and ash. A former warehouse on the central quay has been converted into a small museum of rural life.

The coast on either hand should be allowed 400m clearance, heading in for the centre of the bay only when it is fully open. Anchor south or southeast of the small quay in about 10m over rock and sand. The quay has steps, a ramp and a small crane.

Water is available by can, and there are several cafés and restaurants serving the village and nearby campsite, a small supermarket and a bank with ATM.

Looking southwest across the central quay at Urzelina. A pine tree breaks the skyline near the centre of the photo, flanked by small red and white windmills *Anne Hammick*

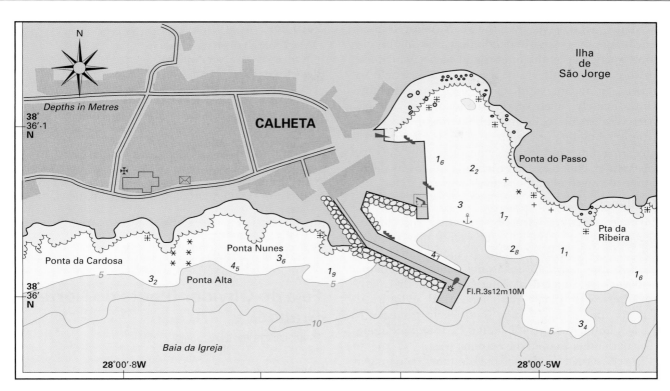

# Calheta

38°35'·98N 28°00'·56W (breakwater head)

**Lights**
**Breakwater** Fl.R.3s12m10M
  Red column, white bands 6m

### Quiet harbour behind short breakwater

Formerly a small rocky bay sheltered by high cliffs from northwest through north to east, the completion in 2003 of an entirely new outer breakwater – with a rather curious 'stepped' projection at its outer end – provided both ferry landing and much improved shelter from the southwest. Even so, some swell is nearly always present, especially at high tide.

The otherwise pretty Baía da Calheta is somewhat marred by the very derelict fish cannery at its head, said in 2015 to be due for conversion into a museum. Coincidentally, the Santa Catarina Cannery, the largest tuna cannery in the Azores, occupies a modern factory at the other end of town. Its produce has won international awards and is recommended.

The terraced and wooded slopes behind the old factory are most attractive and seem to be the haunt of many songbirds, while a fine view over the harbour and the Pico channel may be had from the conspicuous stone cross, a short, steep walk up the *Ladeira Velha* – an ancient cobbled lane between high, lava-block walls.

Walking westwards into town along the seafront road one passes Calheta's two most important landmarks, the 16th century Matriz de Santa Catarina and the Museu de São Jorge. Although victim of numerous fires and earthquakes over the years, the church's stone-bordered doors are a beautiful example of local baroque architecture. The museum (open 0900–1730 weekdays) is located inside a large and handsome house built in 1811. It contains two exhibition halls, and a library and bookshop specialising in the island's history and traditions.

### Approach and anchorage

The coast on either side is clear to within 200m of the shore, but a rocky, steep-to shoal runs south from Pta da Ribeira on the eastern side of the entrance, which should not be approached until the end of the breakwater bears at least 290°.

The quay and sort breakwater at Calheta, seen from cliffs to the northwest *Anne Hammick*

Many yachts have, over the years, enjoyed good anchorage over sand and boulders east of the old inner quay, but as the inter-island ferries which use the breakwater turn inside the harbour, it would be unwise to anchor south of its southern extremity. Unfortunately much of the sand appears to have been covered by rocks and rubble, possibly detritus from the building of the breakwater, but location of any remaining sand patches will be aided by the very clear water. Dinghies can be left on the slipway north of the old quay, or at the nearby steps.

### Berthing

Visiting yachts are normally permitted to secure to the breakwater, though larger yachts may need to move if a ferry is due, usually no more than twice a week – see page 48 regarding timetables. Large bollards are situated at intervals along the quay, together with black rubber vertical cylindrical fenders intended for ships (and likely to mark a yacht's hull). At least 4m should be found all along its length other than in the extreme west.

In very settled conditions the old inner quay might be a better bet, but inspect first by dinghy as, although around 2·5m should be found along its eastern face, parts are slightly undercut, said to have been caused by storm damage in the early 1990s causing some blocks to shift. There are steps near the crane, which is in frequent use and must not be impeded, and bollards and rings at intervals along its length.

### Formalities

Not a port of entry, though if going ashore it might be wise to take ship's papers and passports as in the past skippers have occasionally been sent back aboard to collect them – even when the yacht has only sailed from Velas.

### Facilities

*Water* From a tap on the old quay.
*Electricity & fuel* Not available.
*Bank* Several in the town, with ATMs.
*Shops/provisioning* Several small supermarkets, sufficient for day-to-day needs.
*Cafés, restaurants & hotels* Numerous restaurants and cafés, plus two or three small hotels.
*Medical services* Pharmacy near the harbour, and hospital, ✆+351 295 416498, on the main road above.

### Communications

*WiFi* There is said to be good (free) WiFi in the harbour area.
*Car hire & taxis* Both available, with a taxi stand just west of the harbour.
*Buses* Daily service to Velas and elsewhere.
*Ferries* Infrequent service to Velas and Horta.

## Fajã do Ouvidor (Ponta do Norte Grande)

38°40'·68N 28°03'·03W (quay)

**Lights**
**Ponta do Norte Grande** Fl.6s34m12M
White tower, red bands 5m

### Pretty bay open to the north

In settled light southerlies intrepid cruisers may be tempted to visit Fajã do Ouvidor, close east of Ponta do Norte Grande and believed to be the only viable anchorage on the north coast of São Jorge. Little more than a quay overlooked by a summer café, the surroundings are particularly beautiful even by the high standards of the Azores. Some swell is almost certain, ruling out the possibility of lying alongside, but there are ladders and steps at which a dinghy might be secured. The rocks close west of the harbour have been joined to form a seawater swimming pool, making Fajã do Ouvidor worth a detour if touring the island by car in hot weather. There are toilets on the quay but, apparently, no tap, and no other facilities except for the café already mentioned.

The pretty bay at Fajã do Ouvidor on the north coast of São Jorge, looking a little west of north *Anne Hammick*

The inner quay at Calheta, backed by high wooded hills – almost the reciprocal of the view overleaf. The small blue crane has been moved since this photo was taken
*Anne Hammick*

# Graciosa

Between 39°00'N–39°06'N and 27°56'W–28°04'W

## Introduction

The most northerly, and isolated, of the central group, Graciosa is a small oval island approximately 13km long by 7km wide with an area of 62km$^2$ – only Corvo is tinier. It is also the least mountainous of the Azores, Alto do Sul on the rim of the *caldeira* and Pico Timão in the centre both reaching around 400m and Pico do Facho a mere 350m. Thus it does not possess the drama of Flores or Pico, though the lower, rounded hills, covered in woodland or large regular fields and separated by wide fertile valleys, are indeed 'gracious' and at one time supported a population second only to São Miguel's in density.

Clearly visible from Terceira, by tradition the first Portuguese settlers came from there and landed at Carapacho on the southeast coast, probably in May 1450. From the first the island was prosperous, Santa Cruz receiving its town charter in 1485 and Vila da Praia some 60 years later, with the hardworking immigrants from Portugal and Flanders cultivating wheat and barley and growing vines on the *biscuitos* (lava fields) to produce high quality wines and brandy for export. Little seems to have changed – maize is grown in place of wheat, and cattle-rearing has become an important part of the economy, but 'Graciosa White' is still reckoned among the best wines produced in the Azores, though with the shrinking population (down from 12,000 in 1900 to less than half of that 100 years later) many of the tiny fields and terraces lie neglected. Each island has it's own favourite local

foodie treat, and Graciosa's are the tiny tartlets known as *queijadas* – sickly sweet and not to everyone's taste, but something every visitor should try once!

Until the late 20th century the timelessness of Graciosa's way of life was made clear by the number of horses and donkeys, and occasionally even cows, used for both work and transport. Walking in the countryside in the 1980s at least half the 'traffic' one

Whale rock, off Ponta da Barca at the northwest tip of the island  *Anne Hammick*

encountered was fuelled by grass – only logical in an island where it grows in abundance whilst every drop of petrol or diesel must be imported. A decade later, by which time the 5,500 or so islanders were said to own some 2,500 vehicles, no more than 10% of traffic had hooves, and by 2015 it was rare to see an animal in use on the roads. Even so there are still far more water troughs than filling stations and many doorways offer a ring, or simply a hole in a projecting stone, to solve the parking problem. Glancing upwards, though, the roof is quite likely to be adorned with a reception dish for satellite television ...

Almost all this fertile island is or has been cultivated, although there are few springs and fresh water has always been in short supply. The damp sea air and wells up to 60m deep combine to keep the lower fields green, but stone walls rather than thirsty hydrangeas mark out the dry hill pastures and banks of tamarisk fringe the sandy coastal roads. As a result Graciosa often appears browner from seaward than its sister islands. Also, and possibly due to the long years of intense cultivation, Graciosa does not seem to have the profusion and variety of wild flowers to be seen on some of the other islands.

Windmills dot the landscape, and though only one is still in working order many of their sturdy stone trunks have been converted into barns or houses. Each island has its typical style, those in Graciosa having a pointed wooden dome reminiscent of a giant onion to which the lattice sails are attached. A long pole allows this upper part to be manoeuvred towards the wind. Surprisingly, these very Dutch buildings did not arrive with the early Flemish settlers and were only introduced in the early 19th century when milling ceased to be a licensed activity using machinery driven by water or animal power.

Ponta da Barca lighthouse keeps guard at the far northwest of Graciosa *Anne Hammick*

### Navigation

**Magnetic variation**
9°30′W (2016) decreasing by 9′E annually

**Tidal Streams**
Tidal streams set northeast on the flood and southwest on the ebb, seldom exceeding 1 knot.

**Lights**
**Ponta da Barca** Fl.7s71m20M
   029°-vis-031°, 035°-vis-251°, 267°-vis-287°
   White tower, black bands and building,
   red lantern 23m
**Vila da Praia** Fl.G.3s13m9M
   White tower, green bands 4m
   *Note* Obscured 231°–264° by Ilhéu da Praia when seen
   from offshore
**Ponta da Restinga**
   Fl(2)10s188m15M 165°-vis-098°
   Grey tower and building, red lantern 14m

The waters around Graciosa seem almost as productive as the land, and a good number of larger fishing vessels are based in Praia. The stretch of rocky coast running south to the Ilhéu de Baixo is a favourite place for smaller craft using hand lines. Tourists are not yet an industry in Graciosa. Apart from the Graciosa Hotel at Portinho da Barra there are only a few *residencials* (guest houses) on the island, plus a few rooms available in private houses, and visitors are treated with polite interest. Offers of assistance and information may be proffered in strong American or Canadian accents, and on enquiry it generally turns out that the helpful local is a returned emigrant, who left as a young man (or woman) to make their fortune in the New World. Otherwise less English is spoken than in most of the larger islands, and one gets the impression that many of the educated young people leave to seek wider horizons.

One of the first yachtsmen to call at Graciosa, in 1879, was Prince Albert of Monaco, who led several hydrographic expeditions to Azorean waters in his yacht *Hirondelle*. Like many later visitors he was intrigued by the Furna do Enxofre (sulphur springs), a rare geological phenomenon inside the *caldeira* in the southwest of the island. A hundred years ago the crater could only be gained by a steep climb over the rim and an even steeper descent inside, but the modern visitor passes through a tunnel to emerge deep in the beautiful *caldeira* on a road which winds amongst pine and eucalyptus down to the floor of the old volcano some 300m below its rim. One may often see, hovering around the crater rim, the hawks or buzzards – *açôres* in Portuguese – from which the islands took their name.

Inside the *caldeira* several dark fissures cut into the earth, one guarded by a locked gateway giving access to a stone staircase spiralling 75m down the

The *Imperio do Espírito Santo* (chapel of the Holy Ghost) at Vila de Praia, decorated for the festival *Anne Hammick*

An old cottage on the west coast of the island, topped by a characteristically long and angular chimney *Anne Hammick*

rock face to the mouth of a huge cavern. It must have been a tiring climb for the adventurous prince, for whom a rope ladder was provided. The cave, probably formed by a lava collapse, is immense – some 150m by 100m and over 20m high – and contains a lake 130m across and at least 15m deep. For many years visitors were able to paddle around the lake in a small rowing boat, but the area is now cordoned off following an accident in which two people died. Several fumaroles emit a strong smell of sulphur, which has condensed into yellowish patches on the surrounding rock, and there are cauldrons of hot, bubbling mud, although the lake is cold and tasteless and presumably fed by rainwater.

There is a small charge for entry to the cavern, which is open 1000–1800 daily between mid June and mid September, otherwise 0930–1300, 1400–1700 Tuesdays to Fridays and 1400–1730 Saturdays. It is best visited around noon when sunlight streams down the narrow entrance to light the cave mouth, though electric lighting has now been installed. A Visitors' Centre (with information in English as well as Portuguese) opened in April 2010, both to explain how the Furna do Enxofre came into being and to give some background regarding the dramatic geology of the Azores as a whole. Real-time CCTV cameras give virtual access to those unable to handle the many steps.

On the south coast, near Ilhéu de Baixo, is the little spa of Carapacho, whose subterranean mineral springs must be associated with those of the Furna. Many years ago a medicinal bathhouse was built on a natural terrace overlooking the sea where the hot yellowish water wells up. That this is still not merely functioning as a spa, but has recently been renovated at considerable expense, is surely an anachronism in the 21st century – but then so, in many ways, is Graciosa.

## Holidays and festivals

In addition to the national holidays listed on page 50, Graciosa celebrates the Festival of *Espírito Santo* about six weeks after Easter, the Feast of *Senhor Santo Cristo Milagres* on 8 August and its official holiday four days later.

## Approach

Although Graciosa is the least mountainous island of the archipelago it is often visible from 40M or more when, from almost all directions, its three major peaks (which form a rough triangle) give the impression of at least two separate islands. Much of the coast consists of high cliffs fringed by inshore rocks, and if approaching from the south or east an offing of 0·5M leads clear of all dangers other than the two islands of Ilhéu da Praia and Ilhéu de Baixo. A deep-water passage more than 0·5M wide runs between Ilhéu da Praia and Graciosa on a heading of 329°/149°, parallel to the trend of the coast. A passage some 650m wide leads inside Ilhéu de Baixo, with greatest depths about two-thirds of the way towards the smaller island. If staying outside either island maintain at least 0·5M clearance. Off Graciosa's north coast, the Baixa do Pesqueiro Longo, with 5m depths, lies between 0·5M and 0·75M offshore and should be avoided if any sea is running.

Three marine reserves have been created around Graciosa – on the northwest coast around Ponta da Barca, surrounding Ponta da Resinga and its offlying islands in the southeast, and around Ilhéu da Praia off Vila da Praia, as shown on the plans on pages 107 and 111. See page 57 for details of restrictions, etc.

II. THE AZORES

## Harbours and anchorages

# Vila da Praia (São Mateus)

39°03'·16N 27°57'·95W (breakwater head)

### Tides
Time difference on Ponta Delgada: +0001
Mean spring range 1·3m
Mean neap range 0·6m

### Lights
**Vila da Praia** Fl.G.3s13m9M
    White tower, green bands 4m
    *Note* Obscured 231°–264° by Ilhéu da Praia when seen from offshore
**Ldg Lts on 307°** 293°-vis-321° *Front* Fl.R.2s8m6M
    Red tower, white bands on root of breakwater 4m
    *Rear*, 70m from front, Iso.R.4s13m6M
    Red column, white bands 9m
**Fishing harbour breakwater**
    Fl.R.3s10m6M Red column, white bands 7m
**Fishing harbour north quay**
    Fl(2)G.6s6m3M Green column, white bands 4m
**Approach buoy** Q(3)10s3M
    East cardinal buoy, ♦ topmark 5m
    *Note* Withdrawn as of August 2015, but likely to be reinstated
**Two red pillar buoys** both Q(3)R.4·5s3M
    Red pillar buoys, ■ topmarks
**Praia cables**
    Fl(2)R.8s13m9M (daylight range 1·7M) 264°-vis-292°
    White lantern on wall. Marks submarine cables

### Harbour communications
**Fishing harbour**
    ☎+351 295 712044, *mobile* +351 919 827647
    *Note* Both phone numbers are harbour manager Lázaro Silva's own, so should be used sparingly outside office hours
    pescadores_graciosa@hotmail.com
**Port Authority**
    ☎+351 295 712257,
    aptg.graciosa@aptg.pt
    www.aptg.pt

### Port limits
A rectangle extending 2·5M from Vila da Praia breakwater light – see Port limits, page 57.

The classic view northeastwards over Vila da Praia, as seen from the vantage point of Senhora da Saúde *Anne Hammick*

## Fishing harbour with anchorage

Until the main breakwater was completed in the early 1980s Vila da Praia remained an isolated fishing village – as in some ways it still is, despite the construction of a small fishing harbour which, is should be stressed, is NOT a marina. It took another thirty-odd years for the breakwater to gain a RoRo ramp, doubtless to the relief of the islanders who must have been very tired of craning everything from cars to cows ashore in slings, but the downside is that yachts are no longer permitted to lie alongside.

Neither is the town particularly attractive, with many of its frontage of terraced white houses with pink tiles now holiday or weekend homes – perhaps not surprisingly, since they overlook the island's only sandy beach. It appears to have expanded very little over the past thirty years, and still offers very limited facilities, though a visit to Santa Cruz will supply all day-to-day shopping needs.

Vila da Praia's principal charms are its total lack of sophistication and its people – it would be rare to pass anyone in the street without exchanging a

An unusual view of Vila da Praia from the southeast, courtesy of a commercial aeroplane *Anne Hammick*

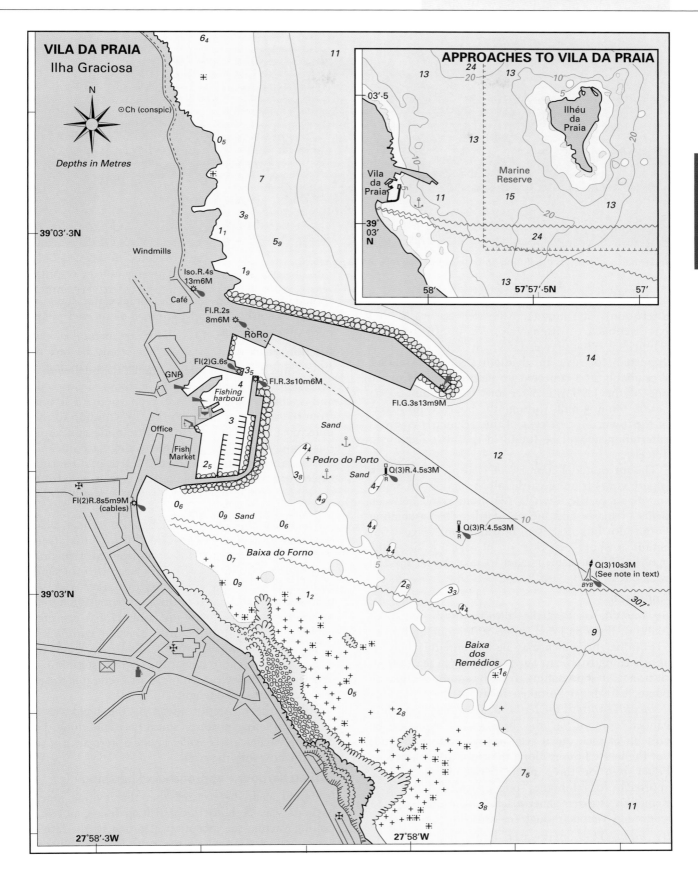

VILA DA PRAIA
Ilha Graciosa

N

⊙Ch (conspic)

*Depths in Metres*

39°03'·3N

Windmills

Iso.R.4s
13m6M

Café

Fl.R.2s
8m6M

RoRo

Fl(2)G.6s

GNR

Fl.R.3s10m6M

Fishing
harbour

Fl.G.3s13m9M

Office

Fish
Market

Sand

Fl(2)R.8s5m9M
(cables)

Sand

+ Pedro do Porto

Q(3)R.4.5s3M
R

Sand

Q(3)R.4.5s3M
R

Baixa do Forno

Q(3)10s3M
(See note in text)
BYB

307°

39°03'N

Baixa
dos
Remédios

27°58'·3W

27°58'W

**APPROACHES TO VILA DA PRAIA**

Ilhéu
da
Praia

03'·5

Marine
Reserve

Vila
da
Praia

39°
03'
N

58'

57°57'·5N

57'

II. THE AZORES

A German yacht enters the fishing harbour at Vila da Praia  *Anne Hammick*

smiling *bom dia* (good morning) or *bõa tarde* (good afternoon). In summer the streets, walls and pavements are often covered in (fortunately odourless) red seaweed, which after drying is exported for use in medicines and cosmetics. Presumably it is collected up before festivals, when one of the favourite diversions is the *tourada da corda*, running bulls through the boarded-up streets of the town. More details of this peculiarly Azorean entertainment will be found in the introduction to Terceira.

The surrounding countryside is also unspoilt, with superb views from the little hill of Senhora da Saúde southwest of the town, a two hour stroll between fields of maize and piebald cattle. The fascinating Furna do Enxofre (see Introduction, page 108) entails a short taxi-ride or pleasant walk – the majority of yachtsmen seem to take a taxi up and walk back.

### Approach

*By day* Vila da Praia lies directly inside the small island of Ilhéu da Praia, some 500m long and up to 51m in height, which may be left on either hand if approaching from eastwards allowing at least 300m clearance. If approaching from the south via Ilhéu de Baixo, care must be taken to avoid the Baixa dos Remédios south of the harbour. The green and white banded column on the breakwater end can be difficult to pick out if seen against cultivated land, but the white houses along the front are distinctive. Either two or three pillar buoys demarcate the approach for shipping, but provided Baixa dos Remédios is given generous clearance these can be ignored by yachts (though see Anchorage, opposite).

*By night* The breakwater light may safely be approached from the north or northeast when bearing between 159° and 220°, while from the south it would be wise to remain 0·5M offshore until one has picked up the leading lights on 307°. These should be followed until the breakwater light is abeam to starboard and the inner of the red pillar buoys abeam to port.

### Anchorage

Most ships berth port side-to against the breakwater, necessitating a turn inside the harbour on arrival, and yachts should therefore keep south of a line from the southeast corner of the RoRo ramp to the innermost buoy. Unfortunately fibre-optic cables run out from the beach south of the fishing harbour, and it is equally important to remain north of a bearing of 264° on their light (mounted on a projection from the white-painted harbour wall, a little south of the archway which gives access to the beach).

Much of this 'usable triangle' – which also contains the rock Pedro do Porto, not itself dangerous to most yachts but notorious for snagging anchor chain – carries 5–7m over large areas of sand alternating with smaller patches of darker rock. A number of small boat moorings (apparently seldom occupied, but not up to the weight of a cruising yacht) may be laid in the area, together with semi-submerged fish cages, while a loop of armoured cable has been reported near the northwestern buoy. The water is very clear, and it is far preferable to set the anchor in good daylight.

Despite the protection given by the breakwater, swell from either north or south may run along the coast, in which case consider laying a stern anchor to hold the bow into the swell.

### Fishing harbour – approach and berthing

It should again be stressed that the inviting inner harbour was built for local fishing boats, not for visiting yachts, the reception afforded to the latter depending very largely on the attitude of the person currently in charge. As of 2015 this was Lázaro Silva, who is far more welcoming than his predecessor and reckons to be able to fit in four or five yachts of normal size (11m/12m) at any one time – though he once berthed a yacht of 27m LOA and 3m draft (5m with her centreplate down). It is, however, essential to give advance warning, the ideal being to e-mail several days ahead from the previous port, then call Lázaro on his mobile when approaching. An alternative to the latter would be to anchor outside and go ashore by dinghy. It bears repeating that the numbers quoted under Harbour communications are Lázaro Silva's own, not those of his office, so particular consideration should be shown outside normal working hours. While Lázaro's English is limited, such is his desire to assist that straightforward communication is unlikely to be a problem.

Having made verbal contact, approach along the leading line (see plan), turning just short of the RoRo ramp to line up for the relatively narrow entrance into the harbour. Considerably more water is likely to be found in the final stages than is indicated on most charts, with at least 4m in the entrance itself. Yachts may be berthed almost anywhere, depending on the current situation, with the northeasternmost pontoons particularly long and robust. Larger and heavier yachts may be placed against one of the quays, the short extension to the east breakwater having much improved protection on the north quay which was previously exposed to easterly wind and swell. In the unlikely event that neither Lázaro nor any of his staff appear to direct operations and take lines, choose any suitable-sized berth as a stop-gap, but be prepared to move at short notice should its rightful owner return.

There is no security around the harbour other than a barrier for incoming cars, probably because Graciosa's crime rate is so low.

### Formalities

Formalities are very relaxed compared to most Azorean harbours. If in the harbour area Lázaro is almost certain to appear, otherwise his office lies at the north end of the block which backs onto the town wall. His official working hours are 0830–1200, 1300–1630 weekdays, 0800-1200 Saturday, but he claims to spend time at the harbour pretty well every day.

The only mandatory visit – whether berthed in the harbour or at anchor – is to the *Guarda Nacional Republicana (GNR)* in their corner office opposite the old fishing harbour. They require sight of the ship's papers and all passports, and being open 24/7 this should be done within an hour of stepping ashore (and again before departure). In 2015 all the officers were notably pleasant and helpful and spoke some English, but even so it may speed things up if a computer printout from one of the islands' true marinas is available, as this carries answers to all the standard questions.

Graciosa is not a 'border post' under the Schengen Agreement – see page 51. If arriving from outside the Schengen area clearance should, in theory, first be obtained at Faial, Terceira or São Miguel, though flexibility is nearly always exercised in the case of a short visit.

### Charges

There is no charge for berthing in the fishing harbour, possibly because visitors were not catered for in the original game-plan. This situation should not be exploited, however, and though yachts have on occasion stayed for several weeks, in the high season it is only fair to move on after a few days to make way for newcomers.

### Facilities

*Travel-lift* An 80-tonne capacity hoist equipped with two pairs of slings serves the harbour. Though obviously intended for fishing boats, if a yacht in trouble were to enter there is little doubt that all available assistance would be given.

*Water* On the pontoons but not on the quays, with reasonable usage permitted.

*Showers* Two (free) showers are planned for the block which backs onto the town wall (and which already houses six immaculte toilets). They may well be operational by the time this book is printed

*Electricity* Sockets on the pontoons, though it would be tactless to help oneself without permission.

*Fuel* The large green tank at the end of the fishing harbour breakwater contains diesel for the fishing boats, but it is untaxed and cannot be sold to yachts. The nearest filling station is in Santa Cruz, that on the road from Praia towards the *caldeira* having closed.

*Bottled gas* Nothing available other than GALP's own cylinders.

*Bank* Single bank, with ATM.

*Shops/provisioning* Small general store plus café/bakery on the front, with the larger Supermercado Melo a few minutes further south. Several hardware and other shops, but for anything else it is necessary to visit Santa Cruz.

*Café & restaurant* The café/bakery mentioned above plus several other cafés and snack bars, but no hotel.

*Medical services* Hospital, ①+351 295 730070, in Santa Cruz.

### Communications

*WiFi* Available free on the street behind the harbour, though not in the fishing harbour itself.

*Car hire* Both companies based in Santa Cruz (see page 116) will deliver to Vila da Praia.

*Taxis* Can be ordered by phone to come from Santa Cruz.

*Buses* To Santa Cruz and elsewhere.

*Ferries* An Atlânticoline RoRo ferry calls every two or three days, as does the occasional small cruise ship.

*Air services* Small airport close west of Santa Cruz.

**II. THE AZORES**

# Cais da Barra

39°05'·03N 27°59'·82W (quay)

### Shallow bay and planned marina site

A small, shallow bay at the extreme northeast of Graciosa, once a whaling station and barely 10 minutes' walk from Santa Cruz. The *Clube Naval do Ilha Graciosa* have a workshop on the south side of the harbour although their main premises are at Barro Vermelho some distance west of Santa Cruz. Several whaleboats – or *canoas* – are stored undercover, with a traditional towboat outside. Since 2009 the north side of the bay has been marred by a frankly hideous hotel and conference centre – an almost inexplicable lapse, when so much Azorean architecture is notably harmonious and beautiful.

Cruising yachts have occasionally used the bay as a fair-weather anchorage but, despite giving good protection other than from the east, it is not place where any skipper would want to leave a yacht unattended for very long. However, this is due to

Cais da Barra, where Graciosa's first marina is likely to be built, seen from Monte d'Ajuda to the southwest
*Anne Hammick*

change. Plans for a marina to be run by the *Câmara Municipal da Santa Cruz da Graciosa* (effectively the town council) were already well in hand when the 5th edition was published in 2011, when a completion date of 2015 was mentioned. Perhaps

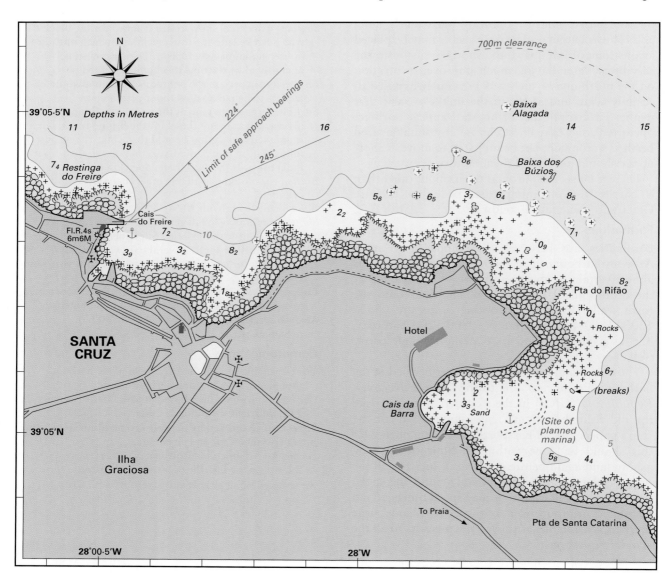

not surprisingly given the economic climate, this proved to be optimistic and in May 2015 work had still to begin, though it was anticipated for later that year.

The main breakwater will make use of the rocks which already give some protection from the northwest – the '*barra*' from which the bay takes its name – but even so construction will plainly be very weather-dependent. All being well it is hoped that the marina will accept its first boats – both locals and visitors – during 2018. There are likely to be between 80 and 90 berths, but possibly only five or six large enough to take the average cruising yacht. All will be alongside finger pontoons and supplied with water and electricity, with toilets and showers ashore. WiFi is anticipated, but it is unlikely there will be a fuel pump.

### Approach and entrance

From the south, an offing of 400m clears all dangers; from north and northwest about 700m is necessary to clear the Baixa Alagada. Enter when the tall white crane on the quay bears due west, by which time it should be quite clear whether work has started on the marina described above making it wiser to pass on by.

### Anchorage

Although a crescent-shaped patch of sand with 3m depth lies well into the bay, this has been reported to cover the underlying rock so thinly as to afford scant holding. An iron eye let into the rock (dating back to Cais da Barra's whaling days) may be recommended by local people, but the metal is old and sharp and if a warp is used it must be checked frequently for chafe. A few smallboat moorings may be in evidence, but it is unlikely that any would be up to the weight of a cruising yacht.

### Facilities

Currently none, other than water from a tap beside the gateway opposite the *clube naval* workshop. However, Santa Cruz is no more than 10 minutes' walk away.

## Santa Cruz

39°05'·33N 28°00'·46W (northwest mole)

**Tides**
Predictions for Santa Cruz are available via Admiralty *Easytide* – see page 54

**Lights**
**Santa Cruz** Fl.R.4s6m6M
   Red lantern on post 6m
*Important* For information only – totally unsuitable for
   night entry

### Pretty town best visited by land

With the building of first the airport and then the breakwater at Vila da Praia, Santa Cruz's importance as a port has largely died, leaving the picturesque little harbour with its four tiny boat quays deserted except for a few small fishing craft. Even the whaling industry is a thing of the past. A small, traditional harbour open to the north and east and nearly always affected by swell, it cannot be recommended other than as a daytime stop in exceptionally calm weather. Most yachtsmen will prefer to leave their boats at Vila da Praia and visit by road.

Looking southwest into the rocky harbour at Santa Cruz, from a plane lining up to land at the island's tiny airport
*Anne Hammick*

The pretty pink and white town is laid out around two small ponds – which originally provided water for both people and animals – and a spacious tree-lined square, giving Santa Cruz an almost Mediterranean air. Parts of the *matriz* (parish church) date back to the 16th century, though the rest is 18th century as are most of the surrounding houses with their distinctive wrought-iron balconies. There is a particularly good museum of island life, as well as a whaling museum in an old boathouse on the waterfront.

A steep road zigzags up the 130m Monte d'Ajuda behind the town, where three tiny chapels perch on the rim of a miniature crater in which nestles the island's equally miniscule bull ring. If driving, follow the signs and don't take fright at the short stretch of rough cobbles, which soon give way to tarmac. If walking, turn left off the cobbled stretch and take the old path – part steps, part steep slope – to the summit from which, until well within living memory, a permanent watch was kept for whales. As so often in the Azores, physical effort is rewarded by lovely views.

### Approach

From south and east an offing of 700m clears all dangers including the breaking Baixa Alagada. The Cais do Freire (which is inconspicuous from seaward) may be approached when bearing no more than 245°. From west or north the 5m Baixa do Pesqueiro Longo is best avoided, but 400m clearance is sufficient for all other hazards. The dangerous Restinga do Freire rocks north of the Cais do Freire will be cleared if the latter is not closed until bearing at least 224°, when the tiny Santos chapel will be seen just clear of the mole end.

### Berthing and anchorage

In very calm conditions yachts have occasionally berthed alongside the eastern part of the Cais do Freire, but depths shoal rapidly near the steps. Another possibility would be to secure 'all-fours' south of the quay (with lines to it and to rocks under the fort, and an anchor to the southeast) but this blocks access to the manual crane used to launch and recover small fishing boats and would be impossible with any swell running.

Alternatively anchor southeast of the mole end in 7–10m. The bottom is very rocky with poor holding and a tripline is essential.

### Facilities

*Water* Tap at the root of the Cais do Freire.

*Fuel* By can from the filling station near the root of the west quay.

*Bottled gas* Nothing available other than GALP's own cylinders.

*Banks* Three, all with ATMs.

*Shops/provisioning* Three or four small but adequate supermarkets in the town (the largest open 0900–1500 Sunday and holidays, otherwise 0800-2000). Although shopping and other facilites cannot compare with those of the larger islands, they are very much better in Santa Cruz than throughout the rest of Graciosa.

*Produce market* Small and rather sleepy market next to the Cultural Centre.

*Cafés, restaurants & hotels* Numerous cafés and snack bars, and several *residencials* (guest houses), in addition to the Hotel Graciosa at Portinho da Barra.

*Medical services* Small hospital, ☎+351 295 730070.

### Communications

*WiFi* Free service, plus power sockets in the *Biblioteca Municipal* (public library) overlooking the main square, where there are also several computers for general use, open 0900–1700 weekdays only. The signal extends over most of the square.

For computer hardware, software and consumables try Inforclick ☎+351 295 732325, *mobile* +351 919 523823, www.inforclick.com, on Rua Dr. João de Deus Vieira near the parish church, open 0900–1230, 1400–1800 weekdays, 1000-1200 Saturday. The helpful staff speak good English.

*Car hire* Two companies – Medina & Filhos Lda, *mobiles* +351 919 289538, +351 969 996644, www.medinarent.net, on Rua da Misericórdia in Santa Cruz; and Rent-a-Car Graciosa Lda ☎+351 295 712274, *mobiles* +351 918 449954, +351 967 869218, www.rentacargraciosa.com, at the airport.

*Taxis* Taxi rank on the main square.

*Buses* Services to Vila da Praia and elsewhere.

*Air services* Small inter-island airport west of Santa Cruz. Most services are routed via Terceira.

The miniature crater of Monte d'Ajuda with it's three tiny white chapels, which overlooks Santa Cruz from the south
*Anne Hammick*

# Folga

39°01'·06N 27°59'·99W

**Lights**
**Folga** LFl.5s30m4M
   White column, red bands on hut 5m
*Important* For information only – totally unsuitable for night entry

**Port limits**
A rectangle extending 1·5M from Folga light – see Port limits, page 51

## Rocky bay exposed to the west

A deep rocky bay on the southwest coast of Graciosa which used to be a regular port of call for the steamer from Terceira, Folga provides protection of a sort from northwest through northeast to southeast. Definitely a fair weather daytime stop only, usually with some swell, where a yacht should not be left unattended. Waves break on the rocky beach in even the calmest weather and it is hard to imagine how the steamer ever unloaded its passengers and cargo without mishap.

Folga is easily recognised by the village and windmills on the slopes behind. Once identified the approach is quite straightforward and the light structure can be closed on a bearing of between 353° and 095°. Anchor southeast of the slipway in 10–15m over rock – a tripline would be a wise precaution. There is a small stone landing with steps, but no possibility of lying alongside. The buoys in the harbour are understood to mark fish pots, and in no circumstances should a yacht be attached to one of them.

A seasonal restaurant overlooks the landing, where there is a water tap and some rubbish bins but nothing else. The village of Folga, some distance inland, has basic shops.

The small and rocky bay at Folga, on Graciosa's southwest coast, seen from the southeast *Anne Hammick*

# Carapacho

39°00'·75N 27°57'·53W (baths)

**Lights**
**Ponta da Restinga**
   Fl(2)10s188m15M 165°-vis-098°
   Grey tower and building, red lantern 14m
**Carapacho cables** Fl(2)R.8s18m5M 325°-vis-045°
   White post, red bands 3m. Marks submarine cables

## Anchorage open to the south

Unfortunately much of this attractive settled-weather anchorage off the *Termas de Carapacho* (thermal baths – see page 109) has been rendered unusable by the recent decision to route fibre-optic cables ashore at Baia do Carapacho. The light – which stands behind a thick hedge close west and slightly above the low white bathhouse, and is clearly visible in the photograph below – covers an 80° arc from 145° to 225°, and though it is unlikely that the cables spread more than 20° either side of 185°, testing this could prove very expensive.

It might be possible to tuck in to the east of the protected area, very close under Ponta do Carapacho, but it would be a case for eyeball pilotage in overhead sun. It appears from the chart that 7–8m might be found over sand with isolated rocks.

Taking a dinghy to the tiny quay below the baths is not permitted, as the area is reserved for swimming, but in flat weather – and Carapacho should not be visited in anything else – it is possible to land at steps let into a small quay, identifiable by its white-painted walls, about 400m to the southwest. There is a tap at the campsite overlooking the thermal baths and a café/restaurant nearby, but little else.

Looking southwest over Carapacho, with the red-roofed bath house, its tiny quay, and the post marking the fibre-optic cables in the foreground and the white walls mentioned in the text just visible in the distance *Anne Hammick*

**II. THE AZORES**

# Terceira

**Between 38°38'N–38°48'N and 27°02'W–27°23'W**

## Introduction

Meaning 'third' in Portuguese, Terceira was the third island to be discovered and is also the third in order of size, approximately 30km long and 18km wide with an area of just under 400km². Its western end is composed of a high volcanic peak, the Caldeira de Santa Barbara, with a height of 1,020m. It has a large deep crater – the largest *caldeira* in the Azores – and a lower plateau and fringing ranges lying further east. High cliffs and rocky bays comprise much of the coastline. The last major volcanic eruption occurred in 1761 when lava poured northwards towards the village of Biscoitos, but earthquakes have been a recurring problem with severe destruction in 1641, 1841 and latterly on New Year's Day 1980 when the capital city, Angra do Heroísmo, was particularly badly hit.

Terceira was first recorded in 1450 and soon afterwards settled by immigrants from the Low Countries whose fair-haired descendants can still be seen. The first villages were built in the southeast and the parish churches at Praia da Vitória and São Sebastião both date back to the 15th century. However, Angra do Heroísmo rapidly grew in population and prosperity due to its superior natural anchorage, for centuries being the most important town in the Azores and capital of the archipelago until 1832. According to Portuguese accounts, from it Martin Homem and João de Cortez-Real sailed to discover Newfoundland, Barcelos for Greenland, and João Fernandez Labrador as pilot with the English fleet led by John Cabot in the discovery and exploration of Labrador. In 1499 Vasco de Gama stopped briefly to bury his brother on their return

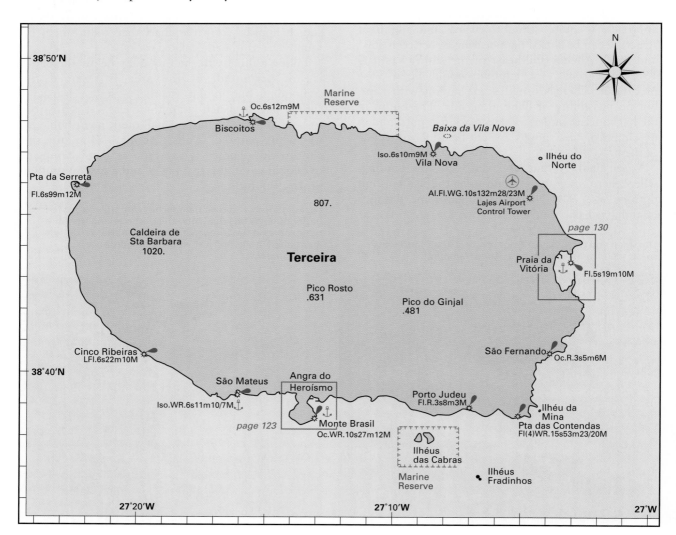

voyage from India. Only very recently has the harbour of Angra do Heroísmo been rivalled by that at Praia da Vitória.

During the 16th century Angra continued to grow, being granted city status in 1534, the same year that a bishopric was set up by Pope Paul III. In 1580, when mainland Portugal was dominated by Spain, Terceira became the last major centre of resistance. A Spanish force was prevented from landing on the beach at Praia in 1581 when the locals, lacking proper weapons, drove their wild cattle down from the hills and against the invaders, but the island finally fell in 1583. Phillip II of Spain quickly built the impressive fortress of São João Batista, commanding both the town of Angra and its harbour, to provide safekeeping for the gold and silver brought to the island by galleons returning from the New World, always a tempting target for pirates and privateers. Amongst the latter were Sir Francis Drake, who attacked Angra in 1587, and the Earl of Essex who attempted to seize an entire fleet of Spanish treasure ships at anchor in the harbour.

Even after Portugal regained her independence in 1640 and the Spaniards were expelled, small forts continued to be built around the island as a defence against the pirates – Spanish, French, English, Dutch and North African – who plagued all the Azorean islands in the 16th and 17th centuries. The deposed King Alfonso VI was imprisoned in the fortress of São João Baptista in the 1660s, a foretaste of its much later use as a prison for captured German

Porto Martins on Terceira's east coast does not have its own lighthouse. Instead it has a bus shelter... *Anne Hammick*

troops during the First World War. Terceira's last major role in Portuguese politics was its support of the Liberalists in 1829. The right-wing Absolutists were prevented from landing at Praia – earning its *da Vitória* title – swiftly followed by the award *of do Heroísmo* to the city of Angra by the Liberalist Regency established there.

The lessening importance of Angra as a port was to some extent compensated by the construction at

Lagoa das Patas (lake of the ducks) in the foothills of Monte Santa Barbara  *Anne Hammick*

**II. THE AZORES**

Every country village in Terceira has its *Imperio do Espírito Santo*, often painted in bright primary colours
*Anne Hammick*

Lajes of the Azores' first major airport, built by the RAF in 1943. Part was leased to the US in 1947 when the airport at Santa Maria was returned to the Portuguese and many American servicemen are still based on the island. As well as being an important NATO airfield it serves as the headquarters of the Portuguese Azores Air Command and as Terceira's civil airport.

Although Terceira, with a population of around 60,000, is one of the more densely populated islands, the impression from a distance – and particularly from the sea – is one of spaciousness. This may be partly due to the wise decision, taken some years ago, not to permit unnecessary building above the 200m contour. The south and east have long been cleared for farming, while the upper slopes were unfenced grazing until the 18th century when walls were built by government order – and promptly destroyed by the locals. As a result the fields are large and regular, in contrast to the small and generally random effect prevalent in the other islands. Pastoral farming remains an important industry.

Further north and west more of the native forest of pine, laurel and eucalyptus survives, with moorland and scrub on the upper slopes which are often blanketed by mist or low clouds even though at sea level it may be pleasantly sunny and warm. Thus the majority of villages are near the coast, characterised by low whitewashed cottages with odd wedge-shaped chimneys vented near the top by a few missing bricks. Particularly around Angra, casement windows give way to sash frames, often in three overlapping parts, while cottage gardens are obviously a source of pride with roses and chrysanthemums vying for space with hibiscus and bougainvillaea.

On the north coast around Biscoitos vines are grown in tiny plots surrounded by protective lava-block walls. Even the soil seems to be mostly pumice, and apparently it is the iron oxide in the stone which gives the wine its distinctive smell and flavour – making it something of an acquired taste. The wine museum, set up in an old farmhouse and displaying tools, documents, photographs and even dried rootstocks, is well worth a visit.

Also worth visiting are the caverns at Algar do Carvão, about 14km north of Angra do Heroísmo, and the nearby fumaroles at Furnas do Enxofre. Not fully explored until the 1960s, the caves extend at least 100m underground and, as in Graciosa, contain a small subterranean lake. Originally access was via a narrow vertical shaft, but in 1996 a tunnel was dug and electric light laid on. Steps and galleries allow the visitor to move around easily, though since the earthquake of 1980 it has not been possible to reach the further part of the system. The caves are open daily from June to September inclusive, with a small entrance fee.

All over Terceira one sees brightly painted *Imperios do Espírito Santo* – literally Empires or Theatres of the Holy Ghost – tiny chapels with windows on three sides and often a balcony, used for displaying the silver crown, dove and sceptre associated with the festivals of *Espirito Santo* which mainly take place during June. The other typically Azorean entertainment is the tourada da corda, the local version of the Portuguese bullfight, when the animals are allowed to career through the village streets whilst the local youths show off their courage and daring, cheered on by spectators from safe vantage points. Two or three men check the bull's movements by means of a long rope, and although it is teased to the point of exhaustion – brightly coloured T-shirts and umbrellas are the modern substitute for the cape – no bull is killed or seriously injured. It has been suggested that the *tourada da corda* goes back to the day over 400 years ago when the Spanish invaders were driven back into the sea from the beaches at Praia da Vitória. *Tourada da corda* can be held any time from May until October, with dates and venues available from tourist offices.

Certainly Terceira is an island with a proud history, and it was a tragedy that so many of its ancient buildings were severely damaged by the earthquake referred to previously. Fortunately most people were outside celebrating the New Year and escaped injury, but 64 people died and three-quarters of Angra's buildings were affected. Now all are repaired and the atmosphere is prosperous, perhaps due partly to the American presence on the island, though this is unobtrusive.

## Holidays and festivals

In addition to the national holidays listed on page 50, Angra do Heroísmo celebrates its official holiday on 24 June. Known as *Sanjoaninas*, these festivities can lead to serious congestion in the marina, which does not accept advance reservations. If planning to attend it is wise to arrive several days in advance.

The local holiday at Praia da Vitória occurs on 20 June, with the Mid Atlantic Gastronomic Festival taking place over ten days in early August, complete with bands on the promenade and events on the beach.

Festivals of *Espírito Santo* take place all through the Azores about six weeks after Easter, but are particularly popular in Terceira where the *Imperios do Espírito Santo* are decorated and filled with offerings, and bread and wine offered to passers by.

## Approach

Terceira is one of the higher islands in the Azores, and the hills which lie close behind much of its coastline make it visible from a considerable distance. Even before the advent of GPS Terceira was considered a relatively easy landfall, although there are a few offlying hazards, most unlit. When closing the southeast coast the Ilhéus Fradinhos, some 10m in height and lying about 2M offshore at 38°36'·66N 27°06'·64W, are clearly visible by day but unlit at night though covered by a red sector of Ponta das Contendas light, as are the Ilhéus das Cabras. (A passage exists between the two Ilhéus das Cabras carrying a least depth of some 8m, but caution should be exercised due to strong and unpredictable currents). Other possible hazards are the Ilha da Mina, close off the headland of that name, the Ilhéu do Norte just over 0·5M offshore from Lajes on the northeast coast, and the breaking shoal known as the Baixa da Vila Nova, off the town and tiny inlet of that name a few miles to the west. In rough weather it would also be wise to avoid the Baixa da Serreta, 2M off Ponta Serreta on the west coast and shoaling to 8m, where bad seas might be expected.

According to a note in the *Avisos aos Navegantes*, published online by the Portuguese Hydrographic Institute, in late 2012 intense volcanic activity was taking place near Ponta da Serreta. Volcanic outcrops and gas releases were to be expected, as well as changes in minimum depths and floating obstacles to navigation. The activity has not been

## Navigation

**Magnetic variation**
9°11'W (2016) decreasing by 9'E annually

**Tidal Streams**
Tidal streams set north or east on the flood and south or west on the ebb, but seldom reach 1 knot.

**Lights**
**Ponta da Serreta** Fl.6s99m12M
    White tower, red bands 14m
**Lajes Airport** Aero
    Al.Fl.WG.10s132m28/23M Control tower 19m
**Praia da Vitória**, north breakwater Fl.5s19m10M
    White column, black bands with 'basket' top 9m
**Ponta das Contendas** Fl(4)WR.15s53m23/20M
    220°-W-020°-R-044°-W-072°-R-073° 079°-R-093°
    (Obscured 073°-079° by Ilhéu das Cabras)
    Square white tower and building, red lantern 13m
**Monte Brasil (Ponta do Farol)**
    Oc.WR.10s27m12M 191°-R-295°-W-057°
    White column, red bands 5m
**Cinco Ribeiras** LFl.6s22m10M
    White pyramid, red bands 2m
*Note* The lights of Porto Judeu and São Fernando (Ribeira Seca), both on the southeast coast, and Vila Nova, on the north coast, are omitted due to their total unsuitability for yachts

mentioned again, but take particular care if in the area. As if that were not enough, Admiralty chart 1956 bears a note that 'Aircraft may occasionally jettison external loads within the area indicated on this chart', the area concerned being a circle 10M in diameter centred just over 10M north of the eastern end of Terceira. Exactly what these 'external loads' may consist of it not specified, but some may prefer to avoid the area on principle.

Finally, careful navigation is essential if on passage towards Terceira from São Miguel, particularly in poor weather, as the unmarked Banco Dom João de Castro shoal lies only 5M west of the direct course between the two (see plan page 38). Although the shoal – the tip of a subterranean volcano – has broken the surface at least once during the last 500 years it is currently charted at 12m. This was confirmed in 1999 by the crew of a yacht who carried out several dives on the bank, but as there is ongoing seismic activity in the area depths could decrease at any time. They pinpointed the least depth to be at 38°13'·37N 26°36'·36W, and within 100m of this spot were off soundings. As one might expect, seas break heavily on the bank in strong winds.

Three marine reserves have been created around Terceira – on the north coast between Biscoitos and Vila Nova, around the Ilhéus das Cabras off the south coast, and a smaller area around Monte Brasil, as shown on the plans on pages 118 and 123. See page 57 for details of restrictions, etc.

## Harbours and anchorages

# Angra do Heroísmo

38°39'·05N 27°12'·93W (Porto das Pipas molehead)

### Tides
Predictions for Angra do Heroísmo are available via Admiralty *EasyTide* – see page 54
Time difference on Ponta Delgada: –0004
*Mean spring range* 1·4m
*Mean neap range* 0·6m

### Lights
**Monte Brasil (Ponta do Farol)**
Oc.WR.10s27m12M 191°-R-295°-W-057°
White column, red bands 5m
**Ldg Lts on 341°** *Front* Fl.R.4s20m7M
Red post near church 2m
*Rear*, 505m from front, Oc.R.6s61m7M
Yellow metal structure, red top 2m
**Porto das Pipas molehead** Fl.G.3s13m6M
White column, green bands 5m
**Marina south mole** Fl(2)R.6s8m3M
White cone, red bands 3m

### Harbour communications
**Marina d'Angra**
VHF Ch 09, 16
☏+351 295 540000, +351 295 212304
0800–2000 from 15 May to 15 September, 0800–1700 at other times
marinaangra@portosdosacores.pt
**Port Authority**
VHF Ch 11, 14, 16
☏+351 295 540000
0900–1200, 1300–1700
aptg.sa@aptg.pt
www.aptg.pt

### Port limits
A rectangle extending 2·5M from Porto das Pipas molehead light – see Port limits, page 51.

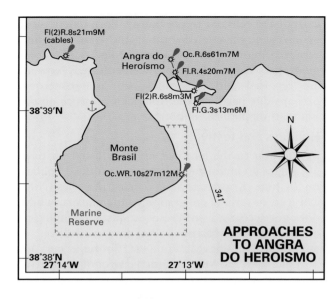

**APPROACHES TO ANGRA DO HEROISMO**

## Marina adjoining UNESCO World Heritage city

One of the most handsome natural harbours in the Azores, Angra do Heroísmo is protected by high land from all directions other than southeast, though swell sets in with winds from anywhere between south and east. Yachts at anchor had always to be ready to leave the harbour at short notice, often curtailing exploration beyond the immediate city, but that is now a thing of the past thanks to the long, narrow marina which lies directly beneath the old sea wall. Plans for the marina were approved in the mid-1990s, but work had barely started when a historic wreck – thought to be that of a 16th- or 17th-century galleon – was discovered on the harbour bed and operations were suspended while archaeologists investigated the site. Construction resumed in 1999 and by June 2001 it was effectively complete, though without much of its shoreside infrastructure.

From early days the harbour was used by vessels trading to Africa, India and the Americas, bringing wealth and importance to the settlement which was

Marina d'Angra seen from the west, with the Porto das Pipas boatyard on the right and the city to the left. The angular white Angra Marina Hotel is visible from several miles offshore *Anne Hammick*

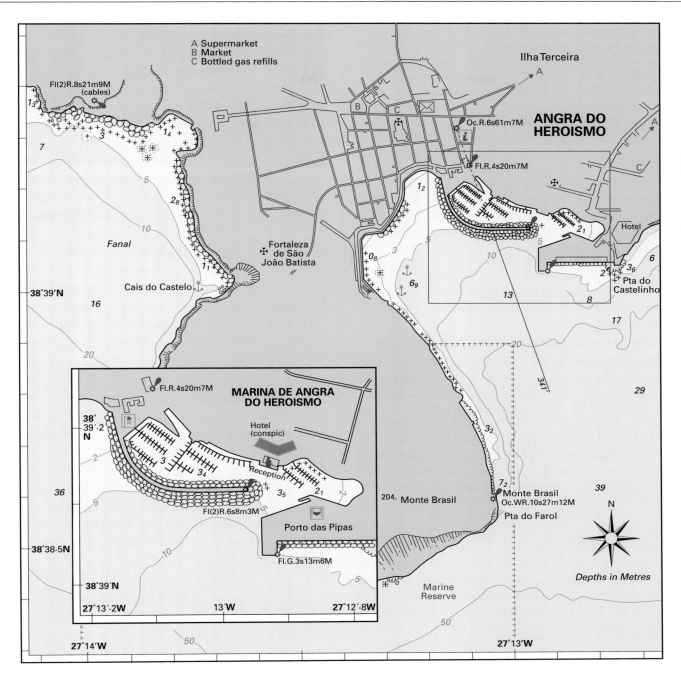

A Supermarket
B Market
C Bottled gas refills

Ilha Terceira

ANGRA DO HEROISMO

Fl(2)R.8s21m9M
(cables)

Oc.R.6s61m7M

Fl.R.4s20m7M

Fanal

Hotel

Fortaleza
de São
João Batista

Pta do
Castelinho

38°39'N

Cais do Castelo

**MARINA DE ANGRA
DO HEROISMO**

Fl.R.4s20m7M

38°
39'·2
N

Hotel
(conspic)

Reception

38°38·5N

Fl(2)R.6s8m3M

Porto das Pipas

Monte Brasil
Oc.WR.10s27m12M

Pta do Farol

38°39'N

204· Monte Brasil

Fl.G.3s13m6M

Marine
Reserve

27°13'·2W      13'W      27°12'·8W

N

Depths in Metres

27°14'W                      27°13'W

II. THE AZORES

raised to city status in 1543. During the Spanish occupation in the 16th century it was twice attacked by British fleets, one commanded by Sir Francis Drake, and the fort of São João Baptista was built for harbour defence and the safekeeping of valuable cargoes – as well as to keep the townspeople in a suitably submissive frame of mind. The harbour is much quieter these days, all commercial traffic other than occasional inter-island ferries using purpose-built wharfs at Praia da Vitória instead. The harbour is remarkably clean with very clear water, recognized by the award of an EU 'Blue Flag' each year since 2006.

The city is notable for its fine buildings and well-kept public gardens, and a particularly informative city guide is available free from the tourist office on Rua Direita (open 0900–1200, 1400–1700 weekdays, 0900–1200 Saturday). Angra was declared a UNESCO World Heritage Site in 1983 while restoration following the 1980 earthquake was still under way – the high proportion of bright terracotta roofs visible from Monte Brasil indicate buildings which sustained damage – and remains a most attractive city with considerable atmosphere. The west end of the marina is overlooked by the imposing 15th century *Alfandega* building and the magnificent 18th century Misericordia church, both now restored. Between them, a handsome double stairway sweeps around an artificial waterfall and descends to the ancient Cais Alfandega. Below the harbour wall and south of the fountain a modern, glass-panelled building houses a restaurant, bar and the marina services block.

The city museum in the former monastery of São Francisco (open 0930–1200, 1400–1700 Tuesday to Friday, 1400–1700 weekends, closed Monday) is well worth a visit, even though many of the captions are in Portuguese only. Two particularly enjoyable walks are up to the pyramid monument which overlooks the city from the north, and out to Monte Brasil, the entrance to which is through the main gateway of the fort. Both offer splendid views over the city and harbour. Those with younger crew-members might like to know that this passes a particularly imaginative children's play area, with something for every age group and the bonus of a great view.

### Approach and entrance

*By day* Monte Brasil, rising to over 200m, is easily identified from a considerable distance and approach is straightforward, though the marina entrance itself is narrow. The massive Angra Marina Hotel has recently been completed directly behind the glass-fronted reception building, itself fronted by a 40m pontoon also used for fuel. Rubble extends some distance beyond the end of the marina mole (buoyed in previous years, but currently unmarked), but 3·5m should be found in the centre of the entrance and at least 3m at the reception pontoon.

*By night* If approaching from the west, Monte Brasil light will not be visible until bearing less than 057°. Both sides of the marina entrance are lit, though that on Porto das Pipas is some distance from its northwest corner. The considerable ambient light from the city makes night entry perfectly feasible in light conditions, though see the note re rubble, above. Alternatively follow the leading lights until Porto das Pipas mole is abeam to starboard, when a course of about 287° will lead into the anchorage. Do not venture inside the 8m contour in darkness. There is a signal mast with red and white lights on the roof of the marina reception building, but it is understood to belong to the *Capitania* and is never used.

### Berthing

On arrival, yachts should secure at the reception/fuel pontoon directly opposite the marina entrance to be allocated a berth. Alternatively, call on VHF Ch 09 or by mobile phone during the approach. At least 3·5m should be found in the entrance, at the reception pontoon and at the larger berths. All the 260 or so berths are alongside finger pontoons, with 25 berths reserved for visitors of over 10m though

A small motorboat enters Marina d'Angra, swinging wide to avoid rubble off the end of the marina mole *Anne Hammick*

up to 50 visiting yachts have occasionally been squeezed in. The marina can take a few yachts of 18m LOA, though it would always be wise to check whether space is available before leaving one's previous port.

The pontoons immediately west of the fuel and reception pontoon, where larger visiting boats are normally berthed, were replaced a few years ago by heavier ones with concrete floats and steel (rather than aluminium) framework, able to take a dozen boats of up to 15m (50ft) LOA and 4·6m (15ft) beam. These new pontoons move much less than their predecessors in the almost continuous surge, but even so, if any swell is running it is worth requesting a spot in the western part of the harbour where the movement is least, though even then mooring line snubbers are highly recommended. A generous 3·5m will be found at least half way up the harbour, though depths decrease to 1m at its head.

Security is excellent – in addition to card-activated pontoon gates, the entire marina is overseen by CCTV cameras and security guards are on duty day and night.

### Anchorage

In suitable weather it is possible to anchor off the prominently marked *clube náutico* in the western part of the harbour. Depths (over sand) shoal gradually, but until Baixa da Prainha, awash at HW springs, has been identified it would be unwise to venture into less than 6m, even in good daylight.

Three areas close to the shore of Monte Brasil form an underwater archaeological park, where anchoring is prohibited. In theory each of these sites – of 19th-century wrecks and an anchor graveyard – should each be marked with a yellow buoy, though none were in evidence in May 2015. Remaining inshore of a line between the light structure on the marina mole and the yellow-walled chapel on Monte Brasil (the higher of the two buildings) clears the southernmost marine reserve – the remains of the wreck of the

Angra do Heroísmo's imposing *Câmara Municipal* (town hall) is fronted by a vividly paved square  *Anne Hammick*

*Lidador* – with the other two further inshore. Information on the sites, scuba excursions and equipment can be obtained from local dive shops.

Although no charge is made for anchoring, skippers of anchored yachts are asked to visit the marina office on arrival to check in with the authorities. Thereafter, dinghies can be left at the Cais Alfandega at the head of the marina – but take care on the ancient steps, which can be slippery. A long painter will be needed as lines must be taken up to the quay, some 5–6m above the water at low tide. Crews of anchored yachts may also use the marina toilets and showers – see Facilities below.

There are currently no mooring buoys in the bay, nor plans to lay any.

### Formalities

All formalities are carried out in the marina office, which overlooks the reception pontoon opposite the marina entrance. Marina manager Roldão Duarte and his staff could not be more helpful, and speak excellent English and French. The handsome modern building also contains offices intended for *Alfândega* (Customs), *Serviço de Estrangeiros e Fronteiras* (Immigration) and *Polícia Marítima* (maritime police), but these are seldom manned. Check-in is carried out quickly and efficiently by the marina staff and the information passed on to the authorities, who may occasionally visit a yacht if they think it necessary.

Together with Faial and São Miguel, Terceira is a 'border post' under the Schengen Agreement – see page 51. Fortunately this does not entail extra paperwork, as clearance into Portuguese waters and the Schengen area are handled concurrently.

Non-EU citizens considering an extended stay in Terceira should be aware that under European law the 18-month VAT exemption period – see page 51 – may be extended by a further six months, provided a yacht is ashore or otherwise immobilised. This extension is at the discretion of the local *Alfandega* (Customs), however, and as of 2015 the officials in

Terceira differed from their counterparts in the other Azorean islands in choosing not to make it available.

### Charges

Marina d'Angra is part of the *Portos dos Açores SA* chain, and shares their basic price structure – see page 55. Payment can be made using most major credit/debit cards other than American Express. There is no charge for anchoring.

### Facilities

Like MAYS in Horta and Boat & Sail Service in Ponta Delgada, Angra do Heroísmo has its own 'Mr Fixit' who appears to have contacts in all the right places, works in close harmony with the marina staff, and speaks excellent English and some French. Initally Pedro Parreira, who trades as ParreiraAzor, ☎+351 295 401280, *mobile* +351 912 355308, geral@parreiraazor.com, opened a chandlery in one end of the family hardware and agricultural store at Atalaia, Ribeirinha, a few kilometres east of the city, but his range of services has broadened and he now employs six staff. ParreiraAzor can handle repairs to GRP and timber, engineering (including generator sales and repair), electrical work, installation and checking (but not repair) of electronics, hull cleaning and painting, minor sail repairs, and fit new rigging made up elsewhere.

*Boatyard & laying up* A secure gated area of hardstanding with 24-hour security occupies the east end of the Porto das Pipas mole (which is high enough to provide reasonable shelter from south winds). Water and electricity are laid on, and a range of skills is available, including engineering and aluminium welding – enquire at the marina office or contact Pedro Parreira, above. The yard has received high praise from a number of boat owners, some of whom have laid up there for several winters. There is no restriction on DIY work, or on living aboard while a boat is ashore.

*Travel-lift* 50-tonne capacity hoist on the Porto das Pipas mole, with a least depth of 3m in the dock. Organise via the marina office, where proof of insurance will probably be requested. Should a yacht be too large, or wide, for the travel-lift a mobile crane can be brought

Yachts laid up on the wide quay at Porto das Pipas  *Anne Hammick*

in. ParreiraAzor hire out well-made metal props and cradles, and Pedro Parreira will oversee the shoring-up in the owner's absence, as well as providing guardinage once the yacht is ashore.

*Engineers* Arrange via the marina office or Pedro Perreira (who will translate if necessary). The machine shop operated by Gil Sousa e Filhos Lda at Zona das Combustiveis 6 ℡+351 295 213629, is highly recommended by MAYS in Horta.

*Chandlery* ParreiraAzor (see above) is currently Terceira's only chandlery. The company handles boat and engine sales (as a Yanmar agent) and also stocks International Paints (including antifouling), anodes, hardware including nylon and bronze plumbing, general chandlery, rope and Portuguese charts of local waters. Items not in stock can be ordered from the major catalogues. Open 0900–1200, 1330–1800 weekdays, 0900–1200 Saturday.

*Showers* The services block at the west end of the marina houses immaculate showers, sinks and toilets, accessible 0830–1200 and 1300–2000. There is a large jacuzzi, and even a babycare room complete with bath. With six ladies' showers and 11 for men there should seldom be a queue.

*Launderette* In the shower block, with two washing machines and one dryer. The machines are operated by tokens, available from shower reception during office hours. An iron and ironing board are available on request.

*Fuel* Pumps for both diesel and petrol at the east end of the reception pontoon, operational 0900–1200, 1300–1900 15 May – 15 September, 0900–1200, 1300–1600 at other times. Payment can be made using most major credit/debit cards other than American Express.

*Bottled gas* Exchanges of any cylinders other than GALP's own have been discontinued throughout the Azores. Fortunately most bottles, including Camping Gaz, can be refilled (with butane only) at Comércio Agricola Lda on Rua João Vaz Corte Real, a short walk from the marina, open 0900–1200, 1300–1700 weekdays only. Allow at least two working days.

*Banks* Many in the city, plus ATMs seemingly on every corner.

*Shops/provisioning* Small supermarket opposite the Cathedral, the larger Guarita supermarket on Rua da Guarita about 10 minutes' walk northeast of the marina, plus a huge Modelo hypermarket about 10 minutes beyond that – worth the walk/taxi fare if stocking up for a long passage. A wide variety of other shops are to be found, as befits the Azores' second largest city.

*Produce market* Thriving and spotlessly clean market (see plan) on two levels and selling everything from fish to carpets!

*Cafés, restaurants & hotels* The Aquaemotion restaurant at the head of the marina is unexpectedly good (though not particularly cheap), or for more traditional dining try the Hotel Beira Mar beside the *Alfandega* building. These are the tip of the iceberg, however, with a range to suit all pockets. The same diversity appies to residential accommodation.

*Medical services* Large hospital just outside the city, ℡+351 295 403200, plus doctors, dentists and opticians.

The Hotel Beira Mar on Angra's waterfront has been serving *Sopa de Camarão* – prawn soup served in a crusty loaf – for decades. Highly recommended! *Anne Hammick*

### Communications

*Mailing address* C/o: Marina d'Angra, Porto das Pipas, 9700–154 Angra do Heroísmo, Terceira, Açores, Portugal.

*WiFi* Free service in and around the marina, for which a password is required, with three Skype-enabled computers (also free) in the services (not the administration) block.

*Car hire & taxis* Readily available.

*Buses* Services around the island – details from the tourist office.

*Ferries* The (relatively) small catamaran ferries berth on the quay at Porto das Pipas once or twice a week, but the much larger and more frequent Atlânticoline vessels use the commercial harbour at Praia da Vitória. See Transportation, page 48.

*Air services* International and inter-island flights from the airport near Praia da Vitória, about 24km distant by road.

## Cais do Castelo

38°39′N 27°13′·75W (anchorage)

> **Lights**
> **Silveira cables**
> Fl(2)R.8s21m9M (daylight range 1·7M) 024°-vis-052°
> White post, red bands 4m. Marks submarine cables

### Anchorage for easterly winds

When wind or swell from the eastern quadrant make the anchorage at Angra do Heroísmo uncomfortable, shelter may be found under the cliffs west of Monte Brasil. Good holding in 5–10m has been reported at the mouth of the small inlet southwest of São João Baptista fort, near the distinctive white steps. Note the presence of cables, which run out from a point close west of a large pink and cream hotel, but fortunately these trend southwest so do not affect the anchorage.

The bay and steps at Cais do Castelo, on the west side of Monte Brasil, seen from the northwest  *Anne Hammick*

# São Mateus da Calheta

38°39'·33N 27°16'W (west molehead)

**Lights**
**São Mateus** Iso.WR.6s11m10/7M
   270°-R-296°-W-067°
   White column, red bands 3m
**Northeast mole** Fl.G.3s6m3M
   White post, green bands 3m
**Southwest mole** Fl(3)R.6·1s9m3M
   White post, red bands 3·4m

### Small fishing harbour

For many years protected only by a short southwest mole, the small fishing (and formerly whaling) harbour at São Mateus was improved a few years ago by the addition of a new east mole, an inner spur near the end of the old southwest mole and new pontoons inside. Two ruined forts and an impressive church overlook the town, which has basic facilities including water on the quay, limited shopping and the usual restaurants and cafés.

An excellent reason to call at São Mateus, whether by sea or land, would be to visit the small whaling museum in the *Casa dos Botes* (part of the *Clube Naval de São Mateus*) just behind the quay. Formally opened in September 2009, it houses three beautifully kept whaleboats on the ground floor, surrounded by harpoons and other equipment as well as photographs of the harbour during the 19th and 20th centuries, with more photographs and models upstairs. In 2015 two traditional towboats were undergoing restoration just outside. Entry is free, and while there are no formal opening hours it is accessible most days, with two or three elderly men sitting chatting in the doorway.

### Approach and anchorage

The enlarged harbour is clearly intended for local boats and it is uncertain how a yacht would be received should one enter, but there is space for a well-handled yacht of 12m or so to manoeuvre while assessing the situation – and the reception. It might be possible to lie alongside for an hour or two when

**II. THE AZORES**

Looking into São Mateus da Calheta from the northeast, with the town's imposing church on the right
*Anne Hammick*

Looking northeast across the southern basin at São Mateus da Calheta. The wide-angle lens makes the harbour appear larger than it really is  *Anne Hammick*

Preparing bait at São Mateus da Calheta – it remains very much a working fishing harbour *Anne Hammick*

things are quiet, and there is nothing to prevent the more adventurous anchoring outside, in about 10m over sand and large boulders.

The prominent white church is visible from several miles off, dwarfing the surrounding village, but the rock-fringed coastline on either hand should be given an offing of at least 500m until the end of southwest mole bears between 330° and 000°. About 9m will be found in the entrance, shoaling rapidly to 3–4m. The water is very clear.

# Biscoitos

38°48'·05N 27°15'·59W

Lights
**Biscoitos** Oc.6s12m9M
    White column, two red bands 3m

### Attractive north coast anchorage

In settled southerly weather Biscoitos offers a pleasant daytime anchorage in 8–10m over rock. The mole was extended by 35m about 15 years ago, apparently to increase its appeal as a swimming area, but though about 2m will be found at its head and 1m its root the bottom is rocky and it is not suitable for lying alongside. There is a slipway and steps near the root of the mole, as well as three ladders inside the angled head, at which one could land by dinghy. Nearby facilities are limited to a café/bar and swimmers' (ie. cold) showers, with shops in the village about 1km inland.

The anchorage is overlooked by a miniature three-cannon fort and a monument commemorating Biscoitos' place in Portuguese history when, in the run-up to the Miguelite uprising of autumn 1828: 'it was through the Port of Biscoitos da Cruz that weapons and ammunition arrived from other islands in the Central Group, aiding the Royalist militias

Looking south into the small bay at Biscoitos from a commercial aeroplane *Anne Hammick*

and troops who supported King Miguel'. With commendable honesty the caption (in English as well as Portuguese) continues: 'These weapons were neither great in number nor in a very good state, but they were enough to cause enormous commotion and dread among the Constitutional troops stationed in Angra'.

There are several other possible daytime anchorages east of Biscoitos which might be visited in calm southerly conditions, including Quatro Ribeiras and Vila Nova (Iso.6s10m9M, black and white column with red lantern 2m). However, none of the three can be recommended other than in very settled weather, being deep, poorly protected and fringed by rocky cliffs. All should offer excellent snorkelling and diving.

The vicious Baixa da Vila Nova lies off the town of the same name (see plan page 118) *Anne Hammick*

# Praia da Vitória

38°43'·58N 27°03'·06W (north breakwater head)

### Tides
Predictions for Praia da Vitória are available via Admiralty *EasyTide* – see page 54
Time difference on Ponta Delgada: +0007
*Mean spring range* 1·4m
*Mean neap range* 0·6m

### Lights
**North breakwater** Fl.5s19m10M
   White column, black bands with 'basket' top 9m
**North breakwater obstruction**
   Q(6)+LFl.10s3m6M
   South cardinal buoy, ⚑ topmark
**Sectored entrance light**
   Fl(2)WRG.5s24m10M (daylight range 0·7M)
   255°-G-260°-W-270°-R-275° Post 7m
**South breakwater** Fl.R.3s22m8M
   White tower, three red bands 9m
**Marina southeast mole** Fl(3)G.10s6m3M
   White post, green bands 3m
**Marina southeast pontoon** Fl(2)G.10s1m2M
   White post, green bands 2m
**Marina northwest mole**
   Fl.R.2s4m2M White post, red bands 2m
   *Note* The high level back-lighting from the town
   when coming from seawards can make the marina
   lights difficult to pick out
**Fishing harbour mole** Fl.G.5s5m3M
   White post, green bands 2·5m

### Harbour communications
**Marina da Praia da Vitória**
   VHF Ch 09, 16
   ☎+351 295 540219
   1 June–31 August: 0830–1930 weekdays, 0830–1200,
   1300-1630 weekends; otherwise 0830–1630
   weekdays, closed at weekends. The VHF may be
   answered by a security guard outside office hours
   marina@cmpv.pt
   www.cmpv.pt/marina
**Capitania**
   VHF Ch 11, 16
   ☎+351 295 542500
   0900–1230, 1400–1730
   capitania.pvitoria@amn.pt
   www.amn.pt

### Port limits
A rectangle extending 2·5M from Praia da Vitória north breakwater light – see Port limits, page 51.

Looking south over the wide bay at Praia da Vitória. Early in the season the yacht lay-up area is almost full although the marina itself is relatively empty *Anne Hammick*

## Friendly marina and sheltered anchorage

Once an open bay, Praia da Vitória is now one of the best protected harbours in the Azores, with breakwaters extending from both north and south to enclose well over half a square mile of water. Following severe storm damage in 2002 both breakwaters were heavily reinforced and the southern part of the harbour developed as a commercial area for fishing and cargo handling.

The well-established marina in the northwest corner of the harbour has grown by stages. First a few pontoon berths were created inside the short mole which protected the old – and very shallow – fishing harbour, but it soon grew to its current 210 berths and has gained a deserved reputation for being friendly and welcoming with particularly good domestic facilities. At least 245 yachts are said to have visited in 2014, so perhaps it is as well that less than half the berths are occupied by local boats. The marina is a local initiative, owned and administered by the *Câmara Municipal da Praia da Vitória* (the town council).

Marina da Praia da Vitória is unique in the Azores in being surrounded by excellent sandy beaches – that to the east is a pepper-and-salt mixture of black and golden grains with a fine texture, unexpectedly clean and gently shelving, complete with small beach café, while to the west lies the town's main beach, its yellower tone indicating that local sand has been augmented by Saharan imports. Also nearby, though not so close as to be obtrusive, is Lajes International Airport, making the marina particularly handy for crew changes. One of the flight paths runs directly over the harbour, but there is still relatively little traffic and no commercial flights between midnight and 0800 – though the military are, of course, free to fly at any time.

An important settlement from early days, Praia da Vitória has some fine buildings including the 16th-century parish church and 17th-century town hall, both of which survived earthquakes in 1841 and again in 1980, though not without considerable damage. Completion of a promenade opposite the marina has added to the town's charm and atmosphere, and there are several good restaurants. The marina office has a particularly good variety of

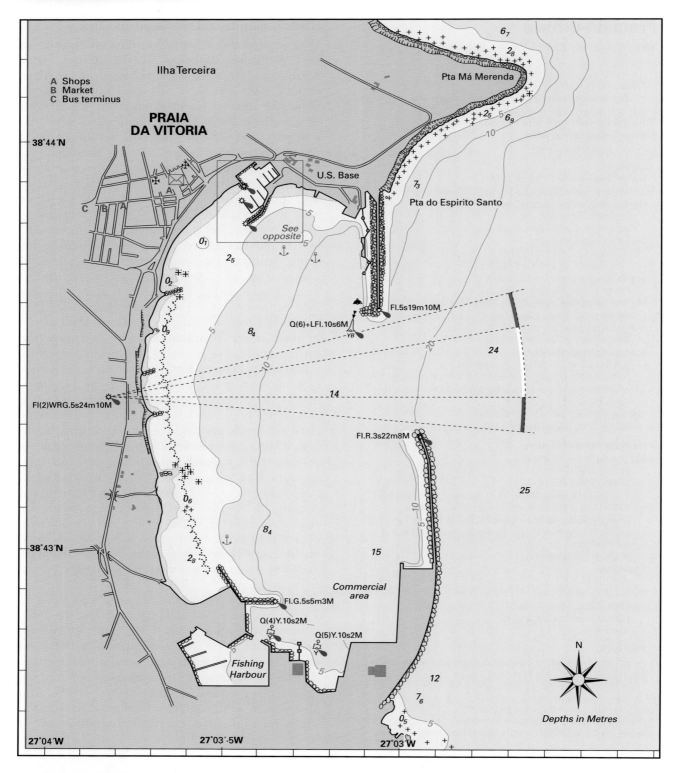

A Shops
B Market
C Bus terminus

Ilha Terceira

**PRAIA DA VITORIA**

Pta Má Merenda

U.S. Base

Pta do Espirito Santo

38°44'N

See opposite

Fl.5s19m10M

Q(6)+LFl.10s6M

Fl(2)WRG.5s24m10M

Fl.R.3s22m8M

38°43'N

Commercial area

Fl.G.5s5m3M

Q(4)Y.10s2M

Q(5)Y.10s2M

Fishing Harbour

27°04'W        27°03'·5W        27°03'W

N

Depths in Metres

tourist and general information – maps, bus timetables etc. – available for the asking. It is well worth walking up the switchback path to the statue of *Nossa Senhora Maria da Conceição* on the ridge north of the harbour which is lit at night. For variety, follow the gently sloping road back down to the harbour (or vice versa).

### Approach and harbour entrance

*By day* Quite clear. The pale concrete of the breakwaters shows up well from a distance, with the tall red and white banded tower on the south breakwater removing any possible doubt (that on the north breakwater is less conspicuous). The storm damage of 2002 left debris extending some distance from the end of the north breakwater, marked by a

The entrance to Praia da Vitória, guarded by its two lit breakwaters. The south cardinal buoy marks rubble which extends southwest from the head of the north breakwater
*Anne Hammick*

south cardinal buoy – do NOT cut inside it. The marina's solid southeast mole will be seen about 0·5M to the northwest, with no hazards between.

*By night* Bright shore lights, both from the town and around the US base in the northeast corner of the harbour, provide a handy beacon from several miles off. Both breakwaters are lit, as are the south cardinal buoy and the marina's southeast mole, both mentioned above. Entrance by night should therefore present no problems even in moderately heavy weather, though in such conditions it might be wise to anchor off the beach until daylight rather than continue directly to the marina reception pontoon.

### Anchorage

In northerly or westerly winds good anchorage is to be found anywhere inside the northern arm of the breakwater over clean sand, but depths shoal suddenly well off the beach so a careful eye must be kept on the echo sounder. Holding is surprisingly patchy, and other than in very light winds the *Polícia Marítima* recommend that two anchors should be laid. A wreck (or other debris) liable to foul anchors has been reported at 38°43'·8N 27°03'·3W.

There is no charge for anchoring, but even so skippers should visit the marina office for clearance on arrival and departure. The crews of anchored yachts are allowed to fill water cans from the pontoon taps, use the marina's toilets, showers and laundry, and leave dinghies between the outer marina pontoon and the protective mole.

When the tanker which delivers aviation fuel is in port (she berths close to the US Army base) the anchorage is temporarily closed to yachts. At these time, or during strong southerly or southeasterly winds, equally protected though less convenient anchorage can be found in the southern part of the bay, provided care is taken not to impede fishing or cargo vessels. However, this is not officially

sanctioned and yachts are likely to be told to move when conditions improve. There is a short pontoon in the corner of the fishing harbour where a dinghy might be left for limited periods, and a few shops in the small village almost hidden behind the new, port-related buildings to the south.

### Marina entrance and berthing

On arrival, secure to the (clearly-labelled) reception berth at the outer end of the southwest pontoon to be assigned a berth, or contact the office on VHF Ch 09 or by mobile phone on entering the outer harbour. Deep-draught yachts should take particular care, as despite the marina entrance and reception area being dredged to 3·5m every spring, silting remains a problem and by late summer no more than 2·5m may be found at low water springs (the marina has its own small suction dredger which appears to work almost continuously). During summer a string of yellow buoys cordons off the swimming beach on

Marina da Praia da Vitória, seen from the statue of *Nossa Senhora Maria da Conceição* to the northeast
*Anne Hammick*

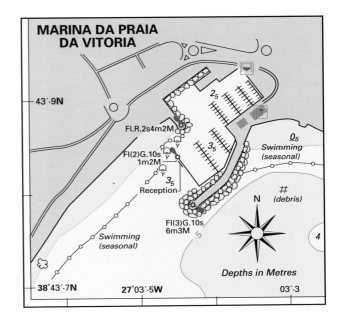

Seven yachts occupy the anchorage at Praia da Vitória, though it has sometimes held three or four times that number. Few would deny its status as the best anchorage in the archipelago *Linda Lane Thornton*

the northwest side of the entrance, with three larger ones directly opposite the reception area, but none are lit and they are unlikely to be in place out of season. Take particular care if approaching at night, when larger yachts may be better advised to anchor, moving to the reception pontoon in daylight.

The outer two pontoons are reserved for visiting yachts, the inner with finger pontoons and the outer for larger and heavier yachts to lie alongside. The fingers are relatively short, making for considerable pontoon overhang, but fortunately remedial work to the bluffs southwest of the marina (which had become badly eroded) is said to have made reflected waves and currents much less of a problem than previously. Even so, manoeuvring a yacht into a berth on the northeast side of the inner pontoon tends to be a communal activity with plenty of fenders and lines in all directions. The innermost pontoon – no more than a stump in 2015 – berths smaller yachts, usually long-term. 'Long-term' does not always mean 'local', however, as Praia da Vitória has become a popular spot for over-wintering, with a small community of liveaboards who return each autumn after cruising elsewhere in the islands.

There is no obvious size limit on the southwest pontoon, and yachts of up to 18m have visited the marina, though it will probably be necessary to raft up at busy periods. This is particularly likely in mid to late June, when yachts ashore need to be relaunched before the start of the *festa* season – see Laying-up, below.

Security is provided by gates operated by magnetic cards (for which a refundable deposit is payable) which also give access to the services block, combined with CCTV coverage. No incidents of theft or damage have been reported either ashore or afloat during the marina's entire existence.

## Formalities

All formalities – for those at anchor as well as marina users – are carried out in the office near the root of the marina mole. Good English and French are spoken and Paulo Vitória, who has worked there since the marina accepted its first yachts in 2000, greets many skippers as returning friends. Both marina and staff receive consistent praise from visitors, 'very friendly and efficient', 'excellent and friendly little marina' and 'as always, most helpful and welcoming' being typical. The *Serviço de Estrangeiros e Fronteiras* (Immigration), *Guarda Nacional Republicana* (GNR) and *Polícia Marítima* all have offices in the same building and receive copies of the computerised form, and non-Schengen area citizens entering the Azores for the first time may be asked to step across the corridor get their passports stamped (together with Faial and São Miguel, Terceira is a 'border post' under the Schengen Agreement – see page 51.)

Departure clearance is also required, whether at anchor or in the marina, and yachts intending to leave outside office hours are requested to check out before 1900 on summer weekdays (1600 at weekends or holidays), or before 1600 Friday throughout the rest of the year.

Non-EU citizens considering an extended stay in Terceira should be aware that under European law the 18-month VAT exemption period – see page 52 – may be extended by a further six months, provided a yacht is ashore or otherwise immobilised. This extension is at the discretion of the local *Alfandega* (Customs), however, and as of 2015 the officials in Terceira differed from their counterparts in the other Azorean islands in choosing not to offer it.

## Charges

As mentioned previously, Marina da Praia da Vitória is owned and administered by the *Câmara Municipal da Praia da Vitória* (the town council) and is not part of the *Portos dos Açores SA* chain. Despite its good facilities, its prices have always been the lowest in the Azores.

By 2016 the overnight fee for a visiting monohull of 10–12m LOA is expected to be €10.10 and that for 12–15m €11.93, including water, electricity, IVA (VAT, currently 18%) and a 4% 'residue' charge to pay for garbage disposal. Multihulls pay a 50% surcharge. Only showers, and of course laundry, are charged on an 'as used' basis. Considerable discounts are available for longer periods, and most winters see a small community of residents wintering afloat. For further details check the marina's website www.cmpv.pt/marina, in Portuguese and English. No charge is made for anchoring.

## Facilities

*Boatyard & laying up* The Marina da Praia da Vitória has become a popular place to lay-up ashore, due to a combination of favourable prices, excellent security record and proximity to a major airport. The main area of hardstanding is available from 1 September – 20 June only, however, and must be vacated by the latter because it is used for the city's *festas* and a gastronomic fair. A small extension has been enclosed to allow a dozen or so boats to remain ashore during the summer, but once made the decision is irrevocable as access to the travel-lift dock will be blocked by tents and marquees until the end of August.

Both lay-up areas have access to water and electricity, with security provided by wire fences and 24-hour surveillance. During the winter all yachts are placed on a northeast/southwest axis, the line of the strongest winds, but even so all sails should be removed and stowed below.

There is no boatyard as such, but the marina office can advise on whom to contact for various types of work, as can Pedro Parreira of ParreiraAzor – see page 125. There is no restriction on DIY work, or on living aboard while a boat is ashore.

*Travel-lift* 35-tonne capacity hoist, with props available for hire from ParreiraAzor – the care taken over shoring-up a newly lifted yacht is impressive. The travel-lift dock is prone to silting, however, and deeper yachts may have to be lifted at high tide.

Should a yacht be too wide for the travel-lift (5m maximum) a mobile crane can be brought in (arrange via Pedro Parreira) or for minor work multihulls can dry out on the wide slipway (arrange via the marina office).

*Diving services, engineer & minor sail repairs* Can all be arranged via the marina office or Pedro Perreira.

*Chandlery* Nothing closer than Angra – see page 126.

*Showers* Immaculate showers – and even a bathtub – in both the ladies and gents sections of the services block, which may also be used by those at anchor. Note that these are only accessible during office hours.

*Launderette* Equally immaculate launderette, with three each washers and dryers, plus iron and ironing board, again open to those at anchor, and again limited to office hours.

*Fuel* No fuel berth and no plans for one. Small amounts of diesel can be collected by can from a filling station outside the town, otherwise the office can arrange for quantities of 200 litres (about 44 UK / 55 US gallons) or more to be delivered by road tanker to a point near the travel-lift dock. Twenty-four hours' notice is required, with no deliveries on Sunday.

*Bottled gas* Exchanges of any cylinders, including Camping Gaz, have been discontinued throughout the Azores, but most bottles can be refilled within two working days if left at the marina office. Only butane is available – no propane.

*Banks* Several in the town, all with ATMs.

*Shops/provisioning* Several small supermarkets in the town, plus two vast hypermarkets on the western fringes. There is a frequent bus service which connects both stores and the marina.

*Produce market* Small but active produce market on Rua de Jesus.

*Cafés, restaurants & hotels* Several hotels and many restaurants and cafés at all price levels, some overlooking the bay. Small beach café just over the wall from the marina.

*Medical services* Hospital, ☎+351 295 540970, plus doctors, dentists and pharmacies.

## Communications

*Mailing address* C/o Marina de Praia da Vitória, 9760 Praia da Vitória, Terceira, Açores, Portugal.

*WiFi* Free signal throughout the marina (and often the anchorage as well), plus three free computers in the services block (where there is also a book-swap). No password is required.

*Car hire & taxis* Readily available, the former from the nearby airport.

*Buses* Services around the island – timetable from the marina office or the *turismo* on Rua de Jesus.

*Air services* Direct flights to Lisbon, the US and Canada, as well as frequent inter-island flights, from Lajes International Airport some 3·5km away.

Launching a 13·4 x 7·5m catamaran by crane. Terceira is currently the only island in the Azores where multihulls can be laid up ashore *Anne Hammick*

II. THE AZORES

# São Miguel

Between 37°42'N–37°55'N and 25°08'W–25°51'W

## Introduction

At just over 750km² (65km by about 16km) São Miguel is the largest island in the Azores by a considerable margin and also has the largest population, at around 140,000. Its two areas of high ground to west and east are separated by a lower saddle which has long been cultivated, but the local name of '*A Ilha Verde*' (the Green Island) owes its origins as much to the dense natural woodland as to the acres of carefully tended crops and pasture. Many of those born and bred elsewhere in the Azores unhesitatingly choose São Miguel as their favourite island, both for its natural beauty and for the attractions of Ponta Delgada, the archipelago's commercial centre and largest city.

First settled about 1440 under the captaincy of Conçalho Velho, São Miguel must often have been visible on the northern horizon to the few people already living on Santa Maria. Landing was made on the beach at Povoação ('village') on the southeast coast, and the new island named in honour of São Miguel Arcánjel – Michael the Archangel. As in all the Azores dense natural forest inland encouraged villages along the coast, and even now probably three-quarters of São Miguel's towns are within 3km of the sea. In addition to Portuguese and Madeiran emigrants there were more than a smattering of French (commemorated in the parish of Bretanha on the northwest coast), transported convicts, and African and Moorish slaves.

The first capital was established at Vila Franca do Campo in the mid 15th century, probably because of the good anchorage behind its small off-lying island. By 1522 the town was thriving with some 5,000 inhabitants under the governorship of Rui Conçalves da Câmara, son of the *capitão donatório* of Madeira. However, eastern São Miguel was suffering a period of seismic activity, and in October that year an earthquake triggered a mudslide and avalanche which completely destroyed the town and killed many of its inhabitants. The government moved westwards, first to Lagoa and then to the slightly more protected bay at Ponta Delgada, which by 1546 had been granted full city status and become the island's new capital.

Even so Vila Franca do Campo figures the more prominently in history, suffering several pirate raids during the 16th and 17th centuries which prompted solid stone fortifications to be built. However, these proved insufficient when in July 1582 a French and Portuguese fleet was attacked just offshore by the forces of King Phillip II of Spain, by then ruler of mainland Portugal, with the town soon falling victim to the victorious Spaniards. Fifteen years later, while still under Spanish rule, the English Earl of Essex attacked one night at the head of 2,000 men. The inhabitants had sufficient warning to flee the town, but not to save it from being plundered and burned.

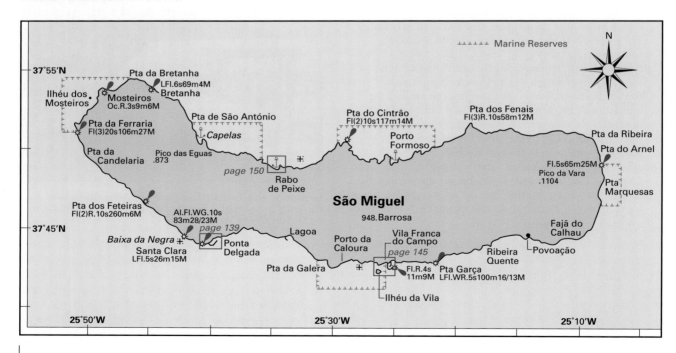

São Miguel was undoubtedly in need of its ports by this time, with wheat, sugar cane, wine and dairy products being exported. During the 17th and 18th centuries sweet potatoes, flax and oranges were added to the list, with the latter proving one of the most profitable crops the island has ever known. The high stone walls which still dominate the northwestern part of the island date from the 'orange days', having been solidly built to protect the groves from both thieves and winter gales. Many of the domestic and religious buildings of those days have also survived, characterised by carved black ashlar, heavy ornate woodwork and the glazed tiles so loved by the Portuguese, while some of the older houses in Ponta Delgada still have their rooftop lookouts, possibly going back beyond the days of peaceful trade to the time when pirates and privateers were an ever-present threat.

São Miguel played its part in the 19th century struggles between the Absolutists and the Liberals, with the latter landing in the northeast of the island in 1831. Ponta Delgada was chosen as their port of embarkation for the mainland the following year, at the start of the campaign which led to the declaration of Dom Pedro IV as King of Portugal, and at least 3,500 Azoreans are thought to have joined the Liberal cause. Island life must usually have been much quieter, however, with agriculture, stockbreeding or fishing the occupations of the vast majority. Oranges for England and America remained a major export until disease struck in the 1880s, by which time tobacco, sugar beet, tea and pineapples had been introduced. The latter two, both highly labour-intensive crops, did particularly well in the mild climate and rich volcanic soil, and it is said that in 1878 two Chinese experts were engaged to teach the skills of tea picking and preparation to the local people. Even in São Miguel's benign climate pineapples have to be grown under glass, and as the old greenhouses fall into disrepair their cultivation may soon, sadly, become a thing of the past. Currently only the Arruda plantation at Fajã de Baixo, just outside Ponta Delgada, still welcomes visitors to see the fruit being grown. On-site sales include, in addition to the fruit themselves, pineapple-flavoured confectionery and a highly regarded liqueur – the latter a little sweet for many people's taste, but delicious on ice cream.

To describe São Miguel's two other major tourist attractions in such terms seems rather inappropriate, since both are natural features on the grand scale which owe little to man's intervention. Probably most famous is the Caldeira das Sete Cidades with its twin lakes, Lagoa Verde (Green Lake) and Lagoa Azul (Blue Lake). On a sunny day the view from Vista do Rei over the emerald and sapphire lakes is breathtaking. Legend has it that they were created by the tears of a princess and a shepherd boy who were forbidden to meet, their separate weeping forming the two lakes which cannot mix, in spite of a common junction now spanned by the road bridge. The more prosaic insist that either dissolved minerals or algae are the true cause.

For several centuries the village on the crater floor was inaccessible other than on foot, and doubtless generations lived their lives there without ever leaving it or seeing the sea. However, a road now plunges down the steep slopes to the east and exits through an impressively engineered cutting to the west, and the 19th century park full of azaleas, hydrangeas and exotic trees is a justifiably popular picnic spot with locals as well as visitors. Fortunately the *caldeira* is large enough to absorb a good many picnic parties and still stay hushed and peaceful, though its quietness must have been shattered during the First World War when the 3km expanse of Lagoa Azul is said to have been used for seaplane landings – surely a horribly difficult approach and takeoff.

São Miguel's second natural wonder, though this time showing a little more of man's influence, is the thermal springs of Vale das Furnas in the east. Approaching from Ponta Delgada by way of Vila Franca do Campo one first passes a large and attractive lake with a small Gothic church on its shores – most unexpected in this bastion of manueline and baroque. A road leads around the northern end of the lake to the famous 'natural kitchens' where complete meals are sealed into pots and buried in the hot earth for several hours to produce the local delicacy known simply as *cozido* (cooked), strongly flavoured with sulphur and something of an acquired taste. (The recipe for *poule au volcan* is said to begin with the words: 'Take a volcano…'.)

A few kilometres further up the valley, dotted around the village of Furnas, lie the more spectacular thermal springs and boiling mud pools, 22 in all and each said to have its own particular medicinal property, which attracted the health-conscious Victorians of the 19th century. In 1838 two English brothers, Joseph and Henry Bullar, wrote a book entitled *A Winter in the Azores and a Summer at the Springs of Furnas* (see Further Reading, page 438), but by then the area was already known as a health spa, soon to gain elegant bath houses and its own hospital. One of the first foreigners to discover Furnas was Thomas Hickling, the first American Consul to the Azores, who built his country home here in the late 18th century – his town house in Ponta Delgada is now the Hotel de São Pedro, itself worth visiting. It is said that he employed English gardeners to plan his grounds, now the celebrated Terra Nostra Park. As well as a naturally warmed swimming pool which is open to the public (iron deposits discolour the water and can stain pale swimsuits), for a nominal fee one can explore the winding paths of the park, almost tropical in its lushness and a haven for bird life as well as all varieties of exotic flowers and trees.

It is tempting to think of Ponta Delgada purely as a convenient base from which to explore the island of São Miguel, but this is perhaps not doing the old town justice. While lacking the relaxed atmosphere of Horta or the architectural distinction of Angra do Heroísmo, and already sporting the first high-rise buildings in the Azores, it is very much a thriving city and the busiest port in the archipelago. Work on the breakwater started in 1861, though it did not reach its present 1·5km length for over a century, but successive waves of building have covered up most traces of the old port. The latest – and, since the building of the breakwater itself, surely the most ambitious – has seen the construction of a new cruise ship terminal, the *Portas do Mar*, in the centre of the old harbour with a large marina immediately to the west.

Further west again lies São Miguel's international airport, opened in 1969 to replace a small airstrip on the north coast in use since 1946 and enlarged several times since. Another source of pride is the island's university, which achieved full status in 1980 as the first Portuguese university outside the mainland. It is perhaps not a bad thing to be reminded that, behind the old world charm and courtesy prevalent in São Miguel as throughout the islands, Ponta Delgada is very definitely a thriving 21st-century city, with a life of its own and a particularly high proportion of well-educated young people.

### Holidays and festivals

In addition to the national holidays listed on page 50, Ponta Delgada holds its official holiday on 1 April, Lagoa on 11 April, Ribeira Grande on 29 April, Povoação on 23 June, Vila Franca do Campo on 24 June and Nordest on 17 July. The Festival of *Espírito Santo* and Feast of *Senhor Santo Cristo* are celebrated about six weeks after Easter, with the Festival of St Peter following on 29 June.

### Approach

In daylight Pico da Vara (1,104m) to the east or the lesser Pico das Eguas (873m) to the west will be visible from many miles off if not obscured by cloud, which may itself reveal the island's presence. From the north or south São Miguel appears to lie in two parts – a long island of several linked peaks to the east, a gap, and a single lower island to the west. At some 25M off the serrated skyline of the lower hills in the centre of the island rises above the horizon.

The coastline is largely steep-to, with few off-lying dangers. However, many headlands are fringed by rocks and all should be given at least 500m

A recyled 'phone box has become a miniature library on one of Ponta Delgada's many squares  *Anne Hammick*

clearance. Particular care should be taken in the vicinity of Baixa da Roida between Vila Franco do Campo and Caloura, Baixa da Negra about 0·5M south of the airport control tower, Ilhéu dos Mosteiros off the town of that name on the northwest coast, and Baixa do Morro bearing 065° from Rabo do Peixe and just under 2M distant. None of these hazards are lit. Currents set southerly around the ends of the island, and can sometimes produce a confused sea close to headlands.

Careful navigation is essential if on passage towards São Miguel from Terceira, particularly in poor weather, as the unmarked Banco Dom João de Castro shoal lies only 5M west of the direct course between the two (see plan page 38). Although the shoal – the tip of a subterranean volcano – has broken the surface at least once during the last 500 years it is currently charted at 12m. This was confirmed in 1999 by the crew of a yacht who carried out several dives on the bank, but as there is ongoing seismic activity in the area depths could decrease at any time. They pinpointed the least depth to be at 38°13'·37N 26°36'·36W, and within 100m of this spot were off soundings. As one might expect, seas break heavily on the bank in strong winds.

Five marine reserves have been created around São Miguel – on the south coast west of Vila Franca do

Campo, around Ponta Marquesas in the east, around Porto Formoso and Porto das Capelas, both on the north coast, and finally around Mosteiros in the northwest – as shown on the plan on page 134. See page 57 for details of restrictions, etc.

## Navigation

**Magnetic variation**
8°29'W (2016) decreasing by 9'E annually

**Tidal Streams**
Tidal streams run eastwards on the flood and westwards on the ebb at less than 1 knot, but may set up eddies around headlands particularly when meeting the southerly-setting current.

**Lights**
**Bretanha** LFl.6s69m4M
  Lantern on red post 1m
**Mosteiros** Oc.R.3s9m6M
  090°-vis-155° White column, red bands
**Ponta da Ferraria**
  Fl(3)20s106m27M 339°-vis-174°
  Square white tower, red lantern, and building 18m
**Ponta dos Feteiras** Fl(2)R.10s260m6M
  White column, red bands 5·5m
**Airport control tower**
  Aero Al.Fl.WG.10s83m28/23M 282°-vis-124° (occas)
**Santa Clara** LFl.5s26m15M 282°-vis-102°
  Red metal framework tower 8m
**Ponta Garça** LFl.WR.5s100m16/13M
  240°-W-080°-R-100°
  Red lantern on grey tower and building 14m
**Ponta do Arnel** Fl.5s65m25M 157°-vis-355°
  Octagonal white tower and building 15m
**Ponta dos Fenais** Fl(3)R.10s58m12M
  White column, red bands 7m
**Ponta do Cintrão**
  Fl(2)10s117m14M 080°-vis-324°
  Red lantern on grey tower and building 14m

**Coast Radio Station**
**São Miguel** 37°45'N 25°29'W remotely controlled
  from Lisbon
**VHF** Ch 16, 23, 26, 27 (24 hours)

**Maritime Rescue Coordination Centre**
**Ponta Delgada** 37°44'N 25°41'W
**DSC MF/VHF** MMSI 002040100, ☏+351 296 281777
  (emergency only), mrcc.delgada@marinha.pt
  (This station does not accept public correspondence other than distress and safety traffic)
**VHF** Ch 11, 16 (24 hours)

**Azores Communications Centre**
**São Miguel** 37°48 5'N 25°33'W, ☏296 101180, *mobile* 910 104165, cca.supervisor@marinha.pt
**Weather bulletins**: VHF Ch 11 Storm and bad weather warnings, synopsis and 24 hour forecast in Portuguese, repeated in English when possible. At 0830, 2000 for waters within 20 miles of São Miguel and Santa Maria; at 0900, 2100 for waters within 20 miles of Faial, Graciosa, Pico, São Jorge and Terceira); at 1000, 1900 for waters within 20 miles of Flores and Corvo.
**Navigational warnings**: VHF Ch 11 Local warnings in Portuguese, repeated in English when possible. At 0830, 2000 for São Miguel and Santa Maria; at 0900, 2100 for Faial, Graciosa, Pico, São Jorge and Terceira; at 1000, 1900 for Flores and Corvo.

**Navtex**
Formerly transmitted from Horta, but with times and frequencies unchanged. The Azores fall within NAVAREA 11.
Transmissions in English (F) are on the standard Navtex frequency of 518kHz, those in Portuguese (J) are on 490kHz. Ponta Delgada 'F' transmits storm and gale warnings, synopsis and 24-hour forecast in English for Areas 3, 5, 7, 30, 31 (see plan page 8) on receipt and at 0050, 0450, 0850, 1250, 1650 and 2050. Navigational warnings follow the weather bulletin. Ponta Delgada 'J' transmits the same information in Portuguese at 0130, 0530, 0930, 1330, 1730 and 2130.

II. THE AZORES

Exuberant wall art – one could not call this graffiti – near the harbour at Lagoa, east of Ponta Delgada  *Anne Hammick*

## Harbours and anchorages

# Ponta Delgada

37°44'·18N 25°39'·37W (breakwater head)

### Tides
Ponta Delgada is the standard port for the Azores, with either Admiralty or Portuguese tide tables available – see Tides and tidal streams, page 54. MLWS is listed as 0·3m above datum, but heights are strongly affected by barometric pressure. Predictions for Ponta Delgada are also available via Admiralty *EasyTide* – see page 54.
*Mean spring range* 1·4m
*Mean neap range* 0·7m

### Lights
**Santa Clara**
  LFl.5s26m15M 282°-vis-102°
  Red metal framework tower 8m
**Breakwater** LFl.R.6s16m10M
  White tower, red bands 7m
**Clube Naval** Fl(2)WRG.5s24m10M
  302°-G-306°-W-312°-R-317°
  Lantern on terrace of Clube Naval 15m
**Forte de São Brás** Fl(4)WRG.8s13m10M
  259°-G-261°-W-263°-R-265°
  Lantern on SE corner of fort 14m
**East marina mole** Fl.G.3s12m10M
  White tower, green bands 6m
**Cruise ship terminal, east end**
  Fl(2)R.5s9m3M White pillar, red bands 3m
**Cruise ship terminal, west end**
  Fl(3)G.15s6m3M White pillar, green bands 3m
**Floating breakwater** Q(6)+LFl.15s3M
  South cardinal pillar, ▼ topmark 5m
**Fishing harbour** Fl(4)R.15s5m3M
  White pillar, red bands 3m
**Pópulo cables** Fl(2)R.8s8m9M (daylight range 1·7M)
  349°-vis-031°
  White post, red bands 4m. Marks submarine cables
*Note* Situated nearly 2M east of the harbour entrance

### Harbour communications
**Ponta Delgada Marina** (previously Marina Pêro de Teive)
  VHF Ch 09, 16
  ✆296 281510
  0900–1830 weekdays, 0900–1230, 1400–1730 weekends 15 May – 15 September,
  otherwise 0900–1730 weekdays, closed weekends
  marinapdl@portosdosacores.pt
**Port Authority**
  VHF Ch 10, 16
  ✆ +351 296 285221
  0900–1230, 1400–1730
  dgpsm@portosdosacores.pt
  www.apsm.pt
**Capitania**
  VHF Ch 11, 16
  ✆ +351 296 205240
  0900–1200, 1400–1730
  capitania.pdelgada@amn.pt
  www.amn.pt

### Port Limits
A circle, radius 2M, centred on Ponta Delgada breakwater light – see Port limits, page 51.

## Large 'double' marina inside commercial harbour

The capital of São Miguel and largest naval and commercial harbour in the Azores, Ponta Delgada is well protected behind its high 1,544m breakwater, though heavy swell can set into the harbour with winds from between east and south. Ponta Delgada is a frequent landfall for yachts coming from the UK or mainland Europe, and is a convenient place for crew changes. It is one of the stops in the AZAB race. It has good facilities for storing-up and is an excellent base from which to explore the beautiful and varied interior of São Miguel. The city itself is picturesque, with some fine churches and other buildings dating back to the 16th century. Maps and guides are available from the tourist office on Avenue Infante Dom Henrique.

The relatively small 'old' marina, known until recently as the Marina de Pêro de Teive, was completed in 1992 and soon filled up with local yachts, though visitors were always squeezed in somehow. By 2003 plans were in hand to build a second and much larger berthing area further west, combined with a purpose-built cruise ship terminal, the *Portas do Mar*, a project completed on schedule in July 2008. This increased marina berths four-fold to 670 in all – and at no time during the building work did the harbour lose its EU 'Blue Flag', held without a break since 1999. Although from the administrative angle the old and new berthing areas form a single marina, now known as Ponta Delgada Marina (or sometimes Marina de Ponta Delgada), for clarity and brevity they are referred to in this book as the west and east marinas.

Visiting yachts berth in the west marina which, in addition to many smaller berths, offers 100 berths for yachts of 10–15m, 25 berths for 15–18m, and 12 berths able to take 18m or more. All are alongside finger pontoons, which at the larger berths are anchored to individual piles, making them exceptionally sturdy. In addition long pontoons line the west side of the cruiseship terminal, providing alongside berthing for superyachts of up to 75m in length, in depths of around 10m. It will be a while before the west marina fills up with local boats, but in the longer term at least 25% of spaces are to be reserved for visitors.

The west marina has not been without its problems, however. Completion of shoreside facilities such as showers lagged behind the marina itself, and for several years it suffered from frequent power failures. Both of those have now been rectified, but two major problems remain – swell entering the marina during south and southeasterly winds ... and seagulls. The former is mainly due to the fact that the western arm of the cruise ship pier is not solid but is formed of a series of arches, through which any swell can travel, the proof being that it all

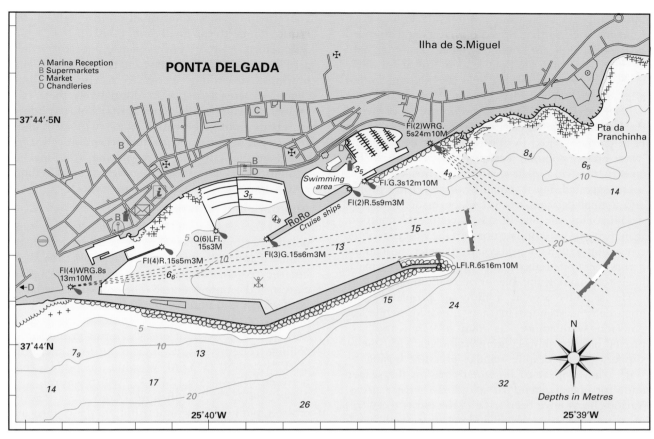

A Marina Reception
B Supermarkets
C Market
D Chandleries

PONTA DELGADA

Ilha de S.Miguel

37°44'·5N

Pta da
Pranchinha

Fl(2)WRG.
5s24m10M

Swimming
area

Fl.G.3s12m10M

Fl(2)R.5s9m3M

RoRo

Cruise ships

15

13

Fl(3)G.15s6m3M

Q(6)LFl.
15s3M

Fl(4)R.15s5m3M

Fl(4)WRG.8s
13m10M

LFl.R.6s16m10M

15

24

N

37°44'N

Depths in Metres

25°40'W

25°39'W

II. THE AZORES

Looking northeast across the two marinas at Ponta Delgada as a motorboat passes between
the west marina and the *Portas do Mar* cruise ship terminal. (The hazy patches are due to
condensation on the window of the commercial aeroplane) *Anne Hammick*

but disappears when a ship is alongside. Longer term residents confirm that ripped out cleats and stranded or broken lines are common, while plenty of anti-chaffing gear and multiple fenders are an absolute necessity. It is essential that lines are adjusted so that adjacent yachts' spreaders cannot touch. Wash from fishing boats which berth in the northwest corner of the harbours also enters the marina, though this has been partially cured by the positioning of a floating 'wave-break' pontoon between the two areas. The construction of a right-angled inner breakwater has been suggested, but it would be an expensive project and a final decision has yet to be made. If built it would follow the line of the 'wave-break' pontoon, then turn east to terminate north of the west arm of the cruise ship terminal. Swell could still enter through the arches mentioned above, however, and the marina is likely to remain unsuitable for overwintering.

The seagulls present a different problem. They apparently descended in their hundreds while the pontoons were empty – as many still are – and have proved hard to shift, coating walkways with smelly, slippery guano despite regular pressure hosing by staff. They appear to be worst early in the season and, fortunately, tend to avoid the busier areas. Various ideas have been tried in the effort to get rid of them permanently, including a trained hawk (withdrawn partly due to fears that visitors would not welcome partially-devoured birds falling down their forehatches), sprinklers (though the logic of using water to drive away seagulls seems open to question), various chemicals, and covering unoccupied pontoons with netting. None have been very successful, and in 2015 the authorities were considering shooting the birds at the inland rubbish tips on which they feed. A final disadvantage for many is loud music drifting from the cafés and restaurants north and east of the marina. It is said to continue into the small hours at weekends, while concerts in the new auditorium on the 'stalk' of the cruise ship berth can go on until 0300.

To return to a more positive note, an extensive lido area has been created between the west and east marinas, providing access to a roped off sea swimming area (see plan). Alternatively there is a treated saltwater outdoor pool just behind the lido, a waterside path between the two providing convenient access to the marina reception office for those berthed in the west marina (the marina administration office near the west marina's shore access does not handle arrival paperwork).

## Approach and entrance

*By day* Very simple, with no hazards. The grey stone breakwater may blend with the concrete esplanade behind if approaching on a bearing of less than 325°, but the red and white banded tower marking its eastern end is unmistakable. The breakwater extends both awash and underwater for a further 50–100m in line with the existing wall – exact depths are not known, but more than one yacht has grounded. If coming from the east, cables run out from the shore at 37°45'·03N 25°37'·07W while an outfall runs between 37°44'·5N 25°38'·9W (onshore) and 37°44'·3N 25°38'W (offshore). Both areas may be crossed, but anchoring and fishing in the vicinity are forbidden.

The relatively narrow gap giving access to the marina reception and fuel quay (see also Berthing, below) lies almost opposite the end of the breakwater, the latter quite unmistakable with its row of flagpoles backed by white buildings surmounted by a squat observation tower complete with conical white roof. Rubble is said to lie some distance off the end of the marina mole and is sometimes, but not always, marked by a selection of small, green, unlit buoys. The swimming area opposite is cordoned off by a string of small red

The unusual curved pontoons of Ponta Delgada's west marina, looking almost due west. The high-rise building on the right is unique in the Azores and is highly visible from offshore *Anne Hammick*

A well-secured Swedish cutter occupies one of the east hammerheads in Ponta Delgada's west marina. At least eight mooring lines hold her in place in the almost incessant swell *Anne Hammick*

buoys, again unlit. The reception quay has at least 3·5m along its entire 60m length.

*By night* Ponta Delgada's city lights are by far the brightest on the coast, with a long row of street lights lining the esplanade behind the harbour. After the light at Santa Clara 1M west of Ponta Delgada, the first harbour light to be identified is likely to be that marking the end of the breakwater, with a range of at least 10M. Sectored lights have replaced both pairs of leading lights, with the white (safe) sector of the outer light spanning 306° to 312° while that of the inner light spans 261° to 263°. An incoming yacht might actually be safer in the red or green zones, and in any case will soon need to veer north to approach the reception quay. Both sides of the access gap are lit, though it would be wise to favour the port side in view of the rubble mentioned above.

## Anchorage

Anchoring anywhere inside the harbour is strictly prohibited – in the event of engine failure, contact the marina via VHF or mobile phone for assistance. A towing launch is available if required.

## Berthing

The east (old) marina is entirely occupied by local boats, so the following refers to the west marina only.

With so many berths still empty it is now accepted that, unless requiring fuel, most skippers prefer to go directly to the west marina without a detour to the reception quay first. Neither are calls on VHF always answered, even during office hours. As well as many smaller spaces there at least 100 berths for yachts of 10–15m and 25 for 15–18m, all alongside finger pontoons (which at the larger berths are anchored to individual piles, making them exceptionally sturdy). Slots are wide, with plenty of manoeuvring space between the curved arms. At least 3·5m will be found at all but the smallest berths. Up to three 18m yachts can berth on the

eastern hammerheads, while megayachts generally lie alongside the pontoon which fringes the west side of the Portas do Mar. Finally, alongside berthing is available for two or three yachts in the 12·5–14m range approximately where the 3·5m depth is shown on the plan, but these may be reserved for specific vessels so should not be occupied before checking with the reception office.

Security is excellent throughout, with pontoon access via card-operated gates (a single one for the west marina, a gate to each pontoon in the east), backed by both CCTV and round-the-clock security patrols.

## Formalities

If the reception quay was not visited on arrival (see above), the skipper should walk over to the marina reception office as soon as convenient. The usual ship's papers and insurance documents will be required, together with all crew passports, though even non-EU crew need not attend in person. Do not forget to note down the berth number before setting off. If outside office hours clearance can be made next moring, though a GNR official checks the pontoons every day so it would be unwise to leave it too long.

The reception office – where Pedro Santos has been welcoming visitors for nearly 20 years – has been reorientated to overlook the reception/fuelling quay at the entrance to the east marina (it used to be somewhat further north in the same range of buildings). The building also houses the offices of the *Guarda Nacional Republicana (GNR)*, *Alfândega* (Customs), *Serviço de Estrangeiros e Fronteiras* (Immigration) and *Polícia Marítima*. After visiting the marina office (where, in addition to excellent English, Pedro and his colleagues between them speak French, Spanish, Italian and some German), it is necessary to call at both the *Alfândega* and *Polícia Marítima*. Together with Faial and Terceira, São Miguel is a 'border post' under the Schengen Agreement – see page 51. Fortunately this does not entail extra paperwork, as clearance into Portuguese waters and the Schengen area are handled concurrently.

On departure the marina office must be visited first to settle the bill, and copies of the receipt presented at the other offices. If planning to visit any of the smaller islands it will be worth preserving the computer printout which one receives of marina and clearing details, as this carries answers to all the standard questions.

A separate marina administration office overlooks the west marina. Situated almost opposite the single access gate it is mainly a source of city maps and information, as well as containing a small book-swap and providing tokens for the nearby marina laundry.

Boat & Sail service is somewhat tucked away in the east marina, hence the need for Thomas's very practical bicycle and trailer  *Anne Hammick*

## Charges

Ponta Delgada Marina is part of the *Portos dos Açores SA* chain, and shares their basic price structure – see page 55. Payment can be made using most major credit/debit cards other than American Express.

## Facilities

Defying categorisation are Thomas and Any Dargel whose Boat & Sail Service, *mobile* +351 963 925707, boatsailservice@gmx.net, www.boatsailservice.com has been assisting visitors to Ponta Delgada since 1997. There seems to be little that they cannot handle – and if they cannot, they will know who can – in fluent English as well as their native German, plus French and Portuguese. Feedback received about Thomas and Any invariably heaps praise on their work in terms of both speed and quality.

Boat & Sail Service has long been established in the northwest corner of the east marina, where Any handles sail repairs and general canvaswork while Thomas more often works in situ aboard yachts in both basins (a smart bicycle and trailer combination has proved ideal for commuting with tools and other heavy items). In 2011 they were able to expand their previously somewhat cramped premises to allow more space for chandlery, with a separate workshop behind. The shop is normally open 0900–1300 and 1430–1730 during the season, but if closed – because both Thomas and Any are working elsewhere – try contacting by mobile phone on the number above. As of 2015 Boat & Sail Service were unable to accept payment by credit/debit card.

Further details of the range offered by Boat & Sail Service will be found below, to which should be added gas installation, plumbing, year-round guardinage and – should it be necessary – de-cockroaching.

*Boatyard* There are several yards where wooden and steel fishing boats are built and repaired, but no boatyard specifically for yachts, though space ashore is usually available on the east marina mole, near the travel-lift.

DIY work is permitted, otherwise Boat & Sail Service (see above) handle osmosis treatment, repairs to wood and GRP, and painting/antifouling (they stock Epifanes, Seajet and Coppercoat), while Tecnináutica ☎+351 296 636401, tecninautica@gmail.com www.tecninautica.pt, based at Azores Parque about 5km northeast of the city, also offer osmosis treatment, and GRP and gelcoat repair.

*Travel-lift* The marina has a 25-tonne capacity lift, and shares the limited area of hardstanding on the east marina mole with the *Clube Naval de Ponta Delgada*. Book via the marina reception office.

*Crane* The *clube naval* also have a 3-tonne crane suitable for removing engines etc., located on the east marina mole. Use is generally arranged directly with the clube, often by the person or company carrying out the work.

*Diving services* Three kiosks offering diving services overlook the east marina, including Nerus Diving Center, *mobile* +351 918 270186, www.nerusazores.eu. Though primarily in the training and holiday business it could doubtless tackle most underwater problems. Diving with tanks in the marina requires prior permission, though there is no restriction on snorkelling.

*Engineers* The first port of call for non-Portuguese speaking yachtsmen will normally be Boat & Sail Service (see above), as if Thomas is unable to do the work himself he is well placed to advise and translate. Otherwise Tecnináutica (see Boatyard, above) is an agent for Yamaha, and also handles engine repairs plus work in stainless steel and aluminium, while Varela & Ca Lda ☎+351 296 301823, volvo.penta@bensaude.pt at Rua dos Velados No.20 is an agent for Volvo, offering spares and maintenance. Finally, Navel SA ☎+351 296 205290, commercial@navel.pt, a long-established firm with premises on Rua Engenheiro Avel Ferin Coutinho a few hundred metres northwest of the root of the main breakwater, handles welding, machining and general engineering, and also sells a wide range of tools and hardware. Some English is spoken.

*Electrical work* Thomas of Boat & Sail Service handles electrical installations as well as trouble-shooting and repairing those already in place.

*Electronic sales and repair* JB Electrónica Lda ☎+351 296 283781, jbelectronica@sapo.pt at Rua do Perú No.73 (three blocks inland from the east marina, on the steep, cobbled Ladeira da Mae de Deus which leads up to a small church), sells, installs and repairs most major international brands including Garmin, Raymarine, ICOM, Simrad etc. The helpful staff speak good English.

*Sail repairs & canvaswork* Any of Boat & Sail Service repairs sails (though she does not make them) and handles general canvaswork and boat upholstery. She has a particularly good range of materials and fittings. Alternatively Rui Soares, trading as Velame, *mobile* +351 966 451161, velameazores@gmail.com offers a similar service from his premises on the lower floor of the *Clube Naval de Ponta Delgada* at the root of the east marina mole.

*Rigging* Boat & Sail Service specialises in rigging and deck hardware, stocking Lewmar, Barton, Seldén, Profurl,

Wichard, Furlex and Sparcraft among others. They have a swage machine and hold stocks of rigging wire from 3mm to 16mm in diameter, plus yacht rope including exotics.

*Liferaft servicing* OREY Técnica Naval ①+351 296 929314, azores.technica@orey.com www.orey-tecnica.pt are based in the Zona Industrial dos Portões Vermelhos about 7km northeast of Ponta Delgada. In addition to servicing and selling liferafts, they also stock Pains Wessex distress signals and other safety equipment. Arrange direct or via Boat & Sail Service.

*Chandlery* Boat & Sail Service stock general chandlery in addition to the rigging items already mentioned. Again, anything not in stock can be ordered from catalogues, a process which usually takes three days or more.

Larger but less convenient is MAP Açores, mapazores@gmail.com www.mapazores.com (the latter detailed and multi-lingual). It has a small shop overlooking the west marina, ①+351 296 282244 (open 1000–1230, 1400–1800 weekdays, 1000–1300 Saturday, closed Sunday) which is mainly given over to sport fishing equipment but also sells rope and fenders. Its main shop, ①+351 296 716400 (open 0900–1230, 1400–1830 weekdays, 0900–1300 Saturday) has moved from its previous position on Rua do Mercado to Santa Clara, about 1·5km southwest of the city centre. Chandlery including International Paints, electronics, safety equipment and stainless steel fittings is held in stock, and items not on the shelves can be ordered from a range of catalogues. Good English is spoken in both venues.

Finally, Honorato Moreira Monteiro Lda, ①+351 296 385047, honoratomonteiro@hotmail.com, www.honoratomoreiramonteiro.pai.pt, at 42 Rua da Boa Nova, 9500-296 Ponta Delgada (east of the old marina and one road inland) stocks some chandlery together with a wide range of fishing equipment.

*Charts* Boat & Sail Service stock Imray charts and books covering nearby waters, and have an agreement whereby unsold older editions are replaced with new ones so that everything is always fully up-to-date. MAP (see Chandlery above) sells Portuguese charts of the Azores, but they are not formal agents so charts will not be corrected to date.

*Showers* One shower block behind the west marina, with 14 showers (four each in the ladies and gents areas, plus six rooms each containing a shower, basin and toilet, one fitted for disabled use), plus another facility containing six showers at the east marina.

*Launderette* Next to the shower block at the west marina (though serving both, as that at the east marina closed) but with only two washers and two dryers, though another washing machine may be added soon. The machines use tokens obtainable from either marina office. Alternatively there is a launderette in the basement of the Solmar shopping centre (see below) open 1000–1700, closed Sunday, or the Sol Nascente laundry in Lagoa, *mobile* +351 910 608060, will collect from and return to either office.

*Electricity* 220v 50Hz at all berths in both marinas, with 380v 3-phase also available at the larger berths in the west marina and on the megayacht pontoon. The west marina suffers from a shortage of power sockets –

worth taking into account if selecting a berth – though a limited number of 'doubling' adapters are available. Yachts must provide their own cable and standard European plug.

*Fuel* Both diesel and petrol are available at the marina reception quay, and yachts are encouraged to fill up on arrival to avoid a return visit. Megayachts can be refuelled in their berths by road tanker – enquire at the reception office. Payment can be made using most major credit/debit cards other than American Express.

*Bottled gas* Exchanges of any cylinders other than GALP's own have been discontinued throughout the Azores. Boat & Sail Service can arrange for most bottles, including Camping Gaz, to be refilled (with butane only) but allow at least two working days.

*Banks* Many in the city, nearly all with ATMs, which will also be found at the root of the cruise ship pier and in the Solmar shopping centre.

*Shops/provisioning* A choice of supermarkets within walking distance of the marinas, including Solmar in the shopping centre of that name, plus several vast hypermarkets further out. Also many souvenir, clothing, pharmacy and other stores, as one would expect in the archipelago's largest city.

*Produce market* The large fruit and vegetable market, with fish market attached, lies two blocks inland from the waterfront on Rua do Mercado. A wide selection of good quality local produce is available, with the best variety early in the day.

*Cafés, restaurants & hotels* Numerous restaurants, cafés and snack bars to suit all tastes and pockets, plus hotels of all categories.

*Medical services* There is a hospital on the northern outskirts of the city, ①+351 296 203000, highly praised yachtsmen and women who have used its services. The marina maintains a list of doctors, dentists and opticians.

### Communications

*Mailing address* C/o Marina de Ponta Delgada, Avenida Infante Dom Henrique Ap.113, 9500 Ponta Delgada, São Miguel, Açores, Portugal.

*Wifi* Although free WiFi is claimed to be available in both sections of the marina, that in the west marina has received a consistently poor press, with slow speeds even when a connection can be made. Fortunately several of the cafés fringing the marina offer free WiFi, some also providing power sockets, while the Solmar Shopping Centre has free WiFi on the ground floor (not associated with any of the cafés), with tables and chairs provided but no power sockets. Two (free) Skype-enabled computers are available to those berthed in the west marina and one to those in the east section.

*Car hire & taxis* Readily available, organised direct or via either marina office.

*Buses* Services run to most towns in São Miguel, though all appear to start and finish in Ponta Delgada.

*Air services* The airport is situated some 4km west of the city and offers frequent inter-island flights, plus several to/from Lisbon each day and more limited links with other major European cities including London and Manchester – see Transportation, page 48.

II. THE AZORES

Looking southeast across the small harbour at Lagoa *Anne Hammick*

## Lagoa

37°44'·48N 25°34'·54W (molehead)

**Lights**
**Lagoa** Fl.R.3s8m6M
White column, red bands 4m
**Lagoa cables**
Fl(2)R.8s6m9M (daylight range 1·6M) 339°-vis-007°
White post, red bands 4m. Marks submarine cables

### Small, scenic fishing harbour

About 4M east of Ponta Delgada and the site of one of São Miguel's oldest settlements, the mole at Lagoa was extended several years ago to create a small harbour where a few fishing boats lie afloat with others drawn up on the slipway. The surrounding shoreline is generally low, but the harbour is easily identified from seawards by the tall grey silo 0·5M to the west.

Several attractive swimming pools have been created among the rocks east of the harbour making Lagoa an interesting daytime anchorage in light conditions, but the area should be approached with care as depths have not been verified. Cables run out from the shore about 600m further to the east.

A small *clube naútico* overlooks the harbour, as do several cafés and restaurants and a large fish market, while shops and a bank with ATM will be found in the adjoining town. There is a regular bus service to/from Ponta Delgada.

## Porto da Caloura

37°42'·81N 25°29'·73W (molehead)

**Lights**
**Mole** Fl.4s6m9M
Square white column, red bands 3m
**Ldg Lts on 333°** Oc.G.3s10/14m5M
White posts, red bands 2m

### Not a port at all

Little more than a slipway protected by a short mole, where half a dozen brightly painted fishing boats are hauled ashore on rollers when not in use, Porto da Caloura is undeniably pretty but not in any way a port. It would be possible to anchor off, perhaps to use the natural swimming pool which lies among the rocks southwest of the harbour, but approach with extreme caution. It is definitely worth including if touring the island by hire car, however. There is a café and public toilets near the slipway, plus a brand new *Posto de Turismo do Mar* (sea tourist office), but little else.

The wide slipway and short mole at 'Porto' da Caloura. Yachts occasionally anchor off in settled weather *Anne Hammick*

## Vila Franca do Campo

37°42'·79N 25°25'·7W (breakwater head)

**Lights**
**Marina east breakwater** Fl.G.4s11m9M
White tower, green bands 7m
**Outer breakwater** Fl.R.4s11m9M
White tower, red bands 9m

**Harbour communications**
**Marina da Vila**
VHF Ch 09, 16
☎+351 296 581488
0830–1230, 1330–1630 weekdays, closed weekends
marinaem@sapo.pt
www.marinadavila.com

### Small, local marina accessed via busy fishing harbour

A small town and off-lying islet (a miniature volcanic crater flooded by the sea) some 11M east of Ponta Delgada, Vila Franca do Campo was once the capital of São Miguel before being destroyed by a landslide in 1522. It is still relatively small and compact, with imposing churches around the attractive town square although sadly the picturesque old fishing quarter has largely disappeared under concrete. Its memory lives on, however, in the pervasive – though surprisingly pleasant – smell from the very old tuna canning factory which still operates nearby.

The tiny Ilhéu da Vila – which has protected status as a 'Natural Park' – contains as perfect a natural swimming pool as one is likely to find and should not be missed. No fishing of any kind is permitted near the island and in theory even rowing dinghies are now banned from entering the island's tiny lagoon. Not surprisingly the island is very popular with local people (a ferry service runs from just south of the marina between June and September) so will be quietest if visited mid-week.

The construction of São Miguel's second marina on the east side of Vila Franca do Campo began in 2000 under the auspices of *Câmara Municipal da Vila Franca do Campo*, effectively the town council. Although the inner basin was largely complete by the following year and received its first yachts in August 2001, it has remained very much a local facility, with all 125 berths in the inner basin let long-term – the outer basin proved too exposed for berthing. Work on the second phase of development, a very substantial outer breakwater to enlarge the old fishing harbour and protect the marina's outer basin, began in 2006 and was largely complete by 2009, providing much improved protection throughout.

The marina has occasionally been reported as noisy on Friday and Saturday evenings, with loud music until late into the night. Though plainly not every weekend, it might be worth checking on this when booking.

**II. THE AZORES**

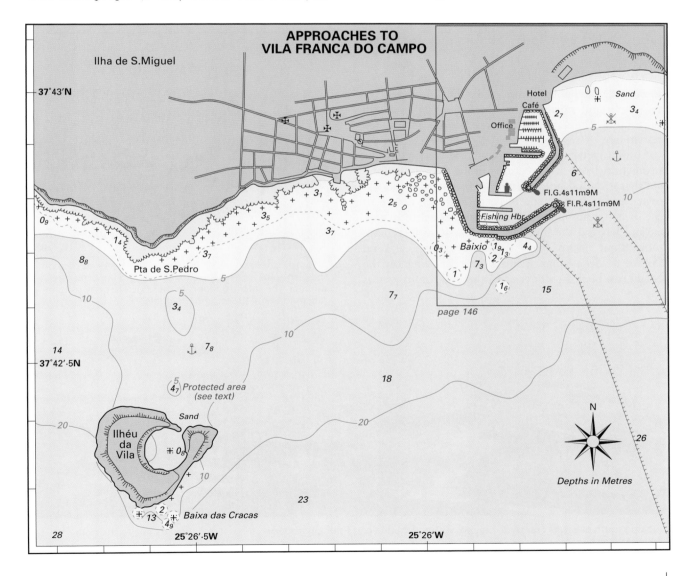

### Approach

Approaching from the west, Ponta da Galera should be given a berth of 500m and a course of 088° then steered for Ilhéu da Vila in order to clear Baixa da Roida. There are several off-lying rocks to the south of the islet, but in good conditions when within 0·5M of the islet a course can be shaped to pass inside. The west wall of the outer harbour follows the line of a long and extremely dangerous shoal which previously ran some 500m south-southeast from the shore. However, the wall covers only the northern part of the shoal, leaving the southern 250m or so exposed and unmarked, with one outlier rising from 13m to 1·6m or less. For that reason it would be wise to remain outside the 20m line until the end of the breakwater bears west of north before heading in.

If coming from the east, an outfall runs just over 0·5M south-southeast from the bay close east of the marina, and fishing and anchoring in the vicinity are forbidden. Vessels are permitted to cross the area, however, and there are no other hazards. A long, arched, cream building – the Hotel Marina – lies directly behind the marina, while the beach close east is backed by a waterpark with slides and other structures.

### Anchorages

In settled, daylight conditions delightful anchorage will be found northeast of Ilhéu da Vila in 6–8m over sand. Note the various restrictions mentioned previously.

Alternatively, the bay east of the marina offers protection from all directions other than south and southeast. Good holding will be found in about 5m over sand, avoiding the large rock in the centre of the beach and its varous offliers, none of which extend beyond the 3m line. It is essential to remain more than 300m from the beach, however, and failure to do so may incur a fine. Landing on the beach can be difficult even in calm conditions as it is

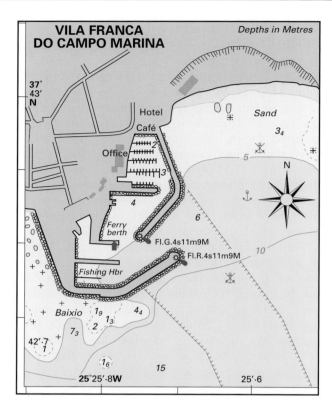

A Swiss yacht lies where the words 'Ferry berth' appear on the plan – not a good place to leave a yacht unattended in summer. The steel trapdoors in the concrete quay contain fuel pumps and hoses  *Anne Hammick*

Looking south over Vila Franca do Campo, with the marina and fishing harbour on the left and Ilhéu da Vila to the right *Anne Hammick*

The marina and fishing harbour at Vila Franca do Campo. Pontoons have long been promised for the central area, but it is not known when they are likely to be installed
*Anne Hammick*

steep and subject to rollers, but there are plenty of corners inside the marina where a dinghy could be left without being in the way.

No charge is made in either location.

### Entrance and berthing

In view of the shortage of space it is necessary to contact the marina office prior to arrival – note the somewhat limited hours, outside which English is unlikely to be spoken.

Final approach to the dogleg entrance should be made from the southeast, a watch being kept for fishing boats leaving or approaching at speed. Once inside a sharp turn to starboard is required, through a gap no more than 30m in width, into the marina's outer basin. In 2015 there were five moorings in this area, laid by the marina and checked annually by the *Clube Naval de Vila Franca do Campo*, which has premises near the marina office. The moorings are said to hold up to 10 tonnes, but it might be wise not to leave the boat unattended until this has been confirmed. In due course pontoons are likely to be laid in this area, which has two shoreside fixing points ready to receive them and 3·5m depths throughout. Plans currently allow for a further 61 berths, of which 48 will be for craft of less than 10m, but bearing in mind the increasing size of locally-owned vessels as well as visiting yachts this may well be revised.

The north side of the short mole which divides the marina from the fishing harbour offers an inviting short-term berth, with relatively smooth concrete and both bollards and steps, but in summer it is used by the Ilhéu da Vila ferry so a yacht should not be left there unattended. Do not be tempted to use the south side, however, as this is the fishermen's fuel berth, a fact easy to miss as the hoses are stored below steel trapdoors when not in use.

The inner basin contains 125 berths on five pontoons. Visiting yachts of up to 13m LOA have lain alongside finger pontoons in the southeast corner of the inner basin – presumably whilst the permanent residents were absent – but found a bare 2m at low water. Shelter is excellent, however, and it is difficult to think of a more protected spot in which to sit out storm-force winds … in the unlikely event that space is available.

Security is provided by card-operated access gates, for which a refundable deposit of €25 is charged, CCTV and a round-the-clock security guards.

### Formalities

The marina office, which overlooks the inner basin, has been run for the past seven years by Berta Aguiar, who is very welcoming and speaks excellent English. Outside office hours and at weekends, however, an arriving yacht is likely to be met by one of the security guards, who are generally helpful but speak almost no English.

Vila Franca do Campo is not a port of entry, and clearance must first be obtained at Ponta Delgada.

### Charges

As mentioned previously, Marina da Vila is owned and run by the *Câmara Municipal da Vila Franca do Campo* and is not part of the *Portos dos Açores SA* chain. In 2015 the daily berthing fee for a visiting monohull of 10–12m LOA was €20.14 and that for 12–15m was €30.15, which included water, electricity and IVA (VAT, currently 18%). No price was quoted for multihulls, probably because there is no room for them. The moorings in the marina's outer basin are charged at €8.38 including IVA, irrespective of size.

For further details check the marina's website at www.marinadavila.com, in Portuguese only but commendably up-to-date.

### Facilities

*Boatyard/engineering* Both run by a local man who speaks no English, so approach via the marina office.

*Travel-lift* 75-tonne capacity hoist which, though primarily intended for fishing vessels (hence the size), can also be used for yachts. There is a reasonable area of concreted hardstanding, but sourcing props of suitable length and strength might be a problem. Local smallcraft are winched ashore on rollers on the wide slipway at the head of the fishing harbour, a method which might also work for a modest multihull. In both cases consult the marina office.

*Diving services* Azores Sub Dive Center, ☎+351 296 583999, divecenter@azoressub.com www.azoressub.com has premises near the marina office open 0830-1800 daily. Though primarily in the training and holiday business it could doubtless tackle most underwater problems and good English is spoken.

*Chandlery* A very limited amount is stocked by a fishing tackle shop opposite the tourist office on Rua Conego Sena Freitas.

*Showers* In the same block as the marina office.

*Launderette* A single washing machine (but no dryer) located behind the marina office.

*Fuel* From pumps on the marina's southwest mole (ie. the one opposite the east mole) though well hidden in storage areas below steel trapdoors. Arrange via Azores Sub Dive Centre (see Diving, above).

*Banks* Several in the town, all with ATMs, plus one outside the marina office.

*Shops/provisioning* Sizeable and well-stocked supermarket on the Rua do Penedo, which leads west from near the Hotel Marina, plus a good range of other shops.

*Produce market* On Rua Teófilo de Braga (the main Ponta Delgada road).

*Cafés, restaurants & hotels* Several hotels and numerous cafés and restaurants, including one overlooking the marina's inner basin. The large Hotel Marina, by the root of the east breakwater, has a pleasant bar and restaurant – the entrance is at the east (beach) end of the building.

*Medical services* Small hospital in the town, plus pharmacies etc.

### Communications

*Mailing address* C/o Marina de Vila, Rua Eng. Manuel António Martins Mota, 9680-909 Vila Franca do Campo, São Miguel, Açores, Portugal.

*WiFi* Free WiFi at the café overlooking the marina's inner basin.

*Car hire & taxis* Available in the town, or arrange via the marina office.

*Buses* Services to Ponta Delgada and elsewhere.

*Ferries* Regular summer foot ferry to Ilhéu da Vila, but nothing coastal.

## Ribeira Quente

37°43'·98N 25°17'·93W (molehead)

**Lights**

**Breakwater** Fl.G.4s5m5M
White column, green bands 3m

### Active fishing harbour

Ribeira Quente is very much a working harbour, but even so the (very) few yachts which have visited have generally been permitted to lie alongside the breakwater, at least while the larger fishing boats are at sea. It is also home port to several whale-watching RIBs. However space is limited – many of the smaller boats are brought ashore – and with little shelter from the southwest some swell is almost inevitable. Much of the harbour appears to carry 3m or more. There is a large travel-lift and a wide slipway, but watch out for inconspicuous buoys around and inside the entrance.

Looking east across the harbour at Ribeira Quente harbour – in torrential rain  *Anne Hammick*

The harbour has an attractive terraced backdrop, but there is little in the village other than a few small shops and cafés, and a bank with ATM.

## Povoação

37°44'·66 25°14'·81W (east molehead)

**Lights**
**West breakwater** Oc.R.4s6m3M
White column, red bands 5m
**East mole** Oc.G.4s6m6M
White column, green bands 5m

### Small, quiet harbour

Understood to have been built in about 1995, the small harbour at Povoação has been the recipient of considerable work – and doubtless funds – with the east mole extended in 2008 and further extended in 2013/4. Despite this, the harbour appears to be little used even by local fishermen

The pretty though somewhat isolated town is thought to be the oldest settlement on the island – a date of 1432 is proudly displayed on a column in the attractive town square, which gives onto a cobbled pedestrian area. Both town and harbour are noticeably tidy and well-kept.

The town and harbour at Povoação, seen from the northwest  *Therese and Howard Beswick*

## Approach and berthing

Straightforward, once the town has been identified – it lies in a valley with cultivated slopes on either side. The harbour is backed by the long, white Hotel do Mar with a low tower at its eastern end, close east of which is a large cream building (a sports hall). The entrance is dog-legged but reasonably wide, the substantial enclosing breakwaters marked by tall banded columns.

In settled conditions it would be possible for a yacht to lie against the inside of the west breakwater. There is one set of steps plus several ladders, and no shortage of bollards. Exact depths are not known, but there appears to be several metres alongside the outer half. Plans for dredging were mentioned in 2015 – though unlikely to take place until at least the following year – to remove debris washed down into the harbour by heavy winter rain.

## Facilities and communications

No facilities at the harbour, not even water. Neither are there fuel pumps, though a filling station will be found near the east end of the bridge. The town has several small supermarkets, a bank with ATM and no shortage of cafés and restaurants. A regular bus service connects Povoção with Vila Franca do Campo and Ponta Delgada.

## Porto Formoso

37°49'·43N 25°25'·55W (east mole)

**Lights**
**Porto Formoso** Fl.4s6M
Lantern on building with red and white bands 3m
**West mole** Fl.G.4s4m3M
White post, green bands
**East mole** Fl.R.4s5m3M
White post, red bands

## Possible anchorage off tiny harbour

A neat little semicircular harbour has been built in the tiny rock-fringed bay, possibly more to protect the beach behind than with any expectation of serving the needs of boats. It would be possible to anchor well off in very settled weather, protected from southeast through south to northwest, but extreme caution would be needed in the approach. There is a café/restaurant nearby, but the town is some distance inland.

# Rabo do Peixe

37°49'N 25°35'·11W (breakwater head)

**Lights**
**North breakwater** Fl.R.5s10m6M 338°-vis-252°
White column, red bands 2·6m
**North breakwater spur** Fl(2)R.5s7m2M
248°-vis-135° White column, red bands 2·5m
**West breakwater** Fl(2)G.5s7m2M
White column, green bands 2·5m
*Note* The above two lights are synchronised
**Inner (east) mole** Fl.R.2s4m1M
White column, red bands 3m

## São Miguel's only north coast harbour

Formerly a wide bay giving protection from east through south to southwest, in 1999 a breakwater was added north of the old quay, and in 2013–14 an entirely new harbour built in the southern part of the bay. Even so, the town which overlooks it has a very different atmosphere to most others on the island – noticably poorer and with very little English spoken, it appears largely untouched by the 20th century, let alone the 21st. This may change if, as rumour suggests, one or more whale-watching enterprises base themselves in the harbour. Currently very much off the tourist route, a modest influx of visitors could only be good for the town, which Azoreans from elsewhere in São Miguel have described as 'inward-looking' and 'unfriendly'. In the meantime it is suggested that a yacht visiting Rabo do Peixe should not be left unattended, at least for the first day or two.

## Approach, entrance and berthing

In common with much of the north coast, Rabo de Peixe should not be approached in northerly winds of any strength as the shelving bottom causes steep seas which may break off the entrance. Otherwise, if approaching from the west an offing of 0·5M clears all dangers. Coming from the east a course of no less than 250° should be maintained after rounding Ponta da Ribeirinha in order to avoid the 4·8m Baixa do Morro, 1·5M northeast of the harbour, not turning for the breakwater end until it bears due south. 6m will be found off the 35m-wide entrance and 5m immediately inside, though depths further in have not been verified.

No provision has been made for yachts in the new harbour, local or visiting, and though plans displayed locally show a '*zona de recreio*' it is clearly intended only for dinghies and smallcraft. There is no shortage of space, however, particularly in the southern harbour where at least 3m is likely to be found near the head of the west breakwater.

Looking northeast across the recently-completed harbour at Rabo do Peixe – 'the tail of the fish'. The white building in the centre houses the *Club Naval  Anne Hammick*

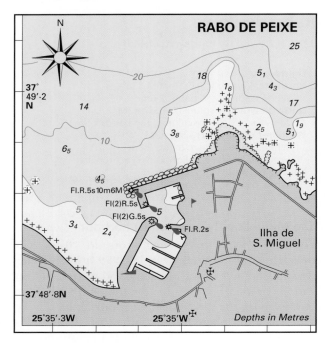

*RABO DE PEIXE*

Alternatively the spur running south from near the end of the breakwater has vastly increased protection along its 100m inner face, and though likely to be busy with fishing vessels it would offer safe sanctuary to a yacht in an emergency. Exact depths are not known, but there is no obvious reason why the 3–5m previously to be found there should have changed.

The smart new premises of the *Club Naval Rabo de Peixe*, ☎+351 296 492911, geral.cnrp@gmail.com www.cn-rabopeixe.com are situated almost opposite the harbour entrance, and its mission statement to: 'encourage nautical recreation in the community of Rabo de Peixe, promote maritime activity in the area, promote environmental education policies, and be a catalyst for social change by interacting with the local community in order to promote good citizenship' sounds extremely hopeful. The office is normally open 0900–1300, 1400–1800 weekdays (closed Wednesday morning), and 0900–1300 Saturday.

### Anchorage

In settled weather it would be possible to anchor west of the entrance in 5–6m over sand and rock, in good protection other than from northwest to northeast.

### Facilities

Travel-hoist at the root of the mole, with a second dock further south, but no boatyard as such – the *Club Naval* mentioned above would undoubtedly be the first place to ask if assistance were needed. Taps on the old inner quay and elsewhere, and shops and banks (with ATMs) in the town.

# Porto das Capelas

37°50'·55N 25°41'·2W (quay)

**Lights**
**Morro de Capelas** Fl(2)R.12s114m8M
   153°-vis-281° White post, red bands 7m

## Attractive north coast anchorage

Not so much a 'port' as a narrow bay surrounded by sheer cliffs giving protection from east through south to west, but totally exposed to northerly winds and swell. The rocky headland to the east is penetrated by several long narrow inlets and would be fascinating dinghy territory, while the anchorage itself is exceptionally pretty with very clear water.

## Approach and anchorage

If coming from the west, Ponta de São António should be given at least 800m clearance and Capelas quay and slipway approached on a bearing of no less than 175°. From the east, the anchorage will be completely hidden until around the Morro de Capelas, at least 200m clear. An isolated breaking rock (Calhau dos Burras) lies some 100m offshore in the southwest corner of the bay, but there are no other outliers. There is a light on the cliffs above the bay, but night entry is not recommended.

Anchor in 5–8m over sand and rock with the tiny quay and slipway bearing about 120°.

## Facilities

There is a small town on the cliffs above the anchorage, with fresh water and fuel available by can, several small food stores, and a bank with ATM.

Porto das Capelas – a misnomer, being no more than a natural bay – looking northeast *Anne Hammick*

# Santa Maria

**Between 35°56′N–37°01′N and 25°01′W–25°11′W**

## Introduction

Santa Maria is the southernmost of the Azores group by almost a full degree, and other than the Ilhéus das Formigas is also the furthest east. It is one of the smaller islands, 17km long by up to 8km wide, with an area of 97km². Like the other islands it is of volcanic origin, but is unique amongst the Azores in also having sedimentary rocks. The western plateau is formed of limestone rich in marine fossils, with useful deposits of red clay.

Santa Maria was the first of the Azores to be settled by the Portuguese, probably in 1427, when Gonçalo Velho Cabral landed on the beach at Praia do Lobos. Herds of pigs and goats were put ashore to ensure a ready food supply for the men who followed, and the native forest burned and felled to make way for cultivation. Scattered villages already existed throughout the island by February 1493, when Columbus anchored off the tiny village of Anjos (Angels) on the northwest coast whilst returning from his first voyage to enable his crew to attend Mass. Wisely, he allowed only half his men ashore where they were promptly imprisoned, probably either on suspicion of spying or because they were in the employ of the Spanish crown. After a quick appeal to higher authority in São Miguel Columbus returned to negotiate their release, and it would seem likely that he sailed round to anchor off Vila do Porto, already the island's capital. The islanders' suspicion of strangers was certainly justified, with repeated attacks from French, Turkish and Moorish pirates, who burnt crops and buildings and frequently made off with slaves. The tiny chapel at Baía dos Anjos still preserves a 17th century iron whip, reputedly from a slaving ship which took eleven local people into captivity.

Although the island's major port from early in its history, the open bay at Vila do Porto did not gain any form of quay until 1874, when a short protective wall was built in the northwest corner of the harbour, now incorporated in the large reclaimed area. A whaling station, since abandoned, once thrived some 10km east at Ponta do Castelo.

One of the most formative events in Santa Maria's history occurred during the Second World War, when Britain invoked the ancient Treaty of Alliance – signed with Portugal in 1373 – to enable the Allies to build a large military airport. US forces arrived in 1944, completing an enormous sprawl of three runways, a hotel, cinema, sports facilities and dozens of smaller buildings the following year, and taking over a large part of the flat western plateau to do so. However, in exchange for the loss of some infertile heath and scrublands Santa Maria gained the largest civilian airport in the islands when it was handed over in 1947. While the other islands still had grass strips only capable of handling local flights Santa Maria served as the gateway to the Azores, but the prosperity it brought waned with the expansion of airports elsewhere, and until very recently there was little tourist development on Santa Maria itself. Now it is becoming a popular weekend destination for Azoreans living in São Miguel, who see the smaller island as a peaceful area in which to own a holiday home.

Doubtless another attraction is Santa Maria's beaches, which are far superior to most of those on São Miguel, while its lower topography tends to result in less cloud, mist and rain than is typical of its northern sister. Like all the islands, Santa Maria has seen high rates of emigration several times during its history. In the 1960s and '70s Canada became the destination of choice for many, some of whom have returned to spend their later years with extended family in their native island. Even so, nearly half the 6,500 or so inhabitants live in or close to the capital, Vila do Porto.

Throughout the rural areas farming is still the major occupation, the steep volcanic slopes patterned with a chequerboard of tiny fields growing sweetcorn, wheat, bananas, vines and all the usual garden vegetables. Some of the old estates boast high

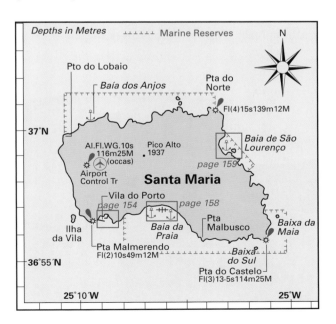

## Navigation

**Magnetic variation**
8°18′W (2016) decreasing by 8′E annually

**Tidal Streams**
Tidal streams set northeast on the flood and southwest on the ebb, but are generally weak.

**Lights**
**Airport control tower**
    Al.Fl.WG.10s116m25M 021°-vis-121° (occas)
**Ponta do Norte** Fl(4)15s139m12M
    White tower, red band 3m
**Ponta do Castelo (Gonçalo Velho)**
    Fl(3)13·5s114m25M Aeromaritime 181°-vis-089°
    Square white tower and buildings 14m
**Ponta de Malmerendo**
    Fl(2)10s49m12M 282°-vis-091°
    White tower, red band 6m

Ponta do Castelo lighthouse at the southeast tip of Santa Maria – and of the Azores as a whole  *Anne Hammick*

walls and gateways surmounted with coats of arms carved from the soft volcanic rock, though the typical village architecture owes much to the Algarve region of southern Portugal from which many of the early settlers came. Most cottages are low and whitewashed, with an outside baking oven complete with tall round chimney and pointed conical cap. Everywhere rough lumps of pumice are piled into low stone walls. Eucalyptus and pine trees scent the air and wild flowers of all colours and varieties, both familiar and exotic, run rampant over walls and verges.

A rough road climbs almost to the top of Pico Alto rewarded – in clear weather – by stunning views of the island spread below. This was the site of Portugal's worst airline disaster when, on 8 February 1989, an American Boeing 707 hit the top of the mountain while coming in to land. All 144 passengers and crew were killed. The crash is said to have been caused by a combination of poor visibility, pilot error and confusing transmissions from air traffic control. Two memorials mark the site.

Even without a car or taxi the island is small enough to explore by local bus and on foot, with well-signed paths all over the island. Take a picnic – the island is dotted with attractive picnic spots, often complete with both view and barbecue!

### Holidays and festivals

In addition to the national holidays listed on page 50, Santa Maria celebrates its official holiday on 15 August, with the August Tide Festival taking place from 22–25 August and the Harvest Festival in September. As throughout the Azores, the Festival of *Espírito Santo* is celebrated about six weeks after Easter.

The wide courtyard at the Forte de São Brás, built in the mid 16th century to protect Vila do Porto from pirate raids *Anne Hammick*

## Approach

Santa Maria can easily be seen in clear weather from the hills of São Miguel, though approaching at sea level from the north or south, the higher eastern part appears as a single cone until the lower plateau to the west rises above the horizon.

Steep cliffs form much of the coastline and there are few off-lying dangers. However, if sailing past the south coast of the island care must be taken to avoid Baixa do Sul, about 0·5M southwest of Ponta do Castelo, and if making a landfall from the east Baixa da Maia is a potential hazard. This latter lies close to 36°56'·66N 25°00'·5E, about 500m off the headland of the same name. It comprises at least two separate rocks on an east/west alignment, and very possibly others, and has reportedly been omitted from some charts, both paper and electronic. Both Baixa do Sul and Baixa da Maia are low, isolated, unmarked and unlit. Take particular care if traversing the southeast coast of the island in poor visibility or at night.

Three marine reserves have been created around the island – one covering much of the north coast, another much of the south coast, and a third at Baia de São Lourenço in the east, as shown on the plans on pages 151 and 159. See page 57 for details of restrictions, etc.

A monument to Portuguese maritime heroes in Forte de São Brás, also visible in the photo opposite *Anne Hammick*

## Harbours and anchorages

# Vila do Porto

36°56'·63N 25°08'·92W (marina molehead)

### Tides
Predictions for Vila do Porto are available via Admiralty *EasyTide* – see page 54
Time difference on Ponta Delgada: +0002
*Mean spring range* 1·4m
*Mean neap range* 0·7m

### Lights
**Ponta de Malmerendo**
Fl(2)10s49m12M 282°-vis-091°
White tower, red band 6m
**Marvão** Fl.G.5s41m3M
010°-vis-190° White tower, green bands 3m
**Breakwater** LFl.R.5s15m5M
White tower, red bands 11·5m
**Clube Naval** Fl(2)WRG.8s17m10M
346°-G-351°-W-354°-R-359° Post 5m
**Marina mole** Fl.G.3s10m3M
White post, green bands 3m
**Starboard hand buoy** Iso.G.6s
Small conical green buoy
*Note* Laid and maintained by the Port Authority, and
normally in place June – October

### Harbour communications
**Vila do Porto Marina**
VHF Ch 10, 16
☎+351 296 882282
15 May – 15 September 0800–1200, 1300–2000,
closed Sunday; 16 September – 14 May: 0800–1200,
1300–1700, closed weekends
arinavdp@portosdosacores.pt
**Port Authority**
VHF Ch 11, 12, 16
☎+351 296 882282
0800–1200, 1400–1700
portovdp@apsm.pt
www.apsm.pt
**Capitania**
VHF Ch 11, 16
☎+351 296 882157
0900–1230, 1400–1700
capitania.vporto@amn.pt
www.amn.pt

## Friendly marina offering excellent shelter

A breakwater some 350m in length was built in the mid 1980s across the western part of what had previously been an open anchorage, to increase protection and facilitate the landing of cargo. It affords good shelter to the western half of the bay, though swell from the south or southeast sets up considerable surge, and for many years visiting yachts had no option but to anchor.

In 2003 work to build a RoRo ferry terminal began in the northwest of the harbour, and then in early 2007 construction started on Vila do Porto Marina, the fifth in the Portos dos Açores SA chain. This was effectively finished one year later, although some related facilities took several more years to

II. THE AZORES

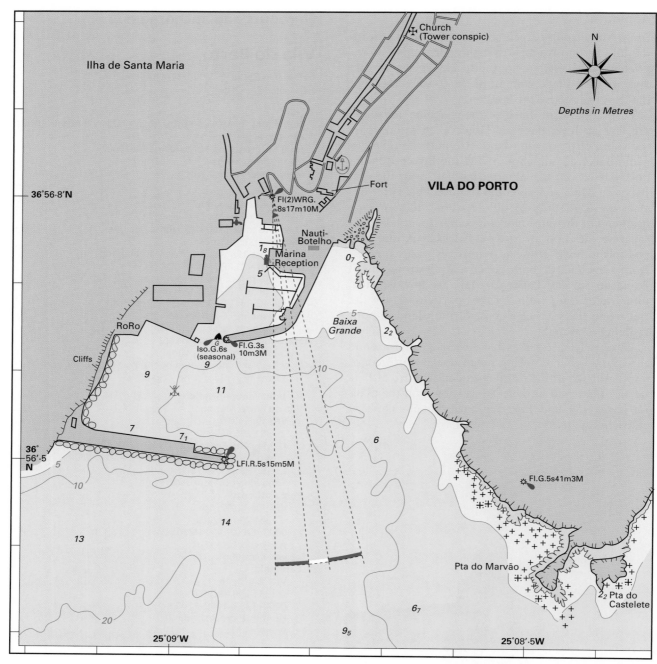

Ilha de Santa Maria

Church (Tower conspic)

36°56·8'N

Fl(2)WRG. 8s17m10M

Fort

**VILA DO PORTO**

Nauti-Botelho

Marina Reception

N

Depths in Metres

RoRo

Iso.G.6s (seasonal)

Fl.G.3s 10m3M

Cliffs

Baixa Grande

36° 56'·5 N

LFl.R.5s15m5M

Fl.G.5s41m3M

Pta do Marvão

25°09'W

25°08'·5W

Pta do Castelete

appear. The artistic will be happy to know that wall-painting is encouraged, with a great deal of virgin concrete still crying out to be decorated (brushes and paint are available at several shops in the town). Santa Maria has long been praised by the growing number of yachtsmen who visit the island, and the marina has likewise received the thumbs up.

The older part of the town is attractive, with parts which are very old indeed. White or pastel-washed houses under red tiles, their large windows picked out in darker colours, line the long cobbled main street which curves up a gently sloping spur away from the harbour. Until recently the lower town was marred by a number of derelict buildings – apparently their owners could not be traced, having emigrated many years ago – but in the last few years

several have been renovated. One has been transformed into a large and very popular youth hostel, much appreciatated by younger visitors from São Miguel, while another further up the hill is earmarked to become the town museum.

The typical Portuguese inlaid pavements feature a pattern of rope, fish, ships and shells, and there are several fine examples of ornately carved baroque and manueline architecture including the town hall buildings, formerly a Franciscan monastery, open to the public during office hours and well worth a visit. Excellent views over the harbour can be enjoyed from the 16th-century Forte de São Bras, the three-flue chimneys of which are said to represent the Father, Son and Holy Ghost.

Approaching Vila do Porto from slightly east of south, with the end of the marina mole just open of the breakwater  *Mike Eastman*

Looking south over Vila do Porto harbour from the Forte de São Brás  *Anne Hammick*

Finally, a new sports centre has opened at the top of the village, complete with tennis courts, astro-turf football field, running track, indoor swimming pool etc. Though not always open during the hours advertised, visitors are welcome and charges are low.

### Approach

*By day* Quite straightforward, with no off-lying dangers, but call on VHF before entering the outer harbour, as if a ship (including the inter-island ferry) is berthing or manoeuvring a yacht may be asked to stand off for up to 30 minutes.

The light grey concrete of the breakwater contrasts sharply with the dark cliffs behind. A

Looking northeast through the marina entrance in June 2015, with the seasonal green buoy in place for the summer. Forte de São Brás and the lower part of the town provide an interesting backdrop  *Sean Milligan*

bearing of 018° on the conspicuous white church tower on the skyline leads past the breakwater, which has 15m close off its end, but the north side of the wall should be given a wide berth as concrete rubble lies up to 30m from its base. There is a wind farm on the skyline a short distance east of the harbour.

*By night* Perfectly feasible in good weather conditions, but perhaps best avoided for first-time entry by the less experienced even though both harbour and marina are generously lit.

### Anchorage

Anchoring is not permitted north of a line between Ponta Malmerendo to the west and Ponta do Marvão to the east – effectively ruling out the entire harbour. The only real alternative is Baía da Praia (Praia Formosa) about 3M further east – see page 158.

### Marina entrance and berthing

The gap which gives access to the marina is distinctly narrow, with limited space for manoeuvring once inside. Even with a ship at the RoRo berth the entrance remains of usable width, however, and a small summer-only buoy (see left) encourages yachts to keep clear of outliers off the marina mole. There is a 3 knot speed limit in the marina and harbour, but this is interpreted somewhat flexibly by local fishermen and an approach line which gives early warning of departing vessels is recommended.

If entering the marina at night, note that the green light on the mole is some distance from its end – take particular care early in the season before the (lit) starboard-hand buoy has been laid. Neither of the two projections on the east side of the entrance are lit, other than by ambient light from the commercial area, but both are tall and sheer and should be easy to make out.

Once inside protection is excellent and, like the main breakwater, the marina mole has proved itself equal to the challenge of winter storms and large seas. At least 5m should be found in the marina entrance, with 4m as far as the reception quay which doubles as the fuel berth.

Many of the marina's 124 berths remained unused as of 2015, and it is likely to be some time before space becomes a problem. Visiting yachts are normally placed on the second (ie. longest) pontoon, the outer five fingers of which are reserved for larger yachts. The fingers are long and the bays unusually wide, but even so berthing can be tricky in cross winds. During office hours a member of the marina staff will normally be on hand to assist. Although the marina can, in theory at least, accommodate at least one yacht of up to 32m on the northern hammerhead, in practice it may be preferable on both sides to berth visitors of this size on the main breakwater if this is not required for commercial vessels. Contact well before arrival to discuss.

### Formalities

The marina office overlooks the reception/fuel pontoon, and as in all marina front offices throughout the Azores the staff are friendly and helpful with several speaking good English. Harbourmaster Armando Soares takes a close interest in the marina, despite also being responsible for the commercial harbour, with João Alves handling day-to-day reception duties.

The usual ship's papers plus crew passports will be required, as may proof of insurance. The offices of the *Guarda Nacional Republicana* (GNR), *Polícia Marítima*, *Serviço de Estrangeiros e Fronteiras* (Immigration) and *Alfândega* (Customs) are located in the marina building, but the *Capitania* remains in the town (up the steep hill past the Forte de São Bras). The *Polícia Marítima* take their duties seriously, and may visit a yacht to inspect safety equipment such as flares and fire extinguishers.

Santa Maria is not a 'border post' under the Schengen Agreement – see page 51. If arriving from outside the Schengen area clearance should, in theory, first be obtained at Faial, Terceira or São Miguel, though flexibility is nearly always exercised in the case of a short visit.

### Charges

Vila do Porto Marina is one of the *Portos dos Açores SA* chain, and shares their basic price structure – see page 55. Payment can be made using most major credit/debit cards other than American Express.

Vila do Porto is one of the few Azorean harbours to actively collect 'lighthouse tax' – *Taxa de Farolagem e Balizagem* – which is payable at the *Capitania* rather than at the marina office. The skipper's passport as well as the yacht's papers must be presented, and though at €2 for the first six months it is not too onerous it is still worth keeping the receipt. The office is open 0900-1230, 1400-1700, closed weekends, but the tax can be paid at any time before departure.

Vila do Porto Marina seen from the northeast, with NautiBotelho's grey building at the bottom of the slope on the right and nearly a dozen yachts ashore between it and the marina office *Harald Sammer*

## Facilities

*Boatyard* NautiBotelho is a small but growing concern, established in 2012 and owned and run by Ricardo Botelho, *mobile* +351 965 785477, geral@nautibotelho.pt, www.nautibotelho.pt (currently a single page), whose family own a car repair business and dive centre. Ricardo speaks excellent English, and either he or one of his four staff can also communicate in French and German. Open 0800–1200, 1300–1700 Monday – Saturday.

Services include metalwork and engineering (agent for Suzuki and Yanmar), repairs to GRP and timber, electrical work, installation and checking (but not repair) of electronics, hull cleaning and painting, and inflatable repairs. Guardinage is offered in or out of the water. Although the travel-lift is too large to enter the 357m² workshop, outdoor work – including osmosis treatment and major paint jobs – can be carried out inside a plastic 'tent', allowing the mast to remain in situ. Owners are permitted to live on their boats while ashore, and there is no restriction on DIY work.

*Travel-lift* A 75-tonne capacity hoist (capable of lifting fishing boats as well as yachts) was installed in 2012 by *Portos dos Açores SA*. It can take a maximum beam of about 5m. There is enough hardstanding for 15 or 20 yachts and smaller craft, with – at least in 2015 – plenty of tri-footed metal props but no cradles. This should not be a problem, however, as the area is very well sheltered from winds other than southeast to southwest.

As in the marina there is no security other than a few faded notices, almost certainly for the simple reason that none is considered necessary.

*Diving services* One of the several commercial dive schools close to the marina would doubtless be willing to sort out any underwater problems, though permission should be sought from the marina office.

*Chandlery* Nautipescas, ☏+351 296 883381, *mobile* +351 919 368481, www.nautipescas.pt, behind the *clube naval*, stocks a small amount of general chandlery (paint, fenders, rope etc) amongst an array of fishing equipment. Owner Paulo Chaves speaks English and will order from Ponta Delgada if necessary. Open 1000–1200, 1300–1800 weekdays, 1000–1300 Saturday during the summer (May to September).

He is soon to receive competition from NautiBotelho, which plans a small chandlery next to its workshop in the northeast corner of the harbour, see *Boatyard*, above.

*Showers* For several years the marina relied on the *clube naval* for toilets and showers, not always with happy results, but by 2010 new toilets and (six) showers had been built, still in the *clube naval* building but with access by key. All are cleaned daily, but the two toilets are reported to be insufficient when the marina is busy. Plans are in hand for a new shower and laundry block near the marina office, hopefully operational by 2017.

*Laundry* Next to the showers in the *clube naval*, again with with access by key. There are no objections to laundry being dried aboard.

*Fuel* A single pump dispensing both diesel and petrol has has been installed in front of the marina office. The quayside is high and lacks a floating pontoon, but two ladders and a hefty 'grab rope' are provided. The pump is normally reserved for yachts, with fishing boats bunkering on the commercial quay opposite, but delays can occur if the latter is out of action and large trawlers need to refuel from the small-capacity marina hoses.

Very large yachts may need to refuel from a road tanker, a somewhat complicated process as – in addition to arranging the delivery via the marina office – a form must be completed at the *Capitania*, who will arrange for the *Polícia Marítima* to be on hand.

*Bottled gas* Nothing available on the island other than GALP's own cylinders.

*Clube naval* The *Clube Naval de Santa Maria* occupies the light blue building at the head of the harbour, with the offices and bar on the upper floor, the latter giving onto a large terrace. It has long been friendly and welcoming towards visiting yachtsmen, and some English is spoken. Shut on Mondays.

*Banks* Several in the town, all with ATMs, but not at the harbour itself.

*Shops/provisioning* Five or six supermarkets, including a large and well-stocked SolMar on the main street (open 0830–2000 daily), plus a good range of other shops. Ricardo Botelho – clearly an entrepreneur – intends to sell limited amounts of fresh food etc at his new chandlery shop, an innovation likely to prove popular.

*Produce market* Large market behind the Hotel Praia de Lobos, on two levels with fruit and vegetables above and a good meat section below.

*Cafés, restaurants & hotels* Several hotels plus a growing number of restaurants and cafés, several of the latter run by returned emigrants who speak excellent English.

*Medical services* Hospital, ☏+351 296 820100, and several pharmacies, though serious cases are normally flown to Ponta Delgada.

## Communications

*Mailing address* C/o Marina Vila do Porto, Apartado 41, 9580-909 Vila do Porto, Santa Maria, Açores, Portugal.

*WiFi* Fast, reliable, free WiFi at all berths from an antenna on the roof of the marina office, plus a computer in the building below.

*Car hire* At least four companies, one of which also hires out motorbikes.

*Taxis* Taxi rank outside the town hall (a steep walk up from the harbour).

*Buses* Hourly bus (to the town and airport) from a stop at the west end of the small bridge. Bus routes cover much of the island, an excellent (and economical) way to explore

*Ferry* Regular (but not daily) link with Ponta Delgada.

*Air services* Regular inter-island flights.

II. THE AZORES

# Baía da Praia (Praia Formosa)

36°57′·1N 25°06′·6W (ruined fort)

**Lights**
**Formosa cables**
 Fl(2)Y.8s12m9M (daylight range 1·7M) 000°-vis-040°
 White lantern on wall 4m. Marks submarine cables
**Baixa da Pedrinha** Fl.Y.4s
 Cylindrical yellow buoy
*Note* Laid and maintained by the Port Authority, and
 normally in place from June to October

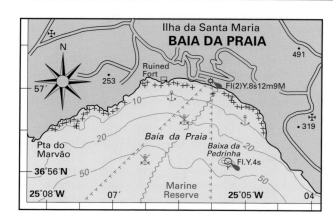

## Beach anchorage open to the south

A crescent-shaped bay almost 1·5M in length, situated 2·5M east of Vila do Porto and protected from northwest through north to east. Being entirely open to the south it provides a daytime anchorage only, with good swimming and an attractive backdrop of cliffs and terraced vineyards. Anchoring (or fishing) in the centre of the bay is now prohibited due to submarine cables (see plan), though there is no restriction on passage through the area and it should still be possible to anchor on either side. Baía da Praia falls within Santa Maria's southern marine reserve, so it would be wise to seek permission to anchor from the *Polícia Marítima* in Vila do Porto before doing so.

The extent of the beach itself varies from year to year, as the sand apparently disappears during the winter, only to reappear – sometimes! – in late spring. For much of the 21st century the beach has been narrow to virtually nonexistent, with the sea reaching almost to the road – certainly the case when visited in May 2015.

## Approach

From westwards, Ponta do Marvão may be rounded 200m off and a course of 102° steered for Ponta Malbusco before edging northwards into the bay itself. If approaching from the east care must be taken to avoid the Baixa da Pedrinha, a rocky ledge rising almost sheer from around 30m. The relevant Admiralty chart gives Baixa da Pedrinha a least

Looking southeast over Baía da Praia in May 2015, before the buoy marking Baixa da Pedrinha had been laid for the summer *Anne Hammick*

depth of 5·5m, though it has been reported to carry considerably less. The buoy listed above was first laid in June 2015, and though expected to be relaid annually this is not guaranteed.

## Anchorage

It is essential to avoid anchoring within the area through which the cables run, though this is not made easier by the fact that the light – a bank of LEDs rather than a conventional lens – is very difficult to identify. In fact it lies close east of a single Norfolk pine which grows on a small promontory near the centre of the beach. Fortunately the best anchorages are at either end of the beach – see plan – in 5m or so over sand. If opting for the western end, however, a wreck with depths of less than 1m lies at around the 4m line, making good light and a sharp lookout essential (the colourful fish which inhabit the wreck add to the snorkeling appeal).

## Facilities

Cafés and a few small shops in the nearby village, but otherwise very little.

# Ponta do Castelo anchorages

**West anchorage** 36°55′·7N 25°01·2′W (pa)
**Northeast anchorage** 36°55′·9N 25°00′·9W (pa)

### Two possible anchorages at the southeast tip of Santa Maria

A possible anchorage has been suggested immediately west of Ponta do Castelo light at the southeast corner of the island. No details are available, however, and it would be tenable only in daylight and near-perfect weather conditions.

In a west-northwesterly force 7, which was wrapping swell around Pta do Norte and into Baía de São Lourenço, the owners of a 12·5m yacht report finding good shelter in a small bay northeast of the lighthouse. The owners approached on a westerly course looking for sand in which to drop the anchor, found good holding in 8m over sand and small round boulders, and enjoyed a reasonably comfortable night before continuing to Vila do Porto.

The village of Maia, a little further north, has a tiny harbour and a single snack-bar, but little else.

# Baía de São Lourenço

36°59'·52N 25°03'·35W (front leading light)

**Lights**
**Ponta do Espigão** Fl.6s208m12M
White column, red bands 6m
**Ldg Lts on 273·3°** *Front* Iso.R.6s23m7M
White post, red bands, in front of white house with blue arches 6m
*Rear*, 64m from front, Oc.R.7·5s36m6M
Red lantern on white house with verandah 2m

## Scenic beach anchorage open to the east

High surrounding cliffs (the semi-circular remains of a volcanic cone) give the 0·75M Baía de São Lourenço good protection from southeast through west to north, but leave it totally open to easterly winds or swell. Thus it should only be considered as an overnight anchorage in very settled weather. The sandy beach at the southern end gives way to stones further north, where a small stone quay offers possible dry-shod dinghy landing.

The Baía de São Lourenço provides one of the loveliest anchorages in the entire Azores, with cliffs terraced into a lacing of black lava walls and tiny green vineyards where the locally famous vinho de cheiro is produced. The island of São Lourenço (also known as Ilhéu do Romeiro) at the southeastern horn of the bay has some fine sea caves and many nesting birds. The water is exceptionally clear to considerable depths. Unsurprisingly, the entire area is a marine reserve, and it would be wise to seek permission to anchor from the *Polícia Marítima* in Vila do Porto before visiting.

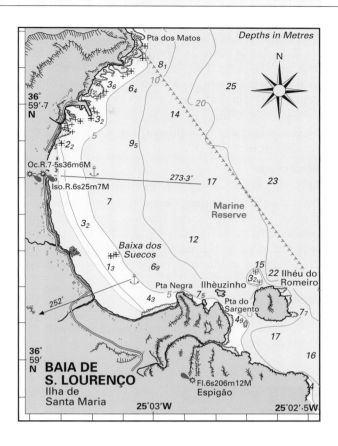

Looking north over the wide Baía de São Lourenço on Santa Maria's east coast. Somewhat unusually the Baixa dos Suecos is not breaking, but its yellowish tinge can be seen in the middle of the bay *Linda Lane Thornton*

II. THE AZORES

### Approach

*By day* Islands fringe both ends of the bay, but there are no outliers. The leading marks (which are difficult to make out in daylight) lie just north of two distinctive – very tall and very thin – pine trees.

*By night* The leading marks are lit and in offshore or light winds could be followed into a suitable depth for anchoring.

### Anchorage

In 4–5m over sand opposite the leading marks, or in the southern corner of the bay with the unmistakable rising road bearing about 252°. The breaking Baixa dos Suecos – which extend further to seaward than indicated on Admiralty 1959 – lies about 200m offshore between the two suggested anchorages.

### Facilities

*Water* Tap on the quay and two summer restaurants, but no shops. The houses fringing the beach are mostly holiday homes.

The tiny chapel at Anjos, on Santa Maria's northwest coast, where Columbus and his men are reputed to have prayed in February 1493 on their return from their second Atlantic crossing *Anne Hammick*

# Baía dos Anjos

37°00′·32N 25°09′·52W (molehead)

**Lights**
**Fábrica dos Anjos** Fl.4s13m10M
   White column, red bands 6m
   (close to red and white banded radio mast)
**Ldg Lts on 173·4°** *Front* Fl.3s12m10M
   *Rear*, 25m from front, LFl.6s20m10M
   White posts, red bands 5m

*Important* For information only – totally unsuitable for night approach

### Attractive fair-weather anchorage

Columbus called here in 1493, but yachtsmen may prefer to visit by land. The tiny rock-fringed bay is protected from east through south to southwest, with a short concrete pier at its western end. An imaginative, semi-enclosed swimming area has been created, into which a small rowing dinghy (NO OUTBOARDS!) might be taken. Alternatively, land at the short mole, which has two sets of steps.

The village is also miniature and very peaceful, and the ancient chapel visited by Columbus's crew (though largely rebuilt in the 17th century) can still be seen. The door is usually locked, but the key is held by the lady who lives next door.

### Approach, anchorage and facilities

The red and white leading marks which lie behind the old quay are readily seen against the hillside and can be followed into 5–8m to anchor, probably over rock and large stones. Although lit, a night approach should not be attempted under any circumstances.

Most of the nearby houses are holiday homes and facilities are very limited. Water taps – and sinks – will be found in the barbecue area above the swimming pools and there is a summer café, but there are no shops for several miles.

The small and rocky bay at Anjos seen from the east  *Anne Hammick*

# Ilhéus das Formigas
## 37°16'·26N 24°46'·82W (lighthouse)

## Introduction

The Ilhéus das Formigas – literally 'The Ants' – are reputed to have been the first of the Azorean islands to be sighted by the Portuguese, in 1426. They now form a marine reserve in which all forms of fishing, scuba diving, and the collection of shells, plants and geological specimens are forbidden and rubbish must not be dumped (which of course applies to the marine environment generally). The reserve covers an area formed by two overlapping circles, both 5M in radius, centred on the Ilhéus das Formigas light and Dollabarat Shoal.

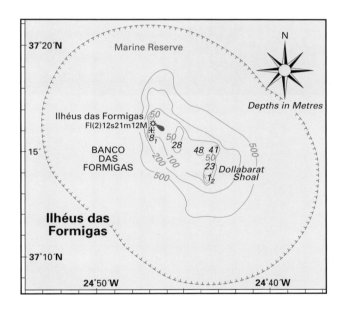

## Navigation

**Magnetic variation**
8°10'W (2015)

**Tidal Streams**
Tidal streams set northeast on the flood and southwest on the ebb but - as is usual in what is effectively mid-ocean - are generally weak.

**Lights**
**Ilhéus das Formigas** Fl(2)12s21m12M
White conical tower with double lantern 19m, situated near the northern end of the visible rocks

## Approach

The Ilhéus das Formigas lie 34M from São Miguel and just over 20M from Santa Maria, bearing 147° and 040° respectively. A short chain of dark rocks no more than 11m in height, they mark the northwestern edge of a bank nearly 5·5M long and 2·5M wide, with average depths of 50–100m. A narrow shoal with breaking patches extends almost 0·5M south from the rocks themselves.

The unmarked Dollabarat Shoal with a least charted depth of 3m (though reputed locally to be as little as 1·2m) bears 133° from the Ilhéus das Formigas at a distance of 3·5M, near the southeastern edge of the bank. Even moderate swells break on the shoal, and bad weather creates ferocious seas. The whole area should be given a wide berth when on passage.

## Anchorage and landing

The bank is composed mainly of rock, with areas of pale sand, shell and coral debris. Yachts have occasionally anchored off in exceptionally calm weather, but should not be left unattended due to poor holding and unpredictable currents. Landing is reported to be possible on the east side of the rocks, from where there is access to the lighthouse.

The Ilhéus das Formigas seen from the southeast
*Fernando Tempera*

II. THE AZORES

Funchal harbour photographed from Madeira's impressive *Jardim Botânico* to the northeast (see page 182) *Harald Sammer*

Looking southwest across the Enseada das Cagarras at Salvegem Grande (see page 210) *Ed Clay*

# III. The Madeira Group

## The archipelago

The Madeira archipelago consists of the island of Madeira itself, together with Porto Santo, the Desertas and the Selvagens. Although by far the smallest group described in this book, with some of the islands little more than large rocks, there is a wide diversity of land forms and related weather patterns, closely reflected in the differing flora and fauna. More detailed descriptions will be found under each individual island heading.

Many thousands of tourists visit Madeira annually and it says much for the character of the archipelago that, other than in the main hotel area around Funchal, both the islands and their people have remained remarkably unspoilt by the influx. The tiny terraced fields are in the main well tended, the forests protected rather than exploited, and the Madeiran people friendly and welcoming towards visitors.

## History

Like the Azores, the islands of the Madeira archipelago drifted on the edge of the known world for many centuries. Genoese explorers were probably aware of their existence by the middle of the 13th century, and they may even have been known to the Arabs hundreds of years earlier. Recorded history begins in 1418 when João Gonçalves Zarco and Tristão Vaz Teixeira, on passage to Africa as part of Henry the Navigator's

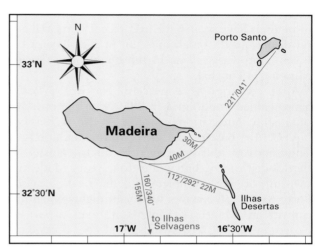

grand design, were driven off course by a gale and eventually sought shelter under the lee of an unknown island. The direction of the gale is not recorded, but it seems likely that it was a northerly, or Porto Santo – 'Holy Port' – might have received a less complimentary name. A rapid passage back to Lisbon was followed by an equally hasty return, this time with orders to colonise the dry, uninhabited island before continuing to investigate the more mountainous one visible to the southwest. Porto Santo's first governor, who accompanied Zarco and Teixeira on their return, was Bartolomeu Perestrelo, a minor Portuguese nobleman chiefly remembered as father-in-law of Christopher Columbus.

Porto Santo had its share of ups and downs over the following centuries. Vines were established,

## Courses and distances within the Madeira archipelago

| Harbour | Course / Reciprocal | Distance |
| --- | --- | --- |
| Porto Santo – Quinta do Lorde Marina, Madeira | 221° / 041° & by eye | 30M |
| Porto Santo – Funchal, Madeira | 221° / 041° & by eye | 40M |
| Quinta do Lorde Marina – Funchal, Madeira | by eye | 13M |
| Quinta do Lorde Marina – Carga da Lapa, Ilhas Desertas | 145°/325° & by eye | 17M |
| Quinta do Lorde Marina – Porto de Recreio da Calheta | by eye | 29M |
| Funchal, Madeira – Carga da Lapa, Ilhas Desertas | 112° / 292° | 22M |
| Funchal, Madeira – Enseada das Cagarras, Selvagem Grande | 160° / 340° | 155M |

together with vegetables and cereal crops, but rabbits introduced by the first settlers ate most of the natural vegetation down to the soil. Occasional pirate raids sent the inhabitants fleeing for safety to the heights of Pico do Facho, but the island's basic poverty was probably its best defence and also served to limit the population to a number which the land and surrounding seas could support. Life was not without excitement, including the wreck in 1724 of the Dutch treasure ship *Slot ter Hooge*, driven onto the north coast during a gale. Although much of her cargo of silver bars was recovered at the time, more finds have been made over recent years and are on display in the small museum in Vila Baleira on Porto Santo, as well as in the Quinta das Cruzes Museum in Funchal.

After centuries as a peaceful backwater, Porto Santo gained importance in 1960 with the opening of a large international airport – also a Reserve NATO Air Base – the first in the archipelago. Thousands of tourists arrived by air to transfer to the Madeira ferry, but within four years Madeira's own airport was complete and the traffic ceased. Porto Santo still receives long-haul flights when the runway at Madeira's Santa Catarina Airport is closed by strong crosswinds, and the occasional military exercise may take place, but the island is usually quiet and the pace of life slow. Having said that, the growth in the tourist industry even since the turn of the 21st century has been dramatic, with much of the long beach now backed by hotels and holiday developments, and a golf course in the northwest of the island. The authorities are to be commended, however, for ensuring that Vila Baleira retains its considerable charm – in fact the basic layout of the tiny capital can have changed little since Columbus lived there in 1480. Another thing which has not changed is the prevailing wind, and those who enjoy a touch of history in their cruising should take a leaf from Zarco and Teixeira's book and plan a landfall on Porto Santo before sailing on

Cristovão Colombo (Christopher Columbus) keeps an eye on Funchal harbour from his plinth in the city's *Parque de Santa Caterina  Anne Hammick*

to Madeira. Even after five centuries of progress, the island of Porto Santo still lies over 20M dead to windward of its larger sister.

Zarco and Teixeira landed on Madeira in July 1419, near where Machico now stands, claimed the island for Portugal, and returned the following year with the first permanent settlers. Within a few years sugar cane was introduced and quickly became an important export crop, followed in 1460 by vines from southern Europe. The sugar trade was responsible for attracting their most famous resident, Christopher Columbus, who lived in the islands for several years after marrying Perestrelo's daughter – though whether he met her in Lisbon or on his first visit to Madeira in the 1470s is not clear.

A vast amount of labour was needed to prepare the land for agriculture after the native woodland – the *madeira* from which the island gained its name – had been burned off, and to tend crops and build irrigation ditches. So in addition to immigration

A dramatic mountainscape in central Madeira  *Mungo Morris*

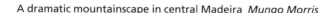

from the Portuguese mainland many slaves were brought from north and west Africa to work on the land, though little trace remains of them today. Funchal, with its relatively protected harbour, quickly grew in size and was granted city status in 1508, the cathedral being completed six years later in 1514.

Quiet prosperity and progress was interrupted by occasional setbacks, including an attack by French pirates in 1566 when Funchal was burned and many people killed, and the domination of the island by the Spanish between 1581 and 1640 following King Philip II of Spain's invasion and occupation of mainland Portugal. Many of the island's small protective forts were built at this time. After the restoration of the Portuguese monarchy British interest in the island, and particularly its unique wine, quickly returned, forging links which have only recently begun to weaken. Captain Cook visited Madeira twice around 1770, and in 1801 British troops were briefly stationed there to help protect it from the French. The defence force returned in 1807 during the Peninsula Wars and this time stayed for seven years, after which many of the soldiers chose to remain on the island to farm or grow vines. Unfortunately their prosperity was short-lived, with a succession of diseases attacking the vines in the 1850s coupled with a serious cholera epidemic, and then blight in the sugar crop in 1882.

However, Madeira's major modern industry was already becoming established with the beginnings of tourism, initially as a health resort for tuberculosis sufferers due to its clear air and mild but damp winter climate. During the First World War, in which Portugal joined the Allies, Funchal was twice attacked by German submarines – one of their victims still lies outside the harbour, ready to snag the anchors of unwary yachts. In 1921 the first aeroplane arrived in Madeira, a small seaplane which landed in Funchal harbour, but it was not until 1949 that a commercial seaplane service was established for passengers from Britain and northern Europe. However, less than a decade later two serious accidents brought flights to a halt, and for several years there were no air services to the islands until first Porto Santo and then Madeira gained airports in the early 1960s.

Since then tourism has grown at a pace which has threatened to drown more traditional ways of life, particularly the labour-intensive farming and viniculture. Sugar cane, although still grown, has become less important but Madeira wine is famous the world over with more than 13 million litres being produced annually, about half of which is fortified with brandy for export. In past years the barrels were transported in the holds of sailing ships

Spectacular cliffs bisected by a delicate waterfall, at Paúl do Mar on Madeira's southwest coast
*Anne Hammick*

which crossed the Atlantic before returning to Europe, the long, warm voyage giving the wine a distinctive flavour which is now produced artificially by gentle heating. Wine-tasting at an *armazem* is an essential part of any visit to Funchal, and the knowledge that bottles of Madeira taken back aboard have a proven history of travelling well under sail provides further incentive to buy.

Other industries are wicker and basketwork, made from locally grown osiers, and strikingly lovely embroidery. This last had long been made by the women of the island for their own use, but became a commercial concern around 1850 when an English lady, Mrs Phibbs, saw the opportunity for island women to supplement the family income while still remaining in their homes. Madeiran embroidery is said to have been on display at the Great Exhibition held in London in 1851. These small beginnings have led to a cottage industry employing women of all ages, some of whom one may still see on fine days in the villages outside Funchal, sitting on their doorsteps or by windows busily stitching away to produce what are probably Madeira's most original and genuine souvenirs.

Portugal's membership of the EU has brought some notable changes to Madeira, the two most obvious being the extended airport runway, a vast concrete apron supported by massive pillars rising up from the sea – under which lies the Água de Pena

boatyard, see page 192 – and the dramatic road system linking Caniçal in the east to Ribeira Brava, west of Funchal. However, while the *Via Rápida* network – see Road transport, page 169 – certainly makes life easier for the islanders, for the visitor in no particular hurry there is much to be said for getting off the beaten track. Madeira is full of contrasts, and it is worth making an effort to glimpse the older island which is rapidly disappearing.

## General information

### Nationality and language

The Madeira archipelago is an autonomous region of Portugal, and therefore part of the European Union, with a governor resident in Funchal. Portuguese is spoken, but many Madeirans (particularly those concerned with the tourist trade) also understand Spanish, French, English or German.

### Portuguese representation abroad

See page 46 of the introductory notes to the Azores.

### Diplomatic representation in Madeira

The following are consulates – embassies are to be found in Lisbon:

*UK*: British Honorary Consulate, Avenida de Zarco 2, CP 417, 9000-956 Funchal, Madeira
  ☎+351 291 212860,
  brit.confunchal@mail.eunet.pt
  Office hours 0900–1300, 1430–1730

*USA*: There is no longer a US Consular Agency on the island.
  Visit portugal.usembassy.gov/service.html for further information.

### Personal documentation

Passport and visa requirements are the same as for the Azores – see page 46.

### Time

The Madeira group uses UT during the winter, as do both mainland Portugal and the UK, adding one hour (the equivalent to BST) during the summer. Changeover dates are normally the same as in the UK – ie. the last weekends of March and October.

### Money

See page 46 of the introductory notes to the Azores. Though almost ubiquitous, as of 2015 ATMs had yet to be installed at either Porto Santo or Quinta do Lorde marinas.

A stall on the upper floor of Funchal's *Mercado dos Lavradores* (produce market) specialises in herbs and spices of every kind. A great way to enliven the sailing diet! *Anne Hammick*

Funchal by night, with two well-lit cruise ships alongside the breakwater *Anne Hammick*

## Shopping

As in most countries, town centre shopping is being eclipsed by out-of-town superstores – *hipermercado* in Portuguese – at least as far as foodstuffs are concerned. Otherwise, by far the best general shopping in the Madeira group is to be found in Funchal, which boasts a vast number of tourist-orientated shops as well as those to be found in any city of medium size. Most of the major Portuguese chains are represented in Madeira, including Pingo Doce, SA, Continente and Modelo. The larger supermarkets provide almost everything that one might expect to find in their British or American equivalents, and plenty that one might not, though tinned meats, other than frankfurters, corned beef and luncheon meats, are seldom to be had. Alcohol, of which a wide choice is available, is considerably cheaper than in the UK.

Funchal's produce market remains superb, both visually and practically. Locally grown fruit and vegetables of all kinds are sold at very reasonable prices on the ground floor and in the gallery above, but not all vendors supply bags – or egg boxes. One local vegetable worth trying is chayote or christophene, known locally as *pimpinela*, which resembles an oversized and sometimes spiky pear and has a consistency midway between cucumber and courgette. It can be eaten raw or cooked and will keep for at least six weeks, adding some crunch to the often rather bland ocean-crossing diet.

Surrounding the produce market are stalls selling fresh meat, with a large fish market to the rear of the building – worth a visit even if not intending to buy. A local delicacy is *espada* (scabbard fish), an evil-looking creature which lives at great depths and tastes delicious, with the added advantage of apparently having very few bones. For a few extra cêntimos the fish of one's choice will be gutted, cleaned and filleted, ready to be taken back aboard and sautéed gently in a little olive oil and garlic.

Some notes regarding ships' stores – principally fuel, bottled gas and chandlery – will be found on page 174.

## Communications

### Mail

All four marinas will hold mail for yachts whose arrival is anticipated. Addresses will be found in the Communications section of the relevant harbour details, and it is worth stressing that the word 'Portugal' should always be included. Mail from the UK usually takes about a week, longer from the USA.

Post office opening hours vary, but stamps (*selos*) can also be bought at newsagents and souvenir shops where the green *correio* sign is seen, or from vending machines, which list current rates but do not give change. There are two classes of mail, *correio azul* and *correio normal* – effectively express and fairly slow – with the former also noticeably more reliable.

### Incoming packages

Much the same problems may occur as in the Azores – see page 47. Consult the marina office for advice.

### Telephones

As in many countries, public telephones are seen as a lower priority with the widespread use of mobile (cell) phones, but are still to be found in most towns. Not all, however, take coins, some requiring cards purchased from post offices, supermarkets and bars. Mobile phone coverage throughout both Madeira and Porto Santo is generally excellent, though there are 'holes' in some of Madeira's mountain valleys. Unsurprisingly, coverage fades as one heads offshore and does not extend to either the Ilhas Desertas or Ilhas Selvagens.

The international dialling code for Portugal, including the Madeira group is +351, and the area code for both Madeira and Porto Santo 291. This latter prefix must be included when dialling any

A brightly-painted fishing boat in Porto Moniz...
*Anne Hammick*

... on which the crew waste no time in salting down the catch
*Anne Hammick*

landline number, even when calling from within the same island. Any telephone number not starting with this sequence can be assumed to be a mobile.

For further information see page 48 of the introductory notes to the Azores.

### Internet access

With email the communication method of choice for the majority of cruising sailors, free WiFi is now available at or near all four marinas, provided by the marina itself, by the local council, or by nearby cafés. See individual harbours for details.

### Electricity

Mains electricity is 220v 50Hz, as is standard throughout mainland Europe, and yachts from elsewhere should beware a probable difference in both volts and cycles. Mains power is provided in all the archipelago's marinas but is unlikely to be available elsewhere. All Madeira's electricity (though not Porto Santo's) is generated by hydro-electric plants, making it so cheap that street lighting can be left on with impunity. Thus Madeiran towns often appear to be lit like beacons when seen from offshore at night.

### Transportation

#### International and inter-island flights

Many airlines, both scheduled and charter, provide flights to Madeira from departure airports throughout Europe and North America. Schedules change frequently and the best deals will be found via the internet. Most flights are direct, though a few may be routed through Lisbon or Porto. Live arrivals and departure information is given in Portuguese and English on the *Aeroportos da Madeira* website at www.anam.pt/English-254.aspx. Most flights to/from Porto Santo take a detour via Funchal, but a few fly direct to the Portuguese mainland – there are currently no international flights from the island.

If planning crew changes it is worth bearing in mind that Madeira's Santa Catarina Airport (technically now called either Madeira International or Funchal Airport, but still referred to locally by its old name) is a long and expensive taxi-ride from Porto de Recreio da Calheta or even from Funchal, but much closer to Quinta do Lorde Marina and only a few kilometres from the anchorage at Machico. The airport on Porto Santo is near the town and harbour.

#### Ferries

Porto Santo Line's 112m car ferry *Lobo Marinho* provides a daily service between Funchal and the smaller island. In summer she normally departs Funchal at 0800 and Porto Santo at 2200, fitting in a second return trip on Friday and Sunday afternoons; otherwise leaving Funchal at 0800 every day except Friday, returning at between 1900 and 2100, with an evening service on Friday. The crossing takes just under 2½ hours and there is generally no need for foot passengers to book. Check the company's website for current schedules: www.portosantoline.pt (in four languages including English).

No other ferries call at, or operate from, Madeira. The Portimão to Funchal service previously run by Spanish company Armas Naviera, was discontinued in 2012 and as of mid 2015 nothing had replaced it; neither are there regular services to the Ilhas

Desertas or Ilhas Selvagens, though several kiosks overlooking Funchal Marina advertise day trips to the former.

A great many cruise ships call at Funchal, but are unlikely to be of interest to yachtsmen except as a potential hazard.

## Road transport

At least a dozen car hire agencies vie for custom in Madeira, most with offices at the airport and in Funchal, while those in Porto Santo are mainly located at the airport. Cars can also be delivered to, and collected from, a marina or other location for an additional fee. All car hire firms accept major credit cards and will require a credit (not debit) card number to be left as 'deposit'. Either national or international driving licences are accepted, provided the former has been held for at least one year, and note that it is a legal requirement to carry one's passport and driving licence at all times when at the wheel. Most petrol stations (at least one in each town of any size) still have attendant service, but note that even in the 21st century some still do not accept credit cards.

There have been vast improvements to the road system in Madeira over the past 30 years, most notably the growth of the *Via Rápida* expressway system which now runs from Caniçal to Ribeira Brava, a succession of soaring concrete bridges and seemingly endless tunnels. If time is not important, however, far more will be seen by choosing the 'old' road, now mercifully relieved of fast through traffic,

as it snakes its way around the valley sides – but do allow for the fact that, despite the lack of width and blind bends, most pedestrians and all dogs appear to take immortality for granted. Driving on Porto Santo is considerably easier, with roads generally wide, straight and fairly empty, but once again other users – whether on four legs or two – may act unpredictably on occasion.

Buses run throughout Madeira and are an excellent and economical way to see the interior. The eastern part of the island is covered by SAM (*Sociedade de Automóveis da Madeira*) and the western by Rodoeste, with websites at www.sam.pt and www.rodoeste.pt respectively. Neither website has a functioning English version, but both are easy enough to follow with route maps and downloadable timetables (*horários*). Most buses run to and from Funchal, departing from a depot on the front a few minutes' walk east of the marina where timetables are on display. Roadside bus stops (marked *Paragem* or *Paragem de Autocarro*) do not usually display timetable or routes. Funchal has its own bus company, Horários do Funchal – visit www.horariosdofunchal.pt (in Portuguese, English and German) for times, routes and fares of Funchal's urban and suburban buses. All three companies' routes feature on David and Ros Brawn's highly recommended *Madeira Bus & Touring Map*, published by Discovery Walking Guides. The bus terminal in Porto Santo is on the road into Vila Baleira from the harbour, with departures about

III. THE MADEIRA GROUP

Vertiginous vineyards on the northwest coast of Madeira  *Anne Hammick*

once an hour plus a service timed to coincide with the ferry's arrival and departure.

Taxis in both islands are yellow with a broad blue stripe (the colours of the Madeiran flag) and are generally plentiful. Fares in Funchal and its environs are pre-set, but all taxis should be fitted with automatic tariff counters. Porto Santo's only taxi rank is on the road leading into Vila Baleira from the harbour, though the arrival of the ferry is always well attended. All four marinas will phone for taxis on request.

### Walking and hitchhiking

Madeira is famous for its mountain walks along the *levadas*, the island-wide irrigation and drainage system which provides level paths through the otherwise untouched forests. Those intending to explore seriously on foot should buy a copy of *Madeira: Car Tours and Walks* by John and Pat Underwood in the *Sunflower Landscapes* series (www.sunflowerbooks.co.uk) now in its 12th edition. For those without a hire car it is often possible to get a bus to a viewpoint or place of interest and walk part or all of the way down. Hitchhiking does not seem to be common, though the chances of a lift may be better once off the beaten track.

### Medical

The emergency number throughout the EU, including Portugal and its islands, is 112. It is claimed that calls are answered within six seconds and an English-speaker is always on hand if required.

The only immunisation required in Madeira is against yellow fever if coming from certain Central American and African countries, though many yachtsmen will also choose to keep vaccinations against tetanus and polio up to date. Funchal has a number of hospitals, including at least two with round-the-clock emergency departments, plus numerous clinics and health centres (and veterinary surgeons). Both Machico and Porto Santo have small hospitals, but serious medical emergencies are normally taken to Funchal. Many of those with medical training speak English, often fluently. Pharmacies abound, and usually appear to have good stocks of both non-prescription medicines and general items such as suntan creams and shampoo, often under familiar brand names. There are opticians in the larger towns, and wearers of glasses would be wise to carry a copy of their prescription (in addition to at least one reserve pair).

In late 2012 an outbreak of dengue fever was reported on Madeira, though by July 2013 it appeared to have died out (like malaria, dengue fever is spread by mosquitoes and cannot be transmitted from person to person). By 2014 the few remaining cases were all in recent arrivals from West Africa or central America, where the disease is endemic.

Otherwise, much of the advice in the Medical section referring to the Azores – see page 49 – holds good, particularly that covering the European Health Insurance Card (EHIC).

### National holidays

Much the same as in mainland Portugal. The four holidays marked with asterisks were officially suspended in 2012 due to the economic crisis, with re-evaluation scheduled for 2018, but Madeirans enjoy their public holidays as much as anyone so it is likely that most will still be observed.

In addition, each town or area celebrates its own municipal holiday, Porto Santo's on 24 June and Funchal's on 21 August. Almost everything except cafés and restaurants is likely to be shut, but there may be the bonus of a festa (festival) with processions or one of the ever-popular firework displays.

| | |
|---|---|
| 1 January | New Year's Day (*Solenidade de Santa Maria, Mãe de Deus*) |
| moveable | Good Friday (*Sexta-feira Santa*) |
| moveable | Easter (*Páscoa*) |
| 25 April | Freedom Day (*Dia da Liberdade*) |
| 1 May | Labour Day (*Dia do Trabalhador*) |
| moveable | *Corpus Christi (*Corpo de Deus*) (60 days after Easter Sunday) |
| 10 June | Portugal or Camões Day (*Dia de Portugal, Dia de Camões*) |
| 1 July | Madeira Day (*Dia da Madeira*) |
| 15 August | Feast of the Assumption (*Assunção de Nossa Senhora*) |
| 5 October | *Republic Day (*Implantação da República*) |
| 1 November | *All Saints' Day (*Dia de Todos-os-Santos*) |
| 1 December | *Restoration of Independence Day (*Restauração da Independência*) |
| 8 December | Feast of the Immaculate Conception (*Imaculada Conceição*) |
| 25 December | Christmas Day (*Natal do Senhor*) |

### Useful websites

A list of websites offering practical information about the Madeira archipelago will be found in Appendix II. Websites – see pages 434–435.

# Regulations and taxes

## Entry and regulations

All four marinas are now official ports of entry. All formalities are handled by marina staff, who enter details on the port control authority's database. Requirements for EU and non-EU flagged vessels may differ so far as the attendance of officials is concerned, and ideally a non-EU flagged vessel should give its intended port of entry 24 hours notice of arrival. Skippers of yachts arriving from the Canaries – which are not part of the EU – have to complete an additional declaration of ship's stores and other items.

As in the Azores it is necessary to clear into and out of each island individually, obtaining outward clearance before leaving Porto Santo and going through the process again on reaching the larger island.

## Pets

See page 51 of the introductory notes to the Azores for general requirements. Madeira's only formal 'travellers' point of entry' for pets arriving from outside Europe is Funchal, but again some flexibility is normally exercised, particularly given the lack of space for visiting yachts in the high season. As in the Azores the final decision rests with the local *Guarda Nacional Republicana*, and it would be wise to keep the pet below until they have been consulted.

## International Certificate of Competence

The same rules apply as in the Azores (see page 51) though, as in the former, it is rarely inspected.

## Port limits

Formal port limits, where various local byelaws apply, are in place around Funchal and may be extended to other harbours. Scuba diving is forbidden on security grounds, although swimming and snorkelling is generally permitted, and if wishing to scuba dive – perhaps to check the yacht's propeller or hull – it is essential to seek permission from the authorities first.

## Permits to visit the Ilhas Desertas or Ilhas Selvagens

Both these archipelagos are nature reserves, and if intending to visit either it is ESSENTIAL to obtain a permit before leaving Madeira or Porto Santo. These are issued, without charge, by the *Parque Natural da Madeira* (Natural Park Department) from their office at the Botanical Gardens northeast of Funchal (well worth a visit in its own right). Although one can apply in person, all four marina offices will handle the paperwork on request, in which case allow at least two working days for the permit to be received. Note that this is NOT a formality. Wardens guard both archipelagos zealously, and those arriving without a valid permit are most unlikely to be allowed to land.

In addition to the Ilhas Desertas and Ilhas Selvagens, three marine reserves fringe the coasts of Porto Santo and Madeira – see the plans on pages 176 and 182. More exact perimeters will be found on current Portuguese and Admiralty charts. A summary of what is – and what is not – permitted within their limits will be found on page 57 of the Azores introductory notes.

## Value Added Tax (*Imposto sobre o Valor Acrescentado*, or *IVA*)

Value Added Tax, commonly referred to as VAT, is known in Portuguese *as Imposto sobre o Valor Acrescentado* (IVA). Madeira enjoys a slightly reduced rate, currently 22% on most items, as against 23% in mainland Portugal and 20% in the UK. Various purchases including water, fuel, food and pharmacy items pay lower rates. Refer to page 52 of the introductory notes to the Azores regarding documentation, time limits for which relief is available, etc.

## Lighthouse tax (*Taxa de Farolagem e Balizagem*)

See page 52 of the introductory notes to the Azores.

## 'Long-stay' tax (*Imposto Unico de Circulação*)

See page 52 of the introductory notes to the Azores.

# Cruising

For many years the Madeira group was viewed by cruising yachtsmen as little more than a convenient stopover en route to either the Canaries or the Caribbean. Until Funchal Marina was built in the early 1980s there was nowhere that a yacht could shelter from poor weather, and within a very few years of opening the marina was so full of local craft that once again visiting yachts were forced to anchor outside. From the late 1980s yachts began to be welcomed into the large NATO-built harbour at Porto Santo, and for a number of years most yachtsmen who visited the larger island did so by ferry.

By 2011 the pendulum had swung back, with Quinta do Lorde Marina in the east and Porto de Recreio da Calheta in the west both welcoming cruisers for stays ranging from a day or two to a year or more. Outside the busy autumn season a few cruising yachts were still able to berth in Funchal, though the anchorage was much reduced. By 2015 space was again at a premium, storms in 2013 having caused damage to both Quinta do Lorde Marina and Porto de Recreio da Calheta, not all of which had been made good and which resulted in fewer berths being available, particularly for visitors.

Meanwhile Funchal was in a state of flux, with the anchorage effectively obliterated. At the same time, a 6% increase in VAT in January 2012 put up berthing fees, though the Quinta do Lorde group mitigated these somewhat with generous discounts to many.

Despite the cost, the availability of safe berthing has doubtless encouraged some cruisers to arrive earlier and stay longer, but the vast majority will continue to visit between September and November. Unfortunately for them most rainfall occurs between October and February inclusive, peaking in November and December, with the mountains of Madeira receiving the lion's share and the much lower Porto Santo very little. Temperatures are mild throughout the year, averaging 24°C in summer and 16°C in winter, while water temperatures average 22°C in summer and 18°C in winter.

### Barometric pressure and winds

The Madeira group lies on the northern fringe of the true trade winds, but at the southern extremity of the northerly Portuguese trade winds. Thus north to northeasterlies prevail for at least 60% of the year, and are slightly more likely in summer than in autumn and winter when the passage of depressions across the North Atlantic can produce strong west or southwesterly winds. The trades generally blow at 10–25 knots, although there is a fairly high incidence of calms throughout the whole year, and in most years true gales are rare.

The south coast of Madeira, however, and Funchal in particular, often experiences local weather conditions which bear no resemblance to those further out to sea. The high mountains which form the island's spine effectively block the north and northeasterly winds, often leaving the south coast calm at night with fresh onshore winds building up during the day from between southwest and southeast. These usually die by sunset but can leave an onshore swell running for the rest of the night.

The eastern end of the island is lower and narrower and thus experiences a truer wind – usually northwest in Machico where it funnels down the valley, and north in Baía d'Abra due to a saddle in the narrow peninsula which runs out toward Ilhéu de Fora. Quinta do Lorde Marina lies in the windshadow of high cliffs and may frequently experience light breezes even when it is fresh to strong offshore.

Having said that, the past six years have seen some of the worst weather ever recorded in Madeira, in terms of rain, winds and swell. In February 2010 the south coast of the island was hit by floods and landslides in which at least 40 people died, though neither Quinta do Lorde Marina nor Porto de Recreio da Calheta were directly affected. After two years of quieter weather, March 2013 brought southwesterly gales which caused damage in the eastern part of the island, though nothing compared to the havoc wrought the following December, when Madeira was hit by southerly storms which caused severe damage to many harbours. GRIB files for the previous week had given a good indication of what was to come, allowing yachts to be moved from the most vulnerable areas, but over the two days the winds lasted they built up very large and powerful seas which broke over most harbour breakwaters, wrecking pontoons and in some cases shifting moles and breakwaters – see individual harbours for details. Somewhat surprisingly, Porto Santo Marina escaped damage by either of the 2013 storms, testament perhaps to the substantial construction of the NATO-built breakwater which shelters the harbour.

### Visibility

Sea fog is almost unknown around the Madeira group, though it is frequently misty in the mountains and particularly on the high plateau of Paúl da Serra which occupies much of the western end of Madeira. Poor visibility at sea is most likely between July and September, when a dry, dusty, easterly wind known as *l'este* sometimes cuts visibility to within a few miles.

### Currents

Ocean currents flow south or southwest past the Madeira group at about 0·5 knots. However, an anticlockwise current runs inshore along the southwest coast of Madeira itself, meeting the main flow off Ponta da Cruz (close west of Funchal) and creating a clockwise eddy which may extend up to 4M offshore.

### Tides and tidal streams

Volume 2 of the Admiralty Tide Tables: *The Atlantic and Indian Oceans including tidal stream predictions (NP 202)*, published annually, covers the Madeira group with Casablanca as standard port. Much the same information is available from the UK Hydrographic Office's excellent *EasyTide* program at easytide.ukho.gov.uk which gives daily tidal data for Porto Santo, Funchal, Porto da Cruz, Porto de Moniz and the Ilhas Selvagens.

Maximum mean spring range is no more than 2·2m and, while there is variation, high water can be reckoned to occur about three hours after high water Dover at springs and 3½ hours after high water Dover at neaps. Tidal streams run northeast or east-northeast on the flood and reverse direction on the ebb, attaining 1·25 knots at springs and 0·5 knots at neaps.

Quinta do Lorde Marina, surrounded by rugged, empty slopes near Madeira's eastern tip. This photo was taken in winter, when the hillsides are green – more usually they are rusty brown *Anne Hammick*

## Magnetic variation

Variation throughout the archipelago ranges from 5°13'W in Madeira itself to 4°54'W in the Islas Selvagens, in 2016 averaging 5°02'W and decreasing by 7'E annually. Exact figures will be found together with the other Navigation data for each island.

## Weather forecasts

Madeira and Porto Santo are covered by Navtex transmissions from Porto Santo in English as well as Portuguese (see page 177). In addition, weather bulletins and navigational warnings for Madeira and Porto Santo are broadcast twice daily from the *Centro de Comunicações da Madeira* in Porto Santo – see page 177.

## Radio communications

Since the withdrawal of the very *useful NP289: Maritime Communications, United Kingdom and the Mediterranean*, those wishing to carry details of all official radio communications in the Madeira archipelago now need to invest in three UKHO volumes – *NP281(1) Maritime Radio Stations*; *NP283(1) Maritime Safety Information Services* and *NP 286(1) Pilot Services, Vessel Traffic Services and Port Operations*.

## Buoys and lights

All buoys and lights in the Madeira group follow the IALA A system, as used in western Europe. Whilst those on the major islands have a good operational record, maintenance of outlying lights – in particular those on the Ilhas Selvagens – is sometimes rendered difficult if not impossible by severe weather so that they may occasionally remain unlit for weeks at a time.

Note also that not every light listed in the text can be shown on the plans, in particular on the small-scale 'island' plans. Refer instead to the relevant – and preferably corrected – chart.

## Charts

The most detailed charts of the Madeira archipelago are those published by the Portuguese *Instituto Hidrográfico*, www.hidrografico.pt, which covers the islands on seven sheets, two of them new editions in 2012. These consist of a small-scale chart of the entire archipelago, two medium-scale charts again covering all the islands at a slightly larger scale, and fourteen approach and harbour plans on various scales. A *Catálogo de Cartas Náuticas* listing both paper and electronic charts can be downloaded from the Portuguese version of the *Instituto*'s website by clicking, *Produtos*, *Cartografia Náutica* and *Catálogo de Cartas Náuticas*, but unfortunately they cannot be bought online. It is a legal requirement for Portuguese-owned boats to carry relevant charts, but even so it appears almost impossible to buy either BA or Portuguese *Instituto Hidrográfico* publications once in the islands.

British Admiralty charts, www.ukho.gov.uk, cover the archipelago on five sheets, comprising two small-scale charts (one including an inset of the Ilhas Selvagens, updates in 2012) and six approach and harbour plans on various scales.

Finally Imray's *Imray-Iolaire* series covers the archipelago on a single sheet, E3, at scale of 1:170,000, with four inset approach and harbour plans. Imray is also an Admiralty chart agent and will mail corrected charts worldwide. www.imray.com.

See Appendix I, page 432, for chart lists.

### Chart datum and satellite derived positions

Not all British Admiralty charts of the Madeira group are based on WGS84 Datum – e.g. positions taken from Admiralty *1831, Arquipélago da Madeira*, must be moved 0·22 minutes north and 0·25 minutes west to comply with both WGS84 and the plans in this guide. Other charts should be checked individually. For a fuller explanation see Horizontal chart datum on page 11 of the Passages section.

### Guides, pilots, etc.

The Madeira group is covered in the British Admiralty's *West Coasts of Spain and Portugal Pilot (NP 67)* which is of course written with very much larger vessels in mind. In addition, the 6th edition of *The Atlantic Crossing Guide* includes brief passage planning notes, with additional harbour details for Porto Santo and Quinta do Lorde Marinas. The archipelago is also mentioned – even more briefly – in Rod Heikell and Andy O'Grady's *Ocean Passages and Landfalls*, and in *World Cruising Routes* and *World Cruising Destinations* by Jimmy Cornell.

### Hauling out and laying up

There are only two places in the Madeira group where a yacht can be laid up ashore at any time of the year – in the boatyard at Porto Santo (25-tonne capacity travel-lift) and at RepMarítima Estaleiro at Água de Pena (35-tonne capacity). Neither can haul multihulls, which are limited to the boatyard run by the fishermen's co-operative at Caniçal (200-tonne capacity travel-lift, plus Syncrolift), and also to the months of April to October, as it is fully occupied by local fishing craft during the winter. One further possibility is Estaleiro Linha Sextante Lda, west of Funchal, but space for long-term lay-up is very limited. Further information on each will be found under the individual harbour details. Although it is hoped that Funchal's Varadouro São Lázaro may reopen in due course, it is almost certain to be for local boatowners only.

A yacht could be laid up afloat at any time of year in either the Porto Santo or Quinta do Lorde marinas, both of which have good reputations for looking after yachts in their care. Ongoing problems with surge in the Porto de Recreio da Calheta mean that it cannot be recommended as a safe place to leave a yacht unattended during the winter, but it should be acceptable at other times or if crew are living aboard. There is no room to lay up in Funchal Marina.

### Ships' stores

#### Water and electricity

In marinas, both of these are assumed to be available at all berths – where this is not the case it is stated in the text. If a public tap exists conveniently near an anchorage this will normally be mentioned, but the absence of available fresh water may not be.

#### Fuel

Diesel (*gasóleo*, pronounced *gas-OH-leo*) is available alongside in all four operational marinas, petrol (*gasolina*, pronounced *gas-ol-EE-na*) from all except Porto Santo. Note that credit cards are not always accepted when buying fuel for either yachts or cars, and where they are an additional fee may be levied – check before filling to avoid embarrassment! If buying fuel at a filling station it is worth paying particular attention to pronunciation, as if the stress falls on the final vowels of *gasóleo* a Portuguese-speaker may well hear it as *gasolina*, with disastrous consequences. Confusion can also arise with paraffin or kerosene (*petróleo*, pronounced *petr-OH-leo*, though both *parafina* and *querosene* are likely to be understood) though less potentially dangerous than if the situation were reversed. Paraffin is available in two grades – poor quality from some filling stations (suitable for cleaning machinery but not for lamps or stoves) and a more expensive grade from chemists which burns well. Methylated spirits is *álcool metílico* (*AL-cool met-IL-ico*) and surgical spirits *álcool etílico* (*AL-cool et-IL-ico*).

#### Bottled gas

Butane is obtainable in both Porto Santo and Madeira, but in Camping Gaz rather than Calor Gas bottles. Calor Gas cylinders, as well as most American and Scandinavian bottles, can be refilled in Madeira (where it may take three working days) but not in Porto Santo or in the Calheta area. Further details are given in the text for each harbour. Propane is not available, but no safety risk is incurred by refilling propane bottles with butane.

There have been recurrent problems with getting gas bottles refilled in parts of the Canary Islands – see page 220 – so some may wish to get them refilled in Madeira even if they are not completely empty.

*Chandlery*

By far the widest stocks are held by Maré in Funchal and RepMarítima Estaleiro at Água de Pena (near Machico). Good English is spoken at both, and items not in stock can be ordered from catalogues. No duty is payable on spares or equipment coming from within the EU, but importing parts from elsewhere (including the US) can be a lengthy process involving a variable import duty plus administrative and handling charges. In some cases it may prove not only faster, but also considerably cheaper, to pay the airfare of a friend or relative willing to act as 'courier' of the essential item.

Madeira's three smaller chandleries – mainly concerned with fishing equipment – comprise Imersão and Nautileste overlooking the marina at Funchal, and Oficina Náutica at Porto de Recreio da Calheta. There is no chandlery availble on Porto Santo, though items can be ordered from both Maré and RepMarítima for delivery by ferry.

## Caution

Any writer of pilot books takes a calculated risk when it comes to describing unfinished projects. The optimistic remarks regarding the Marina do Lugar de Baixo which appeared in the 4th edition proved to be unfounded, whereas those about Porto de Recreio da Calheta were substantially correct. Somewhat the same situation prevails at Funchal harbour in this edition. Changes are an ongoing challenge to both author and user, the latter because work in progress frequently remains unlit, posing a hazard to those approaching after dark, while new features are often slow to be reported through the official channels. Thus even a brand new chart, fully corrected, should not be assumed to be fully up-to-date in all respects.

Although native to South Africa, for many the Bird of Paradise flower (*Strelitzia reginae*) is synonymous with Madeira  *Anne Hammick*

Preparing to set off down the hill from Monte in one of Funchal's famous basket sledges (see page 196)
*Anne Hammick*

An attractive corner in Funchal's semi-tropical *Jardim Botânico*  *Anne Hammick*

An airy bridge on Madeira's *Via Rápida* expressway system (see page 169) passes over a valley with terraced sides. Very little of Madeira's fertile soil is wasted  *Anne Hammick*

III. THE MADEIRA GROUP

# Porto Santo

Between 32°60′N–33°08′N and 16°17′W–16°25′W

## Introduction

Although discovered the year before Madeira and the only other inhabited island in the archipelago, Porto Santo has always been something of a poor relation due to its much smaller size and arid climate. Like Madeira it is of volcanic origin, and though much of the lower land consists of sandstones several of the higher peaks are unmistakably volcanic cones. It is barely 5% of the size of its sister island, with dimensions of around 11km by 6km giving it a land area of only 41km² – apparently much of that sandy beach.

Porto Santo is totally different from Madeira in both appearance and character and is well worth exploring. A taxi tour of the island, visiting the viewpoints at Portela overlooking the harbour, Pico do Castelo high in the centre, and Cabeco do Zimbralinho in the extreme southwest, plus the freshwater springs at Fonte de Areia (literally 'Fountain of Sand') perched halfway up the cliffs to the northwest, takes two hours or more. Alternatively, the energetic can walk and scramble over much of the island, with the views from the summits of Pico do Facho (506m) and Pico de Ana Ferreira (281m) said to be well worth the climb. Be warned, though, by a couple who went for a ramble soon after making landfall in late November and were disconcerted not to find a single bar or café open outside the town – so take plenty of liquids with you.

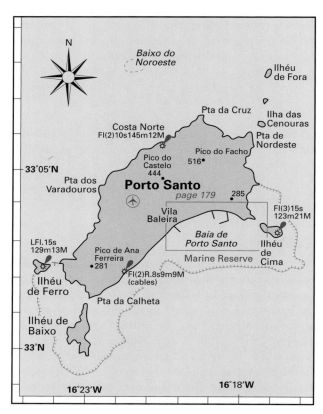

Vila Baleira is an attractive little town with a distinctly Mediterranean air of whitewash, palm trees and dust. Flower gardens lead from the old pier up to a tiny square overlooked by the venerable *câmara municipal* (town hall) and 15th-century

Porto Santo beach and Pico do Castelo, looking northwest from the recommended anchorage area just west of the harbour *Mungo Morris*

## Navigation

**Magnetic variation**
4°59'W (2016) decreasing by 7'E annually

**Tidal streams**
Tidal streams run northeast on the flood and southwest on the ebb at 0·5 to 1·25 knots.

**Lights**
**Ilhéu de Cima** Fl(3)15s123m21M
  Aeromaritime 163°-vis-042°
  Square white tower and building, red lantern 15m
**Cabeço cables** Fl(2)R.8s9m9M (daylight range 3M) 308°-vis-328°
  White post, red bands 4m. Marks submarine cables
**Ilhéu de Ferro** LFl.15s129m13M 302°-vis-318°, 338°-vis-036°
  Round white tower and building, red lantern 14m
**Ponta da Cruz (Costa Norte)** Fl(2)10s145m12M 064°-vis-243°
  White tower, red bands 4·5m

**Coast Radio Station**
**Porto Santo** 33°05'N 16°19'W, remotely controlled from Lisbon
**VHF** Ch 16, 23, 28 (24 hours)

**Centro de Comunicações da Madeira**
**Porto Santo** 33°04'N 16°21'W
**VHF** Ch 11, 16 (24 hours) ☎+351 +351 291 213110
  czmmadeira.com@marinha.pt
**Weather bulletins** VHF Ch 11 at 1030, 1630. Storm and bad weather warnings, synopsis and 24 hour forecast for waters within 20M of Madeira and Porto Santo in Portuguese and English.
**Navigational warnings** VHF Ch 11 at 1030, 1630. Local warnings for Madeira and Porto Santo in Portuguese, repeated in English when possible.

**Navtex**
Porto Santo's long-promised Navtex station finally came on air early in 2013, though as of August 2015 remained unlisted by most sources. The Madeira archipelago falls within NAVAREA 11.
Porto Santo 'P' transmits storm and gale warnings, synopsis and 24-hour forecast in English for the Madeira archipelago and adjacent African coastline, followed by navigational warnings for the seas within 20M of Madeira and Porto Santo, at 0230, 0630, 1030, 1430, 1830 and 2230. Porto Santo 'M' transmits the same information in Portuguese at 0200, 0600, 1000, 1400, 1800 and 2200.

> **Caution**
> In March 2015 a submarine outfall was reported to have surfaced about 275m offshore southwest of Vila Baleira at 33°02'·72N 16°20'·74W. It is presumed to be unlit and otherwise unmarked.

church, with Columbus's reputed home on the island, now the *Casa Colombo* museum, www.museucolombo-portosanto.com, up a narrow lane behind the latter. Open Tuesday to Saturday, 1000–1230, 1400–1730, Sunday 1000–1300, with longer hours from July to September.

However, for many the biggest attraction of Porto Santo is its superb beach, the equal of anything the Caribbean has to offer except perhaps in the matter of water temperature. As Madeira itself has no beaches to speak of, and much cloudier weather due to its extra height, it is easy to see why so many Madeirans crowd off the ferry at weekends or own holiday homes on the island.

### Approach

Porto Santo and its off-lying islets lie just over 21M northeast of Madeira itself, and appear from a distance to consist of several steep and isolated hills. Unlike Madeira, Porto Santo is very arid and there is little vegetation to be seen, though attempts are being made at reforestation.

The northwest, northeast and east coasts mostly consist of steep cliffs fringed by rocks within 0·5M of the shore, plus several small off-lying islands which are easily visible in daylight but are totally unlit and could be hazardous at night. In bad weather the Baixo do Noroeste, which lies about 5·5M northwest of Ponta da Cruz, breaks heavily and should also be avoided, but in fair weather its least depth of 9m will not concern a yacht. There is reputed to be good fishing over the bank.

If approaching from the northeast, as do the vast majority of yachts, Ilhéu de Cima with its powerful light may be rounded within 0·5M to bring the long sandy beach which forms the southeast coast of Porto Santo into view. When arriving from the northwest, Ilhéu de Ferro and Ilhéu de Baixo (unlit) can be left close to port before rounding up into the bay. Submarines occasionally exercise in the waters between Porto Santo and Madeira.

A marine reserve has been created on the south coast of the island, as shown on the plan opposite. See page 57 for details of restrictions, etc.

Golden sands stretch for more than four miles (7km) along the south coast of Porto Santo. In contrast, its larger sister island has almost no natural beaches at all *Anne Hammick*

## Harbours and anchorages

## Baía de Porto Santo

33°03'·49N 16°18'·86W (south breakwater head)

### Tides

Predictions for Porto Santo are available via Admiralty *EasyTide* – see 172
Time difference on Funchal: +0020
*Mean spring range* 2·2m
*Mean neap range* 1·0m

### Plans

Admiralty *1689* (1:20,000 & 1:7,500)
Portuguese *36401* (1:15,000 & 1:5,000)
Imray-Iolaire *E3* (1:25,000)

### Lights

**South breakwater** Fl.G.4s16m6M
    White column, green bands 4m
**West breakwater** Fl.R.4s12m7M
    White column, red bands 4m

### Harbour communications

**Marina do Porto Santo / Port Authority**
    VHF Ch 08 (marina), 11, 12, 16

    ☎ +351 291 980180
    0900–1200, 1300–1700, closed weekends
    marina.portosanto@apram.pt
    www.portosdamadeira.com

**Harbourmaster**
    VHF Ch 11, 16
    ☎ +351 291 980070 / 1
    0900–1230, 1400–1730, closed weekends
    cp.portosanto@marinha.pt

**Capitania**
    ☎ +351 291 984523,
    capitania.psanto@amn.pt
    www.amn.pt

### Ferry harbour, marina and moorings

The entire southeast coast of Porto Santo comprises a shallow bay some 3·5M in length, backed by a near-perfect golden sand beach and well sheltered from winds between west and northeast. The harbour – which was built to take support ships during the island's time as a Reserve NATO Air Base – withstood the storms referred to on pages 171 and 172 with no damage to the marina, which is tucked well inside. The entrance faces west, however, and swell from that quarter can set up a roll inside.

It is used by the Madeira ferry as well as cargo vessels, all of which berth on the south breakwater, and by a small fishing fleet which uses the southern half of the west wall. The northern section of the wall, which overlooks the marina, displays the names of many of the yachts to have visited Porto Santo in recent years. At least 550 yachts pass through the harbour annually.

Porto Santo harbour lies nearly a mile east of Vila Baleira – a hot walk or cycle ride, though just a few minutes by car.

### Approach and entrance

*By day* Straightforward. In calm conditions both Ilhéu de Baixo and Ilhéu de Cima may be rounded at 400m or less and the gently shelving beach closed anywhere along its length. The concrete breakwaters enclosing the harbour will be seen near the eastern end of the bay. The 112m car ferry *Lobo Marinho* arrives at about 1020 daily (not Fridays outside the high season) and departs between 1900 and 2200 according to the time of year, so yachts should take care if entering or leaving the harbour at these times. There is a 3 knot speed limit in the marina, with 6 knots in the rest of the harbour.

*By night* Again straightforward, with powerful lights on both Ilhéu de Cima and Ilhéu de Ferro (though nothing on Ilhéu de Baixo). All three may be rounded within 0·5M. Much of the beach is backed by hotels and other brightly-lit developments. The harbour's port and starboard lights are not prominent, but there are orange street lights at regular intervals along the west breakwater (but not the south), and on the road into Vila Baleira and on the hillside above. The ferry runs a late schedule on Friday evenings – see previous paragraph.

*Porto Santo's large harbour seen from hills to the northwest* Anne Hammick

## Berthing

After many years as part of the Quinta do Lorde group, as of late 2015 Marina do Porto Santo was being run by the *Administração dos Portos da Região Autónoma da Madeira (APRAM)* based in Funchal, but other than contact details and pricing structure it is understood that little has changed. It continues to offer 142 berths, including 42 for yachts up to 10·5m and 12 for yachts up to 15m. A few larger vessels (up to 30m) can berth alongside the concrete spur and the marina has once hosted a 40m megayacht – though not without considerable warning.

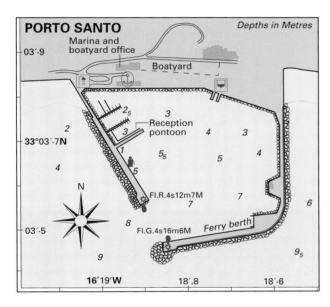

Looking northeast along the west breakwater, with the spur on the right and a yacht alongside the reception pontoon beyond *Anne Hammick*

If arriving in office hours, call the office on Ch 09 15–20 minutes before arrival and a berth – if available – will be allocated. Otherwise the reception pontoon is on the north side of the short concrete spur. Though more than 70m long it may sometimes fill up totally, with yachts rafted two or three abreast. Least depth at the pontoon is 3m, but a shallow spot has been reported about 15m off the end of the concrete spur. Depths throughout the marina decrease from 2·5m on the south pontoon to 2m or less further in, but are generally more than sufficient for the size of yacht in each area. Unlike in many marinas there is generous manoeuvring space between the pontoons.

III. THE MADEIRA GROUP

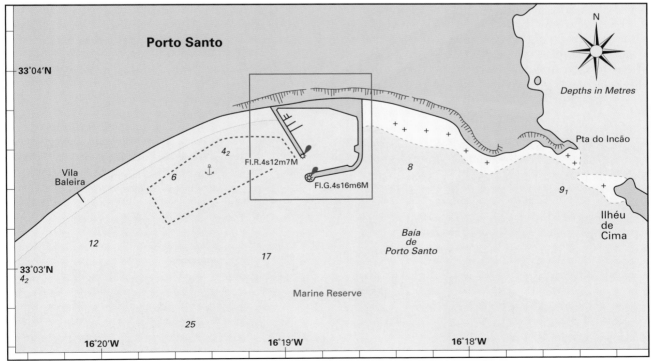

The marina is fitted with a video surveillance system, but has no gates or visible security presence outside office hours, presumably because they are considered unnecessary.

### Harbour moorings and/or anchorage

In late 2015 the marina administered six or eight conventional swinging moorings, and once these were filled newcomers were instructed to drop anchor in the northern part of the harbour, well clear of the commercial and ferry area. Holding is reported to be good over sand. Dinghies can be landed at the slipway near the administration offices north of the marina, or at the marina itself provided no berth is impeded.

### Anchorage off the beach

An official 'small craft anchorage' has been established close west of the harbour, a popular place with visiting yachts in settled conditions for many years, where excellent holding is found in 8–10m over firm sand. Note, however, that northerly and northwesterly winds tend to whistle down Porto Santo's central valley in heavy gusts making a second anchor, both for security and to limit sheering, a wise precaution at these times. It is essential to show a light during the hours of darkness, even if well clear of the harbour entrance.

### Formalities

In office hours the first visit should be to marina reception. The usual documents will be needed (including proof of insurance) and the ship's papers may be held until departure. Outside office hours, but between 0700 and 0100, the Guarda Nacional Republicana (GNR) should be visited soon after arrival at their office close to the root of the mole, followed by the marina office and the Serviço de Estrangeiros e Fronteiras (Immigration), located near the GNR, the following morning. The Polícia Marítima will be forwarded copies of the paperwork and may visit the yacht, though this appears to be the exception rather than the rule.

If planning to depart directly for the Ilhas Desertas or Ilhas Selvagens it is necessary to obtain a permit from the Natural Park Department in Funchal (see page 171). The marina staff can arrange this, but it may take up to 48 hours for it to come through.

Marina do Porto Santo, a welcome landfall for yachts after the passage from northern Europe or the Mediterranean *Anne Hammick*

## Charges

In late 2015 the daily (noon to noon) charge for a marina berth for a yacht of 10–12m was €24.40, rising to €39.04 for yachts of 12–14m and €62 for more than 14m. This was understood to include water, electricity, showers and IVA (VAT) at 22%. Somewhat strangely, berths for an entire month were advertised as costing only €122, €134.20 and €152 respectively, making this an attractive proposition for those planning to stay more than a few days. No mention was made of the pricing structure for multihulls, or whether payment could be made by credit/debit card.

Yachts at anchor, whether in the harbour or off the beach, pay €6.56 per day if under 15m and €10.49 if 16–30m, which includes use of the marina showers (though a deposit is required for the key).

## Facilities

A number of services previously available on Porto Santo are no longer available closer than Madeira, including electronic and radio repairs, sail repairs, rigging and liferaft servicing.

*Boatyard* Understood to remain operational following the change of management, with fenced space for 50 monohulls of up to 15m LOA and 4·4m beam plus some undercover space, and can handle repairs in GRP, wood and metal (including s/s). DIY work is permitted, and owners can live aboard while ashore. There is access to water and electricity and the yard has its own toilets and showers. Security is good, with key-controlled entry.

The hardstanding is clean and very tidy but distinctly dusty, and yachts are secured very carefully – including with guys down to rings or concrete blocks – since storm-force winds toppled several boats in the late 1990s.

*Travel-lift* 25-tonne capacity lift at the boatyard (max beam 4·35m, max draught 3·2m), with supports and ladders provided. A crane is available for removing masts.

*Engineering* Diesel mechanic at the boatyard with others throughout the island.

*Chandlery* No chandlery as such, though the Casa Leao hardware store in Vila Baleira stocks stainless steel fastenings and household paint.

*Showers* In the west end of the building which also houses the Café da Marina, and also in the boatyard. A deposit may be required for the key.

*Laundry* Washers and dryers on site, but as of late 2015 the pricing structure was yet to be confirmed.

*Electricity* Throughout the marina and in the boatyard. 220v 50Hz is standard, but 380v may be available at some larger berths. Yachts must normally provide their own cable and plug, plus adaptor if necessary. After ongoing problems with power surges, all pontoon sockets are now fitted with trip switches.

*Fuel* Diesel from the fuel berth on the southern section of the west breakwater. Depth is not a problem, but an overhang on the wall makes it wise to visit near high tide. Arrange via the marina office, who will set a time with GALP (not Saturday afternoon or Sunday).

Payment must be made in cash. No petrol, which can be obtained from the filling station passed as one enters the town.

*Bottled gas* Camping Gaz exchanges are readily available, but there is no possibility of getting other bottles refilled on Porto Santo.

*Banks* Several in the town, all with ATMs, but nothing at the harbour.

*Shops/provisioning* Several supermarkets in the town, including a well-stocked Pingo Doce on the left as one approaches Vila Baleira from the harbour (open 0800–2200, entrance via the slope at the back), and Ilha Fresca (willing to deliver orders of €40 or more) a short way up the road opposite, plus the usual pharmacy, hardware and many souvenir shops.

*Cafés, restaurants & hotels* The Café da Marina near the root of the west breakwater is open 1200–1500, 1900–2200, with a wide variety of other venues in Vila Baleira and throughout the island (though not all remain open all year – see the island Introduction).

*Medical services* Small health centre, ✆+351 291 980060, on the road between town and harbour, though serious cases are normally flown to Funchal (a Portuguese Air Force aeroplane or helicopter is on permanent standby).

## Communications

*Mailing address* Marina do Porto Santo, Est. Jorge Eduardo M. Caldeira de Freitas, Sitio do Penedo, 9400-240 Porto Santo, Madeira, Portugal.

*WiFi* Outside the marina office and in the nearer parts of the marina, as well as at the Café da Marina.

*Car hire* In the town, or can be arranged through the marina office for collection/return at the harbour. Scooters and bicycles are also available.

*Taxis* Available in the port area when the ferry is due, plus a taxi rank as one reaches the town from the harbour.

*Buses* Bus terminal is next to the taxi rank with departures about once an hour, plus a service coinciding with the ferry's arrival and departure.

*Ferries* Daily car ferry to Funchal – see Ferries, page 168.

*Air services* Regular flights to Madeira and the European mainland – see Transportation, page 167.

Yachts laid up ashore at Porto Santo have been impressively well secured ever since several boats were blown over by storm-force winds in the 1990s *Anne Hammick*

# Madeira

**Between 32°38'N–33°53'N and 16°39'W–17°16'W**

## Introduction

By far the largest island in the archipelago, Madeira – correctly called Madeira Grande – has a maximum length of 57km and maximum width of 22km, giving it an area of about 741km², a great deal of that mountainous. The volcanic peaks which form the island rise sharply out of very deep water, with depths of 2,000m less than 4M offshore, often continuing upwards from sea level as steep cliffs. However, unlike in the Azores, Canaries and Cape Verde islands there have been no eruptions since its discovery in the 15th century, and although many of the mountain tops reach above 1,500m there are no individual giants such as exist in the other groups. Its massive form largely dictates Madeira's climate, with generous rainfall on the north coast and in the highlands, while the south coast including Funchal normally lies in a rain shadow, protected from the northeasterly winds.

The natural forest vegetation was largely destroyed by the early settlers who burnt off the lower slopes for cultivation, but with its rich volcanic soil and mild climate an amazing variety of flowers, trees and shrubs thrive at different altitudes, with fruit, vines and sugar cane cultivated on laboriously constructed terraces. Over 200 species of birds have been identified on Madeira, about one-fifth of which breed locally, though land animals are less varied and almost entirely introduced by man. Even non-enthusiasts should make the effort to visit at least one of the many lovely public gardens, of which the *Jardim Botânico* (which also houses a small museum) is undoubtedly the best known.

Another source of income for the islanders was whaling, with lookout points covering the entire coastline. This is all vividly recreated at the *Museu da Baleia* (whaling museum), ℂ+351 291 961858, www.museudabaleia.org, located on the western outskirts of Caniçal at the southern end of Rua da Pedra da Eira having moved from its old premises near the harbour in 2010. Its vast collection of old photographs, engravings, models, retired whale-boats and audio-visual displays combine to tell the story first of killing and now of conservation, and are backed up by scientific research and educational projects, which also extends to cover other cetaceans

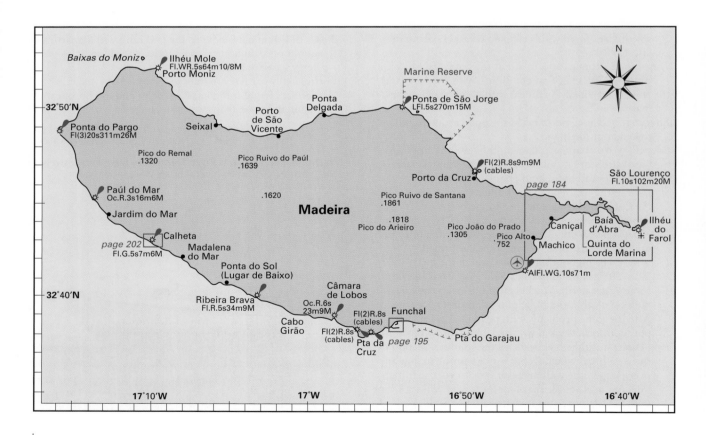

and seals. The informative captions are in Portuguese, English, German, Spanish and French. Open 1000–1800 Tuesday to Sunday (1700 from November to February), and under 5km on foot from Quinta do Lorde Marina (or take the bus), the *Museu da Baleia* is very highly recommended.

Madeira has long had a thriving tourist industry largely centred on Funchal, which continues almost year-round. In addition, a growing proportion of the permanent population of about 260,000 are 'incomers', mainly from northern Europe. Even so, for two decades following the completion of Funchal's small marina in the early 1980s facilities for visiting yachts showed little sign of further improvement – misleadingly, many of the *portos* marked on the chart are little more than rough, stony beaches up which a few local fishing craft are dragged each evening.

The new millennium saw major changes, with Quinta do Lorde Marina near the eastern end of the island receiving its first yachts in 2002 and swiftly becoming established as the island's premier marina. In addition, two new yacht harbours were under construction on the southwest coast. Of these, while Marina do Lugar de Baixo, near Ponta do Sol, was beset with problems from the start and seems most unlikely ever to open, Porto de Recreio da Calheta some miles further west appears to be thriving, despite its somewhat isolated position, though apparently used more by islanders than visitors. In light of these developments, the island's harbours and anchorages are taken in a clockwise direction, starting in the southeast where most yachts make their landfall.

### Approach

Madeira lies just over 21M southwest of Porto Santo and 10M northwest of the Ilhas Desertas. When seen from the north, the mountain chain which runs the length of island gives the skyline a serrated and somewhat forbidding appearance. Pico Ruivo de

## Navigation

**Magnetic variation**
5°13'W (2016) decreasing by 7'E annually

**Tidal streams**
Tidal streams generally run northeast on the flood and southwest on the ebb at 0·5 knot to 1·25 knots. However, they may occasionally attain 2 knots in the channel between Madeira and the Ilhas Desertas, raising steep seas in wind against tide conditions.

**Lights**
**São Lourenço (Ilhéu do Farol)** Fl.10s102m20M
    127°-vis-097°
    White octagonal tower and building, red lantern 10m
**Santa Catarina Airport** Aero Al.Fl.WG.10s71m
    Lantern on control tower
**Ponta do Pargo** Fl(3)20s311m26M 336°-vis-226°
    Square white tower and building, red lantern 14m
**Porto do Moniz (Ilhéu Môle)** Fl.WR.5s64m10/8M
    116°-R-127°-W-116° Lantern on white building 3m
**Ponta de São Jorge** LFl.5s270m15M 085°-vis-300°
    Red lantern on round ribbed tower and building 14m

**Coast Radio Stations**
**Pico da Cruz** 32°39'N 16°56'W, remotely controlled
    from Lisbon
VHF Ch 16, 25, 27 (24 hours)
**Ponta do Pargo** 32°49'N 17°16'W, remotely controlled
    from Lisbon
VHF Ch 16, 24, 26 (24 hours)

**Maritime Rescue Coordination Sub-Centre**
**Madeira (Funchal)** 32°38'N 16°54'W (24 hours)
**DSC** – MF and VHF MMSI 002550100 (planned)
    ☎+351 291 213112, mrsc.funchal@marinha.pt
    (This station does not accept public correspondence other than distress and safety traffic)

São Lourenço lighthouse and part of Ilhéu do Farol seen from the southeast *Anne Hammick*

Santana, the summit of the chain at 1,861m and lying near the geographical centre of the island, can often be seen at up to 40M in clear weather and may be capped by snow. A great deal of the coast consists of high cliffs – those at Cabo Girão in the south drop almost sheer from 575m – with deep water generally to be found within 0·5M of the shore.

Exceptions to this are in the northwest of the island, where the Baixas do Moniz, a low group of unlit rocks, lie just under 1M offshore, and in the extreme east, where yachts rounding Ilhéu do Farol should allow a least offing of 0·5M to avoid the dangerous, unmarked Badajeira Rock, a breaking shoal which lies 800m southeast of the lighthouse. In heavier conditions this should be increased to a full mile, while in even moderate northeasterly winds overfalls may be encountered up to 7M northeast of Ponta São Lourenço, where depths shoal from around 160m to 80m.

Further west, in strong northeasterlies sudden windshifts of up to 180° can occur along the southeast coast between Santa Catarina airport and Ponta do Garajau. Yachts heading east under spinnaker in light southwesterlies have on occasion been backwinded and/or broached by unexpected northeasterly blasts, though approaching white horses will normally give some warning.

## Harbours and anchorages

## Baía d'Abra
32°44'·67N 16°41'·63W (anchorage)

**Lights**
**São Lourenço (Ilhéu do Farol)**
Fl.10s102m20M 127°-vis-097°
White octagonal tower and building, red lantern 10m

### Attractive anchorage

Lying about 10M northeast of Machico and 2·5M northwest of Ponta da Barlavento in the extreme east of Madeira, Baía d'Abra offers a remote and peaceful anchorage under high cliffs with a single building in sight ashore. The narrow neck of land running eastwards toward Ilhéu do Farol gives protection so long as the wind stays in the northerly quadrant, but the prevailing northeasterly whistles through a saddle in the ridge and may sometimes produce enough chop to make landing on the stony beach difficult, even by inflatable.

The area is popular with walkers – there is a large car park complete with ice-cream vans just over the hill to the west – and it is well worth taking the steep track up to the ridge to admire the contrasting views to north and south. The water is generally quite clear and the swimming and snorkelling good. The rocks and headlands to the east, including a spectacular natural archway, make for interesting exploration by dinghy.

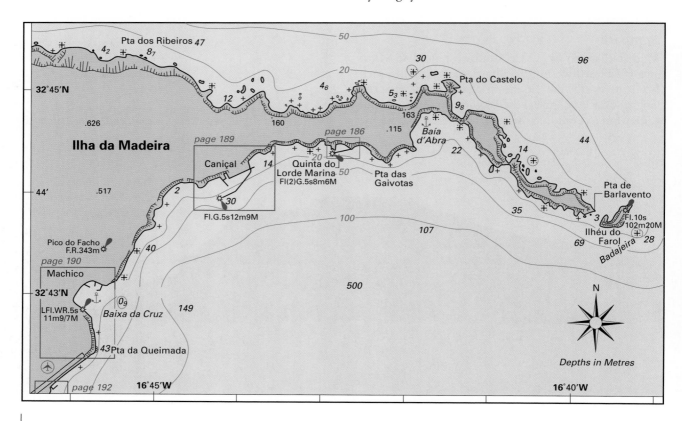

## Approach

*By day* Quite straightforward, though if coming from the west reasonable clearance should be given to Ponta das Gaivotas. If approaching from the east, a large natural arch will be seen before reaching the anchorage. A variety of structures have been moored in the outer part of the bay over the past decade, all seemingly connected with fish-farming research, but over the past few years these have been limited to eight circular fish cages marked by a number of unlit buoys. Fortunately the Baía d'Abra is large and there is plenty of room inside these, but it would obviously be prudent to allow a generous berth on entry.

*By night* Not recommended, in view of both the moored structures and the total absence of lights either afloat or ashore.

## Anchorage and mooring

Holding is good throughout most of the bay and the water crystal-clear. Beware, however, of the three old lorry chassis which lie at 32°44'·66N 16°41'·61W in about 13m, and pose an obvious threat to anchors. Anchoring in 10m or less should keep one clear, though a tripline might still be wise. Right under the steep cliffs to the east and northeast the ground is clear and the holding said to be excellent.

A single, free, mooring has been laid for visitors.

Baía d'Abra, seen from the thin neck of land to the east, is probably the best natural anchorage in Madeira
*Anne Hammick*

# Quinta do Lorde Marina
32°44'·42N 16°42'·84W (south breakwater head)

**Lights**
**South breakwater** Fl(2)G.5s8m6M
  Green and white banded column 6m
**West mole** Fl(2)R.5s6m3M
  Red and white banded column 5·5m

**Harbour communications**
**Quinta do Lorde Marina**
  VHF Ch 09, 16
  ☎+351 291 969607
  office 0900–1800 daily; outdoor staff remain on duty until 2100 from August to November inclusive)
  marina@quintadolorde.pt
  www.quintadolorde.pt
  (in Portuguese, English and French)

## Friendly and well-run marina

Despite its somewhat remote location, Quinta do Lorde Marina is the landfall of choice for most yachts visiting Madeira and almost invariably receives high praise. The staff are consistently mentioned in feedback from cruising yachtsmen as being outstandingly efficient and helpful, with excellent English among other European languages. The marina can accept yachts of up to 25m and 4·5m draught, with the occasional mega-yacht if booked well in advance, though the majority of transients still appear to be in the 12m to 15m range.

A classic marina village development on an ambitious scale, although the marina itself was operational by August 2002 it was several years before its infrastructure – fuel, permanent office, showers, etc. – were completed. The 'village' itself was not finished until 2014, but now features a five star hotel, an attractive square complete with church, and provision for a variety of shops. The marina and its surroundings are well kept, and in 2015 Quinta do Lorde Marina received an EU 'Blue Flag' for the ninth consecutive year. The area's only long-term disadvantage is its remoteness – about 13M from Funchal by sea, but nearer 30km (about half an hour) by road – though this is offset to some extent by the regular bus service (see Facilites, below) and availability of taxis and hire cars.

Quinta do Lorde suffered badly in the winter storms of 2013. These occurred first in the early part of the year, when southwesterly gales combined with severe swell and high tides to create massive waves which broke over the breakwater and onto the long visitors' pontoon which lined its north side, damaging the pontoon and its securing cables and washing away electricity and water outlets. Yachts berthed further into the marina were unaffected, and the damage was made good later in the year.

Sadly this was nothing compared to the storms of December 2013 – described locally as 'the worst in living memory', during which the visitors' pontoon

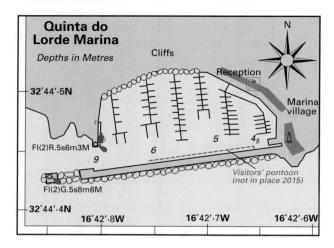

**Quinta do Lorde Marina**

*Depths in Metres*

Cliffs

Reception

Marina village

N

32°44'·5N

Fl(2)R.5s6m3M

9

6

5

4₅

Fl(2)G.5s8m6M

32°44'·4N

16°42'·8W    16°42'·7W    16°42'·6W

*Visitors' pontoon (not in place 2015)*

was effectively destroyed, the fuel pontoon displaced and several of the hammerheads damaged. A large commercial vessel broke loose causing further damage and for a short while the marina was unable to accept bookings, but the staff worked tirelessly both to safeguard yachts during the storm and to start repairs as soon as the waves had subsided. By March the fuel pontoon was operational again, and the hammerheads repaired with water and electricity restored. The visitors' pontoon had not been replaced as of late 2015, but is expected to be in service again for the 2016 autumn season.

Serious damage twice in one year has highlighted the need for many more wave-breaking blocks outside the breakwater, effectively an artificial reef. This is at the planning stage, though it will clearly be very expensive.

## Approach and entrance

*By day* The marina lies in the bay immediately west of Ponta das Gaivotas. Its pale concrete breakwater is 6m or more in height and is conspicuous against the dark volcanic cliffs behind. The approach from offshore is straightforward in reasonable weather, though there are various rocks and shoals fringing the coast on either side. A low neck of rubble extends from the south breakwater, terminating in a large concrete block on which the light is placed.

The entrance, which faces west, is narrow and requires a sharp turn to starboard not far from the cliff face. It would clearly be hazardous in strong onshore conditions – and even in light winds if a heavy southerly or southwesterly swell is running. Katabatic squalls have also been reported as 'falling off' the hills to the north, though these present no danger to yachts inside the marina. The centre of the entrance is reported to carry at least 9m, with more in the bay to the west, but the channel sides are much shallower. There is a 2 knot speed limit throughout the marina.

*By night* The marina entrance is narrow, but in reasonable conditions should present no difficulty. The small church on the cliff due north of the marina entrance is floodlit and (unlike many harbours) the entrance lights can be relied upon. Once inside there is no shortage of ambient light.

Quinta do Lorde Marina seen from near Ponta das Gaivotas ('point of the seagulls') to the east  *Anne Hammick*

Approaching the west-facing entrance to Quinta do Lorde Marina, with the marina's RIB leading the way  *Simon Fraser*

### Berthing

Arriving yachts are requested to give notice of their arrival by VHF or phone, and will often be met by the marina RIB to be escorted through the entrance and directly to a berth. If arriving outside office hours secure to the fuel pontoon immediately to port inside the entrance.

Early in the marina's history surge was sometimes a problem, particularly in strong winds with any westerly component, though never to the point of making it untenable. The addition of tetrapods around the end of the breakwater, to reduce the energy of any surge rebounding inside the marina, worked well. Some were displaced by the December storm referred to above – as was the block on which the light stands – but remedial work was given priority.

Security is good, with access to the pontoons via card-operated gates for which a €25 deposit is required.

### Formalities

Visit the marina office on the north side of the basin taking all the usual paperwork – ship's papers, passports, insurance, etc. Office hours are 0900–1800 daily throughout the year and the staff speak fluent English, French and Spanish in addition to Portuguese. As noted previously, they enjoy an excellent reputation for efficiency and helpfulness, as do the outdoor staff, most of whom also speak English and/or French.

The marina is an official port of entry, collecting the necessary information and forwarding it to the relevant authorities. Non-EU flagged vessels should try to give 24 hours notice of arrival, so that the correct officials can be requested to attend for clearance.

If planning to depart directly for the Ilhas Desertas or Ilhas Selvagens it is necessary to obtain a permit from the Natural Park Department in Funchal (see page 171). The marina staff are happy to arrange this, but allow at least 48 hours.

### Charges

In 2015 the daily charge for a visiting yacht of 10–12m was €39.73, rising to €61.12 for yachts of 12–15m, which included water, electricity, showers and IVA (VAT) at 22% and a 10% 'TECM fee' to cover repair and maintenance of the marina facilities. Multihulls pay a 50% surcharge and discounts were available for longer stays. Payment can be made using most major credit/debit cards other than American Express.

Members of various clubs including the Ocean Cruising Club, Cruising Association, RORC, TransOcean and Voiles Sans Frontières, as well as those taking part in the Atlantic Rally for Cruisers, are eligible for generous discounts. The marina accepts reservations, which can be made by telephone or email.

III. THE MADEIRA GROUP

Looking east-southeast along Quinta do Lorde Marina's south breakwater, with the visitors' pontoon not yet back in place
*Anne Hammick*

## Facilities

*Boatyard & travel-lift* Quinta do Lorde's boatyard is situated about four miles away at Água de Pena, sheltered by the runway of Santa Catarina airport – see page 192 – arrange via the marina office. A *guardinage* service is available for unattended yachts in the marina, which includes checking fenders and lines at least once a day and bilge and battery levels weekly or monthly.

*Engineers* Work can be carried out on yachts while afloat, including engine removal etc. Arrange via the office.

*Electronic & radio repairs* The Maré chandlery in Funchal – see page 198 – is agent for Raymarine and Simrad among other makes. Visit in person or arrange via the marina office.

*Sail repairs & rigging* A local company handles sail repairs and rigging, and is said to offer a reliable and professional service (though unable to handle very heavy materials). Contact via the marina office.

*Liferaft servicing* Available at the Água de Pena boatyard (see above).

*Chandlery* Rep Marítima at the Água de Pena boatyard and at Maré in Funchal.

*Showers* Excellent showers on the north side of the marina, with access via key pad.

*Launderette* Near the marina office, but with only one washer and one dryer so queues may form. Although initial access is limited to office hours, once in progress there is no time limit and users shut the door behind them. A full laundry and ironing service is also available.

*Fuel* Diesel and petrol available from the fuel pontoon to port on entry during outdoor staff hours (see Harbour Communications). Payment can be made in cash or by card, though an additional 2·5% is charged for the latter.

*Bottled gas* Camping Gaz cylinders can be exchanged at the marina office, which will also arrange for other bottles to be refilled. The latter normally takes 48 hours but can take three working days. Read also page 174 if continuing to the Canaries.

*Bank* In Caniçal, about 4km along the coast. An ATM has long been on the wish list, but is unlikely to be in place before 2016.

The attractive interior of Quinta do Lorde Marina. The tower on the right (not a lighthouse!) can be seen for several miles offshore *Anne Hammick*

The Mediterranean-style 'village square' at Quinta do Lorde, with the church on the right and shops and a hotel on the other sides *Anne Hammick*

*Shops/provisioning* The long-promised mini-market finally opened in 2014, a few doors along from the marina office (open 1000–1800 daily, though visit before 1200 if wanting fresh bread). It carries a sufficient range to meet daily needs, but not to store up for a passage. A well-stocked wine emporium leads off the mini-market, with a small shop selling clothes and good quality souvenirs nearby. More shops are planned for the 'village'.

The nearest large supermarkets are in Machico – served by the 113 bus, see below – while for major provisioning it may be worth visiting the Continente hypermarket in the Madeira Shopping Centre west of Funchal.

*Cafés, restaurants & hotels* The Lord's Club restaurant and the Captain's Bar café, both in the 'lighthouse' building at the east end of the marina, are open from 0900 until 2200 daily. The latter offers a 15% discount to visiting yachtsmen. There are two more restaurants in the resort hotel.

*Medical services* Hospital in Machico, with simpler first aid facilities in the marina complex.

## Communications

*Mailing address* c/o Quinta do Lorde Marina, Sítio da Piedade, 9200–044 Caniçal, Machico, Madeira, Portugal.

*WiFi* Fast, fibre-optic service throughout the marina.

*Car hire* The marina staff can arrange car hire for collection and return on site. Online booking may be slightly cheaper but will probably entail collection/return either in Machico or at the airport.

*Taxis* Can be ordered by phone at the marina office.

*Buses* SAM *(Sociedade de Automóveis da Madeira)* service 113, which runs between Funchal and Baía d'Abra, stops on the road near the east end of the development. Eight buses run on weekdays, fewer at weekends, the first departing for Funchal at 0920 and the last leaving the city at 1815. Timetables can be downloaded from the company's website at www.sam.pt/ or may be available from the marina office.

*Air services* The large and spectacular Santa Catarina Airport is about 12km westward down the coast – no more than 20 minutes by road, thanks to the *Via Rápida* which runs west from Caniçal.

# Caniçal

32°43'·96N 16°44'·12W (southeast breakwater head)

### Lights
**Southeast breakwater** Fl.G.5s12m9M
   White column, green bands 6m
**West breakwater** Fl.R.5s8m6M
   White column, red bands 3·5m
**Ship mooring buoys** Four yellow buoys, one
   Fl(5)Y.10s4M, one Fl(4)Y.10s4M, and two Fl.Y.3s4M lie
   southeast of Caniçal centred on 32°44'·3N 16°43'·4W.
   Used for mooring tankers four-square for pipeline
   transfer

### Harbour communications
**Port Authority**
   VHF Ch 08, 11, 16
   ☎+351 291 208600
   0800–2400
   www.portosdamadeira.com
**Capitania**
   VHF Ch 11, 16
   ☎+351 291 213110
   0900–1200, 1400–1730
   capiporto.funchal@telepac.pt

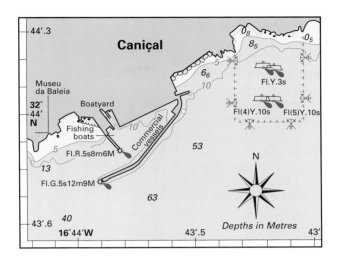

## Commercial harbour with boatyard

Until 1981 the centre of Madeiran whaling, Caniçal
is now the island's main commercial port, allowing
Funchal to specialise in the lucrative cruise ship
trade. Harbour works – including a 350m extension
to the southeast breakwater – were completed late in
2006, providing three container berths, a quay for
grain vessels and a RoRo facility. There are floating
pontoons for small fishing boats, but no space for
yachts and casual visitors would not be welcome.

The port boasts its own *zona franca* (free trade
zone) while the town is thriving if not particularly
scenic. Hampered for many years by poor
communications, the *Via Rápida* network now
serves Caniçal via a two-lane tunnel. A *festa* takes
place on the third Saturday in September, during
which decorated fishing boats circle the harbour,
one of which is chosen to carry the image of *Nossa
Senhora da Piedade*, brought down from the chapel
on the nearby hilltop. The following Sunday there is
a second procession, after which the patron saint is
returned to the chapel.

Madeira's *Museu da Baleia* (whaling museum) –
see page 182 – lies only 600m or so west of the
harbour and is highly recommended.

The large commercial harbour at Caniçal seen from the southwest,
with Quinta do Lorde Marina in the background  *Anne Hammick*

III. THE MADEIRA GROUP

### Approach, entrance and berthing

The only reason for a yacht to enter Caniçal would be to haul out at the boatyard. This will need to be organised well in advance, almost certainly involving a prior visit by land.

Approach and entry are straightforward, though there are various off-lying rocks and shoals along the coast on either side. It would be best to head in from the southeast, keeping a listening watch on VHF Ch 09 and 16 in case of ships manoeuvring. From offshore, the harbour is dominated by a block of enormous concrete silos, with acres of grey solar panels a small wind farm to the east.

### Anchorage

The best – indeed the only – anchorage is off the beach about 600m west of the entrance, near the *clube náutico*. The area is generally calm in summer and provides good anchorage in the right conditions. Dinghies can be left at the club and it may be possible to use the showers, etc. It is only a short walk into the town.

### Facilities

*Boatyard* Large boatyard run by the fishermen's co-operative, long popular with multihulls and those who wish to live aboard while working on their vessels (neither of which are accepted at Água de Pena – see page 192). Unfortunately, and perhaps due partly to the closure of the boatyard at Funchal, from November to March inclusive the large area of hardstanding is fully occupied by local fishing craft, with no space for yachts. The yard is fenced off and guard dogs patrol at night, but security might still be an issue. The staff are said to be very competent, but little English is spoken and arrangements are best made via the office at Quinta do Lorde marina.

*Travel-lift* 200-tonne capacity hoist with three sets of slings – certainly the largest travel-lift in Madeira and very probably in all the Atlantic islands – owned by the fishermen's co-operative, plus a Syncrolift capable of handling vessels of up to 100m and of considerable beam.

*Engineers* Available at the boatyard, though help with translation might be required.

*Showers* In the boatyard compound, but said to be very basic.

*Fuel* By can from a filling station on the main road.

*Bank* On the main road, with ATM.

*Shops/provisioning* Basic shops, though unusually well camouflaged.

*Cafés, restaurants & hotels* No shortage of the former, with several overlooking the harbour square, but little residential accommodation.

*Medical services* In Machico.

### Communications

*Taxis* Surprisingly prolific.

*Buses* On the route of the 113 (see page 188).

*Air services* The airport is about 6km to the southwest, though much further by road.

# Machico

32°43'·02N 16°45'·62W (east molehead)

**Lights**
**Machico (São Roque)**
LFl.WR.5s11m9/7M 230°-R-265°-W-230°
Red column, two white bands on red hut 4m
*Note* Not on the headland (Ponta da Queimada) but tucked well into the bay, hence the limited arc of visibility
**East mole** Fl(3)G.8s6m6M
White column, green bands 3·5m
**Northwest mole** Fl(3)R.8s6m5M
White column, red bands 3·4m
**Pico do Facho** F.R.343m TV mast 22m

### Wide sandy bay with short mole

Until relatively recently Machico was a small, somewhat remote community dependent largely on agriculture and fishing. However the opening of the massive and unlovely Hotel Dom Pedro Baía in the mid 1980s, followed some 20 years later by the extension of the *Via Rápida* (which crosses the upper valley on a massive bridge), has brought development to the area with a vengeance. A very old town, it was the landing place of João Gonçalves Zarco in 1419 and for a while the capital of the eastern part of Madeira under Tristão Vaz Teixeira, his fellow captain. Its 15th-century parish church is certainly the oldest in Madeira, and the tiny, triangular, whitewashed fort facing the beach and dated 1706 probably the smallest (it now houses the tourist office). Machico's other old fort, on the

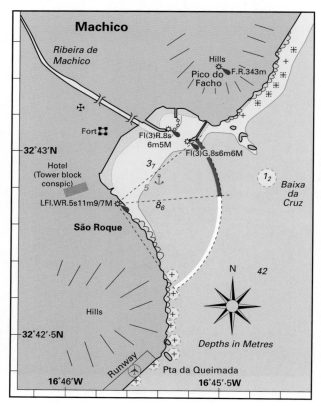

Looking southwest across the bay at Machico with the airport's long runway in the distance *Anne Hammick*

slopes east of the mole and dating back to 1708, is being converted into a hotel, though work has ground to a halt, doubtless for financial reasons.

About 3M southwest of Quinta do Lorde Marina and 6M northeast of Funchal – or 10·5M by water – the bay offers good protection from southwest through west to northeast. Until recently just a wide, sandy bay with a short eastern mole fully occupied by fishing boats, in 2005 work started to extend the mole and lay smallcraft pontoons in its shelter. At the same time a swimming area was created to the west – the fine golden sand is said to have been imported from Morocco – cordoned off by a string of orange buoys and floats. Sadly the pontoons did not survive the storms of December 2013, but

The small 'harbour' tucked into the northeast corner of the bay at Machico, seen from a commercial aeroplane which had just left Santa Catarina Airport (see plan opposite) *Anne Hammick*

though this has freed up more space for anchoring, the likelihood of old mooring chains and other detritus should not be forgotten. The whole area lies almost directly under the flight path to/from Santa Catarina Airport, but the noise is seldom intrusive and there is little flying at night.

A medieval festival is held in the town during June, and a gastronomic festival in August.

### Approach and entry

*By day* Ponta da Queimada to the south may be rounded in deep water with 200m clearance. However, if coming from the east generous allowance should be made for the outlying rocks which run at least 400m southeast from the northern headland. The outermost (Baixa da Cruz) is particularly treacherous, its 1m clearance precluding telltale breakers unless a considerable swell is running. Rubble – visible only at low tide – lies around the end of the east mole, doubtless a by-product of the December 2013 storms, so it would be unwise to cut it too close.

*By night* The white sector of the São Roque light leads clear of Baixa da Cruz, but the light may be difficult to identify against the many bright shore lights. A careful watch is required for unlit boats and mooring buoys.

### Berthing

Yachts frequently secure to the inside of the mole, sometimes three or four abreast. Surprisingly, there seems to be no official objection to this, and neither is there any charge. Yachts generally use the outer part of the mole, which has depths of around 3m, but may sometimes lie further in, alongside fishing boats laid up out of season. It is important, however, not to block the fairway or obstruct the turning area, so this option is effectively limited to yachts of no more than 13m or so.

### Anchorage

Good holding in 7–10m over sand and gravel will be found throughout the bay, with the best shelter north of the mole (though this a rapidly being re-colonised by moorings). Winds are usually offshore, the prevailing northeasterlies being deflected down the broad valley which shelters the town, but even so an easterly swell often works around the end of Madeira and sets into the bay.

In winds from west or southwest a more protected anchorage would be found further south towards the São Roque light, while in very light conditions a stern anchor laid out to the southeast will cut down rolling by keeping the yacht's stern into any swell. The mole has four sets of steps at which to land by dinghy, though an inflatable might be best carried ashore up the slipway at its root.

### Formalities

There are no longer any officials stationed at Machico, which has never been a port of entry even for yachts arriving from Porto Santo. Even so, yachts – and particularly those wearing non-EU ensigns – are occasionally visited by either the *Polícia Marítima* or the *Serviço de Estrangeiros e Fronteiras* (Immigration), so prior clearance at one of the island's larger harbours would be wise.

### Facilities

*Water* From a public tap at the north end of the (largely empty) block containing the café/restaurant.

*Toilets* Public (but reasonably clean) facilities let into the wall opposite the tap.

*Showers* Beach showers (ie. cold) at intervals along the beach.

*Fuel* By can from one of several filling stations in the town.

*Banks* Several in the town, with ATMs.

*Shops/provisioning* Two large supermarkets near the river about 0·5km inland, with a good range of other shops including hardware, pharmacies etc.

*Produce market* Back in operation after several years out of commission.

*Cafés, restaurants & hotels* Seasonal café near the root of the mole, with plenty more throughout the town. Relatively few hotels other than the large Dom Pedro Baía at the southwest end of the beach.

*Medical services* Small health centre on the airport road, ☎+351 291 969130. Serious medical emergencies are normally taken to Funchal.

### Communications

*WiFi* At the large Forum building near the west end of the waterfront, and at many other cafés and restaurants.

*Car hire* At the airport.

*Taxis* No shortage.

*Buses* Regular service to Funchal etc.

*Air services* Santa Catarina Airport lies about 4km to the southwest.

# Água de Pena

32°42'·04N 16°46'·08W (southeast molehead)

**Lights**
**Southeast mole** Fl.R.5s9m3M
White post, red bands 4m
**North (inner) spur** Fl.G.6s9m3M
White post, green bands 4m

**Harbour communications**
**RepMarítima Estaleiro**
VHF 16, moving to a working channel
☎+351 291 969800, *mobile* 925 790857
0900–1800 weekdays, 0900–1300 Saturday
marioolim@repmaritima.com
www.repmaritima.com

## Uniquely positioned boatyard

The tiny harbour at Água de Pena lies adjacent to, and (heading west) about a third of the way along, the runway of Madeira's Santa Catarina Airport. It shelters the lifeboats and firefighting vessels which are always on standby, and would be of no possible interest to yachts were it not for the RepMarítima Estaleiro (boatyard) to which it gives access. Owned and operated by the same company as the marinas at Quinta do Lorde and Porto Santo, it lifted its first yacht in April 2010 and is probably unique in that its extensive hardstanding lies beneath the airport runway, though with an air height of around 100m.

*Chefe de Operações* Mário Olim speaks fluent English and has been highly praised in feedback from a number of yachtsmen. Though generally booked to capacity for the winter – by December 2014, 122 yachts had been squeezed into an area intended for 100 – the floor is impressively clear, with none of the trip-hazards to be seen in many yards. Proof of insurance is required when booking and security is excellent, with high, robust fencing, CCTV and two guard dogs.

Água de Pena harbour and the RepMarítima boatyard were largely unaffected by the December 2013 storms, with no damage to either the harbour or to yachts laid up ashore.

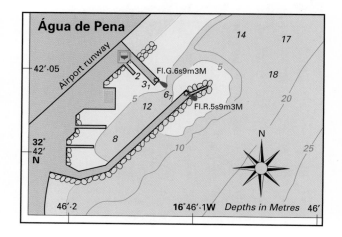

The tiny harbour at Água de Pena seen from an aeroplane passing to the southeast. The boatyard behind it – though not the harbour itself – lies under the extended runway of Santa Catarina Airport *Anne Hammick*

## Approach, entrance and berthing

Yachts coming from Quinta do Lorde Marina are normally either escorted by the marina RIB, carry a member of the marina staff aboard, or both. Once identified beneath the airport columns the approach is straightforward, but the entrance itself is extremely narrow at just 25m. Depths are good, though larger yachts may need high water to enter the travel-lift alcove.

It is absolutely essential for all arrangements to be made in advance and for the yacht to be expected, as there is little area to lie alongside (the mole is generally occupied by a lifeboat and a small tug). It is often be possible to enter the travel-lift dock immediately on arrival, for which warps and fenders should be prepared.

## Facilities

*Boatyard* As already stated, RepMarítima Estaleiro has become popular as a place to lay-up, whether or not work is required, and it is advisable to book well in advance. In addition to a wide range of technical work, standard services such as painting and guardinage (including a monthly hose-down) are available. Great care is shown during lifting and chocking-up, and the metal props – made on-site – are particularly substantial. DIY work is permitted, but owners cannot stay aboard overnight. See www.repmaritima.com for charges, which have been described as 'expensive but not prohibitive'.

The owner of a 15m (49ft) yacht which has wintered in the yard on three successive years notes: 'Not much UV so the (teak) deck loved it, but some raw kerosene from the jets gave a WD40-style treat to the rig – I had to slide down the headfoils with a rag before putting on the headsails. The only things we couldn't get the stains off were the scoops of our Dorade vents – it really sticks to soft plastic.'

*Travel-lift* 35-tonne capacity, and able to lift up to 16m LOA x 5·25m beam.

*Engineers* Agents for Yanmar, but with a machine shop equipped to handle all kinds of mechanical repairs, plus stainless steel and other welding.

*Electronic & radio repairs* Can be arranged if required.

*Liferaft servicing* The only liferaft (Portuguese: *jangada*) inspection centre in Madeira. Though currently certified only for Plastimo and RFD, in practice all makes carried by non-commercial vessels are handled.

*Chandlery* Large stock with a leaning towards the practical – Hempel, International and Jotun paints, Sikaflex, glass mat and cloth, epoxy resins, etc. Open to 'non residents'.

*Water, electricity and compressed air* At each lay-up slot.

*Showers* Well-kept, in keeping with the whole yard.

![More than 100 yachts share space with the massive support columns for the runway above]()

More than 100 yachts share space with the massive support columns for the runway above *Anne Hammick*

Interesting paint jobs! The props are made by the boatyard, and are some of the best-designed the writer has ever seen *Anne Hammick*

# Smallcraft harbours on the southeast coast of Madeira

## Santa Cruz
32°41'·24N 16°47'·07W (molehead)

Situated at the southwest end of the Santa Catarina Airport runway, the single mole at Santa Cruz shelters a miniature harbour, apparently popular with local line fishermen despite appearing to carry no more than 1m at LW. It was badly damaged by the storms of December 2013, but even before that was of no possible interest to visiting yachts.

## São Pedro
32°41'·05N 16°47'·59W (east molehead)

A small, shallow harbour behind an 80m mole and opening to the northeast, São Pedro is overlooked by an active *clube náutico* from which children are taught to sail dinghies, plus a hotel and restaurant complex. An assortment of smallcraft occupy a single pontoon – badly damaged, as was the southeast mole, in the December 2013 storms – and is unsuitable for even the smallest cruising yacht.

Rather surprisingly the harbour is lit, Fl.R.4s6m3M on a red and white banded post on the southeast mole, and Fl.G.4s3m2M on a white block with a green band on the north (inner) spur, though the latter is obscured other than from the southeast. There is a small chandlery, stocking mainly dinghy fittings, plus the ubiquitous café/bar.

## Porto Novo
32°39'·62N 16°48'·4W (west quay)

A port in name only, with a stony beach flanked by two small unlit quays and a rough boatyard for wooden fishing craft, the whole overflown – literally – by a vast concrete bridge, part of the *Via Rápida* system. The quays are used to unload black sand dredged from the seabed and used in building. No protection of any kind and certainly no place for a yacht.

# Funchal
32°38'·51N 16°54'·41W (breakwater head)
32°38'·72N 16°54'·54W (marina mole, angle)

### Tides
Predictions for Funchal are available via Admiralty *EasyTide* – see page 172. Alternatively Portuguese tide tables are available for Funchal, with Casablanca as the standard port – see Tides and tidal streams, page 172. MLWS is about 0·4m above datum and time difference on Casablanca: –0026
*Mean spring range* 2·0m
*Mean neap range* 0·8m

### Lights
**Breakwater** Fl.R.5s14m8M 275°-vis-075°
   Red and white banded column 5m
**Esporão** Fl.G.5s5M
   Green and white banded column 6m
**Cruise ship berth east** L.Fl.G.5s
   Green and white banded column
**Cruise ship berth west** Fl.G(2)10s
   Green and white banded column
**Marina south mole** F.G.6m2M
   White tower, two green bands 5m
**Marina west mole** F.R.10m3M
   White column, three red bands 3·5m
**Naval radio station** F.R.137m Radio mast 20m
**Pico da Silva** F.R.1183m TV mast
**Gorgulho cables** Fl(2)R.8s22m9M (daylight range 1·7M)
   330°-vis-025°
   Lantern above white and red banded wall. Marks submarine cables
   *Note* Situated west of Funchal harbour

### Harbour communications
**Funchal Marina**
   VHF Ch 09, 16 (24 hours)
   ☎+351 291 232717
   0900–1800 weekdays
   marinafunchal@sapo.pt
   www.marinadofunchal.com (Portuguese and English)
**Port Authority**
   VHF Ch 08, 11, 16
   ☎+351 291 208600
   0800–2400 hours
   portosdamadeira@apram.pt
   www.portosdamadeira.com
**Capitania**
   VHF Ch 11, 16 (24 hours)
   ☎+351 291 213110
   capitania.funchal@marinha.pt
   www.amn.pt

### Port limits
Extend from Ponta do Garajau in the east to Ribeira do Socorridos in the west, and 3M out to sea – see Port limits, page 171.

## Small marina inside large commercial harbour
Funchal is a busy commercial harbour and a favourite with the cruise lines, often having three or four ships alongside the breakwater at any time. They tend to arrive in the early morning and leave at dusk, a point worth remembering on approach. The harbour is well protected from the north and west by the high ground on which the city is built, and to the south by the 1,000m breakwater. However, it is fully

open eastwards, allowing wind and swell from southeast or east to enter unimpeded.

The small marina tucked in west of the old Cais de Cidade gives total protection, but is packed with locally-owned boats, day-charter vessels and game fishing boats, leaving little room for transient yachts which raft up six or eight abreast against the western part of the marina's south mole. Like that at Porto Santo, the inside of the marina wall has become a favourite place for crews to leave their yachts' names or portraits.

Considerable work has taken place around the harbour in the past few years. The marina's west mole and port-hand light have been rebuilt, with the small river beyond diverted further west, but sadly it appears no extra space has been added to the marina in the process. The dock beyond has been retained, however – at one time it looked likely to be filled in –

and the old travel-lift remains in place, surrounded in 2015 by acres of empty concrete.

The bulk of the money has been spent along the seafront to the east of the marina, previously the site of a restaurant centred around a large stranded ketch with a dark-sand beach beyond. Off this lay the notoriously roly yacht anchorage. The eastern part of this one kilometre stretch has been transformed by the building of a series of small bays, separated by concrete moles reinforced by thousands of tetrapods. Their beaches are formed of large stones, presumably imported, because it was recognised that sand would not survive the first gale. At the extreme eastern end of this stretch lies the Forte de Santiago, which now houses the *Museu de Arte Contemporânea*, with the Hotel Porto Santa Maria next door. Both buildings are yellow/orange.

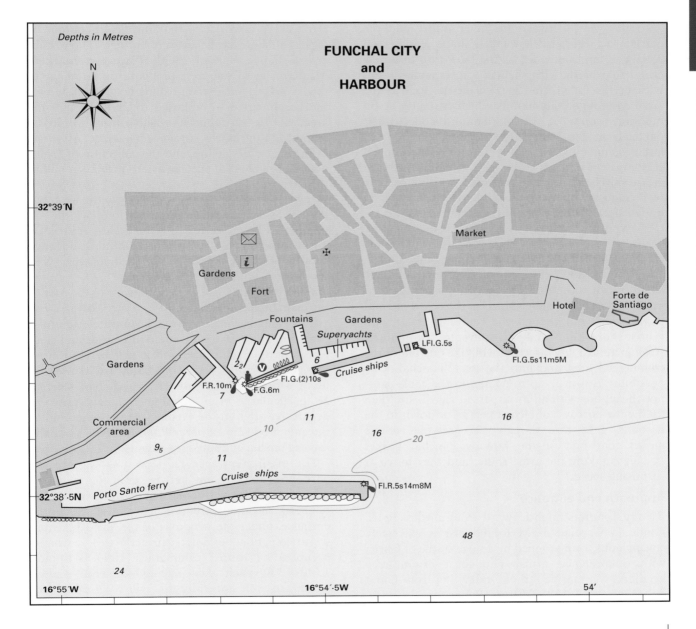

**III. THE MADEIRA GROUP**

The Funchal waterfront looking north from the main breakwater,
while work on the new cruise ship berth was still in progress *Anne Hammick*

To the west, between the river outlet and the marina, a large park has taken shape, entirely on reclaimed land, intended as the backdrop to a new cruise ship berth. This shelters a rectangular basin, with berths for visiting megayachts as well as the large day-tourist catamarans which currently lie on moorings south of the marina and collect their payloads at the marina fuelling berth. While the latter sounds like a major improvement for all concerned, it remains to be seen whether the 330m cruise ship berth – which was used for the first time on 1 August 2015 – will be usable year-round. Many knowledgeable locals are of the opinion that it is far too exposed, and that it will sometimes be hazardous both for the ships and for their often elderly passengers negotiating lurching gangplanks.

For those whose vessels are smaller, however, there is still much to be said for spending a few days in Funchal if at all possible. Much of the city is old and picturesque, and though the centre is thick with tourist shops full of dubious souvenirs, 15 minutes' stroll in almost any direction will take one out of the commercial area and into the 'real' Funchal. One possibility is to ride up to Monte in the cable car – not cheap, but with an unsurpassed view – and then follow the narrow cobbled streets back down to the harbour. Take care though – a growing rumble means that one of the famous Funchal basket sledges is taking the same route, and they move at surprising speed.

### Approach and entrance

*By day* Totally straightforward from all directions. Ponta do Garajau 3·5M to the east is extremely conspicuous, being topped by a huge statue of Christ with outstretched arms. The coast around the headland is a marine reserve, extending from Ponta da Oliveira (16°49'·8W) to Ponta do Lazareto (16°53'·3W) and out to the 50m depth contour or 600m offshore, whichever is further. Three unlit yellow buoys marked *PNM (Parque Natural da Madeira)* lie to the west of Ponta do Garajau. In theory vessels (other than fishing boats launched off the beach) are not supposed to pass through the area, but it is doubtful whether this would be enforced in the case of a yacht on passage. All forms of fishing, scuba diving, and the collection of shells, plants or geological specimens are forbidden within this area.

Fewer yachts approach Funchal from the west, but this is also without hazards so long as the oil terminal at Praia Formosa (which is close inshore) is given reasonable clearance. Light and buoyage details for Praia Formosa are listed together with those for Câmara de Lobos on page 200. A tunny net is occasionally laid close southwest of the root of the main breakwater.

It has long been necessary to keep watch for cruise ships and other vessels manoeuvring inside and close to the harbour entrance, and it will be clear from some distance off whether the 'landward' cruise ship berth is occupied. Fortunately cruise ships seem to be particularly keen on sound signals prior to departure, often in the evening. At the other end of the day, the 112m car ferry *Lobo Marinho* normally leaves Funchal at 0800 – see page 168.

The marina entrance faces west – i.e. into the harbour – and remains narrow, even following the rebuilding of the west mole. There is an arrivals/fuel pontoon on the starboard hand just inside the entrance, under the windows of the small blue and white reception building. Currently this is usually occupied by tourist catamarans 1000–1030 and 1300–1330 each day, taking on and landing passengers, but hopefully this will soon take place inside the new 'cruise ship' basin.

*By night* The statue on Ponta do Garajau is floodlit and is quite unmistakable within a mile or two, whilst the city lights of Funchal are far brighter than any others on the island and most attractive from offshore. The breakwater is lit at its eastern end (though this can be difficult to pick out against the shore lights), plus there are tall floodlights at intervals along its length, but the inner *cais* is unlit other than by street lamps. The marina entrance is conventionally lit on either side.

## Anchorage

As of late 2015 there was effectively no yacht anchorage at Funchal, the very narrow strip indicated on official plans being so far east as to effectively receive no shelter whatsoever. It might be usable for the occasional day or two in flat calm (most likely in summer), but the Atlantic Ocean is very seldom still and even a northerly swell seems to hook around the ends of Madeira and run along the south coast.

It has been suggested that when the day-charter catamarans move into the new basin, the area south of the marina which they currently occupy will become a yacht anchorage – alternatively, the six or eight mooring buoys already there may be renovated and added to. If the former, a tripline will be essential due to well over a century's worth of discarded ground tackle and other detritus. The marina has always allowed dinghies from anchored yachts to be left in out-of-the-way corners and their crews to use the showers and toilets.

Anchorage is most unlikely to be free – see Charges, overleaf.

## Berthing

It would be most unwise to arrive at Funchal Marina without having previously made contact to ensure that space is likely to be available, though it cannot be reserved. The four pontoons with individual fingers provide permanent berths for around 150 local craft, with more berthed stern-to inside the eastern part of the south wall. Visiting yachts lie alongside the western part of the south wall, sometimes up to eight abreast and often with the smallest trapped on the inside. Although it is claimed that up to 25 visiting yachts can be accommodated, half this number seems more likely.

The fuel/reception pontoon is immediately to starboard on entry, but is occupied by tourist catamarans for about 15 minutes each day – see Approach and entrance, opposite. The pontoon has no bollards, just eyes projecting from each end, and one has to wonder if this is because the non-sailing passengers tripped over them!

After a period during which the harbour, and not least the marina, had a reputation for particularly dirty water, it has now achieved EU 'Blue Flag' status and major efforts are being made to keep it clean. Disposal bins are provided for used engine oil, and a repeated plea is made not to use marine toilets whilst berthed alongside. Even so, an occasional oil problem may be inevitable when the wrong combination of wind direction and vessels bunkering in the head of the harbour occurs.

Funchal harbour from the northeast, with the new cruise ship berth on the left and marina on the right – see also page 162 *Harald Sammer*

## Formalities

On arrival call at the small blue and white building overlooking the marina reception berth, where the *Serviço de Estrangeiros e Fronteiras* (Immigration), the *Polícia Marítima* and the *Guarda Nacional Republicana (GNR)* will be found during office hours. Clearance – which is necessary even if only arriving from Porto Santo – averages less than ten minutes, though slightly longer for a yacht not registered in the EU.

The marina office is some distance away, in the centre of the range of buildings backing onto the road, and should be visited after inward clearance has been obtained and again before leaving the marina, particularly if planning to remain at anchor outside. Sr Costa and his staff all speak good English, in addition to other European languages. The other three officials should also be revisited before final departure.

If departing for the Ilhas Desertas or Ilhas Selvagens it is necessary to obtain a permit from the *Parque Natural da Madeira* (see page 171). The marina staff can arrange this, but allow at least 48 hours.

## Charges

In 2015 the daily charge for a marina berth for a yacht of 10–12m was €25.39, rising to €41.87 for yachts of 12–15m. This included water, electricity, showers and IVA (VAT) at 22%. Multihulls – for which there is in any case very little room – paid double these amounts. Payment could be made using most major credit/debit cards. Advance bookings were no longer accepted.

If a usable anchorage is recreated, charges are almost certain to be set by *APRAM (Administração dos Portos da Região Autónoma da Madeira)* and identical to those along the beach at Porto Santo, currently €6.56 per day for yachts of up to 15m and €10.49 for 16m–30m.

## Facilities

*Boatyard* It is hoped that the Varadouro São Lázaro west of the marina may reopen in due course (the 25-tonne capacity travel-lift is still in place), but if so it is likely to be run by the Port authority rather than the marina, for local boatowners only. Apoia Rumos Lda, *mobile* 965 011101, apoiarumos@gmailcom, based northwest of the city, offers a wide range of services including repairs in timber and grp.

*Engineers* A wide range of skills are available in the commercial harbour – ask at the marina office.

*Electronic & radio repairs* The Maré chandlery (see below) is agent for Raymarine and Simrad among other makes, and has technical expertise to match.

*Sail repairs* Vitor Norbrega and Toribio Melim both handle sail repairs and are said to offer a reliable and professional service. Enquire at the marina office.

*Chandleries* Faria & Afonso Lda, trading as Maré, ☎+351 291 236858, mare.madeira@gmail.com, open 0900–1230, 1500–1830 weekdays, 0900–1300 Saturday, have a small but well-stocked shop at 26 Rue Fontes, across the road from the marina. (Go up the slope at the marina's western end, over the zebra crossing, turn right and go over a second zebra crossing, then head down the slope beside the main road. Maré's shop is on the left, beneath the Casa do Turista.) Stock includes electronics – Maré is an agent for Raymarine and Simrad among other makes, and has technical expertise to match – yacht paints and general chandlery, plus pump spares and bottled gas fittings. Excellent English is spoken and they hold a good range of catalogues, with items not in stock generally obtainable from Lisbon by express in three working days.

Nautileste, mobile ☎+351 966 558916, geral@nautileste, www.nautileste.com, has a small shop in the marina complex stocking mainly sport-fishing equipment plus fenders, line and some stainless steel fastenings and fittings where reasonable English is spoken. Loja do Mar, ☎+351 291 620646, lojadomar1@sapo.pt, also selling mixed chandlery, will be found at No.246 in the 'Marina Shopping Centre' (see Shops/provisioning, opposite). Again, some English is spoken.

*Charts* Imersão stock Imray charts and publications, though generally limited to Madeiran waters plus the Canaries and Cape Verdes. Maré stock Imray charts for Madeira and the Canaries, and are happy to order further afield on request. Neither stock BA or Portuguese *Instituto Hidrográfico* publications.

*Launderette* Supervised launderette next to the ladies' showers, operational 0900–1300, 1400–1800 weekdays, 0900–1200 Saturday. Turnaround is

Funchal's colourful *Mercado dos Lavradores* (produce market) is popular with local people and tourists alike
*Anne Hammick*

usually a couple of hours, though up to 24 hours at busy periods. There are several other launderettes in the city.

*Electricity* Numerous 220v 50Hz power points along the marina wall – provided one is within reach. Yachts must provide their own cable and plug, plus adaptor if necessary.

*Fuel* Diesel and petrol are available 0800–1800 daily on the reception pontoon. Payment is made on the spot, in cash. See Berthing, page 197, regarding the use of the pontoon by tourist catamarans.

*Bottled gas* The Maré chandlery (see above) is one of many places in the city offering Camping Gaz exchanges. They can arrange for most other bottles to be refilled, but allow up to three working days. Alternatively go direct to Gasinsular ①+351 291 201450, gasinsular@netmadeira.com at Rua da Ribeira de João Gomes No 53 (about 1·7km from the marina up the road past the produce market) which is able to refill nearly all types of cylinder with propane or butane.

*Banks* Many in Funchal, nearly all with ATMs (though none in the marina complex itself).

*Shops/provisioning* Several well-stocked supermarkets within walking distance of the marina, including a large one in the 'Marina Shopping Centre' opposite. If storing up for a longer period, try either the enormous Pingo Doce hypermarket on the road down to the lido or the equally large Continente in the Madeira Shopping Centre in São Martinho on the western outskirts of Funchal. Both are open long hours, including Sundays.

Almost all general shopping needs can be met, as might be expected in a large and thriving city catering for many thousand of tourists each year.

*Produce market* An excellent fruit, vegetable and fish market has been thriving in the city since its formal opening in 1940. The building – complete with central courtyard, large tiled panels and a tower topped with the city's coat of arms – merits a second look, while flower-sellers in traditional Madeiran costume throng the entrance. Take a camera as well as a shopping bag!

*Cafés, restaurants & hotels* A vast number of all standards, prices and styles. A cluster of somewhat touristy restaurants will be found near the seafront east of the cable car terminal, but it may be necessary to range further afield to track down traditional Madeiran specialities.

*Medical services* Several hospitals, including at least two with 24 hour emergency departments, plus numerous clinics, health centres, dentists and opticians. Funchal Hospital ①+351 291 705730 / 705600.

## Communications

*Mailing address* c/o Marina Funchal, 9000–055 Funchal, Madeira, Portugal. Mail will be held for yachts at anchor as well as those berthed in the marina itself.

*WiFi* Although there is no signal in the marina itself, free WiFi is available on the wide paved area overlooking the marina buildings, in the city's main square and in other public venues. Several provide seating and tables, but none offer any source of power.

*Car hire & taxis* A multitude of both – the marina staff are happy to arrange if necessary.

*Buses* Cheap and reliable, though slightly complicated for out-of-town routes. Three companies cover the island – see page 169 for details and websites.

*Ferries* Regular service to Porto Santo and beyond – see page 168.

*Air services* Santa Catarina Airport, with frequent international flights as well as inter-island hops to Porto Santo, is situated some 18km east of Funchal.

Funchal Marina, crowded as always, seen over the city's rooftops *Harald Sammer*

# Linha Sextante boatyard
32°38'·66N 16°58'·23W (travel-lift molehead)

### Boatyard with 70-tonne hoist

In 2009 a new boatyard – Estaleiro Linha Sextante Lda, *mobile* +351 962 485975, 964 556930 – opened between Funchal to Câmara de Lobos, sandwiched between a substantial seawall and an almost sheer cliff face, with the main road passing some 100 feet above. Though intended primarily to serve the fishing fleet, yachts also use the yard and charges are reported to be reasonable. Boss Jorge Nunes Oliveira speaks some English.

The entrance faces just south of east and is extremely close to the rocky shoreline, and a southerly swell would make the area hazardous. Although the approach from due south is unimpeded, breaking shoals extend up to 100m offshore to the southwest, and during the winter a shingle bank may build up close east of the entrance. The travel-hoist is only used at high water, when depths in the dock are in the 3–4m range. Anyone considering hauling will need to visit the yard first to

III. THE MADEIRA GROUP

Linha Sextante boatyard west of Funchal. Not to be approached without prior arrangement or in anything but perfect weather *Anne Hammick*

The unusually long travel-lift dock at the Linha Sexante boatyard is tucked right behind the breakwater and served by a 70-tonne hoist *Anne Hammick*

make an appointment, a good chance to examine both the approach and the dock itself.

Security is good behind substantial gates, normally open 0800–1800 weekdays, 0800–1300 Saturday. DIY work is permitted and there is no objection to owners living aboard (toilets and showers are provided on site), but the limited hardstanding makes it unsuitable as a place to haul other than for immediate work. Water and electricity are available throughout and the general impression is of a clean, well-kept yard.

Several businesses have workshops on site, including InoxLobos Lda, *mobile* +351 965 754508, geral@inoxlobos.pt, www.inoxlobos.pt, which has its main works northwest of Câmara de Lobos and specialises in stainless steel fabrication, but also handles general metalwork. Other workshops offer carpentry, painting etc.

# Câmara de Lobos
32°38'·88N 16°58'·5W (slipway)

**Lights**
**Formosa cables** Fl(2)R.8s12m9M (daylight range 1·6M)
  027°-vis-055°
  White post, red bands 4m. Marks submarine cables
**Vitória cement jetty**
  Q(6)+LFl.15s13m9M White column 2m
**Câmara de Lobos** Oc.R.6s23m9M 304°-vis-099°
  Red and white truncated column on white block 2m
**Cabo Girão** F.R.691m TV mast 42m
  Three yellow buoys, one Q(4)Y.10s2M, one
  Q(5)Y.10s3M and one Fl.Y.3s2M form a triangle
  centred on 32°38'·3N and 16°58'·1W (between Praia
  de Vitória and Câmara de Lobos)

### Picturesque inlet best visited by land

A very small and busy fishing harbour which lies 4M west of Funchal and 1M west of the oil terminal and prohibited anchorage off Praia Formosa, Câmara de Lobos is very scenic despite the inevitable construction work and well worth visiting – by land. The narrow bay is far too crowded with moored local boats to allow a yacht swinging room, with dozens of smaller craft hauled up on the stony beach to be launched as needed. It might be possible to lie briefly alongside the stone quay on the western side of the bay, but this too is in constant use by fishermen and it would be far better to leave the yacht elsewhere and enjoy the scenic coastal road.

All Madeiran fishing boats seem to be brightly painted, but none more so than in Câmara de Lobos where the crowded foreshore is a mass of primary colour, interspersed with the more muted tones of traditional wooden vessels under repair. Unlike many picturesque villages there is also plenty going on – a catch being landed, boats built or painted and nets repaired. Sir Winston Churchill returned here several times to paint – as the tourist literature repeatedly informs you. Don't miss the little fishermen's chapel right beside the harbour, complete with 1587 gravestone and scenes from the life of St Antony of Padua (born in Lisbon and a follower of St Francis of Assisi) which depict him apparently preaching to some *espada*!

# Ribeira Brava
32°40'·07N 17°03'·8W (molehead)

**Lights**
**Ribeira Brava** Fl.R.5s34m9M
  Square red building 3m
**Mole** Fl.R.5s9m6M
  White tower, red bands 3·5m

**Marine farm**
A marine farm, marked by four yellow buoys with x topmarks, all Fl.Y.6s3M, lies about 0·6M to the southeast centred on 32°39'·5N 17°03'·4W.

## Small harbour and possible anchorage

Ribeira Brava lies just under 9M west of Funchal, from which it is reached via a long tunnel. The area suffered badly in the floods of February 2009 and again in the storms of 2013, but the town itself survived relatively unscathed, and all the usual shops, banks, hotels and restaurants will be found close to the seafront road.

Ribeira Brava's tiny harbour (not to be confused with the semi-enclosed swimming area off the beach) is reached via a tunnel through the headland to the east, but is too small to provide any real shelter from the usual afternoon onshore winds. The south arm is sometimes used by a tourist ferry from Funchal, making it an unsafe spot to leave a dinghy, and the outer section has a low concrete overhang. There is reported to be good if deep holding over sand in the bay to the east, but rolling would be inevitable.

# Marina do Lugar de Baixo

32°40'·7N 17°05'·55W (south breakwater head)

### Lights
As of 2015 there were no functioning lights at Marina do Lugar de Baixo, and it seems most unlikely that this will change

### Large, derelict marina, doomed from the start

Almost every possible mistake appears to have been made in the sad saga of Marina do Lugar de Baixo. Built in the wrong place – reputedly for political reasons – against local advice, even before completion in 2005 serious damage had been caused to the breakwater by winter gales and breaking swell. The root of the problem appears to be the relatively shallow depths which exist along that stretch of the coast, the seabed shoaling smoothly to around 5m off the breakwater. This causes swell to build to double its original height, a fact not lost on local surfers who bemoaned the destruction of one of their favourite waves and predicted – correctly – that it would overpower any breakwater built in its path.

Despite money poured in on a massive scale, efforts to resuscitate the marina have repeatedly been defeated by the elements and by 2015 there were large breaches in the breakwater and the amenities block near the entrance was in ruins. Argument – and the apportionment of blame – continues.

# Porto de Recreio da Calheta

32°42'·99N 17°10'·3W (west breakwater head)

### Lights
**East breakwater head** Fl.G.5s7m6M
    White tower, green bands 4·5m
**West breakwater head** Fl.R.5s8m6M
    White tower, red bands 4·5m
**East breakwater root** Fl(2)G.5s7m2M
    002°-vis-042°-obsc-075°-vis-125°
    Green and white post on wall 1·5m
**West breakwater elbow** Fl(2)R.5s7m2M
    130°-vis-320° Red lantern on wall 2m
**East inner breakwater**
    Fl(3)G.5s6m2M Green lantern on wall 2m
**Pico do Arco de Calheta** F.R.887m TV mast 42m

### Marine farm
A marine farm, marked by four yellow pillar buoys with bells and x topmarks, two lit Fl.Y.3s2M and two unlit, all fitted with bells, lies off Punta da Galé less than 1M west of the marina entrance, centred on 32°43'·2N 17°11'·3W.

### Harbour communications
**Porto de Recreio da Calheta**
    VHF Ch 16 transferring to Ch 09
    ✆+351 291 824003
    0900–2200 daily
    prc@SociedadesDesenvolvimento.com
    www.sociedadesdesenvolvimento.com/porto-de-recreio-da-calheta (Portuguese only)

### Quiet marina under dramatic cliffs

Porto de Recreio da Calheta, which opened to visitors in September 2004, is beginning to show its age. Although somewhat remote – 16M from Funchal by sea and considerably more by road – it is popular with local boat owners and game fishing operators and there is very limited space for visitors, not least due to the loss of its western pontoons to the December 2013 storms. Nearly 18 months later these had yet to be replaced. Around 300 berths remain available for vessels of 6–25m in depths of up to 3·5m, but most are occupied long-term. Rather surprisingly the storms of March 2013 left Porto de Recreio da Calheta unscathed, and though in December several pontoons were wrenched from their fixings and severely mangled, the breakwaters were unharmed and the marina sustained much less damage than did harbours further east.

The marina lies beneath spectacular cliffs in what is claimed to be the sunniest part of Madeira, and a protected swimming areas with large expanses of golden sand (imported from Morocco) have been created on either side. Rock-falls have been an ongoing problem, with damage to some of the marina buildings and the road east of the complex closed for months at a time, but hopefully a recent program of stabilisation will prove successful.

Initial problems with surge were partially rectified by the addition of angled outer moles, but it has not been eliminated entirely and for that reason Porto de

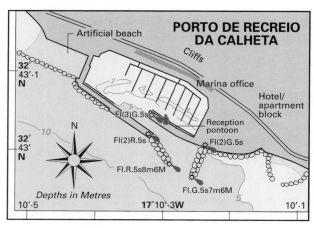

Recreio da Calheta cannot be recommended as a safe place to leave a yacht unattended during the winter. The natural surge is said to be exacerbated by motorboats and jet skis, which frequently ignore the marina's 3 knot speed limit.

### Approach and entrance

Straightforward from offshore, although unpredictable squalls off the cliffs should be anticipated. The large white building behind the marina and the square hotel/apartment block to the east can be seen from some distance, with the pale grey breakwaters becoming obvious on closer approach. The entrance itself is narrow with a tight dog-leg, but though deeper draught yachts are advised to keep to the middle of the channel, particularly at low tide, it should present no problems in reasonable weather. Although well lit, first time entry at night is probably best avoided.

Yachts are requested to call up on VHF before arrival, not least to check that space is available.

Porto de Recreio da Calheta, flanked by protected swimming areas on ether side, seen from high cliffs to the northwest. The horizontal stripes of the hotel/apartment block just east of the marina are visible from well offshore *Harald Sammer*

Porto de Recreio da Calheta, somewhat dwarfed by the large protected swimming area immediately to the northwest – a major attraction for some visiting cruisers, of course! *Harald Sammer*

### Berthing

A berth is often allocated via VHF, but otherwise secure to the long pontoon inside the east mole in depths of 3m or more. To reach it, a U-turn to starboard is required immediately after passing the second pair of lights and, if the pontoon is full (it is often occupied overnight by game fishing boats), a long-keeled yacht might have problems reversing back into clear water. An alternative would be to secure to the inside the southwest breakwater just inside the entrance, where bollards and steps are provided. The long pontoon beyond is used by tourist boats (though if empty and tempted to use it, beware the 6 inch (15cm) gap between the metal edge and the boards in which it would be easy to break an ankle if arriving in darkness).

Security is good, with CCTV and access to the pontoons via card-operated gates for which a €19.50 deposit is payable. There are occasional security patrols during the hours of darkness, but no berthing advice or assistance.

### Formalities

Take all the usual paperwork to the marina office at the northeast corner of the basin, where several of the helpful staff speak English and/or French. The marina is an official port of entry, with all paperwork handled in the main office and forwarded as necessary. If planning to depart in the evening, formalities must be completed before the office staff leave at 1730.

## Charges

For the 2015–16 season the overnight berthing fee for a visiting yacht of 10–12m was €24.98, rising to €32.94 for 12–15m, making it the cheapest berthing in Madeira, particularly for larger boats. This included showers, and IVA (VAT) at 22%, but not electricity or water, for which pre-paid cards are required. Multihulls pay a 70% surcharge, though a discount may be negotiated, and sizeable discounts are available for longer stays. The marina accepts bookings by email and payment may be made by Visa or MasterCard as well as in cash.

## Facilities

Porto de Recreio da Calheta has no boatyard or travel-lift and very limited services on site, though divers, engineers, electronic/radio repairs and sail repairs can normally be arranged via the marina office or through Oficina Nautica, below.

*Chandlery* Oficina Náutica, *mobile* +351 912 178277, comercial@oficinanautica.com, www.oficinanautica.com offers a variety of services in addition to being a Honda agent with fishing gear and limited chandlery on display. Their website implies that wider stocks are held elsewhere.

*Showers* Next to the marina office.

*Launderette* No launderette in the marina, though laundry left at the office will normally be returned dry within 24 hours. The laundry in the town does not allow DIY.

*Fuel* Fuel pontoon (petrol and diesel) just inside the east breakwater, open 0900–2200. Payment may be made by Visa, MasterCard or cash.

*Bottled gas* Camping Gaz exchanges are available in the town, but there is no chance of getting a cylinder refilled closer than Funchal.

*Bank* Beside the Pingo Doce supermarket on the road behind the marina.

*Shops/provisioning* Small convenience store in the marina complex, plus a large Pingo Doce supermarket on the road behind, no more than 250m away.

*Hotels, restaurants & cafés* The Calheta Beach Hotel lies just west of the marina, with a choice of cafés and restaurants overlooking the basin itself.

## Communications

*Mailing address* C/o Porto de Recreio da Calheta, Av. D Manuel 1°, 9370-133 Calheta, Madeira, Portugal.

*WiFi* All the cafés fronting the marina offer free WiFi, but there is no service covering the pontoons.

*Car hire* Available via the travel agent next to the supermarket or the Calheta Beach Hotel.

*Taxis* Usually to be found outside the supermarket, though if bound for Funchal (±30km by road) or the airport (±60km by road) a rental car may well prove cheaper.

*Buses* Infrequent buses to Funchal and elsewhere from a stop outside the hotel – ask at the marina office or consult Rodoeste's timetable at www.rodoeste.pt. Many more buses pass through Estrela, a steep 3km along the cliffs heading west.

*Airport* Calheta is a long way from the airport in terms of both time and distance – see *Taxis*, above.

# Jardim do Mar
32°44'·25N 17°12'·78W (southwest beach)

### Exposed beach anchorage

A stony beach backed by a high promenade with a slipway at its eastern end, Jardim do Mar has been suggested as a potential anchorage in settled weather. Most of the time, however, it would appear to have more appeal to surfers than to yachts. There is an artificial reef about 0·65M northwest of the town where fishing, anchoring and scuba diving are prohibited.

# Paúl do Mar
32°45'·06N 17°13'·45W (molehead)

**Lights**
**Paúl do Mar** Oc.R.3s16m6M
Lantern on post on rooftop 2·5m

### Small fishing harbour

The most westerly of the possible anchorages along Madeira's southwest coast, Paúl do Mar is an old fishing village where a paved slipway is protected by a short, angled mole, the whole backed by spectacular cliffs. It might be possible to lie alongside the mole for a short period with the agreement of local fishermen, the only alternative being to anchor southeast of the entrance – there is no space for a yacht to anchor inside the harbour. The small town has cafés, restaurants and a cash machine as well as basic shops.

Pretty little Paúl do Mar – also to be seen on page 165 – is the most westerly harbour on Madeira's south coast. Even so, a yacht would almost certainly have to anchor outside
*Anne Hammick*

**III. THE MADEIRA GROUP**

The wide breakwater at Porto Moniz looking almost due north, with the dark bulk of Ilhéu Mole behind  *Anne Hammick*

## Porto Moniz

32°51'·93N 17°09'·82W (breakwater head)

**Tides**
Predictions for Porto de Moniz are available via Admiralty *EasyTide* – see page 172

**Lights**
**Porto Moniz (Ilhéu Môle)** Fl.WR.5s64m10/8M
   116°-R-127°-W-116° Lantern on white building 3m
*Note* As of 2015 the mole remained unlit

### Fair-weather harbour in scenic surroundings

Porto Moniz lies in the extreme northwest of Madeira, and is a favourite tourist attraction due to the bathing pools created by concreting some of the western rocks together. A substantial 120m breakwater was built about ten years ago on the southeast side of the headland, intended primarily for tourist ferries and fishing craft. It is seldom busy, however, and yachts occasionally lie alongside for a day or two in summer, when it is reported to remain quite tenable even with a considerable northeasterly swell running outside. At least 3m should be found near the breakwater end, shoaling towards the root. Although the quay is high – at least 5m above sea level – there are several sets of steps and plenty of bollards. Another possibility would be to anchor off and land by dinghy on the steps or slipway.

Facilities are limited, but include a tap at the fishmarket fronting the old quay at the head of the harbour and a cold (outdoor) shower next to the old slipway. Fuel is available by can from a filling station a short distance down the road to the southwest. The village has a small supermarket, a bank with ATM, several restaurants and hotels, and numerous tourist shops.

There is a daily bus to/from Funchal – Rodoeste's 80 service, see www.rodoeste.pt – an excellent way to visit the area if not intending to do so by yacht.

## Smallcraft harbours on the north coast of Madeira

### Seixal

32°49'·31N 17°06'·07W (molehead)

**Lights**
**Seixal** Fl.G.5s11m5M
   White tower, green bands 4·5m

A 100m concrete mole, orientated approximately east/west, was built early this century to protect a smallcraft launching ramp, a black-sand beach and a few small fishing boats which appear to be stored ashore when not in use. Within a few years the *Clube Naval do Seixal* was also up and running, with premises overlooking the natural swimming pool to the west. Presumably it limits its activities to dinghies, as considerable surge enters the bay and depths are reported to be no more than 2m, shoaling further in.

The small bay at Seixal seen from hills to the south. Like the other small harbours on Madeira's exposed north coast most will prefer to visit by land  *Anne Hammick*

In very settled conditions it would be possible to anchor to the east and land either on the slipway or at the single set of steps, but it would be strictly a case for eyeball navigation as the area is poorly charted. The nearby village has basic facilities only.

### Porto de São Vicente
32°48′·83N 17°02′W (west molehead)

A minuscule circular harbour fully exposed to the north, but nevertheless boasting its own *Clube Naval*. The narrow launching ramp must be unusable for much of the year, and the eastern arm is already largely demolished less than eight years after construction. Certainly no place for a visiting yacht.

### Ponta Delgada
32°49′·68N 16°59′W (molehead)

A short breakwater on a northwest/southeast alignment was built about six years ago to provide protection for a few moored smallcraft, with a large swimming pool behind. There is no more than 2m depth and the rough inner face of the mole allows no possibility of lying alongside. Best visited by land.

A prominent white church with a richly decorated interior overlooks the harbour, a focus for the *arraiais* (religious festival) of *Senhor Bom Jesus*, held on the first weekend in September and one of the largest in the Madeiran calendar.

Ponta Delgada, midway along Madeira's north coast, seen from cliffs to the east *Anne Hammick*

The tiny inner harbour at Porto da Cruz. Yachts occasionally anchor in the bay to the east when the weather is very settled *Anne Hammick*

### Porto da Cruz
32°46′·51N 16°49′·6W (dinghy harbour)

**Lights**
**Lagoa cables** Fl(2)R.8s9m9M (daylight range 1·7M)
188°-vis-216°
White post, red bands 4m. Marks submarine cables

A port in name only, the tiny harbour and miniature slipway at Porto da Cruz are tucked in behind a high curved wall, opening onto a bay fully exposed to the northeast trades. The eroded strata on the seaward face of the promontory bear witness to the force of elements.

The village, with its ultra-modern church (unusual in Madeira) is quite unmistakable, dominated by the sheer cliffs of massive Penha de Aguia (590m) to the west and with several rocky islets offshore. Running out towards them is a lower tongue of land, with a black sand beach to the northwest and an equally black stony beach and several rock-edged swimming pools to the southeast.

In calm or light southerly conditions it would be possible to anchor off the southeast beach and land by dinghy at the steps inside the harbour, but the yacht should not be left unattended. The northeast bay is a prohibited anchorage due to cables fanning out from the light detailed above.

The town has cafés, a few shops and a post office.

III. THE MADEIRA GROUP

# Ilhas Desertas
### Between 32°24'N–32°36'N and 16°28'W–16°33'W

## Introduction

The three islands which together comprise the Ilhas Desertas – Ilhéu Chão, Ilha Deserta Grande and Ilhéu Bugio – lie 10M south-southeast of the easterly tip of Madeira and form a low broken ridge nearly 12M long but less than 1M wide. Maximum elevation is 442m near the centre of Ilha Deserta Grande. All three islands are fringed by rocky cliffs and are largely steep-to, an offing of 0·5M being ample.

Discovered and named by João Gonçalves Zarco in 1419 and once owned by a British family named Hinton, the islands later passed into the possession of the Madeiran government whose attempt to found a permanent settlement was frustrated by the lack of fresh water. In 1972 the Portuguese Government bought the islands from its private owners, and in 1990 the *Parque Natural da Madeira* (Natural Park Department) established a nature reserve comprising the Ilhas Desertas and their off-lying rocks and islands, plus their surrounding waters out to the 100m contour, to protect the many breeding birds as well as the endangered monk seals (*Monachus monachus*) of which there are now some two dozen, an encouraging rise from the eight known individuals of twenty years ago.

Fishing, scuba diving and the collection of shells, plants or geological specimens are forbidden within the nature reserve, as are lighting fires and the leaving of rubbish of any kind. Additionally, Ilhéu Bugio and the southern tip of Ilha Deserta Granda should not be approached within the 100m line even if just sailing past. If hoping to land at Carga da Lapa it is ESSENTIAL to obtain a permit before leaving Madeira or Porto Santo – see page 171. This is not a formality: two wardens are permanently stationed at Carga da Lapa and the crew of a yacht will usually be met as they come ashore. No permit – no landing!

The Ilhas Desertas seen from eastern Madeira, with Isla Deserta Grande in the centre and Ilhéu Chão and Ilhéu Bugio on either side *Anne Hammick*

## Navigation

**Magnetic variation**
5°04'W (2016) decreasing by 7'E annually

**Tidal streams**
Tidal streams around the Ilhas Desertas set northeast on the flood and southwest on the ebb at up to 2 knots at springs and 1 knot at neaps.

**Lights**
**Ilhéu Chão (Farilhão)** LFl(2)15s111m13M 031°-vis-321°
  Red lantern on white tower and building 14m
**Ilhéu Bugio (Ponta da Agulha)** Fl.4s71m13M
  163°-vis-100° White tower, red bands 4·5m

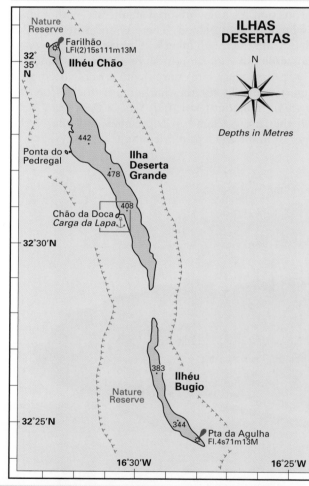

# Carga da Lapa, Ilha Deserta Grande

32°30'·71N 16°30'·53W (anchorage)

**Tides**
Time difference on Funchal: +0011
*Mean spring range* 2·0m
*Mean neap range* 0·8m

## Small and scenic anchorage

Carga da Lapa – literally, *load of limpets* – lies 21·5M from Funchal on a course of 112°, slightly north of the centre of the chain. The tiny bay is protected from north and east by Ilha Deserta Grande, and from northwest by Chão da Doca, a rocky islet and narrow spit of boulders, awash at high water, extending from a rock fall at the base of steep cliffs. Inside this runs a second reef with estimated depths of between 6m and awash. It is a favourite destination for tourist boats from Funchal and elsewhere, to the point that a yachtsman visiting in 2010 described it as 'not deserted at all, but pretty crowded!'.

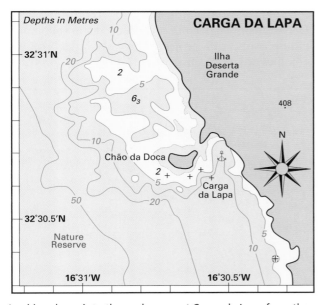

A true deserted anchorage at the Ilhas Desertas, with Ilhéu Bugio visible in the distance  *Harald Sammer*

Looking down into the anchorage at Carga da Lapa from the northeast. Sadly, a landslip has since blocked access to the cliffs  *Henry Adams*

Until about ten years ago it was possible for the fit and energetic to gain access to the plateau almost 400m above via rough steps cut into the cliffs. Sadly the track has since been blocked by a landslip not far above the beach and is now considered too dangerous to attempt, making the excellent photograph below left among the last of its kind. Shore access is now limited to a path of just a couple of hundred metres.

### Approach

Chão da Doca is surrounded by off-lying rocks, including a group immediately to the south of the islet which are covered at high water and should be given a wide berth. The prevailing northeasterly wind may back to blow parallel to the coast in heavy gusts and no shelter will be found from the resultant swell until very close in. Final entry should be made from the south, where there is deep water close to the cliffs, while high sun will aid in detecting underwater hazards – the water is very clear. On no account should the anchorage be approached in poor light or after dark.

### Mooring and anchorage

With no shelter from between southeast and west there is an obvious need to keep a close eye on the weather, as the bay would rapidly become uncomfortable and possibly dangerous in deteriorating conditions. Even so, yachts regularly spend the night there in established northeasterlies, and the anchorage has been described as 'amazingly calm, despite the 25 knot northeasterlies with stronger gusts blowing outside'.

Several moorings have been laid, but reports suggest that they should not be relied upon and most prefer to anchor. The favoured technique is to approach the beach as close as one's nerve will allow, whilst leaving adequate room to swing. Alternatively, it may be possible to drop a bow anchor and take one or more stern lines ashore. Space is not quite as tight as one might expect – though note that the yacht in the photograph is a 25ft Folkboat and not a 50-footer! – and about 10m will be found in the centre of the bay. Holding is patchy over large stones and sand, but as both are black one cannot 'eyeball' a good spot, despite the clarity of the water.

# Ilhas Selvagens

### Between 30°08′N–30°09′N and 15°51′W–15°52′W

## Introduction

The Ilhas Selvagens (which translates as 'savage islands' and has nothing to do with salvage, the Portuguese for which is *salvamento*) consist of three small islands in two main groups nearly 10M apart, close to the direct course between Madeira and Tenerife. Lying nearly 160M from the former but less than 100M from the latter, Spain has cast a covetous eye over the islands with a view to expanding its Exclusive Economic Zone, and in particular its fishing grounds. It appears that if the islands were to be reclassified as 'rocks' they would be deemed to be part of the nearest occupied landmass, and would thus become Spanish. However, Portugal shows no sign of wishing to relinquish its most remote remaining territory, possibly for the same reason. The islands became a Nature Reserve and bird sanctuary in the early 1970s, largely due to the efforts of a Madeiran businessman, Paul Alexander (Alec) Zino. More recently the surrounding waters inside the 200m contour have also been protected. The Zino family maintain a close connection with the islands, Dr Francis (Frank) Zino owning the only private house in the Islas Selvagens where he spends several weeks each year.

Selvagem Grande is the largest of the islands at about 2·5km². Steep cliffs rise to a small plateau with a saddle between two hills, Pico da Atalaia at 153m in the west and Pico dos Tornezelos at 136m further east. Although it looks barren and dry from a distance there is in fact some vegetation – with a much better chance of survival since 2003 when the *Parque Natural da Madeira* (Natural Park Department) carried out a very successful rabbit and mouse eradication project. There are large breeding colonies of Cory's shearwater (*Calonectris diomedea*

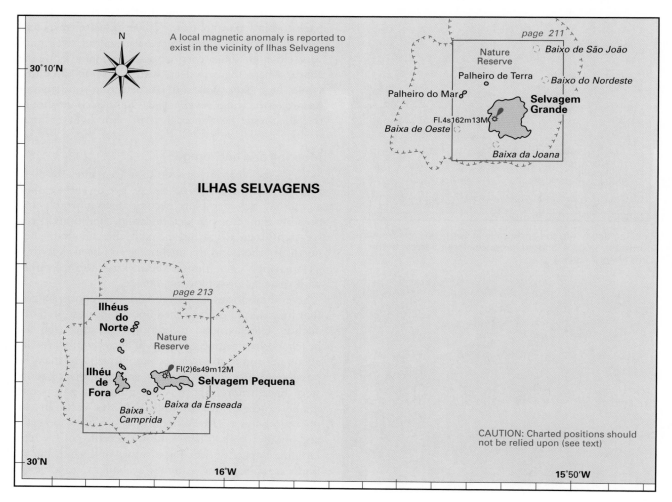

## Navigation

**Magnetic variation**
4°54'W (2016) decreasing by 7'E annually

**Tides and tidal streams**
Predictions for Ilhéu de Fora, west of Selvagem Pequena, are available via Admiralty *EasyTide* – see page 172. Tidal streams around Ilhas Selvagens set northeast on the flood and southwest on the ebb at 0·5 to 1·5 knots.

**Lights**
**Selvagem Grande (Pico de Atalaia)**
    Fl.4s162m13M White tower, red bands 10m
**Selvagem Pequena (Pico do Veado)**
    Fl(2)6s49m12M Lantern on concrete block 1m
    *Note* Both lights are reported to be weaker than stated, and may not operate for extended periods following severe weather

**CAUTION**
On no account should any part of the Ilhas Selvagens be approached in darkness or poor visibility, when they should be allowed an offing of several miles. There are extensive off-lying dangers, the hazards mentioned in the text being only the worst amongst many. Although GPS co-ordinates are now believed to be correct – the current Portuguese chart was prepared in 2009/10 and uses WGS84 datum – prior to that numerous shoals were incorrectly charted in terms of position, depth or both and it is entirely possible that one or more error remains.

Both lighthouses are automatic, maintained by visiting engineers once a year, and inevitably fail at times due to stress of weather. Such failures may not be reported immediately and may last for several weeks.

A *cagarra* chick – more commonly known to British yachtsmen as a shearwater – in its burrow on Selvagem Grande, quite unworried by the camera. The entire archipelago has been a nature reserve since the early 1970s
*Andy Scott*

*borealis* and somewhat larger than their Mediterranean cousins *Calonectris diomedea diomedea*), with lesser numbers of little shearwater (*Puffinus assimilis baroli*), Bulwer's petrel (*Bulweria bulwerii*), white-faced storm-petrel (*Pelagodroma marina*), Madeiran or band-rumped storm-petrel (*Oceanodroma castro*), Atlantic yellow-legged gull (*Larus michahellis atlantis*), common tern (*Sterna hirundo*) and roseate tern (*Sterna dougalli*). The islands are also visited by the rare Madeiran petrel (*Pterodroma Madeira*), known locally as *friera* but in English as Zino's petrel, having been rediscovered by Alec Zino in 1969 when it was considered extinct. It is endemic to the Madeira group and only breeds around Pico do Areeiro in Madeira's central mountain massif. Without any natural predators the birds are remarkably unafraid of people, and in the past many eggs fell victim to fishermen who would sail down from Madeira to collect them. Further depredations were made in the late 19th century when no lady's hat was considered complete without a few feathers to finish it off – as it nearly did the resident avian population. An interesting account of a visit to the Ilhas Selvagens by yacht in 1889 will be found in EF Knight's *The Cruise of the Alerte*.

Two wildlife wardens are stationed on Selvagem Grande, which are also visited regularly by Portuguese Navy patrols, and before departing Madeira or Porto Santo for the Ilhas Selvagens it is ESSENTIAL to obtain a permit – see page 171 – which the wardens will inspect on arrival. Anchoring is forbidden other than in authorised areas – effectively the two anchorages indicated on pages 211 and 213. In theory there is a third permitted anchorage at Fundeadouro das Galinhas, south of Selvagem Grande, but it is too exposed to be viable for a yacht. Anchoring is no longer permitted at Enseada das Pedreiras on the east coast. There is reported to be excellent snorkelling in the very clear waters of Enseada das Cagarras, but all forms of fishing, scuba diving, and the collection of shells, plants or geological specimens are forbidden. So are shooting and lighting fires, and wildlife must not be disturbed or injured. Plants and animals must not be landed from visiting yachts, and prior authorisation must be obtained from the Regional Government before undertaking photography, filming or sound recording for commercial use.

Selvagem Pequena and Ilhéu de Fora lie about 10M southwest of Selvagem Grande, separated from it by a deep, safe channel. Selvagem Pequena has an area of less than 0·25km² centred around 30°02'·1N 16°01'·6W, and is generally sandy and low-lying. Its most prominent feature is Pico do Veado in the extreme north – a single conical hill rising to 49m and topped by strange volcanic shapes. The island is a breeding area for white-faced storm petrels, with an estimated population of some 30,000. Rather than build nests they excavate burrows into the sand, and for that reason visitors should stick to the shoreline or marked paths and NOT walk over the sandhills.

Selvagem Pequena is about as far away from assistance as it is possible to get whilst still near land. The island has been variously described as 'desolate', 'spooky' and 'very lovely', doubtless depending as much upon the observer as on the island itself. Few places can be so totally at the mercy of changing weather conditions and free from the influence of man.

III. THE MADEIRA GROUP

Ilhéu de Fora, about 1M west of Selvagem Pequena, is the southernmost and, at 17m, the highest of a long bank of small islets, rocks and breaking shoals extending about 2M on a north-south axis between 30°01'·7N and 30°03'·7N, and either side of 16°02'·8W. There are no outliers beyond 0·5M in any direction.

The author would particularly like to record her thanks to Dr Frank Zino and Dr Manuel José Biscoito, Curator of the Funchal Museum, for their assistance in correcting and updating this section.

### Approach

Numerous shoals, many both steep-to and unmarked, litter the area. Selvagem Grande's most dangerous outliers are the Baixa de São João, lying 1·3M off to the north-northeast with a charted depth of 2·6m that may be significantly lessened by an ocean swell without breaking; Baixo do Nordeste, just over a mile to the northeast with a charted depth of 4·5m; Baixa da Joana, 400m south of Selvagem Grande with less than 1·8m; and Baixa do Oeste, awash, 0·8M west of Ponta da Atalaia.

Selvagem Pequena is also fringed by rocks, reefs and islets, particularly to the west and east. Its most dangerous shoal is undoubtedly the Baixa Comprida, a long bank reaching more than 0·75M offshore to the southwest, with a breaking rock at its seaward end. Baixa da Enseada, also awash, lies about halfway between Baixa Comprida and Selvagem Pequena.

# Selvagem Grande

## Enseada das Cagarras
30°08'·44N 15°52'·2W (dinghy landing)

**Tides**
Time difference on Funchal: –0018
*Mean spring range 2·2m*
*Mean neap range 1·0m*

### Remote and memorable mid-ocean anchorage

A small cove in the extreme southwest, sheltered from east through northeast to north but open from south to west and untenable in any swell. No more than four or five yachts can anchor at any one time.

### Approach

Definitely a case for 'eyeball navigation' in good overhead light. From Madeira shape a course for 30°10'N 15°50'·1W (about 0·5M from Baixo do Nordeste and 1·6M from Selvagem Grande itself. Alter onto 201° to clear Ponta de Leste by at least 0·5M and maintain that distance offshore around the east and south coasts. Turn in towards the anchorage when Ponta da Atalaia bears due north, so avoiding Baixa da Joana and its associated shoals. Depart on a south or southwesterly course for the same reason.

Looking southwest across the Enseada das Cagarras, with the concrete landing ramp in the foreground. The peak of Selvagem Pequena can just be made out on the skyline at left *Andy Scott*

## Anchorage and mooring

Early arrivals can anchor in the centre of the cove in around 10m, latecomers being forced to stay in greater depths, though watch out for back-draughts which can push a boat inshore. The bottom consists largely of slabs of rock with sand and gravel accumulations in the low spots, and anchors are said to hold by hooking the overlaps between slabs. A quick inspection with swimming goggles is strongly recommended, no real hardship in the very clear water. A tripping line is essential, allowing the anchor to be pulled out at the same angle it went in. Landing by dinghy at the rough slipway in the northeast corner of the bay is usually easiest at half tide or lower, especially if the weather is less than perfect.

Crystal clear water in the Enseada das Cagarras, though a swell can be seen across the entrance  *Andy Scott*

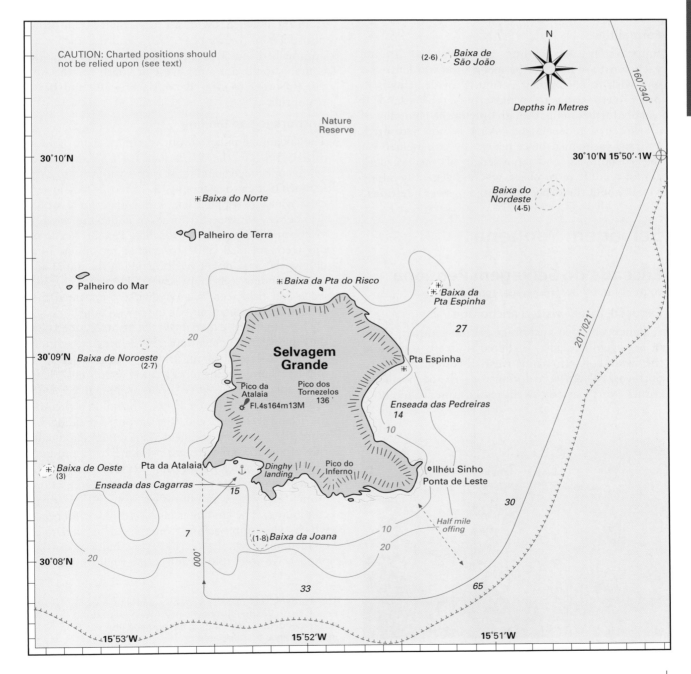

CAUTION: Charted positions should not be relied upon (see text)

N

Depths in Metres

Nature Reserve

(2·6) Baixa de São João

30°10'N

30°10'N 15°50'·1W

‡ Baixa do Norte

Baixa do Nordeste (4·5)

◦⊂⊃ Palheiro de Terra

Palheiro do Mar

‡ Baixa da Pta do Risco

‡ Baixa da Pta Espinha

27

30°09'N  Baixa de Noroeste (2·7)

**Selvagem Grande**

Pta Espinha

20

Pico da Atalaia ⚓ Fl.4s164m13M

Pico dos Tornezelos 136

Enseada das Pedreiras 14

10

‡ Baixa de Oeste (3)

Pta da Atalaia

Dinghy landing

Pico do Inferno

Ilhéu Sinho Ponta de Leste

Enseada das Cagarras

15

30

7

(1·8) Baixa da Joana

10

Half mile offing

20

30°08'N  20

000°

33

65

201°/021°

160°/340°

15°53'W

15°52'W

15°51'W

Lizards get their bearings on Selvagem Grande – for those facing northwest the next land is America *Andy Scott*

A large spherical ship's mooring buoy exists for the use of the Portuguese Navy, but yachts should not secure to this even if unoccupied. In any case, it is well out and somewhat exposed.

### Formalities

Immediately on landing at Selvagem Grande yachtsmen are likely to be met by the wardens who will wish to check their permit. Provided this is in order, permission to walk around the island is usually forthcoming, though only in the company of a warden – independent hiking is not permitted. Visiting yachtsmen have repeatedly commented on the friendliness and knowledge of the wardens and/or wildlife researchers, who are generally happy to talk about their specialities and answer questions.

# Selvagem Pequena

## Enseada do Selvagem Pequena

30°01'·9N 16°01'·5W (anchorage, approx)

### Exposed, rarely-visited anchorage

A somewhat open anchorage off the southern shore of Selvagem Pequena, sheltered by reefs, rocks and the island itself from west through north to northeast. There is a drying rock in the northeast corner. Northeasterly swells tend to run around both

ends of the island, making the anchorage and landing unusable except in near calms. It is occasionally used as an overnight stop by Madeiran fishermen working the banks around Ilhéu de Fora (which itself has no possible anchorages).

Few yachts will arrive without a prior visit to Selvagem Grande, where the wardens may offer to radio their colleagues on the smaller island to say that visitors are on their way. The wardens' hut is in the western part of the island, near the dinghy landing described below.

### Approach and departure

Selvagem Pequena should only be approached in good overhead light which, combined with the very clear water, should allow impending hazards to be seen. In such conditions it can safely be approached from the northeast with no more than 500m offing until Pico do Veado bears 340°, and the anchorage approached on this bearing. On departure, the course should not stray west of south for the first mile in order to clear Baixa da Enseada and Baixa Comprida.

### Anchorage and landing

The anchorage indicated on Admiralty chart *3133* at 30°01'·5N 16°01'·4W is nearly 0·5M south of Selvagem Pequena, and most yachts will want to close in much further to anchor in 12–15m over rock in very clear water. A tripping line is essential, but it would also be wise to inspect from in, or under, the water. A visitor in 2013 reports approaching Pico do Veado on the recommended 340° to anchor in about 14m, despite the 3m+ ocean swell rendering the island and its surrounding reefs 'quite scary'. The anchor caught a ledge and held well, but on diving it appeared that around the 20m contour one might find sand.

The same very experienced yachtsman added that the dinghy landing mentioned in the previous edition, near the east end of the island, appeared 'close to impossible even in the most modest conditions'. They were fortunate to have been accompanied from Selvagem Grande by Dr Zino, who piloted them to the island's western end, the favoured landing for wardens and their equipment. This required a dinghy ride of about a mile around breaking reefs and little islets. With masterly understatement, he added: 'The swell builds up high on the shoals, so that even in our 3·6m dinghy it was all rather wet and exciting,' continuing, 'The landing itself is on a nice sand beach which, when approaching from the sea, appears to be divided into two halves by a big black rock (see photo). We were told to aim to the right of, but very

The wardens' shelter on Selvagen Pequena seen from near Pico do Veado light to the northwest, with the recommended dinghy landing beyond and Ilhéu de Fora in the distance *Harald Sammer*

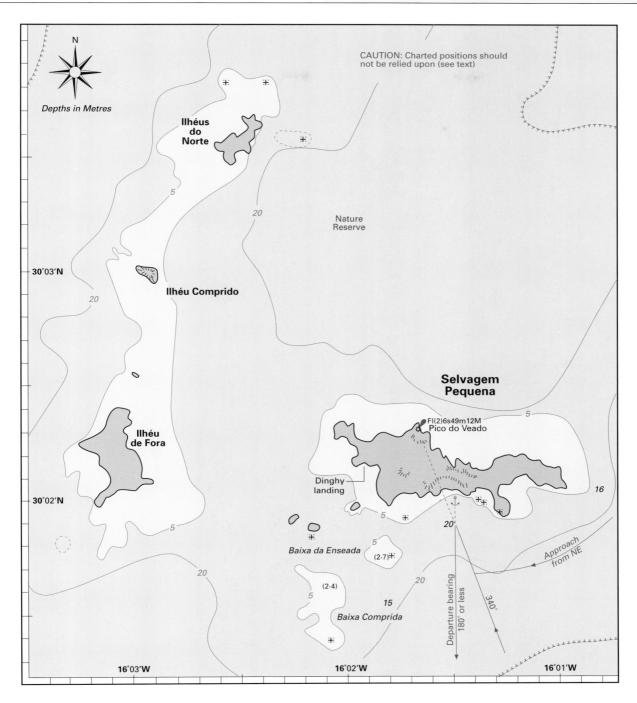

close to, the rock. It seems this spot is free of underwater hazards'. Dr Zino advises that landing is best at high tide, especially if using an outboard. Once ashore, note the point on page 209 regarding the breeding habits of the white-faced petrels and the need to avoid disturbing them or causing damage to their burrows.

My thanks to Harold Sammer and Dr Frank Zino for effectively contributing the final paragraph.

The recommended dingy landing spot on Selvagen Pequena – and the wardens' own dinghy – next to the big black rock mentioned in the text *Harald Sammer*

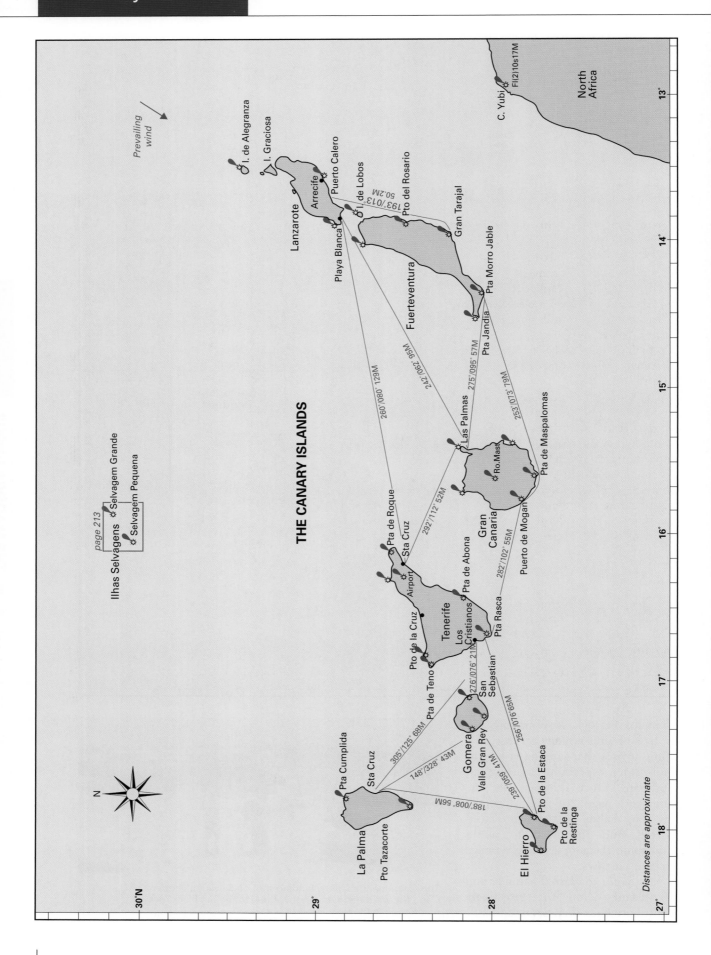

THE CANARY ISLANDS

Ilhas Selvagens
*page 213*
☆ Selvagem Grande
☆ Selvagem Pequena

*Prevailing wind*

I. de Alegranza
I. Graciosa
Lanzarote
Arrecife
Puerto Calero
Playa Blanca
I. de Lobos
Pto del Rosario
193°/013° 50.2M
Fuerteventura
Gran Tarajal
Pta Morro Jable
Pta Jandia

260°/080° 129M
242°/062° 95M
275°/095° 57M
253°/073° 79M

Las Palmas
Pta de Roque
Sta Cruz
292°/112° 52M
Airport
Pta de Abona
Gran Canaria
Ro.Mast
Pta de Maspalomas

Tenerife
Pto de la Cruz
Los Cristianos
Pta de Teno
Pta Rasca
282°/102° 55M
Puerto de Mogan

305°/125° 68M
276°/076° 21M
San Sebastian
256°/076° 65M
Gomera
Valle Gran Rey

148°/328° 43M
239°/059° 41M

La Palma
Pta Cumplida
Sta Cruz
Pto Tazacorte

188°/008° 56M

El Hierro
Pto de la Estaca
Pto de la Restinga

C. Yubi
Fl(2)10s17M
North Africa

N

*Distances are approximate*

30°N

29°

28°

27°

13°

14°

15°

16°

17°

18°

# IV. The Canary Islands

## The Canaries Archipelago

### A group of islands thrown up from the depths of the Atlantic

The Canary Islands are just the tips of volcanoes that originally emerged from the depths millions of years ago. And they are still evolving, not just because weather and mankind are chipping away at them but because four are still volcanically active. A new crater, Volcán de Teneguia, appeared at the southern tip of La Palma in 1971, while as recently as 2012 there were underwater eruptions off the south of El Hierro.

The landscape is one of contrasts, high volcanic cones and cliffs, deep ravines, called *barrancos*, and eroded craters; stretches of arid semi desert to the south and in the rain shadow of the peaks, while the more northern and higher slopes are lush and fertile. Ancient sedimentary geological formations show that these islands were once part of the African continent and the famous beaches of Fuerteventura are thanks to wind-blown sand from the Sahara. The eastern isles lie just 100m from the coast of Morocco.

Mount Timanfaya on Lanzarote, is still active and 8ft below ground level the temperature is 500°C  *Hilary Keatinge*

## Courses and distances within the Canaries

| Harbour | Course / Reciprocal | Distance |
|---|---|---|
| Arrecife, Lanzarote - Puerto de Rosaria, Fuerteventura | 209° / 029° | 33M |
| Playa Blanca, Lanzarote - Santa Cruz de Tenerife | 260° / 080° | 129M |
| Playa Blanca, Lanzarote - Puerto de las Palmas, Gran Canaria | 242° / 062° | 95M |
| Morro Jable, Fuerteventura - Puerto de las Palmas, Gran Canaria | 275° / 095° | 57M |
| Morro Jable, Fuerteventura - Puerto de Mogán, Gran Canaria | 253° / 073° & by eye | 79M |
| Puerto de las Palmas, Gran Canaria - Santa Cruz de Tenerife | 292° / 112° & by eye | 52M |
| Puerto de Mogán, Gran Canaria - Los Cristianos, Tenerife | 282° / 102° & by eye | 55M |
| Los Cristianos, Tenerife - Santa Cruz de la Palma | 305° / 125° | 68M |
| Los Cristianos, Tenerife - San Sebastián de Gomera | 276° / 096° | 21M |
| Los Cristianos, Tenerife - Puerto de la Estaca, Hierro | 256° / 076° | 65M |
| Valle Gran Rey, Gomera - Santa Cruz de la Palma | 328° / 148° & by eye | 43M |
| Valle Gran Rey, Gomera - Puerto de la Estaca, Hierro | 239° / 059° | 41M |
| Santa Cruz de la Palma - Puerto de la Estaca, Hierro | 188° / 008° & by eye | 56M |

The native Dragon Tree has a reddish resin and coral-coloured berries
*Hilary Keatinge*

Do the islands live up to their nickname as 'the islands of eternal spring'? Given their position in the path of the Canary Current, which is driven by the relatively cool NE trades, probably 'yes'. There is a distinct difference between the climate in the north of an island - more temperate, more rainfall - while in the south it is generally warmer and dryer.

The flora and fauna varies with altitude, temperature and rainfall. Laurel forests thrive in the cloud line of several of the islands while the Dragon Tree, once worshipped by the natives of Tenerife, and the Canary Island Date Palm, a symbol of the islands, are subtropical. There are more than 200 species of birds, many breeding in the archipelago and some unique to it. The Canaries' most famous bird *Serinus canaria*, or Wild Canary, is another symbol of the islands. Taken back to Europe by the Spaniards the bird was named after the islands, rather than vice versa.

Off the coasts is one of the better fishing grounds of the world, but while the commercial fishing fleets are suffering from over-fishing and reduced quotas the sports fishing fleets are on the increase with several prestigious championships attracting international competitors.

## History

The islands were known from ancient time, these were the Fortunate Isles, the Islands of the Blest, the Happy Isles, maybe, some thought, the lost land of Atlantis. They were at the edge of the known world, albeit a flat one. Ptolomy put the zero of Meridian of Longitude off El Hierro and it would remain there until, finally, all geographers accepted Greenwich.

The earliest known inhabitants came to be known collectively as Guanches whose origins appear to be Cro-Magnon, Berber and Semite though their practice of mummifying their dead, and the roots of their language, suggest an early Egyptian connection. Phoenician traders collected the purple dye orchil from the Canaries and Pliny the Elder (circa 60AD) reported on an expedition sent by King Juba II of Mauritania (Morocco) to the Fortunate Islands as early as 60BC. His troops discovered large dogs roaming the islands and brought two of them back to the king. The typical Canary dog, the *Presa canario*, is now much smaller but the name Insulae Canium – The Islands of Dogs – lives on in the Islas Canarias of today.

French, Genoese and Portuguese navigators were well received by the inhabitants when they landed in the 13th and 14th centuries. They found that the local people existed comfortably and were well supplied with the necessities of life. What was strange was that these early settlers had no knowledge of navigation and, with no boats, there was apparently no inter-island communication – though presumably this had not always been the case. They were primarily cave dwellers, using tools and weapons of wood and bone with obsidian cutting edges. In the western islands long smooth poles were used for vaulting from rock to rock and over gullies when travelling on the mountainsides. And the Gomerans communicated across their deep valleys with a whistling language, Silbo Gomera, still practised today.

It would take Juan de Bethencourt, a Norman Baron in the service of Spain, and his successors over 90 years to completely subdue the islands, in spite of the invaders' superior weapons. The Spaniards suffered heavy losses before Fernandez de Lugo finally crushed the Guanche resistance at the battle of Acentejo on Tenerife on 25 December 1495. An early attempt was made to ship Canarians back to Spain as slaves, but Isabel la Catolica, Queen of Castile, took steps to see that they were returned to their islands and it appears that there has, over the years, been successful integration between Europeans and the original inhabitants. Christopher Columbus put the islands firmly on the world map when in 1492 he sailed into Las Palmas de Gran Canaria on his first trip to the Americas. Before setting off for the New World, he attended Mass at San Sebastián de la Gomera in a church that still stands (albeit much modified). On future voyages he returned several times to the islands, particularly to the Gomeran home of the beautiful widow Beatriz de Bobadilla whom he had met previously.

Tenerife and Gran Canaria became essential staging posts for those of many nationalities on voyages between Europe and the Americas, while

Stepping back in time in La Laguna, the 15th Century capital of Tenerife  *Hilary Keatinge*

Lanzarote and Fuerteventura were frequently subject to attack by pirates and slavers. Dutch and English ships also raided the islands and Drake lost his flagship in one attack. Two centuries later, in 1797, a reluctant Nelson was ordered to mount an attack on Santa Cruz de Tenerife; he and his men were repulsed, with 350 casualties and the loss of Nelson's arm; that occasion is still celebrated annually, by the victorious side.

In 1927 the islands were divided into two provinces, Las Palmas with the capital on Gran Canaria and Santa Cruz de Tenerife, with its capital of the same name. In 1936 a new military governor arrived, General Francisco Franco, and from the Canaries he planned and then led the nationalist revolt that sparked off the Spanish Civil War. His control over the islands lasted until his death in 1975. Autonomy was granted to the Canaries in 1983.

Where there is land there is a way of growing; the productive Valle Gran Rey on La Gomera  *Hilary Keatinge*

## Island economy

The mainstay of the economy had been sugar, but with increasing competition from Spain's southern American colonies and a fall in the price, there was severe recession and thousands from the islands emigrated westwards across the Atlantic. The economy was partially saved by the expansion of a new crop, cochineal; Cacti were easy to grow on the islands and the tiny cochineal insects feed off the sap. But that industry did not last long either and finally, early in the 19th century the most sustaining industry of all had its beginnings with the arrival in Puerto de la Cruz on Tenerife of a steam ship with the first European, mainly English, tourists seeking a beneficial climate for health and tranquillity. By the end of that century a busier more modern tourism had arrived. Exportable crops are still an important source of GDP with bananas leading the way. But agriculture is visibly being rolled back as the resorts, like reverse lava flows, sprawl further and further inland.

IV.  THE CANARY ISLANDS

# General information

## Regional boundaries and language

In constitutional terms the archipelago is one of Spain's 17 autonomous regions. There are two provinces: Santa Cruz de Tenerife, which includes the islands of Tenerife, La Gomera, La Palma and El Hierro; and Las Palmas de Gran Canaria, which includes Lanzarote, Fuertaventura and Gran Canaria. Since the 1927 division, the position of capital of the autonomous region has been shared by the two on a rotation system.  For those not familiar with the islands, some of the names can be a little confusing and care needs to be taken not to confuse the island of La Palma (capital Santa Cruz) with Las Palmas de Gran Canaria (the province and the capital of Gran Canaria), and between Santa Cruz (capital of La Palma) and Santa Cruz de Tenerife (the province and capital of Tenerife). Mainland Spain is referred to as The Peninsula, and although part of Spain the Canaries are not in the EU (similar to the Channel Islands, Gibraltar etc.). The principal language, Spanish, is closer to Hispanic Spanish than Catalan.

## National and regional holidays

In addition to those listed, each town is also allowed two fiesta days of their own choosing – often the feast of a patron saint or commemorating a historical event. Local festivals, and in particular Carnival in February or March, can lead to serious congestion on roads, in marinas and anchorages. If planning to attend it is wise to arrive days or even weeks in advance. Note: the Thursday before Easter is a Public Holiday, but the Monday after is not.

|  |  |
|---|---|
| 1 January[1] | Anõ Nuevo (New Year's Day) |
| 6 January[2] | Epifanía/Día de los Reyes Magos (Twelfth Night/Three Kings Day) |
| 19 March[2] | Día de San Juan (St John's Day) |
| moveable[2] | Jueves Santo (Maundy Thursday) |
| moveable[1] | Viernes Santo (Good Friday) |
| 1 May[1] | Fiesta del Trabajo (Labour Day) |
| 30 May[1] | Día de las Islas Canarias (Canary Islands Day) |
| moveable[2] | Corpus Christi |
| 25 July[2] | Día de Santiago Apóstol (St James's Day) |
| 15 August[1] | La Asuncíon de la Virgen |
| 8 September[2] | Día del Pino (Pine Tree Day) |
| 12 October[1] | Día de la Hispanidad (National Day) |
| 1 November[1] | Todos los Santos (All Saints' Day) |
| 6 December[2] | Día de la Constitución |
| 8 December[1] | La Inmaculada Concepcíon |
| 25 December[1] | Navidad (Christmas Day) |

[1] National  [2] Regional

Every town enjoys their own special fiesta
*Steve Goldsmith*
*(steve.cms@ntlworld.com)*

### Spanish representation abroad

*Spanish embassies and consulates*
London (Embassy) 39 Chesham Place, London SW1X 8SB
☎ +44 207 235 5555, emb.londres@maec.es
(Consulate) 20 Draycott Place, London SW3 2RZ
☎ +44 207 589 8989 or 871 376 0023
cog.londres@maec.es
www.exteriores.gob.es/consulados/londres/en
*Edinburgh* (Consulate) 63 North Castle Street, Edinburgh EH2 3LJ ☎ +44 131 220 1843
*Washington DC* (Embassy) 2375 Pennsylvania Avenue NW, Washington DC 20037, USA
☎ +1 202 452 0100, +1 202 833 5670
emb.washington@mae.es
See www.exteriores.gob.es/embajadas for a full list of Spanish Embassies and consulates.

*Spanish national tourist offices*
London 64 North Row, London W1K 7DE
☎ +44 207 317 2011 (Mon-Thurs 0900-1600, Friday 0900-1400)
*New York* 666 5th Avenue #3502, New York, NY 10103 ☎ +1 212 265 8822

### Diplomatic representation in the Canary Islands

There are two British consulates in the Canary Islands, the embassy is in Madrid.
*Las Palmas Consulate* Calle Luis Morote 6-3°, 35007 Las Palmas de Gran Canaria
☎ +34 902 109 356 or
+34 913 342 194 (international/alternative)
*Tenerife Consulate* Plaza Weyler 8, 1°, 38003 Santa Cruz de Tenerife
☎ +34 902 109 356 or
+34 913 342 194 (international/alternative)
*The US Consulate General* Edificio ARCA, C/ Los Martínez Escobar 3, Oficina 7, 35007 Las Palmas de Gran Canaria
☎ +34 928 271 259
Ireland has Honorary Consuls in Las Palmas, Lanzarote and Tenerife.

### Time

The Canaries use UT (as do the British Isles), with local daylight saving (+1 hour) from late March until late September.

### Currency and banking

Spain, including the Canaries, is part of the Eurozone (despite the Canaries themselves not being inside the EU) and the currency is the euro. Most visitors rely on credit/debit cards, both for purchases and to withdraw cash – dispensers, locally referred to as *cajeros*, or *automáticos* – are widespread and accept all major cards. Many offer instructions in a choice of languages, including English.

Shopping in the market at Santa Cruz de la Palma
*Anne Hammick*

Banks normally open 0830–1400 weekdays only, though some do open one evening a week or on a Saturday morning. Major currencies are readily exchangeable. Most restaurants, shops, car rental companies and other concerns welcome payment by most of the major credit cards. Some more remote outlets, and some of the smaller fuel stations will only take cash. Where possible this has been noted in the text.

### Shopping

A good range of food is easily obtainable in the larger supermarkets, though at somewhat higher prices than in mainland Europe. Locally grown fruit and vegetables are often excellent in terms of both quality and value, with traditional markets in most of the larger towns and cities, and in some places the local fishermen sell a part of their catch straight from their boats at very reasonable prices. Wines and spirits are readily available and are generally inexpensive. Vines are cultivated on several islands and it is worth trying the sweet whites from Lanzarote and Fuerteventura, the reds from Tenerife and La Palma. Shop opening times vary greatly. The bigger stores, and many shops in the resorts, are now open from 0900 or earlier until 2000 or later. Many close for lunch between 1300–1600, and are then open until 2000. Saturday is generally a half-day and unless in a big resort, most are closed on Sundays. The range of merchandise available generally reflects the size and antecedents of the place in question, be it a major city, a tourist resort or a modest fishing village

Parakeets enjoy a cosy chat in the trees of Los Gigantes
*Hilary Keatinge*

## Water

The eastern islands are dependent on desalination plants for their water supply; the western ones have substantial groundwater storage but this is under stress. Visitors continue to flock in, up to 10 million per year and as a result the local population has also risen, being just over 2 million. Subsequently water and power needs have risen considerably, and so has the need for alternative energy. Water on all the islands is safe to drink, though that from the desalination plants is not to everyone's taste. As a general rule the quality improves as one sails west. Bottled mineral water can be obtained almost everywhere.

## Electricity

Mains electricity is 220v 50Hz, as is standard throughout mainland Europe, and yachts from elsewhere should beware a probable difference in both volts and cycles. Several marinas provide 380v to berths for larger yachts – see individual harbours for details. Domestic plugs for connecting ashore are two-prong (round) as on the European mainland.

## Gas refills

In general those using butane (blue) cylinders will be able to exchange them fairly widely throughout the islands, propane cylinders (orange) are more difficult and these will have to be taken to a gas distribution company (www.disagrupo.es) for refilling. Note the cylinder has to be in good condition and should be marked with full industrial verification. Individual marina offices will be able to advise.

## Communications

Mobile (cell) phone coverage throughout the islands is generally excellent, with only a few 'holes' in the more mountainous western islands.

Calls to the United Kingdom begin with the prefix +44, followed by the area code (without the initial zero) and number. Calls to the United States and Canada begin with the prefix +1 followed by the area code and the number.

The international dialling code for Spain, including the Canaries, is +34. If telephoning within the islands the area code is 928 for the three eastern islands, 922 for the four to the west. This forms an integral part of the phone number (nine digits in all) even when calling from within the same island. Any telephone number not starting with one of these sequences can be assumed to be a mobile. If planning to spend some time in the Canaries it will be cheaper to purchase a pay-as-you-go SIM card from one of the big providers. Ask locally as to which one has the best coverage.

### Internet access

WiFi is now available in many marinas, though not many offer it for free. However there will invariably be a local café or bar with free connection on offer with your coffee. For many the chosen method of connecting will be some form of MiFi device, with a local SIM, or a Hotspot through a mobile. Throughout El Hierro and in some of the larger towns they advertise a free service, but inevitably it is very, very, slow.

### Incoming packages

If ordering parts from outside the islands – or anticipating any other parcel – ensure that the package is clearly marked 'BOAT IN TRANSIT' and that a contact telephone number (possibly of a marina office) is prominently displayed. Where possible, passport details of the addressee should be included in the paperwork. Failure to observe these precautions may result in the package being held up by Customs on arrival, sometimes without the addressee even being informed that it has reached the islands.

Small parcels from the UK are best sent via the Royal Mail's International Tracking and Signature services, but the best way to import large shipments is said to be via a freight forwarder. The goods should be shipped to the airport only and a local agent organised in advance to clear them through Customs and deliver locally. The agent's details should be on the airway bill, and the goods MUST be addressed TO THE BOAT IN TRANSIT, NOT to an individual, on ALL the paperwork. Global parcel delivery companies typically ship goods only as far as the airport, where they are handed over to a local delivery firm who may or may not be efficient. If wanting to import to Fuerteventura or Lanzarote (and possibly the other islands) from UK, Ireland or Mainland Europe a recommended company is Woodside Cargo, www.woodsidecargosl.com

## Travel and transportation

### Flights

*International flights leave from:*

Arrecife Airport on Lanzarote, Fuerteventura Airport (also known as El Mattoral), Gran Canaria Airport (also known as Gando Airport and, incorrectly, as Las Palmas Airport), Tenerife South Airport and La Palma Airport.

*There are also inter-island flights from:*

Tenerife Norte Airport, La Gomera Airport, El Hierro Airport.

If transferring from an international flight arriving in Tenerife South Airport to an internal flight in Tenerife Norte airport the transit will take about an hour by road.

### Ferry services

There is a frequent service between most of the islands run by two ferry companies, Fred Olson with the fast car ferries www.fredolsen.es/en and Naviera Armas www.navieraamas.com/en. There are two companies running a regular service to La Graciosa from Orzola, Lanzarote.

### Road transport

There are good bus services on all the islands. Buses (Guagua) are inexpensive and link most of the major sites and towns on each island. Note that there is often a reduced service at weekends.

Car Hire is readily available and reasonably priced. The major roads on the islands are of a high standard, though side roads can be more challenging. The islands are basically mountainous and what looks easy on a map may be more exciting in reality, but the sights are so wonderful it is definitely worth exploring inland. There are plenty of filling stations; some have attendant service, almost all accept credit cards.

## Regulations and taxes

### Personal documentation

The same rules apply as in mainland Spain. Nationals of EU (and some other European) countries can travel with nothing more than a national identity card or passport. Visitors from elsewhere in the world require valid passports and some – principally those from outside Europe, North America and Australasia – also need visas. It is a legal requirement to carry identity of some kind at all times whilst on Spanish territory, though this is seldom enforced.

The following is important if wishing to stay in Spanish territory for more than 3 months (90 days): Under Spanish law an EU citizen, intending to stay in Spain (including The Canaries) for more than 3 months must register for formal non-residential status, *Certificado de Registro*. Ask in the marina office for more information or go to the local police station. This website has good information in English on many aspects of living, visiting the islands www.canaries.angloinfo.com. See also 'Long-term visits' below.

### Boat documentation

As well as the originals, it is often helpful to carry several copies of: boat registration papers, insurance documents, a list of the boat's basic dimensions (LOA, width, etc.), blank crew list form, travel documents (boarding card, tickets etc.).

### Entry and regulations

On arrival from abroad those coming from within the EU will find that many marinas will handle all the required paperwork including formalities for the Border Police. Those arriving from countries outside the EU will need to obtain clearance from the immigration and port authorities in a designated Port of Entry. Marina staff will normally give guidance. The Border Police make sporadic checks. It is not necessary to clear in and out when moving between harbours or islands.

Arriving at any marina, staff will expect to see passports as well as ship's papers, and proof of insurance. If making an advance booking for a berth in a marina run by Puertos Canarios, copies of passports, ship's papers and insurance cover will have to be scanned or posted with the application.

Outward clearance is not compulsory for EU citizens or boats, but it is worth carrying stamped receipts of crew lists and the berthing contracts paid on arrival and, particularly, departure from the Canaries as proof of last port visited. Some effort to get formal clearance before departing the Canaries is more pertinent to non-EU registered boats or crew as it is likely to be required at the next port of

IV. THE CANARY ISLANDS

The volcanic peak of El Tiede dominates the islands, seen here along the north coast of Tenerife  *Hilary Keatinge*

arrival, be it in the Cape Verdes, Brazil or the Caribbean. Neither La Gomera nor El Hierro are official 'border posts', but clearance can be obtained on your way through the islands in either Tenerife (Santa Cruz de Tenerife or Los Cristianos) or Santa Cruz de la Palma; note these offices work a five-day week and close every day at 1400.

### Long-term visits: vessels registered in the EU

*The Matriculation Tax or ISDMT (Impuesto Sobre Determinados Medios de Transporte)*
Under Spanish law, if a foreign – including EU-registered – yacht spends more than 180 days (cumulative, not consecutive) in any 365-day period in a Spanish harbour with her owner living aboard, the latter, i.e. the owner, may be considered to be a resident 'de hecho' (meaning 'in fact', as opposed to 'by law', as would be the case with a person who officially holds residency). Should this occur he (or she) would become subject to local taxes and other legislation. If the boat is of more than 9m LOA the owner will be obliged to import it at a cost of 13% of its value and then to pay 11% registration tax. The boat's registration of origin may not have to be changed. Anyone who might be affected by the above would be wise to seek professional advice.

It appears that the legal ways to avoid this highly undesirable scenario are either to move the yacht from time to time, thus preserving the 'right of innocent passage' or, if the boat is to be laid up while the owner leaves Spanish territory, to retain evidence of leaving and re-entering the country (flight boarding cards should be acceptable).

In practice this law has rarely been applied in the Canaries, and then only to vessels belonging to those who, by any normal definition, are indeed long-term residents. The law regarding commercial – including charter – vessels, is different, and is outside the scope of this book.

### Long-term visits: vessels registered outside the EU

Vessels registered outside the EU may only remain in Spanish waters for up to 183 days in any 365-day period. If an owner wishes to leave his boat unattended beyond this time he can employ a Customs agent to apply for a voluntary seal – a *precinto voluntario* – which allows the boat to remain 'outside time'. The boat cannot be moved while under seal – usually a small document taped to a window – but can be accessed for service work or for living aboard for short periods by the owner. The agent's fee for sealing and unsealing the boat will normally be around € 100.

## Taxes

There has been considerable confusion in the last few years and many yacht owners avoided using the state ports where there were heavy taxes levied. The situation has been rationalized (2015) and while there are still taxes to be paid they are not excessive and they are more fairly apportioned. It is still not a level playing field and for the moment the taxes are only levied in State marinas, not in local government-owned marinas. The taxes, calculated on a daily basis, only apply to boats over 12m and are not as onerous as they sound; it amounts to about €0.80 per day for a boat over 12m.

For the visiting yacht owner there are three taxes involved:

*IGIC (Impuesto General Indirecto Canario)*

The Canary Islands (though part of an EU member state) lie outside mainland Europe and so VAT is not applicable. However a sales tax of 7% known as IGIC is applied to most bills, including marina fees.

*T5 Recreational Vessel Tax (Tasa de Embarcación de Recreo)*

A vessel over 12m, staying in a state owned marina under the jurisdiction of regional Port Authorities is charged €0.05 per m² per night. Vessels over 12m on long-term visits pay €0.04 per m². It is less for those under 12m. IGIC of 7% is added to this.

*T0 Navigational Assistance Tax (Tasa de Ayuda a la Navegación)*

A vessel of more than 12m LOA (this does not apply to vessels of or under 12m) in Spanish waters, including the Canaries, that is considered to be based here, i.e. this is their home port (or with occupancy of over 6 months), is liable to pay the T0 annually at €9.12 per m². A transient vessel of over 12m LOA in Spanish waters, including the Canaries, is liable to pay the daily sum of €0.025 per m² (This tax is for the maintenance and improvement of navigational installations, lights, buoys etc,). No IGIC added.

## Fishing permits

A fishing licence is required of local boats and it is said that those fishing without one may incur a fine. There is good information online in English at www.canaries.angloinfo.com

# Cruising and navigation

For the sailor there are many reasons to choose to visit, whether just passing through en route across the Atlantic, coming to the Canaries for some adventurous cruising or making it a long term base. There are excellent sailing courses on offer, though a relatively small charter fleet. Protected anchorages may be few and far between but there are numerous marinas with good facilities that are secure for those boat owners wanting to explore inland, or return home for a month or two. However, as news of the increase in the popularity of the Canaries amongst yachtsmen increases, so too comes a warning – in the busy autumn season, September through to Christmas – there is often a shortage of space in the more popular marinas and it is essential to plan well ahead.

Since Columbus first crossed the Atlantic, most vessels leaving Europe and the Mediterranean have taken a downwind leg to stop off on the islands to top up supplies before the long haul west, taking full advantage of the trade winds. Most would still agree that those returning east from the islands will also find the easiest route back is actually via the Caribbean; though the number of yachts returning to Spain, either direct or via Madeira, is steadily increasing.

The islands are situated around 28°N, spread over a distance of 240M in an east-west line, washed by the Canary Current, the average monthly temperature seldom varies more than 5° either side of 25°C and the water temperatures throughout the year range from about 19°–22°C. When sailing between islands it is generally possible to leave and to arrive in daylight – advisable when visiting for the first time as harbour lights can be inconspicuous against the many hotels and apartment blocks.

The coastline is generally steep-to and, with a few exceptions, dangers do not extend for more than 0·5M offshore. Exceptions are mentioned under the information for specific islands and harbours.

### Guides, pilots etc.

The archipelago is covered in the British Admiralty Africa Pilot (NP 1) 17th edition 2014 and in the US National Geospacial-Intelligence Agency's Sailing Directions for the West Coast of Europe and North West Africa (Pub 143), 13th edition 2011, both of which are, of course, written with very much larger vessels in mind. In addition, the 6th edition of the RCC Pilotage Foundation's The Atlantic Crossing Guide covers the islands briefly, with additional harbour details for Puerto de Las Palmas (Gran Canaria) and Marina Santa Cruz (Tenerife). They are also mentioned – even more briefly – in Rod Heikell and Andy O'Grady's Ocean Passages and Landfalls, and in World Cruising Routes and World

The west coasts of the islands are dramatic viewing, but better from the shore. This is El Golfe on the west coast of Lanzarote  *Hilary Keatinge*

Cruising Destinations by Jimmy Cornell. The 5th edition of the Canary Islands Cruising Guide was published by World Cruising Club  in 2006 and it is understood that the 6th edition is being prepared (www.worldcruising.com). Primarily intended for those taking part in the ARC rally (which World Cruising also runs), it is particularly strong on facilities and companies providing services to cruising yachts.

### Sources of further information

Further information is available from a number of sources – the British Admiralty Routeing Charts, North Atlantic Ocean, the US National Geospacial-Intelligence Agency Pilot Charts of the North Atlantic Ocean, James Clarke's Atlantic Pilot Atlas, now in its 5th edition and Imray's Chart 100, North Atlantic Ocean Passage Chart.

### Charts

By far the most detailed charts of the Canary Islands are the 28 sheets produced by the Spanish Instituto Hidrográfico de la Marina, based in Cádiz. These comprise five small-scale island charts and 23 sheets of larger-scale plans. There are currently two official agents for Spanish hydrographic publications in the Canaries – JL Gándara y Cía SA in Las Palmas (see page 276) and the Centro Geofísico de Canarias in Santa Cruz de Tenerife (see page 302). Most chandleries either stock some Spanish charts or are willing to order as necessary. Spanish charts are not normally supplied corrected.

British Admiralty charts (www.ukho.gov.uk) cover the archipelago on five sheets, with two small-scale plans and 12 approach and harbour plans. Suisca SL in Las Palmas (see page 276), hold the only official agency in the islands, though again most chandleries hold a limited stock. Imray are also official agents and will mail Admiralty charts worldwide. Note that while Admiralty charts obtained from an official agent should be supplied corrected to the date of dispatch, those bought from other sources are unlikely to be.

The US National Geospatial-Intelligence Agency devotes five sheets to the islands. Though no longer available directly from the NGIA, they can be ordered online from approved suppliers. See page 430 for further details.

Imray's Imray-Iolaire series covers the archipelago on a single sheet, E2, at scale of 1:600,000, with 10 inset approach and harbour plans. Official distributors for Imray charts and pilots in the Canaries are Rolnautic Las Palmas, Gran Canaria, and Blancomar Nautica SL and Nordest in Tenerife (see pages 276 and 302 respectively). They can be ordered online at www.imray.com.

See Appendix I, page 430, for chart lists.

### Magnetic variation

Variation throughout the Canary Islands decreases by about 1°45' from west to east. In 2014 averaging 5°20' and decreasing by 7'E annually. Admiralty charts 1861 and 1862, and *Imray-Iolaire* E2 mention local magnetic anomalies. Most noticeably in the strait between Lanzarote and Fuerteventura and 7 miles SW and 15 miles ENE of La Palma. See table for magnetic variation for each island.

### Particularly Sensitive Sea Areas (PSSA) and Traffic Lanes

On 1 December 2006 large areas of Canarian coastal waters were designated 'Particularly Sensitive Sea Areas' (PSSAs) recognised by the International Maritime Organisation. This is in addition to the sizeable areas already set aside by the Spanish Government as Marine Reserves.

At the same time, Traffic Lanes were established between Fuerteventura and Gran Canaria, and between Gran Canaria and Tenerife. If crossing these shipping lanes obey the rules, heading at right angles regardless of wind or current. A radar system monitors the zones and if observed off course a boat will be called up on Ch 16. Inshore zones are not monitored. Full details will be found on current editions of British Admiralty charts 1861 and 1862, and they are clearly marked on Imray-Iolaire E2.

### Buoys and lights

The few navigational buoys and many lights in the Canaries adhere to the IALA A system, based on the direction of the main flood tide, as used throughout mainland Europe.

All major lights have good operational records. Harbour lights and those of the marine farms are not so consistent. News of alterations to lights and other navigational marks, whether planned or arising from defects, can take months to percolate through the reporting system and the navigator should be aware that marks may not appear as described, if in place at all. Light characteristics are marked on the plans are as per the Spanish Lights catalogue Part 1, 2014.

### Currents

The Canary Current is a wind-driven surface current associated with the northeast trades and sets through the islands in a southwesterly direction at around 0·5 knots, increasing to 2 knots at times in the summer. A strong southerly gale can cancel or even reverse this current.

### Tides and tidal streams

Volume 2 of the Admiralty Tide Tables: The Atlantic and Indian Oceans including tidal stream predictions (NP 202), published annually, covers the Canaries, with Casablanca as standard port. The UK Hydrographic Office's excellent EasyTide programme at http://easytide.ukho.gov.uk, gives daily tidal data for the main commercial harbour on each island. The maximum mean spring range varies with slightly higher rises round the eastern islands, 2·2m in Lanzarote and Fuerteventura and less in the west, with 1·8m in La Palma, while mean neaps decrease from 1·1m to 0·7m over the same area. The Canary Current (see above) flows southwest with an increase round the southern ends of the islands and in the channels between La Graciosa and Lanzarote and between Lanzarote and Fuerteventura. The southwest going tidal stream (ebbing), combined with the Canary Current can set down the east coast of La Gomera at up to 4 knots up to 4 miles off and while the reverse stream will be weaker there can be a tidal race off Punta de San Cristóbal, La Gomera, in the prevailing winds.

### Visibility

Visibility is normally good throughout the Canaries and once landfall has been made at least one island will nearly always be in sight. However, visibility can be reduced to 0·5M when a strong easterly brings a reddish haze of fine sand from the Sahara, and in these conditions – known locally as a *Calima* – navigators will be glad to rely on GPS, radar or both.

### Barometric pressure

The northeast trades predominate throughout the Canaries and are associated with high pressure established over the Azores. On a few occasions, usually in the winter months, an Atlantic low-pressure system may move southwards to cross close north of the Canaries, replacing the Azores high. When this occurs the barometer will fall rapidly from the norm (usually about 1025mb). A fall of 10mb or more heralds winds of at least 35 knots from anywhere from south through southwest to northwest. A barometer rising to 1030mb or more indicates high pressure over the Sahara and a strong easterly can be expected and seas are likely to be steep and uncomfortable.

### Winds

When consulting forecasts for the area it is wise to treat them with caution as the weather can be very localized, wind strengths in particular; when preparing for a passage, local sailors usually add another 10-15 knots to the advertised wind strength in the acceleration zones.

*NE winds (prevailing)*

The northeast trades predominate throughout the Canaries and are associated with pressure systems over both the Atlantic and the Sahara. These north easterlies prevail during spring and autumn and are at their most intense in July and August. If there is more east in the wind it can create a short steep sea, but it tends to back to the north in the evening and the sea settles providing perfect conditions for evening sailing. Katabatic winds are also evident throughout the islands, and there can be strong land breezes particularly off the lower lying islands like Lanzarote and Fuerteventura.

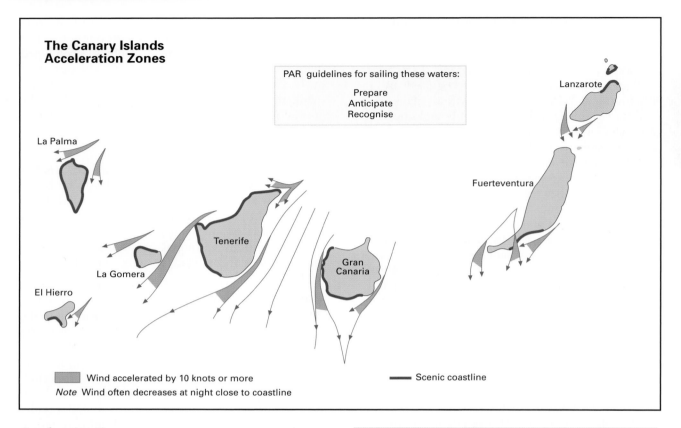

**The Canary Islands Acceleration Zones**

PAR guidelines for sailing these waters:

Prepare
Anticipate
Recognise

Wind accelerated by 10 knots or more

Scenic coastline

*Note* Wind often decreases at night close to coastline

## Acceleration Zones

When the brisk northerly spectrum of winds meet high volcanic peaks and cliff faces they have no option but to go up and over or divide and funnel around and between the islands, increasing in strength. This produces a combination of horizontal acceleration and vertical acceleration zones. These can push the wind force up by 25 knots in a matter of 200m. So only half a mile off shore suddenly conditions can be quite different from a balmy 5 knots in the shelter of the marina.

The plan showing these acceleration zones should be studied carefully. The strongest winds are likely to be encountered off both the northwest and southwest coasts of Gran Canaria, south of Fuerteventura, and south of Tenerife

### E winds

This is likely to be a strong, hot wind, gusting from the African coast. The main cause of this is an extension of the Azores High moving towards the Iberian Peninsula, this creates high pressure north of the Canary Islands. Visibility is often reduced but is rarely less than 1M.

### SE winds

A south easterly is often quite light on the east coast of Lanzarote, but on the west coast it can produce off shore winds of Force 6–9. It brings Saharan dust towards the Canaries, cooling whilst it crosses the water, which leads it to separate from the water

**PAR** The maxim is to Prepare, Anticipate and Recognise:

**Prepare** Forecasts are often for the wider area in general but will not warn you about local conditions in the acceleration zones. It is wise to prepare boat and crew before entering the zone.

**Anticipate** Put reefs in in good time; locals will have their crews ready with safety gear on, even if all appears benign; warning is minimal.

**Recognise** Keep an eye out for the very distinctive lines of low white water. However, the seas are usually moderate so that if you are well prepared the sailing can be exhilarating.

surface and gain altitude. Touching down in the middle of the islands, and descending forcefully and with strong gusts towards the west coast, creating offshore winds. These winds will be variable in strength during day and night. Overnight there will be considerable condensation, and visibility will be reduced, particularly in the mornings.

Both E and SE winds give rise to what is known as a *Calima* (sometimes confused with a *Sirocco*, which is similar but blows from the Sahara northwards across the Mediterranean). Conditions will be hot and very dry and, as the saying goes: 'When the wind is from the east, 'tis neither good for man nor beast.'

It is not difficult to recognise the entry line into an acceleration zone  *Hilary Keatinge*

### SW, S and SE winds

Mainly affecting Fuerteventura, also known as Southern Winds or *Majoreros*. When southerly winds are not warm it is usually because they are the product of storms to the west of the Canaries. These storms bring wind and rain creating confused seas. Such conditions are easy to predict and the forecasters will usually have issued warnings in good time. These conditions are most likely from autumn through winter, although relatively infrequent.

### NW and N winds

When the pressure is high, northerly winds, of varying strengths, cross the islands. Also if a low over the Iberian Peninsula moves to the west and/or south, combined with the Azores high moving west, winds over the islands will back north-to-northwest. It will be cooler, and there is sometimes rain.

### Swell

Atlantic swell is generated outside the local weather patterns and therefore the local wind conditions will not always be the correct indication of the sea state.

For safety and for comfort, if you plan to anchor overnight, or when entering some of the harbours round the islands, it is important that you monitor swell forecasts. There are several excellent websites that show predicted swell direction and height over several days and most local marinas will display forecasts. Note that you will need to factor in any more locally generated waves and any tidal effects to gain a more complete picture of what the local sea state is likely to be.

See Introduction page 10 for further information.

### Weather forecasts

The Canaries are covered by Navtex transmissions from Las Palmas in English as well as Spanish. The table on page 228 is from the Salvamente Maritimo website.

It is recommend that Spanish speakers follow both broadcasts, as it is reported that there is sometimes mis-translation into English (backing / veering is the commonest) while the English text can be missing detail, have different pressure data, or even omit parts of the Spanish synopsis.

### EMERGENCIES

**Salvamente Maritimo** The Spanish Maritime Safety Agency

**Maritime Rescue Coordination Centre (MRCC)**

*Centro de Coordinación de Salvamento
Las Palmas*
VHF Ch 16 & 10
☏ +34 928 467 757 / 928 467 955
laspalmas@sasemar.es

*Centro de Coordinación de Salvamento Tenerife*
VHF Ch 16 & 74
☏ +34 922 597 551 / 922 597 552
tenerife@sasemar.es

www.salvamentomaritimo.es
click on the word WELCOME to read about the organisation (in English).

Round the islands they have a fleet of 10 rescue vessels, up to 21m LOA, a patrol boat of 32m and 2 larger vessels for oceanic rescue. They have two helicopters in the service, one based on Gran Canaria, and one on Tenerife.

**Global Maritime Distress Safety System (DMDSS)**

|  | *Las Palmas* | *La Isleta* | *Tenerife* |
|---|---|---|---|
| **VHF Ch** | 10, 16 | 10, 16 | 74, 16 |
| **Call sign** | *Las Palmas Traffic* | *Las Palmas Traffic* | *Tenerife Traffic* |
| **DSC VHF MMSI** | 002240995 | 002240995 | 002241007 |
| **RT (MF) SSB (Transmit/ receive)** | 2182Khz | 2182 Khz | 2182 Khz |
| **Tel. (+34)** | 928 467 757 928 467 955 | 928 467 757 928 467 955 | 922 597 551 922 597 552 |
| **General emergencies** | 112 | 112 | 112 |

### Coast radio stations

Each island has a station but all are operated from Tenerife on a 24 hour basis. Full details are listed in the introduction to each island.
☏ +34 922 826 324, ccr.tenerife@abertistelecom.com

## Red (Network) Nacional de Centros NAVTEX

| Station | Language / Frequency (kHz) | Ident. Transmitter | Navigational warnings (UTC)* | Meteorological Forecast (UTC)* | Meteorological Areas |
|---|---|---|---|---|---|
| Tarifa | English / 518 | G | 0100, 0500, 1300, 1700 | 0900, 2100 | San Vicente, Cádiz, Estrecho, Alborán, Palos, Argelia, Agadir, Casablanca |
| | Spanish / 490 | T | 0310, 0710, 1110, 1510, 1910, 2310 | 1110, 2310 | |
| Coruña | English / 518 | D | 0030, 0430, 0830, 1230, 1630, 2030 | 0830, 2030 | Gran Sol, Pazzen, Iroise, Yeu, Rochebonne, Cantábrico, Finisterre, Porto, Charcot |
| | Spanish / 490 | W | 0340, 0740, 1140, 1540, 1940, 2340 | 1140, 2340 | |
| Las Palmas | English / 518 | I | 0120, 0520, 0920, 1320, 1720, 2120 | 0920, 1320*, 2120 | Canarias, Madeira, Casablanca, Agadir, Tarzaya, Capblanc |
| | Spanish / 490 | A | 0000, 0400, 0800, 1200, 1600, 2000 | 0000, 1200*, 1600 | |
| Valencia (Cabo La Nao) | English / 518 | X | 0350, 0750, 1150, 1550, 1950, 2350 | 1000, 2200 | Palos, Cabrera, Baleares, Menorca, León, Cerdeña, Alborán, Argelia |
| | Spanish / 490 | M | 0200, 0600, 1000, 1400, 1800, 2200 | 0750, 1950 | |

* Coastal waters

## Weather Forecasts

A. Gale warnings, synopsis and forecast for: channel between Gran Canaria and Tenerife, and the coasts of Tenerife, La Gomera, La Palma and El Hierrro, in Spanish and English (www.salvamentomaritimo.es)
B. Forecast in Spanish for coastal waters
C. Navigational Warnings in Spanish for coastal waters
D. Forecast in Spanish and English (Spanish Meteorological Service, www.aemet.es)

| Ch | Lanzarote | Fuerteventura | Gran Canaria | Tenerife | La Gomera | La Palma | El Hierro |
|---|---|---|---|---|---|---|---|
| 74 15 | | | | 0015, 0415, 0815, 1215, 1615, 2015(A) | | | |
| 20 | | | | | | 0833,1333,2033(B) | |
| 20 | | | | | | 0340.1340,1903 (D)0340, 1903 (C) | |
| 22 | | 0340, 1340, 1903 (D) 1833, 1333, 2033 (B) | | | | | |
| 22 | | 0340, 1903 (C) | | | | | |
| 23 | | | | | | | 0340, 1340, 1903 (D) 0833, 1333, 2033 (B) |
| 23 | | | | | | | 0340, 1903 (C) |
| 24 | | | | | 0340 ,1340, 1903 (D) 0833, 1333, 2033( B) | | |
| 24 | | | | | 0340, 1903 (C) | | |
| 25 | 0340, 1340, 1903 (D) 0833, 1333, 2033 (B) | | | | | | |
| 25 | 0340, 1903 (C) | | | | | | |
| 26 | | | 0340, 1340, 1903 (D) 0833, 1333, 2033 (B) | | | | |
| 26 | | | 0340, 1903 (C) | | | | |
| 27 | | | | 0340, 1340, 1903 (D) 0833, 1333, 2033 | | | |
| 27 | | | | 0340, 1903 (C) | | | |

For more information on worldwide weather forecasting, including internet forecasts, see pages 7-9. In addition, maritime forecasts are available from Spain's Instituto Nacional de Meteorología at www.aemet.es (Predicción Marítima), Spanish only.

## Radio communications & INMARSAT-C

Those wishing to carry details of all official radio communications in the Canary Islands will find The Admiralty List of Radio Signals Volume 1 (286(1) invaluable.

## Medical

There are no special requirements coming to the Canaries. Have all routine vaccinations up to date. If keen surfers or swimmers consider having Hepatitis A and B.

There are reasonable medical facilities in the major towns and tourist resorts, and many of those with medical training speak some English. Pharmacies abound, and usually appear to have good stocks of both prescription and non-prescription medicines. There are dentists and opticians in the larger towns, and wearers of glasses would be wise to carry a copy of their prescription (in addition to at least one reserve pair).

If an EU citizen, apply for a free EHIC (European Health Insurance Card); for those from the UK this can be done online via an NHS website or www.ehic.org.uk, by phone or by post. An EHIC will enable you to access state-provided healthcare either at a reduced cost or for free, though it may not be accepted by all clinics or practitioners. Neither does it cover the cost of repatriation, should that become necessary. It is not a substitute for medical insurance. Needless to say, anyone with a chronic or recurring condition should take a good supply of medication with him or her even though, unlike its precursor the E111, the EHIC does cover the cost of treatment for a pre-existing condition. The emergency number to call is 112, a hospital Casualty Department is signed *Urgencias*. If hiking above 2500m, as at El Teide in Tenerife, be aware that altitude sickness may be a risk.

## Ports, harbours and marinas

### Ports and who runs them

There are state run (commercial and ferry) ports controlled by the two provincial authorities: Autoridad Portuaria de Las Palmas de Gran Canaria and Autoridad Portuaria de Santa Cruz de Tenerife. Some, but not all, have marinas within the port.

The classification of the ports and marinas throughout the islands is not entirely straightforward. Those marked with * are official ports of entry though not all of these have facilities for yachts; most marinas will handle the entry paperwork required. It is crucial that you keep the receipts for the first and last marina visited in the islands.

### Booking berths in Puertos de Canarios harbours, administered by the Canarian Governments

*For harbours in Lanzarote, Fuerteventura, Gran Canaria* ✆ +34 928 452 209
avegsan@@gobiernodecanarias.org.

## Ports, harbours and marinas in the Canary Islands

| Island | State run ports | Ports run by local authorities as Puertos Canarios in Gran Canaria (GC) or in Tenerife (T) | Other marinas run by private companies as concessions from either Autoridad Portuaria, or Puertos Canarios |
|---|---|---|---|
| Lanzarote | Arrecife* | (GC) La Graciosa, Orzola, Puerto del Carmen, Playa Blanca | Marina Lanzarote, Puerto Calero, and Marina Rubicón |
| Fuerteventura | Puerto del Rosario* | (GC) Corralejo, Gran Tarajal, Morro Jable | Puerto del Castillo |
| Gran Canaria | De La Luz/Puerto Las Palmas*, Puerto Arinage, Puerto de Salinetas | (GC) Arguineguin. Puerto de las Nieves (Agaete) | Pasito Blanco, Anfi del Mar, Puerto Rico, Puerto Mogán |
| Tenerife | Santa Cruz de Tenerife*, Los Cristianos, Puerto de Granadilla | (T) Garachico, Playa San Juan, Puerto de la Cruz | Marina Tenerife, Radazul, La Galera, Puerto Güimar, San Miguel, Marina del Sur, Puerto Colón, Los Gigantes |
| La Gomera | San Sebastian de la Gomera* | (T) Las Vueltas, Playa Santiago | Marina La Gomera |
| La Palma | Puerto de Santa Cruz de la Palma* | (T) Tazacorte | Marina La Palma (Calero Group) |
| El Hierro | Puerto de la Estaca* | (T) Restinga | NA |

A passion for the environment, César Manrique had a huge influence on the architectural planning and development throughout the islands, this is one of his 'Wind Toys' outside his studio on Lanzarote  *Hilary Keatinge*

*For harbours in Tenerife, La Gomera. La Palma, El Hierro* ① *+34 922 475 028*
   *itormed@gobiernodecanaries.org*
In addition, both sets of officials are said to access solicitudpuertoscanarios@gmail.com (maybe copy to this address, making clear that it is a copy, not a separate booking).

### Future plans

On the drawing board are plans for development, expansion, and/or construction of marine facilities at: Puerto de Playa Blanca, Lanzarote; Puerto de Corralejo on Fuerteventura; Puerto de Playa Santiago and Puerto de las Nieves (Agaete), Gran Canaria; Puerto de la Cruz and Guía de Isora, just north of Playa San Juan, on Tenerife.

www.gobiernodecanarias.org/citv/puertos (Spanish only.) Under *Puertos Gestionados* can be seen plans for the above developments plus basic information about each individual harbour/marina.

### Anchoring and berthing

Anchoring round the islands is far from ideal and there are few if any bolt hole anchorages. By and large the west and northern coasts are rough untenable lee shores and, throughout the islands, most of the bays and coves that look inviting on the

Ever present, El Tiede towers above the cloud line, as seen across the strait from La Gomera  *Hilary Keatinge*

Bougainvillea cascades from archways in a pedestrian street in Puerto Mogán, Gran Canaria *Anne Hammick*

chart may suffer from swell if not wind. So in very settled conditions there are possibilities, but many will be just day anchorages; it is useful to seek local advice. The nature of the bottom varies, but usually consists of sand and/or round volcanic stones and boulders; beware, there is often a beguiling layer of sand over the latter. The modern anchors, such as Bugels or Rochas work well, and should be equipped with a minimum of 50m of chain and the same of warp; mostly the depths in the anchorages will be 10m or less. There may be occasions when it will be useful to put out a kedge amidships, with chain and or warp, to haul off a harbour wall. A fender board could be useful.

Surge works its way inside many harbours, making mooring, not just to a wall, an art to be acquired by practice. Chaffing gear for line protection and snubbers to dampen the swell are necessary; the strain on warps and fenders can be severe. Make sure that you have enough lines to double up on all in the event of a storm or if leaving the boat unattended for some time.

Most commercial harbours have strict 'no anchoring' rules, details of which will be found in the text. The best anchorage in the islands is Playa Francesca off Isla Graciosa, across from the north coast of Lanzarote. Permission is needed to anchor there because it lies within the Parque Natural del Archipiélago Chinijo.

## Shelter from heavy weather

There has long been a legal requirement throughout the Canaries for all harbours and marinas to provide shelter for a boat at risk from the weather, however full they may already be. This obligation generally appears to be honoured, though the vessel will probably be requested to leave as soon as conditions have moderated. However, there appears to be no formal definition of 'heavy weather', presumably leaving a decision to the discretion of harbour staff who may themselves not be sailors, nor be willing to take the size and crew strength of an individual yacht into consideration.

Before the breakwaters were built, a storm forecast would see fishing boats being hauled out and yachts were advised to seek shelter in bays on the north sides of the islands. Although the situation has now improved greatly, a high proportion of harbours and marinas are open to the south and some will have their breakwaters and walls breached in storm conditions – generally the swell is far more destructive than the wind. Local opinion holds that southerly gales have increased in both frequency and severity over the past two decades, with the likelihood of damage to structures and property. Any harbour with a known problem during such weather is mentioned in the text and owners leaving for any length of time should leave their boats well prepared.

## Laying up

The number of harbours where a yacht might be laid up ashore, at least for a limited period, has increased over the past few years. The most obvious choices are: Marina Lanzarote, Puerto Calero or Marina Rubicón in Lanzarote; Pasito Blanco, Puerto Rico in Gran Canaria; Varaderos Anaga in Santa Cruz or Puerto Radazul in Tenerife; Puerto Tazacorte in La Palma and Puerto de la Restinga on the south coast of El Hierro. All have powerful travel-lifts and a reasonable amount of hardstanding. There is even more choice if wishing to lay-up afloat, at least for a month or two, though space is likely to present the greatest problem and not all marinas accept advance bookings. The level of facilities and security varies greatly, as does the cost. In some marinas you will be required to appoint a local guardian for your boat. Refer to the text for further information.

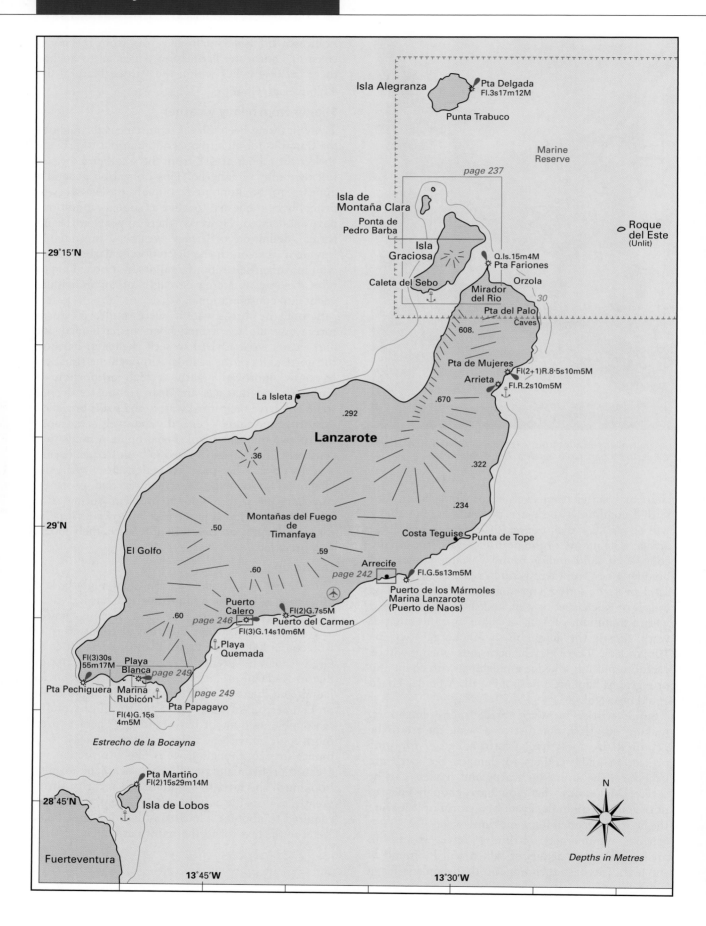

Isla Alegranza
Pta Delgada
Fl.3s17m12M
Punta Trabuco

Marine
Reserve

*page 237*

Isla de
Montaña Clara
Ponta de
Pedro Barba
Isla
Graciosa

Roque
del Este
(Unlit)

Q.Is.15m4M
Pta Fariones

Orzola

Caleta del Sebo
Mirador
del Rio
Pta del Palo
Caves

*30*

608.

Pta de Mujeres
Fl(2+1)R.8·5s10m5M
Arrieta
Fl.R.2s10m5M

La Isleta
.292

.670

**Lanzarote**

.36

.322

.234

Montañas del Fuego
de
Timanfaya

Costa Teguise
Punta de Tope

El Golfo

.50

.59

Arrecife
*page 242*

Fl.G.5s13m5M

.60

Puerto de los Mármoles
Marina Lanzarote
(Puerto de Naos)

.60

Puerto
Calero
*page 246*
Fl(2)G.7s5M
Puerto del Carmen
Fl(3)G.14s10m6M

Playa
Quemada

Fl(3)30s
55m17M
Playa
Blanca *page 249*

Pta Pechiguera
Marina
Rubicón
Pta Papagayo
*page 249*

Fl(4)G.15s
4m5M

*Estrecho de la Bocayna*

Pta Martiño
Fl(2)15s29m14M

28°45'N
Isla de Lobos

Fuerteventura

29°15'N

29°N

N

*Depths in Metres*

13°45'W
13°30'W

# Lanzarote

**Between 28°50'N–29°14'N and 13°25'W–13°53'W**

## Introduction

A very unique landscape sets Lanzarote apart from the other islands; a quarter of its landmass was shaped by two periods of massive volcanic eruptions in the 18th and 19th centuries. The island has some 300 volcanic peaks and at the national Timanfaya Park the magma is still close enough to the surface to set twigs alight; not surprisingly Lanzarote is also known as The Fire Island.

The island is 60km long and 26km across, lying NE – SW, the same direction as the prevailing wind. It has over 210km of coastline, but only about 32km of beach; the rest is rugged rock. The white sand beaches on the east coast are thanks to wind-borne sand from the African deserts less than 90 nautical miles to the east.

But despite the dramatic geology the island has a charm of its own and prides itself on its carefully controlled sustainable economic blueprint, both in agriculture and tourist development. This is a philosophy inspired, and for a time controlled, by local artist and architect César Manrique (1919-1992). To this day there is hardly any high-rise; buildings are mostly painted white with blue, green or brown paintwork and the impact of two million tourists a year is carefully controlled. Thanks to Manrique there are a number of sites well worth a visit including the restored Jameos del Agua: this 7km long lava pipe has been converted into a spectacular café, night club and concert hall, and look out for the unique species of tiny blind crab that exists in a shallow pool in the cave. The Taro de Tahiche, where the great man once lived, is equally fascinating and his design for several Miradors (scenic viewing spots) adds to the spectacular sights round the island.

Manrique was also the designer of the restaurant at the heart of the Parque Nacional de Timanfaya. This park, in the southwest, is the island's biggest attraction. Here the reality of volcanic action warms and flames before the visitor, the twigs are burnt, lunch is cooked over a heat hard to imagine; the lava bubbles just 4km below the surface. The scenery is powerful, awe-inspiring, well worth a day inland to experience.

Volcanic peaks and fertile farming are parts of this unique landscape *Hilary Keatinge*

IV. THE CANARY ISLANDS

Vines growing on Lanzarote protected by the lava
*Edward and Megan Clay*

## Navigation

For information on **Magnetic Variation**, **Tides** and **Tidal** Streams see pages 224-225.

Full **Emergency Service** information is on page 227

**Weather** and **Navigational Broadcasts** are listed on page 228

**Coast Radio Stations**
There are two controlled from Tenerife, both operate 24 hours
**Arrecife** 29°13'N 13°28'W
**VHF** Ch 26, 72

**Yaiza** 28°55'N 13°47'W
**VHF** Ch 03, 74
**DSC** VHF MMSI 002241026

**Lights**
**Punta Delgada (Isla Alegranza)**
    Fl.3s17m12M 135°-vis-045° Dark grey conical tower and building, white lantern 15m
**Punta Fariones** Q.15m4M
    Black over white tower 8m
**Punta de Mujeres** Fl(2+1)R.8·5s10m5M
    White tower, blue bands 6m
**Puerto de los Mármoles**
    Fl.G.5s13m5M Green structure
**Puerto de Arrecife breakwater**
    Q(6)+LFl.15s11m3M
    South cardinal tower 6m
**La Tiñosa (Puerto del Carmen)**
    Fl(2)G.7s5M Green tower
**Puerto Calero** Fl(3)G.14s10m6M
    Octagonal stainless steel tower 4m
**Marina Rubicón**
    Fl(4)G.15s4m5M Green post 3m
**Punta Pechiguera**
    Fl(3)30s55m17M White tower 50m

On Lanzarote traditional agriculture lives side by side with the lava flows, and the volcanic ash is used to good purpose as it provides essential nutrients, absorbs the humidity at night and prevents the heat of the sun from evaporating the moisture during the day. The island has precious little rainfall and now relies on desalination plants for all its water. Nevertheless the land has always been quite productive. Famous for its wines since George, the

Duke of Clarence, likely 'drowned in a butt of Malmsey', a special variety of malvasia grape is grown with each low vine protected from the wind by a *zoco*, a curve of volcanic bricks. All over the island you will see these crescents of laval rock around small depressions in the ground, these act as dew traps and funnel moisture to the plants protected within. The white El Grifo wine is worth a try.

### Ports

There are five ports, from the small harbour of Orzola on the northeast tip of the island to the ferry port of Playa Blanca on the south coast. Half way down the east coast is Arrecife, the island's capital city and commercial centre, home to the new Marina Lanzarote that lies within the port complex. Further along the coast are marinas at Puerto del Carmen and Puerto Calero, while round the south east corner is Marina Rubicón. The west coast is a rough and exposed shoreline where the hamlet of El Golfe makes for a scenically dramatic lunch spot but is best to approach by car rather than by sea.

### Approach and Navigation

*From the north to Arrecife*

The light at Punta Delgada on Isla Alegranza (Fl.3s17m12M) may be raised first. This is directly north of Isla Graciosa and if heading for the east coast of Lanzarote it is most important to identify

Looking west to the imposing northeast corner of Lanzarote, Farión de Tierra *Hilary Keatinge*

the unlit Roque del Este, 29°16'·6N 13°20'·3W which is 6·25M northeast of Punta del Palo on Lanzarote. In daylight this is a useful landmark. While it is tempting to call in to La Graciosa, particularly if coming in from west of north, bear in mind that Caleta del Sebo is not a Port of Entry and the anchorages close by are within the national park and need a permit (see page 236).

Much of the east coast of Lanzarote shelves steeply but there are several shallow banks – generally lava flows – that extend up to 0·5M offshore. Coming from the north stay outside the 100m contour to clear Punta de Tope, off Costa Teguise (see plan page 232). Making for Marina Lanzarote, head towards the E cardinal off Arrecife (see plan page 242), until the lights of the modern port entrance become visible to starboard. Note that an E cardinal marks the reef off the old port of Arrecife, just over 1M south of the modern harbour entrance, (This could be overlooked if relying on Admiralty chart 1870).

### From the west or south to Arrecife

The tall lighthouse of Punta Pechiguera (Fl(3)30s55m17M White tower 50m) is conspicuous on the southwestern point of the island; Marina Rubicón is 3M to the east of the lighthouse.

Off Punta Papagayo on the southeast corner, a breaking reef extends some 500m to the south, southeast of the headland.

Most marine farms have been removed but mid 2015 there was one south of Playa Quemada centred on 28°55'N 13°41'·5W, 28°53'·5N 13°44'·2W and 28°51'·2N 13°51'·1W.

Southwest of Arrecife, at approximately 28°56'N 13°36'W three large, unlit mooring buoys lie about 0·5M offshore southeast of the airport.

## Harbours and anchorages

## Isla Alegranza

Between 29°23'N-29°25'N and 13°29'W–13°32'W

#### Lights
**Punta Delgada** Fl.3s17m12M135°-vis-045°
Dark grey conical tower and building, white lantern 15m

The uninhabited island of Alegranza is 6 miles almost due north of Lanzarote with a light at Pta Delgada on its eastern end. It is under the jurisdiction of the Parque Natural del Archipelego Chinijo and any aquatic activity, including anchoring, requires prior permission (see page 236). There is a possible anchorage in Bahía El Veril, west of Punta Trabuco, but this is only feasible in very settled weather.

## Isla de Montaña Clara

Between 29°18'·43N, 13°32'10W and 29°17'·37N, 13°32'·37W

This tiny island (0·5M²) is off the northwest corner of Graciosa. It is uninhabited except as a refuge for marine birds and is part of the Parque Natural del Archipelego Chinijo; no anchoring is permitted.

IV. THE CANARY ISLANDS

Looking over the Estrecho del Río towards Isla Graciosa, with Isla de Montaña Clara and Isla Alegranza beyond. The photograph was taken from near the *Mirador del Río  Anne Hammick*

# Isla Graciosa

Between 29°13′N–29°17′·5N and 13°27′W–13°33′W

## An island to treasure

Was this the island where Long John Silver buried the treasure? Some say it was. The island lies close to the NW of the northern tip of Lanzarote across the narrow El Río strait. The strait was on the route of the 18th century fleets heading across the Atlantic while today this passage is said to be favoured by migrating pilot whales. This channel creates a funnel for the prevailing wind and one can expect downdrafts from the high cliffs on the Lanzarote side. The current is generally west-setting. At the northern point of Lanzarote there is a spectacular viewpoint on the edge of a vertical 500m precipice, El Mirador del Rio, created by César Manrique and looking across the strait to the island and beyond.

Ashore on Isla Graciosa, four eroded volcanic cones, the highest is 265m, rise from a mostly arid flatland, though there are still some attempts to bring the land to life with small allotments. However the only source of water is what is piped across the strait from Lanzarote's desalination plants. For all that, it is charming, this island of sevens: in 2015 there were about 700 residents, 7 restaurants, and the 7 taxis that run visitors to the two wonderful white sand beaches along unmade roads; of these the Playa de las Conchas on the northwest coast is totally unspoilt and stunning.

There are a number of holiday homes but most visitors just come for the day and walk or hire bicycles. A walk to the top of one of the hills will reward you with the discovery that the ground here is littered with ancient seashells – testament to the fact that it was once on the seabed before being thrust upwards by seismic activity. Access to 'mainland' Lanzarote is waterborne and, subject to weather conditions, and ferries ply regularly from the tiny island village of Caleta del Sebo to Orzola, on the northeast corner of Lanzarote.

## Anchorages

Much of Isla Graciosa lies within the Parque Natural del Archipiélago Chinijo, and anchoring is now limited to one bay only, Playa Francesca. The bays on either side, Bahía Cocina and Bahía del Salado, are reserved for diving. To anchor off Playa Francesca it is necessary to apply for permission, well in advance, from Servicio de Medio Ambiente (see boxed information). There is no charge. Permission can be granted for a maximum of 10 days.

Playa Francesa is delightful and as one of the few, mostly protected, anchorages in the Canaries, it is worth doing the paperwork. The bay is protected by an extensive reef to the east and Punta Marrajos to the west. Best holding is to be found in the western or central part – to the east are stones covered by a thin layer of sand. The bay is large enough for at least two dozen yachts and the water is very clear, but take care on landing, particularly near low water, as there are submerged rocks off the shore. It is a popular swimming beach where propulsion is limited to oars and paddles. There are no facilities, though a reasonable track leads through the scrub towards Puerto Caleta del Sebo (a 50-minute walk, or call one of the taxis, see page 240). Tour boats and jetskis and the like may be busy further offshore.

There is a patrol boat in the area and if the permission is not correct expect to be told to leave. With any queries phone ☏ +34 928 810 100 ext. 2280, some English is spoken. With strong southwesterly winds and swell the anchorage is untenable and in strong east or southeast winds it may also become untenable but in these conditions it may be possible to find some shelter on the Lanzarote side of the strait off Playa del Rojo, west of La Punta.

Playa Francesca, Isla Graciosa's only legal anchorage
*Andy Scott*

---

**PARQUE NATURAL DEL ARCHIPIELAGO CHINIJO ANCHORING PERMIT**

**To apply for the anchoring permit** Either go in person or post a form to the following address in Arrecife: Cabildo de Lanzarote, Av. Fred Olsun s/n, Arrecife 35500

**To receive a copy of the form by email** solicitudeslp@puertoscanarios.com This will come as a pdf, so it would be best to request it when you are somewhere with good internet availability and where you are able to download, print, and then post. It would also be acceptable to copy the form into an email (either by scanning or copying out the information headings) and sending it to the address given above. This could all be prepared some months in advance. When you have checked into the Canaries just fill in the dates to be requested, but allow a minimum of ten working days before the specified dates. Note that copies of the boat's registration papers and passports of all crew members are also required.

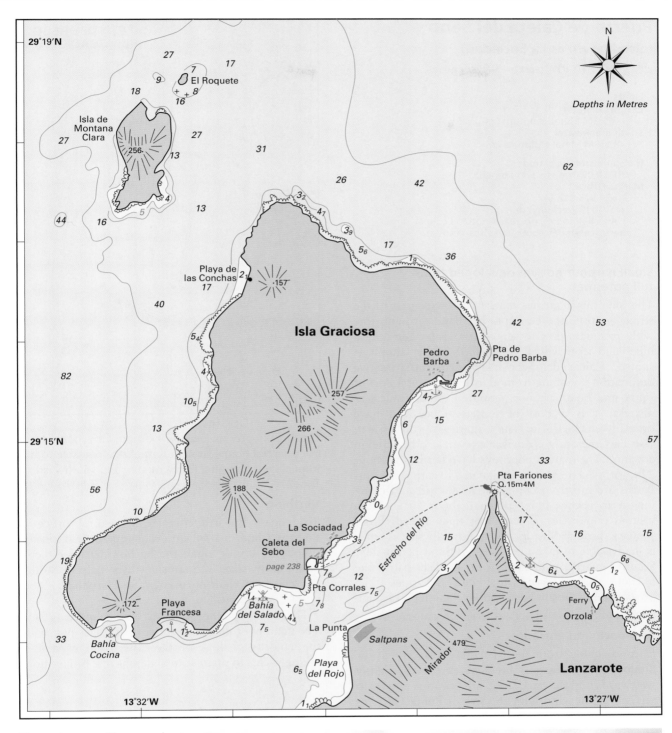

**29°19'N**

27

9    7    17
El Roquete
18    16    8
+    +

Isla de
Montana
Clara
27    256.    13

44    16    5    13

82    40    17
Playa de
las Conchas    21    ·157·
17

5₄

**Isla Graciosa**

4

10₅

13    257

266 ·

**29°15'N**

188

56    10

19    172·

Playa
Francesca    5
1₄

La Sociadad    3₃
Caleta del
Sebo
*page 238*    7₆    12
Pta Corrales    7₅
Bahía
del Salado    +
4₄    7₈
La Punta
33    Bahía
Cocina    1₂    7₅    5    Saltpans
6₅    Playa
del Rojo
1₁

Pedro
Barba    Pta de
Pedro Barba
4₇    27
6    15
12
33
Pta Fariones
Q.15m4M
15    17    16    15
0₆    2    6₄    6₆
1    1₂
0₅    Ferry
Orzola

3₃
3₁

Estrecho del Río

Mirador    · 479

**Lanzarote**

N
*Depths in Metres*

27    17
9
16
18
256.    13    27    31

26    42    62

4₇    3₂
3₉    5₆    17    36
1₉

1₄
42    53
57

**13°32'W**    **13°27'W**

The anchorage with rave reviews,
Playa Francesca, La Graciosa
*Hilary Keatinge*

IV. THE CANARY ISLANDS

# Puerto de Caleta del Sebo
## (also known as La Sociedad)

29°13′·6N 13°30′·09W (east breakwater head)

**Lights**
**East breakwater**
Fl.G.5s3M Metal sculpture 2m
**South breakwater**
Fl.R.5s3M Metal sculpture 2m

**Harbour communications**
VHF Ch 09 (not always manned)
**Marina Office**
☎ +34 928 842 147
0745–1415 weekdays only
lg_juan@yahoo.es, hb_juan@hotmail.com or
puertoscaletadelcebo@puertoscanarios.es

## Small harbour not yet developed to its full potential

This small harbour lies on the narrowest part of the strait, opposite the La Punta headland on Lanzarote with its square grey tower, clearly visible for several miles and from which the island's power supply is routed. Caleta del Sebo may seem an attractive destination if coming from afar but it is not a Port of Entry and boats are not permitted to stay unless in distress; it is a Port of Refuge. Once you have officially clocked in to The Canaries, if you wish to visit La Graciosa it is advisable to make a booking in advance. The marina pontoons have berths for about 214, of which 20 are designated 'visitors' berths. Berths are mostly occupied by local craft and many long-term yachts; it is said that about 50% of the visitors remain for a very long time indeed. From January through March there are usually spaces but it is inadvisable to take up a berth without permission. Security guards, with little or no English, patrol the harbour and they do not bend the rules. The breakwater is mostly busy with excursion and fishing boats and there is usually a reserve ferry alongside.

## Approach and entrance

If approaching from the east the entrance may be hidden, as the eastern breakwater curves slightly westwards and the dark stone breakwaters appear to merge together and with the spit of Punta Corrales running out beyond. If approaching from the west beware the reefs to the west and south of Pta Corrales (see plan page 237).

On approach it is worth calling up on VHF Ch 9, but this is not always manned. There are good depths to be found off the breakwater entrance.

Though relatively narrow, once identified the entrance, with its striking angular sculptures, presents no problems other than the possibility of a fishing boat or the Orzola ferry leaving at speed.

Entry in darkness is feasible though not recommended. The designated 'Reception Berth' on

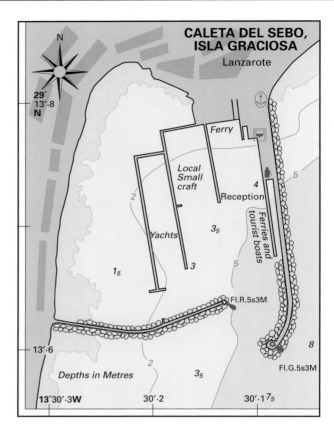

the breakwater is usually occupied by one of the commercial boats, though it might be possible to raft alongside overnight. Entry in a strong southwesterly is not recommended.

## Berthing

To request a berth contact the central office of Puertos Canarios, solicitudeslp@puertoscanarios.es; or phone, fax or email the harbourmaster directly. Some knowledge of Spanish will be helpful though the charming harbourmaster, Sr Hernandez, does speak some English.

The layout of the pontoons has changed (2015). The main pontoons have substantial finger pontoons, the majority of those on the eastern side capable of taking yachts of up to 15m in depths of 2·5m or more.

The waterfront of Caleta del Sebo  *Hilary Keatinge*

Manoeuvring space is tight between the pontoons, and there are no *marineros* to help with lines.

## Formalities

The harbour office is white and blue and situated at the root of the east (main) breakwater. The harbourmaster is not always in his office, but will usually be found there at the beginning and end of the day. Be ready with the usual ship's papers, insurance and passports.

## Charges

In early 2015 the approximate charge for a 12.1 x 4m boat with water and electricity was € 13.27 per night.

## Facilities

*Water and Electricity* Is due to be installed on the pontoons (2015).

*WiFi* Free WiFi at the burger bar *Los Mateos* and *Rosa's café*.

*Showers* Next to the port office. No hot water.

*Rubbish bins* Near the boatyard, recycling bins dotted round the village.

*Fuel* Diesel pumps next to the crane on the east breakwater serve the needs of the whole island, as well as visiting yachts. Hours are limited to 1000–1300, 1600–1800 weekdays only and payment must be made in cash.

*Medical Services* There is a small pharmacy and a doctor available 24hrs. Call on the general emergency number 112. There is also a post of the ambulance and rescue service (EMERLAN) at the harbour. Serious problems are transferred to Lanzarote.

*Bank* Open 0930-1330 on Monday and Thursday only. ATM at the bank 24/7.

*Shops/provisioning* Adequate for day-to-day needs. Two supermarkets, one open 0900-2100.

*Cafés, restaurants, hotels* A variety of cafés and restaurants round the harbour. Several small hotels and guesthouses.

*Car* Hire No car hire.

*Bicycles* including mountain bikes (advisable as there are no roads) very reasonably available for hire.

*Taxis* Several off-road vehicles, usually near the Harbour Office when the ferry comes in. One of the drivers, Sigi, speaks English and German, ☎ +34 630433110. There are water taxis too.

*Ferry* Two ferry companies running out of Orzola on Lanzarote, Biosfera Express and Lineas Maritimas Romano about € 20 return for the 30 minute trip.

*Buses* There are buses to Arrecife from Orzola.

## Boatyard

*Travel-lift* The 64-tonne hoist operated by the Cofradía de Pescadores (fishermen's cooperative) is not really tuned to handling yachts, though help would almost certainly be forthcoming in an emergency.

*Chandlery* None as such, though the FerroBox, a hardware store (*ferretería*) near the harbour, stocks tools, paint and limited chandlery.

## Anchorage

It is possible, though exposed, to anchor to the east of the Caleta del Sebo breakwater in 6-8m sand. There is no charge for anchoring.

# Orzola

29°13'·6N 13°27'·15W (breakwater head)
See plan page 237

### The ferry port for La Graciosa

Orzola is the most northerly village on Lanzarote and it is somewhat off the beaten track unless taking the ferry across to La Graciosa. The breakwater follows the line of the reefs in a northwesterly semicircle, finishing with a straight section running northwest to close slightly with the mainland shore. The outer parts are awash at high tide, but nevertheless it provides some protection for the harbour and the short quay from which the ferries depart. A N cardinal beacon marks the outer part of the breakwater. Much of the harbour's inner area is taken up with local smallcraft on moorings and is very shallow. On no account should the area be approached at night or in less than very settled weather.

The inner harbour at Orzola, looking north *Hilary Keatinge*

# Punta de Mujeres

29°08'·62N 13°26'·81W (headland, SE angle)
See plan page 232

**Lights**
**Punta de Mujeres** Fl(2+1)R.8·5s10m5M
   White tower, blue bands 6m

## Anchorage in settled conditions only

Punta de Mujures is a small village, with a few restaurants and shops. The main part of the village occupies a square peninsula with a small quay on its southern corner, southwest of which there are extensive sand patches, still largely free of moorings. The smaller bay to the northeast has a greater density of local smallcraft moorings – possibly because it offers better shelter – and a rocky bottom. There are steps and a ramp by the short quay though the latter can only be accessed at half-tide and above.

It is the closest feasible anchorage to the famous Jameos del Agua and Cueva de los Verdes, about 3km along the road to the northeast. These are part of a 6km long lava tube that were developed by César Manrique and well worth a visit, though maybe not from this anchorage as it is only tenable in rare and very settled conditions.

# Arrieta

29°07'·71N 13°27'·76W (lop-sided quay, head)
See plan page 232

**Lights**
**Arrieta** Fl.R.2s10m5M
   White tower, blue bands 7m

Casa Juanita is one of the few buildings on Lanzarote *not* influenced by Manrique's 'white only' influence
*Hilary Keatinge*

## Day anchorage in open bay

A typical Canarian fishing village with surprisingly limited tourist development, situated at the north end of the Rada de Arrieta on the east coast and less than a mile south of Punta de Mujeres. This bay is some 2M across with no outlying dangers on approach. It may be worth a daytime visit in calm conditions. A small stone quay lies near the north end of the town, with an unusually (for Lanzarote) distinctive red and blue house, Casa Juanita, with a double-pitched roof on its own separate peninsula close northeast. At the southern end of the town is a wooden jetty terminating in a strange, lopsided stone quay – apparently a swimming platform – with underwater projections, south of which is a sand and stone beach. Anchor either close south of the quay (if moored small craft allow), or off the beach to the south in 5m or so, both over sand and stones. The swell is significant with any east in the wind and breaks along the length of the bay.

Looking down to Punta de Mujeres and Arrieta *Hilary Keatinge*

# Costa Teguise

28°59'·75N 13°29'·14W (south molehead)
See plan page 232

### Offering little possible shelter

Developed in the 1970s and '80s Costa Teguise is a massive tourist development whose low white buildings were influenced by Manrique. It is visible from well offshore and is not to be confused with the historic town of Teguise that is some distance inland. The crowds come for the windy white sand beaches and the nightlife. If the trades are from northwest or north, the bay with its very solid breakwater appears a sheltered haven compared with the waves breaking on the reef off Orzola. However, when the wind comes anything east of north, sailboarders flip in rollers that break right across the entrance. The reef off the north head of the bay extends up to 500m offshore and must be given a generous berth. The two rough, lava-block breakwaters, built primarily to provide shelter for a long and crowded bathing beach, curve southeast and northeastwards respectively. Two pillars, conspicuous on the southern breakwater head, are the artistic work of César Manrique, totem poles of rusty artifacts welded one on the other. A course of 310° for this breakwater should find sufficient water for an approach, but do so with caution, a lookout and an eye to the echo sounder. Do not be misled by the very shallow harbour to the north – make certain to be heading for the totem poles. The breakwater is more substantial than many of its ilk, with a solid top and sheer inner wall with bollards and ladders and it might well be possible to lie alongside – check first by dinghy. Otherwise anchor in 3m or so near the head of the breakwater. Local small craft lie on running moorings in its angle, and the rest of the bay is shallow.

# Arrecife

Arrecife is the capital of Lanzarote, the island's major ferry, fishing and container port with an extensive new facility for yachts, Marina Lanzarote. Arrecife itself is dominated by the only high rise building on the island, very conspicuous from the sea, the five-star Gran Hotel. Originally built in the 50s, it was an empty shell for many years but has been renovated to star quality. There are two castles: Castillo San Gabriel (16th century), housing an archaeological museum, and in the main port complex, Castillo San Jose (18th century), now a contemporary art gallery. Both are somewhat obscured by more recent development.

# Puerto de los Mármoles, Arrecife

28°57'·85N 13°31'·69W (breakwater head)

**Lights**
**Puerto de los Mármoles breakwater**
  Fl.G.5s13m5M
  Fl(2)G.7s6m1M
  Fl(2+1)R10s6m3M

**Harbour Communications**
  VHF Channel 16, 09
**Port Authority**
  ☎ +34 928 598 301 or +34 928 598 305
  arrecife@palmasport.es

### The hub for Lanzarote's commercial traffic

Unsuitable for yachts. Puerto de los Mármoles is a busy commercial harbour to the northeast of the city. The area between the main breakwater and the container wharf is heavily used by commercial shipping berthing on both sides. The outer breakwater is due to be extended another 350m, but no date has yet been set for this. A new dock for cruise ships has been developed to the west of these. Yachts should be on the lookout for constantly moving traffic and keep well clear. In historic Puerto Naos there is the large new Marina Lanzarote.

# Marina Lanzarote, Puerto de Naos, Arrecife

28°58'·16N 13°31'·98W
(approach port hand channel marker)

**Harbour Communications**
  VHF Ch 09 (24/7)
**Marina Office**
  ☎ +34 648 524 649 or +34 928 663 263
  0800-2000 every day
  Marina Lanzarote, Oficina de Capitania, Avenida Olof Palme s/n, 35500 Arrecife
  *reservations* marinas@caleromarinas.com
  *marina office* marina@marinalanzarote.com
  *general enquiries* info@caleromarinas.com
  www.caleromarinas.com

### Marina making a name for itself among those crossing 'the pond'

This new marina (almost completed in 2016) has 400 berths on finger pontoons for boats of up to 80m. It is close to the centre of Arrecife in the southeast corner of Puerto de Naos and has a very good range of shore side services. On the marina complex there is a gym and swimming pool, plus a number of cafés, restaurants and shops. Most details are to be found on the well set out website www.caleromarinas.com/marinas/lanzarote. (When this comes up in the browser it is better not to click the 'translate this page', but rather open the Home

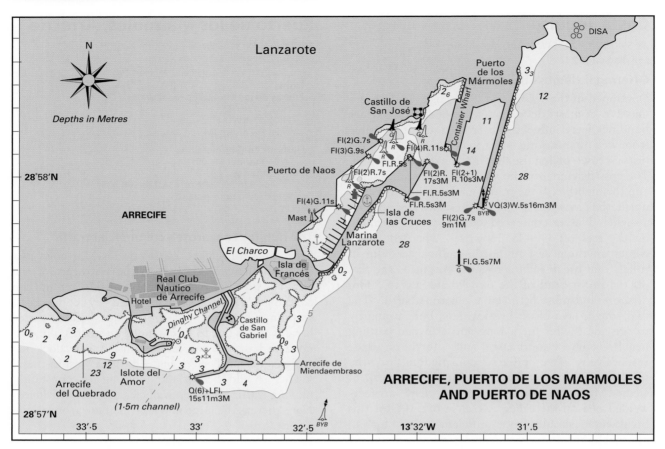

**Lanzarote**

DISA

Puerto de los Mármoles

Castillo de San José

Container Wharf

2.6

3.3

12

11

14

28

Fl(2)G.7s
Fl(3)G.9s
Fl.R.5s
Puerto de Naos
Fl(2)R.7s
Fl(4)R.11s
Fl(2)R. 17s3M
Fl(2+1) R.10s3M
Fl.R.5s3M
Fl.R.5s3M
Fl(4)G.11s
VQ(3)W.5s16m3M
BYB
Mast
Isla de las Cruces
Fl(2)G.7s 9m1M
Marina Lanzarote
28
Fl.G.5s7M

**28°58'N**

**ARRECIFE**

El Charco

Isla de Francés

0.2

Real Club Nautico de Arrecife

Hotel

Dinghy Channel

Castillo de San Gabriel

0.9

3

3

5

3

0.5   2   4   3

9

2

12   5

23

3   3

3

3

Islote del Amor

Arrecife de Miendaembraso

Arrecife del Quebrado

3

4

Q(6)+LFl. 15s11m3M

*(1·5m channel)*

**28°57'N**

*Depths in Metres*

N

**ARRECIFE, PUERTO DE LOS MARMOLES AND PUERTO DE NAOS**

33'·5      33'      32'·5   BYB      13°32'W      31'·5

The new Marina Lanzarote   *Calero Marinas*

page and at the very top there is an option EN/ES, for the English text click EN.)

## Approach

If coming from the northeast, the power station and the two towers of the DISA fuel plant will be seen to the northeast, keep half a mile offshore until the breakwater is identified. From the south, again keep at least half a mile off shore to avoid the reefs, the airport is distinctive south of the city and the tower of the Gran Hotel is conspicuous. An E cardinal buoy marks the edge of the reef 1M south of the port entrance.

Head for the new green starboard hand approach buoy (Fl.G.5s7M) shown on the plan, which will clear you of the planned extension works to the Mármoles outer mole. Then head north towards the end of the container wharf, leaving the outer mole off to starboard. The eastern corner of the outer mole end is marked with an easterly cardinal beacon (VQ(3)W.5s16m3M). The inside of the mole end is marked with a green mast (Fl(2)G.7s6m1M).

To port is the new cruise ship dock, marked at the SW point with a red cylindrical tower (Fl.R.5s6m3M) and at its NE point with another red cylindrical tower, flashing Fl(2)R.7s6m3M.

Ahead to starboard, on the SW corner of the container dock is a Green (FL(3)G.9s6m3M). From the wharf end head NW for the first of two pairs of channel buoys, red lateral (F(3)R.9s1M) and green lateral (FL(4)G.11s1M).

Follow the channel as it curves to the SSW, keeping three more red buoys (total of 4 in the channel) to port. The marina is on the port hand side. IT IS IMPORTANT TO KEEP WITHIN THIS CHANNEL. The fishing dock on the northern side of the channel is marked with a Fl(3)G.9s9m1M. There are plans to dredge the channel to 5m.

## Berthing

Call up Marina Lanzarote on VHF Ch 09. The marina staff will be on hand. Once completed, there will be a reception and fuelling dock immediately to port between pontoons M & L. As with most marinas it is advisable to contact the marina some time before arriving to request a berth.

## Formalities

The forms for both the marina and the Border Police can be printed out in advance from the marina website, or it can be done in the marina office. Hand in the forms with copies of the boat's registration document, insurance and passport of the owner/skipper. All formalities can be handled by the marina staff.

## Charges

In 2016 the charge for a 12·1m x 4m boat was approximately €18 for one night. There is a very clearly set out page on tariffs, including information on taxes, on the website. After some years of confusion the tax position is now simplified and is not excessive. There are discounts for longer stays.

## Facilities

*Water* On the pontoons. The water is potable but it does come from a desalination plant.

*Electricity* On the pontoons. Either single or three-phase 220v/380v.

*WiFi* Free, ask at the office. The code will be attached to an email address.

*Showers* Two shower blocks. Ask at the office for a key.

*Laundrette* Behind Pontoon G. Coin operated. For a full laundry service check at the office or call Smartie Pants Launderette and Dry Cleaners, ☎ +34 928 512 440.

*Fuel* Not yet in place.

*Bottled Gas* Camping Gaz available at two of the chandleries (see below) other makes of canister can be filled via the marina office (allow 2 days) or at the DISA depot, open weekdays to 1500.

*Medical services* there is a large health centre in the Valterra area, opposite Hiperdino hypermarket, a 20-minute walk and the General hospital is just outside the city centre. For onboard consultation the Dr. Mager clinics provide a private medical service with English, German and Dutch speaking doctors. They have three clinics on the island, Puerto del Carmen: ☎ +34 928 512 611, Costa Teguise and at Playa Blanca ☎ +34 928 517 938.
Emergency 24/7 ☎ +34 649 973 366

*Banks/ATM* No ATM yet on the complex. Many banks in the town.

*Shops/provisioning* Hiperdino Express in the complex. Saturday morning market in the San Ginés square. Several large supermarkets in the city.

*Cafés, restaurants, hotels* Wide variety.

*Tourist information* There is a large Tourist Office on the complex open 1000-2200, behind Pontoon J

*Car hire* Cabrera Medina operates from the Tourist Office.

*Bicycle hire* Request this service from the Tourist Information Office. Bikes can be delivered to the marina.

*Taxis* Taxi rank on the site, behind pontoon G.

*Buses* Good service to the main tourist centres. Routes and timetables on www.intercitybuslanzsarote.com

*Airport* The airport for international and inter island flights is 4km south of the town 20-minutes by road.

*Ferry services* Two ferry companies. Fred Olsen and Naviera operate interisland services and to Cadiz. Check the websites for up to date details: www.fredolsen.es/es, www.navieraarmas.com/en/home

## Boatyard

Marina Lanzarote
☎ +34 928 510 158
0800-1300, 1400-1700
varadero@puertocalero.com

A most impressive facility has been built beside the marina. There is a 100-tonne travel hoist and a massive 820-tonne one, the biggest in Spain. The latter is capable of accommodating large multihulls of up to 14·5m. Two deep keel pits have been constructed and there is a large area of hardstanding.

Looking back at the approach to the marina, the yellow buoy on the right of the picture is where the reception and fuel dock will be *Hilary Keatinge*

There are numerous specialists who work as a team based at either Marina Lanzarote or Puerto Calero. The distance between the two is no more than 20km. The yard already has a good reputation with the visiting ocean racing and multihull fleets. In charge of both boatyards is the very capable Sergio (Queco) Morales. First call for any enquiries regarding the boatyard or its services should be through the Marina Office, ask for Christian who speaks English.

There are also a number of workshops in the area round the marina.

The massive 820-ton hoist at work in the new Marina Lanzarote boatyard *James Mitchell, Calero Marinas*

*Engineers* Wes Lunday of Catlanza combines ownership of a successful business running excursions from Lanzarote and Fuerteventura on a large catamara with an equally successful engineering business. His workshop offers full machining, welding and rigging services. ☎ +34 629 145 294, wes@catlanza.com, www.catlanza.com
Jean-Michel Alliott, who is French, has the reputation of being able to do 'virtually any repair on a boat'. He also speaks fluent English and Spanish. ☎ +34 616 286 574

*Electronics* Working with Wes Lunday is Jan Hayward; he specializes in all makes of watermaker, as well as the installation and repair of electrical systems.
Marco works on general electrical and electronic repairs, and refrigeration. ☎ +34 678 807 803

*Sail repairs* John Beamish, from the UK, handles repairs for all sail types, weights and colours. He also makes and repairs sprayhoods, biminis and covers. varadero@puertocalero.com or contact John through the boatyard office (see above).
M SAILS, Gonzalo and Alejandro Morales.
Sale and repair of sails, covers, biminis, sprayhoods, ropework. They speak Spanish, English and Italian. Normal working hours, weekdays 0900-1600. A stock of second-hand nautical items for sale. ☎ +34 606 897 111, C/Extremadur 5, 35500, Arrecife.

*Liferaft servicing* This can be arranged through the marina office, as there is no facility on the island.

*Chandlery* Lava Tienda Náutic, situated at the west side of the marina office. ☎ +34 651 867 721 uwe.krambs@lavacharter.com. They speak English, German and Spanish. Stockists for Garmin, Jabsco, Lwemar, Hempel, Vetus, Waeco etc. and they hold a good stock of Imray charts.
There are six other chandleries within easy reach of the marina:

1. Efectos Navales Duarte, Calle Agustin de la Hoz (one road north of Puerto de Naos) carries a wide stock, including rope, paint, stainless steel shackles, etc., plus general hardware. ☎ +34 928 811 117

2. The Rio Centre, opposite, is also part of the Duarte operation selling smallcraft (including inflatables) and outboards.

3. Duque Hnos SL, next door to Efectos Navales Duarte, carries generators, outboards, hardware, tools, etc.

4. The Cofradía de Pescadores, a little further along towards the fishing wharf, sells mainly hardware and practical items.

5. InoxNaval Lanzarote, Calle Puerto Naos 3, specializes in stainless steel and other metalwork, and carries a wide range of paints and general hardware. ☎ +34 928 814 620

6. Effectos Naval San Gines, Avenida Naos 22, Arrecife 35500. A large hardware superstore. ☎ +34 928 806 849

## Arrecife anchorage

It is no longer permitted to anchor in the old harbour southwest of the reef, Arrecife de Miendaembraso; the port police will move on any boats doing so.

# Puerto del Carmen

28°55'·2N 13°40'·56W (breakwater, southern elbow)

### Lights
**La Tiñosa (breakwater spur)**
Fl(2)G.7s5M Green tower 3m
**Breakwater angle** VQ(6)+LFl.10s3M

### Harbour Communications
VHF Ch 09
### Marina office
☎ +34 928 515 018
0800-1430 weekdays only
*Harbour Official* Juan Gabino Cáceres Batista
puertodelcarmen@puertoscanarios.es
www.puertoscanarios.es

## On the edge of the tourist resort

Puerto del Carmen is situated at the south end of a ribbon of the island's largest tourist development, though no high-rise buildings thanks to César Manrique. The port area still retains a certain old fashioned charm amidst a mass of cafés, bars and restaurants. The harbour itself is the base for an increasing number of excursion and dive boats as well as small local fishing boats.

## Approach and entrance

The approach from the south is straightforward, from the north the harbour is almost at the end of the holiday beaches and development. The end of the angled breakwater head is now lit (Fl(2)G.7s5M) and there is a S cardinal post on the elbow.

## Berths

There are 117 berths for boats of up to 12m on seven pontoons, with finger pontoons. There is a minimum of 2·5m depth, good depth if going to the fuel dock only. To check for a berth it is advisable to contact the harbour office first. It is possible to arrange a long-term stay. No English is spoken and the office is not always attended.

## Formalities

The harbour office is to the right of the small boatyard. If the harbour official is not there try in the nearest café.

## Charges

In 2015 the cost for one night, for a 12m boat, was approx. €12 including water, electricity and ICIG tax.

## Facilities

*Water and electricity* on pontoons
*Showers* It may be possible to use the shower at the diving school.
*Security* 24/7. The guards have a base at the barrier entrance to the harbour area.
*Fuel* 0800-2300
All other general facilities in the town.

## Boatyard

There is a 70-tonne hoist and some hardstanding.
Some general repairs on request.
*Diving Services* Ask in the office. There are several companies based in the harbour complex.

# Puerto Calero Marina

28°54'·92N 13°42'·42W (breakwater head)

### Lights
**South breakwater** Fl(3)G.14s10m6M
Octagonal stainless steel tower 4m
**Port hand buoy** Fl(2)R.8s3M Red can buoy
**North mole** Fl.R.15s3m3M
Set into the wall and very inconspicuous

### Marine farm
A marine farm, marked by four yellow pillar buoys with × topmarks, all Fl.Y.5s5M, lies southwest of Puerto Calero, centred on on 28°53'·5N 13°44'·2W.

### Harbour Communications
VHF Ch 16, Ch 09 (24 hours)
### Marina Office
☎ +34 928 511285
0800–2000 Monday to Saturday, 0900–2000 Sunday
Edif. Antiguo Varadero 2°, 35571 Puerto Calero – Yaiza, Lanzarote
*reservations* reservas@puertocalero.com
*marina* marina@puertocalero.com
*general* info@caleromarinas.com

Approaching the west facing entrance to Puerto del Carmen, the new fuel dock is at the head of the harbour *Hilary Keatinge*

IV. THE CANARY ISLANDS

Puerto Calero, looking east along the coast to Puerto del Carmen *Calero Marinas*

### In an attractive setting, a well-run marina

A marina surrounded by stylishly designed residential apartments, offices, shops, restaurants and bars, Puerto Calero was designed by the artist and architect Luis Ibañez, a close friend of Manrique's. No detail has been overlooked. Even the bollards and manhole covers are of polished brass, the ladders of stainless steel and many of the buildings finished in marble. The marina, opened in 1989, has 450 berths, of which over two hundred are used by transients. They can also accommodate mega yachts of up to 85m. The complex continues to be very well run and spotlessly clean; it has been awarded the EU Blue Flag for over 20 years. Security is excellent, with outdoor staff on duty around the clock. The international airport is only about 15 minutes away and it would be a secure and convenient place to leave a yacht unattended for any length of time. Go to the excellent website for all the details.

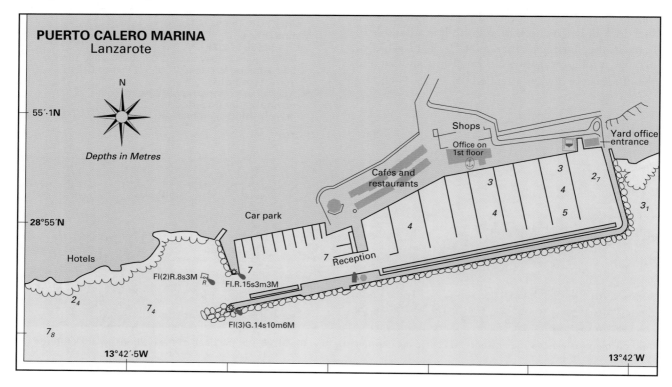

Keeping the spirit of a golden age of yachting alive – part of a classic fleet
alongside in Puerto Calero *James Mitchell, Calero Marinas*

## Approach and Entrance

The entrance is partially open to the west but is protected to some extent by the curve of the coast towards Punta Gorda and Punta Papagayo. There are no particular hazards and in normal conditions entrance is straightforward by day or night. On closing the coast towards the entrance the bottom shelves very steeply from 200m to 20m in less than 500m, so with a southerly swell seas build up and it is wise to take advice, particularly before leaving the marina in such conditions. The grey octagonal tower on the south breakwater forms a useful landmark, though since the latter was extended in the late 1990s it no longer stands at the tip.

## Berthing

Before arrival yachts are requested to make contact on VHF Ch 09, or call, even with a prior reservation, and most will be directed straight to an allocated berth. CCTV cameras are also installed to monitor arriving and departing traffic, so someone should always be on hand to greet an arriving yacht and take their lines. There are finger pontoons and depths are ample (between 3-7m). There is a Reception pontoon on the port side opposite the breakwater tower.

## Formalities

As soon as convenient after arrival, visit the marina office on the 2nd floor of the building overlooking the 'main square' (see plan) with the usual paperwork. Crews must fill out both arrival and police forms. Although this is not officially a Port of Entry, for non-EU crew who want their passports stamped, this can be arranged by the marina office (allow 48 hours) or carried out on the spot in Arrecife, near Puerto de los Marmoles. The very helpful office staff all speak English, as well as a variety of other European languages.

## Charges

In 2015 a night for a 12.1m x 4m boat was approximately €30. See the website for a full list of tariffs, there are several bands of discounts. Water and Electricity included for craft up to 25m.

## Facilities

*Water* At every berth. The water is potable but it does come from a desalination plant.

*Electricity* At every berth. Either single or three-phase 220v/380v.

*WiFi* Available throughout the marina, ask in the office for the code.

*Showers* Two blocks, one behind the administration building and the other near the breakwater's right-angle bend, a total of seven showers for men and five for women. Well-maintained and open 24 hours a day, €10 deposit for an access card.

*Launderette* Located at the back of the main building (also accessible via the Galería Comercial Náutica), with two coin operated washers and one dryer. For a full laundry service call Smartie Pants Launderette and Dry Cleaners ✆ +34 928 512 440.

*Weather forecasts* At the marina office

*Security* 24/7 and CCTV cameras throughout the complex.

*Fuel* The fuel dock is open every day from 0830–1930 and sells diesel and lead-free petrol. Payment can be made by cash or credit card. If the attendant is not in the office, call the Marina Office (VHF Ch 09).

*Bottled gas* Camping Gaz canisters can be exchanged at the local fuel station about 3km away. Other types can either be taken directly to the DISA depot (open weekdays until 1500) or left with the boatyard reception staff who will organise a collection and refill service. NB Allow two days for this.

*Medical services* In Puerto del Carmen. Private medical service can be arranged with English, German, Dutch doctors.

*Banks/ATM* Nearest bank in Puerto del Carmen, but two ATMs in the complex

*Shops/provisioning* Small but quite well-stocked supermarket, open 0800–2000 daily, on the ground floor of the building which also houses the marina's administrative offices. While fine for day-to-day living (with many familiar brands for homesick Brits) it would not be equal to storing ship for a long passage. The Hiperdino Supermercado on the main Arrecife road (ask for directions in the marina office) is recommended, and they will deliver. There is a EuroSpar about 7km away. Frozen items and meat (vacuum packed on request) together with a good selection of fruit and vegetables will be found at Congelados Roper, near the airport.

*Cafés, restaurants & hotels* Two hotels and a wide choice of cafés and restaurants, most with views over the marina.

*Car hire* Rental company in the complex.

*Taxis* Taxi rank at the main entrance, next to the security guard's hut.

*Buses* Bus stop at the exit roundabout.

*Airport* European and inter-island flights from Lanzarote Airport, about 14k by road.

*Ferry* To Puerto del Carmen from the marina.

### Boatyard

Varadero Puerto Calero
✆ +34 928 510 158
0800–1300 and 1500–1700 weekdays, closed weekends
varadero@puertocalero.com

There is a 90-tonne travel-lift but hardstanding in the gated area is limited, effectively ruling out long-term layup, but DIY work by the owner and crew is permitted and there is no objection to owners living aboard whilst their yacht is ashore.

As mentioned above (see Marina Lanzarote) the yard at Puerto Calero is also managed by Sergio (Queco) Morales and most of the specialists operate in both, some with their workshops in Puerto Calero. Refer to Facilities for Marina Lanzarote page 243 for the full list.

*Chandlery* Currently there is none on site. There is said to be a good general hardware store in Tías, about 10km along the road towards the airport.

## Playa Quemada

28°54'·3N 13°44'·1W (anchorage)

### Anchorage open to east through southwest

The small-undeveloped seaside village of Puerto Quemada lies about 1·6M southwest of Puerto Calero; enthusiasts can actually walk to it from the marina. It is tucked in behind the headland of La Puntilla and about 5M north of Punta de Papagayo. Cruising yachts occasionally visit, but there is no pier or breakwater. The beach is black sand and stony. Local small craft are moored off or they are hauled out on the stony beach. Ashore there are three restaurants and little else.

A marine farm, clearly marked by four yellow buoys with × topmarks, all Fl.Y.5s5M, lies south of Playa Quemada centred on 28°53'·N 13°44'·2W.

## Punta Papagayo to Punta del Aguila

28°50'·3N 13°47'·3W to 28°51'·3N 13°48'·7W

### Open beach anchorages

Situated just west of the arid southern tip of the island is a protected area called the Monumento Natural de Los Ajaches, There are a number of golden sand beach areas between the Punta Papagayo and Playa Blanca. These are popular with sun worshipers, divers and windsurfers, while the more secluded are frequented by naturists. They are reached on land by a rough dirt track from Playa Blanca and tourist boats and water taxis come and go during the daytime. Some have laid moorings that could be used when the tourist boats finish their day, but be away by 0900.

In settled conditions this stretch of coast offers a couple of possible anchorages sheltered by Punta Papagayo from the prevailing northeasterly winds. All call for careful eyeball navigation on approach and to find a sandy patch for the anchor. If planning to stay overnight, check the swell forecast.

The open beaches west of Punta Papagayo, looking towards the tourist sprawl from Playa Blanca *Hilary Keatinge*

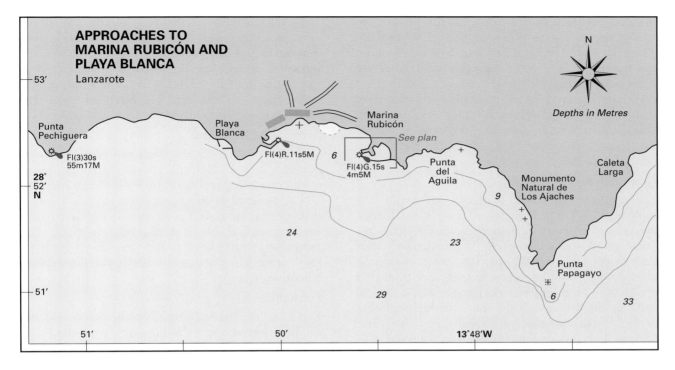

## Puerto Deportivo Marina Rubicón

28°51'·46N 13°49'·18W (breakwater head)

**Lights**
**Breakwater head**
Fl(4)G.15s4m5M Green post
**North mole, outer**
Fl(4)R.15s2m5M Red post
**Breakwater spur**
Fl.G.5s1M Green lantern on breakwater wall 1m
(obscured from seaward by the breakwater)
**North mole, inner**
Fl.R.5s2m1M Grey post, red lantern
**Interior pontoon** Fl.G.2s Post 6m

**Harbour Communications**
VHF Ch 09 (24 hours)
**Marina Rubicón**
☎ +34 928 519 012
Open 7 days a week, 0900–1800 (winter),
0900–1900 (summer)
Urbanización Castillo del Aguila, Calle el Berrugo 2,
35580 Playa Blanca
info@marinarubicon.com
www.marinarubicon.com

### Large marina close to expanding tourist resort and beaches

Marina Rubicón gets its name from the flat gravel plain that lies inland. It is overlooked by the not very high (194m) dormant volcano, Montana Rojo and the more distant but active Montañas del Fuego (the Fire Mountains). These last erupted in the 18th Century. The marina itself lies on the relatively sheltered southern coast of Lanzarote where it is being increasingly subsumed in the ever-expanding tourist resort of Playa Blanca. Even the once

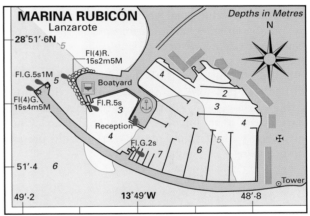

prominent Castillo de las Coloradas, on Punta del Aguila, which dates from the 1740s and lies within a few metres of the root of the breakwater, is difficult to pick out against the developments behind. Note that all lights other than that on the breakwater head are obscured from seaward.

Many of the berths are of good size, doubtless due to its comparatively recent construction. There are 185 berths for yachts of 10–13m, 125 for those in the 13–22m range, while a further 30 take yachts of 22–70m. Depth at berths for smaller boats – in this context up to 13m or so – is around 3m, and there is up to 7m at the larger berths. Neither is there any of the cramping typical of older marinas, and manoeuvring space between pontoons is generous. All berths are against robust fingers of generous length.

Both the marina and the surrounding area are well maintained and secure, and a number of boat owners satisfactorily leave their boats afloat here while they return to northern Europe or the US. There is a wide variety of bars and restaurants round the waterfront and while these inevitably generate some noise, particularly in the summer months, they are required to close at midnight; any excessive disturbance is quickly stamped on by the management. Finally, note that the extreme end of the main breakwater is a designated helicopter-landing pad. (See photo below.)

### Approach and entrance

The entrance to Marina Rubicón lies about 2M northwest of Punta Papagayo, facing Playa Blanca across a wide bay. In daylight the long, smooth outer breakwater is quite distinctive. The tall lighthouse of Punta Pechiguera 3M to the west makes a conspicuous landmark when approaching from that direction. The entrance is northwest facing. Depths shoal gradually towards the shore, with a minimum of 4m in the entrance. If arriving at Low Water Springs with a deep draught boat, it is advisable to consult marina staff before entering. Off the beach to the northwest of the entrance there are various unlit buoys – the usual yellow string to indicate a swimming area, a channel for jetskis leaving the beach, plus an assortment of small buoys laid by the local sailing school.

If approaching after dark the marina lights can be difficult to pick out against the almost continuous string of shore lights. But even in the dark, the long, dark sweep of the breakwater still shows up. Once identified with certainty, night entry should present no problems.

As the entrance is relatively narrow, a heavy southwesterly swell can result in considerable movement and may make it uncomfortable to enter or depart. In such conditions check in advance with the marina staff on VHF Ch 09. The addition of a small 'nose' to the end of the breakwater has improved conditions inside the marina considerably.

### Arrival and berthing

Call up on VHF Ch 09. Staff are reported to be competent and helpful, particularly in gusty conditions when problems are most likely, and they will be on hand to direct and assist arrivals. Coming through the entrance continue past the first basin, with the travel lift and boatyard to port. The reception and fuel dock is then immediately to port, underneath the distinctive dark tower (resembling a lighthouse).

### Formalities

Report to the marina office, on the far side of the small square near the 'lighthouse', with the usual paperwork, including evidence of insurance. The staff are friendly and helpful, and speak several European languages.

### Charges

In 2015 a night for a 12·1m x 4m boat was approximately €32.50. Water and electricity included for craft up to 25m. See the website for a full list of tariffs, there are several bands of discounts.

Marina Rubicón, looking east *Marina Rubicón*

## Anchorage

In settled weather, northeast of the entrance channel there is space for a few yachts to anchor in 3–4m over sand, though holding is poor. Keep clear of the jetski channel markers and sailing school buoys and the line of swimming area yellow buoys.

A riding light would be advisable and considerable rolling can be expected, generated by ferries departing and approaching Puerto de Playa Blanca. A short-term (overnight) stay is normally permitted, particularly if waiting to enter the marina. Call up on VHF Ch 09.

## Facilities

*Water* On the pontoons.

*Electricity* On the pontoons. 220v throughout the marina, with 3-phase 380v also available at berths intended for yachts of 18m or more.

*WiFi* Free WiFi throughout the marina. High-speed connection can be arranged for a charge. Also available in many of the bars and restaurants.

*Showers* Four or five shower blocks dotted around the marina, convenient to all berths, also in the boatyard area. Ask for key at the Marina Office, small deposit.

*Launderette* Located in the centre of the marina complex and containing two washers and two tumble dryers. Machines take €2 coins. Laundry service available through the Marina Office.

*Weather forecast* Posted every 12 hours at the marina office and shower blocks.

*Security* 24/7

*Fuel* Diesel and petrol at the Reception pontoon south of the 'square', available 0700–1900 daily.

*Bottled gas* Camping Gaz exchanges at the office. It can be arranged for most other types to be filled via the office; allow at least a week for their return. Or take cylinders by road to the DISA plant in Arrecife.

*Medical services* A health centre on the road leading out of Playa Blanca, open 24 hours and with multilingual doctors, see details at www.lanzamedic.com/es/

*Banks/ATM* 3 ATMs in the marina complex. Full banking facilities in Playa Blanca.

The reception pontoon under the 'One Bar' lighthouse
*Hilary Keatinge*

*Shops/provisioning* There is a HiperDino supermarket on the road leading out of the marina, open 0830–2200 daily, with others in Playa Blanca. Alternatively leave the marina heading east along the paved coastal way towards the Centro Commercial El Pueblo, where there is a branch of Congelados Roper which, despite its name, stocks fruit, veg, fish, meat and groceries. The walk takes about 20 minutes, but it is reported to be well worth the effort and the pathway fine for a trolley.

*Cafés, restaurants & hotels* Several hotels in the complex with dozens more in Playa Blanca, plus a tempting variety of cafés, bars and restaurants. For on-board catering phone ☎ +34 928 519 012.

*Car hire* Cabrera Medina has offices in the marina complex.

*Taxis* The marina office will telephone for a taxi on request.

*Buses* A shuttle bus runs into Playa Blanca, from where services run to Arrecife and elsewhere.

*Airport* European and inter-island flights from Lanzarote airport, some 30km away by road.

*Ferries* From Playa Blanca to Fuerteventura.

*Miscellaneous services* For guardinage, boat cleaning and lock-ups ask at the Marina Office.

*Diving services* Enquire at the boatyard or at the marina office. There is a PADI diving school near the boatyard for those wishing to gain a formal qualification.

## Boatyard

The boatyard is run by the marina as a separate division. Yard manager is Augusto Escolar Escuder, ☎ +34 660 556 349, though initial contact is likely to be made with Cecilia on ☎ +34 928 519 012 ext.3 (0900–1330, 1430–1800 weekdays only). varadero@marinarubicon.com

Cecilia, whose office is immediately to the right on entering the yard area, is Dutch but also speaks fluent English, German, French and Spanish, and is happy to translate if required.

There is spacious hardstanding with solidly constructed adjustable cradles, with water and power points available, making long stays ashore feasible. DIY work is permitted, and owners are welcome to live aboard while their boat is ashore. The boatyard has its own toilets and showers and a key is provided for the gate, which is locked at night.

Boatyard staff can handle all kinds of repairs and maintenance. Standards are reported to be high and costs reasonable.

*Travel-lift* 90-tonne hoist plus trailer-type yacht transporter, both capable of handling up to 7·4m beam.

*Engineers, electronics & radio repairs, rigging, metal fabrication* There are specialists on site, specialising in Raymarine, Simrad, Lorens, B&G, Volvo, Yanmar. Enquire at the boatyard office.

*Sail repairs* An independent sailmaker, Jorge Cabrera, can carry out canvas work and sail repairs.

*Chandlery* Seahorse Actividades Nauticas (in cooperation with Accastillage Difusion). Opened next to the boatyard entrance in July 2015.

# Puerto de Playa Blanca

28°51'·57N 13°49'·94W (breakwater head)

**Lights**
**Breakwater**
Fl(4)R.11s5M Red brick tower 7m
**Dolphins** Four dolphins. Each lies between the pontoons and the ferry channel carries a single blue flashing light, similar to those on British emergency vehicles

**Harbour Communications**
VHF Ch 08
**Harbour office**
☎ +34 928 517 540

## Ferry and small craft harbour

Puerto de Playa Blanca does not accept yachts at present – mainly because there is absolutely no space. The five short pontoons are packed tight with local boats. Plans for the development of the harbour, including a marina have been on the drawing board for many years, and there is said to be some hope that the project will be carried out in the foreseeable future. The southern part of the harbour handles the car ferries that run an almost continuous service across the Estrecho de la Bocayna to Corralejo on the north eastern corner of Fuerteventura.

## Anchorage

There is no possibility of anchoring in the harbour itself, but in settled northerly weather good anchorage can be found a little further east – though well clear of the entrance in order to allow ample room for the ferries to make their turn. Also keep clear of the line of buoys marking a swimming area. A riding light would be advisable and considerable rolling can be expected, generated by the departing and approaching ferries.

The ferry port of Puerto Blanco is due to be transformed with a new marina  *Hilary Keatinge*

# Fuerteventura
### Between 28°03'N–28°45'N and 13°49'W–14°30'W

## Introduction

The second largest island in the Canary group, Fuerteventura is a windsurfer's paradise and hosts many international wind and kiteboarding championships. Sun worshipers flock here in ever increasing numbers to enjoy the 30 miles of fine white-sand beaches, courtesy of the desert sand blown from the African deserts just 60 miles to the east. This volcanic island is 75M long and just 15M at its widest. The interior is arid and desert-like, the coastline rugged. The topography is more the result of erosion than eruptions, as it is millions of years since the last one. The local struggle for subsistence living in this harsh environment has been alleviated with the advent of waterside tourism. And there is a special charm in the white-washed, flat-roofed village dwellings, the controlled holiday developments, the protected landscape. This island has a chill out factor hard to find on the other islands.

So what for the sailor? Much of what Bernard Moitessier famously loved about the island still holds true today '… this island impressed us with a sense of grandeur, with its solitude, its vast deserted beaches, its high dunes of white sand, its clear waters…'

Those wishing to explore the island and leave their boat with reasonable peace of mind will head for the marina at Grand Tarajal on the southeast coast. For the adventurous there are some anchorages in that area too. Other ports of call might be Corralejo at the northern end of the island, Puerto del Castillo, and in the far south Morro Jable, but these have limited berthing for visitors. The west coast is dramatic from the land, rugged and inhospitable for the sailor.

## Navigation

For information on **Magnetic Variation**, **Tides** and **Tidal Streams** see pages 224-225.

Full **Emergency Service** information is on page 227

**Weather** and **Navigational Broadcasts** are listed on page 228

**Coast Radio Stations**
**Fuerteventura** 28°24'·4N 14°02'·7W
   Controlled from Tenerife, 24 hours
**VHF** Ch 06, 22
**DSC** VHF MMSI 002241926

**Lights**
**Punta Tostón (Punta Ballena)**
   Fl.8s35m14M White tower, red bands 30m
**Punta Martiño (Isla de Lobos)**
   Fl(2)15s29m14M 083°-vis-353°
   Yellow tower and building, white lantern 6m
**Punta Gavioto (Puerto del Rosario)**
   Fl.5s48m20M Reserve light 9M White tower 43m
**Punta Lantailla** Fl(2+1)18s196m21M
   Stone tower on building 12m
   *Note* Obscured when bearing less than 228°
**Morro Jable** Fl(2)10s62m20M White tower 59m
**Punta Jandia** Fl.4s33m22M 276°-vis-190°
   Dark masonry tower on building on low spit 19m
**Punta Pesebre** Oc(2)6s11m10M
   Grey and white truncated tower 5m

Betencuria, the ancient capital, was well hidden inland but even then the pirates eventually found it *Hilary Keatinge*

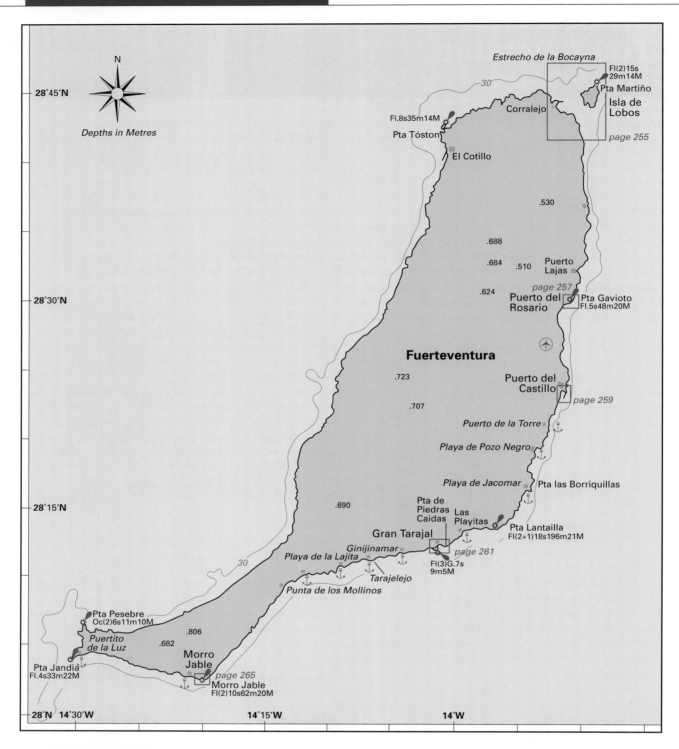

N

Depths in Metres

28°45′N

Estrecho de la Bocayna

30

Fl(2)15s
29m14M
Pta Martiño

Corralejo

Isla de
Lobos

Fl.8s35m14M
Pta Tóston

page 255

El Cotillo

.530

.688

.684    .510    Puerto
Lajas

.624    page 257

28°30′N    Puerto del    Pta Gavioto
Rosario    Fl.5s48m20M

**Fuerteventura**

.723    Puerto del
Castillo

.707    page 259

Puerto de la Torre

Playa de Pozo Negro

Playa de Jacomar    Pta las Borriquillas

28°15′N    .690    Pta de
Piedras    Las
Caidas    Playitas

Gran Tarajal    Pta Lantailla
Fl(2+1)18s196m21M

Ginijinamar    page 261

Playa de la Lajita    Fl(3)G.7s
9m5M

Tarajelejo

Punta de los Mollinos

30

Pta Pesebre
Oc(2)6s11m10M

Puertito    .806
de la Luz    .682    Morro
Jable

Pta Jandía    page 265
Fl.4s33m22M    Morro Jable
Fl(2)10s62m20M

28°N 14°30′W    14°15′W    14°W

## Approach and navigation

The north coast of Fuerteventura becomes a dangerous lee shore in the prevailing northerly winds. Approach Corralejo only in suitable weather, as there are numerous rocks and rapidly shelving depths. There is often a large ground swell running between Isla de Lobos and Fuerteventura itself and yachts are advised to avoid the area if the swell is over 2m. Wind acceleration zones exist along the south coast of the island, one lying between 2M and 12M west of Gran Tarajal and another 3M west of Morro Jable. The two may sometimes combine – see the Acceleration Zone plan on page 226.

## Harbours and anchorages

## Isla de Lobos

Between 28°44'N–28°46'N and 12°48'·5W–12°50'W
28°44'·33N 13°49'·53W (bar to lagoon entrance)

### Natural park and marine reserve

This tiny island lying just off the northeast corner of Fuerteventura across the El Río channel has been a nature reserve, the Parque Natural de las Dunas, for over 30 years. It remains largely unspoilt, wildlife abounds and the surrounding waters offer excellent diving and snorkelling, with many colourful reef fish. Roughly triangular, the highest point is Montaña de la Caldera (107m) near the western apex but much of the rest is low-lying, including Punta Martiño in the extreme north. The island is named after the sea wolves, or monk seals, who once lived there. There is only one tiny hamlet, El Puertito, on the southern shore of the island. It boasts a restaurant but little else – nearly all visitors return to the mainland at the end of the day. Just west of the village is a stone pier used by the ferries, on the east side of the pier it is possible to land at some steps but it is not very secure. The only permitted entry to the island is via this pier. Further west is a shallow lagoon guarded by a bar that dries 1·2m at springs. The beach inside offers totally protected swimming. In settled north conditions it is possible to anchor off the lagoon in good holding 7–8m over sand and rock and experience only slight swell. There are a couple of mooring buoys owned by the tour boats that are used during the day.

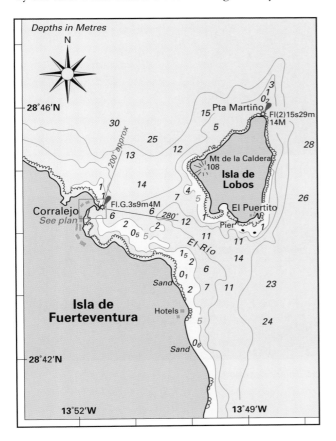

## Corralejo

28°44'·43N 13°51'·64W (breakwater head)

**Lights**
**Punta Martiño (Isla de Lobos)**
   Fl(2)15s28m14M 083°-vis-353°
   Yellow tower and building, white lantern 6m
**Breakwater**
   Fl.G.3s9m4M Green column 5m

**Harbour Communications**
   VHF Ch 09, 16
**Harbour office**
   ☎ +34 928 866 524
   0700–2100 daily
   puertocorralejo@puertoscanarios.es

### Ferry and fishing harbour with lively shoreside atmosphere

Corralejo is on the northeastern corner of Fuerteventura, with the islet of Lobos a mile and a half to the east. Given that Lanzarote's southeastern tip is just 7m away, if conditions for entry to Corralejo are uncertain many yachts tend to head for Marina Rubicón. A former fishing harbour, Corralejo is now busy with the frequent car ferries plying across the channel (Estrecho de la Bocayna) to Playa Blanca on Lanzarote. Many smaller tourist boats take groups back and forth to Lobos. Corralejo is not a Port of Entry. The once small village has expanded greatly as a tourist centre and the development behind the port, though not high-rise, can make the entrance difficult to identify on approach. Two large windfarm-type windmills are prominent on the shore west of the harbour. Some years ago an ambitious government-funded marina was planned, providing at least 600 berths, but the plans remain on the drawing board.

### Approach

*From the north* There are reefs and shallows on both sides of the entrance and caution must be exercised. Be aware that when the wind is from northwest it funnels through El Río, the channel between Isla de Lobos and Fuerteventura. The west coast of Lobos has no hazards and plenty of depth so it is prudent to stay reasonably close to it.

There are dangerous rocks (0.5m at CD) to the north of the breakwater and another (0.9m) to the NNW. Stay outside the 10m contour until the bearing to the green light at the end of the breakwater is at a minimum of 200°T and a maximum of 285°T. The breakwater head can be passed fairly close-to, keeping a watch for manoeuvring ferries.

**Note** A tall blue column with a triangular top is situated on the ferry quay, and should not be confused with the breakwater light structure.

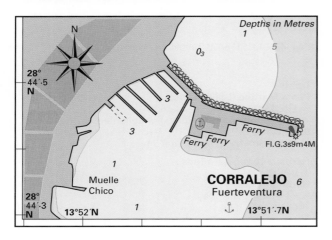

*From the south* Approaching the strait, the coast of Fuerteventura resembles a low desert. Several large apartment blocks have joined the two conspicuous hotels at the southern entrance to the strait. With the hotels abaft the beam, if the strait is passable, steer for the south of Isla de Lobos. South of Montaña de la Caldera (107m) the island is low-lying with El Puertito on the southern tip. Just west of this group of houses is a small stone pier. Bear due north to avoid rocks to the east, and when approximately 300m from the stone pier, the port of Corralejo will be on a bearing of 280°. Rollers breaking on the shallows on both sides can be unnerving and the entrance to Corralejo may be difficult to identify from this distance. This bearing, however, if adhered to carefully, avoids all dangers. If unable to identify the stone pier on Lobos, leave the island to port and approach Corralejo from the north. If a swell of over 2m has developed in the Estrecho de la Bocayna it would be unwise to attempt to enter Corralejo or to pass through El Río. Likewise if the northeasterly prevailing wind is over F7. It is not recommended to enter after dark.

### Entrance and berthing

Final entrance is straightforward. Four pontoons run out directly from the shore, with a fifth angled southwest from the breakwater, containing a total of around 115 berths. Nearly all are permanently occupied. Unless a slot has been pre-booked a yacht is unlikely to find space during the high season; use the email address listed above to place a booking.

### Anchorage

Anchor in 5–6m southeast of the breakwater, leaving ample room for manoeuvring ferries. Official policy fluctuates, but it appears that a yacht is most likely to remain undisturbed if a marina berth has been requested but is unavailable. Much of the harbour bed is said to be foul with rope and ground tackle, making a trip line necessary. A small charge is made for anchoring. The anchorage is not tenable in strong winds from east to southeast.

Well reefed on the approach to Corralejo Harbour with the eastern end of Islas Lobos in the background *Hilary Keatinge*

Montaña de la Caldera on Lobos looms above the harbour of Corralejo *Hilary Keatinge*

### Formalities

The skipper should visit the harbour office (next to the post box on the ferry quay) bearing the usual ship's papers and passports. Although advertised hours are 0730–2100 daily, the office is frequently unattended. Very little if any English is spoken.

### Charges

In early 2015 the cost for one night, for a 12m boat, was approx. €12 including water, electricity and ICIG tax

### Facilities

*Water and electricity* On the pontoons. Electricity is not always turned on.
*WiFi* In many of the bars and cafés
*Showers* None.
*Launderette* Conveniently close in the town, but closes at 1500.
*Fuel* By can from a Shell filling station inland from Muelle Chico (10-minute walk)
*Gas* Most gas bottles can be exchanged or filled in the town.
*Banks* Several in the town, with cash dispensers.
*Shops/provisioning* Supermarkets and other shops in the town.
*Cafés & restaurants* Many, some overlooking the harbour and its small sandy beach.
*Medical services* Two medical centres, one with German doctors who speak some English.
*Car hire & taxis* at the ferry terminal
*Buses* Bus station on the northern edge of the town, with services to El Cortillo as well as Puerto del Rosario and beyond.
*Ferries* Car ferries several times daily across El Estrecho de la Bocayna to Playa Blanca on Lanzarote, and foot passenger ferries to Isla de Lobos.

### Boatyard

*Travel-lift* 70-tonne hoist operated by the Cofradía de Pescadores (fishermen's confederation) with an area of hardstanding to the northwest of the harbour, but no boatyard as such.

## Puerto Ventura and Puerto de las Lajas

28°36'·36N 13°49'·49W & 28°32'·3N 13°50'·3W

### Two misnomers

The names 'Puerto Ventura' and 'Puerto de las Lajas' on large-scale maps are all that remains of two ambitious plans which have come to nothing. Work started in the early 1990s on an upmarket tourist development complete with marina, to be called Puerto Ventura, much of the east breakwater still survives, albeit derelict and partially submerged, and a number of smallcraft lie on moorings in its shelter. It is understood that work never even started at Puerto de las Lajas, a tiny village where a few small fishing boats are either hauled up the beach or lie on moorings close off the stony beach. It might be possible to anchor off in settled weather, though there is little obvious reason to do so.

## Puerto del Rosario

28°29'·46N 13°51'·3W (breakwater head)

**Lights**
**Punta Gavioto (Puerto del Rosario)**
  Fl.5s48m20M White tower 43m
**Breakwater, southeast corner**
  Q(3)10s13m3M East cardinal pillar, ♦ topmark 2m
**Breakwater end**
  Fl.G.5s14m5M Green tower 10m
**West mole extension, south end**
  Fl(2+1)R.10s7m3M Red pillar, green band 3m
**West mole, north (old) end**
  Fl(2)R.7s7m1M Red column 4m
**South RoRo ramp**
  Fl(2)G.7s6m1M Green column 3m
**Beach protection mole**
  Fl.R.5s6m3M Red column 6m

**Harbour Communications**
  VHF Ch 12, 16 (24 hours)
**Port Authority**
  ☎ +34 928 860 200 or +34 928 860 201
  0700–1400 weekdays only
  ptorosario@palmasport.es

### Island capital, but no real facilities for yachts

Rosario is the capital of Fuerteventura and Puerto del Rosario is the main commercial port of the island. Container ships, and ferries from Arrecife and Las Palmas, berth on the inner side of the eastern breakwater, which has doubled in size over recent years, while cruise ships use the north-south spur on the west side of the harbour. There is no space for visiting yachts to lie alongside, but the extended breakwaters have created a reasonably sheltered anchorage southwest of the harbour.

IV. THE CANARY ISLANDS

Looking ENE across to the anchorage in Puerto del Rosario  *Hilary Keatinge*

### Approach and anchorage

The town is easy to identify on the low coastline, with four large grey silos on the breakwater and no outlying dangers in the approach. Allow good clearance for ship movements when closing the breakwater end.

In northeasterly winds the area between the cruise ship quay and the mole protecting Playa Chica remains reasonably sheltered and offers good holding over sand in 6–7m. There appears to be no official objection to this, or to dinghies being left on the (artificially created) sandy beach to the west. The cream building on the quay to the north is occupied by the Centro Náutico Insular, a sail-training centre, which has a slipway where a dinghy, with permission, might be left in greater safety.

### Formalities

The port authority office will be found in the large grey and white building just outside the port gates (if closed there is a small police office opposite). It also houses the Immigration Department, which should be visited with the ship's papers if this is the yacht's port of entry to the Canaries. No charge is made for anchoring outside the harbour.

### Facilities

*Water* On the fishing quay, or possibly from the Centro Náutico Insular.
*Fuel* Petrol and diesel pumps on the fishing quay.
*Bottled gas* Camping Gaz or DISA bottles can be exchanged at several hardware stores in the city.
*Medical services* Hospital south of the town, plus a clinic near the church.
*Banks* In the city, all with cash dispensers.
*Shops/provisioning* Supermarkets and other shops, including an enormous hypermarket in the industrial zone northeast of the town.
*Produce market* Near the root of the southwest mole, but relatively small.
*Restaurants & hotels* Wide choice to suit all tastes and pockets.

*WiFi* Free WiFi is said to be available throughout much of the city, including the public parks and along the waterfront. The free service is distinctly slow. Enquire in the nearest Tourist Office.
*Car hire & taxis* In the town.
*Buses* Bus station the north end of the main square, with services throughout the island.
*Airport* European and inter-island flights from the airport about 5km south of Rosario.
*Ferries* Car ferries to Lanzarote and Gran Canaria.

### Boatyard

*Travel-lift* 30-tonne hoist near the fishing quay, but no real boatyard.
*Engineers, electronics & radio repairs* All the skills necessary to service the fishing fleet, but most workshops are outside the port area. Delfin Servicios Nauticos, ① +34 928 530 699, have premises on Calle Almirante Colon 124 and handle engineering and electrical work as well as repairs and fabrications in steel and aluminium.
*Chandlery* Duque Hermanos SL, ① +34 928 851 194, Calle Alfonso XIII, northeast of the city.

# Puerto del Castillo
## (sometimes known as Caleta de Fustes)

28°23'·49N 13°51'·37W (breakwater head)

**Lights**
**Breakwater** Fl(2)G.12s10m5M
  White tower, pale green band 5m
**South cardinal**
  Q(6)+LFl.15s5M Yellow spherical buoy
**Starboard hand buoy**
  Fl(3)G.9s1M Green pillar buoy, ▲ topmark
**Port hand buoy**
  Fl.R.5s3M Red can buoy, ■ topmark

**Harbour Communications**
  VHF Ch 09
**Marina office**
  ☎ +34 928 547 687
  0900–1800 weekdays only
  *Harbourmaster* Hugo Estevez ☎ +34 928 163 514
  marcan@abaforum.es

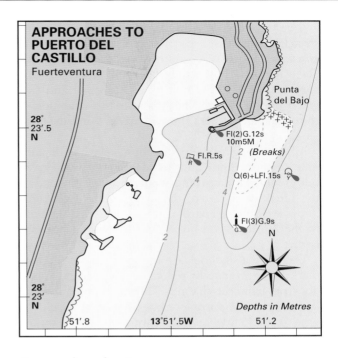

## Part of a busy holiday complex with little space and not recommended for visiting yachts

Puerto del Castillo is now part of Barceló Castillo Beach Resort. Castillo, or Caleta de Fuste, is a purpose built holiday town; even the beach has been imported. However, near the root of the breakwater is a tall round tower of rough brown volcanic rock with a domed roof that dates back to 1743.

## Approach and entrance

Outlying and inshore reefs and sandbanks make entry distinctly hazardous; this is not a harbour to be entered for the first time at night. Once inside, protection from the prevailing northeasterlies is good, but it is essential to check first that space will be available.

The very crowded harbour of Puerto del Castillo with the 18th century tower in the background  *Hilary Keatinge*

IV. THE CANARY ISLANDS

A dangerous reef which has claimed several yachts stretches southeast from Punta del Bajo extending considerably further south than the breakwater, enclosing a shallow sandy bay which opens to the south, its limits indicated by a S cardinal and two green buoys; one red buoy marks the west side of the channel. Others buoys mark windsurf and jet-ski areas.

Approaching from any direction, keep a good half-mile offshore until able to identify the two green buoys and the green and white tower at the end of the breakwater. Leave the inner of the two green buoys well to starboard as it is actually placed close to the 2m line – on no account attempt to cut the corner.

There are also shoals on the west side of the bay, marked by the one lit red can buoy; yachts should not stray from the channel. There is claimed to be at least 3m in the entrance, but even so it would be wise to enter slowly under power with an eye on the depth sounder. Call up on VHF Ch 09 to check on the conditions before entering; wind or swell from the south would make entry difficult and/or dangerous. There is little room for manoeuvering in the harbour itself.

### Berthing

Puerto del Castillo is privately run and is probably the smallest marina in the Canaries, with fewer than 100 berths, of which about 10 are theoretically reserved for visitors – though some appear to be making very long visits indeed. Maximum size, limited by draught (2.5m), as much as length (16m). Berths cannot be reserved, but telephoning to check for space before leaving your previous harbour, and then again via mobile phone or VHF at least 30 minutes before arrival, appears to offer the best chance of success. The reception and fuel berth, with a stated 4m, is immediately to starboard on rounding the breakwater head, or you may be directed straight into a berth.

### Formalities and charges

The marina office is currently located behind the dive school that occupies most of the modern building at the end of the breakwater with a glass-walled bar/restaurant on the upper floor. Some English is spoken. Charges are relatively high at more than €35 per night including tax for a yacht of 13m, but discounts are available for longer periods.

### Facilities

*Water* At all berths.
*Electricity* At all berths.
*WiFi* Not in the marina.
*Showers* Behind the restaurant. Key card from marina office for a €20 deposit.
*Launderette* In the resort, a short walk from the marina.

*Weather forecast* Posted daily outside at the marina office.
*Security* 24hr. with gates to the pontoons. Keys (which also give access to the showers) are available from the marina office (see above)
*Fuel* Not yet available.
*Gas* in hardware shop in the town
*Medical services* Medical centre in the resort.
*Banks* In the resort, all with cash dispensers.
*Shops/provisioning* Close to the tower, with a Eurospar hypermarket about 1km from the harbour.
*Produce market* Weekly produce market in the resort on Saturday mornings.
*Cafés & restaurants* Many in the resort, including a restaurant overlooking the marina.
*Car hire and Taxis* Ask in the hotel
*Buses* From resort to Rosario
*Airport* No more than 15 minutes by taxi

## Anchorages on the east coast of Fuerteventura

Between Puerto del Castillo and Punta Lantailla lie a number of beach-backed coves that can be used in calm weather or light northerlies. Working southwards they include:

⚓ **Puerto de la Torre** 28°21'·8N 13°52'·3W
Just south of Punta del Muellito, with its Guanche ruins

⚓ **Playa de Pozo Negro** 28°19'·4N 13°53'·7W
Protected to the north by Punta del Viento

⚓ **Playa de Jacomar** 28°16'·4N 13°54'·3W
Tucked behind Punta las Borriquillas and some 2·5M north of Punta Lantailla. This anchorage, which has little ashore beyond a small group of fishermen's houses, has shoals in the approach and needs to be closed carefully and in good light. Holding is patchy over small boulders and rocks.

## Las Playitas

28°13'·65N 13°59'·05W (molehead)

### Anchorage sheltered from west to northeast

Lying 2M west of Punta Lantailla, Las Playitas (also called 'El Poris de Las Playas') a small fishing village, occupies a steep-sided valley that offers some protection even in a moderate northeasterly, and provides good anchorage in 3m or more over sand. There are a number of local moorings. A short stone mole with steps lies at the east end of the bay, where there are some facilities including a small supermarket and several fish restaurants. To the west of the bay is a large fitness resort, popular with professional sports teams in training.

# Gran Tarajal

28°12'·32N 14°01'·44W (breakwater head)

**Lights**
**Southeast breakwater**
Fl(3)G.7s9m5M Green tower 7m
**West breakwater**
Fl(3)R.7s9m5M Red metal tower 7m

**Marine farm**
A marine farm, marked by four yellow pillar buoys with
× topmarks, all Fl.Y.3M, lies east of Gran Tarajal, centred
on 28°12'·5N 13°59'·2W.

**Harbour Communications**
VHF Ch 09
**Harbour office**
☏ +34 928 162 151
0730–1400 weekdays only
*Harbourmaster* Domingo Santana Oramas
puertograntarajal@puertoscanarios.es,
solicitudesip@puertoscanarios.es
http://puertoscanarios.es/Inicio/

There is shelter, but often a swell in the anchoraged to the
east of the marina at Gran Tarajal *Hilary Keatinge*

## Fuerteventura's most welcoming harbour for yachts

Gran Tarajal is actually one of the biggest towns on
the island but it is off the tourist track. The harbour
was originally developed for the fishermen and as a
depot from which to ship local produce, mainly
tomatoes. In the last ten years the harbour has been
enlarged and improved and it is well protected from
the prevailing wind. The surrounding area remains
relatively undeveloped, at least by Canarian
standards, and although some might consider Gran
Tarajal's attractions limited it has retained its
'village' atmosphere and offers a real glimpse of how
the island must have been before the tourist boom
took off. The marina may not have all the facilities
yachtsmen have come to expect but it has the
essentials and is friendly and reasonably priced.

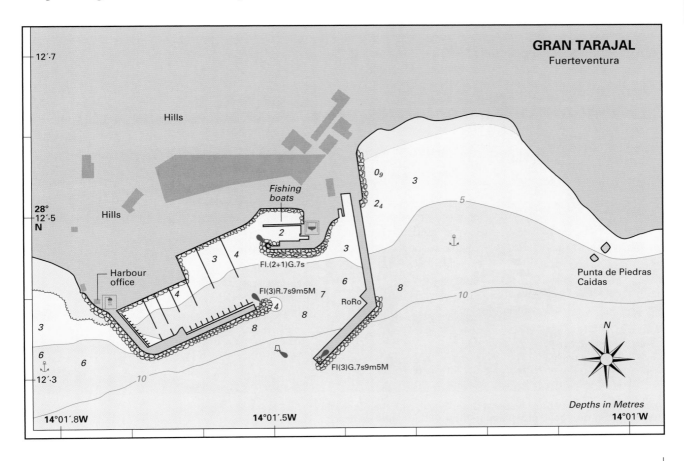

GRAN TARAJAL
Fuerteventura

Hills
Hills
Fishing boats
Harbour office
Fl.(2+1)G.7s
Fl(3)R.7s9m5M
RoRo
Fl(3)G.7s9m5M
Punta de Piedras Caidas
Depths in Metres
12'·7
28° 12'·5 N
12'·3
14°01'·8W
14°01'·5W
14°01'W
N

Gran Tarajal from due east almost round to west  *Anne Hammick*

*Approach from the north* From Punta Lantailla lighthouse to Punta de Piedras Caidas is 3.7M, passing Las Playitas in the curve of the bay. Gran Tarajal lies less than 1M further west in a wide valley with a low coastline. Approach and entry are straightforward, note there is a green buoy off the breakwater, leave to starboard on entering. A minimum of 12m at the entrance. The fishermen's harbour is in the northeast corner, the pontoons for other craft on the port hand.

## Berthing

It is preferable, but not necessary to book in advance. There are currently said to be about 250 berths in total and even in the high season, when other harbours are full to capacity, Gran Tarajal is likely to have space for a visiting yacht. There is no formal reception area, and unless waved into a berth by one of security guards (some of whom speak English), arriving skippers should make their own choice and confirm it with the harbourmaster during office hours. Yacht berths are alongside finger pontoons, with up to 16m LOA possible against the south part of the breakwater and 12m against the western angle. Short-term visitors are normally berthed on one of the two eastern pontoons. In normal conditions these berths are reported to be comfortable, though swell can work into the harbour in southeasterlies and set yachts rolling. The eastern pontoons are also the most convenient for the town, and offer plenty of space to manoeuvre. Local smallcraft occupy the remaining pontoons.

A yacht rounds the W breakwater at Gran Tarajal, with the outer arm of the E breakwater beyond. Together they give good protection to those within  *Anne Hammick*

If planning on leaving the boat for a period it is necessary to engage a local as guardian and the harbourmaster will advise on the best place to secure the boat. The breakwater berths are said to be preferred, particularly the ones against the western wall – winter gales can cause waves to break over the breakwater's south wall.

### Anchoring

Anchor in the bay to the east of the harbour. The bay shelves gently and holding is reported to be good over sand, though the area is often affected by ground swell. A line of small yellow buoys marks the swimming area. Anchoring is prohibited inside the harbour.

### Formalities

The office is in the northwest corner of the harbour. Many yachtsmen have commented on the relaxed way in which the formalities are handled in Gran Tarajal. The skipper should visit the harbourmaster as soon as feasible after arrival, bearing the usual ship's papers and crew passports. Out of hours, and when the harbourmaster is away, the formalities are dealt with by the security guards, but they generally appear unwilling to handle payments.

### Charges

In early 2015 the cost for one night, for a 12m boat, was approx. €12 including water, electricity and ICIG tax.

### Facilities

*Water and electricity* On the pontoons.
*WiFi* at several cafés in the town.
*Showers* Beside the office, normally open, but no hot water yet.
*Security* Security appears to be good with friendly personnel 24/7. Although the pontoon gates usually remain open there are round-the-clock patrols.
*Fuel* Jerry cans can be filled from a filling station on Calle San Diego, about 10 minutes' walk from the harbour.
*Medical services* Health centre in the northern part of the town.
*Banks* In the town, with cash dispensers.
*Shops/provisioning* Several good supermarkets in the town, including a HiperDino on the large main square, but all some distance from the harbour. Good bakery just outside the harbour gates.
*Cafés, restaurants & hotels* Bar/restaurant at the northwest end of the harbour with many more in the town, though apparently no hotel.
*Taxis* Available in the town.
*Buses* Regular bus service throughout the island, including to the airport.
*Ferries* Inter island services from Puerto del Rosario or Moro Jable.

### Boatyard

*Travel-lift* A 70-tonne capacity lift is operated by the Cofradía de Pescadores (fishermen's confederation), inside the curve of the inner mole. However, depth in the hoist dock and hardstanding and props once ashore are all limited.
*Sail repairs* Fuerte Velas, ☎ +34 928 161 027, based at Tarajalejo about five miles down the coast. The Sail Doctor, who lives on his boat in the marina, repairs and does canvas work.
 ☎ +34 661 166 688, info@thesaildoctor.com
*Chandlery* A branch of Duque Hermanos SL (which has its main shop in Puerto del Rosario) lies on the road behind the harbour, Calle Gomera 9. Though mainly serving the fishing fleet, it also has some yacht chandlery and other items can be ordered on request. Comercial Langenbacher SL, Calle Matías López, stocks limited chandlery as well as general hardware.

## Anchorages on the southeast coast of Fuerteventura

From Gran Tarajal the coast runs west for 10M before turning southwest at the Península de Jandia, the highest region of Fuerteventura with Pico de la Zara at 806m. It is a scenic coast to explore, with lovely white sand beaches and several anchorages sheltered from the prevailing winds, though further west the accelerated wind blows from the north across the low neck of land leading to the peninsula.

Possibilities for daylight stops in settled weather include:

⚓ **Ginijinamar** 28°12'·1N 14°04'·4W
A small bay with a stony beach, anchor in 3–5m over sand, holding suspect. There is a restaurant ashore, though landing can be difficult as the beach is steep.

⚓ **Tarajalejo** 28°11'·5N 14°07'·1W
Holding said to be good. There is a stone quay at the east end of the black sand beach and facilities ashore include fresh water, supermarkets, a post office, telephones, restaurants and hotels.

⚓ **Playa de la Lajita** 28°11'N 14°09'·1W
With a beach restaurant.

From Playa de Matas Blancas the coast – named Playa de Sotavento, 'The Leeward Strand' – swings southwestwards as it runs down to Punta de Morro Jable (occasionally referred to as Punta del Matorral). The beaches are stunning, backed by dunes, but along this stretch of coast the only anchorage to offer even vestigial shelter from the prevailing northeasterlies is off the growing tourist resort of Punta de los Mollinos (28°10'N 14°13'·2W). It would be comfortable only in very settled weather and is not recommended for an overnight stop.

IV. THE CANARY ISLANDS

# Morro Jable

28°02'·97N 14°21'·9W (breakwater head)

**Lights**
**Breakwater**
    Fl(4)G.11s10m5M Green metal tower 5m
**Northwest mole, angle**
    Fl(4)R.11s6m3M Red metal tower 5m
**Northwest mole, head**
    Fl.R.5s7m1M
**North inner quay**
    Fl(2+1)R.10s7m1M Red/green/red column 4m

**Marine farms**
Two marine farms lie northeast of Morro Jable, one centred on 28°06'·6N 14°27'·5W and marked by four yellow pillar buoys with × topmarks, all Fl(5)Y.20s3M; the other centred on 28°03'·5N 14°29'·3W and marked by four yellow pillar buoys with × topmarks, all Fl(4)Y.15s3M.

**Harbour Communications**
    VHF Ch 09 (24 hours)
**Harbour authority**
    ☎ +34 928 540 374
    0900–1900 weekdays

## Large, under-developed ferry harbour

Morro Jable, the words meaning 'headland' and 'croze or cooper's gouge' respectively, is essentially a ferry port, currently the only service is to Gran Canaria. It is also home to a large, mainly German, tourist development, La Cebada, that was established in the '80s. It is now difficult to tell where that ends and the old fishing village of Morro Jable begins. Protection inside the harbour was greatly improved in the late 1990s with the construction of a short, angled, northwest mole but despite elevation to the status of 'puerto deportivo' (sports harbour) no progress has been made. There have been plans for the development of the harbour by the Calero group but there is no timescale for any development as yet.

## Approach and entrance

From the west, pass at least 3M south of Punta Jandia to clear shallows and disturbed water southwest of the point. From the east, Punta de Morro Jable appears as a wide sandy beach stretching northeast, with a tall white lighthouse on the point. On rounding Punta de Morro Jable the breakwater will be seen at the west end of the holiday development. Entry, between the breakwater and the northwest mole, is straightforward with 10m depth.

At times – particularly in the winter months when the mountains are covered by a cloud mantle – sudden, vicious gusts can blow down from the hills to the north without warning. These have been reported to reach Force 10 (50 knots), albeit briefly, and one should be prepared for them, particularly when entering or leaving the harbour, which itself is well sheltered from the usual northeasterlies. Should the wind shift to the south or east there is likely to be considerable surge.

## Berthing

The ferries operate from inside the main breakwater making it unusable, in addition to which there is an overhang that may catch stanchions and fenders on a rising tide. Local craft take up most of the space on two of the pontoons in the eastern part, with some spaces said to be available for visitors on the third. Maintenance has been poor. There is a Reception pontoon in the southeastern corner by the fuel pump.

In theory berths should be booked in advance. Due to the chronic shortage of space, visits of more than a few days are discouraged. The single pontoon to

The plans to develop Morro Jable are still 'on hold' *Hilary Keatinge*

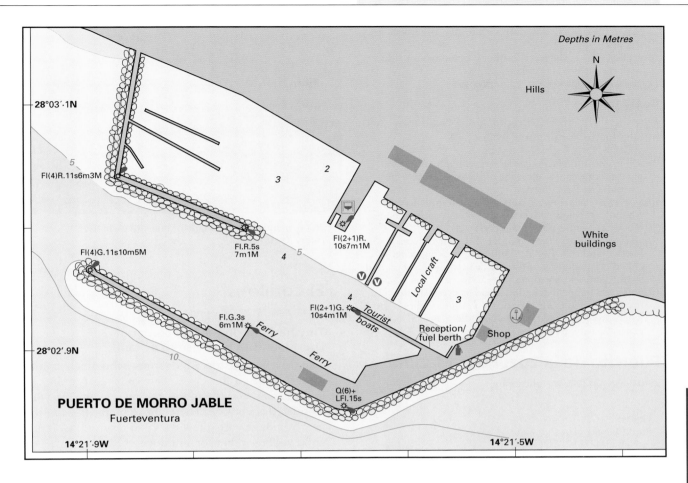

**Depths in Metres**

28°03′.1N

Fl(4)R.11s6m3M

Hills

White buildings

5

3

2

N

Fl(2+1)R.
10s7m1M

Fl(4)G.11s10m5M

Fl.R.5s
7m1M

4

5

4

Local craft

3

Fl.G.3s
6m1M

Fl(2+1)G.
10s4m1M

Tourist boats

Ferry

Reception/
fuel berth

Shop

28°02′.9N

Ferry

10

5

**PUERTO DE MORRO JABLE**

Fuerteventura

Q(6)+
LFl.15s

14°21′.9W

14°21′.5W

the southeast is used by the ubiquitous tourist catamarans and there are two basic pontoons in the western side, these have lazy lines, no finger pontoons, water or electricity.

## Anchorage

Anchoring is no longer permitted in the harbour area.

## Formalities

The port captain's office is on the ground floor of the ferry terminal at the root of the main breakwater. Although nominally open 0900–1900

The tall white lighthouse marking the low sandy promontory 1·5M east of Puerto de Morro Jable could have been taken from a child's drawing
*Tom Hammon*

weekdays only, there is often only one official in attendance and he is frequently elsewhere.

## Charges

In 2015 the cost for one night for a 12m boat was approx. €12 including water, electricity and ICIG tax.

## Facilities

*Water & Electricity* On the pontoons at the east end of the harbour, but still no supply to those in the northwest corner.

*WiFi* None in the harbour area.

*Showers* No showers, though public toilets are open in the ferry terminal.

*Fuel* There is a filling station, which also serves vehicles, at the head of the harbour. The wall is high and although there are several large bollards there are no ladders, so if crew numbers permit, it would be preferable to send a shore party on ahead. In theory sales are limited to fishing boats only, though several yachts have refuelled there without problem in the past few years. Payment must be made in cash.

*Medical services* Medical centre in the tourist resort and hospital outside the town.

*Banks* In Morro Jable, with ATMs.

*Shops/provisioning* Surprisingly well-stocked minimarket next to the fuel pumps on the main breakwater, as well as good general shopping in the tourist resort.

*Cafés & restaurants* Two in or close to the harbour, with many more in the tourist resort.

*Car hire* At least one company operates from the ferry offices.

*Taxis* On the quay to coincide with ferries, otherwise in the town.

*Buses* Bus stop at the ferry terminal, timed to coincide with the latter's schedule.

*Ferries* Car ferries to Gran Canaria

### Boatyard

Operated by the Cofradia de Pescadores, with limited facilities but good security.

*Travel-lift* 80-tonne capacity hoist, with adequate hardstanding but a shortage of props – consult the Cofradia de Pescadores.

*Engineers & electronics* Nautica Puerto Jandia (see Chandlery, below) advertise these services, but their work has not been independently verified.

*Chandlery* Nautica Puerto Jandia SL Lugar Urbanización Puerto Jandía ✆ +34 928 540 512 stocking general chandlery including outboards, electronics and related spares, nauticapuertojandia@yahoo.es.

*Commercial* Langenbacher SL also has premises in the town centre, at Calle Senador Velázquez Cabrera 36, where stocks include limited chandlery as well as general hardware.

## Puertito de la Luz, Punta Jandia

28°04'·23N 14°30'·04W (anchorage)

> **Lights**
> **Punta Jandia**
>   Fl.4s33m22M 276°-vis-190°
>   Dark masonry tower on building on low spit 19m

### Open 'passage' anchorage

Punta Jandia is a long narrow spit of volcanic material off the SW tip of the island. Shoals extend some 3M SSW and the associated disturbed water and whirlpools should be given a wide berth. Whether arriving late from the west or intending to depart at first light, to the east of the spit a wide, shallow bay off the village of Puertito de la Luz makes a useful anchorage in light offshore conditions, but be prepared for gusts and ground swell. It is not suitable in stronger winds from any direction as heavy swell works around the island. In general the holding is good though there are a few patches of rock. At night, a course of 310° for a point on the spit 0·5M northeast of the light will, with soundings, lead to an anchorage in 12m over sand with the lighthouse bearing 270° and the lights of the village due north. The bottom changes to stones inshore, but the water is clear enough to choose a patch of sand in 4–5m for the anchor. The village has a couple of bar/restaurants, but little else.

The bay off the small village of Puertito de la Luz
*Hilary Keatinge*

## El Cotillo

28°40'·84N 14°00'·74W (molehead island)

**Tiny harbour on the NW corner of Fuertaventura best visited by land**

This is a mecca for windsurfers who flock to the rather deserted beaches. The only real point of interest ashore is the old watchtower complete with wooden drawbridge. There are some facilities in the nearby village with a few bars and restaurants. It is a good vantage point for sundowners.

The tiny harbour is formed by the construction of a high breakwater between the shore and a small islet, there are some local moorings for small craft. It is totally unsuitable for yachts, but in the right conditions it would be possible to anchor off and explore by dinghy.

The waves roll in on a calm day off El Cotillo, a favourite with the surfers *Hilary Keatinge*

# Gran Canaria

**Between 27°44′N–28°11′N and 15°22′W–15°50′W**

## Introduction

The third largest of the Canary Islands, Gran Canaria is also the most populous. It is referred to as a continent in miniature, an island of contrasts. It is damp, green and fertile in the north, yet long beaches and banks of dunes line the arid south and southeast coasts. The west coast is rugged and wild. From the mid island peak of Pico de las Nieves (1950m) are deep *barrancos* or ravines that have eroded dramatically over the millennia as they slope downwards to the coasts.

The main commercial activity is centred on the capital Las Palmas and its port whilst visitors in ever increasing numbers make for the southern resorts. Exploring the island is made easy with some fine roads around the coastal fringe, the GC1 motorway from the capital south and west to Puerto Mogán and the GC2 along the north shore.

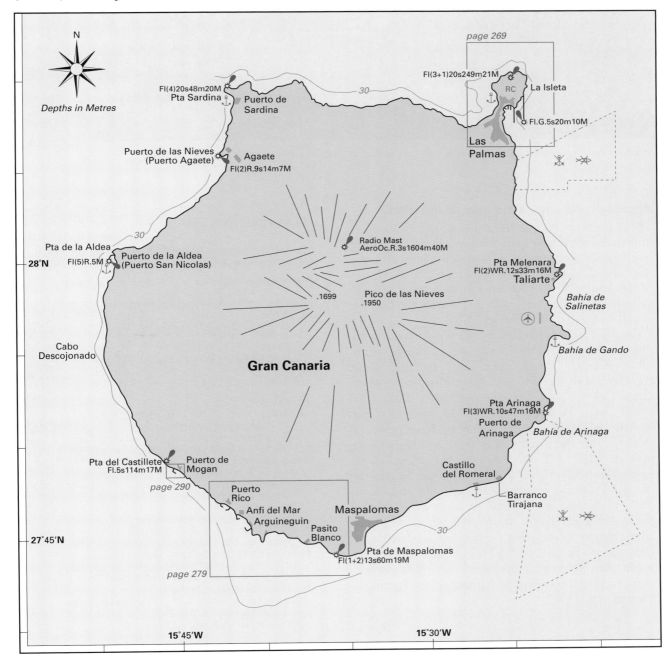

Intensive farming sprawls up the ravine in the more fertile northern reaches  *Hilary Keatinge*

### Approach and navigation around the island

There are no particular hazards in good visibility. If approaching the southern harbours from the east it is advisable to keep 1M off, in soundings of more than 20m, to clear the shallows off the Punta de Maspalomas. If coming up the east coast, in the vicinity of Punta Melenara and Punta de Gando, shoals lie up to 0.5M offshore.

Gran Canaria is affected by the wind acceleration phenomenon and winds from the northerly sector blow strongly down both the east and west coastline, with the strongest in the channel between Gran Canaria and Tenerife (See page 226). The south coast, between Punta de Maspalomas and Puerto de Mogán, often benefits from a wind shadow and there may be a light southerly close inshore while 4M offshore the prevailing north easterly will have 'bent' around the coast. In general the wind will die off somewhat at night and locals often plan their inter-island passages with this in mind. Forecasts should be treated with caution as winds may reverse during the course of a day due to land and sea breeze effects. They are also unlikely to predict the effects of a strong northerly/nor'easterly that can funnel through the *barrancos* (see Puerto de Mogán page 289).

## Navigation

For information on **Magnetic Variation, Tides** and **Tidal Streams** see pages 224-225.

Full **Emergency Service** information is on page 227

**Weather** and **Navigational Broadcasts** are listed on page 228

**Coast Radio Station**
**Las Palmas** 27°57'·5N 15°33'·5W
  controlled from Tenerife (24 hours)
**VHF** Ch 26, 74
**DSC** VHF MMSI 002241026

**Lights**
**La Isleta**
  Fl(3+1)20s249m21M Aeromarine
  White tower, yellow band, and building 10m
  *Note* Shows fixed between flashes within 6M
**Radio Atlantico**
  Aero Oc.R.3s1604m40M Radio mast 55m
**Punta Melenara**
  Fl(2)WR.12s33m12M 270°-W-152°-R-270°
  White tower 17m
**Punta Arinaga** Fl(3)WR.10s47m16M
  012°-R-052°-W-172°-R-212°-W 012°
  White tower, red bands 13m
**Punta de Maspalomas (Punta Morro Colchas)**
  Fl(1+2)13s60m19M 251·5°-vis-093°
  Conical grey tower, white lantern 56m
**Punta del Castillete** Fl.5s114m17M
  Square yellow tower with stair and gallery 20m
**Punta Sardina** Fl(4)20s48m20M
  White tower, red bands 23m

## Harbours and anchorages

## Puerto de Las Palmas de Gran Canaria (also called Puerto de la Luz)

28°07'·28N 15°24'·28W (Dique Reina Sofía, head)
28°07'·69N 15°25'·39W (marina northeast molehead)

### Lights
**Roque del Palo** Q(3)10s12m6M
   East cardinal post, ◊ topmark 6m
**Dique de la Esfinge, head** Q(4)G.10s5M
**Dique Reina Sofía, head** Fl.G.5s20m10M
   Green tower, white bands 8m Racon C 360° 12M
**Dique Reina Sofía, outer angle**
   Q(3)5s13m8M 150°-vis-360° East cardinal post 1m
*Note* Various other lights exist along the 2·1M length of
   the Dique Reina Sofia
**Dique Reina Sofía, inner angle** Q(2)G.6s8m4M
   335·5°-vis-181·5° Green tower 4m
**Dique de Léon y Castillo, east side**
   Fl.R.5s8m5M Red tower 4m
**Dique de Léon y Castillo, southwest head**
   Fl(3)G.12s20m7M 291°-vis-182°
   Octagonal stone tower, white bands 9m
**Marina northeast mole, head**
   Fl(2+1)R.15s5m1M Red column, green band 3m
**Marina west mole, head**
   Fl(2)R.7s5m1M Red post 3m
**Marina north mole, angle**
   Fl(3)10s5m3M 160°-vis-320°
   East cardinal post, ◊ topmark 4m
**Pillar buoy** Fl(2+1)R.10s3M
   Red, green, red
**Real Club Náutico mole, angle**
   Q(3)5s7m1M 180°-vis-090°
   East cardinal tower, ◊ topmark 4m
**Real Club Náutico molehead**
   Q(4)R.10s8m3M Red pyramid 4m
**Muelle del Arsenal, southeast corner**
   Fl(2+1)G.14·5s6m1M Red post, green band 3m
*Note* Many other lights exist in both the Puerto Exterior
   and the Puerto Interior

### Harbour Communications
   VHF Ch 10, 16 (24 hours)
**Port Authority**
   ☎ +34 928 214 400
   palmasport@palmasport.es
   www.palmasport.es
**Muelle Deportivo de Las Palmas (marina)**
   VHF Ch 11, 16
   ☎ +34 928 234 960
   0900–1400, 1600–1900 weekdays,
   0900–1400 weekends
   marina@palmasport.es

### The busiest port in the Canaries

From early beginnings in the 15th century Puerto de Las Palmas has become the busiest port in the Canaries and is ranked as the fourth most important in Spain. It is deep and protected from the prevailing winds, not just by the breakwaters but also by the promontory of La Isleta to the north. It lies conveniently at the crossroads between Europe, Africa and the Americas. In the 19th century one Sir Alfred Lewis Jones founded the Gran Canaria Coal Company to service these fleets and the modern city began to develop. Today almost half the population of the island lives in or near to Las Palmas. This bustling hub is refuelling station, fisheries processor and cold store, container distribution depot and, more recently, cruise ship destination. It is also a busy ferry port with international as well as inter-island routes. There are 14 kilometres of wharfs and huge capacity for storage of all kinds. Despite the focus on commercial shipping and associated industry, such are the controls today that the water quality that was compromised in the past is now so good that the long beaches immediately to the south of the capital are among the most popular on the island.

Las Palmas is also an important transatlantic hub for smaller vessels and from its marina each autumn it hosts the start of the famous ARC (Atlantic Rally for Cruisers). The ARC was awarded the prestigious

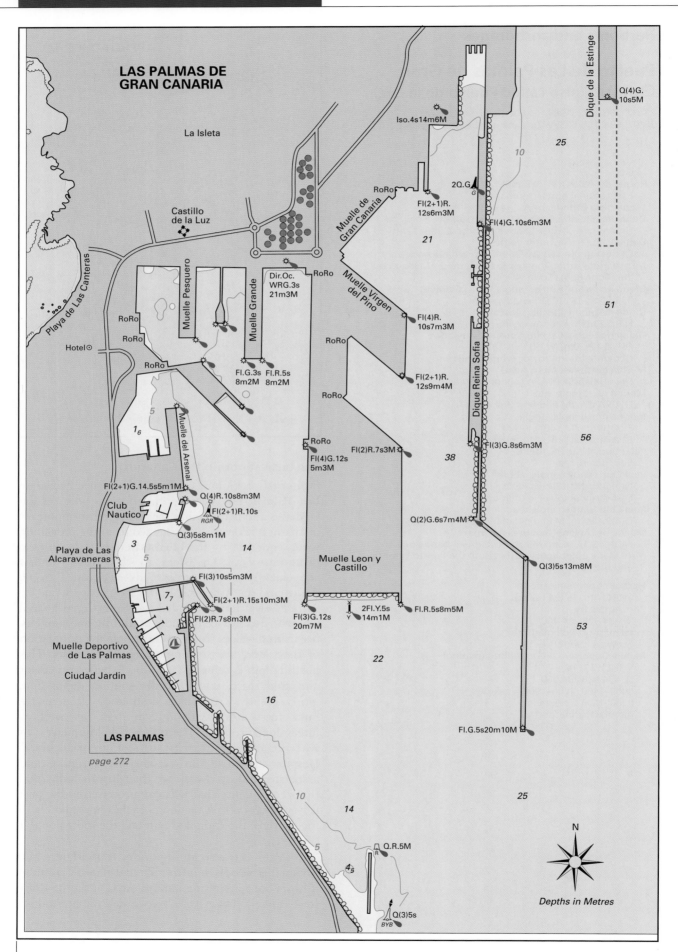

### LAS PALMAS DE GRAN CANARIA

La Isleta

Castillo de la Luz

Playa de Las Canteras

Hotel ⊙

Muelle Pesquero

Muelle Grande

RoRo

RoRo

RoRo

RoRo

Dir.Oc. WRG.3s 21m3M

RoRo

RoRo

Muelle de Gran Canaria

Muelle Virgen del Pino

Iso.4s14m6M

2Q.G
G

Fl(2+1)R. 12s6m3M

Fl(4)G.10s6m3M

21

Fl(4)R. 10s7m3M

RoRo

Fl(2+1)R. 12s9m4M

Dique Reina Sofia

Dique de la Estinge

Q(4)G. 10s5M

25

10

51

56

Fl.G.3s 8m2M

Fl.R.5s 8m2M

Muelle del Arsenal

5

1₆

RoRo

Fl(4)G.12s 5m3M

Fl(2)R.7s3M

Fl(3)G.8s6m3M

38

Fl(2+1)G.14.5s5m1M

Q(4)R.10s8m3M

Fl(2+1)R.10s
RGR

Q(3)5s8m1M

Club Nautico

3

Playa de Las Alcaravaneras

5

14

Q(2)G.6s7m4M

Q(3)5s13m8M

53

Muelle Leon y Castillo

Fl(3)10s5m3M

7₇

Fl(2+1)R.15s10m3M

Fl(2)R.7s8m3M

Muelle Deportivo de Las Palmas

Ciudad Jardin

Fl(3)G.12s 20m7M

2Fl.Y.5s 14m1M
Y

Fl.R.5s8m5M

22

Fl.G.5s20m10M

16

### LAS PALMAS

page 272

10

14

5

25

4₅

Q.R.5M
R

Q(3)5s
BYB

N

Depths in Metres

The Arc Fleet en fête 2015  © WCC / Claire Pengelly

Gold Medal for its 30-year contribution to the city's maritime profile (June 2015).

Coming from any direction yachts are required to make contact with Las Palmas Port Control on VHF Ch 16 at least an hour prior to arrival, following this up on VHF Ch 12 when three miles from the head of Dique Reina Sofia. Port control should also be contacted on VHF Ch 12 when preparing to leave the harbour.

## Approach and entrance

*From the north* La Isleta peninsula is 3km across, the northern half a high conical mound (230m) with steep cliffs, the southern half falling away to Puerto de Las Palmas and the low neck joining it to the mainland. The city and its suburbs appear from seaward as one continuous line of buildings, rising up to the south on the slopes of Cordillera de San Francisco. It is advisable to pass 0.5M off shore and then keep well south of the breakwater head as fast moving ferries may be leaving the port.

*From the south* The cathedral marks the south end of Las Palmas proper and the port lies below La Isleta. Be aware of ships anchoring and or bunkering south of the entrance. There are a number of yellow buoys up to a mile offshore marking protected zones. A little further north, straddling 28°06'·8N, a 400m mole has been constructed a few hundred metres offshore, marked at its southeast end by an E cardinal, Fl(3)5s5M, and at its north end by a square red tower, Q.R.5M. This acts as a port hand marker for commercial traffic. It is recommended not to pass inside.

The marina entrance can be surprisingly difficult to pick out on approach, with the opening not becoming obvious until quite close in. Once located it is straightforward. There is a red port hand light (Fl(2)R.7s3M) on the marina breakwater and on the starboard breakwater a red, green, red pillar buoy (Fl(2+1)R.15s3M) marking the channel for commercial traffic.

IV. THE CANARY ISLANDS

# Muelle Deportivo de Las Palmas

**Harbour Communications**
  VHF Ch 11, 16
**Marina Office**
  ☎ +34 928 214 750 or +34 928 232 378
  0900–1400 & 1600–1900 weekdays,
  0900–1400 weekends.
  Marina staff available daily 0700–2100
  Oficina del Puerto, Calle Jaquín Blanco Torrent s/n,
  35005 - Las Palmas de Gran Canaria
  marina@palmasport.es
  www.palmasport.es

## The Canaries' largest marina

With some 1,250 berths this marina is seldom full other than in the weeks prior to the departure of the Atlantic Rally in late November. Space for participating yachts is pre-booked by the organisers, and those not associated with the event are unlikely to find berths available for the four to six weeks before the start, while those already berthed in the marina may be asked to leave. Space in the anchorage is also likely to be at a premium. The marina has space for several yachts of up to 50m.

The marina has two access points to the city – a south (main) entrance via a vehicle tunnel and pedestrian steps, and a pedestrian ramp at the north end which opens about 0730 and closes at 2200, or sometimes earlier. If berthed in the northern part of the marina the detour via the southern entrance is in

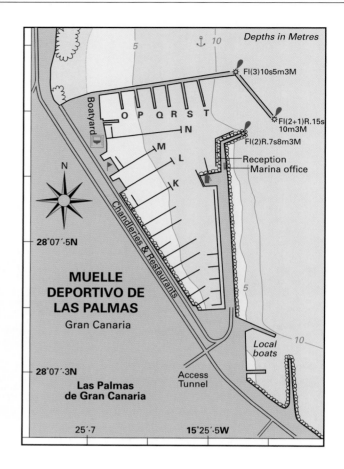

Looking northwest across the *Muelle Deportivo de Las Palmas*, with the (crowded) anchorage at top right  *Puerto de Las Palmas*

the order of 1·2km. Even experienced navigators may experience problems finding their way into and out of the marina complex by car, it is best to seek up to date advice on the route.

## Berthing

A reception pontoon is on the port hand once in the marina proper (the section which faces north in the entrance is the lifeboat berth). Arriving at night it is advisable to call up Las Palmas Marina on VHF Ch 11 before entering. If the Reception pontoon is occupied and it is after 2100 and before 0700, a berth could be taken at the fuel pontoon. At least 3·5m should be found in both places.

Six pontoons (O to T) extend south from the north mole and visiting yachts of medium size are normally berthed on one of the four outer ones. All berths are bow or stern-to, with a buoy and one or two lazy lines provided. A combination of a beam wind and the manoeuvre of backing into a slot - unfamiliar to many northern European yachtsmen - can lead to problems, and it is worth deploying all available crew and placing fenders around vulnerable areas such as self-steering gear. Fortunately there is reasonable space between the pontoons and assistance is available if required.

Security has been improved, partly by moving the main pontoon entry gates to halfway down the ramps, with side panels and spikes above. There is also a substantial police presence in the marina area, particularly prior to the ARC departure. Finally, no less than 22 CCTV cameras have been installed. Sadly the problem is more likely to be caused by those on other boats than outsiders.

## Anchorage

There is an anchorage north of the marina, however from 15 March to 15 September the area is reserved for a wide variety of other watersports and anchoring is not permitted. In the anchorage there is a line of 12 buoys, with mooring rings on the breakwater and these can take craft of up to 20m for a maximum of six months. Prior permission is required; ask in the marina office.

For the six months of the year that anchoring is permitted just south of the Real Club Náutico de Gran Canaria (RCN), a small fee is payable and owners should check in with the marina office. In busy times there may be up to 25 yachts at anchor here. Regular visits from the port police and customs are said to be common. Holding is relatively good over mud, sand and shale, though there is a patch of rock close to the buoyed-off swimming area in 5–6m. The bottom is foul in some areas, making a trip line advisable. A gap must be left clear to the south of the RCN marina mole to allow access to and from the beach – the Playa de las Alcaravaneras. This has been built up with imported sand and is popular with city residents.

There is an ongoing problem with swell – created both by northeasterly winds refracting around the two outer breakwaters which sets up a southeasterly swell in the anchorage, and in a strong southeasterly the anchorage may become untenable. There may also be considerable wash from fast moving pilot boats or other commercial craft – this movement may sometimes make life uncomfortable.

Late autumn gales are relatively common, and precautions (such as laying additional anchors) should be taken if the yacht is to be left unattended. It is not advisable to leave a yacht unattended for any length of time. Dinghies can be left inside the marina on a pontoon at the south end of the marina. Outboards need to be well secured (also a wise precaution on a dinghy left astern).

If there is space, yachts from the anchorage can temporarily use pontoon T (the easternmost on the north mole) to take on water, for which a charge is made, or collect it by can from there or from the reception or fuel pontoons, for free. An access card is needed to use the marina showers and toilets. There are public toilets on the beach though they are reported to be closed on Sundays.

## Formalities

The marina office, where customs and other formalities are also handled, overlooks the reception pontoon just north of the fuel berth. The staff are helpful with good English, though queues can form in the run-up to ARC. Present the ships' papers and skipper's passport. Any crew members who will be leaving the islands by air will need to take their passports to the Frontier Police Office in the main Edificio Autoridad Portuaria (Port Authority Building) near the root of the main breakwater for stamping. The skippers of yachts at anchor also need to visit the marina office, taking the same paperwork with them.

It is wise to reserve a berth by email at least a week, or preferably two weeks, in advance, for which no deposit is required. The simplest way is to send an email as listed above. (There is a form on the website www.palmasports.es, > Ports, Marinas >marinas deportivas > peticion de atraque; Adobe acrobat required and not the easiest to find). There is unlikely to be any possibility of a berth in the weeks prior to the ARC, as much of the marina is reserved by the organisers for participating yachts. No reservation is required if intending to anchor.

## Charges

In early 2015 the cost for a 12m boat, for one night was €9.41 + €10 for water and electricity (this is charged on the first day only), plus taxes. Discounts are available for longer periods. All credit cards accepted.

Sunset over Muelle Deportivo de Las Palmas  © WCC / James Mitchell Photography

## Facilities

*Water* To all berths, it is potable but desalinated.

*Electricity* 220v at all berths, with 380v at the large yacht berths.

*Showers* Three shower blocks, two built into the wall on the west side of the marina and the third situated in the block behind the fuel berth, all with card entry systems.

*Launderette* In the marina. Coin operated and open 24hrs.

*WiFi* Sign up for access at the Aspira office in the Red Cross building on the roundabout near the exit. Most of the cafés which line the west side of the marina offer free WiFi to customers.

*Fuel* Diesel, petrol and a variety of oils at the Cepsa fuel berth near marina reception, open 0800–1800 Monday to Friday, 0900–1400 Saturday, Sunday and holidays (though closed on the Sunday prior to the ARC departure while a party is held).

*Bottled gas* Camping Gas exchanges are available at the fuel dock or in the city, The Disa plant does refills, it is some distance south of the city, open 0900–1300. It will be necessary to hire a car as it is illegal for taxis to transport gas bottles; leave the GC-1 motorway at Junction 12, signposted for Salinetas.

*Weather forecast* Posted daily at the marina office, with copies also on display next to the minimarket and opposite the boatyard.

*Clubs* The Real Club Náutico de Gran Canaria ✆ +34 928 234 566, rcngc@rcngc.com, www.rcngc.com (in English and Spanish) has large premises north of the marina, with a small, private marina which does not accept visiting boats. However, temporary membership may be offered to visitors from recognised clubs, including use of the large outdoor swimming pools, gym, library, computer room and WiFi.

The Club Maritimo Varadero de Gran Canaria overlooks the northern part of the marina ✆ +34 928 249 919 administration@clubmaritimovaradero.es www.clubmaritimovaradero.es. Visiting yachtsmen can become temporary members for around €20 per week.

*Banks* An ATM next to Potencia. Many banks throughout the city with the nearest across the road from the main entrance.

*Shops/provisioning* Two minimarkets in the marina complex, one at the southwest corner, open 0800–2200 daily, and the other behind the fuel berth, open 0800–2000 Monday to Saturday, 0900–1300 Sundays and holidays (though closed on the Sunday prior to the ARC departure while a party is held). Both stock bread, fruit and other perishables, as well as other day-to-day needs.

The closest big supermarket is the HiperDino on Calle Manuel Gonzalez Martin. On foot leave the marina via the ramp at the northern end, cross the main road at the second set of traffic lights and continue west for three blocks. (More than €60 and delivery to the boat is free.)

For major storing it may be worth visiting Carrefour in Centro Comercial Las Arenas at the far end of Las Canteras beach, a pleasant 3km walk north from the marina or catch the No.17 bus at the stop just to the south of the steps near the tunnel. They charge €5 to deliver, about the same as a taxi. Alternatively, about 10km south of the city, near the junction of the GC1 and GC3, is the El Mirador shopping centre with a variety of shops including a good supermarket. For upmarket shopping, visit El Corte Inglés on Avenida Mesa y Lopez in the city centre just north of the marina. Almost everything is said to be available in its supermarket ... at a price.

*Produce market* One on Calle Nestor de la Torre in the old part of the city, the other on Calle Albareda near the commercial harbour, with a fish market behind. The former is highly recommended but only open from 0800–1400 weekdays. Some of the stallholders speak English and at least one (on the top floor) will deliver to the marina.

*Cafés, restaurants & hotels* A wide choice of cafés and restaurants are to be found in the marina complex. The ever popular Sailor's Bar and, particularly recommended, the El Embarcadero Restaurant, in the same building as the Club Marítimo Varadero, with its terrace bar that also serves food and is open to all. Further afield, the city abounds with restaurants and hotels at all levels.

*Medical services* Two main hospitals in the city, as well as many health centres and clinics. The one on the narrow road past the entrance to HiperDino is said to provide free treatment to EU citizens on production of an EHIC (European Health Insurance Card) and passport.

*Car hire* Numerous companies in the city and at the airport.

*Taxis* Readily available, can be booked through the office and will collect from the pontoons

*Buses* Fast services to all parts of the island.

*Ferries* Regular ferries to/from all the islands other than La Gomera, as well as to the Iberian peninsula.

*Air services* The airport, which handles inter-island and European flights, is 19km south of the harbour.

Puerto de las Palmas has some of the best repair and shipwright facilities in the entire Canaries, and at a reasonable price. Although the listing below includes contact details, some personnel at the many companies based outside the marina area speak little English, and non-Spanish speakers would be well advised to enlist the help of Jon Crouch Yacht Services, see details below.

## Boatyard

Rolnautic Varadero, Joaquín Blanco Torrent, 0 S/N, 35004, Las Palmas de Gran Canaria
① +34 928 296 811, jcrodriquez@rolnautic.com

*Travel-lift* 65-tonnes can lift boats up to 82ft. there is a 21·3ft pit. Rolnautic offer a full range of services. The Real Club Náutico de Gran Canaria has its own travel-lift for the use of members, where one might receive assistance in an emergency.

*Diving services* Ocean Shore Canarias has a licensed diver who can carry out hull cleaning, anode replacement, photographic inspection, etc.

*Engineers* There are numerous engineers in the commercial harbour and the city. If in doubt, contact Jon Crouch of Jon Crouch Yacht Services
① +34 609 388 355,
joncrouchyachtservices@hotmail.co.uk.
Jon is an ex-Royal Marine and lives locally with wide experience of solving mechanical, electrical and charging problems. He is the agent for Hydrovane and Schenker watermakers, and Merlin electronic equipment. If a job is outside his field he will advise on where best to take it.

In alphabetical order:

*Mechanics and engineers*
1. Alternators and starter motors – Zurelectrica SL ① +34 928 482 111, tma@zurelectica.com (Spanish only) Atalya 24, Urb. Ind Lomo Blanco, Las Torres.
2. Electric motor repairs - Mecanizados Atlántiko ① +34 928 002 083 (speaks English), mecanizadosatlantiko@hotmail.es, Calle Sao Paulo, El Sebadal, 5 mins from the marina.
3. Hydraulics – Caloplax SL ① 928 466 655, caloplax@infonegocio.com, Calle São Paulo, El Sebadal Seals, bearings, fan belts and windlass gearboxes.
4. Rodamientos Gallardo SL ① +34 928 465 000, Calle Mendoza, El Sebadal.
5. Volvo Penta, Perkins, Mitsubishi, Jabsco – Potencia Marina SL, based in the marina complex (see Chandlery, below) with good English spoken.
6. Watermakers and calorifiers – Rolnautic, based in the marina complex (see Chandlery, below) with good English spoken.
7. Welding and fabrication in s/s and aluminium – Inoxidables Maipez s.l ① +34 928 461 383, ventas@inoxidablesmaipez.com, Calle Sao Paolo 48, Pol Ind El Sebadal
8. Welding, including aluminium – Caribbean Tecnaval SL ① +34 928 465 454, talleres@tecnavin.es Avda de los Consignatarios s/n, Puerto de la Luz
9. Yamaha – Fueraborda SL ① +34 928 270 674 yamaha@step.es, Inés Chemida 69
10. Yanmar – Navales Cazorla SL ① +34 928 721 175 or 660 403 512, yanmargrancanaria@casorla.net or rep.navales.cazorla@hotmail.com, www.tallercazorla.net, Calle Castille y Leon (behind the beach north of the marina), with its main workshop at Puerto de Pasito Blanco.

*Electronic & radio repairs*
11. Apelco, Autohelm, Garmin, Globalstar, Icom – Tesa Nautica SA ① +34 928 223 707, tena@gtc-tesa.com, Albareda 53
12. Electrolysis control – Tech Tronic Nautica ① +34 928 787 744 or 646 675 836 techtronic@terra.es, Calle Torna Golosa 28
13. Furuno, JCR, Sailor – Nautical ① +34 928 474 020, nautical@nautical.es, Esplanada del Pantalan de Cory in the port area.
14. Garmin, Magellan, Plastimo, solar panels – Potencia Marina SL (see Chandlery, below).
15. Garmin, solar panels – Lopacan Electronica SL ① +34 928 290 658, malorenzo@worldonline.es, Calle Alemania 66
16. McMurdo EPIRBs, Skanti – Radio Marítima Atlantico ① +34 928 467 666, Calle Juan Rejon 129
17. Plath, Yaesu – Etel ① +34 928 463 513 or +34 928 463 697, Calle Profesor Lozano 17–2, El Sebadal
18. Raymarine, Mastervolt – Rodritol (see Refrigeration, below).
19. Refrigeration Rodritol ① +34 928 461 384, rodritol@rodritol.com, www.rodritol.com, Avd of Petroleum, S/N 35008, handle refrigeration problems and are agents for Frigoboat, Vetus and Jabsco pumps.
20. In the marina itself Jean-Marie ① +34 695 595 458, a French liveaboard who speaks good English, he works with Rolnautic and is recommended locally.

*Sailmaker/repairs*

21. Velas Linton ☎ +34 928 291 934, 606 555 928 prendergast@wanadoo.es, Alfredo Calderon 37. Makes and repairs sails, handles general canvaswork, and is agent for Profurl and other roller-reefing gears, which they will also repair. Several endorsements for the work of Charlie Linton (who is British) have been received over the past few years.
22. Alisios Sailing Centre SL ☎ +34 928 233 171, alisios-sailing@terra.es, open 0900–1430, 1630–1900, has premises opposite the Club Marítimo Varadero. Sails of all kinds can be repaired or created from scratch using computer cutting.

*Rigging*

23. Alisios Sailing Centre (see above), have rigging wire and terminals of all sizes and a swage machine up to 16mm, together with the necessary skills to deploy them.

*Liferaft servicing*

Three companies in Gran Canaria, each specialising in different makes. Allow at least two weeks although turnaround is often quicker.

24. Liferaft Services, flares, Avon, RFA, Zodiac – Tonogami Canarias SL ☎ +34 928 463 747 info@tonogamicanarias.es, www.tonogamicararias.es Calle Dr Juan Dominguez Perez 44, 35008 Las Palmas de Gran Canaria.
25. Liferaft service, flares, Plastimo – Inprecasa ☎ +34 928 469 422 or 617 447 144, inprecasa@inprecasa.com, www.inprecasa.com which has premises in C/Sucre, 7 Izquierdo, El Sebadal north of the commercial harbour, as well as in Tenerife.
26. RFD, Viking – Ocean Products Espanola SA ☎ +34 928 706 672 or 706 755, info@oceanproducts.es, www.oceanproducts.es based near the airport but willing to collect and deliver.

*Chandlery*

A number of outlets with chandlery of various types now front the west side of the marina. Note: all likely very busy and all may run out of popular items prior to the departure of the ARC in November, particularly those required by the event's safety regulations.

27. Marmare ☎ +34 928 296 352, a supply of charts and pilot books. Selling mainly clothes, shoes and a little 'fancy' chandlery.
28. Potencia Marina ☎ +34 928 463 647 or 928 471 044, mail@potenciamarina.com, www.potenciamarina.es, open 0800–1900 weekdays, 0800–1200 Saturday, with English, French, German and eastern European languages spoken. Large stock of Volvo parts and practical chandlery (pumps, batteries etc.) in addition to its main specialisation in engineering and electrical work.
29. Rolnautic ☎ +34 928 296 811, rolnautic@rolnautic.com, www.rolnautic.com, open 0900–1300, 1600–1930 weekdays, 0930–1300 Saturday, with English, German and Scandinavian languages spoken. Carries a wide range of general chandlery and will order from mainland Europe as necessary. Order online at www.rolnautic.com.
30. Alisios Sailing Centre SL (see Sailmaker/repairs, above) which also stocks rope and deck hardware;
31. Ocean Shore Canarias ☎ +34 928 248 091 or 616 902 599, correo@oceanshoresl.com, open 0900–1300, 1600–2000 weekdays, 0900–1300 Saturday. Primarily a Bénéteau dealer, with spares etc., some

general chandlery is also stocked. Fluent French is spoken, though little English.

32. King Hogar ☎ +34 928 467 304, info@kinghogar.com, www.anidia.com, Calle Dr Juan Dominguez Pérez 10 in El Sebadal, north of commercial harbour (a 15 minute walk). A huge supermarket-type chandlery, tools are a speciality.
33. JL Gándara y Cía SA ☎ +34 928 466 675, laspalmas@gandara-sa.com, www.gandara-sa.com, on the Esplanada Dársena del Castillo, stocks a wide range of safety equipment, also agents for the Spanish Hydrographic Office.

### Charts

Suisca SL is the only Admiralty chart agent in the Canaries, though Rolnautic also stocks some. ☎ +34 928 220 000, laspalmas@suiscasl.com, www.suiscasl.com, Avenida de Los Consignatorios 7.

Rolnautic is an official Imray distributor, though the much smaller Marmare (see Chandlery, above, for both) also stocks a good range of Imray charts and guides for the Canaries and the Caribbean, as well as BA Caribbean Leisure Folios.

## Anchorage west of La Isleta
28°09′69N 15°26′38W

On the west side of La Isleta with shelter from the NE or E there is a possible anchorage, though with any west in the wind or swell it is likely not tenable. There are three mooring buoys reported to be well founded. If approaching from the north keep 0·5m off as there are rocks off the northern corner.

## Ports and anchorages down the E coast

The east coast of Gran Canaria south from Las Palmas has little to recommend it to visiting cruising yachts. Harbours are commercial or military with no facilities for visitors and the few possible anchorages are relatively exposed to strong winds and swell on what is usually a lee shore. The coastline is very built up, with sandy beaches and resort complexes as you approach Punta da Maspalomas, the southern point of the island.

# Taliarte
27°59′·32N 15°22′·13W (breakwater head)

**Lights**
 **Breakwater** Fl.G.5s12m3M
 White tower, green bands 4m
 **West mole**
 White tower, red bands 3m (unlit)

**Marine farm**
A marine farm, marked by four yellow pillar buoys with x topmarks, all Fl.Y.3M, lies south of Taliarte, centred on 27°58′·8N 15°22′·3W. It extends some 550m north/south and 400m east/west.

**Harbour Communications**
**Port Captain** ☎ +34 928 219 300

There is no real space or facilities in Taliarte for a visitor  *Hilary Keatinge*

### Research centre, fishing harbour and dive centre

A small harbour close to the beach of Melanara. Taliarte is home to the Canary Institute of Marine Sciences (Instituto Canario de Ciencias Marinas or ICCM) as well as various commercial companies engaged in marine research. Located just south of Punta Melenara, it remains primarily a fishing harbour occupied by small craft on moorings and five pontoons, all protected by a high concrete wall that gives good protection. A short west mole runs out from the shore opposite the breakwater head and the entrance faces southwest towards Punta de Salinetas.

There are no facilities for visiting yachts, though it might be possible to lie alongside the breakwater for a short period, or to anchor just outside in 7–10m. The Cofradía de Pescadores (fishermen's confederation) operates a 50-tonne capacity travel-lift that is used by local yachts, but there are no facilities on site.

## Puerto de Salinetas

27°58'·52N 15°22'·59W (breakwater head)

#### Lights
**Breakwater, extreme SW**
  Fl.G.4s16m3M Metal post 13m
*Note* Two pairs of leading lights mark the approach, operating only when required

#### Marine farms
Two marine farms lie off Puerto de Salinetas, one to the northeast centred on 27°58'·7N 15°22'·2W and marked by four yellow pillar buoys with × topmarks, all Fl.Y.3M, and one to the southeast centred on 27°57'·7N 15°22'·5W and marked by four yellow pillar buoys with × topmarks, all Fl.Y.5M.

### Commercial quay

This consists of a single mole alongside which commercial ships discharge. Puerto de Salinetas is said to handle more than a million tonnes of cargo a year. The mole was being reinforced (early 2015). A large industrial complex stands on the headland to the north.

## Bahía de Gando

27°55'·9N 15°21'·5W (Punta de Gando)

#### Marine farm
A marine farm, marked by four yellow pillar buoys with x topmarks, all Fl.Y.5s3M, lies in the Bahía de Gando centred on 27°53'·9N 15°22'·7W.

### A military anchorage

Well sheltered from the prevailing winds (though very strong gusts may be encountered around the headland), this is a military area where anchoring is prohibited – and likely to be enforced by heavily armed military police. It lies very close to the island's airport and there is a pipeline in the northern part of the bay, marked by yellow buoy (Fl.Y.3s).

Care must be taken when on passage past the headland to avoid Baja de Gando, 0·5M offshore, NE of Punta de Gando; with a least depth of 0·2m.

## Bahía de Arinaga

27°51'·3N 15°23'·66W (molehead)

### Possible short-term anchorage

Technically, both anchoring and fishing are prohibited in the area south of Punta Arinaga. However, it seems it would be feasible to anchor for a few hours in 4–5m close south or west of the short mole without anyone appearing to object. There are restaurants and shops ashore.

## Puerto de Arinaga

27°50'·53N 15°23'·97W (breakwater head)

> **Lighthouse**
> **Punta Arinaga** Fl(3)WR.10s47m16M
>    012°-R-052°-W-172°-R-212°-W 012°
>    White tower, red bands 13m

### Commercial harbour closed to visitors

In 2004 work started on a commercial harbour less than a mile south of Punta Arinaga. Effectively finished by October 2006 – by which time it was said to have absorbed more than €8 million of EU funds, despite the Canaries being located outside the EU's physical area; Puerto de Arinaga is now admitted to be something of a white elephant. It had apparently been intended that a good proportion of the shipping currently using Las Palmas would be diverted to the new harbour, but this has not happened. It is used by small coastal ships.

The harbour comprises a southeast-running breakwater some 800m in length with a 400m right-angled head, the inner quayside and a RoRo ferry berth protected by 10m concrete walls. It is open to the south, though some shelter is offered from the prevailing winds by Punta Gaviota. Guards man the port gates and unauthorised access from landward is prohibited.

Yachts have occasionally made use of its shelter for overnight anchorage, taking care to keep well out of the way of possible shipping movements. Holding is said to be good in about 15m over sand and rock. A brief stop appears to be tolerated but

there are no facilities whatsoever. A large windfarm lies along the coast southwest of the harbour and, not surprisingly, there are often windsurfers in action along this line of coast.

## Barranco Tirajana (Punta de Tenefé)

27°47'·96N 15°26'·03W (southeast molehead)

> **Lights**
> **Molehead** Q(6)+LFl.15s8m5M
>    South cardinal post, ⊽ topmark 4m
> **Outfall buoy** Q(6)+LFl.15s3M
>    South cardinal buoy, ⊽ topmark

### Not a harbour at all

Although from a distance the hooked mole appears to contain a harbour, in fact it merely provides cooling water for the adjacent power station.

## Castillo del Romeral

27°47'·68N 15°27'·83W (molehead)

> **Marine farm**
> Two marine farms lie southwest of Castillo del Romeral, one centred on 27°46'·4N 15°28'·4W (though extending from 27°46'·1N to 27°46'·6N and 15°28'·1W to 15°28'·6W) and marked by four yellow pillar buoys with × topmarks, all Fl(4)Y.10s3M; the other centred on 27°46'N 15°30'W and marked by four yellow pillar buoys with × topmarks, all Fl(5)Y.15s3M.

### Small, very basic, fishing harbour

Simple even by Canarian standards, the single hooked breakwater at Castillo del Romeral some 1·5M west of Punta de Tenefé shelters a few small fishing boats and local small craft from the prevailing northeasterlies. Some protection would be found if wishing to anchor, reasonable holding.

### Harbours and anchorages on the southwest coast

West of Punta de Maspalomas the coast becomes more protected from the prevailing northeasterlies as you move into the wind shadow created by the central mountains. This area can experience light southerly sea breezes although the wind direction is difficult to predict as the trades can follow the coast around, and a strong N/NE'ly can produce downdraughts which funnel through the *barrancos*. During the day there may be buoys off this stretch of coast used by the jet-ski groups.

Balancing the catch on the sea front in Castillo del Romeral
*Hilary Keatinge*

# Playa de las Meloneras

27°44'·6N 15°36'·8W & 27°44'·8N 15°36'·2W (anchorages)

**Lighthouse**
**Punta de Maspalomas (Punta Morro Colchas)**
Fl(1+2)13s60m19M 251·5°-vis-093°
Conical grey tower, white lantern 56m

## Anchorage off a sandy beach

A sandy beach protected to the east by Punta de Maspalomas and less than 1M southeast of Puerto de Pasito Blanco, Playa de las Meloneras offers daytime anchorage in 5m over sand – work in carefully as parts of the beach have off-lying rocks. For some reason this beach usually seems to escape the worst of the swell, though there can be enough surf to make landing by dinghy difficult. More shelter may be found in the small bay immediately to the east of the entrance to Puerto de Pasito Blanco in 4–5m over sand. Dinghies may be taken into the marina and left at the fuel berth for short periods while visiting the minimarket. There is no charge for anchoring.

# Puerto de Pasito Blanco

27°44'·74N 15°37'·27W (breakwater head)

**Lights**
**Breakwater**
F.R.9m3M Red metal post 3m
**Breakwater spur**
Q(2)R.4s4m3M Red metal post 3m
**Reception mole**
Fl.G.3s4m3M Green metal post 3m

**Harbour Communications**
VHF Ch 12 (24 hours)
**Marina Office**
☎ +34 928 142 194, *mobile* +34 611 615 462
0800–1800 weekdays, 0900–1300 Saturday
English spoken
Club de Yates Pasito Blanco, Ctra GC - 500, Puerto Deportivo Paisto Blanco, Edif. Oficinas, 35160 San Bartolomé de Tirajana
direccion@pasitoblanco.com
www.pasitoblanco.com

## Small, secure, private marina

Pasito Blanco, run by El Club de Yates de Pasito Blanco, is a large, secluded and secure marina with 388 berths. Developed in the early 70s it is one of

The lighthouse on Punta de Maspalomas
*Agustín Martin*

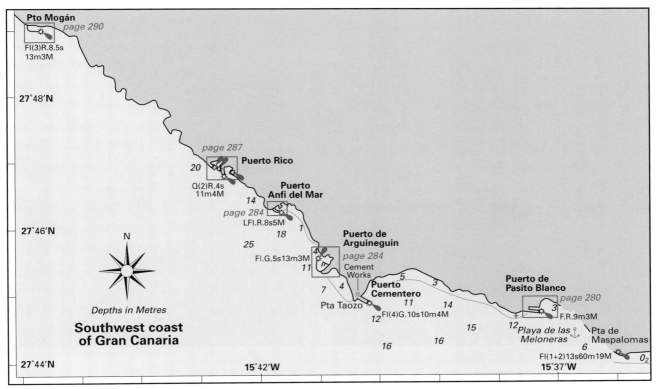

Southwest coast of Gran Canaria

Depths in Metres

IV. THE CANARY ISLANDS

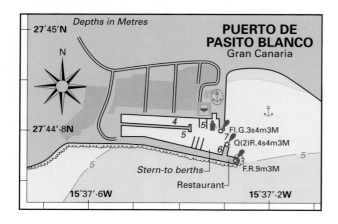

PUERTO DE
PASITO BLANCO
Gran Canaria

Depths in Metres

27°45'N

N

27°44'·8N

Fl.G.3s4m3M

Q(2)R.4s4m3M

F.R.9m3M

Stern-to berths

Restaurant

15°37'·6W

15°37'·2W

the oldest marinas in the Canaries. The surroundings are peaceful if rather isolated. The bungalows and houses are all privately-owned, no two the same and most are second homes of those from Las Palmas or mainland Spain. Only authorized cars may enter the complex. Though very much a private concern, visiting yachts are made welcome, with longer visits preferred to short, and it is an excellent place to leave a boat while returning home or travelling elsewhere. Prior booking is essential, particularly during the busy end of year time (September through December), emails typically receive immediate replies in excellent English. The marina is generally secure from bad weather but worth noting that the wind direction is sometimes at variance with the forecasts as in a strong northerly or nor'eastly it will

funnel down through the *barrancos*. Owners are advised to pull well off the pontoons if a strong easterly is expected. Pasito Blanco has received the EU 'Blue Flag', awarded to marinas with a particularly good record for water quality, and general cleanliness and maintenance standards have always been high.

Pasito Blanco has a good website, in Spanish, English and German, including information on berthing and boatyard rates.

## Approach

*From the east* East of Punta de Maspalomas are impressive sand dunes, beaches and resort buildings. Keep well offshore to avoid shallows off Punta de Maspalomas. The point itself and the conspicuous lighthouse 1·6m to the west are the southernmost points of Gran Canaria. When the lighthouse is abeam to starboard, the Pasito Blanco breakwater will be seen 1·5M up the coast.

*From the west* The cement works on Punta Taozo near Arguineguín are unmistakable. Pasito Blanco lies 3M beyond.

## Entrance and berthing

Call up on VHF Ch 12. The entrance faces east and on entry the reception berth will be seen to starboard by the travel-lift and fuel berth. Outside office hours secure to the reception berth and await instructions. At night the security guard will turn on more light and will advise arrivals where to tie up until

Puerto de Pasito Blanco, looking westwards towards the cement works at Puerto Cementero *Puerto de Pasito Blanco*

morning. The boatyard gate is locked overnight, confining night time arrivals to that area.

The vast majority of berths are for craft of under 8m or so, but there is space for about 60 boats in the 10–13m range on pontoons, and 14 for larger vessels near the end of the breakwater. One or two yachts of up to 40m LOA and 4·5m draught can also be accommodated. Certainly depth would not be a limiting factor with 7m in entrance, 6m at the larger berths and 5m at the yacht pontoons. All berths are bow or stern-to with two pick-up lines.

Security throughout the entire 'gated community' is excellent, from the manned barrier at the single entrance to the round-the-clock security patrols by polite, smartly uniformed guards who appear to be more than usually alert.

### Formalities

Visit the marina office at the rear of the boatyard, taking ship's papers, passports and evidence of insurance. There are normally two or three people in the office, at least one of whom will speak English.

### Charges

The cost in 2015 for a 12m yacht for one night was approximately €21.60. See the website for details, berthing fees do not include water and electricity, which are metered, or the 7% tax. Discounts are available for longer stays if booked in advance. A small deposit is required when booking, but will be refunded if plans change.

### Facilities

*Water* To all berths, metered. The water is potable, but desalinated.

*Electricity* 220v throughout the marina, with 380v available at the larger berths, metered.

*WiFi* available throughout the marina on a pay-to-use basis.

*Showers* Two well-kept shower blocks.

*Launderette* Next to the marina office, coin operated.

*Fuel* Next to the reception berth, available 0800–1800 daily.

*Bottled gas* Camping Gaz exchanges are available at the office, other refills can be arranged through the office.

*Weather forecast* Posted daily at the marina office.

*Banks* No bank or cash dispenser at the marina.

*Shops/provisioning* Small, well-stocked Spar with fresh bread daily, situated just outside the boatyard gates; sufficient for daily needs. If stocking up for a long trip there are good shops in Arguineguín.

*Cafés & restaurants* La Punta Yacht Club – complete with restaurant, sunbeds and enclosed swimming area at the end of the main breakwater.

*Car hire* Can be arranged through the marina office

*Buses* Frequent service along the main road west to Arguineguín, or east to Playa del Inglés/San Agustín and beyond.

*Boatyard* Fair-sized, very tidy boatyard where DIY work and living aboard are permitted (there are also private apartments to rent on the complex). Expert help is available if required. Current prices for all boatyard

services will be found on the marina's website, together with details of five companies or individuals offering a range of services including general repairs and maintenance, osmosis treatment and painting/antifouling.

*Travel-lift* 70-tonne capacity hoist. Boats are shored up using wooden 'box' props, but plenty of them.

*Diving services* A diver is available for both emergency work and hull clearning – enquire at the marina office.

*Engineers* Rep. Navales Cazorla SL ✆ +34 928 721 175 or +34 660 403 512, rep.navales.cazorla@hotmail.com, www.tallercazorla.net has a workshop in the boatyard area run by two brothers, one a transatlantic skipper who speaks some English. The company will handle most engineering problems including gearbox, transmission, steering system etc.
Jorge Ramos ✆ +34 928 142 368, Jorgeramosnav@hotmail.com works from the boatyard, handling both engineering and general repair/maintenance tasks.

*Sail repairs* Sascha Brettschneider ✆ +34 687 368 620, sascha.bretteshneider@yahoo.de, Alisios Sailing Center SL located in Las Palmas, but do work at Pasito Blanco when required.
Tatel Sails: C/Los Pasitos 6. 35140 Puerto de Mogan ✆ +34 928 569 460 or +34 667 850 638, tatelsails@gmail.com

*Chandlery* Not on site, but transport may be available to Náutica Motoracer in Puerto de Arguineguín. Alternatively the office staff will contact retailers in Las Palmas.

## Puerto Cementero, Punta Taozo

27°44'·89N 15°40'·14W (breakwater head)

**Lights**
**Breakwater** Q(2)R.6s12m6M
  White column, red bands
**Inner mole** Fl(4)G.10s10m4M
  Green post

### Commercial harbour

Just as it sounds – a commercial harbour serving a cement works. The dusty grey buildings, silos and chimneys are conspicuous from all directions and quite unmistakable. It is possible to anchor off to the east, keeping clear of the breakwater.

# Puerto de Arguineguín

27°45'·52N 15°41'·19W (breakwater head)

**Lights**
**Breakwater** Fl.G.5s13m3M
  Green tower, white band 5m
**Inner Mole** Fl.R.5s8m3M
  Red tower, white band 5m

**Harbour Communications**
  VHF Ch 09, 16
**Port office**
  ☏ +34 928 736441
  0800–1500 weekdays only
  *Port Captain* Francisco Javier Artiles Jiménez

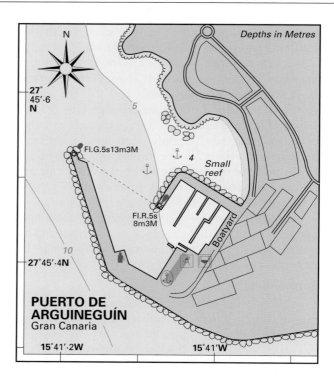

**PUERTO DE ARGUINEGUÍN**
Gran Canaria

## Anchorage off fishing harbour

A small but busy fishing harbour which still retains some vestige of its original character, Puerto de Arguineguín has changed remarkably little over the past two decades. Plans for a marina in the bay north east of the harbour were drawn up in the 1990s, and are thought to be starting in 2016. In contrast to the many tourist resorts on the southwest coast of Gran Canaria, Arguineguín retains a range of 'high street' style shops aimed at – and priced for – local people rather than tourists. There is a very good chandlery in the boatyard (see below).

## Approach and entrance

The cement works on Punta Taozo are very conspicuous from offshore, with Puerto de Arguineguín lying 0·5M to the northwest. The mountainous region of Gran Canaria extends to the west, with the coast running northwest from Arguineguín to Punta de la Aldea lined with high cliffs split in places by steep-sided valleys. The long breakwater runs out to the northwest with a shorter, L-shaped quay opposite. Keep a careful eye out for the fishing boats that are constantly on the move and their fish pot markers. There is also a small ferry that plies regularly from Mogán to Arguineguín.

## Berthing

At present this is really only a refuge for yachts if in need. The inner three pontoons are fully occupied by local small craft. It is said that yachts are no longer permitted to lie alongside the quay. There is often considerable surge in the harbour, and it may well prove more comfortable to anchor.

The harbour and yard at Arguineguín *Hilary Keatinge*

The anchorage off Arguineguín *Hilary Keatinge*

## Anchorage

In normal conditions it is possible to anchor north of the inner mole in about 4m over rock. A patch of sand large enough for two or three boats has been reported as surrounding the more western anchor symbol on the harbour plan. Up to six yachts can also lie stern-to the inner mole, with an anchor out to the northwest and a sternline ashore, which has the advantage of holding the bow into any swell. Even in windless and apparently flat conditions quite a bit of surge can be anticipated. Should the swell become serious, however, or in a strong southerly, it will be necessary to vacate the anchorage. There are a few mooring buoys in the anchorage area, but all are private.

A reef with only 0·8m at LWS extends some 40m northeastwards from the mole almost opposite the root of the outer pontoon, and the southern quarter of the beach is also rocky at low tide. The beach is roped off with the usual string of yellow buoys.

Dinghies can be left on the short pontoon close south of the travel-hoist dock. This is watched over by security guards who may wish to see the passports of those coming and going.

## Formalities

The harbour is run by Puertos de Canarias. The harbour office is at the southwest corner of the large building on the quay, which also houses the Cofradía de Pescadores offices and restaurant as well as the Náutica Motoracer chandlery (see Facilities, below).

The harbourmaster is pleasant and speaks some English. His jurisdiction ends at a line between the end of the breakwater and the end of the inner mole, outside which the Guardia Civil have sway.

## Charges

There is no charge for anchoring.

## Facilities

*Water* Taps on the breakwater and inner mole.
*Showers* No showers, though there are public toilets in the large building on the quay.
*Launderette* In the town.
*WiFi* Ask in restaurants or cafés (not in the harbour area).
*Fuel* Fuel pumps have been installed near the root of the main breakwater, run by the fishermen. They are happy to serve yachts as well as fishing boats. Payment must be made in cash.
*Banks* Several in the town, with cash dispensers.
*Shops/provisioning* Several large supermarkets and a good range of other shops.
*Produce market* Open air market on Tuesdays, the biggest on Gran Canaria.
*Restaurants & hotels* Many nearby.
*Medical services* Medical centre in the northwest of the town.
*Car hire & taxis* Readily available.
*Buses* Bus service along the coast between Puerto Rico and Maspalomas/San Agustín, and on to Las Palmas.
*Ferry* A ferry service plies along the coast from Arguineguín to Mogán stopping at Anfi del Mar and Puerto Rico, seven days a week, seven times a day.

## Boatyard

Run by the Cofradía de Pescadores (fishermen's confederation), though see also Náutica Motoracer, below. Both DIY and owners living aboard are permitted by the Cofradía, though the latter is discouraged. Náutica Motoracer, who have seven allocated slots in the yard, will organise and oversee hauling if they are to carry out the work while the boat is ashore. Round-the-clock security is provided, but no toilets or showers. There is 5m at the hoist slip.

*Travel-lift* Capacity 60 tonnes.
*Engineers & electronics* Náutica Motoracer are Yamaha and Yanmar dealers and agents for Mercury. They can organise engineering, welding in stainless steel and aluminium (contracting out to a local machine shop if necessary), and also have electronics experts available.
*Sail repairs* Náutica Motoracer handle sail repairs and general canvas work.
*Chandlery* Náutica Motoracer ☎ +34 928 736 419 mobile +34 646 896 028
info@automotoracer.com, www.automotoracer.com
open 0900–1400, 1500–1830 weekdays, 1000–1330

Saturday, will be found at the north end of the large building which also houses the harbour authority and Cofradía de Pescadores offices, with workshops below and chandlery above.

It is a family-run business owned and managed by Barrie Simpson, a motorcycle enthusiast who originally intended to meet the needs of fellow bikers, speedboat and jetski enthusiasts. The company remit has since broadened to include boats of all types, and the chandlery includes a useful range of safety equipment, small electronics, specialist paint, etc.

# Puerto Anfi del Mar

27°46'·19N 15°41'·76W (molehead)

**Lights**
**Southwest mole**
  LFl.R.8s5M White post, red bands
**Southwest inner mole**
  F.R.3M White post red bands
**Artificial island, south corner**
  Iso.G.2s3M White post, green bands

**Harbour Communications**
  VHF Ch 09
**Marina Office**
  ① +34 928 150 120 or 639 021 202,
  0900–2000 daily
  Anfi del Mar, Barranco de la Verga 7, 35120
  Arguineguin, Gran Canaria
  marina@anfi.es

### Immaculate marina but very small

During the 1990s a new timeshare resort was built against a spectacular sandstone cliff almost equidistant between Puerto de Arguineguín and Puerto Rico. Although labelled Patalavaca on some older maps, to visitors it is known as Anfi del Mar. The marina and resort have been developed by a

Norwegian, Björn Lyng, and there is quite a Norwegian influence in the whole area. Anfi Tauro, if and when it is developed (with a 500 berth marina) will be part of the same group.

A southwestern breakwater and a short inner mole shelter a small but beautifully-kept marina surrounded by landscaped grounds, with a wide beach of imported white sand close by to the northeast. The entrance faces southeast and the breakwater would appear to give good protection other than from strong southeasterlies. Although most of the 93 berths are reserved for owners of timeshare apartments, space for a short-term visitor may sometimes be available but advance reservation is essential. The harbourmaster's description of the marina as '*muy tranquillo*' seems entirely accurate.

### Approach

As with Puerto de Arguineguín, the most unmistakeable landmark in the vicinity is the cement works on Punta Taozo a mile or so south, though the high-rise buildings of Anfi del Mar itself, backed by even taller orange cliffs, would be hard to miss. The approach is straightforward.

### Entrance and berthing

On rounding the breakwater a wonderfully green and luxuriant 'island', with a pontoon at 90° to shore, will be seen ahead, this is now the reception pontoon. However, the marina should not be entered without prior contact, and the harbourmaster would then be on hand to greet new arrivals. About 9m should be found in the entrance. The entire marina is notably well-kept and security is excellent.

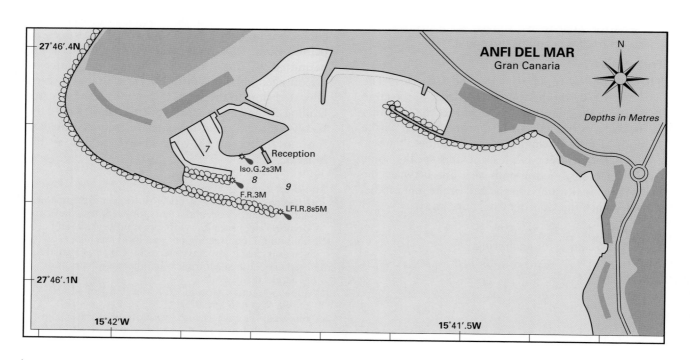

Looking west, the approach to the huge complex and small marina of Anfi del Mar, the reception pontoon is just visible on the right of the photograph  *Hilary Keatinge*

## Anchorage

East of the marina is what is considered by some as the best anchorage round Gran Canaria. The usual line of yellow floats closes off the beach area, but reasonable holding over sand and rock in about 6m is to be found a little further south. Shelter is good in prevailing northeasterly conditions, though the anchorage would become untenable in strong southerly or southeasterly winds or swell. The anchorage is under the jurisdiction of the local Guardia Civil rather than the resort, and they do take an interest in how long a boat stays in the anchorage.

Dinghies may be left for short periods at the reception pontoon in the marina – perhaps while visiting the supermarket or a restaurant – but this is a concession that should not be abused.

## Formalities and charges

Visit the marina office at the root of the inner breakwater. The harbourmaster is pleasant and helpful, and speaks English. The overnight berthing fee in 2015 for a 12m boat was €21.44, including water, electricity and 7% tax. There are discounts for stays of over 5 days.

## Facilities

*Water and electricity* On the pontoons.
*WiFi* In the hotel
*Showers* In the Club Puerto Anfi building behind the swimming pool.
*Fuel* No fuel available.
*Banks* Not as such, but several cash dispensers in the resort, including one next to the supermarket.
*Shops/provisioning* Well stocked (though expensive) supermarket on the ground floor of the resort building overlooking the marina. More varied (and cheaper) shopping in Puerto de Arguineguín.
*Cafés & restaurants* Many in the resort complex.
*Car hire & taxis* Can be arranged via the reception desk.

Looking southeast to the anchorage off Anfi del Mar
*Hilary Keatinge*

IV. THE CANARY ISLANDS

Puerto Anfi del Mar is beautifully laid out and maintained *Hilary Keatinge*

*Buses* Bus service along the main road – a steep walk up from the marina – to Puerto Rico, Maspalomas, San Agustín etc.

*Ferry* Service running seven times a day, daily, from Mogán to Arguineguin.

*Boatyard* No boatyard facilities in place or anticipated.

# Puerto Rico

27°46'·8N 15°42'·66W (Puerto Base east breakwater head)

**Lights**
*Yacht harbour (to east)*
**West breakwater**
  Q(2)R.4s11m4M Red tower 4m
**East mole**
  F.G.11m4M Green tower 3m

*Smallcraft harbour (to west)*
**West mole**
  F.R.11m5M Red tower 4m
**East mole**
  Fl.G.3s6m4M Green tower 4m

**Harbour Communications**
  VHF Ch 08, 16 call *Puerto Rico harbour*
  or *Puerto Base* (basáy)
**Puerto Deportivo Puerto Rico**
  ✆ +34 928 561 141 or +34 928 561 143
  0800–0700 daily – though the office is closed during the changeover period
  Puerto Deportivo Puerto Rico, Avda Juan Diaz Rodrigues s/n, Mogán 35130
  pricomarina@puertoricosa.com
  www.puertoricosa.com/en/puerto

## Large double harbour in tourist resort

Puerto Rico is effectively two separate harbours lying side-by-side but not interconnected. The western – Puerto Escala – is reserved for tourist ferries and local small craft, while both resident and visiting yachts berth to the east in Puerto Base. The town of Puerto Rico is a thriving holiday resort popular with tourists from northern Europe, and both parts of the harbour are owned by the same company. Though pleasantly quiet during the week, loud music continuing into the small hours has been reported at weekends.

## Approach

The most unmistakable landmark is the cement works on Punta Taozo 2·5M to the south. On close approach, the walls of the valley in which Puerto Rico lies are seen to be covered with white apartment blocks. These extend southeast of the port and one must close the shore to identify the marina entrance. Waves are likely to wash over the breakwaters in southwesterly storms.

## Entrance and berthing

A 200m breakwater running southeast separates the western (smallcraft) harbour and bathing beach from the yacht marina to the east. Once identified, the red tower on the end of the breakwater can be closed, but must not be confused with the similar tower on the western harbour molehead. The entrance to the eastern harbour, Puerto Base, opens to the southeast, with the reception/fuel berth immediately to port on entry.

Puerto Base now contains 534 berths, including 68 for yachts of 10–12m, 70 for 12–15m and 21 able to take more than 15m LOA. The breakwater is mainly occupied by tourist boats. Contact with the office several weeks in advance of arrival is essential. Space can generally be found for a yacht of more moderate size, other than in the weeks preceding the ARC departure, but booking three or four weeks before arrival is preferred. The system changes in November, when no bookings are taken. No deposit is required.

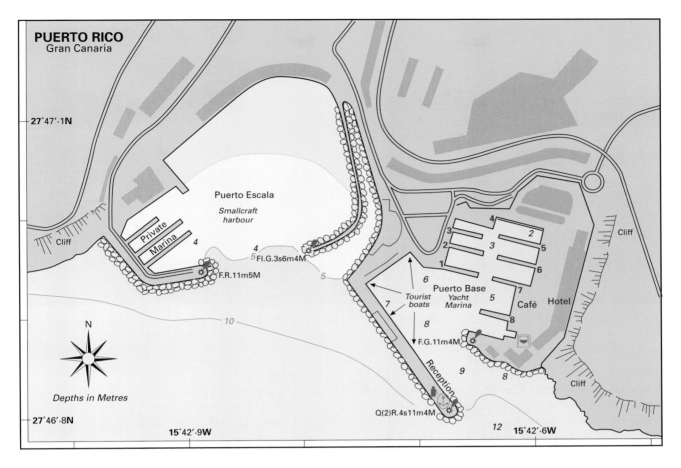

**PUERTO RICO**
Gran Canaria

27°47'·1N

Cliff

Puerto Escala
*Smallcraft
harbour*

Private
Marina

4

4
5 Fl.G.3s6m4M
F.R.11m5M

5

10

N

*Depths in Metres*

27°46'·8N

15°42'·9W

6
Tourist
boats

7

8

9

5

Reception

Q(2)R.4s11m4M

F.G.11m4M

Puerto Base
Yacht
Marina

4
3     2
2     3     5
1           6
          7
5     Café   Hotel
      8

8

12    15°42'·6W

Cliff

Cliff

Berthing is all bow or stern-to with lazy lines, and if wind and swell are strong from the southern quadrant berthing can become challenging. There are no security gates to the pontoons, though the area is patrolled by the marina personnel.

### Formalities

Ship's papers, passports for all crew members and evidence of insurance should be taken to the harbour office, most conveniently done while still at the reception berth. It is claimed to be manned at all times other than during the 0700–0800 'change over' period. The staff are helpful and several speak good English.

The double harbour at Puerto Rico, seen from the northwest  *Anne Hammick*

The entrance to Puerto Rico, with the fuel/Reception dock on the left *Hilary Keatinge*

## Charges

The cost in 2015 for a 12m boat, for one night, was approximately €24.70. This included tax at 7%, but excluded water and electricity, which are both metered. Discounts are available for longer stays. Visitors who hire cars must also pay for parking.

## Facilities

*Water* On the pontoons.

*Electricity* 220v to all berths, with 380v in some areas.

*Showers* Four blocks around Puerto Base. Showers are free, but entry needs a key for which a €30 deposit is required.

*Launderette* Near Pontoon 6, €4 tokens available in the office.

*WiFi* There is a service costing €6 per day. Also available at several of the cafés in the tourist resort.

*Fuel* Diesel and petrol from pumps near the end of the breakwater, available 0800–1645 daily.

*Bottled gas* Camping Gaz exchanges at Seilas, but currently no provision for having cylinders refilled.

*Weather forecast* Posted daily at the harbour office.

*Banks* In the tourist resort, with several cash dispensers in the harbour area.

*Shops/provisioning* Supermarkets and general shopping in the tourist resport, though a wider choice will be found in Arguineguín.

*Cafés, restaurants & hotels* A wide choice, many overlooking the marina. Crews berthed on Pontoon 8 may find the nearby café particularly convenient.

*Medical services* Centro Médico Vulcano ☏ +34 34 928 560 428 or +34 549 281 543, English-speaking staff and a wide range of services. Close to the marina.

*Car hire & taxis* Readily available.

*Buses* Bus service 10 minutes from the marina, along the coast in both directions.

*Ferries* Tourist ferries from the west mole of the smallcraft harbour (a fair walk from the marina) to Puerto de Arguineguín and Puerto de Mogán.

## Boatyard

There is a good-sized, secure yard, though the large undercover work area no longer exists. Time ashore should be arranged at the yard, and most services can be arranged.

*Travel-lift* Capacity 30 tonnes, with props and a ladder provided and a pressure washer available for hire. Arrange via the marina office.

For any work required, electronics, rigging, servicing, maintenance, general repairs, including sail repairs and Liferaft Servicing, check with Enrique and Mai Ly Seilas who own the chandlery in the yard. Open 0830–1800 weekdays, 1000–1300 Saturday ☏ +34 928 561 769, enrique@seilas.es, mai_ly@seilas.es Enrique and Mai Ly grew up in Norway and both speak excellent English as well as Scandinavian languages, Dutch and some German. In addition to being island agents for Harken and Spinlock, Raymarine and Subwing they pack a surprisingly wide range of chandlery, including Imray books and charts, into a small space and are very happy to order anything not to hand (air freight from mainland Europe normally takes 48 hours or less, but does not come cheap). If moving on to another harbour in Gran Canaria they are willing to deliver by road.

*Engineer & electronics specialist* Albert Strik advertises his services for refrigeration and air conditioning. ☏ +34 659 405 888, albert@infomogan.com

## The coast between Puerto Rico and Puerto de Mogán

There are some good day anchorages where a yacht can anchor off and enjoy a swim. But there are no particularly inviting overnight anchorages between Puerto Rico and Puerto de Mogán.

⚓ Sailing northwest from Puerto Rico one passes a large swimming area at **Playa de los Amadores**, enticingly enclosed between natural curved arms but with the ubiquitous line of yellow buoys lying about two-thirds of the way towards the mouth. Yachts occasionally anchor in the entrance while the crew swim, but a longer stay would not be popular.

⚓ Northwest of Playa de los Amadores lies the wide **Playa de Tauro**, backed by a development of the same name under the auspices of the Anfi Group who also own Anfi del Mar. According to company publicity, this is where there will be a 500-berth marina as well as two golf courses and 'an extensive range of leisure facilities'.

⚓ Continuing past Playa de Tauro one passes **Playa de los Frailes** and then a second, nameless indentation. Neither of these have road access or offer much in the way of shelter.

⚓ Finally, about 0·5M southeast of Puerto de Mogán lies **Playa del Taurito**, a holiday complex set slightly back from the seafront, which appears to make up for its narrow beach with generous man-made pools.

# Puerto de Mogán

27°48'·94N 15°45'·81W (breakwater head)

**Lights**
**Punta del Castillete** Fl.5s114m17M
   Square tower with blue and white bands 20m
**Breakwater** Fl(3)R.8·5s13m3M
   White truncated pyramid, three red bands 6m
**Reception mole** Fl(2)G.7s3m4M
   White truncated pyramid, three green bands 2m
**Outfall** Fl(4)Y.1M Yellow buoy

**Harbour Communications**
   VHF Ch 12 (0700–2100 daily)
**Marina office**
   ☎ +34 928 565 151 or +34 928 565 668
   0800–1500 weekdays only
   Torre de Control, 35140 – Puerto de Mogán
   servicios@puertomogan.es
   www.puertodemogan.es

### Attractive, long-established marina

Puerto de Mogán was originally a small fishing village with an adjacent beach, the town itself lies 8km inland. The development of holiday homes and marina was begun in the early 80s and it is one of the older – and therefore better-known – marinas in the Canaries. Nicknamed 'Little Venice', it has matured into a very attractive, colourful complex, with a safe environment for boats. The bars and restaurants overlooking the marina add much to the atmosphere while, reportedly, creating very little night-time noise. Market day is on a Friday and this draws crowds from far and wide. The marina offers

Puerto Mogán with the beach and swimming area to the east *Alan Spriggs*

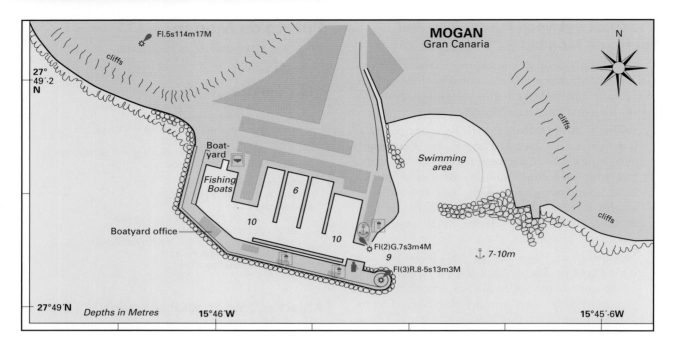

protection from all normal weather conditions, though southerly winter gales have caused severe damage to the breakwater several times over the past decades. It is a marina of choice for charter and training yachts (see RYA courses online) and the inner section of the harbour is set aside for local fishing boats. A small breakwater to the east protects a horseshoe-shaped bathing beach, with a row of small buoys marking the swimming limit. Puerto de Mogán is rightly very popular and its 216 berths, with a range from 10·5 to 45m, are usually fully occupied, many with long-term boat owners. It is advisable to book well in advance, though even then a berth may not be available in the high season (September through to the end of the year).

The lighthouse at Punta del Castillete is now blue and white
*Alan Spriggs*

## Approach

Puerto de Mogán lies at the end of one of the many steep-sided valleys that fissure the high cliffs between Arguineguín and Punta de Aldea. The Lighthouse of Castillete overlooks the marina from the cliffs to the west/north west. It is now painted white with blue bands. Fl.W.5s114m17M. The tall brown bluff on the west side of the harbour surmounted by the lighthouse and several aerials, lit by red lights, is probably the best clue from a distance and the mini lighthouse port hand entrance marker is clear when closer in. Approaching from the south, Puerto Rico will be passed 3·5M northeast of the conspicuous cement works on Punta Taozo, with Puerto de Mogán 3M further up the coast. From the northwest, where the shoreline is steep-to, a close approach can be made to the coast that can then be followed until the breakwater is located.

Under sail, the northeast trades are likely to follow you around the coast but there may be a wind shadow close inshore. To hold the wind expect to keep about 2M offshore until within sight of Puerto de Mogán, at which stage a head wind may well be encountered as the trade wind sweeps around the south coast of the island.

## Entrance and berthing

The marina opens to the east. It is important to call up on Ch 12 for berthing instructions before arrival as the 'reception' berth, on the starboard side under the marina office, is used by the local ferry and tripper boats during the day. Arriving at night the reception berth can be used if there is space available(1800–0900).

The entrance to the marina at Mogán with the office and services building to starboard
*Alan Spriggs*

The staff are helpful and assist in berthing, On approaching an allocated berth you will be handed the bight of two lazy lines attached to the wall or pontoon, there are no finger pontoons.

### Anchorage

It is possible to anchor outside the entrance in 7–10m, good holding, but there is no protection from the south and it would be unwise to leave the yacht unattended for any length of time. It can also be untenably rolly, not least due to the passing tourist ferries and fishing boats. However, shelter is good in normal, northeasterly conditions; local winds tend to blow along the coast and die at night.

Dinghies can be left in the marina for short periods, at the root of a pontoon or elsewhere so long as they do not cause an obstruction. They should not be left at the reception berth or at the outer end of any of the pontoons where they impede

It is not surprising that Mogán is also known as 'Little Venice'
*Hilary Keatinge*

larger craft manoeuvring and from where they are likely to be removed. There is no charge either for anchoring or for leaving a dinghy in the marina. Crews of anchored yachts are not entitled to use the marina facilities. There are public toilets on the beach. Water can be obtained at the fuel station. The anchorage is not part of the marina.

### Formalities

An outside stairway leads to the marina office. Although the staff are helpful not many speak English. The ship's papers and passports will be required, plus evidence of insurance. It is advisable to book at least four weeks in advance – more if the schedule permits. No deposit is required.

### Charges

In early 2015 for a 12m boat for one night it was approximately €23 including tax at 7%, but not water and electricity which are both metered and for which deposits must be paid. Discounts are available for longer stays.

### Facilities

*Water* On the pontoons, metered. Water comes from underground wells and it is not recommended as potable.

*Electricity* On the pontoons, metered.

*Showers* Access to the showers requires a key, obtainable on payment of a small deposit.

*WiFi* A new system with a daily rate charge of €6 for one device.

*Launderette* On the Calle Subida de los Riscos, just past a pharmacy (on the left very close to the marina entrance barrier). Open Monday – Saturday, staffed service 1000-1500, self service, 1500-2000.
☎ Lourdes +34 620 390 271.

*Weather forecast* Posted daily in the entrance to the marina office.

*Security* Security is good in the marina, there are CCTV cameras, marina staff on duty during the day and dedicated security staff take over in the evening at 2100. Note: the boatyard is not part of the mogán and has no security.

IV. THE CANARY ISLANDS

*Fuel* On the main breakwater under the marina office. Open 0900–1300, 1600–1800 Monday–Saturday, 0900–1400 Sunday.

*Bottled gas* Camping Gaz exchanges at the hardware store on Calle del los Riscos as mentioned above. For other brands ask in the office, there is a filling station in Salinetas.

*Medical services* Centro Medico Mogán ✆ +34 928 565 090, Av. de las Artes, 1100–1900 Monday–Saturday, 1100-1300 Sunday. English and other languages are spoken.

*Letters and Parcels* Can be sent to the marina office, address above, including registered parcels.

*Banks* Cash dispensers in the marina complex, bank behind the beach area.

*Shops/provisioning* Well stocked supermarket in the marina complex and more in the village. There is a HipoDino a 15-minute walk away and a large Spar even closer, both will deliver. The popular Friday market around the harbour offers fresh produce as well as tourist souvenirs.

*Cafés & restaurants* Dozens in the marina complex, including the cheerful Dennehys Marina bar and Restaurant that was the first to open in the complex. They also have apartments to rent overlooking the marina. www.barmarina-mogan.com

*Car hire* Via the hotel directly north of the marina control tower.

*Taxis* Readily available.

*Buses* Anti-clockwise around the coast to Las Palmas, including an express service which is claimed to take only 90 minutes.

*Ferries* Regular ferries to Puerto Rico. Check times on the Líneas Blue Bird website.

*Boatyard* Run by the Cofradía de Pescadores de Mogán (the fishermen's confederation) ✆ +34 928 565 438, cofradia.mogan@canarias.org, from their office on the breakwater, open 0800–1400, 1600–1800 weekdays, 0800–1400 Saturday. Check the availability of props. Both DIY and living aboard are permitted, the latter possibly a good idea as the boatyard has little security. Water and electricity are available and metered.

*Travel-lift* 65-tonne capacity and up to 22m LOA x 6m beam. Check that you have full insurance cover.

*Woodwork* Mike Platzer ✆ +34 928 170 551 or +34 628 104 890, mjplatzer@yahoo.de

*Stainless steel* Peter Hobbisiefken, ✆ +34 679 385 106, speaks German, English, Spanish

*Engineer* Jens Petersen ✆ +34 680 821 981, speaks German, English, Spanish and will work in other ports.

*Electronics & air conditioning* Albert Strick ✆ +34 659 405 888, speaks English, German, Dutch, Spanish. Frigoboat Rep. he will work in other ports round the island.

*Sails, rigging & canvas work* Velas Linton, Charlie Prendergast, ✆ +34 606 555 928 speaks English and French. Profurl agent. Based in Las Palmas but works in all ports.

*Chandlery* None on the complex, the ferretería on Calle del los Riscos stocks a good range of tools and other hardware or go to Arguineguín (see above).

For any specialities not listed here check the entries for Las Palmas (above) as most technicians work round the island.

## Day anchorages on the west coast of Gran Canaria

North of Puerto de Mogán towards Cabo Descojonado the coast is largely steep-to, cleft by *barrancos* some of which give onto small beaches off which anchorage is possible in settled weather. These include:

⚓ **Barranco del Parchel** 27°49'·8N 15°46'·8W

⚓ **Barranco de las Secos** 27°51'·1N 15°48'W

⚓ **Playa de Tasárte** 27°52'·2N 15°48'W

⚓ **Playa del Agua Palmito** 27°53'·6N 15°49'·1W
At the mouth of the Barranco de las Lanias, where there is a fresh water spring

⚓ **Playa del Asno** 27°54'·3N 15°49'·8W

All have deep water close inshore and are mostly in the lee of the wind acceleration zone, though these winds sometimes follow the coast around.

North of Cabo Descojonado it is advisable to keep well offshore in all but the most settled conditions. Buoys marking shellfish and other pots may be encountered all along this coast, sometimes several miles offshore in considerable depths of water.

## Puerto de la Aldea (Puerto San Nicolas)

28°00'·34N 15°49'·15W

> **Lights**
> **Breakwater**
> Fl.R.5s5M Red tower 4m

### Anchorage off small harbour

Punta de la Aldea lies some 14M north of Puerto de Mogán by sea, though a great deal further by road. The town of San Nicolas is 4km inland up the Aldea valley, with the pretty village of Puerto de la Aldea in the bay south of the headland. There are a few bars, shops and restaurants, with more shops and a filling station in San Nicolas.

The breakwater at Aldea might offer some protection
*Hilary Keatinge*

The harbour entrance to Puerto Agaete faces southeast  *Hilary Keatinge*

Limited shelter is provided by the short breakwater, which runs southwards parallel to the stony beach, but much of the interior space is occupied by moored small craft. Holding is reported good, either off the beach or inside the end of the breakwater in about 5m, though a second anchor might be wise in view of the limited swinging room. There are some rocky patches close to the beach, visible at low water.

## Agaete and Puerto de las Nieves

28°05'·87N 15°42'·68W (breakwater head)

### Lights
**Breakwater**
Fl(2)R.9s14m12M Red column 10m
**Roque Partido (Baja de la Marina)**
Q(3)G.9s5M White post, green bands 5m
*Note* Stands in the water outside the rocks which it marks
**Breakwater spur**
Fl(3)R.8m3M Red column 5M
*Note* Obscured from seaward by the breakwater

### Harbour Communications
VHF Ch 10
### Port Captain
☎ +34 928 554 227

### Gran Canaria's W coast ferry harbour

Agaete is a small town in the northwestern corner of the island. Just a kilometre from the town is Puerto de las Nieves; confusingly more likely called Puerto Agaete. Previously the island's principle port, it is now the terminal for the ferries linking the island with Tenerife. There is a small but charming fishing harbour with a short quay, a small pebble beach, some good fish restaurants and a small supermarket. Even by Canarian standards the breakwater is notably wide and high, it was extended to give improved protection for the ferries. Three tall blue and white-banded posts with triangular tops support floodlights on the quay.

The coastal scenery is spectacular with high cliffs and rock formations, though sadly the much-photographed Dedo del Dios (God's Finger) just south of the village fell during a storm in late 2005. Puerto de las Nieves is popular with locals from Las Palmas, especially at weekends.

### Approach and entry

The pale grey breakwater is easily seen from offshore, and there are no hazards in the approach – other than the frequent ferries that back into the harbour. The entrance is wide with good depth, and the rocks to the east marked by a green and white striped post. The port officials are mainly involved with the ferry port.

### Berthing

There is very little room for visitors and it is unlikely that you will be able to book in advance. A boat may be able to raft up to a fishing boat, until they want to leave. The authorities are said to allow up to three

The ferry needs plenty of space to back into its berth
*Hilary Keatinge*

yachts to raft up alongside the rough tidal wall overnight. A fender board is advised if 'inside boat' as there is considerable surge from the ferries. The three pontoons in the northwest corner are fully occupied by local boats, though it may occasionally be possible to find space if a regular occupant is absent. If going ashore it is advisable to lock the boat.

## Anchorage

There is good water off the end of the breakwater, with the green and white post marking Roque Partido. Anchor between Roque Partido and the short inner mole in 5–6m over black sand and stones, taking care to remain well clear of the ferry berth. Holding is poor and following repeated rockfalls much of the bottom is foul. The swimming beach is delineated by posts joined by strings of easily-seen floats. There are several sets of steps at which to land, in addition to the beach and a slipway next to the travel-lift dock, but the three pontoons are protected by security gates.

## Formalities and charges

On arrival visit the harbour authorities at their office in the ferry terminal.

## Facilities

*Water & electricity* On the pontoons only.
*Fuel* No fuel station in the port area.
*Banks* In Agaete, but a cash dispenser in the entrance to the Laguete Restaurant (which overlooks the harbour) and another a few streets away.
*Shops/provisioning* A small supermarket.
*Cafés & restaurants* Numerous, with a particular reputation for local fish dishes.
*Bus* Regular service to Las Palmas and elsewhere.
*Ferries* Frequent ferry service to Santa Cruz de Tenerife.
*Travel-lift* 70-tonne capacity backed by ample hardstanding.
*Chandlery* A small and rather anonymous ferretería, which sells some chandlery, one street back from the harbour.

# Puerto de Sardina del Norte

28°09'·14N 15°41'·86W (SE molehead)

**Lighthouse**
**Punta Roque Negro** Fl(4)20s48m20M
    White tower, red bands 23m

## Colourful bay with little shelter

Tucked into an indented and largely unspoilt bay about a mile southeast of Punta Sardina and its distinctive lighthouse situated on the north west corner of the island is the small fishing village of Puerto de Sardina del Norte. The short quay was damaged in storms some years ago and it is no longer possible to lie alongside. Anchor off the sandy beach in 5–6m clear of the many local moorings, fish pots, rocks and swimmers – the bay is very popular with divers who come in search of manta rays. There are steps in the harbour close to the crane that lifts out the fishing boats. Facilities are limited. There are a couple of small fish restaurants beside the harbour plus a few shops in the rapidly expanding village up the hill, but little else.

Looking towards Puerto Agaete along the windy north coast of Gran Canaria *Hilary Keatinge*

# Tenerife

**Between 28°00'N–28°35'N and 16°07'W–16°55'W**

## Introduction

Roughly triangular in shape, Tenerife is the largest island in the archipelago with an area of 2,043km², a population of around 900,000 and the highest mountain in Spain, El Teide, a gigantic volcanic cone, often snow-capped, rising to 3,717m above the frequent sea of cloud.

The backbone of mountains runs east-west and causes a dramatic climatic divide between the north and south of the island. Winds carry moisture up the north face of the range, resulting in high winter rainfall and a humid, temperate climate, ideal for many varieties of crops. The world-famous botanical gardens at the foot of the fertile Orotova valley, on the outskirts of Puerto de la Cruz, were established

on the orders of Charles III of Spain (1716–1788) in an attempt to acclimatise tropical garden plants from the New World before onward shipment to mainland Europe.

There are three major towns in the northern part of the island – the capital, Santa Cruz de Tenerife, which has wide tree-lined streets, art deco buildings and the best produce market in the Canaries. Up behind Santa Cruz is the picturesque university town of La Laguna, the old capital, which dates back to the 16th century and is typified by narrow streets, churches and monasteries. And half way along the north coast is Puerto de la Cruz, the first tourist destination on the islands when in Victorian times it became a favourite English wintering resort. The

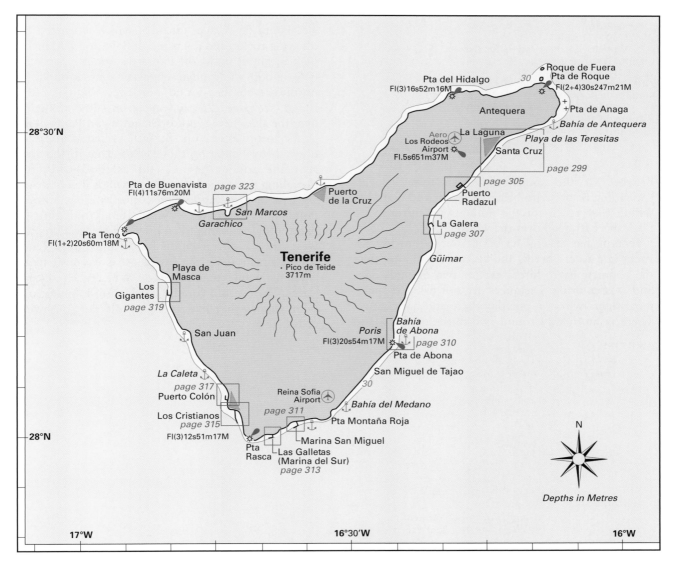

IV. THE CANARY ISLANDS

## Navigation

For information on **Magnetic Variation**, **Tides** and **Tidal Streams** see pages 224-225

Full **Emergency Service** information is on page 227

**Weather** and **Navigational Broadcasts** are listed on page 228

**Marine farms**
Three marine farms, each marked by four yellow pillar buoys with × topmarks either Fl.Y.5s3M or Fl(4)Y.11s3M, lie off the northeast coast of Tenerife, centred on 28°30'·9N 16°09'·6W, 28°30'·6N 16°09'·7W and 28°22'·7N 16°21'W.

**Coast Radio Station** (24 hour)
**Tenerife** 28°18'·4N 16°30'·2W
**VHF** Ch 16, 16
**DSC** VHF MMSI 002241026

**Lights**
**Punta de Roque (Punta de Anaga)**
   Fl(2+4)30s247m21M Grey tower,
   white building and lantern 12m
**Los Rodeos Airport**
   Aero Fl.5s651m37M Metal tower 14m
**Punta de Abona**
   Fl(3)20s54m17M 214°-vis-040°
   White tower, red bands 39m
**Punta Rasca**
   Fl(3)12s51m17M
   White tower, three red bands 32m
**Punta Teno**
   Fl(1+2)20s60m18M
   White tower, red bands 20m
**Punta de Buenavista**
   Fl(4)11s76m20M Square white tower 40m
**Punta del Hidalgo**
   Fl(3)16s52m16M Masonry tower 50m

and the places of interest are well signposted. A characteristic feature are the *barrancos* or ravines. The beautiful Barranco del Infierno belies its name, 'Hell's Gorge' attracting hikers and archeologists alike. The narrow winding road cut into the mountainside between Garachico and Los Gigantes in the north, is slightly more challenging for the driver, with glimpses of the sea through swirling clouds down the dramatic ravines; the drama of it all will not easily be forgotten.

On a clear day a drive along the ridge of the mountain range to view El Teide is breath-taking. There is a cable car that takes visitors to within a few hundred feet of the top, though not if the wind gets up. With an extensive plain of solidified lava to the south there are many opportunities in the area for the walkers and photographers. The surreal landscape is a favourite with film-makers. The ascent to the peak is not advised for those with high blood pressure or heart problems.

### Approach and navigation

There are few hazards on approaching Tenerife other than on the north coast between Punta Teno and Punta de Anaga, much of which is fringed by off-lying rocks, and a 4m shoal, Bajo de La Mancha Blanca, about 0·4M off Punta de Anaga. However, beware both the wind acceleration zones around the northeast, southeast and northwest limits of the island (see page 226) and the strong downdraughts over the cliffs between Los Gigantes and Punta Teno at its northwestern tip. Be well prepared and reef down before entering these areas. Due to the way that the topography of the island bends the prevailing trade winds, northeast winds dominate on the east of the island whereas northwest winds are dominant on the west. Winds tend to reduce at night, often changing to an offshore breeze along the west coast between Punta Rasca and Punta Teno. Sailing north along the east coast is easier at night when the wind strength is likely to be much reduced.

Keep an eye out for the bottlenose dolphins and pilot whales that live and play off the southwest coast.

beaches of the southwest, with today's ever-expanding resorts, are bringing beach and night-life within easy reach for the millions of visitors who flock there from all over the world.

Tenerife has several harbours suitable to leave a yacht in a secure berth, and visitors should not miss the opportunity to hire a car for two or three days and go exploring. Distances are not excessive with most sights within a one day there-and-back range. There is motorway round two-thirds of the island

## Harbours and anchorages down the east coast

Most visiting yachts will make landfall on the steep sided east coast with its almost continuous ribbon of modern development on the shore side of the TF1 motorway and the older towns perched in the heights behind. Worth noting if taking to the roads that the coastal town often takes the same name as the original hillside town, sometimes confusing at roundabouts (San Miguel and Guimar are just two that might confuse the unwary).

## Bahía de Antequera

28°32′N 16°07′·8W (quay)

### Popular open anchorage

A pretty bay about 5M northeast of Santa Cruz, sheltered from northerly quadrant winds by Punta de Antequera but totally open to the south, Bahía de Antequera is a popular destination for the many small motorboats kept in Santa Cruz and San Andrés, and in the right conditions makes a reasonable overnight anchorage. It offers good holding in 5m or more over sand, off a black sand beach. There is a small quay on the east side of the bay from which it is possible to climb a path over the headland. There are sometimes some campers, but nothing whatsoever ashore, not even a road.

## Playa de las Teresitas (San Andrés)

28°30′·21N 16°11′·3W (breakwater south head)

### Daytime Anchorage with beach access

The town of San Andrés with its adjoining tree lined Playa de las Teresitas, lies some 4M north of Santa Cruz city centre. The golden sand beach – imported from the Sahara many years ago - is protected by a long rocky mole running parallel to the shore about 150m off, with an E cardinal off the southeast end. This creates a safe swimming area and space for the many small craft lying on their own moorings. The gaps at both ends are narrow and it would not be possible for a yacht to enter. In settled conditions there is good holding outside in 10–15m and a dinghy can be taken through the southern opening.

Many claim that Playa de las Teresitas is the best beach on Tenerife, very popular with locals, not least because it is remote from the main tourist centres. The small town of San Andrés has shops, a bank and a post office, and is famous for its local fish restaurants, many of them along the beach. There is a tap on the quay and swimmers' (i.e. cold) shower on the beach.

Both the beach at Playa de las Teritas (San Andrés) and the many small boats are sheltered by a long mole, just visible to the right of the photo *Hilary Keatinge*

# Santa Cruz de Tenerife

**Lights**
Full entrance and interior Lights for the Dársena Pesquera and Dársena de los Llanos are listed under those headings. Further Lights exist within the Dársena Este and Dársena Sur.

**Dársena Pesquera (Marina Tenerife)**
**Southwest mole**
  Fl.R.5s13m3M Red post 6m
**Breakwater head**
  Fl.G.5s11m3M Green column 5m

**Dársena Este**
 **Breakwater, northeast angle**
  Q(6)+LFl.15s11m5M
  South cardinal post, ⚑ topmark 3m
 **Breakwater, southwest angle**
  Q(6)+LFl.15s8m2M
  South cardinal post, ⚑ topmark 3m
 **Breakwater head**
  Fl(2)G.7s13m9M Green tower 6m
 *Note* Various other lights exist inside both Dársena Este and Dársena Sur

**Dársena Sur (Dársena de Anaga) Breakwater head**
  Q(2)R.7s19m10M Red tower 5m

**Dársena de los Llanos (Marina Santa Cruz)**
**Breakwater angle** Q(3)10s9m5M
  East cardinal post, ⚑ topmark 2m
**Breakwater head** Fl(3)G.9s13m9M
  Green tower 6m
**Southwest mole** Fl(3)R.10s8m9M
  Red post standing in the water

**Harbour Communications**
  VHF Ch 16, Ch 74 working Ch 12
**Port Authority**
  ☏ +34 922 596 447 (port operations)
  atraques@puertosdetenerife.org

The platforms alongside for servicing are very conspicuous
*Hilary Keatinge*

## Tenerife's capital city and commercial port

Santa Cruz is a bustling, increasingly high-rise city with attractive plazas, lush parks, good shopping and a very cosmopolitan feel. It is the administrative centre of not just the island but also the Province of Santa Cruz de Tenerife that includes the more western islands. Since 1927, jointly with Gran Canaria, it is the seat of government of all the islands (Cabildo Insular); with a Presidency that rotates on a four-year cycle.

Puerto Santa Cruz de Tenerife is by far the largest commercial port of the archipelago. It covers a vast area and has not been fully developed by any means. It is a busy hub for trans-shipping cargoes coming and going from Europe, Africa and the Americas. There is a large oil refinery and often towering into the skyline are oil platforms that have come in for servicing from stations off the length of the African coast. The port is an important commercial fishing centre, it is a ferry port, and is increasingly on the cruise ship schedule. For recreational craft there are four marinas, two of them open to visitors. The two marinas that accept visiting yachts in Santa Cruz de Tenerife are Marina Tenerife and Marina Santa Cruz. They are situated in separate harbours with entrances some 3M apart. The more general information about specialist boatyard services, being common to both, will be listed under Marina Tenerife.

The whole extensive harbour zone is effectively split into four sections behind separate breakwaters:

*Dársena Pesquera and Marina Tenerife* To the north is the Dársena Pesquera. Here are the fishing industry's docks backed by processing and storage buildings. South of the fisheries dock on the land side is Puerto Chico, a private marina and, most importantly, next to it, the only fuel dock in Santa Cruz for pleasure craft. On the outer mole is Marina Tenerife, with facilities for visiting yachts and a boatyard.

*Dársena Este* The next section of harbour, the Dársena Este, encompasses the massive container storage parks.

*Dársena Sur* Cruise ships and ferries berth alongside in the Dársena Sur, with a small harbour for the Real Club Nautico.

*Dársena de los Llanos and Marina Santa Cruz* Most southerly is the Dársena de los Llanos. Entrance to this part of the port is from the south. Commercial shipping berths inside the breakwater, ferries berth on the mainland side. Marina Santa Cruz (previously known as Marina del Atlantico) is through the narrow opening at the northern head of the main basin.

The Auditorio de Tenerife 'Adan Martin' is the architectural symbol of the island. It makes for a
very conspicuous landmark on the approach to Santa Cruz  *Hilary Keatinge*

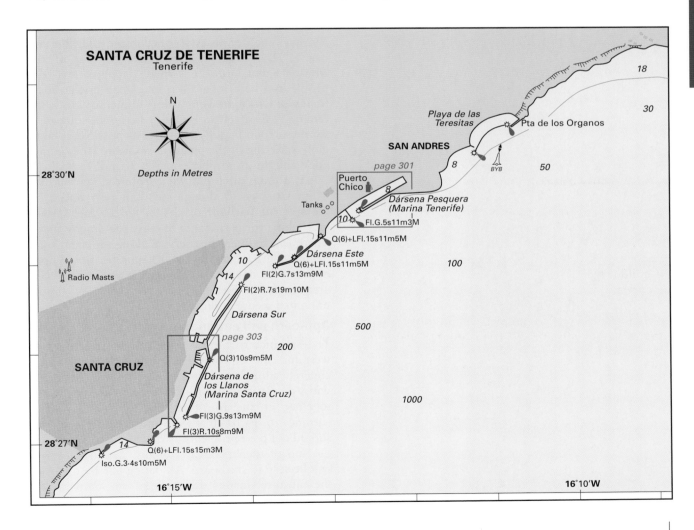

IV. THE CANARY ISLANDS

### Approach to Puerto Santa Cruz de Tenerife

*From the northeast* The high backbone of the island extends from the northeast cape, Punta de Anaga right up to the peak of El Teide. Keeping at least 1M offshore, the rocky peninsula of Punta de Antequera is passed, followed by Punta del Roquete. One mile further southeast is Punta de los Organos, at the northern end of the Playa de la Teresitas. A further mile down the coast will be seen the first of the breakwaters, the Dársena Pesquera. Land has been reclaimed near the root of this and it is still fairly undeveloped.

*From the south* After passing the storage tanks and chimneys of Puerto Caballo and the small headland of Punta Maragallo the entrance to the Dársena de los Llanos will be seen about 0·5M ahead. The very conspicuous white and shining Auditorio de Tenerife lies directly south west of the entrance to the basin, visible from at least 10M off on a clear day.

# Marina Tenerife

28°29'·57N 16°12'·66W

**Lights**
**Southwest mole**
Fl.R.5s13m3M Red post 6m
**Breakwater head**
Fl.G.5s11m3M Green column 5m
**Reclaimed area**
Q(6)+LFl.15s9m2M South cardinal post, ⚑ topmark
**Reclaimed area**
Fl.Y.5s3M Spherical yellow buoy, × topmark
**Entrance, southeast side**
Fl(2)G.7s5m1M
Green column standing in the water
(obscured from seaward by the breakwater)
**Entrance, northwest side**
Fl(2)R.7s5m1M
Red column standing in the water
(obscured from seaward by the breakwater)

**Harbour Communications**
VHF Ch 09 (24 hours)
**Marina Tenerife**
☎ +34 922 591 247
0900–1300, 1500–1900 weekdays,
1000–1400 weekends and holidays
Dársena Pesquera, Vía Auxilliar s/n, 38180
Santa Cruz de Tenerife
marinatenerife@nauticaydeportes.com
www.nauticaydeportes.com

### Quiet, secluded marina in Dársena Pesquera

Marina Tenerife was established in the early 90s and has a very different atmosphere to that of the Marina Santa Cruz. It is much favoured by local people as a base for jet-skis and small power boats (many of which are kept ashore and craned in when required). Every effort is made to keep the somewhat sterile surroundings as attractive as possible, even to daily watering of the plant tubs. Onsite facilities are good and the atmosphere notably friendly.

It is a long, often hot walk from the marina into Santa Cruz itself, though this can be reduced by crossing the harbour by dinghy to the fuel station and asking for permission to leave the dinghy there. There is a frequent bus service along the main road behind the harbour (every 10 minutes throughout much of the day). Alternatively the marina staff can arrange for a hire car or taxi. There is almost unlimited secure parking.

### Approach and entrance

The entrance to the Dársena Pesquera faces south west and can be positively identified close north of a concrete silo, five oil tanks and two large buildings with red and blue roofs respectively, all close together at the northeast end of the city. The entrance to the basin is wide and unobstructed, and should not pose problems by day or night. Rounding the end of the breakwater elbow, Marina Tenerife will be seen to starboard. A floating barrier opposite the entrance shelters the marina from minor debris

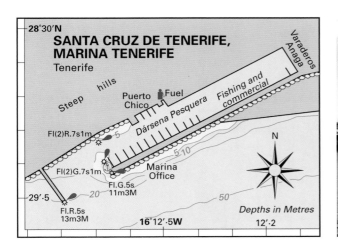

The fuel dock in Dársena Pesquera, next to Puerto Chico marina *Hilary Keatinge*

and oil pollution, though the marina has now expanded beyond this with several more smallcraft pontoons.

## Berthing

There are 220 berths for boats from 6–16m. There is a minimum depth of 9m. The marina is always very full and it is imperative to make contact prior to arrival requesting a berth. There is no reception berth. The pontoons to the southwest berth the smallest boats, with size increasing as one continues northwest. The furthest pontoon can accommodate yachts of up to 16m, all berths being alongside substantial finger pontoons.

## Formalities

The marina office is situated just inside the head of the breakwater next to the slipway and crane. Excellent English is spoken by the office staff but this may not be the case out of hours. Skippers of non-EU registered yachts, or those with non-EU crew, may also need to visit the Policía Nacional in their office in the Fred Olsen ferry terminal overlooking the Dársena Sur.

## Charges

In 2015 one night for a 12.1m x 4m yacht was approximately €18 and includes water, electricity and tax at 7%.

## Facilities

*Water & electricity* On the pontoons.
*WiFi* near the office, but there are plans to extend coverage to the pontoons.
*Showers* Next to the marina office.
*Laundry* No. Can be arranged through the marina office.
*Security* Excellent; behind an electronically operated gate, just past the Guarda Civil post. There are also CCTV cameras installed, and Marina Tenerife would be a good choice if wishing to leave a yacht unattended for several weeks – always assuming a berth is available.
*Fuel* The fuel station is beside Puerto Chico, so opposite the marina, access sometimes difficult due to boats berthed at the marina and wind conditions. Open 0700-2030.

*Bottled gas* At the DISA station in Santa Cruz, close to Corte Ingles.
*Medical services* Several hospitals in the city plus dentists, opticians etc.
*Banks, shops & provisioning* See Marina Santa Cruz, also in San Anrés. There is an outlet in the port selling frozen foods.
*Café* At the marina, Kiosco is open 0930-1800 (closed on Mondays)
*Car hire & taxis* Ask in the office.
*Buses* Frequent buses to the centre of Santa Cruz from a bus stop opposite the wholesale fish market close to the Dársena Pesquera. Island buses depart from the main bus station on Avenida Tres de Mayo to both the island's airports, Los Cristianos (for ferries to the western islands) and many other points.
*Airports* Most international flights come into Tenerife Sur, Granadilla, in the south (40m, about an hour away), Inter-island flights are from Tenerife Norte, San Cristóbal (9m, about 30 minutes)
*Ferry* To all the islands (except El Hierro) and to Huelva in Spain.

## Boatyard

Varaderos Anaga
☎ +34 922 591 313
0900-1700 weekdays only
Good English and German spoken.
varaderosanaga@nauticaydeportes.com
www.nauticaydeportes.com

The company NADETESA incorporates Nautica y Deportes Tenerife, Varaderos Anaga and Marina Tenerife. The boatyard, Varaderos Anaga is situated at the head of the Dársena Pesquera, with a dedicated waiting pontoon and plenty of hard-standing, some undercover work area, and no shortage of yacht-length props. A pressure washer is available and services include engineering, welding and other metalwork, GRP repairs, painting and antifouling. Over the years the yard has received consistent praise from visiting yachtsmen, both for their work and for the careful way in which yachts are lifted and moved. Bookings must be confirmed in

IV. THE CANARY ISLANDS

Looking northeast up Santa Cruz's Dársena Pesquera, with Marina Tenerife in the foreground. The Varaderos Anaga boatyard, which is owned by the same company, lies at the head of the long narrow basin *Marina Tenerife*

advance, two to three weeks' notice is normally sufficient. Prices are very reasonable, particularly if paid in advance.

*Security* Good, with CCTV cameras. Owners can do their work and can live aboard with access to water, electricity, toilets and showers.

*Travel-lift* 70-tonne capacity travel-lift (maximum 23m LOA, 6m beam) at the boatyard. A crane is available for mast removal. There is a forklift for handling smaller boats.

*Engineers* There are four big companies operating in Santa Cruz specializing in servicing boats of all sizes. To save time seek advice at the boatyard. Nearly all major international brands are represented by one or more of those listed, and items not in stock can be ordered. This guide is an outline of the services on offer:

1. Nautica y Deportes Tenerife SA, Dársena Pesquera 18, 38180 SC de Tenerife. ☎ +34 922 549 840.
   They have an office just 100m outside the yard and import and service a wide range of engines, inboard and outboard.
2. Spinnaker Canarias ☎ +34 922 243 975, 1000-1400 weekdays, 1000-1300 Saturday.
   Juan Montalban and Javier Abad (who speaks good English), C/San Juan Bautista 32, 38002 SC de Tenerife.
   Agents for Beneteau, Selden, B&G, Lowrance and others. Wide range of engineering expertise, plus rigging and sail repairs.
3. Nordest C/Antonio Benavides, 91, La Matanza, 38370 SC de Tenerife ☎ +34 922 577 322, nordest@nordest-canarias.com
   Agents for ProFurl, Selden, Aqua signal, Lewmar, Max prop and many other brands. Large range of general chandlery, charts.
4. Blancomar Nautica, C/ Santiago 109, 38001 SC de Tenerife ☎ +34 922 275 058, info@blancomarnautica.es
   Agents for Vetus, Hempel. Contact for sail repair. Good range of general chandlery, charts.
5. La Marina, Transversal 1, Dársena Pesquera, SC de Tenerife ☎ +34 922 549 136, 0800-1300 and 1500-1800 weekdays, 0800-1300 Saturday.
   Or at Celia Cruz 6, 38003 SC de Tenerife ☎ +34 922 209 851 0830-1300 and 1530-1900 weekdays, Saturday 0830-1300, administration@lamarinasal.com
   A general chandlery with an impressive catalogue.

*Charts* The Centro Geofísico de Canarias is official agent for the Spanish Hydrographic Office ☎ +34 9922 287 054, Calle La Marina 20, SC de Tenerife

*Liferaft servicing* Inprecasa ☎ +34 9922 650 131 or +34 617 442 068, inprecasa@inprecasa.com, www.inprecasa.com. Premises at La Laguna about 10km northwest of Santa Cruz is a Plastimo service centre. Most marina offices will arrange liferaft delivery and return.
Liferaft Services SL, ☎ +34 922 620 617 ebm@liferaft-services.com (in Santa Maria del Mar, about 9km south of the city). They service most makes including Avon, Plastimo, Viking, etc.

# Marina Puerto Chico

28°29'·76N 16°12'·55W (central pontoon)

**Marina Communications**
VHF Ch 09
**Marina Office**
Office ☎ +34 922 549 818
pch@marinaalgomera.com

Marina Puerto Chico lies on the northwest side of the Dársena Pesquera. A few of its 42 berths can take yachts of up to 12m, but space is seldom available for visitors.

# Marina Santa Cruz

28°27'·34N 16°14'·82W (breakwater head)

**Lights**
**Breakwater angle** Q(3)10s8m5M
East cardinal post, ♦ topmark 2m
**Breakwater head** Fl(3)G.9s12m9M
Green tower 6m
**Ldg Lts on 354°** *Front* Q.1s8m3M
*Rear*, 75m from front, Q.13m3M
White framework towers, red bands 5/11m
**Southwest mole** Fl(3)R.10s7m9M
Red post standing in the water
**Breakwater head spur** Fl(4)G.11s5m3M
Green post standing in the water 2m
**Obstruction** Fl(4)R.11s7m3M
Red post standing in the water
**Ro-Ro berth** Fl.R.5s5m1M
Red pyramid 2m
**Breakwater interior spur**
Fl.G.5s5m1M Green pyramid tower 3m
**Marina entrance, east side** Q.G.5m1M
Green post, white strut 2m
**Marina entrance, west side, north corner**
Q.R.5m1M Red post, white strut 2m
**Marina entrance, west side, south corner**
Q.R.5m1M Red post, white strut 2m
*Note* The above two lights, which are very close together, have identical characteristics. Should only one be working, and ambient light insufficient to see the mole itself, hug the main breakwater to ensure safe entrance

**Harbour Communications**
VHF Ch 09 (24 hours)
**Marina office**
☎ +34 922 292 184
0900–1900, weekdays, 0900–1300 weekends
Muelle de Enlace, Dársena de Los Llanos, s/n. 38001
Santa Cruz de Tenerife
reservas@marinasantacruz.com
www.marinasantacruz.com

## Large marina with space for visitors

Developed by the Port Authority in the mid '90s this marina is now run as a concession by a private company. The present infrastructure was opened in 2007, housing the marina office and facilities. The marina has about 400 berths for vessels of up to 100m. Despite the very enclosed basin, winter storms that often come from the south can cause a

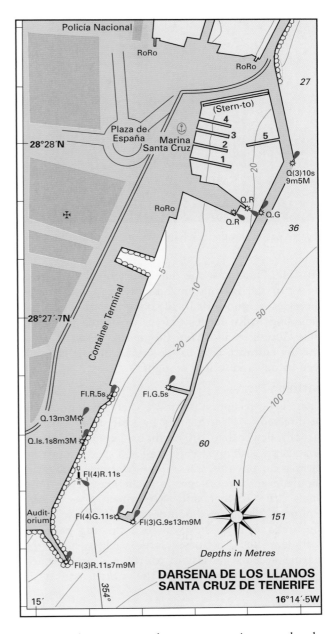

surge in the marina and extra precautions need to be taken. Coiled steel or rubber springs on the dock lines will help to dampen the forces.

## Approach and entrance

Contact must be made with Santa Cruz Harbour Control on VHF Ch 12 at least three miles off, prior to entering the Dársena de los Llanos (and again before leaving the marina basin on departure). On receiving permission to proceed, call Marina Santa Cruz on VHF Ch 09 for berthing instructions.

There are leading marks on the approach to the breakwater (Q.1s3M and Iso.1s3M) though this is by no means essential for most yachts since there are no off lying dangers, except for shipping. The entire harbour carries a minimum of 5m (other than in the entrance to the Barranco de Santos, 28°27'·78N on the mainland side). In most conditions entry is

IV. THE CANARY ISLANDS

A yacht passes through the narrow entrance to Marina Santa Cruz, at the head of the Dársena de los Llanos  *Anne Hammick*

possible. Once past the outer port breakwater it is 0·6M to the marina entrance. Keep a lookout as there is a good deal of commercial shipping, including RoRo ferries that berth on the mainland side. Access to and from the marina basin is via a narrow entrance next to the breakwater. It is easily seen by day and well lit at night.

### Berthing

There is no reception pontoon, yachts will normally be directed to a berth either by VHF, from a rib, or visually. Fewer than 100 berths are occupied by local boats, and with apparently limitless space to raft-up there is no obvious reason why Marina Santa Cruz should ever have to turn a yacht away. The busy times are October and November. Five of the pontoons have finger pontoons, while those lining the north wall go stern-on to a floating pontoon with lazy lines. Seriously large yachts – and the marina accepts vessels up to 100m – are berthed against the quayside to the northeast. It is

occasionally found that berth holders put an extra line to the adjacent pontoon to keep themselves off.

### Formalities

The marina office will be found in the services block, near the root of pontoon No.2, and should be visited taking the usual ship's papers, passports and insurance documents. The front office staff are friendly and speak reasonable English and French. Skippers of non-EU registered yachts, or those with non–EU crew, may also need to visit the Policía Nacional in their office in the Fred Olsen ferry terminal overlooking the main Dársena Sur.

### Charges

In 2015 the charge for a 12·5m yacht for one night in the low season was €27.15. Berthing charges for yachts up to 20m include water and electricity, otherwise metered. There are discounts for longer stays and it is highly recommended to contact the office in advance for full information.

The spacious Marina Santa Cruz de Tenerife with the city in the background  *Marina Santa Cruz*

## Facilities

*Water and electricity* On the pontoons.

*WiFi* Not on the pontoons but in the mostly open area near the drinks dispenser.

*Showers* At the rear of the office. Hot water is dependent on solar panels.

*Laundry* Near the marina office. Coin operated. The office can arrange for a laundry service who will collect and return at €3 a kilo.

*Weather* Forecasts posted daily.

*Security* 24/7. Security gates are fitted to the pontoons, and owners asked to keep them closed, this is not always done. There is also a security barrier from the car park.

*Fuel* Delivery can be arranged through the marina office. The service needs to be booked at least two working days in advance.

*Bottled gas* In the city.

*Medical Service* Seek advice from the office. There are at least three clinics nearby.

*Banks* Nearest off the Plaza de España.

*Shops/provisioning* There are several large supermarkets in the city. Both El Corte Inglés and HiperDino on Avenida Tres de Mayo, there is even a Marks & Spencer on Calle El Pilar.

*Produce market* The excellent Nuestra Senora de Africa market on Calle de San Sebastián is within walking distance of Marina Santa Cruz (cross the Barranco de Santos via the Puente Serador). There is a small supermarket in the basement.

*Café, Bars, Hotels* Nothing at the marina. Huge number in the city.

*Car Hire* Ask in the office. Cicar on Muelle Ribera is likely the nearest.

*Taxi* Ask in the office or try near the ferry terminal

*Airports* Most international flights come into Tenerife Sur, Granadilla, in the south (40m, about an hour away, mostly motorway), Inter-island flights are from Tenerife Norte, San Cristóbal (9m, about 30 minutes)

*Ferry* to all the islands (except El Hierro) and to Huelva in Spain.

For Boatyard and associated services see Marina Tenerife.

# Puerto Caballo and Puerto del la Hondura

28°26'·92N 16°15'·87W (pierhead of the more southerly of the two)

## An oil terminal port

About 1M southwest of the entrance to Dársena de los Llanos there are two piers used by tankers and other bulk cargo carriers. The bigger tankers do not even come alongside but unload from the mooring buoys lying inside three yellow pillar buoys, from the north: with x topmark, Fl.Y.10s2M, Fl.Y.4s3M and Fl.Y.3s4M respectively. There are four pairs of leading lights marking the approach. A refinery with several chimneys, backed by an extensive tank farm lies behind and north of the piers.

# Puerto Deportivo Radazul

28°25'·03N 16°19'·44W (breakwater head)

**Lights**
**Marina breakwater**
Fl(2)G.10s10m5M Green post 6m
**Marina north mole**
Fl(2)R.7s4m3M Red post 2m
**Club do Mar breakwater**
Q(6)+LFl.15s10m3M
South cardinal post, ⚏ topmark 4m
(not associated with the marina – see next page)

**Harbour Communications**
VHF Ch 09 (24 hours)
**Marina office**
☎ +34 922 680 933
0900–1700 weekdays, 1030–1300 Saturdays
Urb. Radazul s/n, El Rosario, 38109 SC de Tenerife
puertodeportivoradazul@gmail.com
www.puertodeportivoradazul.com

## Small, secure, friendly marina

Puerto Radazul is run as a concession with about 200 berths, the largest able to take a 25m yacht. Whether seeking to reserve a long or short-term berth it is advisable to contact the marina office well in advance, by telephone if possible. The marina provides a suitable place to leave a yacht unattended, either afloat or ashore.

## Approach and entrance

The marina lies 6M southwest of Santa Cruz and just south of Punta de Guadamojete. The entrance is west-facing and narrow. There is a group of tall apartment blocks above the marina, which is sited under a high cliff. A short, curved breakwater protects the Club de Mar close east of the marina but is not associated with it. A swimming area, marked off by a string of small yellow buoys, lies off the beach close west of the entrance. There is a 2-knot speed limit in the approach. The end of the short north mole doubles as reception berth.

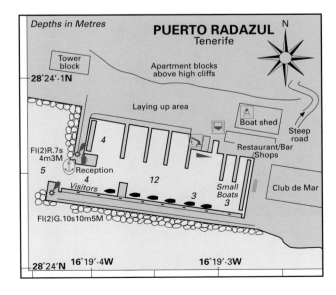

## Berthing

Pontoons with fingers line the north side of the harbour, with stern-to moorings against the south breakwater and the north mole. Short-term visitors are normally berthed on the pontoon alongside the breakwater just inside the entrance, and this is the best place to go if arriving outside office hours.

## Formalities

Visit the marina office on the north mole with the usual paperwork, including evidence of insurance. Good English is spoken.

## Charge

In 2015, one night for a 12m boat for was €18.72 + 7% tax and €1 per crew member. This included water and electricity. Discounts are available for longer stays when paying in advance. Reservations are essential for the boatyard.

## Facilities

*Water and electricity* On the pontoons.

*Showers* Near the office, with several more let into the marina walls. Entry key in return for small deposit.

*WiFi* In the office area and in the local bars and restaurants.

*Weather forecast* Available from the marina office on request.

*Security* There are security gates, and round-the-clock patrols combined with the marina's quiet position provide reliable security.

*Fuel* At the reception berth, open 0800–2000. Payment by credit card is accepted.

*Bottled gas* Exchange of calor gas cylinders possible through the marina. Refilling propane would have to be done in Santa Cruz de Tenerife.

*Shops/provisioning* Large supermarket in the commercial centre up the hill, open 0900-2100 Monday to Saturday, plus pharmacy, etc.

*Cafés, restaurants & hotels* In the holiday complex behind the harbour, several restaurants on the quayside.

*Car hire & taxis* Can be arranged through the marina office.

*Buses* Bus service to Santa Cruz and elsewhere from near the marina entrance.

*Airport* to Tenerife Sur approx. 40 minutes, Tenerife Norte approx. 20 minutes

*Boatyard* Owners can do their own work, though the marina staff can advise on who best to call in for various jobs. It is permitted to live aboard a yacht while ashore.

*Travel-lift* There are two, the larger rated at 60-tonnes, with no shortage of hardstanding.

*Engineers* Large workshop in the marina complex. Cris Motors SL ☏ +34 922 681 814 are agents for Volvo Perkins and Yanmar as well as several makes of outboard. The charter company Alboran can provide a wide range of expertise on site, their office is beside the marina office. They have a good selection of spare parts. Call Fernando Garzón, who speaks good English ☏ +34 629 757 944 (others speak German, Polish, French and Russian). They are happy to help out on weekdays, but are generally occupied on changeover days.

*Chandlery* Cris Motors have a small chandlery. Can order if necessary. See listings for Santa Cruz, only 20 minutes away by bus.

The small well run marina of Puerto Radazul is well tucked in under the east coast cliffs of Tenerife *Puerto Deportivo Radazul*

# Club Náutico y Social La Galera

28°21'·57N 16°21'·92W (breakwater head)

**Lights**
**Breakwater head**
  Fl(3)G.9s6m5M Green post 2m
  **Breakwater spur**
  Fl(3)G.9s3M Green post (synchronised with 2827·931)
**Inner mole**
  Fl(3)R.9s4m3M Red post 1m
  *Note* Obscured from offshore by the breakwater

**Harbour Communications**
  VHF Ch 09
  ☎ +34 922 503 282 or +34 922 500 915
  0900–1300, 1700–2000 weekdays, 1000–1400 Saturday
  Puerto Deportivo La Galera, Avda Maritima 40, 38530
  Candelaria, Santa Cruz de Tenerife
  secretaria@puertodeportivolagalera.com
  www.puertodeportivolagalera.com

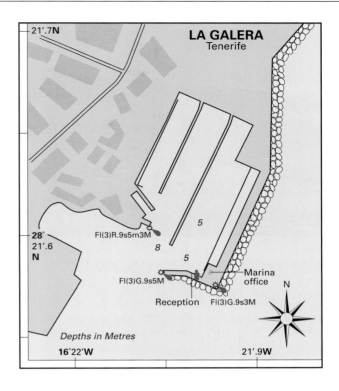

## New Club Náutico marina

In the last ten years Puerto Deportivo La Galera has metamorphosed from a tiny harbour catering for small motorboats and jet-skis, into a small but well-organised marina with 172 berths, though most are for craft of less than 10m. It is essential to make contact well before arrival, confirming a day or two in advance that a space will be available. It is owned by the local authority and operated by the Club Náutico la Galera, but although visiting yachts are welcomed into the marina their crew do not have access to the other club facilities, such as its tennis courts and large outdoor swimming pool. There is, however, a cordoned-off 'swimming channel' between the outermost pontoon and the wall, as well as several small beaches just outside the entrance.

## Approach and entrance

The power station a mile north of the harbour makes a good landmark as does, on closer approach, the church with its tall white tower and red roof a mile to the south. Two harbours front the town, separated by about 300m of dark sand beach, with Puerto Deportivo La Galera to the north and the old fishing harbour of Candelaria to the south. There are no hazards in the approach other than fishing pot buoys, for which a good watch needs to be kept. The entrance itself is narrow, with little more than

Looking NE to the entrance to the small Deportivo La Galera *Hilary Keatinge*

IV. THE CANARY ISLANDS

The new Puerto Deportivo La Galera, seen from just east of north. The tall white tower of Nuestra Señora de la Candelaria, visible just to the right of the entrance, makes a fine landmark *Anne Hammick*

20m between the breakwater head and the end of the central mole, though depths are generous at 8m or so. There is little room to manoeuvre inside the marina. Although the marina is lit, night entry is not recommended.

The small cove opposite is cordoned-off for swimmers with a string of yellow buoys.

### Berthing

The reception berth is immediately to starboard on entry, inside the breakwater head. The three visitors' berths – all bow or stern-to the breakwater and one or two able to take yachts of up to 10m – are adjacent. At least 5m will be found through this area, shoaling further into the marina. Although protected from serious waves, swell rebounding off the beach outside produces some surge, particularly around the reception and visitors' berths.

### Formalities and charges

The marina office overlooks the reception berth, and staff are friendly, helpful and speak good English. In 2015 the charge for one night was approximately €22, which included water, electricity and 7% tax. Cash only.

### Facilities

*Water and electricity* On the pontoons.
*WiFi* Free on the pontoons, code in the office.
*Showers* Permanent shower block is planned.
*Launderette* In the commercial centre in town. Ask at the marina office for directions.
*Weather forecast* On the marina website, which may be printed out at the office on request.
*Security* Security is excellent with a manned gate to the entire complex as well as round-the-clock patrols.
*Fuel* Diesel and petrol pumps at the reception berth. Cash only.
*Bottled gas* Camping Gaz exchanges at the hardware store in town.
*Medical services* Health centre in the town, with all the resources of Santa Cruz to hand if necessary.

*Banks* Several in the town, including one almost opposite the marina approach road, nearly all with cash dispensers.
*Shops/provisioning* Good food and other shopping in the town.
*Produce market* Monday–Friday – ask for details in the office.
*Cafés, restaurants & hotels* Many in Candelaria. The Club Náutico's bar and restaurant are not open to visitors, but a waterside café is planned for the marina.
*Car hire & taxis* Available in the town.
*Buses* Regular services along the coast in both directions.
*Air services* About 45km to/from Tenerife South Airport.
*Boatyard* Small boatyard for local craft only, with a 10-tonne crane but no travel-lift.
*Engineers* Can be arranged via the marina office.

## Candelaria

28°21'·36N 16°22'·09W (breakwater head)

**Lights**
**Breakwater angle** Q(3)10s9m3M
  East cardinal post, ◆ topmark 2m
**Breakwater head**
  Fl(4)G.11s 9m5M Green post 3m
**Inner mole**
  Fl(4)R.11s 7m3M Red post 3m

### Small fishing harbour

Candelaria is a small fishing harbour immediately south of La Galera. Yachts are encouraged to use La Galera (see above). Ashore a striking feature is the church of Nuestra Señora de la Candelaria at the southern end of the town, overlooking a paved square guarded by statues of Guanches, the ancient inhabitants of the islands. The church is a place of pilgrimage as it contains the beautifully decorated shrine of Our Lady of Candelaria, Patroness of the Canaries.

Looking SSE from the fishing harbour of Candelarias towards the white tower of Nuestra Señora *Hilary Keatinge*

# Puerto de Güimar

28°17'·66N 16°22'·36W (fishermen's pier head)
28°17'·18N 16°22'·83W (Club Náutico breakwater head)

**Lights**
**Fishing harbour (to northeast)**
**Pier, head**
　Fl.G.5s7m5M Green post 3m
**Pier, root**
　Fl.G.5s4m3M Green column 4m

**Club Náutico harbour (to southwest)**
**Breakwater**
　Fl(2)G.7s11m5M Green post 6m
**Inner mole**
　Fl(2)R.7s8m3M Red post 4m

**Harbour communications**
**Club Nautico**
　☎ +34 922 528 900
　Camino Las Bajas, 2 38508, SC de Tenerife

## Small, private marina

A little further down the coast is another small fishing village, Puerto de Güimar. The town of Güimar itself lies 5km inland on the slopes of the central range. The port has a short pier with an angled end that gives some protection to local boats. Half a mile further south again is a large sports complex incorporating a *club náutico* and, facing it, a small marina that does not accept visitors. Pontoons provide berthing for an assortment of small motorboats and one or two sailing craft, but depths average less than 2m making it unsuitable for most cruising yachts, even were they welcome.

# Bahía de Abona

28°09'·96N 16°25'·72W (north quay)
28°09'·2N 16°25'·84W (south mole)

**Lighthouse**
**Punta de Abona**
　Fl(3)20s54m17M 214°-vis-040°
　White tower, red bands 39m

## Double anchorage

The Bahía de Abona lies between Punta del Ternero to the north and Punta de Abona with its powerful light to the south. There is a choice of anchorages to suit wind and swell direction – the northern corner, below the tourist village of Poris de Abona, is sheltered from the northwest, while Ensenada del Pedregal in the southern corner provides safe anchorage in southerly and southwesterly winds. It is completely exposed to the prevailing northeasterlies.

## Approach and entrance

Approaching from north or east the bay will open up to the west of the lighthouse. Punta del Ternero has a few outlying rocks and should be given reasonable clearance. Coming from the south, stay well offshore around Punta de Abona to avoid a patch of partly submerged rocks. Beware a spur of lava which extends into the centre of the bay from the west and which could be mistaken for a stone pier.

## Anchorage

*North* Below the village of Poris de Abona will be seen a very old stone quay. Anchor off in 4–5m over sand. Land with the dinghy at the ladder or steps.

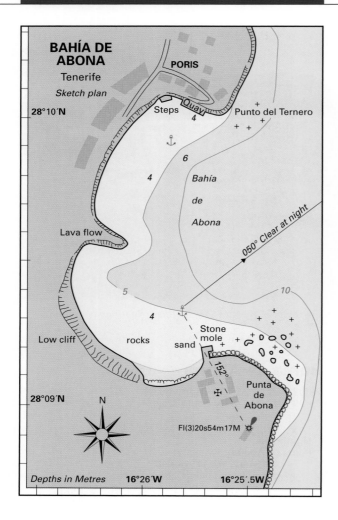

BAHÍA DE ABONA
Tenerife
Sketch plan
28°10´N
PORIS
Steps
4
Punto del Ternero
6
4
Bahía
de
Abona
050° Clear at night
Lava flow
5
10
4
Low cliff
rocks
sand
Stone mole
152°
Punta de Abona
28°09´N
N
Fl(3)20s54m17M
Depths in Metres    16°26´W    16°25´.5W

There are small boats moored off, and the area is popular with swimmers, for whom a good watch needs to be kept. There are cafés and restaurants in the village and basic shopping needs can be met.

*South* In the right conditions the anchorage northwest of Punta de Abona is most appealing, lying off a beach of speckled sand fringed at either end by rocky outcrops. Anchor in 5m over sand off the eastern part of the beach – there are rocks further west – with the lighthouse just open of the short stone mole. Holding is excellent. Although it offers no facilities beyond a small café selling drinks and ice creams, it is worth wandering up the path to view the small, military-style village built around the church and square. The same cannot be said for the long tramp out to the lighthouse on the headland.

# Puerto de San Miguel de Tajao

28°06´·52N 16°28´·2W (breakwater head)

**Lights**
**Breakwater**
  Fl(3)G.9s12m5M Green post 6m

## Possible anchorage off small harbour

A small fishing harbour still relatively unaffected by tourism, Puerto de San Miguel de Tajao lies behind a curved breakwater which opens to the southwest, the entrance partially closed by a short opposing mole. The harbour is packed full of moored small craft, with more drawn up on the black sand beach, and offers no feasible berth for a yacht. In settled weather it might be possible to anchor off but there appears little reason to do so.

# Central Termica de Granadilla

28°05´·8N 16°29´·37W (old harbour molehead)

**Lights**
**Molehead** Q(3)10s9m3M
  East cardinal post, ♦ topmark 4m
**Outfall buoy** Fl.Y.5s3M
  Yellow pillar buoy, × topmark

## Work in progress

Under the chimneys and silos the arms of a large new port are under construction. Just south of the old Puerto de Granadilla, between Punta del Camello and Punta de la Galletita, the plan is to develop a new deep-water port to increase the capability of Santa Cruz de Tenerife by taking the bulk of the LNG, cement and heavy industrial traffic. Two S cardinals and one E cardinal mark the outer limit of the new harbour area at present. The extension should be completed by the end of 2016.

## Anchorages adjacent to Punta Montaña Roja

Punta Montaña Roja appears as a tall red pyramid, forming a small peninsula on the southeast coast of Tenerife. The island's main airport, Aeropuerto de Tenerife Sur (South Airport), lies on the plain northwest of the headland and aircraft can be seen taking off and landing. Southwest of Punta Montaña Roja the coast is low-lying as far as Punta Rasca, the most southerly point on Tenerife.

⚓ **Bahía del Médano** 28°02´·5N 16°32´·3W

A circular bay with a short unlit breakwater close northeast of Punta Montaña Roja. The topology is such that any wind from the south or west makes it an extremely windy place – as evidenced by the number of kite surfers. There can be 20 to 30 knots in the bay yet virtual calm five miles further up the coast. The bottom shelves sharply across the mouth of the bay and it is essential that the anchor be properly set. The village of El Médano in the northern crook of the bay has restaurants, shops and other basic facilities.

⚓ **Playa de las Tejitas** 28°01'·7N 16°33'·3W

Close west of Punta Montaña Roja, a comfortable anchorage in winds from north or northeast in 7–8m over sand. Several large yellow mooring buoys lie off the beach, only one of which is lit, Fl.Y.5s5M. Keep well clear as they are used by tankers bringing aviation fuel for the nearby airport. Two pairs of leading lights guide ships towards the buoys, but are only lit when a vessel is due.

⚓ **Los Abrigos** 28°01'·7N 16°35'·6W

About 2·5M west of Punta Montaña Roja, a once charming fishing village now given over mainly to tourism. A few fishing boats lie on trots secured to the quay, but are hauled out in bad weather. The quay itself bears a green pyramid tower, Fl(2)G.7s10m5M. The waterfront area is famous for its fish restaurants. In the unlikely event of very calm weather a lunch stop might be possible, but the holding is poor.

## Marina San Miguel

28°01'·17N 16°36'·89W

**Lights**
**Breakwater angle** Fl(3)10s11m3M
  East cardinal beacon, ♦topmark 6m
**Breakwater head**
  Fl(3)G.9s12m5M Green column 6m
**Inner mole**
  Fl(3)R.9s6m3M Red column 6m

**Harbour Communications**
  VHF Ch 09
  *mobile* +34 610 777 280 (24 hrs)
**Marina Office**
  ☎ +34 922 785124
  0900–1700 daily
  Puerto Deportivo Marina San Miguel, Torre de Control
  Urb, Amarillo Golf s/n 38639 San Miguel de Abona
  reservas@marinasanmiguel.com
  www.marinasanmiguel.com

### Large marina close to the airport

A private family-run concession (with Puertos Canarias), this marina was started in the early 1990s and is now providing berths for almost 280 boats. It is owned and managed by the Tavio family, who include some serious sailors in their ranks. It is already the biggest private marina in Tenerife with an excellent reputation. It should eventually contain 344 berths for craft of up to 20m, a high proportion intended for visitors and most able to berth 12m or more. Most berths are on finger pontoons, though the largest boats are stern to on lazy lines alongside the breakwater. Dredged spoil from the centre of the

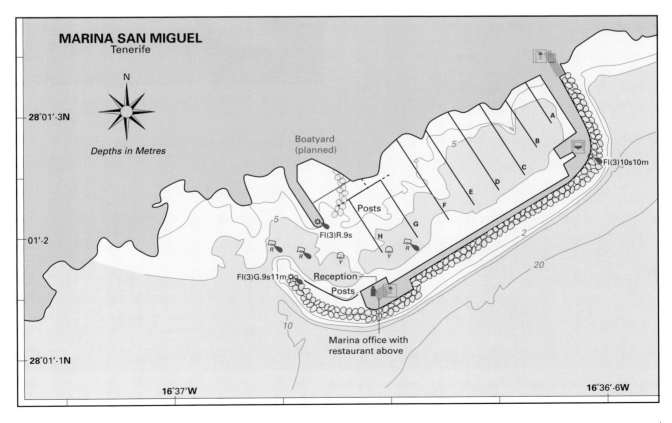

MARINA SAN MIGUEL
Tenerife

N

28°01'·3N

*Depths in Metres*

Boatyard (planned)

Posts

Fl(3)R.9s

5

01'·2

Fl(3)G.9s11m

Reception

Posts

10

Marina office with restaurant above

28°01'·1N

Fl(3)10s10m

5

2

20

A
B
C
D
E
F
G
H

16°37'W

16°36'·6W

IV. THE CANARY ISLANDS

Marina San Miguel's reception building – intended to resemble a ship's superstructure when seen from offshore – aids identification of the marina entrance   *Nigel Mercier*

harbour is being used to infill an area to the northwest, earmarked for the planned boatyard.

The marina has a particularly impressive website, in Spanish, English, German and French, which includes unusual – and thoughtful – items ranging from a Supermercado Virtual (a full 'online shopping list' for delivery to your boat) to the local bus timetable. In the background there is the Amarilla Golf and Country Club, with some attractive landscaping and pleasant restaurants. The busy Tenerife South Airport is less than 5km to the north-northeast, though aircraft are heard as a rumble rather than a roar.

### Approach and entrance

The entrance can be difficult to spot from offshore, though the circular blue tower that is lit, near the end of the breakwater is conspicuous. Low-rise development extends some distance in both directions, with one of the resort's several golf courses backing the marina itself.

A rocky ledge with depths of 5m or less lies across from the end of the breakwater, it is marked by a lit red buoy. The entrance is possible in most conditions but obviously not in a strong southerly gale. If in doubt check on VHF Ch 09. Inside the marina the channel to the pontoons is marked by three flashing red and two yellow buoys.

### Berthing

It is preferable to make contact prior to arrival, at which time the yacht is likely to be directed straight to a berth, avoiding a stop at the reception berth. *Marineros* will be on hand either in a rib or on the pontoon to help arrivals mooring bow or stern to with lazy lines.

### Formalities

After securing at the reception berth, visit the marina office at the head of the breakwater with ship's papers, passports and evidence of insurance, walking through a small tourist shop en route. The office staff are particularly friendly and helpful and several speak good English.

Looking NW towards the marina entrance   *Richard French*

The new pontoon G is now in place, pontoon H (to be installed soon) will attach to the posts on the left of the photo   *Richard French*

## Charges

In 2015, the charge for one night for a 12m boat was approximately €22 and included water, electricity and 7% tax. Discounts are available for longer stays if booked and paid for in advance.

## Facilities

*Water and electricity* On the pontoons.

*WiFi* Free access near the tower or in the restaurant above. Personal Hotspot can be connected for a charge.

*Showers* Well-kept showers and toilets next to the marina office, with more in the services block at the head of the harbour.

*Launderette* At the head of the harbour, with two washers and two dryers all of which take €1 coins.

*Weather forecast* Displayed in the marina office and at the services block at the head of the harbour. Also on the screen in the restaurant above the office.

*Security* Security gates are fitted to the pontoons but are normally left open during the day. There is the usual 24-hour security presence.

*Fuel* Diesel and petrol are available at the reception berth at all times.

*Bottled gas* Camping Gaz exchanges at the marina office, other makes can be refilled within 24hrs.

*Medical services* Medical centre and pharmacy in the resort.

*Banks* Banks and cash dispensers in the resort, but both some distance from the marina.

*Shops/provisioning* Supermarkets and other shops in the resort, all well within walking distance – or patronise the Supermercado Virtual on the marina website, which offers a comprehensive choice of victuals to be delivered to your boat. Bread is made and sold at the café above the marina office.

*Cafés, restaurants & hotels* Outdoor café/restaurant on the upper floor of the marina reception building, a small 'beach bar' in the northeast corner, and many restaurants and hotels in the golf resort.

*Car hire* Several companies have offices in the resort.

*Taxis* Can be ordered at the office for pick-up within the marina.

*Buses* Regular service from the resort. A timetable will be found on the marina website.

*Airport* The South Airport is less than 5km to the northeast.

## Boatyard

The boatyard is currently situated part-way along the breakwater but will eventually move to an in-filled area just inside the north mole. Most services are available – enquire at the marina office. DIY work is permitted and owners are welcome to live aboard while the yacht is ashore.

*Travel-lift* There is a 70-tonne hoist. A vast crane, capable of lifting almost any size, weight and beam, is also brought in as necessary.

*Engineers, electronic & radio repairs* Can be arranged via the marina office.

*Sail repairs* Enquire at the marina office.

*Chandlery* A small chandlery beside the harbour office.

# Marina del Sur, Las Galletas

28°00'·43N 16°39'·69W

**Lights**
**Breakwater head**
  Fl(4)G.7s5m3M Green post 2m

**Harbour Communications**
  VHF Ch 09 (24 hours)
**Marina del Sur** ☎ +34 922 783 620
  0900–1400 and 1600–1900 weekdays,
  0900–1400 Saturday
  Marina del Sur, Torre de Control 2a Planta, CP 38631,
  Las Galletas – Arona
  info@marinadelsur.es
  www.marinadelsur.es

### Small new marina inside old harbour

The harbour of Las Galletas lies 2M to the east of Punta Rasca on the southern tip of the island and to the west of the not very silent white apartment blocks of Costa del Silencio, the first serious tourist development on Tenerife. Marina del Sur opened in August 2007. There are five pontoons providing 196 berths, of which 153 are for yachts from 4–20m. It offers the major advantage, so far as most cruising yachtsmen are concerned, of backing straight on to a bustling traditional Canarian town, though tourism is encroaching, it has not yet overwhelmed Las Galletas.

### Approach and entrance

The curved dark stone breakwater may be difficult to pick out against the shore behind, but the pretty blue and white building at its tip is quite conspicuous and houses the marina office.

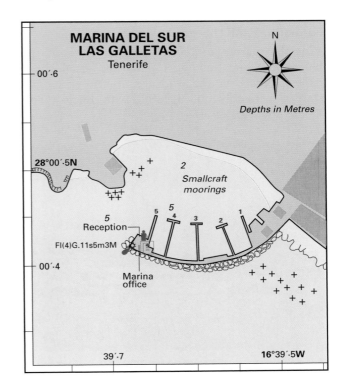

Approaching from the east, keep 0·5M offshore to avoid a reef stretching out from near the root of the breakwater and keep a watch for dive boats. From any direction the final approach should be with the head of the breakwater bearing slightly east of north. Keep well to starboard on entry as a spit of rock runs out from the shore opposite. The marina's reception and fuel berth is immediately to starboard on entry. There is a 2 knot speed limit inside the harbour.

### Berthing

Before arrival call up on Ch 09 and if a berth has been assigned make straight for it rather than tie up on the reception mole. The pontoons are numbered from the eastern end. Mooring is stern-to with lazy lines (no buoys), other than on pontoon No.4 which has fingers on both sides. Depths are generous with at least 5m in the pontoon area, but there is relatively little space between the ends of the pontoons – against which small motorboats are sometimes moored bow or stern-to – and the small craft moorings to the north. It is advisable to reverse between the pontoons. In strong south or southwesterly winds, surge enters the harbour requiring multiple lines, springs, extra fenders, etc. Anyone considering leaving a boat unattended for any length of time should pay particular attention to this aspect, as well as taking precautions against chafe.

### Anchorage

Anchoring is no longer possible inside the harbour and all the moorings are private. Anchoring outside is not permitted and the holding is poor; the Guarda Civil patrol the area.

### Formalities and charges

Visit the marina office on the first floor of the blue and white building, taking the usual ship's papers, passports and evidence of insurance. The staff are friendly and helpful, with English and French spoken.

In 2015 one night for a 12·1m boat was €23.02, including 7% tax. Water and electricity are metered. Discounts were available for stays of longer than one month.

### Facilities

*Water and electricity* On the pontoons.

*WiFi* For a small fee available in the marina.

*Showers* Clean showers with plenty of hot water in the tower below the marina office. Access is by key, obtainable from the office for a small deposit.

*Launderette* In the marina building. Tokens can be bought from the office.

*Weather forecast* At the marina office and on the website.

*Security* There are no gates to the pontoons, accessed off the breakwater, that is open to all, but with CCTV cameras and round-the-clock patrols there is said to be good security.

*Fuel* Diesel and petrol pumps on the quay outside the office, operational 0800–1800 daily. Although not permanently manned, if the *marineros* see a boat tying up one will come over. Credit cards are accepted.

*Bottled gas* Camping Gaz exchanges at the *ferretería* (hardware store) in the town, but no refills available.

*Medical services* Medical centre in the northeast part of the town.

*Banks* Banks with cash dispensers in the town.

*Shops/provisioning* Supermarkets and other shops in the town, all well within walking distance, including a good butcher and a greengrocer. Fish stall just outside the marina. An Iceland store in Las Chafiras, with British favourites including bacon.

*Cafés & restaurants* Restaurants on the breakwater overlooking the marina, offering good food at reasonable prices, with many more in the town.

*Car hire and taxis* Ask in the office.

*Buses* Good bus service around the island, with a stop just outside the marina barrier and a major terminus just outside the town.

*Airport* Tenerife South Airport about 6 miles (15 minutes) away.

*Boatyard* Small boatyard for local craft at the root of the breakwater.

*Travel-lift* No travel-lift and no plans for one. An 8-tonne capacity crane lifts local craft ashore.

*Diving services* Ask at the marina office, or try one of the many SCUBA centres in the town.

*Engineers, electronic & other repairs and services* Ask at the marina office.

The distinctive marina office at Marina del Sur, Las Galletas *Hilary Keatinge*

# Los Cristianos

28°02'·76N 16°43'·03W

### Lights
**Breakwater**
  Fl.R.5s13m5M Red column 6m
**Starboard hand buoy**
  Fl.G.5s3M Green pillar buoy, ▲ topmark
**Breakwater spur**
  Fl(2)R.7s7m3M Red post 4m
**Inner mole**
  Fl(2+1)G.10s6m2M Green column, red band 3m

### Marine farms
Three marine farms lie southeast of Los Cristianos, centred on 28°01'·1N 16°42'·4W, 28°01'·8N 16°42'·6W and 28°01'·9N 16°42'·6W respectively. The first two are marked by four yellow pillar buoys and the latter by six yellow pillar buoys, all Fl.Y.5s.

### Harbour Communications
**Port Authority**
  VHF Ch 16 (24 hour)
  ☎ +34 922 645 354
**Cofradía de Pescadores Nuestra Señora de Las Mercedes**
  ☎ +34 922 790 014
  0800–1500 weekdays, 0800–1300 Saturday
  Muelle Pesquero s/n, Los Cristianos (Arona) 38650
  cploscristianos@gmail.com

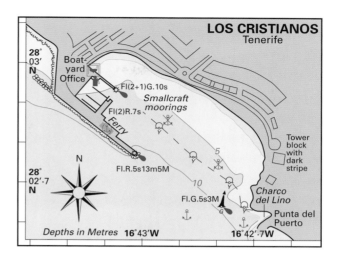

## Busy ferry harbour with no space for visitors

Los Cristianos is primarily a state-run passenger port, with conventional ferries and high-speed hydrofoils running regular services to La Gomera, La Palma and El Hierro. For many years it was one of the most popular departure points for the Atlantic passage until, in the 1990s, the anchorage off the beach was closed to yachts. Today fishing boats and a wide variety of tourist craft operate from the quay. There is a small modern marina with no space for visitors, though as a Port of Refuge, if in trouble they would not turn a yacht away. The ferry harbour is sheltered by a 475m breakwater, facing which is a long sandy beach, centrepiece of the tourist conurbation and ever expanding blocks of high-rise apartments around which the town continues to grow.

## Approach and entrance

Seen from northwest through west to southwest, the 3-mile line of high-rise buildings is most conspicuous. At the extreme southern end is a single tower block with a distinctive dark vertical stripe. Further south there are cliffs and then a small development, Palm-Mar, followed by Punta Rasca, a low-lying point with a 50m light tower. The entrance will be obvious as soon as Punta Rasca is rounded. The southeasterly-facing entrance is wide and without hazards. The beach area is condoned off by a long string of yellow buoys.

Looking towards the entrance to the marina in Los Cristianos *Hilary Keatinge*

**IV. THE CANARY ISLANDS**

Charco del Lino, the only possible anchorage near Los Cristianos  *Hilary Keatinge*

## Berthing

The only reason for a yacht to enter Los Cristianos is to be lifted ashore at the boatyard, in which case temporary berthing would need to be arranged.

## Marina and boatyard

The marina and boatyard are under the authority of the Capitanía Marítima, their office is in the ferry building, see details above. The Cofradía de Pescadores own and operate the travel-lifts. See details above, limited English is spoken.

## Boatyard facilities

Large boatyard that still has extensive concrete hardstanding, Basic facilities, including water and electricity in the boatyard.
*Travel-lift* Three travel-lifts, the largest rated at 110-ton.
*Chandlery* A small amount at the Cofradía de Pescadores, with wider stocks in the town.

## Anchorage

As stated above, no anchoring AT ALL is allowed inside the harbour or off the beach. However, there is a small cove on the eastern approach, behind a green buoy, where yachts can anchor, keeping east of the buoy and out of the way of the ferries and tourist boats. It may offer some protection from the prevailing weather, but not from the wash of the commercial traffic. The holding is said to be poor.

# Puerto Colón

28°04'·81N 16°44'·27W

### Lights
**Breakwater angle** Q(9)15s10m2M
  West cardinal post, ⨉ topmark 2m
**Breakwater head**
  Fl(2)G.7s11m5M Green post 4m
**East mole**
  Fl(2)R.7s8m3M Red post 2m

### Marine farms
Two marine farms lie northwest of Puerto Colon, one centred on 28°04'·7N 16°45'·3W and marked by four yellow pillar buoys with × topmarks, all Fl.Y.11s, the other centred on 28°05'N 16°45'·6W and marked by four yellow pillar buoys with × topmarks, all Fl(5)Y.13s3M.

### Harbour Communications
  VHF Ch 09, 16 (during office hours)
### Marina Office
  ☎ +34 922 714 211 or +34 922 714 163
  0900–1400, 1500–1800 weekdays, 0900–1400, 1600–1800 Saturday, 1000–1300, 1600–1800 Sunday
  Puerto Deportivo Puerto Colón, Edificio Capitania, Playa de las Americas 38660 Adeje – Tenerife Sur
  capitania@puertocolon.com
  www.puertocolon.com

## Private marina fronting a beach resort

This privately run marina is very crowded, mainly with day-charter catamarans, sport fishing boats and small runabouts. Most of the 355 berths were sold when the surrounding holiday development was created and the remaining ones were swiftly taken up by private yachts and commercial concerns. There may be a berth available for visitors but it is essential to book in advance.

The marina is situated at the northern edge of the extensive – and ever expanding – Playa de las Americas development, which has aptly been described as 'a real fish and chip town'. However, the breakwaters are well sited to provide shelter during southerly gales and it is a safe refuge in these conditions.

## Approach, entrance and berthing

Keep 0·5M offshore until the entrance has been identified as reefs extend along the low-lying coast. Once identified, approach the entrance on a course at right angles to the coast and turn to starboard to enter. Several beach-protection moles have been created north of the harbour entrance, but none are as substantial as the marina breakwater nor do they carry buildings.

The reception (and fuel) berth is on the starboard side directly beneath the white control building, though being close to the entrance it has been reported to be almost untenable in a swell; it would nevertheless be unwise to proceed further without permission. Night entry should be avoided, not least because the breakwater lights are almost impossible to pick out against the background of shore lights.

The well-sheltered entrance to Puerto Colón seen from the main breakwater. Although it may be sunny at sea level, Tenerife's higher areas are often covered by dark cloud
*Anne Hammick*

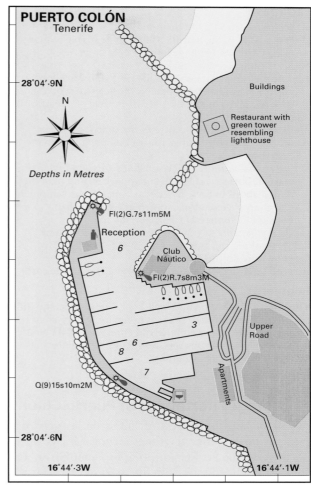

Depths are generous throughout the marina, with 6m in the entrance and 7–8m at reception. It may be possible to overnight at the fuel berth, after 1800 but only until 0900.

### Formalities and charges

Visit the marina office in the white 'control tower' taking the usual ship's papers, crew passports and insurance documents. Some English is spoken. In 2015 one night for a 12m boat was €23 including water and electricity. Discounts are available for longer stays, in the unlikely event that a berth is available.

Puerto Colón is a busy hub for tripper day-boats and is surrounded by the big holiday developments of Playa de las Americas *Hilary Keatinge*

### Facilities

*Water and electricity* On the pontoons.

*WiFi* No WiFi in the marina itself, but available at many nearby bars and restaurants.

*Showers* Built into the breakwater itself.

*Fuel* At the reception berth 0800–1745 daily, available to visitors as well as residents. Nevertheless it would be wise to make contact by VHF or mobile phone prior to arrival.

*Medical services* Health centre in the tourist complex.

*Banks* Several in the nearby tourist complex, plus many cash dispensers.

*Shops/provisioning* A variety of shops surround the marina, plus several small supermarkets and many tourist shops in the Playa de las Americas development and a large Mercadona supermarket in the San Eugenio Commercial Centre up the hill.

*Cafés, restaurants & hotels* Literally hundreds, some overlooking the marina.

*Car hire & taxis* Readily available.

*Airport* Tenerife South Airport, about 17km to the east.

### Boatyard

The boatyard is secure and well-kept, but it is usually full as much of the (limited) space is taken up by day-charter catamarans and other commercial enterprises. DIY work is permitted and various services including engineering and GRP repairs are available.

*Travel-lift* Capacity 24-tonnes, plus slipway.

## Anchorages northwest of Puerto Colón

A pair of bays northwest of Punta de las Gaviotas (Seagull Point) offer daytime anchorage 2M or so northwest of Puerto Colón. If approaching from the south stay outside the 20m line in order to clear the unmarked shoal of Baja de Adeje off the headland immediately north of the small tourist development at La Caleta.

⚓ **Spaghetti Bay** 28°06'·4N 16°45'·8W

The most southern of the two anchorages. Its southern part is backed by a white sand beach off which yachts can anchor in 7–8m over sand. Further in, the seabed turns to rock, while the north part of the bay has large boulders likely to foul an anchor.

⚓ **El Puertito, also known as El Pris**
28°06'·7N 16°46'·2W

About half a mile to the northwest. It is a tiny bay surrounded by high sand-coloured cliffs with a shallow reef on the northwest side of the entrance, easily seen in the clear water. There is a small village at the head of the bay and behind is a church which forms a useful landmark. Best anchorage is to be found near the entrance to the bay in 5–6m over sand and rock. If staying overnight it is best to lay a second anchor to reduce swinging.

## Puerto de San Juan

28°10'·69N 16°48'·85W

**Lights**
**Breakwater**
Fl(3)R.10s13m2M Red column 3m

**Marine farms**
Two marine farms lie southeast of Puerto de San Juan, one centred on 28°07'·2N 16°47'·25W, marked by six yellow pillar buoys with × topmarks, all Fl.Y.5s3M, the other centred on 28°09'N 16°48'·3W, marked by four yellow pillar buoys with × topmarks, all Fl(4)Y.11s3M.

**Harbour Communications**
VHF Ch 09, 16
**Port Captain**
☎ +34 922 865434

### Small, scenic fishing harbour

A small working fishing harbour tucked behind a high breakwater, about 8M up the coast from Playa de las Americas and 5M south of the Los Gigantes cliffs. There is little space for a yacht to enter, but unrestricted – though relatively unsheltered – anchorage outside. The beach inside the harbour is cordoned off by a string of yellow buoys, but it would be possible to land a dinghy on the wide slipway at the head of the harbour. The breakwater is popular with rod-and-line fishermen, particularly in the evenings – keep well clear! There is a plan for the future development of this harbour.

Facilities include a 64-tonne travel-lift operated by the Cofradía de Pescadores (fishermen's confederation). Water is available on the quay and by the slipway, and there is a shower in the boatyard. The village contains several small supermarkets and other shops, and numerous restaurants and cafés.

## Puerto de Santiago

28°14'·22N 16°50'·64W (northwest quay)

### Small fishing village

An attractive fishing village – certainly not a port – less than a mile south of Los Gigantes, with an exposed bay where the fishermen crane their boats onto the wall in bad weather. It is a pleasant place to anchor off in settled weather but beware of rocks inshore. Restaurants and tourist shops surround the bay, with more up the hill.

# Puerto de Los Gigantes

28°14'·94N 16°50'·52W (breakwater head)

**Lights**
**Breakwater angle** Q(9)15s11m4M
West cardinal tripod, ⚡ topmark 3m
**Breakwater head** Fl.G.6s11m3M
Green column 3m
**East mole** Fl(2)R.7s5m1M
Red and white diagonally striped tower and red
tripod 5m
**East mole spur** Fl(2)R.7s6m1M
Red tripod over red and white banded base 2m
**Breakwater spur**
Fl(2)G.7s6m1M Green post 2m
**Breakwater spur, angle**
Fl(3)G.9s6m1M Green post 2m
*Note* If approaching at night – not recommended unless
familiar with the harbour – the angular shape of
Puerto de Los Gigantes causes the entrance lights to
appear reversed

**Marine farm**
Two marine farms lie northwest of Puerto de of Los
Gigantes, each marked by four yellow pillar buoys with
× topmarks, all Fl.Y.5s3M. They are situated close
together, centred on 28°15'·6N 16°50'·6W and 28°15'·8N
16°50'·9W respectively.

**Harbour Communications**
VHF Ch 09 (24 hours)
**Marina Office**
☎ +34 822 199 996 (Note that this number begins 822
rather than 922).
0900–1900 - a security guard will answer calls to the
above number after hours
Puerto Deportivo Los Gigantes, 38683 Santiago del
Teide, Tenerife
puertodeportivolosgigantes@gmail.com
www.puertolosgigantes.com

### Marina with shallow entrance, prone to surge

The marina at Los Gigantes was constructed as part
of the surrounding development that climbs steeply
up the hillside. It is not as developed as the areas
further south and, if conditions allow, it is a good
base from which to explore El Tiede and other
inland sites. The marina is run jointly; the local
residents own 70% and a private concession owns
30% of the berths. There are 362 berths for vessels

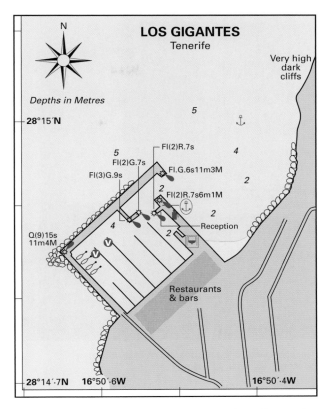

of up to 20m, and a reservation needs to be made,
particularly during peak weekends.

### Approach and entrance

Punta Teno light lies about 8M northwest, situated
on a low-lying spit backed by the northern end of the
spectacular cliffs of Los Gigantes sweeping some 7M
to the southeast. From any direction, it is not
difficult to identify the town on a steeply rising
promontory south of the cliffs. Buildings now rise in
tiers at least halfway up the slope.

At a distance of 2M the marina wall can be made
out under the cliff end, though the dog-leg entrance
faces northeast in an endeavour to provide some
shelter. A watch needs to be kept for craft leaving or
entering the marina and there is a speed limit of 2
knots in the immediate approach.

**CAUTION**

Situated as it is at the southern extremity of a run of
enormous sheer cliffs that reflect incoming swell, the
marina is very prone to surge. If there is a severe storm
forecast boats may be advised to vacate the marina
completely and this should be taken into consideration
if planning to leave the boat for any time, particularly
in the winter months. The harbour also has an ongoing
problem with silting of the approach and entrance, and
can become extremely dangerous at times - it is said not
to be viable for at least 80% of the time in winter. The
entrance is said to carry no more than 2m at low water
springs, which may be significantly reduced by surge. A
swell of 1·5m or more, which is not uncommon, can
make the entrance untenable. Entry should not be

considered unless tide, wind and swell conditions are
near-perfect. Conversely, once inside there is no
guarantee of being able to depart.
Always call on Ch 09, or phone, at least ten minutes
before entering or leaving. When even an apparently
insignificant swell is running down or onto the coast a
yacht may encounter breaking waves BEFORE reaching
the entrance. In such a situation the choice is either to
free off and make the 17M downwind passage to San
Sebastián de la Gomera, head down the coast of
Tenerife to Las Galletas or Marina San Miguel, or heave-
to a few miles offshore in the hope that conditions may
improve.

The approach to the marina at Los Gigantes on a
peaceful day  *Hilary Keatinge*

A speedboat makes the tight turn into Puerto de Los
Gigantes, seen from the cliffs to the northeast. La Gomera,
about 16M away, is very clear on the horizon
*Anne Hammick*

### Berthing

Call on VHF Ch 09 again, while still offshore,
having made contact previously to confirm entry is
possible and that a berth is available. Normally a
yacht will be directed straight into a berth, the
*marineros* are very helpful. The reception pontoon is
located inside the short spur jutting out from the
eastern quay, and is shallow at low water (2m).  A
larger yacht may be placed stern-to the breakwater
in the western corner if a berth-holder is absent.

Space is limited at the entrance to Los Gigantes
*Hilary Keatinge*

The rugged but beautiful coast north of Los Gigantes
*Hilary Keatinge*

## Formalities and charges

Visit the marina office on the end of the east mole bearing the usual ship's papers, passports and insurance certificate. In 2015 the overnight berthing fee for a monohull of 12m was approx. €26 which included water, electricity and 7% tax, with discounts for longer stays.

A deep ravine twists down to the sea to the north of Los Gigantes *Hilary Keatinge*

## Facilities

*Water and electricity* On the pontoons.
*WiFi* Available at many of the bars and cafés.
*Showers* Several shower blocks dotted around the marina. Access by key for which a small deposit is taken.
*Fuel* Diesel and petrol pumps at the reception berth, operational 0700–1800. Check the depth alongside, it varies with the tide.
*Medical services* In the town.
*Banks* In the town, nearly all with cash dispensers.
*Shops/provisioning* A small supermarket fronts the marina, with others (including Lidl) in the town.
*Cafés, restaurants & hotels* Many overlooking the harbour and throughout the resort.
*Car hire & taxis* In the resort.
*Buses* Anticlockwise around the island to Tenerife South Airport and Santa Cruz, etc.
*Airport* Tenerife South airport less than an hour away.
*Boatyard* Limited boatyard space and facilities. Specialists can be summoned if necessary.
*Travel-lift* Capacity 50-tonnes

# Playa de Masca

28°17′·3N 16°51′·8W (anchorage)

### Remote, unspoilt anchorage

In a natural bay surrounded by high cliffs, north of Punta de la Higuera and south of Punta de la Galera, the anchorage at Masca is protected from north around to southeast but can suffer from overnight swell. Approaching from the southwest one notices a white beacon high up on the cliffs, and below it a short pier in the north corner of the bay and a cluster of trees and bushes surrounding a small building. Tourist boats come in to anchor for a swim and lunch stop, and sometimes to pick up walkers who have come down the *barranco*. Anchor in 8m over sand and boulders, the latter making a trip-line a wise precaution.

## Punta de Teno

28°30'·5N 16°55'·1W (anchorage)

**Lighthouse**
**Punta Teno** Fl(1+2)20s60m18M
   White tower, red bands 20m

### Anchorage southeast of lighthouse

There is a possible anchorage – suitable for daylight and settled conditions only – in a small bay southeast of Punta Teno lighthouse in about 7m, protected from northeasterly winds but open to the south. Ashore there is a track and then a road to the lighthouse on the promontory.

### Anchorages on the northwest coast of Tenerife

There are a number of small fishing harbours along this lee shore coast, a few of which offer potential anchorage in the right conditions. However, with a spectacular, though exciting, coast road running between the mountains and the sea there is much to be said for exploring this area by car, leaving the yacht secured in one of Tenerife's more sheltered harbours.

Bird's eye view of the old harbour of Garachico
*Anne Hammick*

## Garachico

28°22'·37N 16°46'·08W (quay)

### The old harbour

Garachico was once a major port until destroyed by a volcanic eruption in 1705 with heavy loss of life. The town has been rebuilt on the lava flow. The old harbour is not a suitable anchorage, and the few fishing boats are hauled up on the wall when not in use. A rocky islet, Roque de Garachico, is conspicuous offshore to the northeast.

Though possible to anchor off in very settled conditions, this is not a spot for the faint-hearted. There is at least one isolated breaking rock in the approach, very possibly more, while a low reef (said to be the semi-submerged remains of a breakwater) obstructs much of the entrance – very much a case for eyeball navigation.

## Puerto de Garachico

28°22'N 16°45'W

**Lights**
**Breakwater**
   Fl(2)G.7s15m6M
   Fl(2)G.7s15m6M
**Harbour Communications**
   VHF Ch 09
   ☎ +34 922 830 791
   0800-1530 Monday, 0800-2100 Tuesday–Friday,
   0800-1530 Saturday
   solicitudestf@puertoscanarios.es

The new marina at Garachico, with Roque de Garachico in the background.
The four entry buoys (circled) are just visible at the entrance *Puertos Canarios*

## New marina in a tricky place

In May 2012 this vast marina, though incomplete, was officially opened. The plans for the project are very ambitious and include a ferry terminus, fishing port, small coastal trader dock and berths for 220 yachts of up to 20m. Considerable expertise was required to build the 630m outer breakwater which has to face the prevailing northeasterlies. It stands 14m high and is said to contain over 1700 concrete blocks weighing 60 tonnes each. The line of filigree frieze blocks added to soften the enormity of the whole structure are not standing up to the conditions and are not likely to be replaced. A huge, very distinctive white angular sculpture marks the entrance. There is plenty of depth at both the entrance, with a minimum of 4·5m, and in the marina itself with 6–7m. However, as with Los Gigantes, it is swell, not necessarily wind, that is the danger. Entry is only possible with any safety if the swell is less than 1·5m. Entry at night is not recommended.

## Approach and entrance

Coming from the west there is reported to be a dangerous unlit rock at 28°22'·53N 16°44'·93W. Having passed the old port of Garachico there is the very visible Roque de Garachico, it is possible to go either side of it.

From the east do not turn in for the entrance too soon as there are several rocky shoals off the coast. On approach keep as close to the breakwater as possible, there are two red buoys to be left well to port and two yellow buoys off the breakwater. It is recommended that you call up on VHF 09 to enquire on the state of swell off the entrance (some Spanish will be needed). Once in the shelter of the marina there is ample room to manoeuvre and the pontoons are well spaced out, all with finger pontoons. Large yachts could be berthed alongside the breakwater. The *marineros* will be on hand to assist.

## Formalities

Bring the usual paperwork to the harbour office, currently in a portacabin opposite the fishing boat pontoons.

## Charges

In 2015 one night for a 12.1m x 4m yacht was approximately €18, including water, electricity and ICIG at 7%.

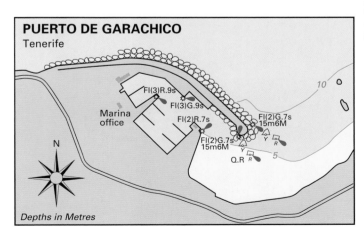

**PUERTO DE GARACHICO**
Tenerife

Fl(3)R.9s
Fl(3)G.9s
Marina office
Fl(2)R.7s
Fl(2)G.7s
15m6M
Fl(2)G.7s
15m6M
Q.R
N
Depths in Metres
10
5

### Facilities

*Water and electricity* On the pontoons.
*WiFi* None. Weak phone signal.
*Showers* Currently in a portacabin.
*Weather Forecasts* At the office.
*Security* Patrolled 24hrs.
*Fuel* (Planned for February 2016.)
*Other services* Ask in the office, as no other services on site yet. Most in the town; a 15 min. walk to the west.

## San Marcos

28°22'·75N 16°43'·52W (quay)

### Possible anchorage in settled southerlies

An attractive bay affording shelter in bad weather from the south. San Marcos lies 2M east of the conspicuous Roque de Garachico. Approach on a southeasterly bearing, taking care to avoid the rocky reef which runs out from the northeast headland on which stands a large cream building with distinctive arcades. Anchor in the eastern part clear of the fishermen's wall and crane, in 4–5m over fine sand. Fishing boats are hauled out on the quay when not in use.

The bay is backed by a black-sand beach on the eastern side and equally dark boulders to the southwest. A line of cafés and restaurants overlook it from the east, fronted by a road from which cars have been swept by northwesterly swells. There is a tap on the quay, but little else is available.

## Puerto de la Cruz

28°25'·19N 16°32'·98W (outer molehead)

> **Lighthouse and lights**
> **Puerto de la Cruz**
>   Fl(2)7s31m16M Square tower 27m
> **Western (outer) mole**
>   Fl(3)G.9s8m4M Green column 3m
> **Eastern (inner) mole**
>   Fl(3)R.9s7m3M Red column 3m

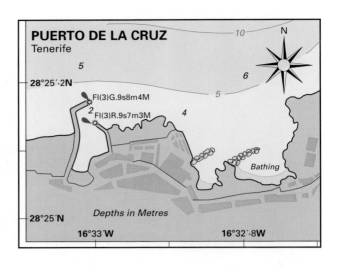

### Tiny harbour best visited by land

In the 18th century Puerto de la Cruz was the trading capital of the island, having taken over from Garachico when a volcanic eruption destroyed that harbour. Fast schooners from Devon loaded soft fruit and much of the island's wine was exported from here. However, the prevailing onshore winds and seas gradually caused the port to lose its trade to the more sheltered Santa Cruz. Following the tourist boom of the mid-20th century the old harbour entrance was closed off to create a bathing area, and though there is a small fishing harbour it is quite unsuitable for yachts. Puerto de la Cruz was the first tourist resort on Tenerife, much loved by the Victorian English who came for the weather and the sophisticated spas. It has now been overtaken by the mass tourism of the Playa de las Américas/Los Cristianos sprawl along the southwest coast, but still retains a measure of its elegance and character. The Botanic Garden, established by King Charles III of Spain in the mid-18th century, is well worth a visit if exploring the area by road.

This is all that remains of Tenerife's 16th century hub _ Puerto de la Cruz
*Puertos Canarios*

# La Gomera
**Between 28°01′N–28°13′N and 17°06′W–17°21′W**

## Introduction

La Gomera is roughly circular with its peak, Alto de Garajonay, rising almost 1500m in the centre. Deep ravines, chiselled out by lava flow and erosion, wend their way down to the shore, and indeed beyond. It is an island that is heavy on the 'wow' factor, as much of it is extremely beautiful and it is worth making an effort to explore inland. Wipers and fog lights are a 'must' driving through the misty, lush forests high in the upper reaches, in contrast to the dry, hot, rugged cliffs round the coast. Columbus made several stopovers here, not least because he is said to have had a special relationship with the First Lady of the island. And from that time La Gomera, with its sheltered harbour, was on the Atlantic map. Mass tourism has not hit the island as it is short on beaches, though it is increasingly popular with serious hikers for whom there are endless challenging trails. La Gomera is the second smallest

A monument to those who use *el silbo* ('the whistle') to communicate across the deep ravines of La Gomera
*Hilary Keatinge*

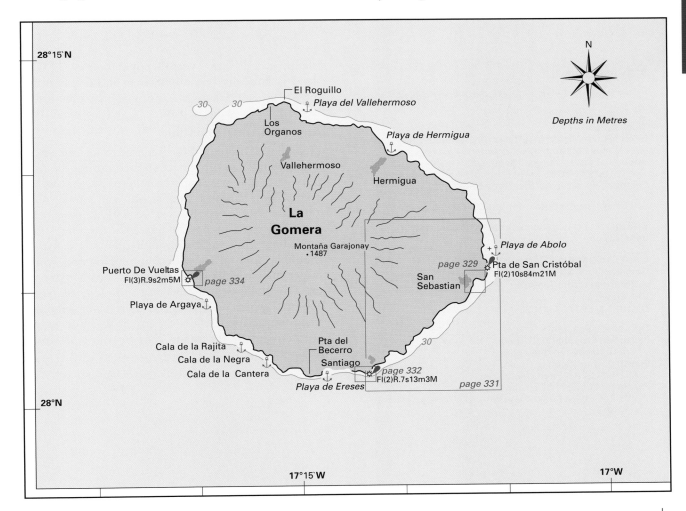

**IV. THE CANARY ISLANDS**

Spectacular scenery, good if exciting driving and nowhere is ever far from the backdrop of El Tiede  *Hilary Keatinge*

## Navigation

For information on **Magnetic Variation** and **Tides** see pages 224-225

**Tidal Stream**
It has been reported that the southwest-going tidal stream may occasionally set down the east coast of La Gomera at up to 4 knots. The reverse stream is much weaker but, even so, a race forms off Punta de San Cristobal when the northeasterly trades are blowing.

Full **Emergency Service** information is on page 227

**Weather** and **Navigational Broadcasts** are listed on page 228

**Coast Radio Station** (24 hours)
**Gomera** 28°05'·8N 17°07'·1W
 Controlled from Tenerife
**VHF** Ch 06, 24
**DSC** VHF MMSI 002241026

**Lighthouse and lights**
**Punta San Cristóbal** Fl(2)10s84m21M
 White tower, red band 15m
**Puerto de Santiago**
 Fl(2)R.7s13m3M Red column 5m
**Puerto de Vueltas (Valle Gran Rey)**
 Fl(3)R.9s2m5M Red column 1m

island, just 375km², with a population of 22,000; there is basically one all-weather harbour here for the sailor, San Sebastián, and it seems some arrive here and never want to leave.

### Approach and navigation

Prepare well if sailing from Tenerife to La Gomera as strong winds are often encountered during the final third of the passage. Northern sector winds predominate around the island with some relief along the southwestern coast. As with all the islands the NNE coast of La Gomera is in the line of the prevailing winds and this high dramatic coastline should be approached with caution. However, worth inspecting, in calm conditions, are Los Organos – the Organ Pipes – a towering cliff face of basalt columns which can only be seen from seaward. They are at 28°13'·06N 17°16'·55W, close to the northern tip of the island, but be wary of strong downdraughts.

## Harbours and anchorages

### Anchorages on the northeast coast of La Gomera

⚓ **Playa del Vellehermoso** 28°12'·3N 17°15'·1W

This might be an interesting day anchorage on one of the rare occasions when there is a strong southerly. If anchoring and the bottom appears sandy care needs to be taken as this often covers hard rock. A stony beach backed by a summer holiday complex with pool, restaurant and swimmers' shower lies at the foot of a steep-sided valley. This leads up to the town of Vallehermoso about 3km inland, where supermarkets and other shops will be found. The renovated Castillo del Mar (actually on the site of an old quay with a derrick for loading bananas) is prominent at the base of the cliff on the west side of the bay.

There is talk of transforming the ruined Castillo del Mar into a café and nightclub *Hilary Keatinge*

⚓ **Playa de Hermigua** 28°11'N 17°10'·9W

Playa de Hermigua is easy to identify from a distance – look for a row of multi-coloured buildings set a few hundred metres back from the beach, and a valley running up to the village of Hermigua a mile or so inland. Best anchorage is to be found on the west side of the bay under a steep hillside covered with banana terraces, where there is reasonable holding in 8–10m over shingle and stones.

⚓ **Playa de Avalo** 28°06'·7N 17°06'·3W

A pretty bay 1·5M north of San Sebastián, facing east and in need of careful navigation because of Roca Bermeja (marked on Admiralty chart 1869) off the headland at the north end of the bay. It is said that military target practice has reduced its height and it is now barely visible even at high water and with less than 2m at low water; it remains unmarked.

Like Playa del Vallehermoso, Playa de Hermigua faces directly into the northeast trades *Anne Hammick*

Vallehermosa was once the economic and cultural centre of the island *Hilary Keatinge*

**IV. THE CANARY ISLANDS**

# San Sebastián de la Gomera

28°05'·01N 17°06'·53W (breakwater head)

**Lights**
**Roque la Hila** Fl(3)10s3M
  East cardinal pyramid, ♦ topmark
**Breakwater**
  Fl.G.5s16m5M Green tower 7m
**Port hand No.1**
  Fl.R.5s3M Red pillar buoy
**Port hand No.2**
  Fl(2)R.7s Large red can buoy, ■ topmark
**Marina west mole**
  Fl(4)R.12s7m3M Slim red pyramid 3m
**Marina east mole**
  Fl(2)G.9s7m3M Slim green pyramid 3m

**Harbour Communications**
**Port Authority**
  San Sebastián de La Gomera Port Control
  VHF Ch 12 (24 hour)
  ☎ +34 922 870 357
**Marina La Gomera**
  VHF Ch 09 (24 hour)
  ☎ +34 922 141 769
  0830–1300, 1600–1800 weekdays, 0900–1300
  weekends and holidays
  Marina la Gomera, Av. Fred Olsen s/n, 38800 San
  Sebastián de la Gomera, Islas Canarias
  info@marinalagomera.es
  www.marinalagomera.es

## Friendly marina, great town and island

San Sebastián is the main harbour of La Gomera, with ferries running to Tenerife and El Hierro. Open to the southeast, it is easy to enter by day or night and provides a good base from which to explore the island. The town has strong links with Columbus, whose house is said to be on Calle Real and is now a museum and art gallery (open 1000–1300, 1530–1730 weekdays). The town hall (Ayuntameinto) was once the home of Columbus' friend (and possibly mistress) Beatriz de Bobadilla. The Iglesia Nostra Senhora de la Asunción a little further up Calle Real was where Columbus and his crew attended Mass before their departure. Also worth visiting is the Museo Arqueológico de la Gomera (open 1000–1800 weekdays, 1000–1400 weekends) housed in an old building next to the church.

The marina is a private concession from the Autodiad Portuaria de S/C de Tenerife. It is owned by the same company as Marina Puerto Chico in Santa Cruz de Tenerife, and has earned continuous praise since it opened in 1995–96. 'Quite the most pleasant marina in the Canaries' and 'without doubt the most helpful, well-run marina that I have come across in five years of cruising' are among the unsolicited comments received over the past decade. Inevitably the marina is very full between September and December, as well as in June when a sport-fishing championship brings thirty or more large motorboats to the island.  At all times it is recommended to get in touch well in advance and make a reservation, reconfirming a few days before arrival. The marina has 335 berths for yachts from 6–20m. There are many long stay yachts in this successful marina.

## Harbour approach and entrance

From the northeast the lighthouse of St.Cristobel is conspicuous, though the breakwater and town are concealed until past the headland. There are no outlying dangers, other than the Roca Bermeja

Colourful San Sebastián climbs ever up the ravine behind the harbour *Hilary Keatinge*

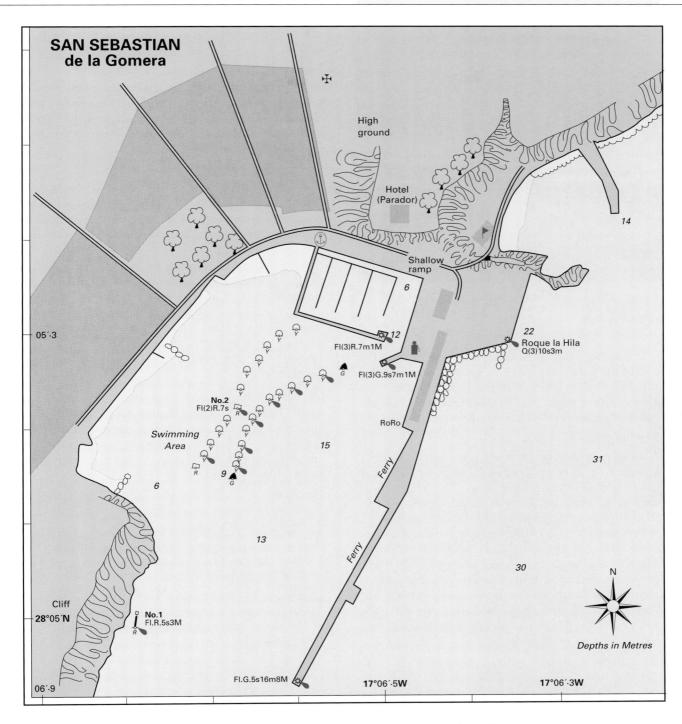

SAN SEBASTIAN
de la Gomera

High ground

Hotel (Parador)

14

Shallow ramp

6

05´.3

Fl(3)R.7m1M

12

22

Roque la Hila
Q(3)10s3m

Fl(3)G.9s7m1M

No.2
Fl(2)R.7s

RoRo

Swimming Area

15

Ferry

31

9

G

6

Ferry

13

30

N

Depths in Metres

Cliff

28°05´N

No.1
Fl.R.5s3M

Fl.G.5s16m8M

17°06´.5W

17°06´.3W

06´.9

mentioned above, though a considerable tide-rip can build up around Punta San Cristóbal. From the south or east the town on the north side of the valley can be seen from some distance, and the breakwater will be raised on closer approach. Again there are no outlying dangers and a course can be set to clear the breakwater end. Call San Sebastián de La Gomera Port Control on Ch 12 to request permission to enter the harbour area. Yachts may be instructed to delay entry if a ferry is entering or leaving. The breakwater is open to the southwest but gives good protection.

## Marina approach and entrance

After rounding the breakwater the buoyed channel leading to the marina will be seen ahead. A port and starboard buoy mark the channel entrance (not lit to avoid confusion for the commercial traffic), pass between the two rows of yellow buoys, some are lit. The purpose of this channel is to keep non-commercial craft clear of the large area that the ferries need for turning. It is important to keep to this channel. There is a somewhat larger (lit) port hand buoy about halfway up the channel. The final green buoy, nearest the marina entrance, is unlit.

Two small fishing boats approach the marina in the designated channel; it is not as difficult as it may sound
*Hilary Keatinge*

The dogleg marina entrance is directly beyond the end of the buoyed channel; skippers of larger yachts should be aware that it is relatively narrow, but with a minimum depth of 9m. Yachts approaching should call the marina on VHF Ch 09, or mobile phone.

### Berthing

A member of staff (a *marinero*, not merely a security guard) is on duty at all times, though English may not be spoken outside office hours. The fuel berth, at the marina entrance, doubles as the reception area, though yachts are often directed straight to a berth.

The eastern part of the marina – which suffers from surge in the infrequent southerly winds – contains the larger berths. All are alongside finger pontoons, including those stern-to the east wall. If allocated a berth in the latter area, beware the shallow sloping ramp in the far corner. Vessels in the 15–30m LOA range may be berthed alongside just

north of the fuel berth, but are likely to have to raft up.

### Anchorage

Anchoring in the harbour is not permitted at any time. If waiting for a berth in the marina and unwilling to raft up, in northeasterly winds good anchorage over sand can be found in one of the bays close southwest of the harbour.

### Formalities

Visit the office at the northwest corner of the marina taking the usual ship's papers, passports and insurance documents. The staff have long had a reputation for being notably helpful and speaking excellent English.

Note that San Sebastián de la Gomera is not a frontier port and one cannot be given an official exit stamp from the Canaries on La Gomera. However many places will accept a copy of a passport stamped by a marina with the arrival and departure dates, plus a receipt for marina dues paid. The nearest post for official clearance would be on Tenerife.

### Charges

In 2015 the cost for one night for a 12m yacht was approx. €26 including water, electricity and ICIG tax at 7%. Discounts available for payment in advance and for longer stays. Other taxes may also be payable.

### Facilities

*Water and electricity* On the pontoons.
   Good drinking water.
*WiFi* Within the marina one connection per boat for free.
   Connection for multiple devises available for a fee.
   Many of the bars and restaurants offer free connection.
*Showers* Well-kept showers next to the marina office,
   access by card, for which a small deposit is taken.
*Laundry* Washing left at the marina office before 0900
   will be returned dry and folded in the evening.
   Alternatively there is a launderette on Calle Real,
   beyond the church and post office.

The channel is to keep lsmall boats clear of the commercial traffic  *Hilary Keatinge*

*Weather forecast* Posted daily at the harbour office.

*Security* Security is good, with round-the-clock staffing and a card-activated gate to the entire marina area. The gate remains open during the day from 0600-2000 after which the appropriate card is needed.

*Fuel* Diesel and petrol available at the inner end of the reception berth, open 0830–1800.

*Bottled gas* Camping Gaz exchanges are readily available in the town. Most other bottles can be filled at the nearby DISA fuel station.

*Medical services* Ask in the marina office. Hospital just outside the town.

*Banks* Several in the town, all with cash dispensers.

*Shops/provisioning* Several supermarkets and bakeries, plus a convenient mini-market at the DISA petrol station across the road, which is run by the marina and open even when other shops are closed for holidays. The HiperTrebol supermarket at the western end of Avenida de Colón carries everything one might need when stocking up for a transatlantic passage. They will deliver to the marina.

*Produce market* Combined produce/fish market outside the HiperTrebol supermarket. The Saturday market here is said to offer a good variety of fresh produce, plus a baker and butcher.

*Cafés, restaurants & hotels* Good selection, including a spectacular four-star Parador Nacional on the hill high above the town.

*Car hire & taxis* In the ferry terminal on the breakwater, as well as in the town.

*Buses* Regular service throughout the island from the bus station next to the market.

*Ferries* RoRo ferries and large hydrofoils from Los Cristianos, sometimes continuing to El Hierro.

*Airport* Air services limited inter-island flights from the airport near Puerto de Santiago.

### Boatyard

Not as such, mainly for small local boats.

*Travel-lift* No. Shallow-draught boats of up to 7m or so are brought ashore by fork-lift truck, but the nearest travel-lifts are at Puerto de Santiago on the south coast, Los Cristianos (Tenerife) and Puerto de la Restinga (El Hierro). See pages 332, 315 and 350 respectively.

*General repairs and maintenance* Various. seek advice at the marina office.

*Engineer and rigging* Andy Altenhofer, who is German but speaks fluent English. ☎ +34 638 766 167, a.yachtservice@yahoo.de, www.a-y-s.eu.
Andy works from small premises on the east side of the marina. His team offer engine repairs, stainless steel welding and general services such as painting and antifouling, plus diving and underwater repairs. He handles rigging with Norseman terminals but does not have a swage machine. Spares can usually be sourced within 48 hours, though it can take ten days to get parts from mainland Europe. Offers guardianage service.

*Sailmaker & repairs* Rubén Chinea, makes and repairs sails, and canvas items. He also has a selection of general spares. He speaks Spanish, English and German ☎ +34 922 141 967 or +34 600 256 239. Rubén works for Canary Sail and can also be contacted through their office (see below).

*Rigging* Darren Lee specialises in rigging but can help with a wide variety of problems. He carries a good supply of stainless steel and rigging materials. He is agent for Nordest the large chandlery in Santa Cruz de Tenerife (agents for Selden, Bluewave, Wichard etc. see relevant listing under Tenerife). Contact Darren through Canary Sail ☎ +34 922 141 967.

*Chandlery* Náutica y Pesca Océano Azul, ☎ +34 922 141 502, on Avenida de Colón has a small amount of chandlery and yacht paint among its fishing equipment and general hardware. Little English is spoken. For advice and local knowledge useful for those afloat (if they are not too busy) speak to the team at Canary Sail, headed by Jim Grey, Apartado 211, Calle Del Medio, San Sebastián. ☎ +34 922 141 967.

*Club náutico* The Club Náutico de la Gomera has premises on the Playa la Cueva close to the root of the main breakwater. Its bar and restaurant are open to visitors, but use of other facilities (including the swimming pool) requires temporary membership.

## Fair weather anchorages on the southeast coast

There are three offering some protection from the prevailing winds, with good holding in 8m or more over firm sand. Nothing much to offer ashore other than dramatic cliffs and dry brown hillsides:

⚓ **Playa de La Guancha** 28°04'·4N 17°07'·7W

⚓ **Playa de Suarez** 28°02'·5N 17°01'W

⚓ **Playa del Medio** 28°02'·2N 17°10'·8W

In addition to the three described above:

⚓ **Playa de El Cabrito** 28°03'·7N 17°08'·5W
At the foot of a wide, wooded valley about 2M south of San Sebastián, Playa de El Cabrito ('goat beach') provides good holding in 6m over sand and stones, but any northerly swell is likely to work its way in. Be prepared for katabatic

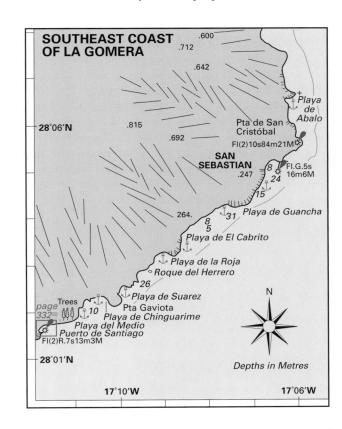

Looking northwest into the secluded anchorage at Playa de El Cabrito, a few miles south of San Sebastián de la Gomera
*Nigel Mercier*

windblasts and be ready to leave at short notice should the wind veer. There is a small settlement ashore, which includes a quiet hotel where facilities are reserved for residents. Land on the beach or at the small jetty in the southwest corner.

### ⚓ Playa de la Roja (Playa de Oroja)
28°03'·3N 17°09'·1W

Just round the headland from Playa de El Cabrito, Playa de la Roja is marked at its southwest end by a distinctive exposed rock resembling a shark's fin, known locally as the Rock of Heroes. There are a few small craft moorings off the dark sand beach and the bay is said to offer particularly good snorkelling, but again swell can be a problem.

### ⚓ Playa de Chinguarime 28°02'·3N 17°10'·5W

A possible night anchorage. Just over a mile northeast of Puerto de Santiago and tucked in behind the protruding Punta Gaviota, Playa de Chinguarime offers some protection both from the prevailing northeasterly winds and its associated swell. There are rocks in several places around the bay and a shallow reef in the northern corner, but the water is very clear making eyeball navigation straightforward. Anchor in 8–10m over sand.

## Puerto de Santiago
28°01'·6N 17°11'·8W (breakwater head)

**Lights**
**Breakwater**
Fl(2)R.7s13m3M Red column 5m
**North (outer) mole**
Fl(2)G.7s9m5M Green column 3M
**Northwest (inner) mole** Fl(2)G.7s1M
Green column standing in the water 1m

**Harbour Communications**
VHF Ch 16 (only during office hours)
**Harbourmaster**
☏ +34 922 895 275
0800–1530 weekdays only
*Note* Early in 2015 the harbour masters of Puerto de Santiago and Puerto de Vueltas were working as a team and when needs must were covering for each other in one port or the other.

### A small but pleasant fishing harbour facing onto a stony beach

A 4-star hotel development occupies the cliff top to the east, with stunning views, swimming pools and a lift connecting it with the bottom of the cliff. The island's airport, connecting only with Tenerife Nord, lies northwest of the town on the road to Valle Gran Rey and Puerto de Vueltas. The harbour breakwater was rebuilt and massively reinforced after damage caused by a southerly gale. Space for yachts along the breakwater is limited, and the bay is open to southerly swell. The harbour office is situated at its root.

Looking southwestwards into Puerto de Santiago
*Hilary Keatinge*

## Approach and entrance

As with the other islands, the hills fall away to the south into a series of low promontories and bays. Approaching from the east conspicuous tall conical evergreens on the east head of the bay present an excellent landmark, as do the low-rise white hotel buildings, the trees can also be seen over the headland when approaching from the southwest. The harbour has no particular hazards in the approach; it opens to the east, with the high breakwater wall running northeastwards from the western headland. The end of the breakwater has been further reinforced with large concrete blocks.

## Berthing and anchorage

Check with the security guard but in very calm conditions it might be possible to lie alongside the breakwater for a short period. (note: with the tidal rise of up to 2m at HWS) Much of the inner length is normally occupied by fishing boats. The quay is well provided with both bollards and ladders, and there is currently no ferry operating out of the port.

It is not possible to anchor within the harbour due to fishing boat moorings. However, in offshore winds a secure, if somewhat rolly, day-anchorage can be found in 5–6m to the northeast of the short stone pier. Holding is good over sand and stones. Dinghies can be left on the beach or at the head of the harbour, where there are convenient steps.

## Formalities

Visit the harbour office (if it is open) at the root of the breakwater with the usual ship's papers and passports, though it is doubtful if much notice will be taken of a yacht at anchor. No charge is made for anchoring.

## Facilities

*Water* Good water from a tap on the harbour wall or a hose in the boatyard.
*Showers* Basic showers in the harbour building (if open).
*Other facilities* There are few other facilities other than along the waterfront and in the town.
*Boatyard* The boatyard is run by Puerto Canarios.
  ☎ +34 922 895 275.
*Travel-lift* 45-tonne capacity, and with a new hoist dock which appears to have overcome the previous problems with turbulence, but few yacht-length props.

The breakwater in Puerto de Santiago with the conspicuous evergreens in the resort above  *Hilary Keatinge*

IV. THE CANARY ISLANDS

## Anchorages on the southwest coast of La Gomera

⚓ **Playa del Ereses**  28°01'·4N 17°14'W

About 2M west of Puerto de Santiago, Playa del Ereses is a scenic open bay east of Punta del Becerro. Anchor in 12–16m over sand, but watch out for rocks.

⚓ **Cala de la Cantera**  28°02'·1N 17°16'·4W

About 3M west of Playa del Ereses lies Cala de la Cantera ('quarry creek'), where a disused canning factory overlooks a small beach. Coming from the east one sees a large cave – the Cuevo del Obispo – and a natural rock arch. From the west first sight is of the factory and its associated stone pier at the southeast end of the beach. The bay sometimes suffers from swell, making it best to anchor in the centre in about 10m. If heading ashore by dinghy the beach is quite steep, and despite the poor condition of the pier it may offer the easiest shore access.

⚓ **Cala de la Negra and Cala de la Rajita**
28°02'·8N 17°17'·5W & 28°03'N 17°17'·9W

These two share a double bay, the latter accessible by road and with a few houses set back from the beach, though the old fish cannery has largely been demolished. Both anchorages offer good holding in about 8m over firm, dark sand and make sure the anchor is well into sand, there is foul ground closer in.

## Puerto de Vueltas (Valle Gran Rey)

28°04'·68N 17°19'·85W (outer breakwater head)

**Lights**

**Outer breakwater, head**
  Fl(3)R.9s1m5M Red column 1m
**Outer breakwater, angle**
  Q(9)15s3M West cardinal post, Ⅰ topmark
**Inner breakwater**
  Fl(2+1)G.21s16m3M Green column, red band 2m

**Harbour Communications**
  No VHF service
  ☎ +34 922 805 476
  0800–1530 weekdays only
  puertodevueltas@puertoscanarios.es

### Enlarged harbour still awaiting development

Puerto de Vueltas, also known as Valle Gran Rey after the impressive valley behind, is an old fishing harbour backed by high red cliffs that enjoys one of the most spectacular settings in all of the islands. One of the main attractions of the area is the walk up (or down) the spectacular Valle Gran Rey ('valley of the great king'). Although the ascent is not steep one possibility would be to take a taxi a few kilometres inland and walk back down the well-maintained tourist path. Close by is the more developed Playa La Calera with many hotels and restaurants. Over ten years ago a long, angled breakwater was built outside the old harbour wall with a ramp for a RoRo ferry. Today the harbour remains little used and there is no ferry service,

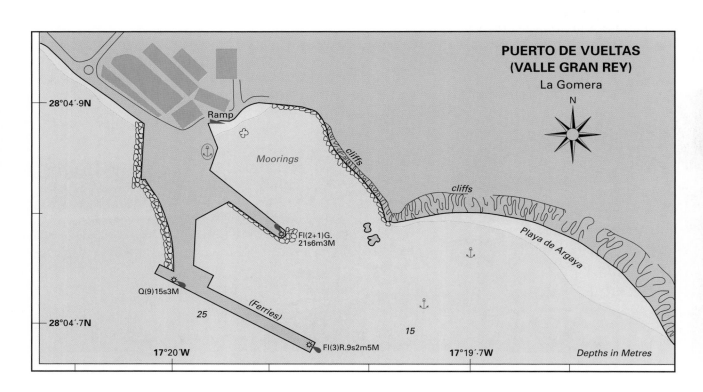

though there has been talk of a marina. It is possible to lie alongside, but seek permission from the harbour office.

### Approach and entrance

High cliffs line the west coast of La Gomera, but the harbour can be identified by the cluster of white houses rising up the valley and the long, pale grey breakwater. From the south the conspicuous rock just off Punta Iguala can be identified 2M southeast of the harbour. There are more outlying rocks just south of the entrance. From all directions keep 0·5M offshore. There are outlying rocks off the breakwater root, though most have been incorporated into the outer arm. There may be a backwash but no particular dangers.

### Berthing

Currently the inside of the inner breakwater is used by fishing and tourist boats. There is usually space for a few yachts with the possibility of a second row rafted out in settled northeasterlies. The facing of the breakwater has been improved and there are plenty of bollards and stainless steel ladders every 20m or so along the breakwater. There are five or six yachts bows-to the western quay on semi-permanent moorings. Note that concrete blocks project about 7m inwards from the end of the breakwater, providing some protection from southerly swell. The bay is full of private small craft on moorings. Anchoring in the inner harbour is not permitted, and the holding is said to be very poor.

The stunning Valle Gran Rey sweeps down to the sea with terraces lining each side *Hilary Keatinge*

Puerto de Vuelas, sometimes called Puerto Valle Gran Rey after the municipality of the area. Note the protective blocks off the end of the inner breakwater *Hilary Keatinge*

A road going nowhere but to the unused harbour area in Puerto de Vueltas *Hilary Keatinge*

## Anchorage

In the prevailing northeasterlies good anchorage can be found off Playa de Argaya, close southeast of the harbour, in 6–8m over sand (inside the 5m line the bottom is of rock and large stones). Holding is good and no charge is made. There can be fierce squalls funnelling down the Barranco de Argaya if a strong northerly is blowing. If the swell makes the bay too uncomfortable yachts may be allowed to anchor in the outer harbour, close to the inner wall. Protection may be good but the holding is said to be poor.

## Formalities and charges

Visit the harbour office with ship's papers and passports. In early 2015 the cost for one night, for a 12m boat, was approximately €12.

## Facilities

*Water* From a tap near the head of the harbour – the quality is usually excellent. For larger quantities the harbourmaster may be able to arrange a metered delivery from one of the manholes on the quay.

*Showers* Yet to materialise. There are patrons' toilets at the café mentioned below.

*Fuel* Available on the quay from a pump controlled by the Cofradía de Pescadores, 0900–1300, 1600–1800 Monday–Saturday. Small quantities by can from the filling station on the main road at La Calera, about 1·5km from the harbour.

*Medical services* Health centre on the main road, about 2km from the harbour.

*Bank* Bank with cash dispenser on Av. El Lano, about 600m from the harbour.

*Shops/provisioning* A good sized supermarket near the bank.

*Cafés & restaurants* Small café/bar at the head of the harbour, with good WiFi connection. Restaurants and hotels along the seafront.

*Car hire* An agency just outside the harbour gates, and others in the town.

*Taxis* In La Calera.

*Buses* To Puerto de Santiago, San Sebastián and elsewhere from a stop on the seafront about 300m from the harbour.

*Boatyard* None.

La Merica towers over Valle Gran Rey – the valley of the great king – just north of Puerto de Vueltas *Andy Scott*

# La Palma

**Between 28°27'N–28°51'N and 17°43'W–18°00'W**

## Introduction

*La Isla Verde* and *La Isla Bonita* are two of the names given to this gem of an island. La Palma is the most mountainous of the Canaries, its skyline is topped by the Roque de los Muchachos that rises to 2,422m above sea level from its base 4,000m below. Surrounded by dramatic heights is La Caldera de Taburiente; this crater has been hollowed out by erosion of the original volcanic crater over many millennia. It was here, in this almost impregnable area, that the indigenous Guanches made their last stand against the invading Spanish. The crater is 27km in circumference and drops dramatically 763m from the rim top. The entire area forms the Parque Nacional de la Caldera de Taburiente. Volcanologists remain busy on La Palma with the last eruption still in living memory (1971). A theory has been advanced that it is only a matter of time before the entire western part of La Palma detaches itself from the rest and slides catastrophically into the Atlantic Ocean. While this may well be correct – it appears that pressure inside the mountain is building all the time – estimated dates vary from any time now to 2515 or beyond. But as it is inconceivable that there would be no warning, it would be a pity to avoid La Palma on this account.

La Palma is the wettest and, therefore, greenest island in the archipelago, with an abundant and rich plant life thanks to the banks of clouds that swirl moisture in from the Atlantic. High above the cloud level the volcanic ridges rise into crystal pure air and

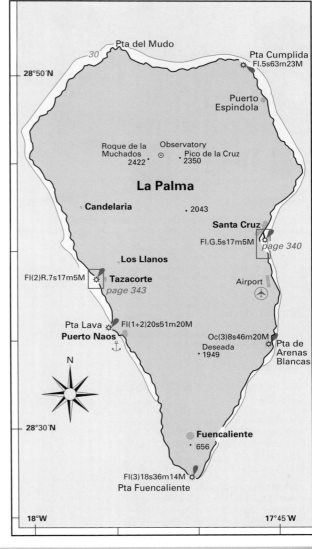

Observatories along the edge of the Calera de Taburiente
*Alan Spriggs*

IV. THE CANARY ISLANDS

Santa Cruz de la Palma is famous for its balconies, many enclosed by glass or festooned with flowers *Anne Hammick*

Dramatic views from the heights of La Palma *Alan Spriggs*

## Navigation

For information on **Magnetic Variation**, **Tides** and **Tidal Streams** see pages 224-225

Full **Emergency Service** information is on page 227

**Weather** and **Navigational Broadcasts** are listed on page 228

**Coast Radio Station**
**La Palma** 28°38'·9N 17°49'·6W
   Controlled from Tenerife 24 hours
**VHF** Ch 06, 20
**DSC** VHF MMSI 002241026

**Lighthouse and lights**
**Punta Cumplida** Fl.5s63m23M
   104·5°-vis-337° Grey tower 34m
**Punta de Arenas Blancas (Punta Salamera)**
   Oc(3)8s46m20M White futuristic tower 38m
**Punta Fuencaliente**
   Fl(3)18s36m14M 230·5°-vis-118·5°
   White tower, two red bands 24m
   *Note* The old light tower still stands nearby
**Punta Lava** Fl(1+2)20s51m20M
   Octagonal white tower, green lantern 48m

**Coast Radio Station**
**La Palma** 28°38'·9N 17°49'·6W, remotely controlled from
   Tenerife
**VHF** Ch 06, 16, 20 (24 hours)
**DSC** VHF MMSI 002241025, 28°39'N 17°50'W, remotely
   controlled from Tenerife

are the place of choice for many astrologers studying the wider universe from some twenty observatories, including the home of the largest optical infrared telescope in the world at the Observatory de El Roque de Los Muchachos.

Most of the population of 86,000 live round the capital Santa Cruz de La Palma and the local economy is based on agriculture, bananas, grapes and other crops that like the rich volcanic soil and, inevitably, on tourism; though with no beaches to talk of tourism is quite specialized, attracting the serious hikers and divers.

The coastline is such that there are only two harbours suitable for yachts, one on each side of the island; both contain marinas in which a yacht can safely be left while exploring by car. A road runs around the crater's northern edge to serve the observatories – as well as a stunning viewpoint well worth the tortuous drive up – while another leads to La Cumbrecita, on the southern rim.

### Approach and navigation

La Palma's great height – second only to Tenerife – makes it easy to identify from many miles off in reasonable visibility. The vast majority of yachts will approach from the north or east, and will encounter no off-lying hazards until close inshore. Northern sector winds predominate around La Palma and acceleration zones may be encountered off the northeast, northwest and southern tips of the island.

## East coast

### Puerto Espíndola

28°48'·71N 17°45'·81W (mole hammerhead)

#### Tiny harbour on exposed coast

Once a small trading port, the village of Espindola (sometimes written as Spíndola) is north of Santa Cruz de la Palma and 2M south of Punta Cumplida, the northeast corner of the island. It has a fleet of small local fishing boats and it attracts the sports fishing enthusiasts too. There is a crane on the hammerhead mole that lifts out the local boats but the small area of sheltered water is both too small and too shallow for most yachts. Although it would be possible to anchor off in exceptionally calm weather, be warned that there are several rocks in the approach and depths are not known.

### Playa de Santa Cruz

28°41'·26N 17°45'·52W (northern end of hammerhead)

Outside the harbour of Santa Cruz de la Palma and immediately north, there are two new breakwaters, one as a hammerhead, both roughly parallel to the shore and protecting a new beach. Either end of the hammerhead is lit, the northern one Fl.Y.5s8m3M and the southern light VQ(3)5s8m3M.

## Santa Cruz de la Palma

28°40'·27N 17°45'·84W (breakwater head)

**Lights**
**Breakwater**
  Fl.G.5s17m5M Green tower 8m
**Port hand 'A'** Fl.R.5s2M
  Red pillar buoy, ▪ topmark
**Port hand 'B'** Fl(2)R.7s2M
  Red pillar buoy, ▪ topmark
**Port hand 'C'** Fl(3)R.9s2M
  Red pillar buoy, ▪ topmark
**Port hand 'D'** Fl.R.5s2M
  Red can buoy, ▪ topmark
**Fishing harbour angle**
  Fl(4)R.11s9m3M Red post 4m
**Fishing harbour molehead**
  Fl.R.5s9m3M Red post 4m
**Container terminal** Fl(2+1)R.21s9m3M
  Red column, green band 4m
**Marina entrance, port side**
  Fl(2)R.7s5m3M Red pyramid 5m
**Marina entrance, starboard side**
  Fl(2)G.7s5m3M Green pyramid 5m

**Harbour Communications**
**Port authority**
  VHF Ch 16, 06 (24 hour)

#### Friendly city with good facilities

Santa Cruz de la Palma is situated mid-way down the eastern coast of this long island. It is one of the most attractive towns in the Canaries. Below and behind the new apartment blocks that line the shore much of the old city remains, with its cobbled streets, original Canarian houses and their ornately carved wooden balconies leading to shady squares, with a café or two. The city has a busy, friendly atmosphere and good facilities for storing up. Over the years many thousands of vessels have filled up on water and stores in Santa Cruz in preparation for an

The commercial harbour at Santa Cruz de la Palma, seen from the cliffs to the southwest. The marina lies behind the grey mole with white uprights at the head of the harbour
*Anne Hammick*

Atlantic crossing. Ferries, which berth on the breakwater and the southern wall of the marina, run to Tenerife, La Gomera and El Hierro. A constant stream of cruise ships dock on the outer breakwater and there is a dedicated walkway for their passengers into the city via the marina. On the inner side of the harbour is a container terminal and next to it a small harbour, the Dársena Pesquera, for local fishing vessels and other smallcraft. Yachts should pass on to the Marina La Palma.

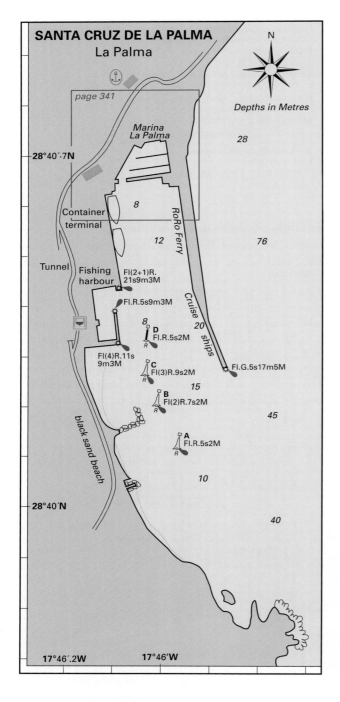

SANTA CRUZ DE LA PALMA
La Palma

page 341

Marina La Palma

28°40′.7N

Depths in Metres

28

Container terminal

8

Tunnel

Fishing harbour

Fl(2+1)R. 21s9m3M

RoRo Ferry

12

76

Fl.R.5s9m3M

8 **D** Fl.R.5s2M

Cruise ships

20

Fl(4)R.11s 9m3M

**C** Fl(3)R.9s2M

Fl.G.5s17m5M

15

**B** Fl(2)R.7s2M

45

black sand beach

**A** Fl.R.5s2M

10

28°40′N

40

17°46′.2W        17°46′W

### Harbour approach and entrance

The island is mountainous and the fall-away to the southeast is less pronounced than on Gran Canaria and Tenerife. In most weather conditions the white buildings of Santa Cruz are conspicuous at the foot of the mountains, though these are often cloud covered.

Santa Cruz is a large harbour by Canarian standards, with a wide entrance opening to the south and no natural hazards in the approach. A close watch needs to be kept for ferries and cruise ships, both in the approach and while proceeding up the harbour, where space is tight. The ferries that berth on the breakwater reverse into the RoRo slots, while the smaller hydrofoil berths against the marina mole. In addition there is a container berth on the west side of the harbour, and often a cruise ship or two for good measure. Following the harbour bye-laws, first contact must be made with the Traffic Control Centre on VHF Ch 06, likely then asked to change to Ch 09, while still two miles from the entrance. No vessel is allowed to enter the harbour without authorisation. Once inside the harbour, yachts must follow a designated – though unmarked – route up its western side towards the marina entrance.

*Entrance and exit of yachts and smallcraft*

After passing the end of the breakwater, yachts and small craft must continue across the harbour and not turn north for the marina entrance until close to buoy C. When leaving the marina they should head for buoy B, and not turn east to cross the harbour until between buoys B and A.

## Marina La Palma

**Harbour Communications**
  VHF Ch 09, 16
**Marina Office**
  ☎ +34 922 410 289 or +34 608 223 345
  0900–1300, 1700–1900 weekdays, 0900–1300 Saturday
  Dársena de Embarcaciones Menores, Puerto de S/C de La Palma, 38700 Santa Cruz de La Palma
  info@marinalapalma.es
  www.caleromarinas.com/marinas/la-palma

### New marina adjacent to traditional Canarian town

Responsibility for the marina's construction, maintenance and management was awarded as a joint venture to Puerto Calero SA of Lanzarote and the Real Club Náutico de La Palma for a term of 35 years. The marina and its complex were formally opened in July 2010, with offices, services and ancillary businesses such as shops and restaurants housed in an attractive curved building at the head of the harbour. The complex is open to custom from the city, just a three-minute walk away, and passengers off the cruise ships, as well as those in the marina.

## Marina approach and entrance

The marina lies at the head of the commercial harbour. Head for the west end of what may appear as a solid barrier. The main E/W breakwater is constructed as a bridge with supporting pillars from the seabed connected by concrete spans. As a result surge has been an ongoing problem in all parts of the marina. Make a call to the marina office on VHF Ch 09 (in addition to an earlier call to the Traffic Control Centre on VHF Ch 06). If a booking has not been made yachts should tie up on the reception berth that is directly ahead on entry, under the windows of the marina office; those who have pre-booked are likely to be directed straight to their berth.

### The surge problem

In early 2013 permission was granted to install an adjustable barrier in the marina entrance such that in times of heavy swell it may be raised; work commenced late 2014. The plan was that in bad weather the gate would be kept closed, with one metre extending above the water. Sensors would control the height depending on the tidal state and staff will be on hand 24/7 to open when required (VHF channel 09). When open the gate would drop to a sill on the seabed, leaving a minimum depth of 5m. Work has been halted indefinitely (late 2015).

## Berthing

The marina contains 180 berths for yachts of up to 18m, 55 of them able to take boats of 13–14m LOA and 34 capable of berthing more than 14m, all in wide bays between long finger pontoons. Often yachts will be allocated a double berth and advised to lie off the pontoons when not on board or at night. Until the surge problem is solved it is advisable, if alongside, to run multiple lines and put out plenty of fenders. Each hammerhead can berth 22m, while there is a single 25m slot in the northeast corner, and at least 25% will be reserved for visitors. Depths throughout the marina are generous, with at least 6m, but 4·5m minimum at the entrance. Pre-booking is preferable, call or email as per the details above.

## Formalities

Visit the marina office with the usual passports, ship's papers and evidence of insurance. The staff are particularly friendly and helpful and speak excellent English. If clearing out of the Schengen zone it is necessary to have a departure (or entry) form stamped by immigration officials. Sometimes, if arranged, this can be done at the marina office, or by visiting the Immigration Office in the ferry building.

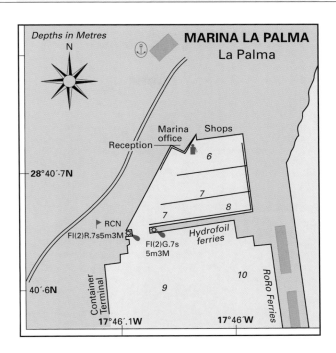

Note: working hours are 0800–1400 Monday to Friday, not at weekends. If planning to arrive or leave The Canaries via the islands of La Gomera or El Hierro it is necessary to obtain clearance here in Santa Cruz de La Palma; ask for guidance from the marina office.

## Charges

In 2015, for a 12m yacht for one night the cost was approximately €25.17 including water, electricity and taxes. Increasing discounts are available for stays of 90, 180 and 365 days. See the website or contact the office for full details.

## Facilities

*Water and electricity* On the pontoons.

*WiFi* Available in the marina, ask for the code in the Office.

*Showers* In the services block, with access by electronic card. Cards from the office, for a small deposit.

*Launderette* Coin-operated washer-dryer in the services block, 2 x €2 coins per cycle.

*Weather forecast* At the marina office.

*Security* 24/7 with CCTV cameras and security guards 0800-0300, after that the Port Police are on watch.

*Fuel* Diesel and petrol pumps at the fuel berth near reception, 0800-2000 Monday–Friday, 0800-1530 Saturday.

*Bottled gas* Camping Gaz exchanges at a hardware store 1·5km from marina. The DISA fuel station, 500m from marina, will exchange the larger NuB bottles.

*Medical services* Doctors in the town and a hospital (which looks more like a five-star hotel) on the slopes to the west.

*Banks* ATM in the marina complex. Banks in the city, all with cash dispensers.

*Shops/provisioning* SPAR on site (closed Mondays). In the city several good supermarkets able to supply all needs if storing up for the Atlantic passage, though perhaps without quite the variety of Las Palmas de Gran

IV. THE CANARY ISLANDS

Looking back down the harbour of Santa Cruz de la Palma from the marina *Alan Spriggs*

Canaria or Santa Cruz de Tenerife. The Boutique del Pan opposite the market is recommended for bread and cakes, and is open daily including Sunday.

*Produce market* The small market on Avenida del Puente near the centre of the city is open 0800–1400 Monday to Saturday. There is a large market on the parking area behind the marina on the first and third Sunday of the month.

*Cafés, restaurants & hotels* Wide choice at all price levels, including some delightful pavement cafés in the town. Several eating and drinking establishments overlook the marina, while the Real Club Náutico has both a bar and a more formal restaurant.

*Club náutico* Since the opening of the marina the Real Club Náutico de Santa Cruz de la Palma has welcomed

A surge barrier at the entrance to the marina has yet to be put in place *Calero Marinas*

crews of yachts berthed in the marina. Use of the club's outdoor pool is free, and it may be possible to use the indoor pool, gym, jacuzzi and sauna for a small charge.

*Car hire* At the ferry terminal on the breakwater and at the airport.

*Taxis* A taxi rank at the port exit. Can be pre-booked.

*Buses* To the airport and throughout the island.

*Ferries* Regular service to La Gomera and Tenerife.

*Air services* European and inter-island flights from the airport about 7km south of Santa Cruz.

### Boatyard

There is a small boatyard area behind the marina building where smallcraft are lifted out by a forklift truck. There is a larger boatyard at the fishing harbour, and though only basic skills are available DIY work is permitted, as is living aboard while ashore. Both are monitored by CCTV cameras. Seek advice and details from the marina office.

*Travel-lift* 70-tonne hoist in the fishermen's harbour, careful supervision would be essential. Best arranged via the marina office, though it may also be necessary to visit the Port Authority building to collect the necessary paperwork. Payment is required in advance.

*Engineers & electronics* Ask at the marina office. Náutica El Chopo (see *Chandlery*, below) is distributor for Volvo Penta engines and can organise work on other makes.

*Sail repairs* Small repairs can be carried out locally – ask at the marina office – but larger jobs would need to be sent to La Gomera or Tenerife.

*Chandlery* Náutica El Chopo in the marina complex. ☎ +34 922 420 076, open 0900–1400, 1600–2100 Monday to Friday, 0900–1400, 1700–2000 Saturday. It stocks a reasonable range of chandlery and fishing gear, including lines, fenders, paint and stainless steel fittings. There is a larger branch in Los Llanos on the western side of the island.

# West coast

# Puerto Tazacorte

28°38'·46N 17°56'·63W (inner breakwater, west head)

### Lights
**Marks work on new outer breakwater**
Q.R.5M Red pillar buoy 3m
**Outer breakwater**
Q(9)15s7m3M West cardinal post, ⟂ topmark 7m
**Inner breakwater, west head**
Fl(2)R.7s17m5M Red post 2m
**Inner breakwater, east head**
Fl(2)R.7s6m5M Red post 2m
*Note* The above two lights are synchronised and have
identical characteristics
**East mole**
Fl(2)G.7s7m1M Green post 3m
**Inner harbour, port side (marina reception)**
Fl(3)R.9s7m1M Red post 6m
**Inner harbour, starboard side**
Fl(3)G.9s5m1M Green post
**Old harbour mole**
Q(9)15s3M West cardinal post 3m
*Note* Not associated with the main harbour – see
below

### Marine farm
Three marine farms, each marked by four yellow pillar
buoys with × topmarks, either Fl(3)Y.9s3M, Fl(4)Y.11s3M
or Fl(5)Y.13s3M, lie northwest of Puerto Tazacorte,
centred on 28°39'·1N 17°57'·3W, 28°39'·2N 17°57'·8W
and 28°39'·4N 17°57'W respectively.

### Harbour Communications
VHF Ch 09, 16 (0800–2100 June–Sept. As per office
hours for the rest of the year)
### Marina office
☎ +34 922 480 386
0900–1300 & 1500–1800 weekdays,
0800–1300 Saturday
Puerto Deportivo s/n, 38779 Tazacorte
informacion@puertotazacorte.com
www.puertotazacorte.com

## A possible last port before crossing

Puerto Tazacorte lies halfway down the west coast of
La Palma, about 0·5M south of the original harbour
whose derelict breakwater was rebuilt in the late
'90s and enlarged to shelter a popular swimming
area off a small, black-sand beach. The end of the
restored breakwater is lit. Both harbours occupy the
mouth of the steep-sided valley that originates in the

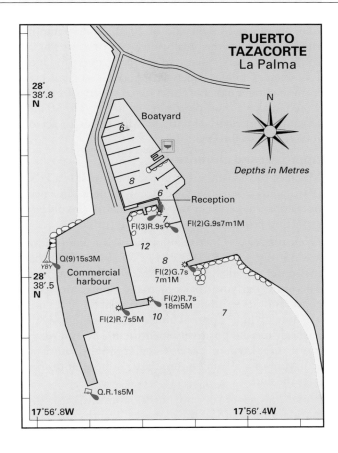

Taburiente crater (well worth a day trip inland to
explore). There are cliffs to the north of the valley
mouth, while to the south the coastline is lower with
the land behind sloping gently up to the base of the
central spinal range. Terraces of bananas line all but
the steepest inclines.

Work to enlarge the main harbour started late in
1997 and the massive breakwater extension was
officially opened in December 2002 but not completed
until 2014. Then development stalled, though
negotiations with the ferry companies are said to be
ongoing. However, the inner harbour was converted
into a modern, full-service marina. The marina was

*Beyond the sea of bananas, the outer breakwater gives
protection to Puerto Tazacorte and its marina, it has no
commercial business as yet* Hilary Keatinge

**IV. THE CANARY ISLANDS**

fully operational by the end of 2010. Nine pontoons run inwards from the breakwater, with two more in the southeast corner of the harbour earmarked for local fishermen. Though somewhat remote – isolated even from the bright lights of Santa Cruz – Puerto Tazacorte would make a fine departure point for an Atlantic crossing, particularly for those who prefer to set off relaxed and well-rested.

### Approach and entrance

Much of the coastal area off the southwest is a PSSA (Particularly Sensitive Sea Area) though this need not concern a yacht as it is mainly involves a reporting procedure for commercial traffic.

*From the south* Once the lighthouse on Punta Lava (28°35'·8N, 17°55'·5W, Fl(1+2)W.20s) is identified the outer breakwater is 2·8m to the northwest. There are outlying rocks at many points along the coast and it is advisable to keep at least a mile offshore while approaching Tazacorte until the harbour can be positively identified. The end of the inner breakwater carries a large and unusual sculpture of a leaning figure that can be seen peering over the end.

*From the north* do not turn landwards for the marina until south of the entrance. Depths are good, and the double wall configuration offers protection from northwesterly winds and seas for a useful distance before the inner harbour is entered. Crucially, the inner entrance has been greatly improved by overlapping moles and while these make it narrower and something of a dog-leg, they eliminate surge in all but the strongest southerly winds.

### Berthing

The reception and fuel pontoon are to port on entry into the marina, overlooked by the marina office. A call on VHF Ch 09 before arrival is requested, and it is likely that a yacht will be directed straight to a berth by the *marineros*. There is berthing for 341 boats of up to 14m, all alongside finger pontoons; and 70 berths can take boats of 12m or more. Although the marina has never turned anyone away it is advisable to book in advance.

### Anchorage

There is no permitted anchorage and indeed, particularly in winter, it would be dangerous to do so.

### Formalities

Visit the marina office overlooking the reception pontoon with the ship's papers, passports and insurance document. British yachtsmen may have feelings of déjà vu when greeted in perfect colloquial English by Janet Gómez León, who was born within the sound of Bow Bells when her parents immigrated to London; Janet returned to the island on her marriage. Other members of the staff are equally

The remarkable guardian of the inner breakwater
*Hilary Keatinge*

friendly and helpful, if slightly less fluent in English. The marina office staff can provide documentation with formal details of entry and departure.

### Charges

In 2015, the cost for a 12m yacht for one night was approximately €17.90 including water and 7% tax, but excluding electricity, which is metered. Discounts are available for stays of 30, 90 and 180 days.

### Facilities

*Water and electricity* On all pontoons, as well as in the boatyard.

*WiFi* Throughout the marina, check in the office for the code, there is a nominal charge. Also available in several of the cafés round the beach in Tazacorte and more in Los Llanos. In the marina services building there is a business centre with computers, printer, copier and fax machine available.

*Showers* Smart cubicles with shower, wash basin and toilet in the services building. The water is heated by solar panels on the roof, so may be at its hottest later in the day!

*Launderette* Coin-operated machines in the services/office block.

*Fuel* At the reception pontoon in front of the marina office and available during office hours. Most credit cards are accepted.

*Bottled gas* Camping Gaz exchanges in the marina. Other refills in Santa Cruz de La Palma.

*Weather forecast* Internet forecast displayed at the marina office.

*Security* Provided by both electronics gates and CCTV, but one suspects that the threat is fairly minor to start with.

*Other facilities* include covered car parking area, bike hire, recycling bins, and a pumpout station.

*Medical services* Health centre in Puerto Tazacorte with a pharmacy en route.

*Banks* In Tazacorte town (not in the port) and Los Llanos, plus cash dispensers.

*Shops/provisioning* There is a small supermarket near the old north harbour, open 0800–2000 Monday to Saturday, with more shops in Tazacorte and Los Llanos (some of which offer a delivery service).

*Cafés & restaurants* Pleasant outdoor café at the head of the harbour, with several more along the beach to the north and around the old harbour. A bar/restaurant is planned for the upper floor of the marina reception building (where there will be an outstanding view).

*Car hire & taxis* Both readily available, and best arranged via the marina office.

*Buses* Regular service to Los Llanos and Santa Cruz from a bus stop on the beach road leading north from the harbour.

*Ferry* Day excursion boat for whale and dolphin watching.

*Air services* European and inter-island flights from the airport near Santa Cruz. Though only 25 miles along a well-marked route east across the mountains, allow an hour to be comfortable.

### Boatyard

There is a large boatyard area and extensive dry-storage racks for smaller craft on the east side of the harbour, with 24-hour security. Best suited to DIY work, but with some skills available locally. There is a facility for long-term boat storage. Reservation is essential.

*Travel-lift* 60-tonne capacity hoist and a 125-tonne mobile crane. The charges for the hoist and storage are very reasonable.

*Engineers & electronics* Repairs available locally – ask at the marina office.

*Chandlery* Náutica Tazacorte with a wide range of services is situated in the boatyard. ① +34 922 480 330. Open 0900-1300, 1600-1900 Monday–Saturday. Náutica El Chopo, has premises at Los Llanos (8km away) as well as Marina La Palma. They will deliver to the marina. ① +34 922 402 256, info@nauticaelchopo.com

*Charts* It is intended that a limited stock of charts will be on sale at marina reception.

## Puerto Naos

28°35'·06N 17°54'·61W (beach)

### Open beach anchorage

A once small fishing village, south of the new lighthouse at Punta de Lava on the southwest coast, Puerto Naos now forms one of La Palma's mercifully few tourist resorts. The open bay could offer a pleasant enough daytime anchorage in calm weather, perhaps for lunch and a quick swim, but it is seldom really free from swell. Holding is reasonable over sand and rock, but jet skis and parasailing make the area less than peaceful.

Marina Tazacorte is well sheltered with the office and facilities in the building overlooking the marina
*Hilary Keatinge*

IV. THE CANARY ISLANDS

# El Hierro

**Between 27°38'N–27°51'N and 17°53'W–18°10'W**

## Introduction

El Hierro is the most southerly and most westerly of the Canary islands. This volcanic island has some 500 visible cones, including the most recent ones coming through the Atlantic seabed just two miles off the southern tip in 2011 and 2012. But all has gone quiet again (April 2015), though the marine life has improved and increased dramatically following the prolonged warming of the surrounding sea after the eruption. On the road north out of La Restinga there is a new Geoparque, the Centro de Interpretacion Vulcanologico, with an impressive interactive facility where you can see footage that reproduces the recent eruptions.

Before Columbus sailed the Atlantic El Hierro was known as 'the island at the end of the world' because in the 2nd century BC the Egyptian astrologer Ptolemy placed a prime meridian at Punta Orchilla on the western tip (the island is also known as 'The Meridian Isle'). The French scientists under Cardinal Richelieu agreed with this and it would be several decades after the establishment of Greenwich as the Meridian, in 1885, before every nation would change their lines of longitude.

When the northern side of the volcano slid into the sea this is all that was left *Hilary Keatinge*

The capital Valverde is a tortuous drive high inland, 570m up above Puerto de la Estaca on the east coast. The main source of island income is agriculture; tourism is growing, though hampered by travel connections with the island. There is now only one ferry six days a week to and from Los Cristianos on Tenerife, but there are several flights a day to Tenerife North Airport. The tourists come mainly to walk or dive and there are well-organized facilities for both groups.

El Hierro is somewhat triangular in shape, with high forbidding cliffs up to 1,000m round much of the island. The highest peak, Malpaso, in the centre of the island is 1,501m above sea level. 50,000 years ago much of the northern side of the island slid violently into the sea leaving behind a wide amphitheatre of flat and fertile land known as El Golfe; the devastating consequences of this landslide right across the Atlantic can only be imagined.

Scenically the island is magnificent with the fireproof Canary Island pine and 'laurisilva' (laurel) forests high in the centre and roadsides lined with wild flowers. The drier moonscape lava fields flow down to the south. There are a few beaches but several well-known natural rock pools on the rugged north coast attract those in the know in the warmer months.

**There are two harbours** On the ENE is Puerto de la Estaca with a small marina and ferry port, and La Restinga on the southern tip. Neither are Ports of Entry.

There is a free WiFi service advertised throughout the island, but it is advisable to have a personal hotspot system. Several bars and cafés have a free service.

## Navigation

For information on **Magnetic Variation**, **Tides** and **Tidal Streams** see pages 224-225

Full **Emergency Service** information is on page 227

**Weather** and **Navigational Broadcasts** are listed on page 228

**Coast Radio Station**
**El Hierro** 27°47'·7N 17°56'·2W
   Controlled from Tenerife 24 hours
**VHF** Ch 23, 74
**DSC** VHF MMSI 002241026

**lighthouse and lights**
**Puerto de la Estaca**
   Fl.G.5s14m5M Green column 7m
**Puerto de la Restinga**
   Fl(2)G.7s15m1M Green column 1m
**Punta de Orchilla** Fl.5s132m24M
   Octagonal grey stone tower, grey and white building 25m

## Approach and navigation

Northern sector winds predominate around El Hierro, producing an often protected area to the SSW of the island. Acceleration zones may be encountered off the northeastern tip and have also been reported on the east coast between Punta de la Bonanza and Punta Restinga.

Approaching from north or northeast the coast appears low and ragged, with outlying rocks and hills rising steeply inland. The first houses seen will be those of Tamaduste with its seawater bathing area developed among the rocks. A close look will show that the village is at the base of an old crater, half of which has been eroded by the sea. The island's airport lies a short distance to the south, by which time Valverde, the island's capital can be seen high on a ridge inland. If approaching at night its lights will be seen from 20M or more in good visibility, but in unsettled weather cloud is likely to obscure much of the higher land.

IV. THE CANARY ISLANDS

Spring colour at the edge of the world *Hilary Keatinge*

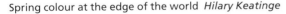

An unforgiving sparsely inhabited coast but awesome at every turn *Hilary Keatinge*

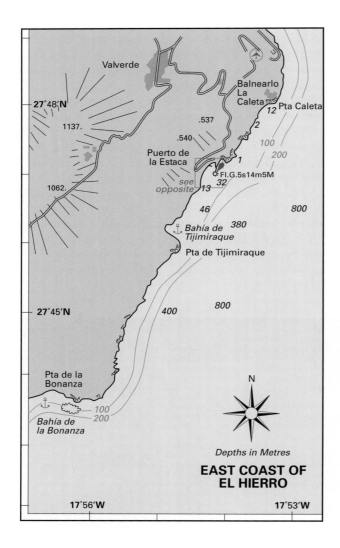

Valverde

27°48'N

1137.

.537

.540

Balnearlo La Caleta

Pta Caleta

12

2

Puerto de la Estaca

100

200

1062.

*see opposite*

13

1

☆Fl.G.5s14m5M

32

46

800

⚓ *Bahía de Tijimiraque*

380

Pta de Tijimiraque

27°45'N

400

800

Pta de la Bonanza

100

200

*Bahía de la Bonanza*

N

Depths in Metres

**EAST COAST OF EL HIERRO**

17°56'W                17°53'W

## Harbours and anchorages

## Puerto de la Estaca

27°46'·83N 17°54'·06W (breakwater head)

**Lights**
**Breakwater**
  Fl.G.5s14m5M Green column 7m
**Port hand buoy** Fl.R.5s2M
  Red pillar buoy, ■ topmark
**Inner harbour entrance, starboard side**
  Fl(2)G.7s5m3M Slim green pyramid 3m
**Inner harbour entrance, port side**
  Fl(2)R.7s5m3M Slim red pyramid 3m

**Harbour Communications**
  VHF Ch 14, 16
**Port Authority/Marina** ☎ +34 922 550 903
  0600–2200 daily
  controlhierro@puertosdetenerife.org
  salvador@puertosdetenerife.org
  www.puertosdetenerife.org

### Ferry port and recently developed marina

Puerto de la Estaca is used by the car ferry from Tenerife. In 2015 work was completed in the inner basin to install three pontoons to accommodate 87 boats of up to 15m, with space for larger craft of up to 40m alongside the breakwater. Anchoring in any part of the harbour is not permitted.

### Approach

**CAUTION**

At 27°47'·2N, 17°53'·6W, 0·5m northeast of the breakwater, there is a shoal, the Bajo de Roca Anegada, that carries only 1·8m at low water. Several charts have inaccurate data.

Coming from the northeast keep at least 0·5M offshore, the breakwater will be sighted on rounding a bluff 2M south of the airfield, though the zigzag wall of the road running up from the harbour may become visible before the breakwater itself. At least 15 minutes before arrival call the harbour authorities on Ch16 to request entry. There may be ferry traffic.

### Entrance and berthing

The entrances opens to the S/SW. Entering the outer harbour is straightforward, with shelter from wind and seas once inside the breakwater. There is a slight dogleg to gain the inner basin, the gap about 35m wide at its narrowest point. Depths are generous with a minimum of 5m throughout. There is ample room to manoeuvre. To book a berth in advance call or email as above.

The new marina being put into place at Puerto de la Estaca. The new marina office and facilities block is just visible on the right. Note that by the time the work was finished there were no longer any moorings nor was anchoring allowed
*Puertos Canarias*

## Formalities

Take the ship's papers and passports to the Marina Office. At least one official speaks good English.

Note that Puerto de la Estaca is not a frontier port, and one cannot obtain an exit stamp here from the Canaries, Spain or the Schengen Area such as may be required on arrival in your next territory. Enquire locally before crossing to El Hierro and mention that you will be stopping there. It may be necessary for the skipper to visit Santa Cruz or Los Cristianos on Tenerife or Santa Cruz de la Palma, on La Palma to obtain official clearance.

## Charges

In 2015 the cost for up to two days for a 12m boat on the new pontoons was €25.83 including taxes, electricity and water.

## Facilities

*Water & Electricity* On the pontoons.
*WiFi* Free WiFi around the island (see above).
*Showers* New facility on the quay to the north west of the pontoons, ask for a key in the office.
*Launderette* Yes.
*Weather forecast* Available at the office.
*Security* The marina is fenced and there is controlled access to the pontoons.
*Fuel* Not at the moment. There is a DISA filling station on the way into Valverde.
*Bottled gas* Camping Gaz exchanges at the filling station in Valverde.

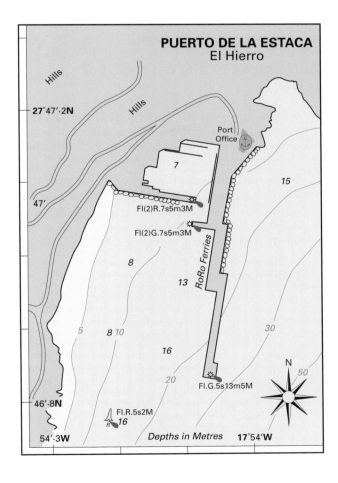

*Medical services* Hospital just outside Valverde.

*Banks* In Valverde, with cash dispensers.

*Shops/provisioning* Two supermarkets and other shops (including an excellent bakery) in Valverde. Both supermarkets are at the far end of the town if coming from Puerto de la Estaca and close for lunch 1300–1630 weekdays. Open until 1400 on Saturday, closed Sunday. Although more than equal to everyday needs, Valverde might not be the best place to provision for an Atlantic crossing.

*Produce market* Saturday morning market in Valverde.

*Cafés, restaurants & hotels* Several in Valverde.

*Taxis & car hire* At the port when the ferry comes in, or can be organised via the office.

*Buses* A bus to Valverde leaves the harbour every 2 hours 0800–1700. From there it is possible to travel onwards to Frontera, Taibique and Puerto de la Restinga.

*Ferries* One service a day, except Saturday, to/from Tenerife.

*Air services* From the small airport about 5km north of the harbour but only to Tenerife North Airport.

*Travel-lift* A travel-lift is planned for the distant future; the necessary dock already exists at the root of the west mole and there is no shortage of hardstanding.

*Engineers* A range of skills is available on the island – enquire at the marina office. Spares would most likely need to be ordered from Tenerife.

Many other facilities in Valverde, which is approximately 9km uphill from the port. Consider booking a hire car for collection from the port (Cicar is a good option), or take a taxi, though outside ferry times you may have to order one by phone.

## Anchorages on the east coast of El Hierro

As with nearly all anchorages round the Canaries these are only comfortable in very settled conditions. Even then one should be alert to local weather conditions such as downdraughts and swell.

⚓ **Bahía de Tijimiraque** 27°46'·2N 17°54'·8W

Nearly 1M south of Puerto de la Estaca and just north of the headland of the same name, is a deeply indented bay formerly used as a refuge by local boats in strong southerlies. There is a small sandy beach.

⚓ **Bahía de la Bonanza** 27°43'·7N 17°56'·6W

The famous arched rock Roque de la Bonanza – 'Fair Weather Rock' – which in northerly conditions is often surrounded by calm water, though there may be breaking waves offshore. South from this headland runs a narrow strip of beach 2M long, backed by an impressive cliff and with the Parador Nacional at its southern end. Although a feasible fair-weather anchorage this stretch is very deep – at least 30m close inshore over rock and stones.

# Puerto de la Restinga

27°38'·32N 17°58'·92W

**Lights**
**South breakwater**
Fl(2)G.7s15m1M Green column 1m
**West breakwater**
Fl(2)R.7s3M Red column 4m

**Harbour Communications**
VHF Ch 09
**Harbour office**
☎ +34 922 557081 or +34 678 797197
0800–1400 weekdays only
jpadpad@puertoscanarias.es

## Much improved harbour

Puerto de la Restinga was originally constructed as a harbour of refuge for fishermen working off the inhospitable southwest coast of El Hierro. Its single, very solid, breakwater gave good protection from the easterly quadrant, but westerly winds – and, more importantly, seas – rolled straight into the harbour. A curved west breakwater was completed during 2006 and two pontoons laid in the northeast corner of the harbour. At the same time the old south breakwater was massively reinforced and embellished. Work then paused before an inner mole was added in 2010. It is planned to add a 25m spur running northwards from the end of the south breakwater, but this has not yet been done.

The impressive steep-sided east coast of El Hierro
*Hilary Keatinge*

Although the town itself has grown surprisingly little over the past decade or more, the adjacent coastline is said to offer some of Europe's best diving and is home to several PADI (Professional Association of Diving Instructors) centres. The Reserva Marina Mar de las Calmas administer the area, from offices near the root of the breakwater.

The coastline is divided into three zones, originally marked by buoys (no longer on station) and distinctive markings on the cliffs: Zone A, an 'Integral Reserve' where everything other than passing through by boat is prohibited; Zone B, a 'Restricted Area', where swimming and Scuba diving are permitted; Zone C, 'Traditional Use', where anchoring, fishing from a boat, spearfishing and shellfish collecting are forbidden. The harbour lies in Zone C, with Zone B and then Zone A about 0·5M to the northwest. These areas are monitored daily from land by wardens with binoculars as well as by boat. If planning to explore the coastline it would be wise to obtain current information from the above office, as there is talk of including the whole of the south and much of the east coast of the island in the reserve area.

### Approach and entrance

A group of low volcanic cones and lava flows form the southern point of the island, and east of the harbour the swell breaks on a reef that runs out 0·75M from Punta Restinga so keep well off and do not to steer for the end of the massive breakwater until it bears due north. The final approach from south or west should also be with the breakwater end bearing due north.

Large concrete blocks are piled loosely along the outside of the breakwater, currently extending around its head and into the harbour, and providing some reduction in the surge along the quay.

### Berthing

The marina can accommodate up to 100 on the pontoons and more on the 220m of quay. Reservations are possible. On approach, call up on Ch 09. There is usually a *marinero* to help with lines. The official reception berth is alongside the western part of the breakwater, ahead of the bright orange Salvamente Maritimo vessel, if it is in, and other government-owned craft. If a berth is available many skippers will prefer to go directly onto the pontoon. There are finger pontoons, but those on the eastern pontoon, for the smaller craft, are not capable of supporting any weight. If it is necessary to go alongside the wall good fendering will be necessary, together with long warps to accommodate the tidal differences (MHWS 2·0m). Although the concrete edge has been smoothed by the bollards, and heavy-duty rubber strips affixed to the side at regular intervals, chaffing gear would still be necessary for all but the shortest stay.

Up to eight yachts of 14m or less can berth on the south end of the west pontoon, though two or three visitors may be allowed to lie against the north side of the 'joining piece' – the most sheltered spot in the entire harbour. However, this area should not be used without prior permission.

There is good depth, minimum 8m, to be found at the main pontoon berths, with 2–3m at the 'joining piece'.

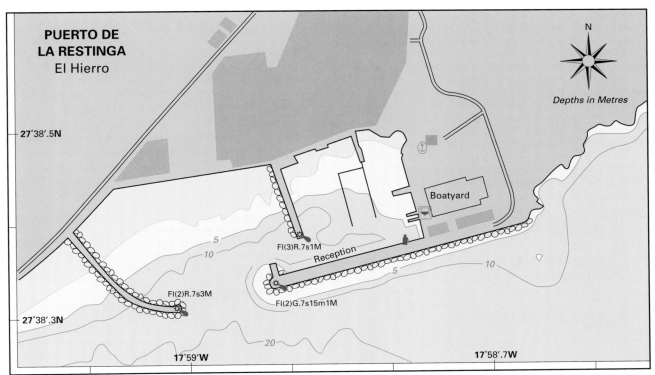

**PUERTO DE LA RESTINGA**
El Hierro

27°38'.5N

*Depths in Metres*

Boatyard

Reception

Fl(3)R.7s1M

Fl(2)R.7s3M

Fl(2)G.7s15m1M

27°38'.3N

17°59'W

17°58'.7W

IV. THE CANARY ISLANDS

The waves on the Art Deco finish of the breakwater tell their own story  *Conor Lindsay (www.conorlindsay.com)*

## Formalities

The harbour office is located in a dark stone building set back slightly and up some wide steps in the northeast corner of the harbour. The port official is pleasant and helpful, and plainly happy to welcome visiting yachts to his harbour, but speaks no languages other than Spanish.

## Charges

In early 2015 the cost for a craft of 12.1m x 4 was €13.27 per night including taxes, water and electricity. Discounts are available for longer periods.

## Facilities

*Water* On the pontoons. There are two taps on the breakwater and one in the boatyard by the travel lift dock.

*Electricity* On the pontoons. Also available in the boatyard and one point on the breakwater.

*WiFi* In theory WiFi is available throughout the island, but in practice it appears somewhat inconsistent. Many of the waterfront bars and cafés provide WiFi for customers.

*Showers* Several local hostelries will hire bathrooms to yachtsmen, including Casa Kai Marino, ☎ +34 922 557 034, on Calle Juan Gutiérrez Monteverde (the road leading inland from the pontoon access quay).

*Launderette* In the town.

*Security* There are now security gates, and a small deposit is taken for a key; this also opens the toilet door. There are *marineros* on duty around the clock and the crime rate in such a remote and peaceful spot is low.

*Fuel* From the Cofradía de Pescadores. Weekdays 0800-1400. The fuelling point is near the crane in the southeast corner of the harbour. Payment by card or cash.

*Bottled gas* No Camping Gaz exchanges closer than Valverde.

*Medical services* Check with the office, a doctor comes from El Pinar twice a week.

*Bank* In the town, with ATM.

*Shops/provisioning* Two small supermarkets, surprisingly well stocked for their size, plus pharmacy and other shops. Fresh fish is available from the co-operative at the root of the breakwater, the best time is after 1300.

*Produce market* A travelling greengrocer selling good quality fruit and vegetables sets up his stall by on the north side of the harbour every Friday 0830–1300. A meat stall likewise in the supermarket building on Thursdays.

*Cafés, restaurants & hotels* Several waterfront restaurants serving local seafood, at least one hotel, and several guesthouses.

*Car hire and taxis* Ask in the harbour office.

*Buses* To Valverde and Puerto de la Estaca – every two hours between 0800–1700.

## Boatyard

Well-kept boatyard with good security and plenty of hardstanding, run by the Cofradía de Pescadores (fishermen's confederation). The office is in the yard open 0900-1400 Monday–Friday. Closed at weekend. ☎ +34 922 557 097.

Welding, painting and other skills are available and DIY work is allowed. Living aboard is permitted in the short-term, but not for long-term projects.

*Travel-lift* Capacity 70 tonnes, but check with the office. Charges for both the hoist and time ashore are said to be very reasonable.

*Engineers* Well accustomed to fishing boat diesels, but not much in the way of yacht spares available.

*Chandlery* Small chandlery in the boatyard office, mainly tuned to the needs of fishing boats (and gardeners, with a rack of 'grow your own seeds'!).

## Now prohibited anchorages on the southwest coast of El Hierro

The southwest coast of the island is really devoid of anchorages despite some fine sandy beaches. It is generally steep-to and is known for its excellent diving and swimming. Hammerhead sharks are sometimes seen in the area – local advice dictates 'if one gets too close, hit it on the nose'!

⚓ **Bahía de Naos** 27°38'·7N 17°59'·9W

About 1M northwest of Puerto de la Restinga and previously recommended as a daytime anchorage now forms part of the Zone A where anchoring is not permitted.

⚓ 27°40'·7N 18°01'·8W

This small unnamed bay backed by a sand and stone beach is in Zone C, where anchoring remains prohibited. With enough crew aboard it might be possible to stop for a swim in the very clear water while the boat drifts. There are submerged rocks to the southeast and a reef to the west.

⚓ 27°42'·2N 18°08'W

A short stone mole wall found about 1M southeast of Punta Orchilla, with a ladder where it might be possible for the intrepid to land by dinghy. However, the mole itself is surrounded by shoals and the surrounding seabed offers poor holding over rock. A track leads up to the lighthouse and there is reputed to be a tap, but absolutely nothing else. For most it will be far preferable to head for the next destination, be it elsewhere in the Canaries or several thousand miles distant.

The Orchillo Lighthouse is the last conspicuous light before 'the other side' (of the Atlantic) *Hilary Keatinge*

The rugged deep Atlantic southwest coast *Hilary Keatinge*

La Restinga is a mecca for the underwater explorers; this narrow gorge is known as 'Chinaman's Boat' *Ciarnan O'Murchu Photography*

**IV. THE CANARY ISLANDS**

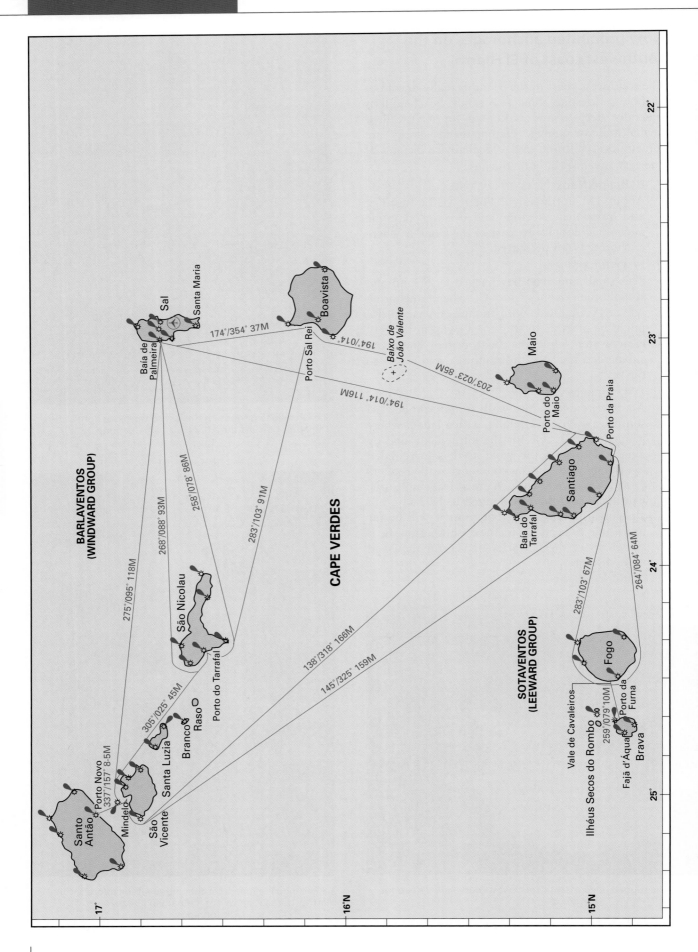

BARLAVENTOS
(WINDWARD GROUP)

SOTAVENTOS
(LEEWARD GROUP)

CAPE VERDES

Santo Antão

Porto Novo
337°/157° 8·5M

Mindelo

São Vicente

Santa Luzia

Branco

Raso

Porto do Tarrafal

São Nicolau

275°/095° 118M

268°/088° 93M

258°/018° 86M

305°/025° 45M

Baía de Palmeira

Sal

Santa Maria

174°/354° 37M

Porto Sal Rei

Boavista

194°/014°

Baixo de João Valente

203°/023° 85M

194°/014° 116M

283°/103° 91M

Maio

Porto do Maio

Porto da Praia

Santiago

Baía do Tarrafal

138°/318° 166M

145°/325° 159M

283°/103° 67M

264°/084° 64M

Vale de Cavaleiros

Ilhéus Secos do Rombo

259°/079° 10M

Porto da Furna

Fajã d'Aqua

Brava

Fogo

17°

16°N

15°N

22°

23°

24°

25°

# V. Cape Verdes

## The archipelago

The Cape Verde archipelago lies just over 800M southwest of the Canary islands and is separated from the West African coast by a channel some 325M wide. Its 4,033km² is made up of 10 larger and four smaller islands, which together form a rough horseshoe open to the west. Taken clockwise they are Santo Antão, São Vicente, Santa Luzia, Ilhéus Branco e Raso, São Nicolau, Sal and Boavista (the *Barlavento* or Windward group), and Maio, Santiago, Fogo, Brava and the Ilhéus Secos do Rombo (the *Sotavento* or Leeward group).

All are of volcanic origin and most are mountainous, with several classic craters. Only Ilha do Fogo has a volcano which is still active (most recently in 2014–15), but earthquakes and tremors sometimes occur throughout the Leeward group, particularly in Ilha Brava. The islands owe their existence to the major weakness in the earth's crust known as the Mid-Atlantic Ridge, and were never part of the African continent. Since their emergence some 130 million years ago new rock has steadily been formed along the Ridge, forcing the older rock outwards at up to 0·5cm per year, until they now lie over 1,200 miles east of the Ridge itself. The eastern islands are mainly low-lying, and according to some calculations the Republic of Cape Verde ranks eighth on the list of nations most threatened by flooding due to climate change.

The islands have always been poor, not least due to lack of rainfall, deforestation and prolonged droughts over the past two centuries. Even so they are primarily agricultural, growing maize, fruit (chiefly bananas and oranges), sugar cane, sweet potatoes, beans and other subsistence vegetables and, until the most recent volcanic eruption in Ilha do Fogo, coffee and grapes. The fishing industry is also important, providing protein for local people as well as some exports, particularly of shellfish. Even so, a large proportion of food must be imported.

After decades of relying heavily on foreign aid, much of it 'in kind' – either in the form of subsidised staple foods such as flour, help with education or assistance with technological projects such as new harbours and airports – in 2008 the Republic became the 153rd member of the World Trade Organisation. Europe is its most important trading partner, taking 60% of Cape Verdean exports and providing 80% of imports. Of these, 33% of exports

## Courses and distances within the Cape Verdes

| Harbour | Course / Reciprocal | Distance |
|---|---|---|
| Palmeira, Ilha do Sal - Mindelo, São Vicente | 275° / 095° & by eye | 118M |
| Palmeira, Ilha do Sal - Tarrafal, São Nicolau (via north coast) | 268° / 088° & by eye | 93M |
| Palmeira, Ilha do Sal - Tarrafal, São Nicolau (via south coast) | 258° / 078° & by eye | 86M |
| Palmeira, Ilha do Sal - Porto da Praia, Santiago | 194° / 014° & by eye | 116M |
| Palmeira, Ilha do Sal - Porto de Sal Rei, Boavista | 174° / 354° & by eye | 37M |
| Porto de Sal Rei, Boavista - Tarrafal, São Nicolau | 283° / 103° & by eye | 91M |
| Porto de Sal Rei, Boavista - Porto da Praia, Santiago (avoiding Baixo de João Valente) | by eye & 194° + 203° 023° + 194° & by eye | 85M |
| Tarrafal, São Nicolau - Mindelo, São Vicente | 305° / 025° & by eye | 45M |
| Mindelo, São Vicente - Porto Novo, Santo Antão | 337° / 157° | 8·5M |
| Mindelo, São Vicente - Porto da Praia, Santiago (via east coast) | 138° / 318° & by eye | 166M |
| Mindelo, São Vicente - Porto da Praia, Santiago (via west coast) | 145° / 325° & by eye | 159M |
| Porto da Praia, Santiago - Vale de Cavaleiros, Ilha do Fogo (via north coast) | 283° / 103° & by eye | 67M |
| Porto da Praia, Santiago - Vale de Cavaleiros, Ilha do Fogo (via south coast) | 264° / 084° & by eye | 64M |
| Vale de Cavaleiros, Ilha do Fogo - Porto da Furna, Ilha Brava | 259° / 079° | 10M |

and 38% of imports are with Portugal. Between 2000 and 2009 GDP increased by an average of 7% per year, unemployment fell rapidly and in 2008 the Republic was upgraded from Least Developed Country to Middle Income Country status – only the second time this has ever happened. A national minimum wage of CVE 11,000$ per month (about €100) came into effect on 1 January 2014, though it is unclear how fully this is honoured. The fast-growing tourist industry was badly hit by the recession of 2008 onwards and many ambitious projects – including several planned marinas – were abandoned, but by 2015 the worst was over, evidenced by the increase in international airports, from two to four within the past ten years.

Much foreign currency is also received from the many Cape Verdeans who have emigrated, temporarily or permanently, but still support relatives at home – it is estimated that more Cape Verdeans live abroad than in the islands themselves. The greatest number of emigrants (more than 400,000) are in the USA, with around 150,000 in Portugal, 45,000 in Angola and significant communities in Senegal, São Tome and Príncipe, France, the Netherlands, Spain and Italy. Recently the trend has begun to reverse itself, however, with the country's stability and relatively high per capita income making it attractive to many from West Africa, while its low cost of living and climate holds obvious appeal to those from northern Europe.

The average age is just under 25, an increase from 18·5 at the millennium. Life expectancy at birth in the islands now stands at 73 for men and nearly 79 for women – the highest in Africa and a dramatic increase from the 50 years at the time of independence in 1975. At 18·5 per 1,000 live berths, infant mortality is very low compared to much of Africa, but even so, population growth has levelled and few women choose to have more than four children.

Free education is available for children from ages 6 to 14, with primary education supposedly mandatory though in practice about 15% of children in the more remote country areas are believed to slip through the net. More than 90% of those over the age of 15 are literate, many are multi-lingual, and nearly 25% hold degrees from one or other of the country's ten universities – a record which far outshines that of most neighbouring countries. Even so, unemployment and downright poverty – particularly in country districts – are still major problems and likely to remain so for the foreseeable future. In contrast the cities, and particularly Mindelo, are growing fast. Most houses are built on bank mortgages, often with the owner doing his own work – even down to making breeze-blocks on site! This practical approach – typical of much Cape Verdean thinking – has resulted in a marked absence of the shanty towns so common in many parts of Africa and the Caribbean. The government is justly proud of its first place ranking in the United Nations Development Programme's Human Development index for West Africa.

The islands are visited by relatively few English-speaking yachtsmen, the vast majority being French or Scandinavian though with a growing number of Dutch and Germans. After a few decades following independence in 1975 during which visiting yachts typically spread their time over four or five islands, the opening of the archipelago's first – and only – marina in 2007 at Mindelo on São Vicente inevitably proved a magnet for yachts which might otherwise have spent at least some time elsewhere. In 2010 one cruiser remarked that, of the skippers he had spoken to, most of those at anchor had made their landfall at Ilha do Sal and visited at least one other island (usually Boavista or São Nicolau) before reaching Mindelo. In contrast, most yachts berthed in the marina had made their landfall at São Vicente and did not plan to visit any other island.

Other than Mindelo the best harbours are Porto da Palmeira (Ilha do Sal), Porto do Tarrafal (São Nicolau) and Porto da Praia (Santiago), with the anchorages at Baía do Tarrafal (Santiago), Porto de Sal Rei (Boavista) and Fajã d'Agua (Brava) also very appealing. Most other harbours and anchorages are distinctly weather-dependent. As so often, the smaller the harbour the more enthusiastic the welcome and the safer it is likely to be in terms of theft – said to be a major problem only at Baía do Tarrafal and Porto da Praia, though the situation in the former has improved greatly over recent years. Even so, throughout the archipelago it is wise to observe basic precautions – never to leave the yacht unlocked, and never to leave her unattended after dark until one has assessed the situation in a particular harbour. Once ashore youthful pickpockets are an acknowledged problem, particularly in the larger towns, but violent crimes such as muggings are very rare. The one yachtsman who experiences a problem is far more likely to publicise the fact than are the 50 who do not, and it should be stressed that the vast majority of Cape Verdeans are friendly and hospitable towards visitors.

Apart from the interest of visiting a fascinating and relatively little-known area, the practical advantages of breaking the transatlantic passage in the Cape Verdes are obvious. If en route to the Caribbean the distance to Barbados is cut to under 2,000M, compared with 2,700M from the Canaries or 2,900M from Madeira, and as the islands lie well within the trade wind belt a direct course can usually be steered. For the typical small cruising boat this

The emigrants' memorial at Porto Novo, Santo Antão. It is thought that more Cape Verdeans live abroad than in the islands themselves *Anne Hammick*

may mean at least a week less spent at sea, with a passage of around 16–18 days as against 25 or more. Other yachts visiting the Cape Verdes are heading for Brazil – the shortest possible crossing in these latitudes is Ilha Brava to Fernando do Noroñha – with a few on their way to West Africa, most often Senegal or The Gambia.

## History

In common with the majority of the Atlantic islands discovered by the fleets of Prince Henry the Navigator, the Cape Verde islands were already rumoured to exist before the arrival of the first Portuguese in the mid-15th century. There is some evidence that the Romans and Carthaginians were aware of their existence, while Arab seafarers may have visited in the 12th century. The year of their official discovery is in doubt, being placed anywhere between 1451 and 1460, and the truth is probably that they were explored and recorded piecemeal, as happened in the Azores. Almost certainly named after Cap Vert on the African mainland, they were also known to the Arabs as *el ras elkhader* – the green top – and were uninhabited when Diogo Gomes and António de Noli sighted and named Ilha do Maio and Ilha de São Tiago (now Santiago), the island chosen by the first permanent settlers in 1462.

References to the islands over the next century are few, though by 1541 Ribeira Grande on Santiago – now known as Cidade Velha or 'old city' to avoid confusion with the town of the same name in Santo Antão – was sufficiently wealthy to attract the attention of attacking pirates. The period following King Philip II of Spain's invasion of mainland Portugal in 1581 brought even greater troubles, with an attack in 1583 by forces supporting the Prior of Crato, claimant to the Portuguese throne. Neither was the settlement spared by English and Dutch privateers, the traditional enemies of Spain. Sir Francis Drake sacked it in 1585, in 1592 a Dutch fleet attempted a less successful attack, and on visiting the islands the following year Sir Richard Hawkins's opinion was that 'It is wisedome to shunne the sight of them'. After a further attack on Ribeira Grande in 1712, this time by the French, in 1772 the site was abandoned in favour of the more easily defended hilltop position on which Cidade da Praia stands.

As well as providing a base for Portuguese merchants trading with the African continent, many slaves were imported to work in the sugar plantations or to be resold further afield. However, even with free labour, agriculture was never more than marginally successful, and when Charles Darwin visited Porto da Praia in HMS *Beagle* in January 1832 he remarked on 'the novel aspect of an utterly sterile land'. This had not always been the case, however, and until the mid-18th century rainfall was regular if limited. Then in 1747 came the first of a series of droughts, exacerbated by the felling of trees for agriculture and overgrazing by goats. As Darwin pointed out, 'When the island was discovered the immediate neighbourhood of Porto Praya [sic] was clothed with trees, the reckless destruction of which has caused here, as at St Helena and some of the Canary Islands, almost entire sterility.' He also remarked on the 'impalpably fine dust, which … falls in such quantities as to dirty everything on board, and to hurt people's eyes; vessels even have run on shore owing to the obscurity of the atmosphere.' Repeated droughts over the next two hundred years killed well over 100,000 people, with almost no assistance received from Portugal or any other source.

In the later 19th century the islands became a regular port of call for American whaling ships from New Bedford, and were known as a source of skilled crew who would work for little more than their keep. Not surprisingly many Cape Verdean seamen settled in America, founding the sizeable emigrant communities which exist in New England today. The further decline which followed the abolition of slavery in 1876 was alleviated to some extent by the growing importance of Porto Grande (now known as Mindelo), both as a bunkering station for steamships en route to the South Atlantic or Pacific, and as a centre of undersea cable-laying operations, with links to the African continent and the Americas. However, the opening of the Suez and Panama Canals, the demise of coal-burning ships in favour of oil, and later the introduction of radio communications, spelt the end of this short-lived period of relative prosperity.

For several centuries the islands were administered as a colony from mainland Portugal together with Portuguese Guinea (now Guinea-Bissau), an arrangement which was only terminated in 1878. After the split they remained as a colony until 1951 when their status was changed to that of an overseas province or territory. Full Portuguese citizenship was extended to all islanders in 1961, but in spite of this, local desire for independence in company with Guinea-Bissau grew steadily. Guerrilla warfare began on the mainland in the early 1960s, headed by the African Party for the Independence of Guinea and Cape Verde (PAIGC) and led by Amilcar Cabral, son of a Cape Verdean father and Guinean mother. In spite of this neither the PAIGC nor guerrilla fighting ever really took hold in the islands, and Cabral's assassination in 1973 increased the rift. When a new Portuguese government was installed after the Carnation Revolution in April 1974, independence was granted to Guinea-Bissau. Cape Verde chose to maintain a separate identity though still under the PAIGC banner, finally achieving independence from Portugal on 5 July 1975 as the República de Cabo Verde.

The initial intention was for unification with Guinea-Bissau at some time in the future, but after a coup in that country in 1980 all references to a union were removed from the constitution and PAIGC was renamed PAICV (*Partido Africano da Independência de Cabo Verde*). For 10 years the Cape Verdes continued to be governed by the left-wing PAICV, with Amilcar Cabral the hero of many islanders. However, the easy-going Creole outlook fused with Marxist economic principles to produce an unusual but practical situation where state control actively encouraged private enterprise. Although the islands could have been of considerable strategic importance the PAICV wisely vetoed construction of foreign military bases, thus remaining on good terms with countries as diverse as the USA, Russia, Cuba and China – and at one stage said to be receiving aid from all four simultaneously.

Gradually other political parties were allowed to emerge, culminating in elections in 1991 in which the PAICV were defeated and the MPD (*Movimento Para a Democratia*), founded and led by Carlos Veiga, came to power with the PAICV forming the Opposition. A new national anthem and redesigned

flag were adopted the following year. Ten years on the balance of political power changed again, with the PAICV narrowly beating the MPD in the election of February 2001. In 2006 the PAICV again won, followed by a third term in office from early 2011. More than half the population were registered to vote and the result was accepted unanimously. The Republic of Cabo Verde is thus one of the very few African countries to have achieved stable democratic government, and to have done so peacefully and without bloodshed.

The Cape Verde islands have always had a foot in both Africa and Europe. Geographically and ethnically they clearly belong to the former, but centuries of European influence have left their mark in more than just the architecture and the political structure. The country currently has Special Partnership status with the EU, and membership has even been suggested as a goal for the long-term future.

## Natural history and Natural Reserves

The waters surrounding the Cape Verde islands are particularly rich in cetaceans (whales and dolphins) and have bird and plant species found nowhere else in the world.

Amongst the species recorded during a cetacean survey carried out a few years ago were pilot whales, bottlenose dolphins, Atlantic and pan-tropical spotted dolphins, sei, bryde, sperm, fin and humpback whales. Sperm whales, though usually in depths of 500m or more, were found northwest of Ilha do Sal and between Boavista and São Nicolau, as were fin whales (which had not previously been

A locust at São Pedro, São Vicente *Chris Bates*

reported in the area). Humpback whales are thought to calve in the lee of Ilha do Sal, Boavista and Ilha do Maio.

The beaches of Ilha do Maio, Boavista, Sal, São Vicente and Santa Luzia are favourite breeding grounds for several species of turtle. Although most laying takes place in summer when few yachts will be around, they do breed throughout the year. The slightly contradictory recommendations state that one should not disturb or approach turtles too closely while they are out of the water, but equally that one should note down the number on any tag spotted and report it to the natural history museum of one's home country. A number of travel companies offer wildlife-centred holidays, alerting local people to the economic sense of protecting species which might otherwise be exploited for food or considered predators.

Cruisers with a particular interest in birds and plants should refer to Eraldo De Gioannini's long-established website at www.caboverde.com (see page 437), which contains 'Naturalist Pages' including a section entitled *Aves de Cabo Verde* detailing 48 local species of bird complete with pictures, and *Planta Endemicas e arvolres indigenas* covering some 60 plants. However, a dictionary may be necessary, as in both cases the text is in Portuguese only.

The Cape Verde islands contain a number of Natural Reserves, those of most obvious relevance to yachts being Baía da Murdeira on Ilha do Sal, much of the coastline of Boavista, Santa Luzia, and its nearby islands of Branco and Raso. A more complete list will be found at www.kauberdi.net/english. In theory access to Natural Reserves is restricted, and in 2015 the *Polícia Marítima* were advising skippers that anchoring without a permit was forbidden. No one appears to know how such permits can be obtained, however, and as none of the Reserves are patrolled by wardens it is difficult to see how any ban might be enforced. It is fortunate that yachtsmen are among the most environmentally-aware people on the planet – tourists, quad bike owners and local fishermen are likely to pose a far greater threat.

Perhaps not surprisingly, locusts are often found in the islands, though seldom in numbers which constitute a serious problem. They are assumed to come from West Africa, as though relatively poor fliers they can be carried by the wind for hundreds of miles. The last time serious swarms were seen was in 2004, when locusts spread throughout North Africa until controlled by pesticide and other means. In the Cape Verdes they are said to be a favourite snack with local cats, which enjoy both the thrill of the chase and the reward of a crunchy morsel if successful.

## General information

### Nationality and language

The population, estimated at around 525,000 in 2015, is of mixed African and European (mainly Portuguese) descent. The national flag is predominantly blue, with white and red horizontal stripes and a circle of 10 gold stars to represent the 10 larger islands.

The native tongue of nearly all Cape Verdeans is Crioulo or Kriolu – a language with its origins in West Africa but owing much to Portuguese – but the latter is the official language and it is rare to encounter anyone who cannot speak it. For many years considered the language of the uneducated, as Cape Verdeans have come to place more value on their own culture Crioulo has lost its 'second-class' status. However, it remains almost entirely a spoken language, not least because of the major differences between the version spoken in the northern islands and that in the southern chain. See *Portuguese and Creole : Two Old Rivals* in the excellent *Cape Verde Islands* (Bradt Travel Guides) – see page 439 – for a detailed analysis.

Many older people, including shopkeepers and taxi drivers, have some command of French, while English is more likely to be spoken by the young. Many of the street vendors who speak fluent English are immigrants from the African mainland.

A young Cape Verdean helps her mother pound maize as chickens roam around their feet and fishing nets are spread out in the foreground  *Anne Hammick*

Hauling a small fishing boat ashore at Porto da Ponta do Sol, Santo Antão *Anne Hammick*

They don't come much fresher than this! Tuna for sale on the quay at Porto do Tarrafal, São Nicolau *Anne Hammick*

## Cape Verdean representation abroad

*Embassies and consulates*

*London* (Honorary Consul) Mr Jonathan S Lux, ✆+44 7876 232305, capeverde@jonathanlux.co.uk

*Washington DC* (Embassy) 3415 Massachusetts Avenue NW, Washington DC 20007-1446 ✆+1 202 965 6820, www.embcv-usa.gov.cv (contact link on website, but no email address)

*Lisbon*: Avenida do Restelo 33, 1400-314 – Lisbon, Portugal ✆+351 21 304 1440, info@embcv.pt, www.embcv.pt

In Western Europe embassies will also be found in Madrid, Paris, Brussels, Berlin, Rome, Luxembourg and Vienna, and consulates in many other cities.

## Diplomatic representation in the Cape Verde Islands

*US* Rua Abílio Macedo 81, Cidade da Praia, Ilha de Santiago, República de Cabo Verde, ✆+238 261 5551, praiaconsular@state.gov, www.praia.usembassy.gov

*UK* (Honorary Consul) Sr Antonio Canuto, Shell Cabo Verde, Avenida Amilcar Cabral CP4, Mindelo, São Vicente, República de Cabo Verde, ✆+238 232 6625/6/7, antonio.a.canuto@scv.sims.com

Other British interests in the Cape Verdes are looked after by the British Embassy in Dakar, 20 rue du Dr Guillet, Boite Postale 6025, Dakar, Senegal ✆+221 33 823 7392, britembe@orange.sn, www.gov.uk/government/world/organisations/british-embassy-dakar and ukinsenegal.fco.gov.uk

## Personal documentation

All foreigners need passports valid for at least six months and, unless spending every night aboard the yacht for the duration of their visit, most foreigners, including citizens of Europe, the USA and Canada, will also need visas. (It has been stated that, technically, even visiting yachtsmen require visas, but lack of one has yet to cause a problem). If arriving or departing by air a visa will certainly will be required, even if in direct transit to or from a yacht, and visitors from countries where there are Cape Verde embassies or consulates should in theory obtain their visa in advance. In the UK this service is provided by Honorary Consul Mr Jonathan S Lux (see above), at £40 for a 30-day visa or £80 for a multiple-entry one-year visa. Travel companies such as Expedia provide a similar service, but at considerably greater cost. In practice visas are available at all legal points of arrival, by sea and air, for a fee of CVE 2,500$, €25 or US$40. A duplicate passport photo may be required, and it would also be wise to carry a few spare copies of the information page of one's passport.

Insist on a visa being issued if leaving by air or if planning to spend even a single night ashore –

perhaps to go hiking in the mountains of São Nicolau or Santo Antão – even if Immigration officials say that it is not necessary. It is, and it is the hapless visitor who will suffer if an error is made. If departing by air do not leave obtaining a visa until the last moment. While the airport immigration desk is always manned when an international flight is expected, it may not be manned before one departs – and without a visa one is unlikely to be allowed to board one's flight.

As in many countries, the law requires visiting foreigners to carry identification at all times. However, it is accepted that passports are vulnerable to theft, particularly in the cities, so a photocopy of the visa and the 'information' page (on the same sheet of paper), will normally be accepted in lieu.

Finally, if irritated by all the paperwork bear in mind that the Cape Verde government has a serious problem with illegal immigrants, mainly from west Africa. Immigration officials are nearly always polite and many speak some English, but they are clearly trained to treat all arrivals – however poorly they fit the stereotype – in much the same way.

### Time

The Cape Verde islands use UT –1 throughout the year.

### Money

Although the Cape Verdean escudo (*escudo Caboverdiano*) is no longer tied to the Euro, the exchange rate has remained close to CVE 110$ to €1 for more than two decades. Despite this, if using Euros to pay for goods or for services such as taxi fares, the 'local' exchange rate of CVE 100$ to €1 will often be quoted. Although US dollars are usually accepted, an even higher 'penalty' may be imposed. When prices are written the ubiquitous dollar sign is, in theory, used to separate escudos and cents, though in practice the latter are rarely used.

Import and export of CVE is forbidden and it is therefore impossible to get currency through a home bank before departure, but once in the islands it can be withdrawn from ATMs by holders of internationally recognised cards including Visa, or exchanged for other currencies over the counter (when a passport will be required). If changing currency, give each note to the bank clerk individually to demonstrate that it is in good condition, to prevent a damaged note being substituted and politely 'refused'. Travellers' cheques will also be honoured, but commission may be charged.

Banking hours vary according to the size of the community served and are generally given in the text, though 0800–1500 appears to be fairly standard. There is no weekend opening, though some currency exchanges (*câmbios*) operate on Saturday morning

If the Cape Verdes have a national dish it is *cachupa*, a tasty mix of maize, beans and meat or fish. Add a fried egg and *é perfeito*! *Anne Hammick*

and may remain open until 1700 or 1800 during the week. Note that many ATMs are installed inside buildings so are only accessible during opening hours.

There is no limit on the import and export of foreign currency provided it is declared on arrival, though yachtsmen who are carrying considerable amounts of reserve cash aboard will probably prefer not to publicise the fact. In theory it is possible to change excess CVE back into other currency on departure, provided the original exchange receipt can be produced, but in practice not all banks hold a sufficient reserve to change large amounts.

Credit cards are proving relatively slow to catch on with companies in the Cape Verdes and many, including Marina Mindelo, pass on the fee charged by the card company to the customer. If intending to pay by card it is essential to check that it really can be accepted – despite a Visa sign being prominently displayed outside, the machine may be out of order or the power off. Having said that, many car hire firms, larger restaurants and hotels now take payment by Visa, though MasterCard or Amex are rarely accepted.

### Shopping

Shopping, and particularly the variety of foods available, varies markedly from island to island. By far the best choice is available in Mindelo (São Vicente) and Porto da Praia (Santiago) where there are busy produce markets in addition to surprisingly well-stocked supermarkets. Meat of all kinds – fresh, frozen and chilled – is normally available in the larger supermarkets of both cities, as is UHT milk and other basics (though prices are high). In contrast, on some of the smaller islands local shops can barely meet day-to-day needs. In either case, all visiting yachts would be well advised to store up as fully as possible before arrival, not least because prices of most items are much higher than in Madeira or the Canaries.

Shops are usually open 0800–1200 and 1430–1800 Monday to Friday, 0800–1200 Saturday. Market hours are much the same, though the best choice is generally to be found early on. Although in theory market prices are set, a little good-humoured bargaining will sometimes produce results, particularly if buying in quantity. Market-bought fruit and vegetables are generally of a high standard, doubtless due to the fierce competition, though their shop-bought equivalents have often been chilled so will not keep. Although supermarkets usually provide bags, this is not the case in markets where strong bags – and egg boxes – are seldom available and, should they be provided, will generally be charged for.

Almost everything is shut on Sunday – with the exception of the ubiquitous 'Shell Select' convenience stores to be found at most (but not all) Shell filling stations. Prices are somewhat higher than in locally-owned establishments, but the Shell Select stores are air-conditioned, spotlessly clean and, like many of their brethren in the UK, carry an unexpectedly wide range of goods.

Alcohol of all descriptions is for sale almost everywhere, with Portuguese wine a particularly good buy. The locally-made Superbock lager goes down very well, though European brands are generally available if one is willing to pay. However, mixers are expensive and tonic, in particular, may be unobtainable. Cape Verdean rum – known as *grogue*, *aqua-dente* or *Sant' Anton* – is mainly produced in Santo Antão, where the sugar cane may be crushed in cattle or donkey mills with the 'ovens' (stills) nearby, it deserves to be treated with caution.

Who needs a games console when you have friends and a skipping rope? *Anne Hammick*

*Ponche* – rum mixed with a honey syrup – is considerably less potent, or try *coupada* , which lies somewhere between the two.

A variety of local vendors work the more popular yacht anchorages and it is often possible to buy fish at very reasonable prices, less so prawns and crayfish. In other harbours fishermen may sell their catch on the beach. In both cases bargaining appears perfectly acceptable and bartering for fuel or other essentials may also be suggested.

Some notes regarding ships' stores – principally fuel, bottled gas and chandlery – will be found on pages 366.

## Communications

### Mail

The postal service is generally reliable (though very slow), as is *poste restante*. Letters for yachts sent c/o *Poste Restante* to post offices at the larger ports will normally be held for one month pending collection and then returned to the sender. Marina Mindelo – see page 391 – will hold mail for arriving yachts, though it would be wise to make email contact beforehand. Mail usually takes between one and three weeks from Europe, slightly less from the USA or Canada. Outgoing mail generally takes around two weeks to reach Europe or North America.

Note that post offices in smaller towns may be closed all day Saturday, as well as Sunday, and that post boxes for stamped mail appear to be unknown. Mail must therefore be handed in at the post office during working hours.

### Telephones

International calls can be made from most post offices (marked *Correios* or CTT) as well as from CV Telecom offices and an increasing number of *telefono publico* shops (which use the internet and offer the best rates). Nearly all public telephones require phone cards, purchased at post offices and elsewhere, and most accept international calls – or rather claim to, since a high proportion do not actually work. Calls to the United Kingdom begin with the prefix 044, followed by the area code (without the initial zero) plus number. Calls to the United States and Canada begin with the prefix 01 and the area code plus number.

The country code for the Republic of Cape Verde islands is +238, with no individual island or area codes. All phone numbers contain seven digits. If only six are given, add a 2 (for landlines) or 9 (for mobiles) between the country code (if required) and the listed number.

Mobile (cell) phone coverage via CVMovel is generally good throughout the islands, though there are the inevitable 'holes' in more remote areas. Do not rely on texting – this is said to work with some phones in some areas, while in others only voice calls can be made and received. The costs incurred by using a mobile phone abroad are beyond the scope of this book, and individual phones may need 'unblocking' before they will work at all. If planning to spend some time in the country it may be cheaper to buy a new phone or at least a new SIM card.

### Internet access

Internet access is becoming ever more widespread – at cybercafés, using the free WiFi provided by many bars and restaurants, in public areas such as town squares and airports, and via 3G roving dongles or data SIM cards which provide on board internet access in most larger harbours. In 2015 a 3G dongle cost around CVE 800$ (€7) and credit could be added in many shops. Data SIMs were available for tablets, but at that time micro SIMs were not available.

Take care if using a public connection. Not only is connectivity subject to frequent failure but it is demonstrably insecure – more than one yachtsman's laptop has been hacked while in the Cape Verdes. A good firewall and antivirus program with daily updates is essential.

Marina Mindelo offers password-protected WiFi for visitors, charging by the quantity downloaded – see page 398 for details.

## Electricity

Electrical current throughout the Cape Verdes is 220v 50Hz, as is standard in western Europe. The chances of plugging a yacht into mains current are slight other than in Marina Mindelo, though it might be possible to use power tools ashore in other places by arrangement with the *Capitão do Porto*.

## Transportation

### International flights

Amilcar Cabral Airport on Ilha do Sal in the northeast of the archipelago is the Republic's major international airport, handling flights to Lisbon, Paris, Amsterdam, Munich, Rome, New York, Boston and Johannesburg, amongst other destinations. The main carrier is TACV (*Transportes Aéroes de Cabo Verde*, www.flytacv.com) but it is also served by TAP-Air Portugal (www.flytap.com) and others companies, both scheduled and charter. In addition to Ilha do Sal, flights from outside the islands also land at Nelson Mandela International Airport, Santiago, Cesária Évora Airport, São Vicente and Aristides Pereira International Airport, Boavista. Most flights from the UK are routed via mainland Europe, usually Lisbon, though at the time of writing Thomson (www.thomson.co.uk/flights) flew direct from Gatwick, Birmingham and Manchester to Ilha do Sal and Boavista, with additional flights from Glasgow to the latter. Check the internet for current services. TACV also operates services from Providence, Rhode Island as well as several airports in Brazil.

If flying with TACV it is essential to confirm the flight at least 48 hours before departure, but note that most TACV offices, even at airports, are closed at the weekend. It is also wise to check again the day before departure, as last-minute schedule changes are frequent and departure times are as likely to be brought forward as to be put back. Note also that a crewmember leaving by air must have a visa – see page 360. Check-in is nominally three hours prior to departure for international flights and four hours prior to departure for flights to the United States.

### Inter-island flights

There are small airfields on all the islands other than Santo Antão and Brava. TACV currently runs the only scheduled inter-island flights, and the charter aviation company Cabo Verde Express (www.caboverdeexpress.com) offers flights from the African mainland as well as between the islands. TACV offers daily flights linking the four international airports, with less frequent connections to São Nicolau, Maio and Fogo, but inter-island flights are frequently booked up well in advance and if planning a crew change it would undoubtedly be simplest to do it via one of the international airports.

Check-in for inter-island flights is 90 minutes prior to departure, though in practice it may be wise to allow nearer two hours as standby passengers are occasionally given preference if a booked passenger is late to arrive. Inter-island flights seldom depart at the time specified – many are en route from another island, so any delays are cumulative – but every effort is made to ensure that passengers make their international connections, if necessary holding the long-haul flight until the inter-island flight arrives.

### Ferries

The islands are served by a varying fleet of ferries, including the fast catamarans *Kriola* and *Liberdade* and the conventional ships *Sal Rei*, *Mar d'Canal*, *Inter-Ilhas* and *Ribeira de Paúl*.

The São Vicente/Santo Antão route – used by many yachtsmen who want to visit the latter's dramatic interior but prefer to leave their boats safe in Mindelo – is normally serviced by the *Sal Rei* and *Mar d'Canal* (the latter replaced by the *Inter-Ilhas* as of late 2015, though whether temporarily or permanently is unclear) with two return services every day except Sunday, when there is a single return service. Tickets cost CVE 800$ over the counter at the ferry terminal in Mindelo.

Most other routes are covered by Cabo Verde Fast Ferry (www.cvfastferry.com), whose two 160-seat fast catamarans *Liberdade* and *Kriola* both came into service in 2011. Based in São Vicente, *Liberdade* visits São Nicolau twice a week and Santo Antão on the remaining days, while *Kriola*, based in Santiago, runs to Fogo and Brava, and by mid 2016 may also be visiting Maio regularly. The company is based in

A new road under construction in Tarrafal, Santiago. Chipped to shape and firmly hammered home, these blocks will stand decades of use despite being laid without foundations *Anne Hammick*

Praia but it is normally possible to book online. It is fair to say that it has a reputation for frequent cancellations and schedule changes.

Finally the elderly *Ribeira de Paúl*, believed to have been built in Norway in the 1950s and for many years a fixture on the São Vicente/Santo Antão run, provides an irregular service between São Vicente, São Nicolau, Ilha do Sal and Boavista. There is no fixed schedule.

### Road transport

The Cape Verdes are well worth exploring inland. Car hire, though generally available, is expensive compared to the Azores or Canaries and there may be a kilometre charge. It is worth inspecting the vehicle carefully before signing for it, and being seen to photograph it from all angles can do no harm. A British or American (i.e. not international) driving licence is accepted, and payment can generally be made by credit card.

In practice – and particularly given the state of the roads in the smaller islands – it is often simpler and more enjoyable to hire a taxi for the day, agreeing in advance on the number of passengers, approximate

Everyone – and everything – travels by *aluguer* (literally 'to hire') in the Cape Verdes *Anne Hammick*

route, expected hours and fee. A tip can then be added if justified. The vehicles on offer range from the impeccable to the extremely dubious-looking, their drivers likewise. Rates are often set over common routes such as airport to town.

Buses seldom run to a formal schedule, but most of the islands have plentiful *aluguer* (literally 'to hire') pickup trucks and minibuses. These private-enterprise buses do not carry a destination board: simply ask the driver where he is headed, and if not lucky first time around you will almost certainly be directed to the right vehicle. Competition for passengers is such that no driver leaves until his vehicle is full – it then gets fuller, and fuller, and fuller en route. Fares are low and it helps to have the right change. On arrival, be sure to check what time the driver will be leaving for the return trip – asking him to write it down will avoid possible misunderstandings.

### Walking and hitchhiking

There are some superb walks in the Cape Verde islands, notably in the mountains of Santiago, São Nicolau and Santo Antão, many described in detail in the excellent *Cape Verde Islands* (Bradt Travel Guides) – see page 439. A number of specialised walkers' maps are also available. All the above should be bought before reaching the islands where, if on sale at all, they are likely to be expensive.

Finally, if offered a lift, be sure you have not flagged down an unmarked taxi or *aluguer* with a driver who will expect to be paid.

### Medical

The Cape Verde islands are among the healthiest place in Africa, though the usual 'tropical' problems (diarrhoea, infections, ulcers, etc.) can and do occur. The ebola epidemic which ravaged many West African nations in 2014–15 never touched the islands, the incidence of HIV/AIDS is low at around one in 500, and the Cape Verdes have no history of yellow fever (yachtsmen arriving from West Africa may be asked to show proof of vaccination). Although leprosy has been reported in Santo Antão and Fogo and tuberculosis throughout the archipelago, neither are serious risks for the short-term visitor.

A greater threat are mosquito-borne viruses, including dengue fever, the Zika virus and malaria. The first is now endemic, but recent winters have produced few cases, nearly all in Santiago and all among local people. The same *aedes* mosquito which carries dengue fever also transmits the Zika virus, first detected in the Cape Verdes in October 2015. By February 2016 it appeared to be on the wane, although more than 7000 suspected cases had been reported in the interim, mainly in Santiago but also in Boavista, Maio and Fogo – visit www.fitfortravel.nhs.uk for the current status. No

*Carnaval* in Ribeira Brava  *Kath McNulty*

## National holidays

Although Good Friday is not an official holiday, the vast majority of Cape Verdeans are Roman Catholic and some shops may be closed. The same is true in Mindelo and some other towns while *Carnaval* is in full swing.

| | |
|---|---|
| 1 January | New Year's Day |
| 13 January | Democracy Day |
| 20 January | National Heroes' Day |
| *moveable* | Ash Wednesday (46 days before Easter) |
| *moveable* | *Carnaval* (usually one week after Ash Wednesday) |
| 1 May | Labour Day |
| 5 July | Independence Day |
| 15 August | Feast of the Assumption (*Nossa Senhora de Graça*) |
| 12 September | National Day |
| 1 November | All Saints' Day |
| 25 December | Christmas Day |

cases had been reported in Mindelo or elsewhere on São Vicente, which is much drier than the southern islands so has far fewer mosquitoes. Although malaria occasionally crops up in the mountains of Santiago in the 'wetter' autumn months, MASTA (the Medical Advisor Service for Travellers Abroad, www.masta.org) no longer advises visitors to take any form of preventative medication.

It would clearly be wise to take precautions against mosquito bites, including frequent applications of repellent (note that some can damage varnish if spilt), and possibly nets fitted over open hatches from dusk onwards. The latter will also be useful on the west side of the Atlantic, where *aedes* mosquitoes are again prevalent.

Other than in Ilhas Fogo and Brava it is probably best to avoid drinking local water, which in any case is somewhat chlorinated. The yacht's tanks should have been filled in Madeira or the western Canaries and, if possible, this water kept for the Atlantic crossing. Bottled water is available everywhere.

Medical facilities in the Cape Verdes have improved radically over the past few decades, particularly in the major cities. However, the country does not have the infrastructure of Europe or North America and drugs in particular may be in short supply. Needless to say, anyone with a chronic or recurring condition should take a good supply of medication with them, and any yacht passing through the islands should carry a comprehensive first-aid kit put together with tropical areas in mind.

There are pharmacies in most towns and villages where non-prescription medicines and general items can be found, but outside the two major cities their stocks are likely to be limited. Prescription medicines, if available, will be expensive. Both dentists and opticians exist in the larger towns, and wearers of glasses would be wise to carry a copy of their prescription (in addition to at least one reserve pair).

## Sailing and navigation

### Practicalities

#### Entry and regulations

*Arrival* After a short period in the 1990s when entry regulations for yachts arriving in the Cape Verde islands appeared be becoming more relaxed, in July 1999 the law was changed. Since then it has been an offence to make landfall anywhere other than Palmeira (Ilha do Sal), Mindelo (São Vicente) or Porto da Praia (Santiago) – designated 'Official Sea Border Posts' (the republic's four international airports are designated 'Official Air Border Posts'). Breaches can attract fines of up to CVE 5,000,000$ – more than €45,000.

Because entry formalities vary markedly from island to island, full details for each harbour are given in the text. Most commonly it will be necessary for the skipper to visit the *Delegação Marítima* (harbour office) where both the *Capitão do Porto* (port captain) and the *Polícia Marítima* (maritime police) are to be found. However, in Mindelo and Praia the first visit should be to *the Polícia de Fronteira* (effectively Immigration) while in Porto do Palmeira the *Polícia de Ordem Publica* (local police) stamp passports. Ship's papers, crew list and passports will always be required, while the *Polícia de Fronteira* may request an extra passport photo, making it worth carrying a few spares. CVE 500$ (€5) per person is charged for inward clearance.

IV. CAPE VERDES

A pavement in Espargos incorporates tile and flooring offcuts to interesting effect *Anne Hammick*

***Departure*** Until 2011 final departure from the islands had to be made via one of the 'Official Border Posts' listed above, preventing yachts from legally visiting either Fogo or Brava unless they fancied the long beat back to Santiago or São Vicente. Then senior officials in Mindelo's *Instituto Marítimo e Portuário* drafted a more relaxed interpretation for private yachts, making it possible – at least in theory – to clear out via Mindelo or Porto da Praia and then call in at one or more of the smaller islands before leaving territorial waters.

After revisiting the *Polícia Marítima* to retrieve the ship's papers and pay any dues, followed by the *Polícia de Fronteira* to get passports stamped, one can now request a 'next port' (*próximo porto* or *porto seguinte*) document from the latter which permits the yacht to leave for any other inhabited island, checking out with the local *Delegação Marítima* before final departure. Unfortunately, and despite the amended regulations, that request may not always be granted. In 2015 some officials were happy to issue such a document while others denied its very existence, though in several cases they suggested that a short stay – possibly to 'repair damage' – would not be a problem. Once in Fogo or Brava the situation seems far more relaxed, and all feedback concerning local officials has been entirely positive.

As of late 2015 harbour dues, payable to the *Polícia Marítima* in each harbour on departure, were CVE 700$ (€7) throughout the archipelago. One may be asked to show the receipt from the previous harbour on arrival at the next.

See Personal documentation, page 360, regarding passport and visa requirements, particularly the necessity for crew leaving by air to obtain a visa in addition to the 'transit' entry stamp issued to those arriving and leaving by water.

### Laying up

The only place where a yacht could be left unattended with any degree of confidence would be in Mindelo, São Vicente, either in Marina Mindelo – see page 394 – under the watchful eye of Kai Brossmann and his staff or possibly ashore at Lusonave, though the yard's future is uncertain.

### Ships' stores

All kinds of ships' stores are very limited, including water which is in short supply in most of the islands. It must usually be carried from the tap, so plenty of five or 10-litre cans are essential – local children will probably be happy to help carry them in return for a few escudos. Only in Porto da Palmeira (Ilha do Sal), Porto do Tarrafal (São Nicolau), Mindelo (São Vicente) and Porto da Praia (Santiago) is there any possibility of filling tanks by hose, and only in Mindelo would it be straightforward. Other than in Ilha do Fogo and Ilha Brava water may be of doubtful quality, though bottled water is on sale almost everywhere.

Diesel and petrol (*gasóleo*, pronounced *gas-OH-lee-o*) and petrol (*gasolina*, pronounced *gas-oh-LEE-na*) can be found in most harbours, but again will probably need to be collected by can; only in Mindelo is it easy to take on fuel by hose, though it might be possible in Porto da Palmeira, Porto do Tarrafal or Porto da Praia – see under Facilities for each harbour. Paraffin or kerosene (*petróleo*, pronounced *petr-OH-leo*, though both *parafina* and *querosene* are likely to be understood) is generally sold by pharmacies but is expensive, and is becoming increasingly difficult to obtain.

Camping Gaz uses the same fitting as in the UK and Europe, and exchanges are available in most towns (generally at the Shell filling station). Other cylinders can normally be refilled (with butane) by Enacol in Porto da Palmeira, Mindelo and Porto da Praia – see individual harbours for details. It would be wise to carry a selection of valve adaptors if relying on getting cylinders refilled, or possibly a few metres of rubber hose fitted with the necessary connector for the ship's bottles in the (reasonable) hope that the depot will have a connector for their end.

Almost no yacht spares or other chandlery are available outside Mindelo, where boatCV's Ship Shop has stocks of commonly used items and can order if necessary – see page 397. More general items, including electrical goods, hose and some stainless-steel fittings, are readily available from hardware stores in the larger towns, as are a wide variety of tools.

## Cruising

Although still viewed by many British yachtsmen as little more than a convenient stop en route to the Caribbean or Brazil – or perhaps a bolt hole in which to sort out problems – other nationalities are visiting the Cape Verde islands in ever-increasing numbers. It can only be a matter of time before this leads to improved facilities in islands beyond São Vicente, and before the authorities begin to realise that providing basic infrastructure for visiting yachtsmen – and easing the paperwork burden – can do nothing but good both for both the reputation and the economy of the Republic.

From the northern yachtsman's point of view they certainly have the weather in their favour – consistently high but not baking temperatures, combined with very limited rainfall. In Mindelo (São Vicente) this averages only 126mm annually, almost entirely during the months of August to November. Some higher areas may receive up to twice this amount, but droughts of several years' duration are common. Humidity averages about 70% and mid-day temperatures at sea level vary relatively little, from around 31°C in September to 26°C in January, dropping to the low 20s at night. However, it can feel surprisingly chilly at altitude – perhaps if walking in Santo Antão, Santiago or Fogo – when warm clothing will be appreciated.

## Winds and swell

The Cape Verde islands lie squarely in the path of the northeast Trades with over 80% of winds coming from that direction, together with occasional northerlies or easterlies. According to published statistics speeds average around 10–12 knots with a 5% incidence of calms, while true wind speeds of 35 knots or more occur on average only four times a year and are unknown between July and January. However, in practice it generally appears to blow considerably harder than this, particularly in winter and spring, averaging nearer 18–20 knots between December and May and frequently reaching 25–30 knots. Gale or near-gale force winds appear to be much more common in the *Barlaventos* (the northern or 'windward' chain) than in the *Sotaventos* (the southern or 'leeward' chain).

This overall picture is further complicated by local land effects, the most obvious occurring in the channel between São Vicente and Santo Antão, a classic *venturi* (see page 393). In both groups, gusts funnelling down the ravines may create sudden squalls. One yacht reported 55 knot gusts in a true wind strength of 30 knots while sailing down the west coast of Santiago, and gusts of up to 35 knots may occur in mean winds of 10–15 knots. At sea, line squalls may be encountered. These heavy banks of cloud, usually lying on a north/south line and moving westwards at around 25 knots, are often preceded by gusts of up to gale force followed by heavy rain and sometimes thunder.

Wind strengths fall off towards the end of May, with light variables predominating from May to November interspersed with occasional periods of absolute calm, though these seldom last more than twenty-four hours. Southerly or southeasterly winds are common at this time of year, and though seldom exceeding 15 knots may occasionally become strong or even gale force, rising very suddenly with no visual or barometric warning. Local people take this danger very seriously indeed, and in a few harbours ships may move out overnight due to the danger of being trapped by a southerly gale. Both the pier at Santa Maria and the breakwater at Vale de Cavaleiros, Ilha do Fogo, were damaged by summer southerlies, and some years ago winds and swell from this direction put both a yacht and the inter-island ferry ashore at Ilha Brava. A heavy southeasterly swell may also cause problems at Porto de Sal Rei, Boavista, making it difficult to exit the bay.

Many of the most severe hurricanes to hit the Caribbean and southern US begin life near the Cape Verdes, building in strength as they pass over the warm waters of the Atlantic. It is very rare indeed for a hurricane to affect the islands themselves, and only two have occurred since records began in 1851 – one in 1892, and Hurricane *Fred* on 31 August 2015, which struck the northeastern islands and caused considerable damage, particular on Boavista and São Nicolau. A detailed and interesting article is https://en.wikipedia.org/wiki/Hurricane_Fred_(2015)

Swell can arrive from almost any direction for no apparent reason. Local winds may be constant in strength and direction, but storms further north (December to May) or south (June to November) can give rise to a nasty swell capable of running for several hundred miles. Almost any of the anchorages in the Cape Verdes may suffer, but those flanked by good beaches are usually most at risk – after all, something caused the beach to form in the first place!

In light of the above it has been suggested that the best time to cruise the islands is in late September or early October, when there is likely to be less wind and swell than a month or so later, so making some of the smaller anchorages much more inviting. While this may well be true, it would still be unwise to approach the Caribbean before the end of the hurricane season, which can extend into December.

## Visibility

True fog is almost unknown in the Cape Verdes, though visibility may sometimes be cut drastically by dust haze carried from the interior of Africa by a hot, dry wind known as the *harmattan*, and if the northeast trades are (or have been) blowing at 17 knots or more such conditions should be expected. Most common between November and March, the effects of the *harmattan* can extend up to 600M from the mainland, usually cutting visibility to 5M or less (though a reduction to 0·5M is not unknown and 50m has been recorded). Indeed, more than one crew's first sight of the islands has been of surf.

IV. CAPE VERDES

Although GPS has eased the problem of accurate position fixing in such conditions, the possibility of collision with another vessel should not be overlooked. Neither should the fact that charting of the islands is still far from perfect – see Chart Datum and Satellite Derived Positions, below – and that many of the major lights are frequently unlit.

In *harmattan* conditions the horizon may appear quite firm with the overhead sky a clear blue, and without any external reference it is quite possible to remain unaware of the potential problem. In winds of more than 15 knots all yachts, and particularly those without radar, should approach the islands with extreme caution.

## Currents

The Cape Verdes lie in the path of the Canary Current, itself generated by the northeast trades, which sets southwest at up to 1·5 knots. It is heavily influenced by recent wind conditions and can be cancelled or even reversed by a southerly gale.

## Tides and tidal streams

Volume 2 of the Admiralty *Tide Tables: The Atlantic and Indian Oceans including tidal stream predictions (NP 202)*, published annually, covers the Cape Verde islands with Dakar, Senegal as standard port. However, many more yachtsmen will probably turn to the internet and the UK Hydrographic Office's excellent *EasyTide* programme at http://easytide.ukho.gov.uk, which gives daily tidal data for at least one harbour on every island other than Ilha do Fogo. Following a suggestion from the author, the island name is now included in cases where the harbour name alone (e.g. Tarrafal) is insufficient. Note, however, that for some unfathomable reason the Cape Verdes are indexed under the South Atlantic!

Tidal ranges are small, São Vicente having less than 1m at springs (0·4m above datum) and only 0·5m at neaps, and are given for each island. Tidal streams are also negligible offshore but can run strongly in the passages between islands, particularly in the Canal de São Vicente and the Canal de Santa Luzia where, combined with the ocean current, it may attain over 4 knots. A 2 knot east-going tidal stream has been reported to occur off the south coast of Santiago close west of Porto da Praia at mid-ebb.

## Magnetic variation

Variation throughout the Cape Verdes decreases by just over 1° from west to east, in 2016 averaging 10°W and decreasing by 7'E annually.

## Weather forecasts

Since 2006 the Cape Verde islands have been covered by Navtex transmissions from São Vicente in English as well as Portuguese – see page 10 – though their reliability has been questioned.

Various websites carrying worldwide weather information are listed on page 9, and a forecast is normally posted in the office of Marina Mindelo.

## Radio communications

Since the withdrawal of the very useful *NP289 – Maritime Communications, United Kingdom and the Mediterranean*, those wishing to carry details of all official radio communications in the Cape Verde islands now need to invest in three volumes – *NP281(1) – Maritime Radio Stations; NP283(1) Maritime Safety Information Services* and *NP 286(1) Pilot Services, Vessel Traffic Services and Port Operations*.

## Buoys and lights

All lights and the few lit buoys in the Cape Verdes follow the IALA A system, as in Europe. It must be emphasised, however, that in the nearly three decades since this guide was first published numerous yachtsmen and women have reported that many – possibly most – lights simply **DO NOT WORK**. In August 2014 official sources in the Cape Verdes stated that only 39 of the islands' 74 lighthouses and other light structures were operational – barely more than half – and this was clearly not an unusual situation. By far the most common reason for a light being unlit was said to be theft of batteries, solar panels or other electrical equipment, though simple breakdowns also accounted for a significant number. Some lights, even though working, may not exhibit their listed characteristics and even when this is intentional details of changes may take many years to appear in Admiralty *Notices to Mariners* – if they ever do. The light on the breakwater at Porto da Palmeira, Ilha do Sal, is a case in point.

Even the *Admiralty List of Lights*, which chooses its words carefully, states that "Many of the lights have been reported as extinguished, damaged, destroyed, irregular or unreliable" – while if a light on one of the islands' relatively few lit buoys should fail it leaves a large, rusting hazard in the darkness... BE WARNED!

The nine inhabited islands are spread over a distance of 145M in latitude and 155M in longitude, forming a neat horseshoe when viewed on the chart. Most passages between adjacent islands can be completed in daylight, but if sailing between two islands further apart consider night departure, while if making landfall for the first time and unable to arrive in daylight the best course may be to heave-to until first light.

## Charts

All charts of the Cape Verde islands should be used with caution, though a little more confidence can be placed in the current edition of Admiralty *367* (which covers the islands' three primary harbours and their approaches), the Portuguese *Instituto Hidrográfico*'s *66301, 66302, 67501, 67502* and *67503*, and those produced by the *Direcção Geral de Marinha e Portos* (Director General of Marine and Ports) in São Vicente. All other charts are based on surveys which predate electronic position fixing, including a few going back a century or more.

The first locally surveyed and printed Cape Verdean charts became available in 2001 (previously all charts of the islands had been surveyed and printed by Portugal). The first three covered the islands' major harbours – *No 21: Porto da Palmeira, Ilha do Sal*; *No 41: Mindelo (Porto Grande), São Vicente*; and *No 71: Porto da Praia, Santiago*. A further two – *No 31: Porto do Tarrafal, São Nicolau*; and *No 11: Porto Novo, Santo Antão* – followed the next year, but since then work appears to have stopped, and neither are they easy to obtain.

The Portuguese *Instituto Hidrográfico*'s *66301, 66302, 67501, 67502* and *67503* can be ordered online from J Garraio & Ca Lda in Lisbon (www.jgarraio.pt). If any other Portuguese charts are seen, avoid them – they will have been surveyed before the islands gained their independence in 1975 and are seriously out of date.

British Admiralty charts (www.ukho.gov.uk) cover the archipelago on two sheets, one small scale and covering all the islands, the other containing three medium-scale island/approach charts and four larger-scale plans of harbours and anchorages. Imray, www.imray.com, are official agents and will mail corrected Admiralty charts worldwide.

Finally, Imray's *Imray-Iolaire* series covers the archipelago on a single sheet, E4, with 10 inset harbour plans. (The four sheets formerly produced by the US National Geospatial-Intelligence Agency were withdrawn in October 2014 in compliance with international agreements between NGA and other chart producing nations.)

See Appendix I, page 433, for chart lists.

### Chart datum and satellite derived positions

Neither of the British Admiralty charts of the Cape Verdes islands are yet based on WGS84 Datum. Positions taken from Admiralty *366, Arquipélago de Cabo Verde* must be moved 0·1 minutes north and 0·4 minutes east to comply with both WGS84 and the plans in this guide, while Admiralty *367* uses three different datum references for the islands of Sal, São Vicente and Santiago and their related harbour plans. For a fuller explanation see Horizontal chart datum on page 433 of the Passages section.

### Guides, pilots, etc.

The archipelago is covered in the British Admiralty's *Africa Pilot (NP 1)* which is of course written with very much larger vessels in mind. In addition, the 6th edition of *The Atlantic Crossing Guide* includes brief passage planning notes, with additional harbour details for Mindelo, São Vicente. They are also mentioned – even more briefly – in Rod Heikell and Andy O'Grady's *Ocean Passages and Landfalls*, and in *World Cruising Routes* and *World Cruising Destinations* by Jimmy Cornell.

Two guides cover the Cape Verdes in some detail – *Kapverdische Inseln: Der Nautische Revierführer* by André Mégroz and Kai Brossmann, and Donald M Street's Street's *Guide to the Cape Verde Islands*. The full 200-page edition of the former is only available in German, though a 60-page 'light' version is also available in English, French and Italian and can be ordered online from http://www.segeln-kapverden.ch.

*Street's Guide to the Cape Verde Islands* by American author Don Street Jr (Seaworthy Publications, Florida, distributed in the UK by Imray), was published in 2010 following visits over a number of years. Don suggests more than two dozen possible anchorages, many of them not mentioned in these pages – often because they are fully open to the northeast trades. Others, such as those on the south coast of São Nicolau and southwest coast of Santiago, appear far more viable. Most are illustrated with sketch plans, though these often lack soundings. Unfortunately the book also contains some misleading errors, both in the stated positions and in the text – see page 90 regarding 'Puerto de São Pedro' for an example of the latter.

## Caution

Although tremendous progress has been made in the Cape Verde islands over the past 30 years, it is nevertheless essential to remember that they are not an outpost of Europe. They are very much a part of Africa, albeit a remarkably successful one in many ways, and the needs of visiting leisure sailors do not rate highly on the list of government priorities. Local people know their own waters, ships (unless visiting Mindelo or Praia) stay well clear, and search and rescue facilities are minimal.

Paper charts may be dangerously inaccurate in some areas, and years may elapse between changes in light characteristics, harbour developments, etc. taking place and appearing on new editions – if they ever do. Even a brand new chart, fully corrected, should not be assumed to be fully up to date in all respects. The same applies to electronic charts, nearly all of which are based on the paper charts of one or more nations. They may be updated more frequently, but even this cannot be done when basic information is not forthcoming from a country's authorities. See also the remarks regarding the frequent unreliability of lights.

# Ilha do Sal

**Between 16°35′N–16°51′N and 22°53′W–23°W**

## Introduction

The most northeasterly of the Cape Verde islands, Ilha do Sal covers an area of some 216km². Much of this is low and flat, the highest point being Monte Grande (Monte Vermelho at 407m. It is the oldest island in the archipelago at some 50 million years and arguably the least attractive, though there are some fine beaches at Santa Maria in the extreme south. Doubtless due to the latter it is amongst the most developed of the Cape Verdes, with the archipelago's largest airport – Amilcar Cabral International – near the centre of the island. By the 2013 census the population was said to to have reached nearly 31,000, as against 14,000 in 2000 and 6000 in 1980. Together with São Vicente and Santiago it is one of the three islands at which yachts may clear into the Republic of Cape Verde, and is obviously the most convenient at which to rendezvous with crew arriving by air or to wave off departing crew members.

The expanding tourist industry in Ilha do Sal was particularly badly hit by the recession, being aimed almost entirely at foreign holidaymakers and buyers. The wave of new developments begun prior to 2008 had nearly all ground to a halt by 2010 and most had not restarted by 2015, leaving the eastern parts of Santa Maria resembling a wild west film set – flimsy frontages with nothing behind them, and entire blocks defined only by foundations. A few development companies had diversified, including

Cabo Golf SA's imaginative *viveiro* project specialising in plants and garden design for hotels and other developments. By 2015 this was said to have been taken over by an Argentinian company, but at the time of writing it had not been possible to confirm whether the greenhouses and polytunnels had survived the ravages of Hurricane *Fred* in late August. The same company was said to have taken over other projects planned by Cabo Golf SA, including that for a marina village on the southwest coast of the island. If the previous plans are followed – and the project ever gets off the ground – it will contain 188 berths, more than half of them able to take yachts of 12m or more, surrounded by the usual houses and apartments, and will have a small boatyard with travel-lift, fuel and other facilities. All the other planned marinas mentioned in the 5th edition appear to have been shelved.

## Approach

Much of the island is low, with a few isolated hills of which the highest, at 407m, is Monte Grande (Monte Vermelho) in the extreme northeast. Thus it can often be lost in haze until very close in. An offing of 0·5–1M is sufficient around the northern part of the island, but the southern part should be allowed a minimum of 1M due to the long sand spits which extend offshore in several places. The current in the vicinity of Ilha do Sal usually sets southwest at about 0·5 knots but may sometimes be much stronger, particularly when the northeast trades are blowing.

## Navigation

**Magnetic variation**
9°26′W (2016) decreasing by 7′E annually. Local magnetic anomalies are reported to exist west of Ilha do Sal.

**Tidal Streams**
Tidal streams around Ilha do Sal are generally weak. However, allowance should be made for the current, which usually sets southwest at 0·5–1 knot but is strongly influenced in both rate and direction by the wind.

**Lights**
**Amilcar Cabral airport (Monte Curral)**
  Aero Al.Fl.WG.7·5s83m26M Airport control tower (operates only when an aircraft is due)
**Ponta Norte** Fl(3)12s16m8M Metal column 5m
**Pedra de Lume** Fl(5)20s28m8M
  Metal post with gallery 5m
**Rabo Junco** Fl.4s15m8M Metal column 5m
**Ponta do Sinó** Fl(2+1)15s11m8M
  300°-vis-142° Square grey tower 9m

**Coast Radio Station**
**Ilha do Sal** 16°45′·3N 22°56′·3W (remotely controlled from São Vicente)
**VHF** Ch 16 (24 hours), 22, 79
**DSC VHF** Ch 70, MMSI 006170000

## Harbours and anchorages

# Porto da Palmeira

16°45'·16N 22°58'·91W (breakwater head)

### Tides

Time difference on Dakar: 0000, on Mindelo (Porto Grande): +0045. Predictions for Porto da Palmeira are available via Admiralty *EasyTide* – see page 368
*Mean spring range* 0·8m
*Mean neap range* 0·4m

### Lights

**Breakwater** Fl(2)R.5s White tower, red bands 5m
This conflicts with the Iso.R.4s11m5M stated in official sources, but has been confirmed by numerous visiting yachts over the past five years
**Oil pipeline, Lts in line on 044°** (occas)
Fl.3·5s9/15m5/3M Red posts 7/11m (lights 95m apart)
The above pair of lights in line indicates the oil pipeline and tanker berth – they are NOT leading lights

### Anchorage behind extended breakwater

A deeply indented bay on the west coast of Ilha do Sal, Porto da Palmeira offers good shelter from northwest through east to south behind a 150m breakwater complete with RoRo ramp. Work on a second breakwater further west was reported to have started during 2015, with at least two unlit hazard buoys positioned off it. In daylight the pale stone and concrete of the main breakwater is said to be visible from well offshore, as are two derelict wind generators to the northwest and a cluster of aluminium oil storage tanks to the southeast.

The anchorage can accommodate at least two dozen yachts without serious overcrowding, though fishing boats and derelict yachts occupy valuable space, but is somewhat bleak and often subject to swell. The village remains small, but is lively colourful and always full of music, and though some new building has taken place it has changed remarkably little over the past two decades. Barefoot women still carry their loads in great baskets

The main breakwater at Porto da Palmeira seen almost end-on, with the port hand buoy shown on the plan in the foreground *Kai Brosmann*

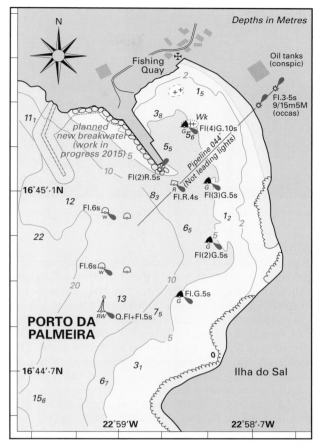

balanced on their heads, whilst children play in the streets. The roads are either cobbled, a legacy of Portuguese colonial times, or dirt tracks. Only the main road to the airport is of tarmac.

There appear to be few problems with security. Most cruisers leave their dinghy astern on a painter (i.e. not a padlocked wire strop), and neither is it considered necessary to employ a yacht or dinghy 'minder' while the crew are ashore.

### Approach and entrance

Straightforward in daylight and feasible at night in good visibility, though note the warning on page 368 concerning the unreliability of lights throughout the archipelago. Four steel buoys mark a tanker berth southwest of the entrance, with the outer two buoys supposedly lit, both Fl.6s3M, though more often they are not. It is best to avoid crossing the area, as the discharge pickup buoy is often awash and difficult to spot even in daylight and there are other unlit buoys in the area.

There is no reason why a yacht arriving from the north should not enter between the breakwater and the northern pair of tanker buoys – the gap is more than 250m wide, with a port hand buoy positioned about 100m south of the breakwater head. This forms part of a buoyed channel which must be left clear for ships approaching and leaving the breakwater (see plan) but can safely be ignored by yachts, for which the channel is of no relevance other than in limiting the westward spread of the anchorage.

Looking southwest across the anchorage at Porto da Palmeira in early 2015  *John Head*

## Anchorage

Best anchorage is to be found in the northeast of the harbour in about 3–5m over sand and stones, though holding is variable (it seems that, once set, an anchor is generally secure). Holding in the middle of the harbour is reported to be good in thick mud, but this area is crowded with local 'yachts', some semi-derelict, as well a two day-charter catamarans. The inside of the mole is in continuous use by cargo boats, ferries and fishing boats and there is no possibility of lying alongside.

The remains of a 40ft steel motor-sailer lie inside the harbour at 16°45'·25N 22°58'·84W – close east of buoy No.7 – and until 2007 its masts broke the surface. It has now settled sufficiently to offer about 2·5m clearance at mean low water, but still constitutes a hazard to anchor and chain.

Dinghies can be left on the beach or at the small quay in the north corner of the harbour, though both consideration and a long painter should be employed as it is used extensively by local fishermen who are generally friendly but do not appreciate being impeded by flocks of dinghies on short painters. Catches are landed and gutted on the stones, often watched by tourists bussed in for day trips on a charter yacht. There is a small slipway at the west end of the quay where it might be possible to carry an engineless inflatable ashore, but beware its lower slopes which are extremely slippery.

## Formalities

Palmeira is currently one of only three ports in the archipelago where inward clearance to the Republic of Cape Verde can be obtained – see Entry and regulations, page 365. Formalities appear to change relatively frequently, but in 2015 the situation was as follows:

*Arrival* The skipper should visit the office of the *Polícia de Ordem Publica*, taking ship's papers and crew passports. (To be found on the street leading from the public toilet/shower to the market and *fontenario*). The *Capitão do Porto* occupies the office on the left and is usually there from 0800–1600 on weekdays – if arriving at the weekend, visit on Monday morning. A crew list must be completed and the ship's papers will be held until departure.

The office on the right is occupied by the *Polícia de Ordem Publica*, where crew passports will be stamped on payment of CVE 500$ (€5) each. This office is claimed never to close, and though no English is spoken the atmosphere is relaxed and friendly. Any crewmembers due to leave by plane must get visas, which can now be issued on the spot (it used to be necessary to visit the *Polícia de Fronteira* at the airport). A fee of €25 is charged and a spare passport photo may be required.

*Departure* Both offices need to be revisited. No charge is made for exit stamps in passports, but CVE 700$ (€7) is payable at the office of the *Capitão do Porto* when reclaiming the ships' papers. Visiting

Shell's cluster of aluminium oil storage tanks – visible from well offshore *Kath McNulty*

The unusual sight of a fisherman sailing out past Porto da Palmeira breakwater, with one of the steel tanker mooring buoys at far left
*Kath McNulty*

another anchorage on Sal is permitted, but if sailing to another island and planning to return it is necessary to clear out and then in again.

## Facilities

Little is available in Palmeira itself and it is generally necessary to visit Vila do Espargos, about 2M inland, for more than routine needs. Athough taxis are rare in Palmeira, *aluguer* minibuses (see page 364) depart regularly from the edge of the town.

*Water* By can from the *fontenario* – a blue concrete structure set back to the north of the main street, which is locked at night and all day Sunday. Water is brought by road tanker from the nearby desalination plant, and there a charge of a few cents per litre. It is claimed to be safe to drink, though many will prefer to play safe and buy bottled water, which is readily available. In 2015 water was also available from a French-run restaurant adjoining the square at the top of the steps up from the beach. It was open evenings and Sundays, but charged a little more than the *fontenario*.

*Showers* A public toilet / shower block – painted blue and labelled *Sentina Municipal* – overlooks the quay and beach. Though nominally open 0700–1800 Monday to Saturday, in practice its hours appear variable and although not the most modern facilities, it is kept very clean by a local lady. There is a small charge for its use – make sure you have change with you.

*Laundry* Nothing in Palmeira other than the *fontenario*, where most local laundry appears to be done. There is said to be a laundry in Espargos near the football field east of the town – ask for Casa de Manuel – but it has not been checked.

*Fuel* Diesel is available by can from the Shell depot to the east of the harbour. However, they do not accept payment, so first it is necessary to visit the office in Espargos, located at the back of the Shell filling station about 200m down the road towards the airport. Vessel details are required together with payment in cash. Back in Palmeira cans will be filled on production of the printed receipt. There is a gate into the depot from the beach, so dinghy access is easy.

*Bottled gas* Camping Gaz cylinders can be exchanged at the tiny bakery (see below), or failing that at the filling station in Espargos. Other bottles may be refilled (with butane only) at the Shell depot – but only if the necessary adaptor is available. Unlike diesel, gas can be paid for in the depot office, where some English is spoken.

*Banks* No bank or ATM in Palmeira, but three in Espargos, all in the centre near the church. Both Caixa Económica de Cabo Verde and Banco Interatlântico have exterior ATMs. There are two more banks at the airport, both with accessible ATMs.

*Shops/provisioning* Several small grocery stores in Palmeira, plus bread from diminutive Padaria Dadô on the main square. A much better choice is available in Espargos, where there are three or four *mini-mercados* with tinned goods, freezers and cold counters. The largest, The Central, also stocks some household items. Also two bakeries, clothes shops, small stationery store, etc., with several Chinese-owned general stores meeting any remaining needs.

*Produce market* In both Palmeira and Espargos. Note that most fruit and vegetables offered in shops will have been chilled so will not keep, making market purchases a better bet.

*Cafés, restaurants & hotels* Several bar/cafés and restaurants in Palmeira, with many more in Espargos where there are also hotels and other accommodation.

*Medical services* Hospital in Espargos, ☎ 241 11130, plus an immaculately-kept pharmacy.

## Communications

*WiFi* In early 2015 free WiFi was available at an Italian-run restaurant on the left side of the street leading into town from the steps up from the beach, at the café in the main square in Espargos (where reception was better outside than in), and at the airport a few miles to the south. Note the warning on page 363 when accessing the internet in the Cape Verdes.

Cyberspace in Espargos – a bright orange building a couple of streets south of the square – is open 0800–2200 daily and has ten computers, paid for by the minute. It also sells local voice and data SIM cards and dongles, though as of early 2015 it was not possible to buy a microSIM for an iPad Air. Prices were very low by European standards.

*Car hire* In Espargos and at the airport. See Road transport, page 364.

*Taxis* Readily available in Espargos, but it may be difficult to find one in Palmeira itself. *Aluguers* (see page 364) are available on an ad-hoc basis, the chief pick-up point in Palmeira being near the edge of the village on the Espargos road.

*Ferries* There is no longer a regular inter-island ferry service, though the elderly *Ribeira de Paúl* – which also carries cargo – visits from time to time.

*Air services* Amílcar Cabral International Airport remains the largest and busiest in Cape Verde, with frequent inter-island and international flights including a few direct from the UK – see page 363. If needing to confirm a TACV flight (recommended at least 48 hours before departure), note that the office at the airport is open 0800–1130, 1400–1700 weekdays only.

IV. CAPE VERDES

# Baía da Mordeira

16°41'·7N 22°58'·1W (NW anchorage)

**Lights**
**Rabo Junco** Fl.4s15m8M Metal column 5m

### Beautiful bay and Marine Protected Area

Baía da Mordeira (or Murdeira) is nearly 3M wide and almost semicircular, with very clear water. Situated on the southwest coast of Ilha do Sal, it gives good protection from northwest through northeast to southeast. Though designated a Marine Protected Area, favoured by turtles which come ashore in summer to lay their eggs, there appears to be no objection to yachts anchoring in the northern corner of the bay, where the bottom shelves gradually and fetch can be reduced by working into 5–6m over rock and sand. A tripline is advisable.

The centre of the bay is a prohibited anchorage due to submarine cables which terminate at a red building on the shore – a line from this building to the northwest point of the bay (Ponta Pesqueirona) marks the northern limit of the cables.

There is excellent snorkelling, but take care when landing as a big surf runs on the beach. There are no facilities ashore, but buses to Palmeira or Santa Maria run along the main road a little to the east.

A tourist resort has been created around a small semicircular lagoon on the southeast shore of Baía da Mordeira, but entry is totally unsuitable even for dinghies – which in any case would probably not be welcome.

Beautiful Baía da Mordeira, looking northwest towards the headland of Rabo Junco *Anne Hammick*

# Baía de Santa Maria

16°35'·6N 22°54'·5W (anchorage)

**Lights**
**Ponta do Sinó** Fl(2+1)15s11m8M
  300°-vis-142° Square grey tower 9m
**Ponta de Vera Cruz** Fl(5)R.20s6m5M 300°-vis-049°
  White tower emerging from building

### Rolly anchorage off excellent beach

Formerly a salt shipping port, Santa Maria is the archipelago's first serious venture into the tourist industry – and hopefully lessons will be learned from the apparently indiscriminate building which has mushroomed over the past decade and far outstripped the town's infrastructure. Nearly all the new construction is of hotels and holiday apartments, and many buildings sport tattered *vende-se* (for sale) notices while others are abandoned and derelict. Most roads remain unsurfaced and unlit.

Having said that, the beach which fringes the western part of the bay is outstanding. Windsurfers and scuba equipment are available for hire from several outlets and it is backed by a multiplicity of bars and restaurants. A long range of cream buildings with pink tiled roofs (the Morabeza Hotel) lies near the head of the bay and is easily seen from seaward. The single jetty was damaged in August 2015 by waves associated with Hurricane *Fred*, but is essential to both fishermen and the tourist trade and has already been rebuilt. The hurricane also saw off the remains of a large schooner which had lain on the reef southeast of Ponta do Sino for the best part of 20 years. It should be noted that the south-going current is gradually causing the sandbank off the headland – now largely built over – to extend, leaving the lighthouse stranded some distance inland.

Kite surfing is a growing sport in Ilha do Sal, though most takes place on the Costa da Fragata, the long bay northeast of Santa Maria where several companies offer lessons and hire out equipment.

### Anchorage

Shelter is good from southwest through north to east, though northeasterly swells frequently work into the bay and some rolling is almost inevitable. Best anchorage is in the middle of the bay southwest of the jetty, outside the local boat moorings, but depths shoal suddenly so approach with care. Holding is good in 5m or more over sand, and some yachts favour a second anchor to hold them into the swell.

Landing on the superb white sand beach is likely to be a wet experience – another reason for the jetty to be rebuilt sooner rather than later, as it was in constant use by fishermen and tourist traffic.

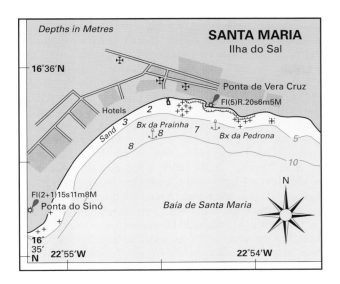

Buying fish on the jetty at Santa Maria  *John Head*

Wherever a dinghy is left, a local boy is likely to appear offering to 'guard' it for a fee, but while the dinghy may be safe its contents will not, so nothing should be left in it to tempt the light-fingered.

## Facilities

*Water* Bottled water is readily available in the shops and bars, but there is no public tap.

*Showers* Several of the hotels have beach showers, for which a small charge is likely to be made.

*Bank* Several, open 0800–1500, nearly all with ATMs.

*Shops/provisioning* Several small supermarkets, plus a bakery at the east end of the main street.

*Produce market* Large covered market – though much of it occupied by souvenir sellers – with fresh fish often available on the beach.

*Cafés,restaurants & hotels* Good choice of the first two, including several on the beach, plus accommodation at all levels.

*Medical services* Small health centre, with a hospital in Espargos.

## Communications

*Car hire* Several companies hiring out both standard and 4-wheel-drive vehicles. See Road transport, page 364.

*Taxis & buses* Plenty of the former, plus frequent *aluguer* minibuses to Espargos via the airport.

*Air services* See page 363.

The picture perfect beach at Santa Maria  *John Head*

Getting ashore dry can be a problem at Santa Maria  *John Head*

# Porto de Pedra de Lume

16°45′·7N 22°53′·45W (molehead)

**Lights**
**Pedra de Lume** Fl(5)20s28m8M
Metal post with gallery 5m
**Quay** Fl.R.4m1M Column on round base 7m

### Fascinating area best visited by road

On the exposed east coast of Ilha do Sal, Porto de Pedra de Lume provides shelter from south through northwest to northeast, but would be uncomfortable and probably dangerous when the northeast trades are blowing. The tiny inner harbour has little more than 1m depthand is criss-crossed with mooring lines. Parts of the bay are rocky, but when the wind shifts into the west it is possible to anchor south of the quay in 7–8m over sand and rock. In January 2005 a very experienced yachtsman reported finding good overnight anchorage in flat seas off Porto de Pedra de Lume, following several days of strong winds from the southwest. He was later told that conditions in Palmeira that night had been 'terrible'.

Porto de Pedra de Lume was the first settlement on Sal and for many years exported salt, which forms naturally in a nearby volcanic crater. Until less than a decade ago the rusting tugs and lighters employed in this trade remained hauled out on the beach, close to the antique and sadly dilapidated processing machinery. Salt production has now resumed, though largely as a tourist attraction, and it is also possible to swim in the very buoyant, salty water.

Between 2007 and 2010 plans for a marina and golf resort were to be seen on roadside hoardings and elsewhere, but by 2015 the former had been dropped and the latter morphed into a few half-built apartment blocks.

Looking south towards the little harbour's entrance *John Head*

Colourful fishing boats in the tiny harbour at Pedra da Lume. Note the mooring lines strung across to the outer mole *John Head*

# Boavista
## Between 15°58'N–16°14'N and 22°40'W–22°58'W

## Introduction

Ilha da Boavista is the most easterly of the Cape Verde islands, lying just over 21M south of Ilha do Sal and 42M north-northeast of Ilha do Maio, and covering an area of some 620km². Much of the eastern part is high, reaching 390m at Pico Estância, but visibility is sometimes deceptively poor and the island hidden by haze until only a few miles distant. Until recently it was one of the least developed of the Cape Verde islands and still has the lowest population density, despite a rise from about 3,500 inhabitants in 1990 to more than 9,000 at the time of the last census in 2013.

With its giant sand dunes and thousands of date palms, Boavista has aptly been described as 'a small piece of the Sahara adrift in the Atlantic Ocean', and it is well worth visiting the unexpectedly attractive interior. After centuries of being virtually ignored, its miles of white sand beach, excellent windsurfing and interesting diving (more than 200 known wrecks litter the shores of Boavista), now attract many thousands of tourists each year – enough to warrant the building of an international airport handling direct flights from northern European countries including the United Kingdom. Several enormous luxury hotels cater for the influx, and many tourist village developments were begun – though not all completed – before the global recession set in.

In addition to the anchorage off Porto de Sal Rei, between January and March it may be possible to anchor off the long white beach at Santa Monica on the south coast of the island, but later in the year swell makes this unpleasant or downright impossible. The so-called 'ports' of Porto Ferreira on the east coast and Porto do Ervatão somewhat further south are complete misnomers – small bays behind headlands offering minimal protection, with nothing whatsoever ashore.

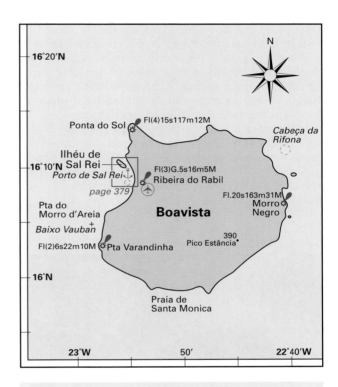

## Navigation

### Magnetic variation
9°37'W (2016) decreasing by 7'E annually. Local magnetic anomalies are reported to exist east of Boavista.

### Tidal Streams
Although tidal streams as such are weak, generous allowance must be made for the strong south-southwest setting current in the channel between Ilha do Sal and Boavista.

### Lights
**Ponta do Sol** Fl(4)15s117m12M
   017°-vis-272° Metal tower 7m
**Morro Negro**
   Fl.20s163m31M 163°-vis-035°
   Square white turret on building 12m
**Ponta Varandinha**
   Fl(2)6s22m10M Lantern on red structure 7m
   Racon V every 30s 310°-194° 24M

### CAUTION
The maintenance of lights around Boavista appears consistently poor, even by Cape Verdean standards. In 2002 the *Capitão do Porto* took pains to stress their unreliability, and things have not improved. In April 2011 only one of Porto de Sal Rei's four lights was working, and three years later there was just one functional light on the whole island, instead of eight!

Approaching Boavista in darkness, even with GPS, chart plotter and current paper charts, would be unwise in the extreme.

### Approach

Ilha da Boavista is most likely to be approached from the north or east, both of which require particular care. Generous allowance must be made for the strong south or southwest-going current, and an offing of at least 4M maintained along the northeast coast to avoid the breaking reefs of Cabeça da Rifona. The island should be closed to within 1M only after Ponta do Sol comes abeam.

If departing Sal Rei's southern anchorage for Ilha do Maio or Santiago it is essential to leave on a bearing of not less than 220° in order to clear the Baixo Vauban, a reef running almost 1·5M offshore west-southwest of Ponta do Morro d'Areia.

In October 2011 two large, unlit, red buoys, said to mark cables, were encountered north of the breakwater head at about 16°11'·8N 22°55'·8W and 16°11'·2N 22°55'·7W respectively. Though not been reported since they are probably still in situ.

'Down at the waterhole' – the water tank and communal laundry near the beach at Vila de Sal Rei in 2003...
*Sue Thatcher*

... and virtually unchanged twelve years later  *Rosie Spooner*

## Anchorages

## Porto de Sal Rei

16°10'·87N 22°55'·73W (breakwater head)
16°09'·9N 22°55'·1W (southern anchorage)

### Tides
Time difference on Dakar: –0020, on Mindelo (Porto Grande): +0025. Predictions for Porto de Sal Rei are available via Admiralty *EasyTide* – see page 368
*Mean spring range* 1·0m
*Mean neap range* 0·4m

### Lights
**Outer (new) breakwater** Fl(5)20s
  Pale concrete column
**Breakwater** Iso.R.4s7m5M
  Concrete column on wall 1m
**Ponta de Escuma** (Ilhéu de Sal Rei, NW)
  Fl(5)G.20s9m7M Lantern on metal post 3m
**Calheta do Velho** (Ilhéu de Sal Rei)
  Fl(5)WR.20s28m11M 220°-R-355°-W-220°
  Column close to grey building 8m
**Inner quay** Fl(3)R.12s8m5M
  Red lantern on building 6m
**Communications tower** F.R. Lattice tower
**Ribeira de Rabil** Fl(3)G.5s16m5M
  010°-vis-120° Metal column with lantern 5m
  (situated at the airport about 1M inland)

### Anchorage close to excellent beaches

Vila de Sal Rei, lying inside the island of the same name, has grown over the past two decades from little more than a village into a town more than 1km across – this despite nearly all the new tourist developments take advantage of the beaches further south. There is a small concrete quay off the town, but all commercial shipping uses the newly-extended harbour to the north.

The beautiful beaches south of Sal Rei are long, clean and almost deserted – other than where they front tourist hotels or other new developments – though landing is often difficult due to the swell. Sailboards are available for hire, and the area has a growing international reputation as an outstanding venue for the sport. There are also several PADI-accredited dive schools.

### Approach and anchorage – southern

Visiting yachts normally anchor in the bight formed by the southern end of the island and the shore, sheltered from north through northeast to southeast, with some protection around to south.

Approach in daylight only, keeping well offshore in 25m or more until Ilhéu de Sal Rei bears due east. A ruined chapel and large cross are clearly visible about halfway along the island. Then close the island to the 10m contour (some 400m offshore) and skirt its southern end, passing inside Baixo Inglez which lies 0·65M off the island at 16°09'·3N 22°55'·9W.

Turn east when the ruined fort comes abeam and hold this course until the town bears due north.

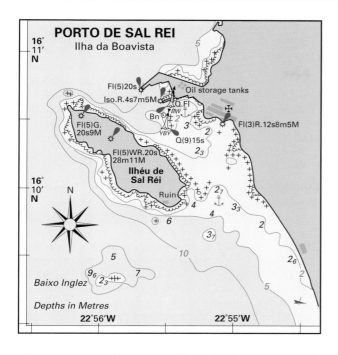

**PORTO DE SAL REI**
Ilha da Boavista

Depths in Metres

22°56'W      22°55'W

Then turn northwards and work into a suitable depth for anchoring – the bottom shelves gradually but does vary – and 4–5m will be found about halfway between the southern point of the island and the shore. Take care not to stray too far west as a reef fringes the southeast coast of Ilhéu de Sal Rei, extending beyond the island to its shallowest point at 16°09'·96N 22°55'·27W. Behind it, at the southeast corner of the island, lies a small but excellent (and usually deserted) beach, where a dinghy can be left while exploring the island. Holding is patchy with rock underlying the sand. It is claimed that this has been disappearing in recent years, together with the dunes which used to fringe the shoreline, and many patches no longer have sand deep enough for an anchor to dig in. It would seem wise to don mask and flippers and dive down to check.

It is not possible to reach the village from the south by yacht due to shoals – access is via a dinghy passage carrying about 1m. Stone steps provide a convenient dinghy landing point, though the dinghy itself would be better left on the small beach just north of the old quay. There does not appear to be a security problem in Boavista, but even so a padlocked wire strop might be wise to deter 'borrowing'. If using an outboard, beware the floating lines used by moored boats tied off to the pier.

Particular care should be taken if visiting the area during summer or autumn when south or southeasterly winds are common. Though seldom strong, they can rise without warning and set up a heavy swell which makes it difficult if not impossible for a vessel to leave the bay. Even in winter when the northeast trades are established, gales further north may set up a northwesterly swell which runs down both sides of Ilhéu de Sal Rei, breaking heavily on Baixo Inglez, causing the reef between the island and

the town to break all the way across, and even producing white water on the 3·7m patch south of the anchorage. The only thing to do in such conditions is to get out while it is still safe to do so – conditions offshore are likely to be much pleasanter.

## Approach and anchorage – northern

Work on a major new breakwater was completed in 2014, though this is of no obvious benefit to visiting yachts as the prospect of lying alongside or anchoring in its shelter appears remote. Weather permitting and subject to space it may be possible for a yacht to anchor south of the inner (old) breakwater, or even lie alongside, albeit briefly, if no ships are expected. Extreme caution is needed, however, as the area can quickly become dangerous if the weather deteriorates and particularly if a northwesterly swell develops.

Do NOT attempt entry other than in light winds and good daylight. Approach the northwest end of Ilhéu de Sal Rei on a southerly bearing, altering course for the entrance channel at approximately 16°11'N 22°56'·2W and then heading southeast towards 16°10'·6N 22°55'·8W. From there the anchorage will lie due east, and can be approached between the inner breakwater and the north cardinal buoy which marks the central reef. Should the buoy be off station, the itself reef is topped by an (unlit) beacon. A number of fishing boats, day charter yachts – mostly large catamarans – and semi-derelicts are normally to be found in residence, either on moorings or multiple anchors, making a tripline a necessity. Note that all the buoys are private – should one be free, a day charter boat is almost certain to return to claim it before the evening.

The reef extends more than 200m south-southeast from the beacon, with a west cardinal buoy positioned southwest of its southwest end. The channel between it and the shore carries 3m or more at its northern end decreasing as one continues south – sufficient for an outboard nearly all the way to the old quay. Alternatively, there is a beach just south of the inner breakwater, and others along the waterfront where local smallcraft are hauled ashore.

## Formalities

In theory, the skipper should visit the *Delegação Marítima* (harbour office) in the commercial port on arrival, taking the usual ship's papers and crew passports. In late 2015 this proved easier said than done, however, with no harbour office identifiable and the local police denying that a visit was necessary. Should the situation change, a fee of CVE 700$ (€7) is likely to be charged for a stay of any duration, irrespective of the size of yacht or number of crew, and the ship's papers retained until departure.

Any crewmembers leaving the yacht by plane will need visas, costing CVE 2,500$, €25 or US$40 each, for which it is necessary to visit the airport about 5km southeast of the town. They should accompany the skipper, taking photocopies of the information

**IV. CAPE VERDES**

pages of their passports plus a couple of passport photos each, although these are unlikely to be needed. Obtaining a visa should not be left until the last moment, as although the airport immigration desk is always manned when an international flight is due to land, it may not be manned before one departs – and without the correct entry and visa stamps they will NOT be allowed to board their flights.

### Facilities

*Water* By can from a standpipe a short walk north of the old town pier (although local people consider the water drinkable, boiling would be a wise precaution). Bottled water is readily available.

*Showers* Try one of the hotels.

*Fuel* By can from one of the two filling stations on the road south out of town. It may be possible to order larger quantities of diesel for delivery to the breakwater by road tanker, but Palmeira and Mindelo are much better options for fuelling up. The large Shell depot in the apex of the two breakwaters is not a retail operation.

*Bottled gas* Camping Gaz cylinders can be exchanged at many outlets, but it is unlikely that other bottles could be refilled.

*Bank* Several in the town, all with ATMs.

*Shops/provisioning* Several supermarkets of varying size with reasonably good stocks, plus a small pharmacy, hardware stores, etc. There is a small tourist bakery, though bread rolls are usually available in the produce market – ask if they cannot be seen, as they may well be covered against flies.

*Produce market* Large, airy produce market on the main square, though prices are much higher than in most of the other islands as almost everything has to be imported. Stocks vary (depending on when the cargo ship last called) but generally include a reasonable variety of tropical fruits and vegetables. Take your own bags.

*Hotels & restaurants* An ever increasing number of hotels at all levels, many of them Italian owned and run, and a similarly good choice of restaurants, both European and local. Booking is generally necessary and check if payment is required in cash.

*Medical services* New and modern health centre with limited hospital facilities, near the main square, ☎+238 251 1167.

### Communications

*WiFi* Several internet cafés, including Internet Center Boavista ☎+238 251 1553, where SIM cards are also available.

*Taxis* Readily available, or negotiate with an *aluguer* driver for a day trip. Car hire is also possible, but given that Boavista's better roads are cobbled and the others no more than dirt tracks, most people will prefer their car to come complete with local driver.

*Ferries* There is no longer a regular inter-island ferry service, though the elderly *Ribeira de Paúl* – which also carries cargo – visits from time to time.

*Air services* The previously tiny airport at Rabil, 5km southeast of the Sal Rei, a dirt-strip until 2007, now handles direct flights to and from northern European countries as well as regular inter-island flights. In 2011 it was renamed Aristides Pereira International Airport after the country's first president.

Looking east across the southern anchorage from the south end of Ilhéu de Sal Réi *Mungo Morris*

Looking east across Porto de Sal Rei's north anchorage. The unlit beacon can be seen near the left side of the picture with its associated reef breaking in the foreground. It is now marked by two (supposedly lit) buoys  *Chris Smith*

# Baixo de João Valente

15°48'·7N 23°09'·2W

### Dangerous shoal, isolated and unmarked

This dangerous unlit shoal lies some 17·5M southwest of Ilha da Boavista, almost straddling the direct course to Ilha de Santiago – see page 354. The shallowest part, itself divided into two distinct reefs, is said to have less than 2m over it at mean low water – not surprisingly, it breaks in all but the calmest weather. Depths of less than 10m extend nearly 2M to the north-northwest, with the 50m contour enclosing an area some 5M in latitude and 3M in longitude.

The bank is formed mainly of hard basalt rock with a thin covering of broken shells and sand. It is home to a wide variety of fish species and local charter boats visit for the diving, some claiming that it is the best dive site in Cape Verde. It is said to be a good place to sight whales on the surface.

The sun sets over Ilhéu de Sal Réi, with moored smallcraft and the old town pier in silhouette  *Mungo Morris*

IV. CAPE VERDES

# São Nicolau
## Between 16°29'N–16°41'N and 24°01'W–24°26'W

## Introduction

São Nicolau, with an area of 388km², is the most easterly of the northwestern group of islands, lying only 9M from Ilhéu Raso but approximately 60M due west of Ilha do Sal. It is very mountainous, reaching 1,304m at Monte Gordo, and is thus wetter and more productive than most of the other islands with fruit, vegetables and sugar cane being grown. Much of the northern and western coastline terminates in sheer cliffs – in 2010 one yachtsman remarked that 'sailing along the north coast, the dramatic scenery was reminiscent of the island at the start of the King Kong film'.

The main town is Vila da Ribeira Brava, near the centre of the island, where nearly half of the island's 13,000 or so people live. For many years this was the seat of the Cape Verde diocese, later moved to Santiago, and was also a notable seat of learning in Portuguese colonial times. The attractive town centre still has much colonial-era Portuguese architecture and is notably well cared for.

If anchored at Tarrafal and happy to leave the yacht unattended, an *alugeur* ride through the dramatic and varied scenery to Vila da Ribeira Brava is highly recommended. After exploring the town, the energetic may enjoy stretching their legs after time at sea by walking back up from Ribeira Brava to the main road at Cachaço – about 4km as the crow flies, but much further on the ground – to catch an *alugeur* back to Tarrafal.

## Approach

The exposed north coast should be given at least 1M clearance, increasing to 1·5M around Ponta Espechim. A generous 0·5M gives a safe margin along the south and southwest coasts, except if sailing from Ponta da Vermelharia towards Porto da Preguiça, when the shoals of Baixo do Pataca should be given a wider offing.

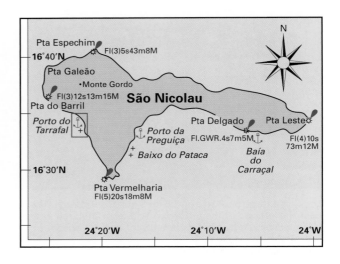

## Navigation

**Magnetic variation**
10°08'W (2016) decreasing by 7'E annually

**Tidal Streams**
Tidal streams set west on the flood and east on the ebb at up to 2 knots.

**Lights**
**Ponta Leste** Fl(4)10s73m11M
  140°-vis-030° White column, red lantern 3m
**Ponta Espechim** Fl(3)5s43m8M
  Metal column 5m
**Ponta do Barril** Fl(3)12s13m15M
  Square white tower and building 9m
**Ponta Vermelharia** Fl(5)20s18m8M
  Metal column 5m
**Ponta Delgado** Fl.WRG.4s7m5M
  Metal column 5m

Parts of the north coast of São Nicolau are very productive, with maize, beans and sugarcane grown on the terraced slopes  *Sue Thatcher*

*Carnaval* in Ribeira Brava  *Kath McNulty*

## Harbours and anchorages

# Porto do Tarrafal

16°34'·06N 24°21'·63W (breakwater head)

**Lights**
**Breakwater** Iso.R.4s8m5M
Red post and lantern 5m

### Popular anchorage off growing town

Situated on the southwest coast of the island, Porto do Tarrafal with its substantial breakwater provides shelter from north through east to southwest. A small village when visited in 1993, by 2015 it had grown into a sprawling town with wide cobbled streets, sporting a contrasting mixture of old and new buildings and able to meet all daily needs.

The local people are friendly and welcoming towards visitors, and security appears to be good. Two crews who visited in 2013 both commented on this aspect as regards themselves, their boats and their dinghies, an opinion endorsed in early 2015. Many yachtsmen familiar with the Cape Verde islands consider Porto do Tarrafal their favourite anchorage.

The local economy revolves largely around fishing, with tuna and other large fish salted on the quay and a fishmeal processing plant (which generates surprisingly little smell) behind the beach. After years of discussion as to whether a tourist centre should be built to exploit the excellent sport fishing in the channel between São Nicolau and Santa Luzia, where a number of international records are held, construction of a large complex about 2·5km northwest of the town finally started in 2007. However, work appears to have ground to a halt without much of the supporting infrastructure being in place. In late 2015 it was described as 'looking reasonably complete, but with no lights and no people'.

Swimming in the harbour would be unwise, but if anchored further out the water is clean. In 2015 the beach opposite the harbour was described as 'disappointing, with lots of broken glass everywhere and the water full of rubbish'. A much nicer beach (complete with local beach bar) will be found at Praia da Telha, about five minutes' walk south.

The wide bay at Porto do Tarrafal, looking west-southwest
*Anne Hammick*

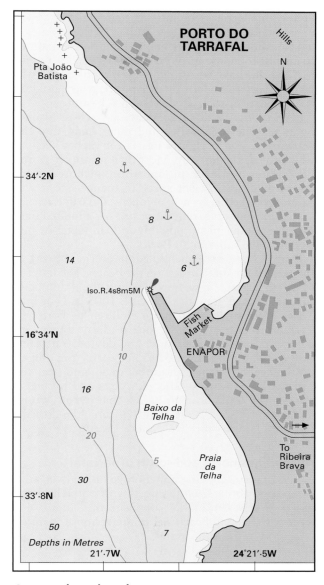

### Approach and anchorage

The breakwater and village are easily identified from offshore with no hazards on approach, though if coming from the south a minimum offing of 300m should be allowed around the Baixo da Telha. It would be wise not to close the breakwater until it bears northeast.

Holding is mainly good in 5–10m over black sand (fortunate, since fierce northeasterly squalls may funnel down the ravines with little warning) but there are reported to be a few soft patches. Consider

IV. CAPE VERDES

laying a second anchor if leaving the boat unattended, even for a few hours. At other times a light onshore wind picks up, making it essential not to anchor too close in. When very crowded – and up to 50 yachts have occasionally been reported – it will be necessary to anchor further north, where holding is variable over rock, stones and black sand.

Ferries and small cargo boats as well as fishing boats use the breakwater and inner quay, and the *Capitão do Porto* rightly insists on yachts keeping well clear of the fairway. Most turn just north of the breakwater and back in, and if an anchored yacht leaves them insufficient space to manoeuvre it will be moved whether or not anyone is aboard. Even so, it might be possible to lie alongside for a limited time by prior arrangement, possibly to load water or fuel – consult the *Capitão do Porto*.

Dinghies can either be pulled up on the slipway at the root of the mole or left on the beach. The latter is likely to attract a posse of young 'boat minders' eager to 'guard' it all day for CVE 100$ (€1) or less. There seem to be even more children in Porto do Tarrafal than in most Cape Verdean towns, all competing to take the painter and demonstrate their skill at tying a bowline, or to help carry the dinghy up the beach. If using an outboard to land near the fish market beware submerged rocks and rubble; if relying on oars bear in mind that when strong northeasterly squalls are blowing it may be difficult or even impossible to make headway in an inflatable.

### Anchorages north and south of Tarrafal

*North of Tarrafal* Good anchorage in 7m over sand is reported about 1½ miles northwest of the harbour at 16°35'·1N, 24°23'·4W, opposite the mouth of a river with a small beach and a single house (painted

The anchorage north of Tarrafal referred to in the text, with the single house clearly visible *Paul and Rachel Chandler*

orange and white) ashore – a very peaceful setting. The water is clear, but the tidal stream can be strong so weak swimmers should take particular care.

The tidal stream here is not as stated on page 382, instead running east-southeast on the flood and west-northwest on the ebb, turning about an hour before high or low water.

*South of Tarrafal* Equally good anchorage is reported at Baiá Baixo de Rocha, about 2½ miles south-southeast of Tarrafal at 16°31'·4N 24°20'·1W, where 9m of crystal-clear water is to be found over sand. The white sand beach is backed by dunes and a cliff formed of vertical tubes of basalt rock which is, not surprisingly, considered one of the most beautiful of the archipelago.

Looking south over Porto do Tarrafal from Monte Gordo, at 1,312m (4,304 feet) São Nicolau's highest point *Chris Smith*

Tarrafal lies between its dark sand beach and a backdrop of equally sandy hills  *Mungo Morris*

## Formalities

The friendly 'one-stop' *Delegação Marítima* (harbour office) is housed in a pink building on the right as you go up the main square towards the church (not, as one might expect, in the pale blue wedge-shaped building prominently labelled Edifício Mira Mar, complete with anchor symbol, which is a shopping centre and apartments). The office is open 0800–1530 Monday to Friday. Entry is quick and straightforward, with some English spoken, and a standard charge of CVE 700$ (€7) payable for a stay of any duration, irrespective of the size of yacht or number of crew. Ship's papers are normally retained until departure. Provided that immigration clearance has already been obtained at one of the three specified islands – see page 365 – there is no further paperwork.

If intending to stop at Santa Luzia en route to São Vicente see the note on page 359.

## Facilities

Facilities in the town have improved vastly over the past two decades and the trend looks set to continue.

*Engineers* The generating station behind the cream wall opposite the beach also contains some engineering equipment, and maintenance staff might be willing to assist in an emergency (provided the language barrier could be overcome).

*Water* Tap in the fish market, though it is best to avoid the times when fishing boats have just returned. Not of drinkable quality, but bottled water is readily available.

For larger quantities visit the ENAPOR office at the top of the breakwater steps. A metered tap will be turned on, controlling a hose at the back of the steps.

*Showers* Several of hotels and *residençials* either provide showers or will rent out an en suite room for a short period for that purpose.

*Fuel* By can from either of the filling stations on the road out of town. The Shell diesel pump on the quay does not serve yachts. It may be possible to get fuel delivered to the quay by road tanker – enquire at the ENAPOR office.

*Bottled gas* Camping Gaz from the Shell filling station (which maintains several other compounds around the town) but no chancing of refilling other bottles.

*Bank* On the main square, open mornings only, closed weekends, with ATM outside.

*Shops/provisioning* Several supermarkets, which in late 2015 were reported to be surprisingly well-stocked and some of which open on Sunday. That in the Edifício Mira Mar (the pale blue, wedge-shaped building on the square where the taxis congregate) has received particular praise.

*Produce market* Small but good quality morning vegetable market in the shed next to the fish market (the one closest to the water). Most of the produce on sale is island grown, however, so choice is limited. Fish can be bought directly from the boats as they unload at the quay.

*Restaurants & hotels* Six or seven small hotels and *pensãos*, most of which serve meals to non-residents (booking is generally necessary and payment may be required in cash), plus various cafés and bars.

*Medical services* Health centre in the town, ☎+238 236 1130, plus small hospital in Ribeira Brava, ☎+238 235 1130.

## Communications

*WiFi* Several cafés offer free WiFi for the price of a coffee, and SIM cards are also available.

*Car rental* One company in Tarrafal and two more in Ribeira Brava.

*Taxis* Congregate on the main square and elsewhere.

*Buses* Shared *aluguer* minibuses offer excellent value. The ride across the mountain ridge to Ribeira Brava shows a completely different side of São Nicolau and is highly recommended.

*Ferries* The catamaran ferry *Liberdade* normally visits twice a week from Mindelo, São Vicente – see page 363.

*Air services* Small airport on the road between Ribeira Brava and Porto da Preguiça, with regular inter-island flights.

# Porto da Preguiça

16°33'·65N 24°16'·81W (molehead)

> **Tides**
> Time difference on Dakar: –0035, Mindelo (Porto Grande): +0010. Predictions for Porto da Preguiça are available via Admiralty *EasyTide* – see page 368
> *Mean spring range* 0·8m
> *Mean neap range* 0·4m
>
> **Lights**
> **Porto Velho**
> Fl(2+1)R.15s25m5M 285°-vis-016°
> Red lantern on white building 7m

## Possible anchorage off old quay

Once the main port of São Nicolau but now entirely eclipsed by Porto do Tarrafal, the more exposed Porto da Preguiça has reverted to life as a small fishing village where boats are drawn up on the stony beach west of a small quay. A large white building on low cliffs to the east is conspicuous from offshore.

In favourable weather it is possible to anchor off in about 10m, and yachts have been known to go alongside the quay for short periods, though it would be wise to check first by dinghy for underwater obstructions. There are steps on the western side to facilitate landing by dinghy. A rock carrying 2·3m or less has been reported as lying 50m from Porto Velho light on a bearing of 255°.

Any attempt to close the beach would be unwise due to moored boats and numerous floating lines. Not a harbour to be recommended, and with very little ashore beyond a couple of bars and a communal water tap.

Looking southwest along the south coast of São Nicolau past the old town of Preguiça and its tiny quay
*Anne Hammick*

# Baía do Carraçal

16°33'·1N 24°05'W (anchorage)
### Remote but interesting anchorage

Suggested as a possible anchorage in the *Africa Pilot* (see page 438) but not visited by the author. The following description was received from Jill Schinas, to whom grateful thanks:

> 'The south coast of São Nicolau is of unremitting orange-brown until one reaches Baía do Carraçal. Here a little clump of palm trees and acacias chokes the mouth and meeting place of two *ribeiras*. The sea has pushed its way into their mouth to form a tiny cove, and the village of Carraçal sits on either side. For a yacht on passage from Ilha do Sal to Tarrafal or vice-versa it would be a good place for an overnight stop.'

Other reports confirm that the village of white houses is easy to spot, but the bay is small with shoals on either side. Though offering shelter from the northeast trades it can be rolly in any swell. There is a disused tuna-canning factory on the shore. There appear to be two possible anchorages – just off Carraçal itself, and slightly further west.

Jill recommends:

> 'Anchor just outside the cove in about 12m, but beware of isolated rocks on either side. It is also possible to anchor inside the cove and take a line ashore (there is insufficient swinging room for normal anchoring). Landing is easy on the black sand beach, and the local people friendly without being pushy.'

Kath McNulty adds:

> 'Good anchorage in 5m over sand will also be found in the first cove to the west of the village, at about 16°33'·3N 24°05'·5W. It is less rolly than off the village and good for an overnight stop, but a longish way from the village if you want to go and visit.'

Baía do Carraçal, on the southeast coast of São Nicolau
*Kath McNulty*

# Santa Luzia

**Between 16°44'N–16°48'N and 24°41'W–24°48'W**

## Introduction

Santa Luzia is separated from São Vicente by the 4·5M wide Canal de Santa Luzia. At less than 12km long it is one of the smaller of the Cape Verde islands and has very little vegetation and no permanent inhabitants, though fishermen from São Vicente may stay for periods of a week or more, camping either in their boats or in the derelict village on the southwest coast. However it is said to be home to a variety of feral animals including donkeys, goats, cats and dogs (though possibly the latter travel to and from the island with the fishermen).

Santa Luzia and the nearby islands of Ilhéus Branco e Raso – see page 389 – are one of Cape Verde's primary venues for the spawning of turtles, and the surrounding waters are home to many species of fish and shellfish. The islands have been designated a Natural Reserve, and in 2015 a management plan was being drawn up to identify which activities – primarily scientific and educational – were compatible with environmental preservation and conservation of the endemic species of reptiles and birds which depend on them. In theory access is restricted, but in practice Santa Luzia in particular is becoming a favourite with cruisers eager to experience a real 'deserted island' – and effectively a desert island, too.

In late 2015 the *Polícia Marítima* at Tarrafal advised departing skippers of the islands' Natural Reserve status and said that anchoring without a permit was forbidden, a stance confirmed by their colleagues in Mindelo. Neither had any idea where such a permit might be obtained, however, and as no wardens are stationed on any of the islands it is difficult to see how such a ruling might be enforced. Plainly the environment must be respected, with no creatures killed or injured afloat or ashore, no fires lit and no litter deposited, but as the four species of turtle which lay their eggs on the islands' beaches all do so in late summer it is unlikely that they will encounter visiting yachts – and far from certain that it would trouble them if they did.

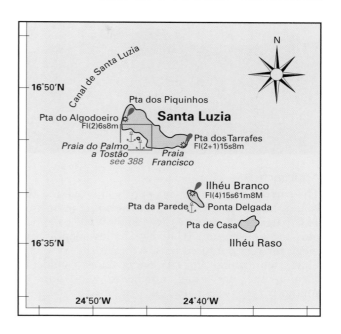

## Navigation

**Magnetic variation**
10°13'W (2016) decreasing by 7'E annually

**Tidal Streams**
Tidal streams can run strongly in the Canal de Santa Luzia, the northeast-going stream beginning about three hours before HW (though in practice the tidal stream overrules the ocean current only after very prolonged periods of light winds) and the southwest-going stream – which combined with the ocean current can reach 4 knots or more – beginning about two hours after HW.

Around the rest of the island tidal streams set west on the flood and east on the ebb at up to 2 knots.

**Lights**
**Ponta do Algodoeiro**
    Fl(2)6s8m Metal column 5m
**Ponta dos Tarrafes**
    Fl(2+1)15s8m Metal column 5m

Approaching Santa Luzia from the southeast *Ed Clay*

IV. CAPE VERDES

Approaching Praia do Palmo a Tostão from the west, with Ilhéu Zinho just visible below the saddle between the hills
*David Caukill*

## Approach

The surrounding waters are poorly charted and the island should therefore be given an offing of at least 1M, particularly at its eastern end. Wind over tide plus the uneven and relatively shallow depths can make for very confused seas. At times the wind can blow right round Ilha da Santa Luzia, suddenly turning the prevailing northeast wind into a southerly.

## Anchorages

## Praia do Palmo a Tostão

16°45'·1N 24°45'·5W (Ilhéu Zinho)

### Tides
Time difference on Dakar: –0040, on Mindelo (Porto Grande): +0005. Predictions for Santa Luzia are available via Admiralty *EasyTide* – see page 368
*Mean spring range* 0·8m
*Mean neap range* 0·6m

### Windy anchorage off deserted beach

A shallow bay on the southwest coast backed by a sandy beach, affording protection from northwest through northeast to southeast. The 12m Ilhéu Zinho, with outlying rocks, lies some 500m offshore in the centre of the bay and anchorage may be made either side of it, or between it and the shore. The shallow shelf broadens considerably towards the southeast end of the beach.

The anchorage is prone to williwaws which may peak at more than twice the average wind speed, one yacht experiencing squalls in excess of 50 knots even though no more than 25 knots was encountered once on passage towards São Vicente. In compensation, there is almost limitless swinging room and another yacht reports laying 70m of chain after which 'the williwaws were not a problem'.

Holding appears to be variable, having been described both as 'basically a thin layer of sand over rock' (though 100m of 13mm chain eventually

helped the anchor take hold) and 'fine – we dropped anchor in 7m inshore of Ilhéu Zinho and held well in winds gusting 30 knots or more and shifting around'. The snorkelling around Ilhéu Zinho is said to be particularly good.

Landing by dinghy can be difficult due to surf, and sometimes only those prepared to swim ashore may be able to set foot on the island. The surf is reported to be least inside Ilhéu Zinho and just northwest of the small rocky shelf which extends towards it from the shore. This appears to have little to do with the island, however, and more to the fact that the area is sheltered from the northeast by a hill bracketed by deep ravines which channel the gusts to either side. Once ashore there is no fresh water or other facilities.

Ilhéu Branco seen from the northeast, with the pale patches from which it gets its name clearly visible *Ed Clay*

# Ilhéus Branco e Raso

## Navigation

**Tidal streams**
See under Santa Luzia, page 387

**Lights**
Ilhéu Branco Fl(4)15s61m8M
    Metal column 5m

## Unihabited island nature reserves

Tiny islets both less than 3km long, Ilhéu Branco lies 4M southeast of Santa Luzia with Ilhéu Raso some 3·5M beyond. Neither is inhabited. Both are nature reserves and in theory permission is required to visit. Great care should be taken not to disturb birds or other wildlife, including the Cabo Verdean giant gecko. Both islets are high and generally steep-to, and can safely be approached to within 0·5M.

## Anchorages

## Ilhéu Branco

Bisected by 16°39'·5N 24°40'·2W

### Challenging island anchorage

Jill Schinas describes Ilhéu Branco as 'magnificent'. The oblong island emerges through the *harmattan* haze as a vast white triangle and only later, as it gets closer, does the surrounding rock come into view. The island's highest point reaches 327m, and much of the coast consists of sheer cliffs. As with Santa Luzia, fishermen visit and camp ashore, both to fish and to collect young birds for food – the latter causing a catastrophic collapse in the endemic Cape

Verde shearwater population. Frigate birds also breed on the island.

It would be possible to anchor anywhere along the south coast of the island, in that it is shallow enough, but in normal trade wind conditions vicious northwesterly gusts (reportedly reaching 50–60 knots) may be encountered between Ponta da Parede and Ponta Delgada in the extreme southeast. More shelter should be found just west of Ponta da Parede in about 8m, where landing can be made on a small, stony beach just east of the white sand patch. The eastern extremity of Branco consists of a flat, low-lying sandy tail where, in very windless conditions, it might also be possible to anchor.

The occasional strong southwesterly gust should be anticipated when anchoring, and any variation on the usual northeast or east-northeast wind would probably allow a swell to work around one or other end of the island.

## Ilhéu Raso

Bisected by 16°37'N 24°35'·5W

### An island for birders

Ilhéu Raso consists of an 8km² plateau raised above the sea on a low cliff (less than 2m in places), surmounted by a number of dull, brown mounds, the tallest reaching only 164m. The southwestern area is flat and rocky, intersected by dry riverbeds. There is little vegetation. The island's only real attraction is the colonies of seabirds which nest there – including the brown booby, red-billed tropicbird, shearwaters and petrels – plus the Raso lark which is found nowhere else in the world and is thought to number no more than 40 pairs.

Visiting fishermen anchor off a tiny inlet with a ancient quay close northwest of Ponta de Casa at the southwest corner of the island, possibly in considerable depths.

Looking southwest towards low-lying Ilhéu Raso *Ed Clay*

# São Vicente
Between 16°46′N–16°55′N and 24°52′W–25°06′W

## Introduction

Much of São Vicente's 227km² is hilly, in contrast to a low-lying peninsula on the northeast coast and extensive sand dunes south and east of Baía do Porto Grande on which Mindelo, the archipelago's second largest city, is situated. When seen from the northeast at 25–30M the western hills appear to be detached from the main mass centred around the 774m Monte Verde, the summit of which is often hidden in haze.

The entire island – including the optimistically named Monte Verde – is very lacking in both natural water and vegetation, and is largely of an unrelieved sandy brown. Almost all its 80,000 population live in Mindelo and its surrounding suburbs.

The island was discovered on 22 January 1462, the feast day of Saint Vincent, hence its name. Being unsuitable for agriculture it remained largely uninhabited until 1838, when a coal bunkering station was established to supply the early Atlantic steamers and Mindelo also became a focal point for transatlantic cables. The attractive old Portuguese customs house on the waterfront in Mindelo, modelled on Lisbon's famous Torré de Belem, still bears witness to the one-time importance of the port.

*Carnaval* celebrations, some of the most lively in the Cape Verdes, take place in Mindelo during the days before Lent. Many shops, banks and other businesses are closed on the Tuesday and Wednesday, and some remain shut all week.

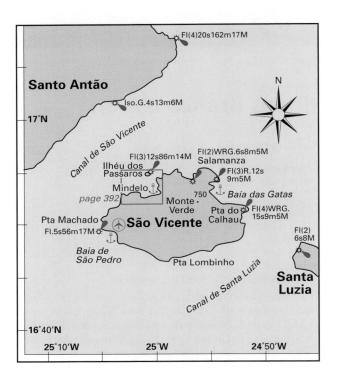

## Approach

São Vicente is separated from Santo Antão to the northwest by the 6·5M wide Canal de São Vicente, and from Santa Luzia to the southeast by the 4·5M wide Canal de Santa Luzia. Both are deep and clear of dangers, but the strong tidal currents can build large seas, particularly on the flood. The small islet of Ilhéu dos Pássaros lies 0·75M northwest of Ponta João Ribeira, close north of Mindelo, and can be passed in deep water on either side. There is also good water close inshore all around São Vicente and an offing of 0·5M is adequate except in the vicinity of Ponta Viana on the east coast where at least 1M should be allowed.

Mindelo in the early years of the 20th century, photographed from almost the same spot as the photo on page 393

## Navigation

**Magnetic variation**
10°15'W (2016) decreasing by 7'E annually

**Tidal Streams**
Tidal streams run strongly in both the Canal de São Vicente and Canal de Santa Luzia, the northeast-going stream beginning 3·5 hours before HW and the southwest-going stream about 2·5 hours after HW. The latter can reach 2·5 knots in the Canal de São Vicente and 4 knots or more in the Canal de Santa Luzia when combined with the southwest-going current.

**Lights**
**Ilhéu dos Pássaros (Dom Luís)**
Fl(3)12s86m14M 057°-vis-091° & 196°-vis-258°
White pyramid, red lantern 5m
Obscured from offshore 091°-196° by Santo Antão and 258°-057° by São Vicente, but visible if passing between the two larger islands
**Salamanza**
Fl(2)WRG.6s8m5M Metal tower 5m
**Baía das Gatas**
Fl(3)R.12s9m5M Metal tower 5m
**Ponta do Calhau**
Fl(4)WRG.15s9m5M Metal tower 5m
**Ponta Machado (Dona Amélia)**
Fl.5s56m17M 302°-vis-172°
Square white tower and building 14m

**Coast Radio Station**
**São Vicente** 16°51'·5N 24°59'·1W
**VHF**Ch 16 (24 hours), 18, 19
**DSC VHF** Ch 70 MMSI 006170000 16°52'·1N 24°56'W
☎+238 232 2158/2263, s.movelmaritimo@cvtelecom.cv

**Maritime Rescue Coordination Centre**
16°52'·1N 24°56'W ☎+238 238 4342/6475,
capitaniasv@cvtelecom.cv
**VHF** Ch 16, 70 (24 hours)
(This station does not accept public correspondence other than distress and safety traffic)

**Navtex**
Ribeira de Vinha, identification letters 'U' and 'P'. Transmissions in English (U) are on the standard Navtex frequency of 518kHz, those in Portuguese (P) are on 490kHz. Ribeira de Vinha 'U' transmits weather bulletins and navigational warnings in English at 0320, 0720, 1120, 1520, 1920, 2320 UT. Ribeira de Vinha 'P' transmits the same information in Portuguese at 0230, 0630, 1030, 1430, 1830, 2230 UT. (Several yachtsmen have commented on the unreliability of this station, which is sometimes off the air for extended periods and at others may transmit the same information for several days running.)

## Harbours and anchorages

# Mindelo (Porto Grande)

16°53'·28N 25°00'·06W (outer breakwater head)

**Tides**
Portuguese tide tables are available for Mindelo (Porto Grande), alternatively the standard port is Dakar – see Tides and tidal streams, page 368. MLWS is 0·4m above datum and time difference on Dakar: –0045. Predictions for Mindelo (Porto Grande) are also available via Admiralty *EasyTide* – see page 368
*Mean spring range* 0·8m
*Mean neap range* 0·5m

**Lights**
**Cabnave Shipyard**
Fl.R.2s8m5M Metal post 4m
**Breakwater, outer arm**
Fl.R.3s10m6M White column 8m
**Breakwater, inner arm**
Fl.G.4s10m5M White column 8m
**Ferry quay** Iso.Y.4s6m5M Post 4m
**Marina, outer pontoon** Iso.3s2m2M
**Marina, access jetty** Iso.4s2m2M
All the above lights are reported difficult to identify against the many lights ashore
**Comando Naval Lts in line on 076° (occas)**
F.R.20/27m5M Buildings (lights 530m apart)
Not leading lights – see Entrance, below
**Fishing harbour detached mole, W end**
Fl.R.5s5m4M
Square white column, red lantern 2m
**Fishing harbour detached mole, E end**
Fl.G.5s5m4M
Square white column, green lantern 2m
**2943·4 Oil tanker berth Lts in line on 147° (occas)**
F.G.13/19m 5M (lights 790m apart)

**Harbour communications**
**Marina Mindelo**
VHF Ch 72
☎+238 230 0032, +238 997 2322
0900–1830 Monday to Saturday, 0900–1200 Sunday from 15 October–15 March, otherwise 0900–1230, 1430–1830 weekdays, 0900–1500 Saturday, closed Sunday
mail@marinamindelo.cv or reserve@marinamindelo.cv
www.marinamindelo.cv
**boatCV**
VHF Ch 72
☎+238 232 6772, +238 991 5878
0900–1200, 1500–1800 Tuesday to Saturday
info@boatcv.com
www.boatcv.com
**Port Authority** VHF Ch 15 ☎+238 231 4492/4144
**Cabnave Shipyard** ☎+238 232 1930, 232 6526
**Lusonave** ☎+238 232 7928

Approaching Mindelo from the northwest, with the city framed between Ponta João Ribeiro and Ilhéu dos Pássaros
*Henry Buchanan*

IV. CAPE VERDES

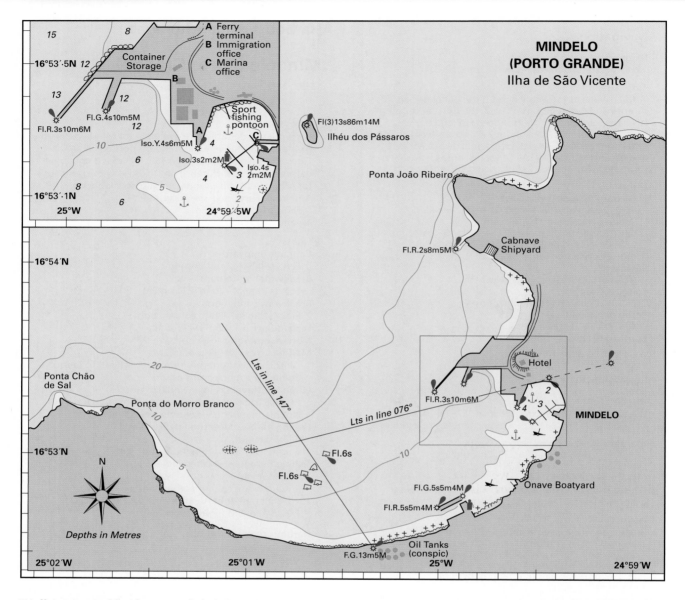

**MINDELO
(PORTO GRANDE)**
Ilha de São Vicente

### Well-protected harbour and thriving city

The harbour at Mindelo – still referred to on some charts by its 'colonial' name of Porto Grande – is amongst the finest in the eastern Atlantic, giving total protection from northwest through east to south, and partial protection (with a fetch of up to 2M) from south around to west. Very occasionally a westerly swell can set in but this is rare, and although strong northeasterlies can produce unpredictable gusts these have little fetch. More often cool breezes of 5–10 knots from northeast or east keep the area well ventilated.

Visitor numbers have increased hugely since the 120-berth Marina Mindelo opened in 2007, and several rallies now visit the harbour most years. The combination of marina and sport fishing boat pontoon – see plan – has inevitably encroached on the anchorage, with the result that most yachts in transit which opt to anchor must remain southwest of the marina, where shelter is much poorer than in the 'bag' to the northeast.

To the east of the harbour lies the city of Mindelo, second largest in Cape Verde with a population estimated at more than 70,000. The tall buildings and narrow cobbled streets near the waterfront date back to colonial days, with an occasional patterned pavement in the style typical of older Portuguese towns, whilst the rapidly expanding suburbs separated by wide, tree-lined roads are a great improvement on the depressing shanty-towns which so often surround the cities of less developed countries.

The atmosphere in Mindelo has changed vastly since the first edition of this book was researched in 1987. While poverty clearly exists in some areas, contrasting with the small percentage of ostentatiously rich residents, both are far outnumbered by a prosperous, educated middle-class. The population is young by European standards – nearly one-third are under 30 – which doubtless promotes the pace of change, and though a few yachtsmen may lament the growing commercialisation of the harbour-front, it is possible they did not experience the hordes of ragged children and starving dogs which used to greet every foreign visitor in hopes of a few escudos or some table scraps – after which even more would appear... There are doubtless areas of Mindelo where it would be unwise for a visitor to venture alone in darkness, but that is true of most cities in most countries. All in all, Mindelo now bears comparison with many of the more interesting cities of southern Europe. Those with an interest in culture should visit the *Museu de Arte Tradicional* on Praça Nova, open 0900–1230, 1500–1900 weekdays, to admire its displays of Cape Verdean art and sculpture. Entry is a modest CVE 100$.

Sadly yachts are not allowed to anchor overnight off the wide sandy beach at Praia da Laginha, the long bay north of Mindelo, but it deserves mention as the nearest good swimming to the harbour. In settled weather it offers a pleasant if slightly rolly short-term anchorage in about 8m of clear water over sand and eel grass. Alternatively it is only a short walk north past the root of the breakwater, leaving the yacht in Mindelo.

An excellent view over the entire area can be obtained from the small hill immediately north of the anchorage, for many years the site of the island's prison but now being redeveloped as a luxury hotel.

## Caution

The Canal de São Vicente, which separates São Vicente and Santo Antão, is notorious for its strong and gusty winds, the two islands combining to produce a classic *venturi* effect. Although true throughout the year, this is particularly noticeable between December and May, when the northeasterly winds may increase from 15–20 knots over the open ocean to gusts of 35–40 knots in the channel. Even during the less windy season from June to November, 10 knots elsewhere may increase to 25–30 knots between the islands. Surprisingly, this fact does not appear in the published statistics but has nevertheless been reported by many yachtsmen over the years.

## Approach

The vast majority of yachts are likely to approach from the north, but it is straightforward from any direction. Ponta João Ribeiro and the breakwater sheltering the Cabnave shipyard to the north, and Ponta Chão de Sal to the west, may both be rounded at 200–400m, and Ilhéu dos Pássaros passed close on either side. Thence a direct course to the end of the grey stone breakwater clears all dangers, including two unmarked wrecks in the southern part of the bay.

After nightfall, bright street lighting in Mindelo and the docks shows as a distinct loom in the sky above the hills when approaching from the north or northeast. The outer breakwater light should be identified without problem, and both the breakwater itself and some oil tanks on the southern shore are brightly lit. The navigation lights themselves, however, may be difficult to identify against the many lights ashore.

## Entrance

Entry in daylight should present no problems and, provided the current edition of Admiralty 367 or an electronic equivalent is to hand, neither should entry in darkness even if – as is quite probable – not all the various lights are operating. Note in particular that the lights in line on 076° lead not into the yacht anchorage or to the marina but straight onto the

Looking south-southeast over the inner yacht anchorage at Mindelo, with the marina beyond and yachts in the outer anchorage on the right. The semi-submerged wreck mentioned in the text can just be made out below the ENACOL tanks
*Paul and Rachel Chandler*

IV. CAPE VERDES

Mindelo anchorage and marina seen from just south of east  *Ed Clay*

corner of the substantial stone quay. While several of the potentially dangerous wrecks to the south of the entry line have been removed, slow speeds and a good bow lookout are essential both day and night to watch for the many anchored vessels, unlit buoys and semi-submerged fish-holding pens.

The marina itself is lit, but the small can buoys which divide it from the inner yacht anchorage to the north and hazards to the south are not. If approaching the southwest corner of the marina be certain to stay inside the buoy which lies near it, as a semi-submerged wreck lurks not far to the south – see photo page 393.

Hosting cruise ships is a growing part of the economy, and the quayside west of the ferry terminal is due to be redeveloped as a cruise ship berth with the fishing boats which currently use the area moved north to the northern end of Baiá de Laginha. It seems that the quay may also be extended, which would help protect both marina and inner anchorage from the swell which sometimes rolls in during January and February. As harbours developments in the Cape Verdes frequently remain unlit until completion – and sometimes well beyond that – take particular care if approaching the northeast anchorage in darkness.

### Anchorage

The 'old' anchorage in the northeast corner of the bay has been squeezed by the marina to the south and a pontoon for sport fishing boats to the north. It is also occupied by a growing number of semi-permanent vessels, both occupied and semi-derelict. Holding in this area is good in 4m or less over firm sand and some mud, though patches of poor holding have been reported close to the beach. Most visiting yachts have little choice but to anchor much further out, however, southwest of the marina in 5m or so over sand. Generous scope, preferably of chain, is required in either position as the prevailing northeasterlies occasionally pick up to gale force (35–40 knots) in the gusts, and the southwest anchorage has a fetch of at least 500m. The water appears to be fairly clean but is far from clear, with visibility seldom more than 2m and less after heavy rain when the entire bay turns brown.

Keep well clear of the ferry terminal. All the ferries need to turn on either arrival or departure – not easy with so much windage and (often) so much wind – and at least one anchored yacht has been seriously damaged during this manoeuvre. Security in the anchorage appears to be much improved, and local officials are reported to have made a serious effort to crack down on harassment and petty crime against visitors both ashore and afloat. Even so, the authorities recommend that someone is always on board at night. There is no charge for anchoring.

Dinghies can be left on the beach, possibly in the care of one of the street vendors for a fee of around CVE 400$ (€4). If heading towards the beach from the northeast anchorage beware the very solid lump which breaks surface from about half tide and could do serious damage to a dinghy propeller. The old photograph on page 390 shows what appears to be a wreck exactly where this lump still lies. For many it will be more convenient to land at Marina Mindelo's combined bar and dinghy area just south of the marina office. In 2015 the same charge of CVE 400$ (€4) per day was payable, though apparently this may be waived if enough is spent at the bar!

### Berthing

Marina Mindelo contains 120 berths on six pontoons for vessels of up to 30m LOA and 4·5m draught. It accepted its first visiting yachts in 2007 and has remained virtually unchanged since then. Yachts berthed to windward of a pontoon have a buoy but no pick-up line; those to leeward have a pick-up line but no buoy – think for a moment of the manoeuvring implications in an area where the wind is nearly always from the same direction and one realises immediately that this marina was designed by a yachtsman! Even so, a bow-thruster would undoubtedly make the whole manoeuver much, much easier. Shore access is via the restored *Cais d'Alfandega Velha*, with the marina office on its outer tip and a security gate alongside, for which a card is obtainable against a CVE 1,000$ (€10) deposit.

Yachts in Marina Mindelo *Kath McNulty*

Even if prior contact cannot be established on VHF Channel 72, yachts arriving in daylight are likely to be spotted, directed straight to a berth and have their lines taken – particularly helpful with the prevailing northeasterly wind taking the yacht sideways. RIB tow and push boats are available if required. Some motion is nearly always evident, with resulting wear on mooring lines, and snubbers (either rubber or steel) are essential even for short stays. If berthed on the windward side of the pontoon it would clearly be wise to reinforce the line through the buoy in chafe-resistant fashion.

### Formalities

Mindelo is currently one of only three ports in the archipelago where inward clearance to the Republic of Cape Verde can be obtained – see Entry and regulations, page 365. There are no plans for the relevant officials to be based at the marina – the *Polícia Marítima* at the rear of the building are concerned with general harbour security, while the office between the showers and toilets is occupied by the marina master – often, and confusingly, referred to as the 'harbourmaster'. Neither need be visited by yachtsmen.

*On arrival*: The two officials who do need to be visited are both in the main port area, in almost adjacent offices. Only the skipper need go, bearing the ship's papers, crewlist and passports. The *Polícia de Fronteira* (Immigration) office (also labelled *Polícia Marítima* and *Guarda Fiscal*), open 0800–1600 weekdays only, is the last on the left as one approaches the main gateway to the port. CVE 500$ (€5) per person is charged for inward clearance. If arriving at the weekend one is expected to clear in on Monday morning.

Any crew member leaving the yacht by plane will need a visa, issued on the spot on payment of CVE 2,500$ (€25), so must obviously accompany the skipper, taking a spare photocopy of the information page of their passport plus a couple of passport photos, though neither are likely to be needed. Note that the office is closed at weekends, and without the correct entry and visa stamps in their passport they will NOT be allowed to board their plane.

Just beyond the *Polícia de Fronteira*, again on the left, is 'Gateway A', complete with uniformed guard. The *Polícia Marítima* will be found behind the first door on the left in the first building on the left – all totally unmarked. Office hours are again 0800–1600 weekdays only, with the same relaxed 'Monday is fine' attitude to weekend arrivals. A form must be completed and the ship's papers will be held pending departure, but no charge is made for entry.

*On departure*: Both the above officials must be visited for the appropriate departure stamps, and the ship's papers reclaimed from the *Polícia Marítima*, for which CVE 700$ (€7) is charged. A receipt will be issued (and should be retained), together with a *Desembaraço de Autoridade Marítima* – particularly important if heading for the Caribbean where proof of one's port of departure is often required. If intending to leave at the weekend the formalities can be completed on Friday afternoon, otherwise one has the usual 24 hours.

If intending to call in at one or more of the smaller islands before leaving territorial waters, request a 'next port' (*próximo porto* or *porto seguinte*) document from the *Polícia de Fronteira* when clearing out – see page 366. As late as 2015, and despite the more relaxed interpretation of clearance

Many of the buildings which line Mindelo's attractive waterfront date back to Portuguese colonial times. The building at far right, once the customs house, was modelled on Lisbon's famous Torré de Belem  *Anne Hammick*

regulations drawn up by senior officials in the harbour's *Instituto Marítimo e Portuário* more than five years previously, some immigration officials denied the existence of such a document. Others, however, were happy to issue it. It would seem wise to leave sufficient time for amicable discussion.

Mindelo is now said to attract at least 60 cruise ship visits each year – one can't help wondering what some of the passengers make of the island! – causing inevitable delays for yachtsmen wishing to clear in or out. Both the *Polícia de Fronteira* and the *Polícia Marítima* are efficient and courteous, and most speak either French or English in addition to Portuguese, but it would obviously be unwise to leave outward clearance until the last moment. Both offices open at 0800 and, as usual, queues are shortest early in the day.

### Charges

The marina berthing fee is calculated on a length x beam basis, and in early 2016 stood at CVE 62$37 (€0·567) per m² per day, including tax (at 15·5%) and 100 litres of water – whatever the size of the boat or the length of stay. A handy ready-reckoner on the website calculates exact prices in seconds. Considerable discounts are available for longer stays, and for visits between 1 April and 30 September. Payment – which must be made on arrival – is accepted in all major currencies, as are credit cards including Visa and Mastercard (though use of a card incurs a surcharge). In common with most marinas, evidence of third party insurance is required.

### Facilities

*Boatyards* Cabnave, ✆+238 232 1930, situated about 0·75M north of Mindelo, can haul and repair almost anything from a 3,000-tonne ship downwards, though interest in yachts appears to fluctuate according to the amount of other work available.

Lusonave (referred to locally as Onave), ✆+238 232 7928, situated about 0·5M south of the anchorage is currently run by Zece Duarte, a local fisherman who speaks some English. It no longer has a GRP moulding shed or, indeed, much else other than two marine railways, one with a carriage onto which a yacht can be floated and lashed. Although distinctly decrepit at first sight, Lusonave hauls the boatCV charter fleet every year, so far without incident. (As a result boatCV – see opposite – has developed expertise in working on rudders, stuffing boxes, seacocks etc while a yacht remains afloat). It may also be possible – and cheaper – for a smaller yacht to be craned ashore, though reports mention poor skills on the part of the crane operator and the lack of a crosspiece in the slings to spread the lateral load. There is no water on site, though power is normally available.

Fibreglass products – mat and resin – are available from Matexplas, ✆+238 232 7928, on the south side of the Praça Estrela and also opposite the Lusonave entrance gate.

*Travel-lift* Despite the purchase of a 50-tonne capacity travel-lift in 2012, 3½ years later boatCV were still waiting for local officials to agree on where the dock should be situated.

*Engineers* Cabnave and boatCV both have diesel engineers, while the former has a metalwork shop which is said to be able to fabricate virtually anything. boatCV holds Volvo spares, though the mechanics will work on any engine, inboard or outboard. It also has a TIG welding machine and stocks a range of outboards.

*Electronic & radio repairs* boatCV has a fully equipped electronics workshop and is a certified Raymarine service agent and distributor, though will work on any make. Kai Brossmann is a fully qualified marine electronics engineer and has had a vast amount of experience of fixing autopilots…

*Sail repairs* boatCV employees handle repairs of all kinds on two professional machines, but do not make new sails.

*Rigging* boatCV has a swage machine for wire of up to 12mm, and a wide variety of swage terminals, including larger sizes. Should it be necessary, entire rigs can be ordered and set up.

*Chandlery* boatCV's ShipShop (open 0900–1200, 1500–1800 Tuesday to Saturday), at the landward end of the marina building, holds some basic items with more in a warehouse ashore. Items not in stock can be ordered from abroad – delivery normally takes five days by DHL (very expensive), or four weeks by ordinary mail (usually no extra shipment cost). Visa and MasterCard are accepted.

Maripesca Lda, on Rua de São João stocks mainly fishing gear plus a little general chandlery. Several hardware stores selling electrical cable and fittings, piping, hose clips and other plumbing items, and all kinds of tools will be found in the city.

*Courtesy flags* Fully sewn flags are made and sold in the African market on Praça Estrela by Mrs Mercy Cole at Stall 127 (near the restaurant end). She makes various sizes, a typical 30cm x 40cm courtesy flag costing CVE 1,000\$ (€10), albeit without lanyard, and can make or repair any flag to order in an hour or so. Mrs Cole, ☏+238 915 2523, +238 914 9125, is Nigerian so speaks excellent English, and will normally be found at her stall from 0900–1830 Monday to Saturday.

*Water* On the marina pontoons – 100 litres is included in the berthing fee – and available to anchored yachts by arrangement at CVE 2\$ (€0.02) per litre. Payment is via a prepaid card which those berthed in the marina can also use in the shower block.

*Showers* Showers and toilets behind the marina reception area, available to marina users only with payment via prepaid card (see *Water* above). The alternative is to use the adequate though elderly (cold) showers at the *Clube Náutico*, for which a charge is also made.

*Laundry* No launderette is planned for the marina, but laundry left at the office before 0900 will be washed and ready for collection the next day. There are several other options, including the full-service Lavanderia Mindelo Express (on the side of the prominent blue building southeast of the Cais d'Alfandega Velha), and the Lavomatic launderette on the southeast side of the Praça Estrela, beyond the produce market.

*Electricity* At all marina berths, charged by the day according to load – 6, 16, 32 or 63 amps.

*Fuel* The fuel berth (diesel only) occupies the western corner of the marina. Arrange times in advance at the office and note that a surcharge is made if paying by credit card. Hours are similar to those of the marina office, but closing 30 minutes earlier at the end of the day. Petrol – and small quantities of diesel, as the marina will not fill cans – is available by can from the Shell filling station on the waterfront south of the *Cais d'Alfandega Velha*. Yachts are no longer welcome at the fuel berth in the fishing harbour.

*Bottled gas* Camping Gaz cylinders can be exchanged at the Shell filling station mentioned above. A standard 3kg exchange costs less than CVE 500\$ (€5), with the cylinders visible appearing to be in a good state.

Other makes of cylinder must be taken to Enacol, at their large orange and grey building at the south end of town for refilling. Only butane is available. The staff are helpful and some speak English, but cylinders can only be refilled if the necessary adaptor is available – the days of a length of rubber hose and two jubilee clips are long past. If filling proves possible it will be done in a matter of minutes, and prices are low.

*Clube náutico* Long established in a low building with two gables, opposite the *Cais d'Alfandega Velha*. After a period of seeming neglect in the 1990s, the *Clube Náutico de Mindelo* is once again thriving as a pleasant and shady yachtsmen's bar and restaurant – aptly described by one visitor as 'the Café Sport of the Cape Verde islands' – though without any sign of actual

The floating bar and dinghy dock at Marina Mindelo, seen in the hazy conditions typical of a *harmattan  Ed Clay*

IV. CAPE VERDES

maritime activity. Local musicians play traditional music most evenings, for which a small charge is added to the bill.

*Banks* Numerous, most equipped with exterior ATMs. If drawing cash against a card inside the bank, or even changing currency, a passport will be required. See also Money, page 361.

*Shops/provisioning* Although vastly improved since the first edition was researched in 1987, the variety of foodstuffs available is more limited than in Praia and almost everything is noticeably more expensive than in the Canaries. There are several small *supermercados*, including a couple open long hours – Fragata on Praça Nova is open 0900–1300, 1500–0000 from Monday to Saturday and 1800–0000 on Sunday and public holidays – but all have limited ranges and it may be necessary to visit several.

There is a Belgian-owned deli in the Ponte D'Agua complex – see *Cafés* etc below – and several bakeries in the city, among which the French-run Padaria Français on Avenida 12 de Setembro is particularly recommended. Other shops include several pharmacies, photographic shops, footwear, clothing, booksellers and stationers.

*Produce market* Bustling produce market in the renovated 19th century *mercado* building on Rua Libertadores de Africa, selling all kinds of fruit and vegetables, familiar and unfamiliar, plus every variety of beans and pulses known to (wo)man. With so much competition the quality is high. The surrounding booths contain several butchers, plus one cubicle apparently selling nothing but eggs (take your own box). Upstairs are assorted boutiques, souvenir and music shops.

The market is open Monday to Saturday from 0800 onwards, though many of the vendors leave by about 1400. Prices are higher than in Madeira or the Canaries and bargaining does not appear to be the custom. Carrier bags, if available, are unlikely to be free.

*Fish market* On the waterfront next to the old customs house. A good, though sometimes unfamiliar, choice at very reasonable prices is to be found in surroundings of somewhat dubious cleanliness (but it's going to be cooked...). Fish is also sold by roadside vendors on the ajacent streets.

*Cafés, restaurants & hotels* No shortage of eating places at all levels, many with live local music, and at least a dozen hotels and *residencials* of varying standards and prices. If intending to leave an anchored boat after dark it is wise to organise a 'minder' – possibly a friend from another yacht.

In January 2011 Marina Mindelo opened a floating bar, the Marina Club, open 0900–2200 daily. Close south lies the Pont d'Agua complex, a Belgian/Cabo Verdean 'leisure club' containing bars, restaurants, boutiques and a small swimming pool.

*Medical services* Mindelo Hospital, ☏+238 231 0312, +238 231 1879, is on the east side of the city and is reported to be of good standard. Many of the doctors and other staff speak some English.

## Communications

*Mailing address* The marina's postal address is C.P. 1191 – Cais Alfândega Velha, Mindelo, São Vicente, República de Cabo Verde. It is essential that the name of the yacht is included. If ordering parts or other goods from abroad the marina office recommends using DHL – other carriers do not appear to be as reliable.

*WiFi* Free WiFi is available at the Marina Club bar, and berth-holders can also pre-purchase set download sizes for use aboard. (If your computer is set up to make automatic downloads it will gobble your allowance, so disable them.) Free WiFi is sometimes available on the Praça Nova (also known as the Praça Amilcar Cabral) where you can sit outdoors under the trees, and is reported to be most reliable in the evenings. Note the warning on page 363, however.

Alternatively, voice and data SIM cards are available at Libertel, about 100m south on leaving the marina, open 0800–2000. Prices are very low by European standards.

*Car hire* Eight or ten companies in the city, though none, apparently, at the airport. See also Road transport, page 364.

*Taxis* Both taxis and communal *aluguers* – see page 364 – are available. As with car hire, rates should be agreed in advance.

*Ferries* Two or three return services to Porto Novo, Santo Antão daily, plus twice weekly service to Tarrafal, São Nicolau – see page 363. The ticket office, where timetables are also displayed, is on the ground floor of the imposing new building at the root of the *Cais Cabotagem* (ferry quay).

*Air services* Frequent inter-island flights from the airfield at São Pedro, 8km southwest of Mindelo – renamed Cesária Évora Airport in March 2012 – plus direct flights to/from Lisbon, Paris, Amsterdam, Boston, Senegal and Brazil (though it may be considerably cheaper to fly via Ilha do Sal). If needing to confirm a TACV flight (recommended at least 48 hours before departure), note that there is only one TACV office on the island, on Avenida 5 Julho in Mindelo, open 0800–1200, 1430–1700, weekdays only.

The view westwards over Mindelo and the Canal de São Vicente, with Santo Antão showing clearly in the background  *Andy O'Grady*

## Baía de São Pedro

16°49'3N 25°03'·8W (anchorage)

### Blowy beach anchorage

Just over 5M southwest of Mindelo, Baía de São Pedro offers shelter from northwest through northeast to southeast, though northeast winds may funnel down the wide valley and swells can work their way in from the east. Best anchorage is off the small village at the southeast end of the black sand beach in 8–10m over a flat sandy bottom with very good holding. The airport buildings can be seen about 0·5M inland (there are no flights at night) with the approach path over the bay marked by four red buoys. As my informant remarks, 'it may be advisable not to anchor just there'. A submerged wreck has been reported in the vicinity of 16°49'·1N 25°04'·6W. It is not known exactly how accurate this position is, nor the depths over the wreck, so the area should be treated with caution.

When deciding on anchor scope, allow for both the *venturi* effect created between the islands of São Vicente and Santo Antão – see Caution, page 393 – and that in the valley between Mindelo and São Pedro. Boardsurfing and speedsailing enthusiasts claim that the bay at São Pedro has the best wind in the world, and many records are set there.

A bar and small general store will be found in the village, together with a French-run restaurant and a daily baker's van – at 0600! The Fajã Branca Hotel complex at the western end of the beach caters for non-residents and provides a good buffet lunch (with free transport to/from Mindelo at weekends). Frequent *aluguers* make the trip into Mindelo, with taxis at the airport.

## Baía das Gatas

16°54'·16N 24°54'·27W (molehead)

**Lights**
**Baía das Gatas**
   Fl(3)R.12s9m5M Metal tower 5m

### Unpromising anchorage but good swimming

A small southeast-facing bay on the northeast coast of São Vicente, flanked by a tiny harbour behind a short mole, Baía das Gatas has been suggested as a possible anchorage. With depths of little more than 2m on the rocky bar, however, it appears suitable only for shoal-draught yachts or multihulls willing to eyeball their way in – and then only when the northeast trades are down.

The Baía das Gatas is well worth visiting by road to enjoy a swim or to wander around the small fishing village. There are several cafés and restaurants, and the area is popular with Mindelo residents, some of whom own holiday homes in the area. An international music festival is held at the Baía das Gatas every August.

# Santo Antão

**Between 16°54'N–17°12'N and 24°58'W–25°22'W**

## Introduction

The northwesternmost island of the archipelago, Santo Antão is both second largest and second highest, reaching 1,979m in the far west at Tope de Coroa. Due to its greater rainfall it is the most productive island agriculturally of the entire group and lays claim to being the most beautiful, particularly in the north where there are deep, dramatic valleys and forests of pine, eucalyptus and cypress. In contrast, the southern part of the island is much lower and dryer, with scrub or desert vegetation. The majority of Santo Antão's 45,000 inhabitants live on the east side of the island, most around either Porto Novo or Ribeira Grande.

The island has no real harbour, though there is a quay at Porto Novo used by small commercial vessels as well as ferries from Mindelo. It is possible to visit by yacht but, with two or three crossings most days it is far simpler to visit by ferry. Numerous *aluguers* meet the ferry at Porto Novo and set off for Ribeira Grande (also referred to as Povoação) and Ponta do Sol. Most public *aluguers* use the new road along the east coast – quicker, but much less scenic – making group hire of a minibus worth considering. The old, cobbled road runs through breathtaking mountain scenery which no visitor should miss.

Finally, check the water temperature at Ponta do Sol! Vulcanologists have been monitoring a steady rise since 1999 which may indicate a forthcoming eruption.

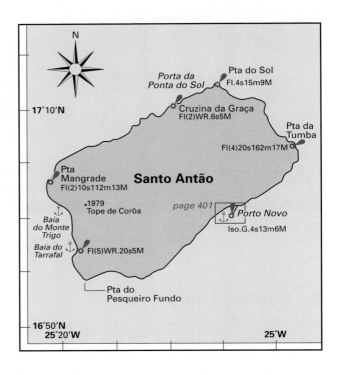

## Approach

Much of the coastline consists of cliffs with deep water within 0·5M of the shore, though headlands should be allowed an offing of at least 1M. The mountains produce a windshadow extending up to 20M to the southwest.

Spectacular scenery in northeastern Santo Antão, where even the precipices appear to have been terraced
*Sue Thatcher*

## Navigation

**Magnetic variation**
10°21'W (2016) decreasing by 7'E annually

**Tidal Streams**
Tides run strongly in the Canal de São Vicente. The northeast-going stream begins 3·5 hours before HW and the southwest-going stream about 2·5 hours after HW, with the latter reaching 2·5 knots when combined with the southwest-going current.

**Lights**
**Ponta do Sol** Fl.4s15m9M
    141°-vis-321° Metal tower 10m
**Ponta da Tumba (Fontes Pereira de Melo)**
    Fl(4)20s162m17M 141°-vis-321°
    White octagonal tower and building 16m
**Porto Novo** Iso.G.4s13m6M
    Metal column on white base 6m
**Tarrafal de Monte Trigo**
    Fl(5)WR.20s5M Metal column 5m
**Ponta Mangrade**
    Fl(2)10s112m13M 005°-vis-200°
    White column, red lantern 3m
**Cruzina da Graça**
    Fl(2)WR6s5M Metal column 5m

## Harbours and anchorages

# Porto Novo

**Lights**
**Breakwater** Iso.G.4s13m6M
    Grey post with angular 'lantern' 6m

### A port in name only

The 'harbour' at Porto Novo is protected from the north by the land and from easterly swell by a 300m breakwater used by the Mindelo ferry, small cargo boats and a few fishing craft, though most of the latter are drawn up on the beach further west. There is little shelter from winds out of the west or south. In 2012 work to widen and reinforce the breakwater was completed, with shoreside infrastructure including a new ferry terminal building, said to feature an escalator!

Fruit for sale under the shade of a tree near Porto Novo
*Sue Thatcher*

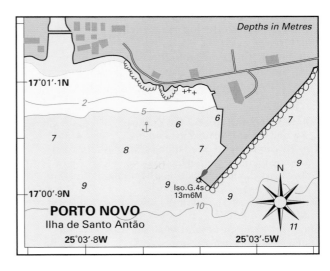

*Aluguers* load up with goods and passengers on the quay at Porto Novo  *Sue Thatcher*

A ferry emerging from behind the breakwater at Porto Novo
*Paul and Rachel Chandler*

IV. CAPE VERDES

The colourful town opens up on rounding the end of the breakwater *Kath McNulty*

## Anchorage and berthing

Best anchorage will be found west of the breakwater in about 6m, though both holding and shelter are poor. Be sure to allow sufficient room for vessels manoeuvring to and from the breakwater – and note that the ferry turns in its shelter on leaving. Allow also for the fact that the prevailing northeasterly wind may die during the night, or even blow onshore.

It is sometimes possible for a yacht to lie alongside near the root of the breakwater in 3–4m, but there is constant surge and both lines and fenders will suffer.

## Facilities

*Water* No public tap – try the market or one of the cafés. Bottled water is readily available.

*Fuel* By can from the Shell filling station on the road leading inland from the harbour.

*Bottled gas* Camping Gas from the filling station, but no refills.

*Bank* At the western end of the town, open 0800–1400 Monday to Friday.

*Shops/provisioning* Several small supermarkets plus numerous tiny general stores.

*Produce market* On the road which parallels the beach, plus separate fish market (though fish can often be bought direct from the boats).

*Restaurants & hotels* Several *residencials*, together with the usual pavement cafés and small restaurants.

*Medical services* Health centre only – the island's only hospital, ☎+238 221 1337 is in Ribeira Grande – though anything serious would undoubtedly mean evacuation to Mindelo.

## Communications

*Car hire* At least one company in Porto Novo, though the roads are such that a local driver may be preferable.

*Taxis* Plenty available, but somewhat expensive. Best value is obtained by group hire of a minibus.

*Buses* The usual public *aluguers* run a frequent service to Ribeira Grande and beyond, generally via the coast road.

*Ferries* Two or three crossings from/to Mindelo most days.

*Air services* The tiny airport at the north end of the island has been closed since 2003.

# Baía do Tarrafal

16°57'·2N 25°18'·7W (anchorage)

**Tides**
Predictions for Baía do Tarrafal do Monte Trigo (Baía do Tarrafal) are available via Admiralty *EasyTide* – see page 368

**Lights**
**Tarrafal de Monte Trigo**
Fl(5)WR.20s5M Metal tower 5m

## Remote anchorage off welcoming village

In the extreme southwest of Santo Antão, the 2M long Baía do Tarrafal is protected from northeast through east to southeast (indeed, located in a complete windshadow so far as the trade winds are concerned) and is reported to offer reasonable anchorage. Swell breaks almost permanently on the beach of large round boulders, and should a northwesterly Atlantic swell start to set in the bay would swiftly become dangerous and should be vacated at once.

Tarrafal, surrounded by green vegetation, is the first village seen when coming from the south. An isolated, semi-derelict building stands at the south end of the bay, which is very scenic with sea eagles and kites flying overhead. In 2015 the local people were described as 'super friendly', with security never a problem.

## Anchorage

Best anchorage is reportedly found about 100m off the beach just south of the small fishing boats, in 9–12m over good holding in dark sand. The recommended 50m of chain necessitates at least 100m clearance between anchored boats, as the windshadow caused by the mountains, combined with occasional katabatic gusts, causes very unpredicatable swinging. The shelf is narrow and the slope quite steep, so ensure the anchor is well dug in. There is no jetty or quay, and landing by dinghy is often difficult, particularly in winter. It may be easier somewhat further south, where there is more sand and a gentler slope.

## Formalities

Rather surprisingly, in late 2015 it proved possible to clear out of the archipelago at Baía do Tarrafal – local schoolteacher Simão Evora can advise. Very helpful, and clearly an entrepreneur as he also runs a bar/guesthouse and is a respected musician, Simão is reported to welcome foreign visitors to his school (set back behind a dark blue gate in a cream wall). Simão speaks Portuguese and French, but not English.

Baía do Tarrafal on the west coast of Santo Antão, with three yachts anchored south of the moored fishing boats
*Ilona Kooistra and Frans Veldman*

## Facilities

The village has a few few small shops (with very limited choice) and a health centre, as well as the usual bars and cafés. There are several possibilities for accommodation ashore, including the small Mar Tranquilidade resort, run by a German/American couple who got sidetracked in the course of a circumnavigation. Needless to say, they are very welcoming to visiting cruisers, who can fill water cans *gratis* and eat in their restaurant. Their WiFi is said to be poor, however, and visiting yachtsmen are asked to use it sparingly. A second option for WiFi is Vista Tarrafal, though this is some distance from the anchorage. Neither will most mobile phones find a signal, even when using a Cape Verde-bought SIM card.

It takes about two hours to reach Porto Novo by road, an *aluguer* normally leaving the village each weekday afternoon to meet the arriving ferry. The road itself is said to have been improved recently, and to provide a spectacular and beautiful excursion (though it may be difficult to return that day). One reason to make the trip could be to fill diesel cans, as fuel is almost impossible to obtain in Baía do Tarrafal.

## Baía do Monte Trigo

17°01'·3N 25°20'W

### The westernmost anchorage in the Cape Verdes

My thanks to Jill Schinas for the following information:

> 'Situated just north of Baía do Tarrafal, Baía do Monte Trigo is smaller and browner than its neighbour. It shares the same, almost permanent, windshadow. In theory it could become a dangerous lee shore if a southerly gale rose, but local people say that such a thing has never happened in this bay.
>
> The shore at Monte Trigo drops off steeply and what looks like a perfect spot to anchor, 100m off the beach in the corner of the bay, is actually off soundings. However there is a 15m patch just outside the breaker line at the west end of the village.
>
> Landing needs to be timed very carefully as the waves are even bigger than at Tarrafal and the beach is of equally unsympathetic large, round stones. However the people are wonderfully friendly, probably because they seldom see any visitors. There is no surfaced road and, as with Tarrafal, the only way out of Monte Trigo is a steep track up the valley – or by boat.'

To which Mary Robinson added:

> 'We found about 10m over sand with good holding to the west of the village, in the area suggested by Jill Schinas. There is a conspicuous white mark on the rocks which looks a bit like a giant gingerbread man, and we anchored just below it. We were in a total wind shadow and needed 360° swinging room, but had no problems. Landing looked hazardous with surf over boulders and we didn't attempt it.'

There are a number of local fishing vessels and moorings to the west of the village close inshore.

Sunlight and shadow as a local fishing boat enters the tiny Boca da Pistola ('gun's mouth') at Porto da Ponta do Sol *Anne Hammick*

# Porto da Ponta do Sol

17°12'·22N 25°05'·65W (molehead)

**Tides**
Time difference on Dakar: –0030, on Mindelo (Porto Grande): +0015. Predictions for Ponta do Sol are available via Admiralty *EasyTide* – see page 368
Mean spring range 0·8m
Mean neap range 0·5m

**Lights**
**Ponta do Sol** Fl.4s15m9M
   141°-vis-321° Metal post 10m

## Small harbour best visited by land

A small and attractive village situated in the extreme north of Santo Antão. Its miniature harbour, the Boca da Pistola, is used by local fishing boats which are then manhandled ashore. The harbour is totally unsuitable for yachts and, though it is possible to anchor off when the wind is from well east of northeast, this is another Cape Verdean harbour which is best visited by land.

## Approach, anchorage and facilities

If approaching from north or east, allow an offing of at least a mile around Ponta do Sol which is fringed by extensive reefs, and do not turn in towards the headland until it bears almost due east, when about 25m over rock and stones should be found some 300m southwest or west of the harbour entrance. The reefs provide some protection from the northeasterly swell, but in the calmer conditions of summer the outer reefs do not break at all and even the reefs close to the shore are scarcely visible.

Landing by dinghy in the tiny harbour can be interesting – once again it is a matter of careful

A small fishing boat is carried ashore inside the Boca da Pistola. An *aluguer* waits in the background, possibly to take the catch to market in Ribeira Grande *Sue Thatcher*

timing as the waves sometimes break across the entrance. However, only accept the help of local fishermen after careful negotiation – it has been reported that they may be very eager to offer lifts ashore, only to demand an exorbitant fee for the return journey.

Facilities are minimal, though there are several tourist restaurants along the front while the town itself has various shops, a couple of cafés offering basic lunches, and at least one *residencial*. For a bank and better shops it would be necessary to catch a minibus or *aluguers* to Ribeira Grande.

# Ilha do Maio
## Between 15°07'N–15°20'N and 23°05'W–23°15'W

## Introduction

Measuring 270km² or less, Ilha do Maio is one of the smaller Cape Verde islands and is also the most southeasterly, its nearest neighbour being Ilha de Santiago 14M to the southwest. Much of the island is arid and low-lying, though a small area in the centre around Monte Penoso (436m) is somewhat higher, and large stretches of the coast are fringed with fine sandy beaches. Fewer than 5,000 people live on Maio, a decrease of at least 2,000 in the past decade, nearly all of them in or near Vila do Maio, the island's only real town. Its name is derived from the date of its discovery – 1 May 1460.

## Approach

An offing of 1M is sufficient all around the island other than in the extreme north, where the breaking Baixo do Galeão extends more than 2M offshore, and the extreme south, where a potentially dangerous wreck lies about 1·25M south of Ponta da Poça Grande. Currents can be strong and erratic and, according to recent GPS readings, charted positions may be suspect. Swell tends to hook around the roughly oblong island, and 2·5m waves have been reported as breaking on the beach at Porto do Maio even in apparently calm conditions.

If approaching from the northeast, refer to the caution regarding Baixo de João Valente on page 381. If sailing at night note also that the light at Ponta Cais, described above, is unlikely to be working.

## Navigation

**Magnetic variation**
9°54'W (2016) decreasing by 7'E annually

**Tidal Streams**
Tidal streams are weak, but the current around Ilha do Maio sets southwesterly at 0·5–1 knot, strongly influenced by the wind.

**Lights**
**Ponta Cais** Fl.7s14m10M
   038°-vis-292° Metal structure 7m
   Reported as 'temporarily extinguished' in April 1996 and still not operational nearly 20 years later
**Calheta** Fl.WRG.4s7m8M Metal column 5m
**Porto do Maio (Forte de São José)**
   Fl(3)R.12s22m9M 349°-vis-090°
   Platform on tower of fort 7m
**Ponta dos Flamengos** Fl(3)12s12m10M
   038°-vis-292° Metal column 5m

The pretty church at Vila do Maio, lovingly cared for inside and out  *Anne Hammick*

IV. CAPE VERDES

## Anchorages

# Porto do Maio (Porto do Inglez)

15°08'·37N 23°13'·24W

### Tides
Time difference on Dakar: –0100, on Mindelo (Porto Grande): –0015. Predictions for Porto do Maio are available via Admiralty *EasyTide* – see page 368
*Mean spring range* 1·0m
*Mean neap range* 0·6m

### Lights
**Porto de Maio (Forte de São José)**
Fl(3)R.12s22m9M 349°-vis-090°
Platform on tower of fort 7m
**Jetty** Iso.G.4s6m5M
Rusty white metal post 3m

### Rolly beach anchorage off 'desert' island

Porto do Maio, formerly known as Porto do Inglez due to the many English vessels which called to load salt, is little more than an open anchorage off a southwest-facing beach. There is nearly always some swell, making the anchorage rolly and landing difficult – though the beach itself is superb. The large church fronted by an attractive square is clearly visible from several miles offshore, with Forte de São José to the south and a long jetty, completed in 1997, to the north.

### Anchorage

Best anchorage is to be found at the southeast end of the beach in 4–8m over sand, directly off the town. If anchoring close in a stern anchor could be wise, as both wind and current may reverse direction with little warning. Good anchorage may also be found near the jetty, in 6–8m over fine sand, where a yacht reports holding well on two anchors despite some strong gusts. The jetty is built of ferro-concrete piles and elevated some 3–4m above sea level, making even the small section which is solid almost to water level unsuitable for a yacht to lie alongside. It has several iron ladders, but take care if approaching by dinghy as there are some sharp concrete and iron projections. The cargo boat from Santiago normally calls each Tuesday, and sometimes makes a second visit later in the week.

Dinghies can be left on the beach – there is generally least swell near the low rocky cliff at its southeast corner – or off the steps at the old quay, in which case a long painter and a holding-off anchor will be needed. If left at the jetty, bear in mind that tidal streams and wind may drag it under the structure and a rising tide – even with a range of less than 1m – could cause damage. Following a theft in early 2016, it is recommended that dinghies are padlocked (using a chain or a wire strop) if left astern overnight or if left unattended on the beach or at the jetty.

Anchored near the jetty at Porto do Maio *Uwe Sander*

Azure waters off the long beach at Porto do Maio, looking a little north of west, with the jetty in the middle distance and the mountains of Santiago clearly visible behind *Anne Hammick*

## Formalities

Visit the *Polícia* near the old quay – there is no *Delegação Marítima* (harbour office) in the town. Yachts are still a rarity at Porto do Maio.

## Facilities

*Engineers* There is a mechanical workshop in the town (even if it is said to look more like a scrapyard!) where outboards etc can be repaired.

*Water* Public water supply just off the main square.

*Showers* May be possible at one of the *residenciais*.

*Fuel* By can from the filling station on the north edge of the town.

*Bank* On the main square, open 0800–1300 Monday to Friday, plus ATM.

*Shops/provisioning* The Mini Mercado Paulo Jorge – continue up from the church, right at the tiny roundabout, first left, first right and in a grey building on the left – is surprisingly well stocked and spotlessly clean. The Chinese-run general store overlooking the roundabout sells everything from clothes to oil lamps.

*Produce market* Near the main square. Informal fish market under a shade tree near the stone cross on the front, though fish and shellfish can often be bought direct from the boats at very good prices.

*Cafés, restaurants & hotels* Several cafés and restaurants, including at least three along the beach, plus several small hotels and *residenciais* in the town.

*Medical services* Health centre on the road overlooking the beach, plus a small hospital, ☎+238 255 1010, with pharmacy. Anything serious would undoubtedly mean evacuation to Santiago.

## Communications

*Car hire* Two companies, both in Vila do Maio, though a taxi may be a better choice.

*Taxis* Available for day tours. Go for an all-terrain vehicle if possible.

*Buses* The usual irregular *aluguers*.

*Ferries* A small cargo ship from Santiago normally visits weekly and carries some passengers. There is talk of adding the island may to Cabo Verde Fast Ferry's itinerary.

*Air services* Regular (but not daily) flights to/from Santiago from the airport north of the town.

Selling fish, Maio style! *Sue Thatcher*

**IV. CAPE VERDES**

# Santiago

Between 14°54'N–15°20'N and 23°25'W–23°47'W

## Introduction

With a surface area of 991km² Ilha de Santiago is the largest island in the group by a considerable margin. Much of the central and northern parts are mountainous, the highest point being Pico da Antónia at 1,392m. Rainfall is higher in these areas than in the south, permitting the widespread cultivation of fruit, maize and sugar cane on the lower slopes and in the valleys.

Santiago was discovered around 1460 and was the first island in the Cape Verdes to be permanently inhabited. The first settlement, at Cidade Velha on the southwest coast – see pages 414 and 415 – was the earliest European colonial outpost in the tropics. Santiago is still the leading island commercially, with Cidade da Praia, the capital and seat of government, situated in the extreme south. It is home to more than half the archipelago's population – an estimated 275,000 of the 502,257 recorded by the census in 2013 – of whom about half live in and around Praia.

Much of the island is very attractive, with stark contrasts between the lush central mountain slopes and the flat and arid land further the south, and if anchored in Praia an excursion by taxi or *aluguer* is highly recommended. Well-travelled cruisers who spent a day exploring by car reported that, 'we had a wonderful time, helped by having a clear day – though a day is not long enough. We missed the Botanical Gardens, and would have liked to spend time walking in the Serra Malagueta Natural Park. We were impressed by the industrious, happy people and the many schoolchildren we saw along the way'.

## Approach

The coast is generally steep-to with 0·5M offing sufficient, except on the east coast from Ponta da Corõa to Ponta do Lobo where at least 1M should be allowed.

The west coast of Santiago lies in a wind shadow, and if unwilling (or unable) to motor it may be better to sail up the east coast if on passage between Porto da Praia and Baía do Tarrafal. At other times gusts funnelling down the ravines can create sudden squalls – one yacht encountered 55 knot gusts in a true wind strength of less than 30 knots off the west coast of Santiago.

If approaching from the northeast, most probably on passage from Ilha do Sal or Boavista, refer to the caution regarding Baixo de João Valente on page 381.

Boat repairs on the beach at Praia  *Anne Hammick*

## Navigation

**Magnetic variation**
10°05'W (2016) decreasing by 7'E annually

**Tidal streams**
Tidal streams are generally weak, though a 2 knot east-going stream has been reported to occur close west of Porto da Praia at mid-ebb. The southwesterly-setting current is felt most strongly around the northern part of the island, where it may run at up to 1 knot.

**Lights**
**Ponta Moreia**
Fl(5)20s97m10M 055°-vis-275°
Red lantern on white hut 4m
**Porto Formoso**
Fl(3)10s10M Metal column 5m
**Calheta de São Miguel**
Fl(4)R.15s10m5M Metal column 5m
**Pedra Badejo**
Fl.G.4s8m6M Metal column 4m
**Praia Baixo**
Fl(3)G.12s10m6M Metal column 5m
**Ponta do Lobo**
Fl(4)15s17m10M 190°-vis-292°
Square tower and building 9m
**Ponta Temerosa (Dona María Pía)**
Fl(2)6s25m15M 258°-vis-095°
White octagonal tower and building 21m
**Mosquito** Fl(2)WRG.6s13m8M
Grey tower 7m
**Porto Rinção**
Fl(5)WR.20s9m8/5M Metal column 4m
**Ribeira da Barca**
Fl(3)RGW.12s6m6M 080°-vis-121°
Grey post 3m
**Chão Bom** Fl(2+1)WRG.15s7m5M
Metal column 5m
**Ponta Pretá** Fl(3)12s34m8M
Square white building 6m

**Coast Radio Station**
**Ilha de Santiago** 15°02'·1N 23°37'·2W (remotely controlled from São Vicente)
**VHF** Ch 16 (24 hours), 20, 21
**DSC VHF** Ch 70, MMSI 006170000

Local ladies still carry their vegetables to market in the traditional way *Anne Hammick*

## Harbours and anchorages

# Porto da Praia

14°54'·31N 23°30'·12W (Breakwater, head)

**Tides**
Time difference on Dakar: –0104, on Mindelo (Porto Grande): –0019. Predictions for Porto da Praia are available via Admiralty *EasyTide* – see page 368
*Mean spring range* 1·1m
*Mean neap range* 0·6m

**Lights**
**Ponta Temerosa (Dona María Pía)**
Fl(2)6s25m15M 258°-vis-095°
White octagonal tower and building 21m
(Can be difficult to identify against shore lights)
**Breakwater**
Fl.G.4s10m5M, White tower, green bands
**Fishing harbour**
Fl.Y.4s4M Yellow metal column 2·5m
**Porto do Praia sectored light**
A new light with red-white-green sectors has been built on the cliff behind the harbour at approximately 14°55'N 23°30'W. It is reported to be operational, but its characteristics are unknown

**Harbour communications**
**Port Authority**
VHF Ch 13, 16
☎+238 261 2382, +238 260 2970

### Rolly harbour anchorage with few facilities for yachts

Porto da Praia lies at the head of a deeply indented bay and is well sheltered from winds from southwest through north around to east, though some swell nearly always works in. The main commercial and ferry quay lies on the east side of the bay, its facilities much improved by the recent completion of a substantial new breakwater. The western end of the quay terminates in a ferry and fishing harbour.

Praia is the capital of the Republic of Cape Verde, with diplomatic representation including a US Embassy – see page 360. British and other European yachtsmen wishing to visit the United States later in their cruise are normally able to get visas issued within a few days, on payment of the standard visa fee to a specified local bank. See also https://ceac.state.gov/genniv/.

The older part of the city – generally referred to as the 'plateau' – stands on a steep-sided area about 30m above sea level to the northwest of the harbour, but building has spread in all directions over the surrounding lower land. The older areas are interesting, with several imposing churches, squares and official buildings as well as a bustling market. Over the past few years the city's mayor has been active in improving security, though casual theft is likely to remain a problem (as it is in most cities), and wallets and other tempting items should always be carried in a secure inner pocket or waist bag. Most visiting yachtsmen now consider Cidade da Praia very pleasant – visibly thriving, with well-

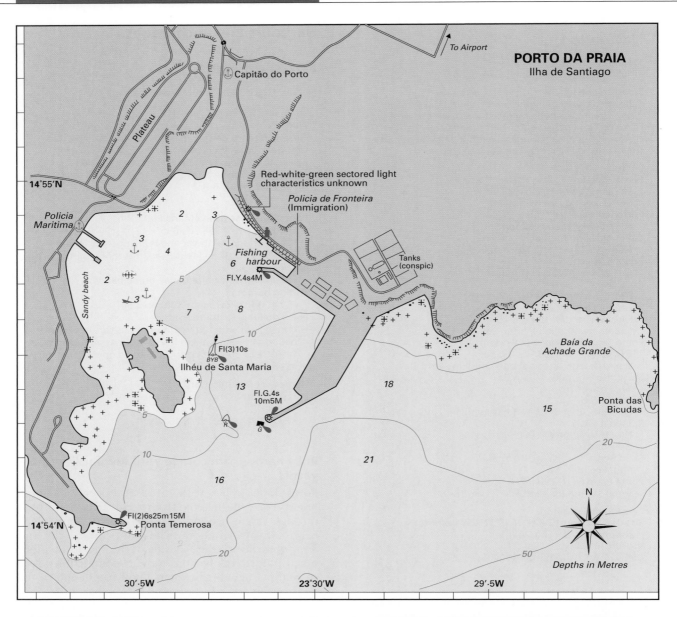

**PORTO DA PRAIA**
Ilha de Santiago

To Airport

Capitão do Porto

Plateau

Red-white-green sectored light
characteristics unknown

Policia de Fronteira
(Immigration)

14°55'N

Policia
Maritima

Sandy beach

2    3
3
4
2    5
3
7    8
10
Fl(3)10s
BYB
Ilhéu de Santa Maria
13    Fl.G.4s
10m5M
5
R
G

Fishing
harbour
6
Fl.Y.4s4M

Tanks
(conspic)

Baía da
Achade Grande

18

Ponta das
Bicudas

15

20

10

16

21

50

N

Fl(2)6s25m15M
Ponta Temerosa
14°54'N

20
20

Depths in Metres

30'·5W          23°30'W          29'·5W

Approaching Porto da Praia from the southeast, with the end of Ilhéu de Santa Maria at far left,
the breakwater at far right and the port-hand buoy near the centre *Mungo Morris*

stocked supermarkets and many new cars in evidence. Perhaps with these in mind, a two-lane highway has been built around the base of the plateau to connect the southern part of the town – which includes most of the better hotels, as well as embassies and other official buildings – with the harbour and airport. However, roads on the plateau are still mainly cobbled, and flanked by pavements which are irregular to the point of being dangerous. Watch your step!

A major problem for the city authorities is its annual population growth rate, due to a combination of improved health care (leading to lower infant mortality and much increased life

Looking southeast across the harbour from the south end of the plateau while work on the breakwater was still in progress
*Paul and Rachel Chandler*

span), immigration (mostly from west Africa), and a drift to the city from rural areas of Santiago as well as from neighbouring islands. This imposes considerable strain on fresh water, sanitation and housing, and a large proportion of the foreign aid received is spent on improving basic services.

Not to be missed while in Praia are the small *Museu do Cidade* (also called the *Museu Etnográfico da Praia*) on Avenida 5 de Julho, and the *Museu de Arqueologia* below the south end of the plateau on Rua Cabo Verde Telecom, behind the large, pale green *Arquivo Historico Nacional*. The former gives an idea of life in the islands in previous centuries, while the latter presents a fascinating selection of artefacts recovered from wrecks around their shores. Exhibits in both museums are well labelled in English, Portuguese and sometimes French, both are open 0900–1200, 1400–1800 weekdays only, and both charge a modest CVE 100$ for entry.

### Approach
Entry in daylight is quite straightforward, with no dangers further than 400m offshore, and although entry after dark is not recommended it is feasible in clear conditions. The harbour is well provided with navigation lights – providing all are functioning – with considerable ambient light from both the breakwater and the city itself.

Since May 2012 all vessels have been required to contact the Port Authority before passing the breakwater, but several yachts who called on VHF Ch 16 report no response, even during normal working hours.

### Anchorage
After many years during which yachts were expected to anchor off the beach on the western side of the harbour – an area notorious for its long fetch, swell, indifferent holding and submerged wrecks – the authorities have now accepted that most prefer to anchor west of the fishing harbour. The cliffs to the northeast provide some shelter from the wind, though the trade winds still funnel down the valley of the Ribeira de Trinidade (and deposit a good deal of dust and grit from the nearby harbour road), and the new breakwater blocks much of the swell. Depths vary from 5m or more and holding is good in firm, sandy mud.

Looking west from the yacht anchorage, with Ilhéu de Santa Maria at far left, the two jetties on the right, and the east cardinal buoy in the foreground  *Mungo Morris*

The fishing harbour, with the very conspicuous fuel tanks behind and the fuel pontoon on the left *Paul and Rachel Chandler*

After many years during which thefts from unattended yachts were so commonplace that the *Capitão do Porto* recommended that a crewmember remain aboard at all times, security appears to have improved. Even so, it would be wise not to leave the yacht empty after dark until several days into a visit, by which time the situation will have been assessed. A 'boat boy' (often middle-aged) is likely to approach each newly arrived yacht to offer his services. Many speak good English and have repeatedly proved their worth in organising local services – particularly for those who speak little or no Portuguese – though it would be wise to ask to see references from other yachtsmen and agree payment, by the day or per 'service', in advance.

Dinghies are best left at the fuel pontoon, where a self-appointed dockmaster assisted by numerous small boys watches them for a small fee, which should be agreed in advance. Outboards should either be securely padlocked, or left aboard the parent craft (similarly padlocked) and oars used for getting ashore.

### Caution

If cruising the islands in August, September or October, be warned that strong southerlies are quite common and send a dangerous swell into the bay. It may be possible to seek temporary shelter inside the new fishing harbour, but it would be unwise to leave an anchored yacht unattended for more than a few hours at this time of year.

### Formalities

Porto da Praia is currently one of only three ports in the archipelago where inward clearance to the Republic of Cape Verde can be obtained – see Entry and regulations, page 365. The rules appear to change every few years but are, very gradually, relaxing. Even so, they must be followed with care – any attempt to circumvent any part of the procedure is simply not worth the likely consequences.

*On arrival*: Having come ashore at the fuel pontoon, the skipper must first visit the *Polícia de Fronteira* (Immigration police) in their office in the new passenger terminal located about halfway between the fuel station and the port gates. Two officials are normally on duty, at least one of whom will speak French, English or both. The passports of all crew members will be required, and possibly the ship's papers, but there is no need for everyone to attend (though see below). CVE 500$ (€5) per person is charged for inward clearance. If the yacht has already cleared at Porto da Palmeira or Mindelo, and all the crew are remaining aboard and departing with her, passports will be stamped and immigration procedures are complete. If not previously cleared into the archipelago, the *Polícia de Fronteira* are likely to visit and inspect the yacht, for which a charge will almost certainly be made. The office is open 0800–1600 weekdays only, and if a yacht arrives at the weekend the *Guarda Fiscal* will notify the *Polícia de Fronteira* who will then come out to the yacht – again, charging for their services. It would be unwise to go ashore before they arrive.

Any crewmembers leaving the yacht by plane will need visas, which can be issued by the *Polícia de Fronteira* on payment of €25 each. They should accompany the skipper, taking photocopies of the information pages of their passports plus a couple of passport photos each, although these are unlikely to be needed. Without the correct entry and visa stamps they will NOT be allowed to board their flights, so it would be tempting fate to rely on a visa being issued in time for a crewmember to leave on a weekend flight.

The second stage of the process appears to change from time to time. After many years during which the skipper was required to visit the *Polícia Marítima* in their office on the root of the northern of the two jetties on the western beach, by 2010 this had been replaced by a visit to the *Capitão do Porto* in his office at the *Instituto Marítimo e Portuário*, a modern building overlooking the dry riverbed between the city and the docks. The following year visiting skippers were once again being directed to the *Polícia Marítima* office, but by 2013 the *Capitão do Porto* had resumed the task, only to have it revert to the *Polícia Marítima* in 2015. Fortunately, all agree that the *Polícia de Fronteira* should be visited first, so check current requirements while doing so. Either the *Capitão do Porto* or the *Polícia Marítima* are likely to hold the ship's papers until departure.

Taxis are readily available for those who do not fancy the dusty walk into town. If considering visiting the *Polícia Marítima* by dinghy, note that both piers are dilapidated and do not offer safe landing. The swell which broke almost unceasingly on the surrounding beach has decreased somewhat with the building of the breakwater, but even so getting ashore may be a wet affair, calling for documents to be protected by several layers of self-seal bags.

*On departure*: Both the previous offices must be revisited (by any member of the crew), the *Polícia de Fronteira* to get exit stamps in the passports and the *Polícia Marítima* or *Capitão do Porto* to reclaim the ship's papers and pay an exit charge of CVE 700$ (€7). They can be visited in either order. A receipt will be issued (and should be retained), together with a *Desembaraço de Autoridade Marítima* – particularly important if heading for the Caribbean where proof of one's port of departure is often required. If wishing to clear out the day before leaving, be sure to make this clear so the exit date is entered accordingly.

If intending to call in at either Fogo or Brava before leaving territorial waters, the skipper would be wise to visit the *Polícia de Fronteira* in person and allow plenty of time for amicable discussion. Although more relaxed rules (see page 366) were drawn up by senior officials in the *Instituto Marítimo e Portuário* at Mindelo in August 2011, it appears that either no one told the officials in Praia or that they oppose the changes, as several yachts have had their requests to call at these islands refused. Others have been given permission for a limited – usually two-day – stopover.

In contrast to the *Polícia de Fronteira*, both the *Polícia Marítima* and the *Capitão do Porto* seem quite relaxed about issuing clearance for the smaller islands.

## Facilities

*Chandlery* No chandlery as such, though there are several hardware stores selling tools and plumbing items such as hose clips, etc. Similarly, non-specialist electrical items are readily available.

*Water* One of the boat boys may be willing to assist with filling cans, but always verify the source as some, if not all, the taps on the breakwater deliver salt water. Larger quantities can be ordered at the fuel station for delivery to the fishing harbour by water tanker – charges are said to be low, but should be confirmed in advance. Bottled water is readily (and cheaply) available, including at the fuel dock.

*Showers* Can often be had at one of the hotels on payment of a fee.

*Laundry* There is no launderette in the city, and apparently only one laundry – Lavanderia Super Limpo in the Palmarejo district about 4km west of the city. Washing/drying normally takes three days and has been described as 'expensive', with an express wash considerably more so.

*Fuel* Diesel only from the fuel pontoon northwest of the fishing harbour, behind the roadside filling station.

Buying fuel duty free requires the garage to arrange for a *Polícia Marítima* representative to oversee the sale (to ensure it is indeed for a yacht), which may take anything from 30 minutes to three hours.

*Bottled gas* Most Shell filling stations exchange Camping Gaz bottles. Other cylinders can be refilled (with butane) at the Enacol plant overlooking the Cais Novo, provided the necessary adaptor is available.

*Banks* Several around the city, plus the Cotacâmbios currency exchange just north of the produce market (open 0800–1800 Monday to Friday, 0900–1300 Saturday) where cash can be drawn against a Visa card (passport required). The Banco Interâtlantico and Banco Comercial do Atlântico on the main square, and the nearby Casa do Cidadão, all have ATMs.

*Shops/provisioning* Several well-stocked supermarkets on the plateau, including the Supermercado Felicidade located beneath the hotel of the same name; the Palácio Fenícia near the corner of the main square (the Praça Alexandre Albuquerque) with an equally impressive 'department store' next door; and Calú & Ângela northwest of the market with electronic and household items on the upper floor. All have good ranges of everything from washing powder to breakfast cereal, spotless chilled and frozen meat counters, and shelves laden with alcohol of all kinds.

*Produce market* Colourful African-style market on the plateau, operating from 0700 or earlier seven days a week and selling a good variety of fruit and vegetables plus all kinds of beans, as well as meat and fish in the buildings in the corners. A greater variety of fish is available at the informal fish market near the fishing harbour, where it may also be possible to buy small quantities of ice-box grade ice.

The market area at Sucupira, northwest of the plateau, handles mainly clothes and shoes, but is also a good place to buy CDs or tapes of Cape Verdean music. All three are areas in which to watch one's purse.

*Cafés, restaurants & hotels* A wide range of cafés and restaurants in the city, with food to suit most tastes and pockets, plus a café in the *Gare Maritimo* building at the head of the harbour near the fuel pontoon. Several dozen hotels and *residençials* at all levels, with more being built each year, generally at the upper end of the price scale.

*Medical services* Hospital ☎+238 246 2130 on the plateau, plus several pharmacies.

## Communications

*WiFi* Free WiFi is available in the city's main square (the Praça Alexandre Albuquerque), though service is slow and fitful. It is necessary to log in with a username and password, both of which are provided on the welcome screen. See also page 363 regarding online security. Computer expendables, including inkjets, are available from Infotel, nearly opposite the post office.

*Car hire* Said to be nearly 20 companies, but inspect the vehicle carefully before signing anything – see Road transport, page 364.

*Taxis* Both taxis and communal *aluguer* minibuses cover routes all over the island. A trip through the mountains by *aluguer* is surprisingly cheap and gives a glimpse of a completely different world.

IV. CAPE VERDES

Free WiFi is available in the main square at Praia, which is well provided with stone benches and shade trees
*Anne Hammick*

*Ferries* The catamaran ferry *Kriola* makes the Santiago-Fogo-Brava circuit several times weekly. Visit http://cvfastferry.com, or call at the Cabo Verde Fast Ferry sales office at Avenida Andrade Corvo 35 on the plateau, open 0800–1800 weekdays, 0830–1230 Saturday. The company has gained a reputation for frequent cancellations and schedule changes.

*Air services* Frequent inter-island flights from Praia Airport about 3km northeast of the city – renamed Nelson Mandela International Airport in 2005 – plus direct flights to/from Lisbon, Paris, the Netherlands, the USA, Brazil and West African destinations. If needing to confirm a TACV flight (recommended at least 48 hours before departure), note that the office on the plateau is open 0800–1300, 1500–1800 weekdays only.

Calheta de São Martinho  *Paul and Rachel Chandler*

## Calheta de São Martinho

14°54'·57N 23°34'·18W (anchorage)

### Narrow inlet with little ashore

A deeply indented inlet about halfway between Praia and Cidade Velha, Calheta de São Martinho still lacks a surfaced road or any other shoreside infrastructure. It is, however, reported to be an intriguing place for those who like to get off the beaten track, with entry requiring eyeball navigation in good light. There are rocks either side of the entrance, so remain well off until it is possible to steer straight for the middle of the cove on a bearing of approximately 340°.

Once inside shelter is good, with anchorage possible in the centre of the inlet in 6m or so, perhaps with a line run ashore (though taking care not to impede local fishermen). There is a small and very elderly marine railway, but neither the carriage nor the rails would be adequate for a cruising yacht. There is no settlement or other facilities ashore.

## Cidade Velha

14°54'·8N 23°36'·5W (anchorage)

### Anchorage off World Heritage site

A popular anchorage at which to break the passage between Baía do Tarrafal and Porto da Praia. The bay is well sheltered from the northeast, though strong gusts off the land have been reported. There is an area of breaking rocks in its southeastern part, but in good light and with the very clear water it is possible to eyeball in behind them, anchoring in 5–6m over sand with some rock. Others may prefer the wider bay to the northwest, in 7–10m over sand. A hooked breakwater enclosing a very small 'harbour' has been built off a hotel development in the next bay westward, but it is of no relevance to visiting yachts.

Cidade Velha was the site of the islands' first capital, at which time it was known as Ribeira Grande and was the first European-built city in the tropics. Despite being recognised by UNESCO as a World Heritage site, to the uninformed visitor little appears to remain of the 'old city' – after successive

Approaching Cidade Velha from south-southwest  *Paul and Rachel Chandler*

Cidade Velha, looking southeast from the anchorage in the northwest bay *Paul and Rachel Chandler*

attacks during the 16th and 17th centuries, in 1712 the capital moved to the steep-sided plateau where Cidade da Praia now stands. For nearly three centuries – certainly until the 1990s – Cidade Velha remained a small village of thatched cottages with few facilities, but over the past two decades it has seen considerable development, with an increasing number of shops, at least one bank, a health centre and a growing number of restaurants and hotels (the Restaurante Pelourinho almost on the beach has received consistently high praise).

Cidade Velha boasts some fascinating relics, including the imposing walls of the original cathedral and the surprisingly well-preserved old church of Nossa Senhora do Rosário on the north side of the village with flagstone memorials dating back to the days of the *conquistadors*. In 2015 visiting cruisers were shown around Forte Real de São Felipe, which overlooks the town, by 'a very knowledgeable local as part of our entry price', the same crew next day walking 'the full length of the verdant green gorge. It was cool out of the sun with papaya, cashews, bananas, coconuts and cane in all directions, clouds of butterflies and dragonflies, and even monkeys on the cliff faces. At the far end we spent a happy half hour watching a kingfisher eating his fill of dragonflies laying eggs, totally unfazed by our presence'. A startling contrast to much of the archipelago!

If not planning to visit by sea, Cidade Velha is well worth an excursion from Praia by taxi or *aluguer*.

Looking northeast into the wide bay at Ribeira da Barca *Paul and Rachel Chandler*

## Ribeira da Barca

15°08'·25N 23°45'·7W (anchorage)

**Lights**
**Ribeira da Barca** Fl(3)WRG.12s6m5M
  080°-vis-121° Grey post 3m

### Anchorage off small fishing village

This small bay on the west coast of Ilha da Santiago, sheltered from north through east to south, is occasionally visited by yachts on passage between Baía do Tarrafal and Porto da Praia. A linked pair of breaking rocks lie in the middle of the bay, with another two rocks awash further south and slightly inshore – keep north of the visible pair.

The northeast trades tend to funnel down the valley and there is usually some swell, and with holding patchy in sand and rock it is prudent to lay two anchors, possibly with a third to prevent the yacht swinging inshore if the wind drops. The northeast corner of the bay contains a small quay with steps where it would be possible to land by dinghy.

The fishing village behind the bay has grown considerably over the past few decades and most basic needs can now be met.

## Baía do Tarrafal

15°16'·83N 23°45'·26W (molehead)

**Tides**
Time difference on Dakar: –0035, on Mindelo (Porto Grande): +0010. Predictions for Baía do Tarrafal are available via Admiralty *EasyTide* – see page 368
*Mean spring range* 1·0m
*Mean neap range* 0·6m

**Lights**
**Ponta Pretá** Fl(3)12s34m8M
  Square white building 6m

### Rolly anchorage in attractive bay

Baía do Tarrafal, on the northwest coast of Ilha de Santiago, provides good shelter from north through east to south. The town with its distinctive blue and white church lies at the southeast corner of the bay, overlooking an attractive white sand beach backed by coconut palms. It has become a popular weekend venue for people from Praia and is regarded locally as Santiago's main tourist attraction.

About 2km along the road leading southeast towards the town of Chão Bom lies the *Museu da Resistência*, created in the cell blocks which from 1936 until 1974 housed political prisoners exiled from Portugal and open daily from 0800–1800.

### Approach

If approaching from the south be sure not to confuse Baía do Tarrafal with Baía do Chão Bom, a wide shallow inlet some 2M further south. Ponto do Atum, which separates them, is comparatively low and can be difficult to identify from offshore. However, the white tower and brown roof of Ponta Pretá light to the north of Baía do Tarrafal is unmistakable, standing on a ledge some 30m above

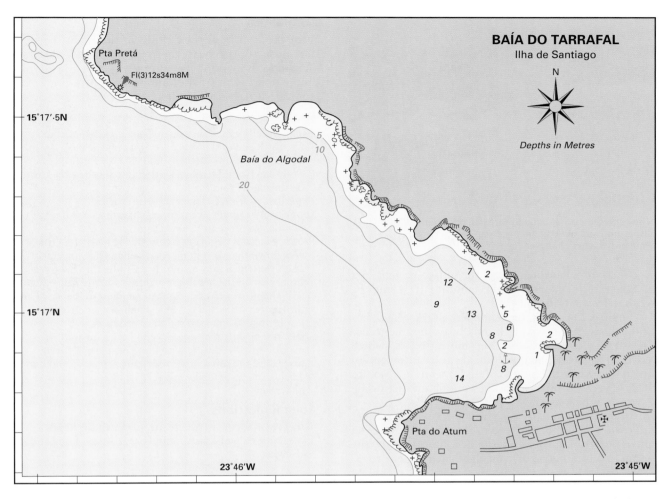

The wide bay at Baía do Tarrafal seen from the southeast, with the old mole and its offlying rocks on the left and Ponta Pretá just right of centre *Anne Hammick*

the water backed by a steep hill which continues upwards to 369m.

Enter the bay on a course just south of east. There are several shoal spots close in and careful watch should be kept both on the depth sounder and over the bow – the water is usually very clear. An increasing number of moorings for local fishing craft have been laid over recent years, with more hauled up on the beach.

## Anchorage

A line of yellow buoys marks an underwater cable which provided power to the Ponte Pretá light, and yachts are expected to anchor inshore of this cable but outside the local boat moorings, in about 6–8m. The sand is thin in patches and much of the bottom rock and boulders, making a tripline a sensible precaution. Gusts come down off the hills in the evening or an onshore breeze may spring up, so two

The superb beach at Baía do Tarrafal, a favourite with fishermen and holidaymakers alike
*Paul and Rachel Chandler*

anchors are advisable, and in the unlikely event of a northwesterly ground swell building it would be wise to leave at once.

Dinghies can normally be landed on the beach, but if much swell is breaking it may be preferable to use the steps on the inside of the mole. Rocks, which cover at high tide, lie both outside and off the end of the mole, while the path leading up from it is said to have severe subsidence and be verging on the unsafe – watch your step!

Although previously a hassle-free anchorage, following a number of thefts it is now considered unwise to leave a yacht unattended after dark. By the same token, dinghies left on the beach appear to be relatively safe in daylight when there are plenty of people around, but the same may not be true in the evening.

### Formalities

Visit the *Policía* at their office in the town (beyond the post office, near the vegetable and clothing market). It would be unwise – and probably impossible – to make initial clearance into the country at Baía do Tarrafal.

### Facilities

*Water* Usually available by can from a communal tap at the north end of the beach, or from one of the hotels/restaurants further south.

*Fuel* By can from the filling station just south of the town on the main Praia road.

*Bank* Bank with ATM near the main square.

*Shops/provisioning* Several small supermarkets, though not a place for major storing-up.

*Produce market* Good covered produce market a little way down the main Praia road selling fruit, vegetables and fish (which may also be bought directly from the fishermen on the beach). If wanting a better range than is available in Tarrafal, catch an *aluguer* to Assomada in the centre of the island where small farmers from the fertile uplands come to sell their produce.

*Cafés, restaurants & hotels* Several hotels on and overlooking the beach, with more *residencials* in the town, and the usual range of restaurants, café and bars.

*Medical services* Small hospital, ☎+238 266 1130, and pharmacy.

### Communications

*WiFi* Free in the main square, or try one of the hotels.

*Taxis* and frequent *aluguer* minibuses to/from Praia and elsewhere.

Looking north across the anchorage at Tarrafal from just west of the mole  *Paul and Rachel Chandler*

# Ilha do Fogo

**Between 14°49'N–15°03'N and 24°17'W–24°31'W**

## Introduction

Ilha do Fogo lies 30M west of Ilha de Santiago, the whole 476km² island comprising a classic and spectacular single volcanic cone. A crater nearly 8km in diameter occupies the middle of the island, with a small cone on its eastern side forming the highest point at almost 3,000m. The volcano's most violent eruption in recorded history occurred in the late 17th century and lasted for several years, during which flames and smoke were said to be visible for more than 100 miles. It was at this time that the island's name was changed from São Filipe to Fogo – 'fire' in Portuguese. Though largely quiet these days the volcano continues to have active periods – in 1951, when lava poured down the steep eastern slopes into the sea, in early 1995, when it spewed ash, lava and molten rock at intervals for over a year, and most recently over the winter of 2014–15, when several villages were destroyed.

The 1995 eruption, which began on the night of 2 April, was largely confined to the interior of the massive crater. Lava flows and 'bombs' of molten rock covered the single access road across its floor and almost obliterated the small village of Boca Fonte, but fortunately no lives were lost as local people fled their homes. Much of the vine-growing area was destroyed, either by lava or by layers of volcanic ash, but despite being provided with new houses on the mountain's southern slopes many people chose to return.

The most recent eruption started on 23 November 2014 and lasted until 7 February 2015. It was more powerful than the 1995 eruption, though once again there were no fatalities as the 1,000 or so inhabitants

of the 'Chã das Caldeiras' were forewarned by preliminary earthquakes and evacuated as soon as the eruption began. Sadly the villages of Portela and Bangeira, which had survived the 1995 eruption, were both destroyed together with the tourism infrastructure and wine production facilities. The agricultural land and the vineyards are now buried under lava, and if local people decide to return to the *caldera* area and rebuild on top of the lava flow, their best hope to earn a living is likely to be geological tourism. For further information, see https://en.wikipedia.org/wiki/Pico_do_Fogo or www.volcanodiscovery.com/fogo/news.html

Probably the most common reason for calling at Ilha do Fogo – 'island of the fire' – is to visit the volcano, which last erupted in 2014–15, destroying several villages
*Anne Hammick*

IV. CAPE VERDES

## Navigation

**Magnetic variation**
10°30'W (2016) decreasing by 7'E annually. Local magnetic anomalies are reported to exist near Ilha do Fogo.

**Tidal Streams**
Although tidal streams are weak, the southwest-going current may attain 1 knot around the north and northeast coasts of Ilha do Fogo, but is strongly wind-influenced.

**Lights**
**Porto dos Mosteiros**
 Fl(3)RW.12s12m5M White pyramid on wall 3m
**Ponta do Alcatraz**
 Fl.4s135m10M 225°-vis-045°
 White column 3m
**São Filipe (Fortim Carlota)**
 Fl(5)R.20s37m8M
 Red lantern on white column near large cream building 4m
**Ponta Salina**
 Fl(3)20s10m8M Metal column 5m

When approaching from the east the island looks totally desolate, but the western side is cultivated with much terracing, though still predominantly brown. Due to Fogo's height a wider variety of crops can be grown than on most of the other islands, including coffee, vines (though wine production was halted by the 2014–15 eruption), and the usual fruit, vegetables, maize and sugar cane. The 40,000 or so population appear to be more evenly spread throughout the island than is usually the case elsewhere in the Cape Verdes, though the majority live in and around the capital, São Filipe.

Fogo has long been popular with yachtsmen, and after more than a decade during which departure regulations effectively precluded a visit by yacht the law has now been relaxed – see page 366 – and private yachts may now request a 'next port' (*próximo porto* or *porto seguinte*) document from the Delegação Marítima when clearing out from Mindelo or Porto da Praia, and then visit one or more of the smaller islands before leaving territorial waters. It is still necessary to clear in and out with the *Capitão do Porto* at the harbour – see page 422.

### Approach

The coast is generally steep-to and 0·5M clearance is sufficient. However, more is required both north and south of Vale de Cavaleiros – see Approach and entrance, on this page.

## Harbours and anchorages

# Vale de Cavaleiros

14°55'·13N 24°30'·24W (breakwater head)

**Tides**
Time difference on Dakar: –0120,
on Mindelo (Porto Grande): –0035
*Mean spring range* 1·1m
*Mean neap range* 0·6m

**Lights**
**São Filipe (Fortim Carlota)** Fl(5)R.20s37m8M
 Red lantern on white column near large cream building 4m
**Breakwater** Iso.R.4s6M
 White column, red bands
**Fishing harbour north mole** Fl.R
 White column, red bands
**Fishing harbour south mole** Fl.G
 White column, green bands

**Harbour communications**
Port Authority ☏+238 281 1264

### Fogo's only harbour

Situated on the west coast of Ilha do Fogo about 1·5M north of the main town of São Filipe, Vale de Cavaleiros provides reasonable shelter from the prevailing northeasterly winds and swell. It is Ilha do Fogo's only harbour, used mostly by small cargo boats and the inter-island ferries which visit several times each week. There is limited space for yachts, which are tolerated rather than welcomed.

### Caution

In 2012 a report was received of a yacht being attacked in the harbour at Vale de Cavaleiros, its crew tied up and threatened with a knife. Others were approached with aggressive demands for money and/or alcohol in return for very minor services. Although a yacht visiting in 2013 encountered no problems, robbery was still said to be an issue in 2014 and skippers were advised not to allow local people aboard and to leave at least one crewmember on the yacht at all times. The harbour is isolated and some may see yachts as easy prey – be warned.

### Approach and entrance

If coming from the north keep at least 1M offshore to avoid Baixo do Rui Pereira which has less than 2m. If coming from the south take care to avoid the reef about 0·5M south of the port, 'marked' by a very angular section of wreck which shows at all times. An offing of 0·75M is adequate.

The harbour was effectively rebuilt a few years ago, but although the breakwater should be lit as above, this should not be relied upon and night entry would be unwise. The small harbour north of the headland is intended for local fishing craft, most of which are brought ashore when not in use, and is entirely unsuitable for yachts.

## Anchorage and berthing

The rebuilt harbour offers less space for visiting yachts than previously, though one or two can still be fitted in. The quays are used by ferries, freighters and even the occasional cruise ship, and any attempt to lie alongside without prior permission would be unlikely to go down well.

The previous system of dropping a bower anchor and then taking a stern line ashore remains prevalent, most often to a ring set into boulder a few metres to the right of the RoRo dock. A very long line will be needed and, as swell-induced chafe is likely to be significant, a chain loop through the ring may be a wise precaution. Be sure to remain well to the east – arriving ships normally turn inside the harbour, and while this is generally done with great skill there would almost certainly be no compensation were a yacht to be damaged in the process.

Yachts occasionally anchor without employing a stern line, but even in 4–5m swinging room could prove a problem. For once, construction work appears to have been completed without the seabed being scattered with concrete blocks and other anchor-snagging debris.

Dinghies can be landed on the beach to the east, and security does not appear to be a problem. Access between beach and road is via a track running outside the fence which encloses the harbour, which has manned security gates. After dark – and when no ships are expected – the ferry dock may be a better bet for a dinghy, coming and going via the main gates. The harbour staff are said to have no problem with this.

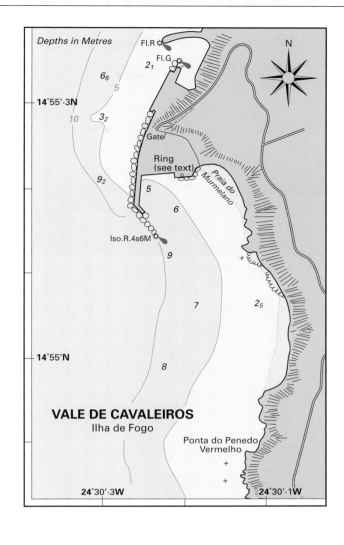

VALE DE CAVALEIROS
Ilha de Fogo

Vale de Cavaleiros, looking slightly south of west. One of Cabo Verde Fast Ferry's catamarans – probably *Kriola* – lies alongside the breakwater, with an anchored yacht and moored sport-fishing boat in the foreground
*Hedley Saunders*

IV. CAPE VERDES

Looking north into the harbour at Vale de Cavaleiros in February 2013, just before construction work was completed   *Paul and Rachel Chandler*

Be particularly vigilant if visiting Vale de Cavaleiros between June and November, a season when the wind may swing into the south without warning. Local people take this danger very seriously indeed, and ships generally move out of the harbour overnight due to the danger of being trapped by a southerly gale. Yachts should be ready to leave at short notice at any time of year, should a southerly swell start to form. Porto da Furna on neighbouring Ilha Brava is a much better bet in these conditions.

### Formalities

All formalities are now handled by the *Capitão do Porto* at the harbour, with no need to visit any officials in the town. In late 2013 the *Capitão* and his staff were said to be friendly and helpful, and spoke some English. The usual ship's papers, passports and crew list (giving name, passport number and place/date of birth) are likely to be required, and the ship's papers may be held until departure. The standard charge of CVE 700$ (€7) is payable on clearing out, which can be done on Friday if intending to leave at the weekend.

### Facilities

Good drinking water from a tap in the gated area beyond the harbour offices, right under the cliffs against the eastern wall. Visiting yachtsmen are normally allowed to fill containers without charge – visit the ENAPOR office to request a guard to unlock the gate – or it many be possible to lie alongside for a short period to take on water by hose.

Small amounts of fuel can be collected by can from one of the filling stations in São Filipe. Alternatively it may be possible to arrange for large quantities (for one or more yachts) to be delivered by road tanker – a short (but hot) walk up the road from the harbour brings one to the main Shell depot and offices – but it would be far preferable to fuel up before leaving Mindelo or Praia.

There is virtually nothing else at the harbour other than a part-time bar (operational only when a ship is in) and the possibility of buying fish direct from the boats. It is necessary to walk some 3km south into São Filipe for shopping, though there is a good chance of getting a ride in an *aluguer* or a private car.

A local fishing boat enters small northern harbour at Vale de Cavaleiros *Paul and Rachel Chandler*

## São Filipe

14°53'·7N 24°30'W

### Poor anchorage but pleasant town

São Filipe is an open and exposed roadstead – the island is almost circular and the prevailing northeast wind and swell work right round it. It is generally untenable during the winter with heavy surf running, though it might be possible to anchor off its dramatic black sand beach in summer when the northeasterlies are light or the wind is in the south. Conditions are too unpredictable to leave a yacht unattended, and for the same reason it is unsuitable as an overnight stop.

São Filipe is Ilha do Fogo's largest town, identifiable by its large church and the old fortress of Fortim Carlota to the south. It is the oldest town in the Cape Verdes other than the largely ruined Cidade Velha in Santiago, and one of the most elegant. Many of the houses and official buildings dating back to Portuguese days are in good condition, and the *Casa da Memoria* (www.casadamemoria.com.cv, open 1000–1200 Wednesday to Friday) and the *Museu Municipal* (open 1000–1500 weekdays, 1000–1200 Saturdays) are both recommended. The atmosphere is pleasantly relaxed, there are several attractive public squares and gardens and local people are notably friendly towards visitors.

A visitor information centre has recently been built on the road leading into town from the harbour, presumably replacing the one in the town centre where a helpful English-speaking lady gave out information about walks on the island.

### Facilities

*Water* Several taps in the town in addition to the one at Vale de Cavaleiros.

*Showers* Try one of the hotels or *residencials*.

*Laundry* Communal washing area with public taps and apparently unlimited water.

*Fuel* Small amounts by can from either of the filling stations. See opposite regarding larger quantities.

*Bottled gas* Shell Gas is available from the filling station in São Filipe and the Shell depot near the harbour, but bottles cannot be refilled.

*Banks* At least three, all with ATMs, but as the latter rely on the same system a single computer glitch can mean they all cease to operate.

*Shops/provisioning* Several grocery stores plus at least one bakery, the former reasonably well-stocked with staples and canned goods, including canned butter and UHT milk. The bakery appears to sell out early, but bread is also available from a vendor near the market. The Shell Select shop, on the road which leads south from the harbour, is open on Sunday.

*Produce market* Good-sized covered market with a reasonable selection of fruit and vegetables, some locally grown. Several vendors also sell eggs, and/or fresh goats' cheese in small rounds wrapped in sisal leaves.

*Cafés, restaurants & hotels* Several restaurants and hotels, but a surprising lack of seafront cafés or bars. The Hotel Xaguate, ☎+238 281 1222, has a swimming pool which is available to non-residents for a small fee.

*Medical services* Small hospital, ☎+238 281 2775, on the road towards the harbour, plus pharmacy.

### Communications

*WiFi* At Eduteca Alf ☎+238 281 1944, in the centre of the town, plus free WiFi in the seafront gardens.

*Car hire* Four companies (prices are said to be relatively high). See Road transport, page 364.

*Taxis* Taxi trips to the volcano are expensive, but if the weather is clear the cost is more than justified. Several local taxi drivers speak good English.

*Buses* The usual *aluguers*, which leave from near the market.

*Ferries* The catamaran ferry *Kriola* makes the Santiago-Fogo-Brava circuit several times weekly. Visit http://cvfastferry.com, or call at the Cabo Verde Fast Ferry sales office on the quay at Vale de Cavaleiros, open 0700–1100, 1800–2100 every day except Sunday. The company has gained a reputation for frequent cancellations and schedule changes.

*Air services* Small airport some 2·5km east of São Filipe, with departures to Santiago most days and less frequently to São Vicente and Ilha do Sal. The old airport at Mosteiros is now closed.

## Porto dos Mosteiros

15°02'N 24°19'·39W (molehead)

#### Lights
#### Porto dos Mosteiros
Fl(3)RW.12s12m5M  White pyramid on wall 3m

### A complete misnomer...

Not a port by any stretch of the imagination – rather a gap in the rocks where a few fishing boats are hauled ashore. Fully open to the northeast trades and quite impossible so far as a yacht is concerned.

# Ilha Brava
### Between 14°48'N–14°54'N and 24°40'W–24°45'W

## Introduction

Ilha Brava is the southwestermost island of the archipelago, separated from Ilha do Fogo by a 10M wide channel. With an area of only 67km² it is the smallest of the Cape Verdes to be permanently inhabited, most of its 7,000 or so people living in or around the island's capital, Vila Nova de Sintra (often referred to as simply Nova Sintra). Very little of Isla Brava is low-lying, its highest point being Monte de Fountainhas at 976m. Nova Sintra, at 520m, lies in a small *caldeira* more than halfway up the mountain's northeastern slope – obviously called after the town which lies in the hills northwest of Lisbon. It is a very beautiful island – frequently described as the prettiest in the archipelago – and unique in that even the west coast, so often dry and desolate in the other islands, is green and fertile with coconut palms lining the shore and good drinking water.

Whether anchored at Porto da Furna or at Fajã d'Agua it is worth catching an *aluguer* up to Nova Sintra, an attractive little town which is nearly always shaded by a cloudcap and, for much of the year, is remarkably green with splashes of red hibiscus and indigo-flowered creeper. The young man employed to dig weeds out of the cracks between the cobblestones must surely have a job unique in the Cape Verdes... If anchored at Furna, the walk back down the old cobbled road is highly recommended for those without knee problems, and offers a chance to admire the scenery at one's own pace. Only the very energetic would wish to walk back to Fajã d'Água, albeit the views are even more spectacular.

## Navigation

**Magnetic variation**
10°36'W (2016) decreasing by 7'E annually. Local magnetic anomalies are reported to exist near Ilha Brava.

**Tidal Streams**
Tidal streams are weak but the current sets southwest around Ilha Brava at 0·5–1 knot.

**Lights**
**Ilhéu de Cima, summit**
    Fl(3)12s80m9M 047°-vis-252° & 304°-vis-010°
    Square white hut and lantern 4m
    Obscured from offshore 010°-047° by Ilha Brava and
    252°-304° by Ilha do Fogo, but visible if passing
    between Ilhéu de Cima and its larger neighbours
**Ponta da Jalunga**
    Fl(2+1)15s24m5M 187°-vis-007°
    Grey column and building 8m
**Ponta Nhô Martinho**
    Fl(4)15s30m9M 237°-vis-106·5°
    Square white column, red lantern 4m
**Ponta de Fajã d'Água**
    Fl(3)5s25m5M Metal column 5m

Following the relaxation in departure regulations detailed on page 366, private yachts may now request a 'next port (*próximo porto* or *porto seguinte*) document from the *Delegação Marítima* when clearing out from Mindelo or Porto da Praia, and then visit one or more of the smaller islands before leaving territorial waters. It is still necessary to clear in and out with the *Delegação Marítima* in Porto da Furna – see page 426.

## Approach

The coast is generally steep-to with 0·5M clearance sufficient all round the island.

Looking eastward over the rooftops of Vila de Nova Sintra, with the shadow of Ilha do Fogo in the distance  *Sue Thatcher*

## Harbours and anchorages

# Porto da Furna

14°53'·2N 24°40'·7W (anchorage)

### Lights
**Ponta da Jalunga**
Fl(2+1)15s24m5M 187°-vis-007°
Grey column and building 8m
**Ponta Badejo** Iso.G. (period unknown)
White column, green bands

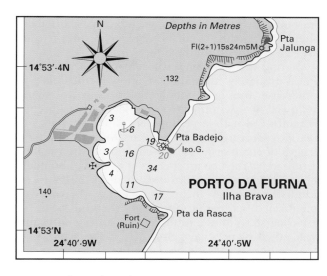

### Small ferry harbour with limited space for yachts

Porto da Furna lies 0·5M southwest of Ponta Jalunga and is well sheltered other than in a southeasterly. It is the island's main harbour and is normally visited several times each week by inter-island ferries, which berth alongside the quay inside Ponta Badejo, as does the occasional cargo ship. The village lies on the west side of the bay, from which a road runs the few kilometres up to Nova Sintra, and consistently gets the thumbs up from visiting yachtsmen for its friendly welcome and lack of security problems (a refreshing change from some of the other islands). This increases the likelihood of visitors eating ashore in the evening and touring the island by *aluguer*, so putting money into the island's economy.

Looking northeast across the bay at Porto da Furna, with the ubiquitous *Kriola* again in shot  *Paul and Rachel Chandler*

### Approach and anchorage

The white buildings of the village are visible from several miles offshore unless hidden by Ponta Badejo. The structures associated with Ponta da Jalunga are more difficult to spot (and resemble farm buldings until close enough to see the lantern), but a single, large wind generator stands on the hill behind. Although Ponta Badejo is supposedly lit, entry in darkness is not recommended.

The bay is sandy, 15m deep in the centre shoaling to 4m about 30m from the shore, and holding is good. There is a single mooring off the slipway, used by a medium-sized fishing boat. Yachts normally lie to the west of it, with one or two bower anchors set to the south-southeast plus a stern line run ashore – although the bay is sheltered by hills from the prevailing northeast trades, the wind may be deflected to southeast or even southwest within the

harbour itself. At least six yachts can be fitted in, though departure could become interesting if each set two anchors from the bow.

Getting the stern line ashore can be a challenge, but fortunately assistance is often forthcoming as otherwise the only viable solution is to swim, followed by a scramble over boulders. The shoreline is reinforced with large boulders and a sea wall, but the latter has holes in it to secure lines etc. Either a length of chain or good anti-chafe protection will be required, as the line must cross some 5m of boulders before being secured to the sea wall. In 2012–13 an English-speaking local known as Berto was mentioned as being extremely helpful both in securing stern lines and in keeping an eye on yachts while their owners were elsewhere in the island.

The only viable dinghy landing is at steps on the quay in the north of the bay, though even this can be close to impossible if there is much swell, particularly around high tide. Small, light dinghies are best lifted out onto the quay, larger ones held off with a stern anchor (though again this may require assistance). Either way, security is not an issue – 'everyone knows everyone else's business in Furna', as visitors in 2013 remarked.

## Formalities

If the *Capitão do Porto* does not appear seek him out at the *Delegação Marítima* (harbour office) in the first building on the right on entering the town – the entrance is up some stairs at the back. The usual ship's papers, passports and crew list are likely to be required, and the ship's papers may be held until departure. The standard charge of CVE 700$ (€7) is payable on clearing out, which should be done on Friday if intending to leave at the weekend as the office will be closed unless a ship is due. There are no immigration authorities on Ilha Brava and no *Polícia* in the village, though an official will come down from Nova Sintra if necessary.

## Facilities

*Water* A tap in the village provides good water, though boiling might nevertheless be wise.

*Fuel* Small amounts by can from the filling station in Nova Sintra.

*Bottled gas* Camping Gaz cylinders can be exchanged, but there is no chance of refilling other makes.

*Bank* With ATM in Nova Sintra.

*Shops/provisioning* Several small stores selling dried and tinned foods – little fresh produce is available other than bread and eggs, plus fish and shellfish directly from the boats. A better choice will be found in Nova Sintra, where there is a well-stocked grocery store with a good range of frozen meats two blocks west of the main square.

*Produce market* None as such, but Nova Sintra boasts many street vendors of fruit, vegetables and eggs.

*Cafés & restaurants* One restaurant and several cafés, but no residential accommodation nearer than VN da Sintra (which also has several more restaurants).

*Medical services* Small hospital, ✆+238 285 1706, in Nova Sintra, where there is also a pharmacy.

## Communications

*WiFi* Available one street up from the harbour at the north end of the town in a clearly signed building.

*Ferries* The catamaran ferry *Kriola* makes the Santiago-Fogo-Brava circuit several times weekly. Visit http://cvfastferry.com, or call at the Cabo Verde Fast Ferry sales office on the quay at Porto da Furna, open 0600–0900, 1900–2200 every day except Sunday. The company has gained a reputation for frequent cancellations and schedule changes.

*Air services* None. The small airstrip constructed on the west coast in the early 1990s only operated briefly before being closed permanently – it was just too dangerous.

Looking down to valley to Porto da Furna, with a hazy Fogo looming in the distance *Paul and Rachel Chandler*

# Fajã d'Agua (Porto da Fajã)

14°52'·4N 24°44'W (anchorage)

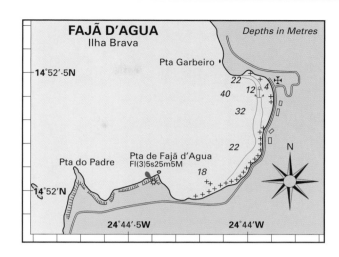

**Tides**
Time difference on Dakar: −0135, on Mindelo (Porto Grande): −0050. Predictions for Fajã d'Agua are available via Admiralty *EasyTide* – see page 368
*Mean spring range* 1·2m
*Mean neap range* 0·6m

**Lights**
**Ponta de Fajã d'Água**
  Fl(3)5s25m5M Metal column 5m

## Scenic bay with little ashore

The small bay at Fajã d'Agua on Brava's west coast is sheltered from north through east to southwest. It offers quiet and pleasant anchorage in the right conditions, and over the years many have chosen it as their final departure point from the Cape Verdes. As elsewhere on the island local people are friendly and helpful without being pushy, though little English is spoken. There are good natural swimming pools at the southern end of the bay.

In the late 1990s an airport was completed about 2km to the south, but unpredictable crosswinds combined with a very short runway proved such a dangerous combination that within a year or two it was closed – fortunately before an accident took place.

## Approach and anchorage

Anchor off the village in the northeast corner of the bay, in 8m or less over sand with a few rocks. One or two local craft plus a few fishcages are moored off the small slipway. The seabed drops steeply to 20m or more offshore and it is essential to be well onto the shelf before anchoring. Swell can work its way right around the island, and the surrounding mountains frequently cause the wind to box the compass.

The beach is mainly boulders with some sand and getting ashore can be a damp experience, particularly with a heavy dinghy, though local fishermen often come to assist. The favoured places are either below the slipway (where a dinghy can safely be left), or further north in the shadow of the pale green church, according wind and swell.

## Formalities

None – there is no *Delegação Marítima* (harbour office) or *Polícia* in the village.

## Facilities

Facilities ashore are limited, but many yachtsmen will appreciate the opportunity to fill their tanks with good water, do their laundry and even take a (cold) shower. (Note that only the tap gives drinking water – the supply to the showers and laundry sinks is brackish). All three facilities cost just a few escudos – ask around for the young man who holds the key.

Looking northeast along the stony beach at Fajã d'Agua. The tilted line in the left half of the picture marks the only road out of the village *Paul and Rachel Chandler*

Fajã d'Água seen from the north, with the parapet of the narrow road in the foreground *Sue Thatcher*

the market in Nova Sintra. The village boasts one small shop and spectacular views, but little else. Even so, the climb up to the village is recommended as worth the effort, the descent being made 'along shady terraces beside irrigation channels to the adjacent valley, which is farmed and grows every fruit known to man – a true Garden of Eden'.

A dozen or more rowing boats are drawn up on the beach at Baía dos Ferreiros, reported as 'launching in the dark at about 0300, each lit by a flaming paraffin torch and crewed by entire families fishing – an amazing sight'. Few yachts visit, but when one appears the village children run down and swim out to it (towing the smaller ones on homemade rafts of empty water bottles!), while fishermen are generally eager to barter part of their catch for fuel or other necessities. Many also offer fruit and vegetables, grown in gardens around the village. More than one crew have described their visit to Baía dos Ferreiros as the highlight of their time in the Cape Verdes.

A small general store sells the usual dry and canned goods, and a limited range of fruit and vegetables is generally obtainable from local people. Fish and fresh bread are sold from a bright green house almost opposite the slipway – it may also be possible to arrange with local fishermen for a langouste or two. More shops, including a relatively well-stocked general store, will be found some distance up the valley at Vila de Señora del Montaña. Taxis are available, though the energetic will enjoy the attractive walk.

Two small *pensãos* overlook the bay, and with prior arrangement a shower followed by meal ashore might be arranged.

## Baía dos Ferreiros

14°49'·9N 24°44'·4W (anchorage)

### Sheltered anchorage in remote, unspoilt bay

This deeply indented bay south of Ponta Praínha offers good anchorage in about 8m good holding over sand some 100m off the beach, opposite the white-roofed building. There are rocks both sides off the head of the bay. It is open only to the south, with limited fetch for the prevailing northeast trades though gusts blowing down off the mountain might well be fierce. South or southeast winds would obviously pose a problem and require immediate departure, but these are said to be rare.

There are no permanent homes at Baía dos Ferreiros and for many years fisherman had to carry their catch up a very steep footpath to the small village of Lomba Tantum perched on a ridge high above. That changed in July 2015 when the country's first (cargo only) cable car was constructed to transport fish and boat equipment up from the beach – rapid progress, seeing that the road connecting Lomba Tantum to the rest of the island was only completed in 2010. Electricity is still something of a novelty, put to good use running a small ice plant to enable the villagers to send fish to

Fishing boats drawn up on the beach at Baía dos Ferreiros in early 2013. Since then the building has received a smart new blue paint job *Paul and Rachel Chandler*

Looking down into Baía dos Ferreiros, with two yachts at anchor *Paul and Rachel Chandler*

# Ilhéus Secos do Rombo

Bisected by 14°58'·4N 24°38'·2W (Ilhéu de Cima) and
14°58'·1N 24°41'·5W (Ilhéu Grande)

## Rocky islets with connecting reefs

This group of four tiny and two somewhat larger
islets, all connected by reefs, lies about 3·5M north
of Ilha Brava and 7·5M west of Ilha do Fogo,
separated from them by deep-water channels. The
largest and highest of the group are Ilhéu de Cima to
the east at 77m, and Ilhéu Grande to the west at
96m.

None of the islets are inhabited, though fishermen
from Brava visit frequently, principally working the
reef-strewn area between Ilhéu Luiz Carneiro and
Ilhéu de Cima. In rough weather they camp out
(there is a small building) rather than make the
journey to and fro in their small open boats. The
entire group is a designated nature reserve, with
large colonies of nesting seabirds including the rare
Bulwer's petrel.

If on passage and not intending to stop at the
islands, the entire area should be given an offing of
several miles.

## Anchorages

Two possible anchorages have been suggested. That
south of Ilhéu Luiz Carneiro is said to be reasonable
in normal conditions and easy to vacate by day or
night should the need arise. It may also be possible
to anchor south of Ilhéu Grande (known locally as
Ilhéu de Baixo) in 7–9m in good holding over sand.
Neither are recommended for overnight stays but
are usable by day in settled weather.

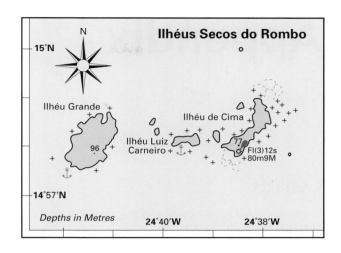

## Navigation

**Magnetic variation, Tides and Charts**
See under Ilha Brava.

**Lights**
**Ilhéu de Cima, summit**
  Fl(3)12s80m9M 047°-vis-252° & 304°-vis-010°
  Square white hut and lantern 4m
  Obscured from offshore 010°-047° by Ilha Brava and
  252°-304° by Ilha do Fogo, but visible if passing
  between Ilhéu de Cima and its larger neighbours

Ilhéu Grande, seen from Ilha Brava on a rather hazy day
*Anne Hammick*

The Ilhéus Secos do Rombo seen from the southeast *Anne Hammick*

IV. CAPE VERDES

# Appendix

## I. Charts

Charts are listed in numerical order within each section. They and other publications may be updated on a regular basis by reference to online *Notices to Mariners* or the national equivalent:

*Admiralty Notices to Mariners* published weekly by the UK Hydrographic Office, www.ukho.gov.uk

*US Notices to Mariners* published weekly by the US National Geospatial-Intelligence Agency, http://msi.nga.mil

*Avisos aos Navegantes* published monthly by the Portuguese *Instituto Hidrográfico*, www.hidrografico.pt

*Avisos a los Navegantes* published weekly by the Spanish *Armada Española*, www.armada.mde.es

*Imray Correction Notices*: contain cumulative corrections for individual Imray charts. Go to www.imray.com, enter the chart number in the home page 'search' box, and click on 'Latest corrections' at bottom left.

Charts produced by the Portuguese *Instituto Hidrográfico* may not be easy to obtain once in the Azores or Madeira, but can be ordered online before departure from J Garraio & Ca Lda in Lisbon (www.jgarraio.pt).

Charts produced by the Spanish *Instituto Hidrográfico de la Marina* are available from JL Gándara y Cía SA in Las Palmas (www.gandara-sa.com). See page 276.

The US National Geospatial-Intelligence Agency (formerly the NIMA/DMA) no longer produces large-scale charts for areas outside US waters, and its passage charts are no longer available for public sale by the NGIA. Instead they are available from OceanGrafix LLC, www.oceangrafix.com, who print them as required thus ensuring that charts are corrected to the date of despatch.

Attention is drawn to the notes regarding Horizontal chart datum on page 11 and on Chart datum and Satellite derived positions on pages 54, 174 and 369.

Imray-Iolaire charts, as well as British Admiralty charts and publications, are available from:

**Imray Laurie Norie & Wilson Ltd**

Wych House, The Broadway,
St Ives, Cambs PE27 5BT, England
☎ 01480 462114

orders@imray.com

www.imray.com

## Passage Charts

### British Admiralty www.ukho.gov.uk

| Chart | Title | Scale |
|---|---|---|
| 3133 | Casablanca to Islas Canarias, including Arquipelago da Madeira | 1,250,000 |
| 3134 | Islas Canarias to Nouakchott | 1,250,000 |
| 3135 | Nouakchott to Bissau and Arquipelago de Cabo Verde | 1,250,000 |
| 4011 | North Atlantic Ocean, Northern Part | 10,000,000 |
| 4012 | North Atlantic Ocean, Southern Part | 10,000,000 |
| 4014 | North Atlantic Ocean, Eastern Part | 10,000,000 |
| 4103 | English Channel to the Strait of Gibraltar and the Arquipélago dos Açores | 3,500,000 |
| 4104 | Lisboa to Freetown | 3,500,000 |
| 4114 | Arquipélago dos Açores to Flemish Cap | 3,500,000 |
| 4115 | Arquipélago dos Açores to the Arquipelago de Cabo Verde | 3,500,000 |

### US National Geospatial-Intelligence Agency
www.nga.mil (but see note left)

| Chart | Title | Scale |
|---|---|---|
| 103 | English Channel to the Strait of Gibraltar including the Azores | 3,500,000 |
| 104 | Lisbon to Freetown | 3,500,000 |
| 120 | North Atlantic Ocean, Southern Sheet | 6,331,100 |
| 121 | North Atlantic Ocean, Northern Sheet | 5,870,000 |
| 125 | North Atlantic Ocean, Southeastern Sheet | 5,281,950 |
| 126 | North Atlantic Ocean, Northeastern Sheet | 3,619,020 |

### Imray Laurie Norie & Wilson Ltd www.imray.com

| | | |
|---|---|---|
| 100 | North Atlantic Ocean Passage Chart | 7,620,000 |

# Bermuda

### NOAA Charts

| Chart | Title | Scale |
|---|---|---|
| 5161 | Newport to Bermuda, including rhumb line | |

### US National Geospatial-Intelligence Agency
www.nga.mil (but see note opposite)

| Chart | Title | Scale |
|---|---|---|
| 26341 | Bermuda Islands | |
| 26342 | The Narrows to Grassy Bay | |
| 26343 | St. George's Harbour | |
| 26344 | Great Sound Plan: North & South Basins | |
| 26345 | Hamilton Harbour | |

### British Admiralty www.ukho.gov.uk

| Chart | Title | Scale |
|---|---|---|
| 332 | Grassy Bay and Great Sound including Little Sound | 12,500 |
| 334 | Bermuda | 7,500 |
| 360 | Approaches to Bermuda | 300,000 |
| 867 | North and South Channels to Great Sound | 17,500 |
| 868 | Eastern and Western Approaches to The Narrows including Murray's Anchorage | 17,500 |
| 1073 | Dundonald Channel to Hamilton Harbour | 6,000 |
| 1315 | Five Fathom Hole, The Narrows and St George's Harbour | 7,500 |
| 4004 | A Planning Chart for the North Atlantic Ocean and Mediterranean Sea | 7,500 |
| 4013 | North Atlantic Ocean Western Part | 10,000,000 |
| 4004 | A Planning Chart for the North Atlantic Ocean and Mediterranean Sea | 10,000,000 |

### Imray Laurie Norie & Wilson Ltd www.imray.com

| Chart | Title | Scale |
|---|---|---|
| E5 | Bermuda | 60,000 |
| | Bermuda Approaches | 350,000 |
| | St George's Harbour | 17,500 |
| | Hamilton Harbour | 15,000 |
| | Dockyard Marina | 4,000 |

# The Azores

### British Admiralty www.ukho.gov.uk

| Chart | Title | Scale |
|---|---|---|
| 1895 | Ilha de São Miguel | 100,000 |
| | Ponta Delgada, São Miguel | 10,000 |
| 1950 | Arquipélago dos Açores | 750,000 |
| 1956 | Arquipélago dos Açores (Central Group) | 175,000 |
| 1957 | Harbours in the Azores (Central Group) | |
| | Canal do Faial | 37,500 |
| | Porto da Horta, Faial | 10,000 |
| | Vila da Praia, Graciosa | 12,500 |
| | Praia da Vitória, Terceira | 12,500 |
| | Angra do Heróismo, Terceira | 12,500 |
| 1959 | Flores, Corvo and Santa Maria with Banco Formigas | |
| | Ilhas Flores and Corvo | 150,000 |
| | Santa Cruz, Flores | 25,000 |
| | Lajes, Flores | 20,000 |
| | Ilha de Santa Maria with Banco das Formigas | 150,000 |
| | Vila do Porto, Santa Maria | 12,500 |
| | Bahia de Sao Lourenço, Santa Maria | 12,500 |

### Portuguese Hydrographic Institute
www.hidrografico.pt

| Chart | Title | Scale |
|---|---|---|
| 41101 | Arquipélago dos Açôres | 1,000,000 |
| 43101 | Arquipélago dos Açôres – Grupo Ocidental | 300,000 |
| 43102 | Arquipélago dos Açôres – Grupo Central | 300,000 |
| 43103 | Arquipélago dos Açôres – Grupo Oriental | 300,000 |
| 46201 | Canal de São Jorge (Ilhas de São Jorge e Pico) | 75,000 |
| 46401 | Ilhas das Flores e do Corvo | 75,000 |
| | Porto das Lajes das Flores | 5,000 |
| | Porto de Santa Cruz das Flores | 10,000 |
| | Porto de Casa | 5,000 |
| 46403 | Ilha do Faial e Canal do Faial | 50,000 |
| | Porto da Horta | 7,500 |
| | Porto da Madalena | 7,500 |
| 46404 | Ilha Graciosa | 50,000 |
| | Vila da Praia | 5,000 |
| | Santa Cruz | 5,000 |
| | Folga | 5,000 |
| 46405 | Ilha Terceira | 75,000 |
| | Angra do Heroísmo | 10,000 |
| | Praia da Vitória | 10,000 |
| 46406 | Ilha de São Miguel | 100,000 |
| | Porto de Ponta Delgada | 10,000 |
| 46407 | Ilha de Santa Maria e Ilhéus das Formigas | |
| | Ilha de Santa Maria | 75,000 |
| | Porto de Vila do Porto | 7,500 |
| | Baía de São Lourenço | 7,500 |
| | Ilhéus das Formigas | 7,000 |
| 47501 | Portos das Ilha de São Jorge e do Pico | |
| | Porto da Calheta, São Jorge | 5,000 |
| | Porto das Velas, São Jorge | 5,000 |
| | Porto de São Roque, Pico | 5,000 |
| | Porto das Lajes, Pico | 5,000 |
| | Porto de Santa Cruz das Ribeiras, Pico | 5,000 |
| 45702 | Vila Franca do Campo, São Miguel | 7,500 |
| | Ribeira Quente | 5,000 |
| | Porto Formoso, São Miguel | 5,000 |
| | Rabo de Peixe, São Miguel | 5,000 |
| | Porto de Capelas, São Miguel | 5,000 |

### Imray-Iolaire Series www.imray.com

| Chart | Title | Scale |
|---|---|---|
| E1 | Arquipélago dos Açôres | 750,000 |
| | Vila das Lajes, Flores | 20,000 |
| | Horta, Faial | 12,500 |
| | Lajes (Pico) | 10,000 |
| | Porto das Velas | 7,500 |
| | Vila da Praia | 10,000 |
| | Praia da Vitória | 20,000 |
| | Angra do Heroísmo | 12,500 |
| | Ponta Delgada | 10,000 |
| | Vila Franco do Campo | 15,000 |
| | Vila do Porto | 10,000 |

APPENDIX

## The Madeira Group

### British Admiralty www.ukho.gov.uk

| Chart | Title | Scale |
|---|---|---|
| 1684 | Machico & Caniçal | 7,500 |
| 1685 | Ponta Gorda to Ponta de Sao Lourenco | 30,000 |
| | Funchal | 10,000 |
| | Canical | 10,030 |
| 1689 | Ports in the Arquipelago da Madeira | |
| | Baia do Porto Santo | 20,000 |
| | Porto do Porto Santo | 7,500 |
| 1831 | Arquipélago da Madeira | 150,000 |
| 3133 | Casablanca to Islas Canarias, including | |
| | Arquipélago da Madeira | 1,250,000 |
| | Ilhas Selvagens | 100,000 |

### Portuguese Hydrographic Institute
www.hidrografico.pt

| Chart | Title | Scale |
|---|---|---|
| 36201 | Ilha da Madeira e Ilhas Desertas | 100,000 |
| 36401 | Ilha do Porto Santo | 50,000 |
| | Baía do Porto Santo | 15,000 |
| | Porto do Porto Santo | 5,000 |
| 36402 | Ponta Gorda à Ponta de S. Lourenço | 30,000 |
| | Porto do Funchal | 10,000 |
| 36403 | Paul do Mar à Praia Formosa | 30,000 |
| | Câmara de Lobos e Praia Formosa | 10,000 |
| 36406 | Islas Desertas | 50,000 |
| | Doca (Carga da Lapa) | 15,000 |
| 36407 | Ilhas Selvagens | 100,000 |
| | Selvagem Grande | 25,000 |
| | Selvagem Pequena | 25,000 |
| 37501 | Portos da Ilha da Madeira | |
| | Portos do Machico e Caniçal | 7,500 |
| | Porto do Moniz | 7,500 |
| | Porto da Cruz | 7,500 |

### Imray-Iolaire Series www.imray.com

| Chart | Title | Scale |
|---|---|---|
| E3 | Arquipelago de Madeira | 170,000 |
| | Porto Santo | 25,000 |
| | Porto de Recreio da Calheta | 6,250 |
| | Funchal | 10,000 |
| | Água de Pena | 5,000 |
| | Porto de Machico | 7,500 |
| | Quinta do Lorde | 20,000 |
| | Ponta de São Lourenço | 30 000 |
| | Enseada da Doca (Isla Deserta Grande) | 25 000 |
| | Selvagem Grande | 30,000 |
| | Selvagem Pequena | 30,000 |

## The Canary Islands

### British Admiralty www.ukho.gov.uk

| Chart | Title | Scale |
|---|---|---|
| 1870 | Lanzarote to Gran Canaria | 300,000 |
| | Approaches to Puerto del Rosario | 75,000 |
| | Puerto del Rosario | 7,500 |
| 1847 | Santa Cruz de Tenerife | 12,500 |
| 1856 | Plans in Gran Canaria | |
| | Approaches to Las Palmas de Gran Canaria | 75,000 |
| | Las Palmas de Gran Canaria | 12,500 |
| | Puerto de Salinetas | 15,000 |

| Chart | Title | Scale |
|---|---|---|
| 1858 | Approaches to Santa Cruz de Tenerife and Santa Cruz de la Palma | |
| | Approaches to Santa Cruz de Tenerife | 75,000 |
| | Approaches to Santa Cruz de la Palma | 75,000 |
| | Santa Cruz de la Palma | 10,000 |
| | San Sebastián de la Gomera | 10,000 |
| 1869 | Gran Canaria to Hierro | 300,000 |

### Spanish Armada Española www.armada.mde.es

| Chart | Title | Scale |
|---|---|---|
| 60A | Lanzarote y Fuerteventura | 200,000 |
| 60B | Fuerteventura y Gran Canaria | 200,000 |
| 61A | Gran Canaria, Tenerife y La Gomera | 200,000 |
| 61B | La Palma, La Gomera y El Hierro | 200,000 |
| 600 | De Arrecife a La Isleta con las islas Alegranza, Montaña Clara y La Graciosa | 60,000 |
| 600A | Pasos entre las islas Alegranza, Montaña Clara, La Graciosa y Lanzarote | 25,000 |
| 601 | Costa occidental de la isla de Lanzarote y costa norte de la isla de Fuerteventura | 60,000 |
| 601A | Estrecho de La Bocayna | 25,000 |
| 602 | De punta de Tostón a punta Amanay | 60,000 |
| 603 | Península de Jandía | 60,000 |
| 604 | Del puerto de Gran Tarajal al puerto del Rosario | 60,000 |
| 605 | De Arrecife (Lanzarote) a Puerto del Rosario (Fuerteventura) | 60,000 |
| | Puerto Calero | 12,500 |
| | Puerto del Carmen | 12,500 |
| 610 | Del cabo Descojonado a la península de Gando | 60,000 |
| 611 | Del cabo Colorado a la bahía de Melenara | 60,000 |
| 612 | Del puerto de Güimar a la punta El Guindaste | 60,000 |
| 613 | Del puerto de los Cristianos al puerto de Güímar | 60,000 |
| 614 | De punta Montaña Amarilla a punta del Guindaste | 60,000 |
| 616 | Isla de la Palma | 60,000 |
| 617 | Isla de La Gomera | 60,000 |
| 618 | Isla de El Hierro | 60,000 |
| 6010 | Puertos de Arrecife, Naos y Los Mármoles | 10,000 |
| 6030 | Puertos de Gran Tarajal y del Rosario | |
| | Puertos de Gran Tarajal | 5,000 |
| | Puerto del Rosario | 5,000 |
| 6100 | Puerto de Las Palmas | 12,500 |
| 6110 | Puertos de Mogán, Arguineguín y Muelle Cementero | |
| | Puerto de Mogán | 7,500 |
| | Puertos de Arguineguín y Muelle Cementero | 7,500 |
| 6120 | Puerto de Santa Cruz de Tenerife | 12,500 |
| | Puerto Caballo | 5,000 |
| 6140 | Puerto de Los Cristianos | 3,500 |
| 6150 | Puertos de Santa Cruz de La Palma, San Sebastián de La Gomera y La Estaca | |
| | Puerto de Santa Cruz de La Palma | 7,500 |
| | Puerto de San Sebastián de La Gomera | 7,500 |
| | Puerto de La Estaca | 7,500 |
| D210 | Gran Canaria | 100,000 |
| | Marina de Las Palmas | 10,000 |
| | Pasito Blanco | 10,000 |
| | Arguineguín | 10,000 |
| | Puerto Rico y Anfi del Mar | 10,000 |
| | Mogan | 10,000 |
| | Agaete / Las Nieves | 10,000 |

**Imray-Iolaire Series** www.imray.com

| Chart | Title | Scale |
|---|---|---|
| E2 | Islas Canarias | 600,000 |
| | Puerto de Santa Cruz, La Palma | 12,500 |
| | Puerto de la Estaca, Hierro | 7,500 |
| | Puerto de San Sebastián de la Gomera | 10,000 |
| | Dársena de Los Llanos (Marina Santa Cruz) | 17,500 |
| | Dársena Pesquera (Marina Tenerife) | 17,500 |
| | Puerto de las Palmas | 30,000 |
| | Morro Jable | 12,500 |
| | Marina Rubicón | 25,000 |
| | Puerto Calero | 15,000 |
| | Estrecho del Río | 50,000 |
| | Puerto de Naos & Los Marmoles (Marina Lanzarote) | 12,500 |
| | Tazacorte | 10 000 |
| | Gran Trajal | 10,000 |

## The Cape Verdes

**British Admiralty** www.ukho.gov.uk

| | | |
|---|---|---|
| 366 | Arquipélago de Cabo Verde | 500,000 |
| 367 | Ports in the Arquipélago de Cabo Verde | |
| | Ilha do Sal | 200,000 |
| | Baía do Palmeira, Sal | 12,500 |
| | Porto do Santa Maria, Sal | 20,000 |
| | Approaches to Porto Grande, São Vicente | 150,000 |
| | Porto Grande, São Vicente | 17,500 |
| | Approaches to Porto da Praia, Santiago | 150,000 |
| | Porto de Praia, Santiago | 15,000 |

**Direcção Geral de Marinha e Portos, Cape Verdes**

| Chart | Title | Scale |
|---|---|---|
| 11 | Porto Novo | 5,000 |
| 21 | Porto da Palmeira, Ilha do Sal | – |
| 31 | Porto do Tarrafal, São Nicolau | 5,000 |
| 41 | Mindelo (Porto Grande), São Vicente | 5,000 |
| 71 | Porto da Praia, Santiago | – |

**Portuguese Hydrographic Institute**
www.hidrografico.pt

| Chart | Title | Scale |
|---|---|---|
| 66301 | Porto da Praia | 7,500 |
| 66302 | Porto Grande | 10,000 |
| 67501 | Portos das Ilhas de São Nicolau e Santo Antão | |
| | Porto Novo, Santo Antão | |
| | Porto do Tarrafal, São Nicolau | |
| | Porto da Preguiça, São Nicolau | |
| 67502 | Portos das Ilhas Brava, Fogo, Santiago e Maio | |
| | Porto Ingles, Maio | 10,000 |
| | Tarrafal, Santiago | 5,000 |
| | Furna, Brava | 7,500 |
| | Vale de Cavaleiros | 10,000 |
| 67503 | Portos das Ilhas da Boavista e do Sal | |
| | Baía de Palmeira | 5,000 |
| | Santa Maria | 7,500 |
| | Porto de Sal Rei | 10,000 |

**Imray-Iolaire Series** www.imray.com

| Chart | Title | Scale |
|---|---|---|
| E4 | Arquipélago de Cabo Verde | 500 000 |
| | Porto Novo (Ilha de Santo Antão) | 10,000 |
| | Mindelo (Porto Grande) (Ilha de São Vicente) | 20,000 |
| | Ilha de Santa Luzia | *sketch* |
| | Porto de Tarrafal (Ilha de São Nicolau) | 8,500 |
| | Porto da Preguiça (Ilha de São Nicolau) | 8,500 |
| | Baía da Palmeira (Ilha do Sal) | 15,000 |
| | Porto de Sal-Rei (Ilha da Boavista) | 30,000 |
| | Porto da Praia (Ilha de Santiago) | 22,000 |
| | Cavaleiros (Ilha do Fogo) | 10,000 |
| | Porto da Furna (Ilha Brava) | 10,000 |

# II. Websites

## Miscellaneous websites of interest

Of the thousands of websites of potential interest to yachtsmen cruising the Atlantic Islands, the following offer something for everybody.

**www.atlantic-islands.com** – German retailer specialising in books and maps for the Azores, Madeira and Cape Verdes (not Canaries). Although most of the former are in German, a map is the same in any language. Site in German and English

**www.bluewaterweb.com** – Bluewater Books & Charts, one of America's largest nautical bookstores and chart agents, including Admiralty and Imray publications.

**www.bradtguides.com** – publishers of *Azores: The Bradt Travel Guide* and *Cape Verde Islands: The Bradt Travel Guide* (both highly recommended) amongst others

**http://easytide.ukho.gov.uk** – free tidal data for ports all over the world, including 38 in the islands covered in this book. Exceptionally user-friendly

**www.imray.com** – publisher of a wide range of cruising guides and charts (correctional supplements on the website), retailer for other publishers and Admiralty chart agent

**www.google.co.uk/maps** – satellite images including good coverage of most parts of the Atlantic Islands. Although every image is labelled 'Map data ©2016 Google' (rolled on each year), this could be misleading – many are several years old and some much older

**www.nauticalchartsonline.com** – supplies US National Geospatial-Intelligence Agency charts (no longer available to buy from the NGA), on a print-on-demand basis, together with a range of other publications

**www.noonsite.com** – originally created to carry updates and corrections for Jimmy Cornell's well-known *World Cruising Handbook* and *World Cruising Routes*, but now run by World Cruising Club Ltd and host to a vast amount of worldwide cruising information

**www.oceancruisingclub.org** – a UK-based club with worldwide membership, backed by a network of port officers and representatives. Categories for Ordinary and Associate membership (the former requiring a port-to-port passage of 1,000 miles or more) ensure it remains THE club for ocean cruising sailors. Application online

**www.oceangrafix.com** – supplier of nautical publications on a print-on-demand basis including Imray charts for the Atlantic and Caribbean islands and US National Geospatial-Intelligence Agency charts

**www.rccpf.org.uk** – homepage of the RCC Pilotage Foundation, containing information about current and future PF titles, supplements etc., as well as access to its *Passage Planning Guide*

**www.ssca.org** – Seven Seas Cruising Association, a US-based club for both serious cruisers and local liveaboards with a worldwide (though mainly American) membership, known for its informative monthly bulletin and 'clean wake' policy

**www.sunflowerbooks.co.uk** – publishers of the highly recommended series of *Landscapes* walking and car touring guidebooks

**www.ukho.gov.uk** – the UK Hydrographic Office. Still the only source of weekly *Admiralty Notices to Mariners* (including a listing of relevant notices by chart) via the 'Products and Services' tab followed by 'Paper Charts'

## Azores & Madeira

The Azores and Madeira are well represented on the internet and the following sites contain general information, some of which may be useful to the visiting yachtsman.

**www.ana.pt** – homepage of *Aeroportos de Portugal*. Click on the Açores or Madeira tabs for live flight arrival and departure information in Portuguese, English and Spanish

**www.flytap.com** – TAP (Transportes Aéreos Portugueses), Portugal's national airline. In Portuguese and English

**www.hidrografico.pt** – the Portuguese *Instituto Hidrográfico*, with details of charts, lights etc. In Portuguese, with (rather clunky) automatic translation to English, French and Spanish. Some items, such as the chart catalogue, will only download from the Portuguese original

**www.meteo.pt** – Portugal's *Instituto de Meteorologia*, which provides immediate, five-day and 10-day weather forecasts (and much more besides) for six cities across the Azores, as well as Madeira's Funchal and Porto Santo. In Portuguese and English

## Azores

**www.andreas-stieglitz.de** – homepage of the author of Azores in the Sunflower Landscapes series. Current information on the Azores and walking areas, in German

**www.atlanticoline.pt** – website of Atlânticoline which, in summer at least, links all the Azorean islands with its three (very different) ferries. In Portuguese and English. See page 48 for further details

**www.azores.com** – a commercial site selling property and holidays in the islands, but also offering a great deal of detailed information on each individual island. In Portuguese and English

**www.azores.gov.pt** – the Azorean Regional Government, in Portuguese only

**www.azores-islands.info** – interesting information backed up by photos and maps. In Portuguese, English and Spanish

**www.birdingazores.com** – compiled by Steffan Rodebrand and The Birding Azores Team, who point out that 'the archipelago has become a popular destination for European birdwatchers in recent years'

**www.destinazores.com** – a model site covering all the islands (with downloadable PDF maps) and many topics of interest, in Portuguese and English, by the publishers of the *destinazores* guide described on page 438

**www.marinasazores.com** – website of the part of *Portos dos Açores SA* concerned with marina operations. Unavailable in early 2016, but expected to reappear in a much-improved format towards the end of the year

**www.sata.pt** – SATA (*Sociedade Açôreana da Transportes Aérios*) the archipelago's own airline, which started small but now offers services to destinations including the US and Canada, the UK and many cities in mainland Europe. In Portuguese and English. See page 48 for further details

**www.semanadomar.net** – Horta's famous Sea Week – see page 81 – in Portuguese only, but readily translatable online siaram.azores.gov.pt/centros-interpretacao/_intro.html – the *Direção Regional do Ambiente* (Regional Environment Directory), a part of the Azorean Government covering everything from invasive plants through caves to snails to marine birds. Fabulous photos, but sadly in Portuguese only

www.theazores.net – cheerful, quirky site with a mixture of quotations, information, photographs and graphics

trails.visitazores.com/en – from that part of *Turismo dos Açores* responsible for encouraging walking in the islands, both as complete holidays and one-off hikes, but apparently not accessible from the parent site

www.visitazores.com – *Turismo dos Açores* - an excellent source of information in six languages including English. Includes travel details, events calendar and an overview of each island, plus real-time webcams from most of the islands/harbours

www.whalewatchazores.com – Whale Watch Azores has been in business since the early 1990s and offers much information about the cetaceans they watch and research in progress. Great photos, of course

## Madeira

www.apram.pt – the *Administração dos Portos da Região Autónoma da Madeira* in Portuguese and English. Concerned mainly with commercial shipping it nevertheless has some pages to interest yachtsmen

www.cm-funchal.pt – the *Camâra Municipal* (the city council) of Funchal, in Portuguese only

www.gov-madeira.pt – the *Região Autónoma da Madeira* (regional government), in Portuguese only

www.horariosdofunchal.pt – times, routes and fares for Funchal's urban and suburban buses, in Portuguese, English and German. Best complemented by a copy of Discovery Walking Guides Ltd's *Madeira Bus & Touring Map* (see page 169)

www.madeiraguide.co.uk – a somewhat commercial site with links to tour operators, hire car firms etc., despite being independently run. In good, though not perfect, English

www.madeiraislands.travel – the islands' official tourism website, in Portuguese, English, French, German and Spanish. Well-constructed and packed with useful and entertaining facts about the two major islands, from history and infrastructure down to 'stop press' news on which *levadas* (foot paths) are currently closed for maintenance. An excellent introduction to the islands

www.madeiraonline.com – a useful reference site containing lists of everything from doctors to someone who can fix your onboard computer, though not all are Madeira-based. In English only

madeira.seawatching.net – fascinating for anyone interesting in avian or marine life (or land creatures from butterflies to bats), with an extensive photo gallery and recorded bird sounds plus specialist pages devoted to the Islas Desertas and Selvagens

www.madeira-web.com – attractive site in a dozen languages including English, covering many topics from 'Madeira old photos' to a 'what's on' guide, plus nearly 20 webcams showing different parts of Funchal, including the harbour and marina

www.madeirawine.com – a complete guide to the island's most famous export, in Portuguese and English, including online sales

www.museudabaleia.org – website of Madeira's excellent *Museu da Baleia* at Caniçal, in Portuguese, English and German

www.museucolombo-portosanto.com – Porto Santo's small but fascinating museum, housed in the building where Christopher Columbus is reputed to have lived

www.netmadeira.com – a government-run site, in Portuguese only but quite easy to navigate. Local radio and TV schedules, live web-cams and a list of duty pharmacies demonstrate its range

www.porto-santo.com – a commercial site with general information and some nice photos, in seven languages including English

www.portosantoline.pt – prices and schedules (for two months ahead) for the car ferry *Lobo Marinho* which plies the route from Funchal to Porto Santo. In four languages including English

www.portosdamadeira.com – the *Administração dos Portos da Região Autónoma da Madeira* (APRAM), including a Tariff list giving current fees for anchoring within port limits. Website in Portuguese and English, Tariff sheet in Portuguese only

www.rodoeste.pt and www.sam.pt – Madeira's two rural bus companies, Rodoeste west of Funchal and SAM (*Sociedade de Automóveis da Madeira*) to the east. Neither has a working English version, but both are easy to follow with route maps and downloadable timetables

www.sata.pt – homepage of SATA (*Sociedade Açóreana da Transportes Aérios*) the Azores airline, which also flies to/from Madeira. See opposite

www.sra.pt/jarbot – Madeira's long-established Botanical Gardens, in six languages including English. Recommended (as is the Jardim Botânico itself)

## Canary Islands

There are many tourist guides dealing with the Canaries and the islands are very well represented on the internet; as a first port of call for any of the islands check the Tourist Board site www.hellocanaryislands.com

Websites relating to specific harbours are listed under Harbour Communications. Below are just some of the many websites covering the islands

www.aemet.es – the Spanish *Instituto Nacional de Meteorología*, in Spanish only but lends itself to auto-translation

www.armada.mde.es –Spain's 'Armada Española', of which their hydrographic office forms a part. Click on Science / Culture, followed by Hydrography – then Notices Io Mariners to download weekly *Avisos a los Navegantes* or Paper Charts from the online chart catalogue. In Spanish, English and French

www.bintercanarias.com – Binter Canarias SA, the Canaries' own inter-island airline based in Gran Canaria

www.navieraarmas.com – Naviera Armas, the Canaries' most wide-ranging ferry company, in Spanish, English, French and Portuguese

www.fredolsen.es – Líneas Fred Olsen SA, which runs ferries through the islands though not linking east to west

www.trasmediterranea.es – Details of Trasmediterránea ferry services from peninsula Spain to the larger islands. In Spanish, Catalan, English, and French

www.dis.ulpgc.es/canarias – University of Las Palmas de Gran Canaria, with pages about all of the islands, each in a different style

www.ecoturismocanarias.com – Acantur, the Canarian Association for Rural Tourism, with information on all seven islands in Spanish, German, English, French and Russian

www.iac.es – Instituto de Astrofísica de Canarias, in Spanish and English. Particularly interesting information on the astrophysical observatories of El Teide on Tenerife and La Caldera de Taburiente on La Palma

**www.iac.es/weather** – clearly an offshoot of the above site, but with no obvious link from it. Weather data gathered from the two observatories, plus satellite images, interpretation etc., but tending toward the theoretical rather than the practical

**www.puertosdecanarias.es** – in Spanish, English, German and French. Information and aerial photos relevant to the 12 State harbours administered by the Department, news of future developments, harbour fees, weather and much else besides

**www.puertosdetenerife.org** – the Port Authority of Santa Cruz de Tenerife, covering the four western islands, most but not all information available in English

**www.palmasport.es** – the Port of Las Palmas, responsible for the larger commercial ports in the three eastern islands as well as the Muelle Deportivo de Las Palmas (Las Palmas Marina)

## Lanzarote

**www.cabildodelanzarote.com** – the island council website, carrying local news and current affairs. In Spanish only but translates well

**www.turismolanzarote.com** – Lanzarote Tourist Board. Interesting and very well constructed in Spanish, English, German and French

**www.centrosturisticos.com** – Lanzarote's *Centros de Arte, Cultura y Turismo* which runs seven very different attractions, from the Montaña del Fuego to the Jardín de Cactus

**www.cesarmanrique.com** – all about the artist and sculptor whose benign influence can be seen throughout the islands

**www.discoverlanzarote.com** – an English language guide. Easy to navigate, with useful information

## Fuerteventura

**www.fuerteventuraturismo.com** –Fuerteventura Tourist Board, in Spanish, English, German and Italian, with a wide range of practical information, photos and links

**www.cabildofuer.es** – the island council website, with local news and current affairs. In Spanish with translation in English

**www.fuerteventura.com** – a good tourist site in Spanish, English, German and Italian, easy to navigate. Includes link to the island weather forecasts

**www.fuerteventurainfo.com** – another general tourist site, but more comprehensive than most on the island's history and natural environment

## Gran Canaria

**www.grancanaria.com** – Gran Canaria Tourist Board, in many languages. A range of downloadable brochures as well as videos, podcasts and eBooks

**www.grancanariainfo.co.uk** – a general tourist site, but more comprehensive than most on the island's history and natural environment. It includes a directory of English websites related to the island

## Tenerife

**www.todotenerife.es** – a good overview of the island from the Tenerife Island Council (Cabildo). Up to date information on special events, local eateries known as *guachinches* (where they serve home made food and wines), festivals and local sports

**www.webtenerifeuk.co.uk** – a full range of information presented by the Tenerife Tourism Corporation

**www.cabtfe.es** – the Tenerife island council, in Spanish, English and German

**www.ost.es/en** –the Tenerife Symphony Orchestra, whose auditorium overlooks the entrance to the Dársena de los Llanos. In Spanish and English

## La Gomera

**www.gomeralive.com** - practical information on activities, transport, eating out; good photographs

**www.gomeraverde.com** – local news in Spanish; can be translated into many languages

**www.m-e-e-r.de** –La Gomera's whale and dolphin research centre, in Spanish, English and German

## La Palma

**www.visitlapalma.es** – La Palma tourist office

**www.ing.iac.es/PR/lapalma** – the Isaac Newton Group's well-researched guide to the island as a whole. For information on the observatory go to **www.ing.iac.es**

**www.islalapalma.com** – an online travel guide created by two emigrants to La Palma who plainly love their adopted home. Information in English, Dutch and German, check out the What NOT to expect link

**www.lapalmabiosfera.es** – the island is a World Biosphere Reserve and is justly proud of it. This comprehensive site, in Spanish, English and German, explains why

## El Hierro

**www.elhierro.es** –the island council website. Not all sections are translatable online

**www.elhierro.travel** – the island council and Office of Tourism, in Spanish, English, German. Sections on geology, flora and fauna and other general interest subjects, as well as general tourist information

**www.elhierro.tv** – El Hierro's own television station, with news and events in Spanish, English and German

# Cape Verdes

The Cape Verdes have an established presence on the internet and the following sites contain general information, some of which may be useful to the visiting yachtsman. If carrying out a search, note that some addresses use the local form of the name, 'Cabo Verde', rather than the English, 'Cape Verde'.

**http://allafrica.com** – in English, carrying current news stories on all African countries including the Cape Verdes

**www.archipelagocapeverde.com** – website of Cape Verde Holidays, including the usual (slightly superficial) information about the islands' history and culture, plus brief details about each of the nine inhabited islands

**www.asemana.publ.cv** – fascinating newspaper-style site carrying a very wide variety of articles, in English as well as Portuguese

**www.bcv.cv** – the unexpectedly interesting website of the Banco de Cabo Verde, in Portuguese and English

**www.bela-vista.net/cape-verde.htm** – tourist information including current ferry schedules and details of the ships which operate them, plus impressive photo gallery and online bookshop. In English and German

**www.boatcv.com** – Mindelo-based boatCV which, according to its home page 'supports and assists yachtsmen visiting Cape Verde'. The 'Navstuff' section, featuring local weather and tidal information, would be useful anywhere in the islands. In English and German

**www.bravanews.com** – the Brava News Network, in Portuguese only which auto-translates poorly, and probably intended as much for the many islanders living abroad as for those at home. Includes news and forthcoming events and impressively up-to-date

**www.caboverde.com** – THE website for the islands, from which almost everything can be accessed. An excellent place to start any kind of research on the islands … or download the recipes for *Cachupa Rica* or *Canja de Galinha* and get a culinary foretaste while listening to local musicians… Highly recommended

**www.caboverdeexpress.com** – Cabo Verde Express, a charter aviation company offering transfers, day excursions, etc. both between islands and to/from the African mainland. See page 363

**www.capeverde.eu** – website of Attila Bertalan, whose 1998 thesis at the Fachhochschule Karlsruhe consisted of producing tourist maps of the islands. Regularly updated, they're still among the best around. Order (together with other maps and books) via the website. In German and English

**www.capeverdetravel.com** – site of UK-based Cape Verde Travel, which has been taking holidaymakers to the archipelago for nearly 30 years

**www.cia.gov/library/publications** – click on The World Factbook and select Cabo Verde for a wealth of current information and statistics covering all aspects of the Republic

**http://cvfastferry.com** – website of Cabo Verde Fast Ferry, which runs the 160-seater catamarans *Kriola* and *Liberdade* between Praia, Fogo and Brava. See page 364

**www.ecaboverde.com** – thousands of photos of the islands captioned in English, Portuguese, French, German or Italian

**www.flytacv.com** – website of TACV – *Transportes Aéroes de Cabo Verde* – the islands' oldest airline. See page 363

**http://fogonews.com** - all the latest news about the island of Fogo. In Portuguese but with good auto-translation

**www.guiadecaboverde.cv** – website of the Cape Verde's *Direcção Geral do Turismo*, in Portuguese, English, Italian and French. Well designed and easy to navigate, if a bit predictable

**www.kauberdi.net/english** – the website of the 'Unofficial Cape Verde Aficionados', apparently a local organisation based in Praia, with some interesting information (including lists of Protected Areas) but few photos

**http://library.stanford.edu/areas/african-collections** – not very user friendly, but searching (under both Cape Verde and Cabo Verde) calls up some interesting pages

**www.maiocv.com** – run by property development company Maio Cape Verde. With far more depth than is typical of the genre, but not always fully updated. In English only

**www.marinamindelo.cv/** – website of the archipelago's only marina, available in English, French, German and Portuguese. See page 394 for further details

**www.mindelo.info** – a French-language site offering news about recent and forthcoming events in Mindelo and, to a lesser extent, the rest of the archipelago. Hundreds of excellent photos

**www.parlamento.cv** – website of the *Assembleia Nacional de Cabo Verde*, the republic's parliament, in Portuguese

**http://virtualcapeverde.net/news2/index.php** – run by the Embassy of Cape Verde in Washington DC, with links to articles on all subjects relating to the islands

**www.volcanodiscovery.com/fogo/news.html** – full (and technical) coverage of the Fogo's 2014-15 eruption, with some striking photos. In English, German and French

**www.wtgonline.com/data/cpv/cpv.asp** – the Cape Verde pages of Columbus Travel Media Ltd, with a wealth of practical detail though some of it a bit superficial

**www.yachtmollymawk.com/cruising-notes** – an interesting take on the islands from long-term cruiser Jill Dickin Schinas, who has visited the archipelago several times over a span of nearly 30 years, with detailed notes on Ilha do Sal and Boavista. Slightly dated – her last visit was in 2011 – but worth studying nevertheless

# III. Further reading

## Passages and general information

*Africa Pilot (NP 1)* (UK Hydrographic Office) Madeira, Canaries and Cape Verdes only

*Atlantic Crossing Guide, The* Jane Russell (RCC Pilotage Foundation/Adlard Coles Nautical)

*Atlantic Pilot Atlas, The* James Clarke (Adlard Coles Nautical)

*Birds of the Atlantic Islands: Canary Islands, Madeira, Azores, Cape Verde* Tony Clarke (Helm Field Guides)

*Cornell's Ocean Atlas* Jimmy and Ivan Cornell (Cornell Sailing Ltd)

*First Aid at Sea* Dr Douglas Justins & Dr Colin Berry (Adlard Coles Nautical)

*Fishing Afloat* Dick McClary (Royal Yachting Association)

*Flight Identification of European Seabirds* Anders Blomdahl, Bertil Breife & Niklas Holmstrom (Helm Identification Guides)

*Ocean Birds* Lars Löfgren (Cristopher Helm)

*Ocean Passages and Landfalls* Rod Heikell & Andy O'Grady (Imray Laurie Norie & Wilson)

*Ocean Passages for the World (NP 136)* (UK Hydrographic Office)

*On-Board Medical Emergency Handbook: First Aid at Sea* Dr Spike Briggs & Dr Campbell Mackenzie (International Marine)

*Reeds Maritime Meteorology* Maurice Cornish & Elaine Ives (Adlard Coles Nautical)

*Reeds Weather Handbook* Frank Singleton (Adlard Coles Nautical)

*Rough Guide Audio Phrasebook and Dictionary: Portuguese* (Rough Guides) Kindle edition with audio/video

*Rough Guide Portuguese Phrasebook* (Rough Guides)

*Rough Guide Spanish Phrasebook* (Rough Guides)

*Rough Guide to Travel Health, The* Dr Nick Jones (Rough Guides)

*Seabirds, an Identification Guide* Peter Harrison (Houghton Mifflin)

*Spanish for Cruisers* Kathy Parsons (Aventuras Publishing)

*Travel Health: Don't let Bugs Bites and Bowels spoil your trip* Dr Jane Wilson-Howarth (Cadogan Guides)

*Travellers' Health: How to stay Healthy Abroad* Dr Richard Dawood (Oxford University Press)

*Whales & Dolphins of the European Atlantic* Dylan Walker & Graeme Cresswell (WildGuides UK)

*Whales, Dolphins and Porpoises* Mark Carwardine (Dorling Kindersley Handbooks)

*Whales, Dolphins and Porpoises* Annalisa Berta (Ivy Press)

*Yachtsman's Ten Language Dictionary* Barbara Webb & The Cruising Association (Adlard Coles Nautical)

## Bermuda

There are a number of tourist guides to Bermuda. Below are some other books that might be of interest to visitors.

*A Guide to the Reef, Shore and Game Fish of Bermuda* Mowbray, LS. 1982. Island Press Ltd.

*A Naturalist's Field Guide to Bermuda* An Exploration of the island's common and important wildlife and geology. 2010. Canadian ecologist Dr. Martin Thomas, professor emeritus at the University of New Brunswick. Published by the Bermuda Zoological Society

*Hiking Bermuda 2003: 20 Nature Walks and Day Hikes* Cecile and Stephen Davidson. 160 pages

*The Bermuda Boater: A Comprehensive Guide to Piloting and Seamanship for Boaters around the Waters of Bermuda* by Bermudian businessman, sailor and author Ralph Richardson. Originally published in 1992, revised in 2015

*Moon Bermuda* (2012) Rosemary Jones. Published by Moon Handbooks

*Reefs, Wrecks and Relics – Bermuda Underwater Heritage* (2007) William B Gilles

*Bermewdian Vurds* (1984) conversational Bermudian (Humour) Peter Smith/ Fred Barritt

## Azores

It took a surprisingly long time for the Azores to become the subject of a tourist guide, but David Sayers' *Azores* (Bradt Travel Guides), now in its 5th edition, fills the gap admirably and is a worthy addition to any cruising yacht's bookshelf. More recently this has been joined by the *Azores Globetrotter Travel Pack* by Terry Marsh, which includes a fold-out map. Walkers will also find *Azores: Car Tours and Walks* by Andreas Stieglitz in the Sunflower Landscapes series, currently in its 7th edition, invaluable.

Once in the islands, a variety of publications are available from local tourist offices. The *Azores Guide for Tourists*, published annually since 1981 by Publiçor Lda, and the equally useful *destinazores* booklet both cover all the islands, containing a mixture of information, advertisements and photographs, plus maps of all the islands and plans of the bigger towns. Both are available free from tourist offices and, sometimes, supermarket checkouts. The *Guide to the Island of ...* series (one for each island, ranging from a dozen pages for Corvo to more than one hundred for São Miguel) produced by the *Direcção Regional de Turismo dos Açores* can be bought individually at the tourist office in Ponta Delgada, though well worth the modest €15 or so charged for the entire set. Local tourist boards have also compiled free walkers' guides to various routes on the islands in the *Açores Percurso Pedestre* series, each comprising a brief description and rating of the 'trail, and a section of large-scale map. Most of the above are available in several languages – be sure to pick up the correct one. Others are multilingual within a single publication.

*Açores em Vista Aérea / Azores in Aerial View* Filipe Jorge, Isobel Soares de Albergaria & Rui Monteiro (Argumentum, Lisbon, Portugal)

*Açores Flores (Azores Flowers)* Erik Sjögren (Direcção Regional de Turismo, Horta, Faial)

*Azores Guide for Tourists* (Publiçor Lda, Ponta Delgada, São Miguel) Published annually

*Azores* David Sayers (Bradt Travel Guides)

*Azores Travel Pack* Terry Marsh (Globetrotter Travel Guides)

*Azores: Car Tours and Walks* Andreas Stieglitz (Sunflower Books)

*Distinazores Tourist Guide* (Destinazores, Ponta Delgada, São Miguel) Available in several languages

*Dolphins and Whales from the Azores* Serge Viallelle (Espaço Talassa, Lajes do Pico)

*Parques e Jardins dos Açores / Azores Parks and Gardens* Isobel Soares de Albergaria (Argumentum, Lisbon, Portugal)

*Peter – Café Sport* Jorge Alverto da Costa Pereira (Quetzal Editores, Lisbon)

*West Coasts of Spain and Portugal Pilot (NP 67)*
(UK Hydrographic Office)
*Winter in the Azores and a Summer at the Baths of the
Furnas, A* Joseph & Henry Bullar (The British Library)

## Madeira Group

Madeira and Porto Santo are the subject of several general tourist guides readily available in the UK and elsewhere. Once in the islands, colourful leaflets and maps can be obtained from the tourist offices in the larger towns.

*Cruise of the Alerte, The* E F Knight (Createspace)
*Faróis da Madeira / Lighthouses of Madeira* Filipe Jorge & J
Teixeira de Aguilar (Argumentum, Lisbon, Portugal)
*Gardens of Madeira, The* Gerald Luckhurst (Frances Lincoln)
*Madeira & Porto Santo: Rough Guide Directions* Matthew
Hancock (Rough Guides)
*Madeira Marco Polo Travel Handbook* (Mairdumont GmbH
& Co)
*Madeira Plants and Flowers* Antonio da Costa & Luis de O
Franquinha (Francisco Ribeira, Funchal, Madeira)
*Madeira: AA Essential Guides* (Automobile Association)
*Madeira: Baedeker* (Mairdumont GMbH & Co)
*Madeira: Berlitz Pocket Guides* (Berlitz Publishing)
*Madeira: Car Tours and Walks* John & Pat Underwood
(Sunflower Books)
*Madeira: DK Eyewitness Top 10 Travel Guides* Christopher
Catling (Dorling Kindersley)
*Madeira: Insight Guides* (Insight)
*Madeira: The Finest Valley and Mountain Walks* Rolf Goetz
(Bergverlag Rudolf Rother)
*Madeira: Thomas Cook Traveller Guides* Christopher Catling
(Thomas Cook Publishing)
*Madeira: Walk and Eat* John & Pat Underwood (Sunflower
Books)
*Pocket Madeira* Marc Di Duca (Lonely Planet)
*Walking in Madeira: 60 Routes on Madeira and Porto Santo*
Paddy Dillon (Cicerone Press)

## Canary Islands

There are many tourist guides dealing with the Canaries. Colourful leaflets about each island, as well as the group as a whole, are also available either from tourist offices or directly from the Spanish Tourist Office. At least one of the car hire companies (Cicar) issues excellent maps and a CD with local information.

*Bananas About La Palma* David M Addison (AuthorHouse)
*Canary Islands: Lonely Planet* Sarah Andrews & Josephine
Quintero (Lonely Planet Publications)
*Classic Geology in Europe: The Canary Islands* Juan Carlos
Carracedo & Simon Day (Terra Publishing)
*Flowers in the Canary Islands* Perez Juan Alberto Rodriguez
(Editorial Everest)
*Flowers of the Canary Islands* Bruno Foggi & Andrea
Innocenti (EG Bonechi, Italy)
*Guanches Survivors, and their Descendants, The* José Luis
Concepción (José Luis Concepción)
*History of the Discovery and Conquest of the Canary Islands,
The* Juan de Abreu Galindo (Elibron Classics) Facsimile of
a 1764 publication
*La Gomera: A Guide to the Unspoiled Canary Island* Tim
Hart (Colley Books)
*La Gomera: Island of Columbus* Kristine Edle Olsen (Thames
& Hudson)
*Sailing the Western Canary Islands* Roland Nyns (Amazon
Media EU) Kindle Edition

*Tenerife and its Six Satellites, or The Canary Islands Past
and Present* Olivia M Stone. Vol.1: Tenerife, La
Gomera, La Palma, El Hierro; Vol.2: Lanzarote,
Fuerteventura, Gran Canaria. (Adamant Media
Corporation / Elibron Classics) Facsimile of an 1887
publication
Series:
*AA Spiral/Essential Guides: Lanzarote; Fuerteventura;
Gran Canaria; Tenerife* (Automobile Association)
*Berlitz Pocket Guides: Canary Islands; Lanzarote and
Fuerteventura; Gran Canaria; Tenerife* (Berlitz
Publishing)
*Car Tours and Walks: Lanzarote; Fuerteventura; Gran
Canaria; Tenerife; Southern Tenerife and La Gomera;
Palma and El Hierro* Noel Rochford (all) (Sunflower
Books)
*Globetrotter Travel Packs: Canary Islands* Andy Gravette;
*Lanzarote* Rowland Mead; *Tenerife* Rowland Mead
(New Holland Publishers)
*DK Eyewitness Guides: Canary Islands* Piotr Paszkiewicz
& Hanna Faryna-Paszkiewicz; *Gran Canaria* Lucy
Corne (Dorling Kindersley)
*Pocket Guides: Lanzarote; Fuerteventura; Gran Canaria;
Tenerife* (Thomas Cook Publishing)
*Rother Walking Guides: Tenerife; La Gomera; La Palma*
Klaus and Annette Wolfsperger (all) (Rother Walking
Guides)
*Rough Guide Directions: Lanzarote & Fuerteventura*
Emma Gregg; *Gran Canaria* Neville Walker; *Tenerife*
Christian Williams (Rough Guides)
*Walk! Lanzarote* David & Ros Brawn; *Walk! Tenerife*
David Brawn; *Walk! La Gomera* Charles Davis; *Walk!
La Palma* Charles Davis (Discovery Walking Guides)
*Walking on: Tenerife; La Gomera and El Hierro; La
Palma, The World's Steepest Island* Paddy Dillon (all)
(Cicerone Press)

## Cape Verdes

At least six travellers' guides cover the Cape Verde islands in varying levels of detail. Booklets and maps are also available on the larger islands, though generally via book and stationery shops rather than tourist offices.

*Cape Verde Islands Berlitz Pocket Guide* (Berlitz Pocket
Guides)
*Cape Verde Islands* Murray Stewart, Aisling Irwin &
Colum Wilson (Bradt Travel Guides)
*Cape Verde Islands* (Great Britain Foreign Office)
Facsimile of a 1923 publication
*Cape Verde* Callie Flood (Other Places Publishing)
*Cape Verde: Crioulo Colony to Independent Nation*
Westview Profiles: Nations of Contemporary Africa,
Richard Lobban (Perseus)
*Kapverdische Inseln : Der Nautische Revierführer* Kai
Brossmann, Nikolaus Hüwe & André Mégroz (MSK
Mediaplanung Schott Klas GbR)
*Street's Guide to the Cape Verde Islands* Donald M Street
(Seaworth Publications)
*The History of the Cape Verde Islands* Abe Hall
(Webster's Digital Services)
*Travellers Cape Verde* Sue Dobson (Thomas Cook
Publishing)
*The History of the Cape Verde Islands* Abe Hall
(Webster's Digital Services)
*Travellers Cape Verde* Sue Dobson (Thomas Cook
Publishing)

APPENDIX

# IV. Glossary

A more complete list of translations can be found in the *Yachtsman's Ten Language Dictionary* compiled by Barbara Webb and the Cruising Association (Adlard Coles Nautical).

## General and chartwork terms

| English | Spanish | Portuguese |
|---|---|---|
| anchor, to | fondear | fundear |
| anchorage | fondeadero, ancladero | fundeadouro, ancoradouro |
| basin, dock | dársena | doca |
| bay | bahía, ensenada | baía, enseada |
| beach | playa | praia |
| beacon | baliza | baliza |
| beam | manga | largura, boca |
| berth | atracar | atracar |
| black | negro | preto |
| blue | azul | azul |
| boatbuilder | astillero | estaleiro |
| bottled gas | cilindro de gas, carga de gas | cilindro de gás, bilha de gás |
| breakwater | rompeolas, muelle | quebra-mar, molhe |
| buoy | boya | bóia |
| bus | autobús | autocarro |
| cape | cabo | cabo |
| car hire | aquilar coche | alugar automóvel |
| chandlery (shop) | efectos navales, apetrachamento | fornecedore de barcos, aprestos |
| channel | canal | canal |
| charts | cartas náuticas | cartas hidrográficas |
| church | iglesia | igreja |
| crane | grua | guindaste |
| creek | estero | esteiro |
| Customs | Aduana | Alfândega |
| deep | profundo | profundo |
| depth | sonda, profundidad | profundidade |
| diesel | gasoil | gasoleo |
| draught | calado | calado |
| dredged | dragado | dragado |
| dyke, pier | dique | dique |
| east | este | este |
| eastern | levante, oriental | levante, do este |
| electricity | electricidad | electricidade |
| engineer, mechanic | ingeniero, mecánico | engenheiro, técnico |
| entrance | boca, entrada | bôca, entrada |
| factory | fábrica | fábrica |
| foul, dirty | sucio | sujo |
| gravel | cascajo | burgau |
| green | verde | verde |
| harbourmaster | capitán de puerto | diretor do porto |
| height, clearance | altura | altura |
| high tide | pleamar, marea alta | preia-mar, maré alta |
| high | alto/a | alto/a |
| ice | hielo | gelo |
| inlet, cove | ensenada | enseada |
| island | isla | ilha, ilhéu |
| islet, skerry | islote | ilhota |
| isthmus | istmo | istmo |
| jetty, pier | malecón | quebra-mar |
| knots | nudos | nós |
| lake | lago | lago |
| laundry, launderette | lavandería, automática | lavanderia, automática |
| leading line, transit | enfilación | enfiamento |
| leeward | sotavento | sotavento |
| length overall | eslora total | comprimento |
| lighthouse | faro | farol |
| lock | esclusa | esclusa |
| low tide | bajamar, marea baja | baixa-mar, maré baixa |
| mailing address | dirección de correo | endereço para correio |
| marina, yacht harbour | puerto deportivo, dársena de yates | porto desportivo, doca de recreio |
| medical services | servicios médiocos | serviços médicas |
| mud | fango | lôdo |
| mussel rafts | viveros | viveiros |
| narrows | estrecho | estreito |
| north | norte | norte |
| orange | anaranjado | alaranjado |
| owner | propietario | propietário |
| paraffin | parafina | petróleo para iluminãçao |
| petrol | gasolina | gasolina |
| pier, quay, dock | muelle | molhe |
| point | punta | ponta |
| pontoon | pantalán | pontáo |
| port (side) | babor | bombordo |
| Port of Registry | Puerto de Matrícula | Porto de Registo |
| port office | capitanía | capitania |
| post office | oficina de correos | agência do correio |
| quay | muelle | molhe, cais |
| ramp | rampa | rampa |
| range (tidal) | repunte | amplitude |
| red | rojo | vermelho |
| reef | arrecife | recife |
| reef, spit | restinga | restinga |
| registration number | matricula | número registo |
| repairs | reparacións | reparações |
| rock, stone | roca, piedra | laxe, pedra |
| root (e.g. of mole) | raíz | raiz |
| sailing boat | barca de vela | barco à vela |
| sailmaker, sail repairs | velero, reparacións velas | veleiro, reparações velas |
| saltpans | salinas | salinas |
| sand | arena | areia |
| sea | mar | mar |
| seal, to | precintar | fechar |
| shoal, low | bajo | baixo |
| shops | tiendas, almacéns | lojas |
| shore, edge | orilla | margem |
| showers (washing) | duchas | duches |
| slab, flat rock | laja | laje |
| slack water, tidal stand | repunte | águas paradas |
| slipway | varadero | rampa |
| small | pequeño | pequeno |
| south | sur | sul |
| southern | meridional | do sul |
| starboard | estribor | estibordo |
| strait | estrecho | estreito |

| English | Spanish | Portuguese |
|---|---|---|
| supermarket | supermercado | supermercado |
| tower | torre | tôrre |
| travel-lift | grua giratoria, pórtico elevador | e pórtico, pórtico elevador, içar |
| water (drinking) | agua potable | água potável |
| weather forecast | previsión/boletin metereológico | previsão de tempo, boletim meteorológico |
| weed | alga | alga |
| weight | peso | pêso |
| west | oeste | oeste |
| western | occidental | do oeste |
| white | blanco | branco |
| windward | barlovento | barlavento |
| works (building) | obras | obras |
| yacht (sailing) | barca de vela | barco à vela |
| yacht club | club náutico | clube náutico, clube naval |
| yellow | amarillo | amarelo |

## Meteorology and sea state

| English | Spanish | Portuguese |
|---|---|---|
| calm (Force 0, 0–1kns) | calma | calma |
| light airs (Force 1, 1–3kns) | ventolina | aragem |
| light breeze (Force 2, 4–6kns) | flojito | vento fraco, brisa |
| gentle breeze (Force 3, 7–10kns) | flojo | vento bonançoso, brisa suave |
| moderate breeze (Force 4, 11–16kns) | bonancible | vento moderado, brisa moderado |
| fresh breeze (Force 5, 17–21kns) | fresquito | vento fresco, brisa fresca |
| strong breeze (Force 6, 22–27kns) | fresco | vento muito fresco, brisa forte |
| near gale (Force 7, 28–33kns) moderada | frescachón | vento forte, ventania |
| gale (Force 8, 34–40kns) | duro | vento muito forte, ventania fresca |
| severe gale (Force 9, 41–47kns) | muy duro | vento tempestuoso, ventania forte |
| storm (Force 10, 48–55kns) | temporal | temporal, ventania total |
| violent storm (Force 11, 56–63kns) | borrasca, tempestad | temporal desfieto, tempestade |
| hurricane (Force 12, 64+kns) | huracán | furacão, ciclone |
| breakers | rompientes | arrebentação |
| cloudy | nubloso | nublado |
| depression (low) | depresión | depressão |
| fog | niebla | nevoeiro |
| gust | racha | rajada |
| hail | granizada | saraiva |
| mist | neblina | neblina |
| overfalls, tide race | escarceos | bailadeiras |
| rain | lluvia | chuva |
| ridge (high) | dorsal | crista |
| rough sea | mar gruesa | mar bravo |
| short, steep sea | mar corta | mar cavado |
| shower | aguacero | aguaceiro |
| slight sea | marejadilla | mar chão |
| squall | turbonada | borrasca |
| swell | mar de leva | ondulação |
| thunderstorm | tempestad | trovoada |

## General and chartwork terms

| Spanish | English | Portuguese |
|---|---|---|
| Aduana | Customs | Alfândega |
| agua potable | water (drinking) | água potável |
| alga | weed | alga |
| almacéns | shops | lojas |
| alto/a | high | alto/a |
| altura | height, clearance | altura |
| amarillo | yellow | amarelo |
| anaranjado | orange | alaranjado |
| ancladero | anchorage | fundeadouro, ancoradouro |
| apetrachamento | chandlery (shop) | fornecedor de barcos, aprestos |
| aquilar coche | car hire | alugar automóvel |
| arena | sand | areia |
| arrecife | reef | recife |
| astillero | boatbuilder | estaleiro |
| atracar | berth | atracar |
| autobús | bus | autocarro |
| azul | blue | azul |
| babor | port (side) | bombordo |
| bahía | bay | baía, enseada |
| bajamar | low tide | baixa-mar, maré baixa |
| bajo | shoal, low | baixo |
| baliza | beacon | baliza |
| barca de vela | sailing boat, yacht | barco à vela |
| barlovento | windward | barlavento |
| blanco | white | branco |
| boca | entrance | bôca, entrada |
| boya | buoy | bóia |
| cabo | cape | cabo |
| calado | draught | calado |
| canal | channel | canal |
| capitán de puerto | harbourmaster | diretor do porto |
| capitanía | port office | capitania |
| carga de gas | bottled gas | cilindro de gás, bilha de gás |
| cartas náuticas | charts | cartas hidrográficas |
| cascajo | gravel | burgau |
| cilindro de gas | bottled gas | cilindro de gás, bilha de gás |
| club náutico | yacht club | clube náutico, clube naval |
| dársena de yates | marina, yacht harbour | porto desportivo, doca de recreio |
| dársena | basin, dock | doca |
| dique | dyke, pier | dique |
| dirección de correo | mailing address | endereço para correio |
| dragado | dredged | dragado |
| duchas | showers (washing) | duches |
| efectos navales | chandlery (shop) | fornecedor de barcos, aprestos |
| electricidad | electricity | electricidade |
| enfilación | leading line, transit | enfiamento |
| ensenada | bay, inlet, cove | baía, enseada |
| entrada | entrance | bôca, entrada |
| esclusa | lock | esclusa |
| eslora total | length overall | comprimento |
| este | east | este |
| estero | creek | esteiro |
| estrecho | narrows, strait | estreito |
| estribor | starboard | estibordo |
| fábrica | factory | fábrica |
| fango | mud | lôdo |
| faro | lighthouse | farol |

| Spanish | English | Portuguese |
|---|---|---|
| fondeadero | anchorage | fundeadouro, ancoradouro |
| fondear | anchor, to | fundear |
| gasoil | diesel | gasoleo |
| gasolina | petrol | gasolina |
| grua giratoria | travel-lift | e pórtico, pórtico elevador, içar |
| grua | crane | guindaste |
| hielo | ice | gelo |
| iglesia | church | igreja |
| ingeniero, mecánico | engineer, mechanic | engenheiro, técnico |
| isla | island | ilha, ilhéu |
| islote | islet, skerry | ilhota |
| istmo | isthmus | istmo |
| lago | lake | lago |
| laja | slab, flat rock | laje |
| lavandería, l. automática | laundry, launderette | lavanderia, l. automática |
| levante | eastern | levante, do este |
| malecón | jetty, pier | quebra-mar |
| manga | beam | largura, boca |
| mar | sea | mar |
| marea alta | high tide | preia-mar, maré alta |
| marea baja | low tide | baixa-mar, maré baixa |
| matricula | registration number | número registo |
| meridional | southern | do sul |
| muelle | breakwater, pier, quay, dock | quebra-mar, molhe, cais |
| negro | black | preto |
| norte | north | norte |
| nudos | knots | nós |
| obras | works (building) | obras |
| occidental | western | do oeste |
| oeste | west | oeste |
| oficina de correos | post office | agência do correio |
| oriental | eastern | levante, do este |
| orilla | shore, edge | margem |
| pantalán | pontoon | pontáo |
| parafina | paraffin | petróleo para iluminãçao |
| pequeño | small | pequeno |
| peso | weight | pêso |
| piedra | rock, stone | pedra |
| playa | beach | praia |
| pleamar | high tide | preia-mar, maré alta |
| pórtico elevador | travel-lift | e pórtico, pórtico elevador, içar |
| precintar | seal, to | fechar |
| previsión/boletin metereológico | weather forecast | previsão de tempo, boletim meteorológico |
| profundidad | depth | profundidade |
| profundo | deep | profundo |
| propietario | owner | propietário |
| Puerto de Matrícula | Port of Registry | Porto de Registo |
| puerto deportivo | marina, yacht harbour | porto desportivo, doca de recreio |
| punta | point | ponta |
| raíz | root (e.g. of mole) | raiz |
| rampa | ramp | rampa |
| reparacións | repairs | reparações |

| Spanish | English | Portuguese |
|---|---|---|
| repunte | tidal range, stand, slack water | águas paradas, amplitude |
| restinga | reef, spit | restinga |
| roca | rock | laxe |
| rojo | red | vermelho |
| rompeolas | breakwater | quebra-mar, molhe |
| salinas | saltpans | salinas |
| servicios médicos | medical services | serviços médicas |
| sonda | depth | profundidade |
| sotavento | leeward | sotavento |
| sucio | foul, dirty | sujo |
| supermercado | supermarket | supermercado |
| sur | south | sul |
| tiendas | shops | lojas |
| torre | tower | tôrre |
| varadero | slipway | rampa |
| velero, reparacións velas | sailmaker, sail repairs | veleiro, reparações velas |
| verde | green | verde |
| viveros | mussel rafts | viveiros |

## Meteorology and sea state

| Spanish | English | Portuguese |
|---|---|---|
| calma | calm (Force 0, 0–1kns) | calma |
| ventolina | light airs (Force 1, 1–3kns) | aragem |
| flojito | light breeze (Force 2, 4–6kns) | vento fraco, brisa |
| flojo | gentle breeze (Force 3, 7–10kns) | vento bonançoso, brisa suave |
| bonancible | moderate breeze (Force 4, 11–16kns) | vento moderado, brisa moderado |
| fresquito | fresh breeze (Force 5, 17–21kns) | vento frêsco, brisa fresca |
| frêsco | strong breeze (Force 6, 22–27kns) | vento muito fresco, brisa forte |
| frescachón | near gale (Force 7, 28–33kns) | vento forte, ventania moderada |
| duro | gale (Force 8, 34–40kns) | vento muito forte, ventania fresca |
| muy duro | severe gale (Force 9, 41–47kns) | vento tempestuoso, ventania forte |
| temporal | storm (Force 10, 48–55kns) | temporal, ventania total |
| borrasca, tempestad | violent storm (Force 11, 56–63kns) | temporal desfieto, tempestade |
| huracán | hurricane (Force 12, 64+kns) | furacão, ciclone |
| aguacero | shower | aguaceiro |
| depresión | depression (low) | depressão |
| dorsal | ridge (high) | crista |
| escarceos | overfalls, tiderace | bailadeiras |
| granizada | hail | saraiva |
| lluvia | rain | chuva |
| mar corta | short, steep sea | mar cavado |
| mar de leva | swell | ondulação |
| mar gruesa | rough sea | mar bravo |
| marejadilla | slight sea | mar chão |
| neblina | mist | neblina |
| niebla | fog | nevoeiro |
| nubloso | cloudy | nublado |
| racha | gust | rajada |
| rompientes | breakers | arrebentação |
| tempestad | thunderstorm | trovoada |
| turbonada | squall | borrasca |

## General and chartwork terms

| Portuguese | English | Spanish |
|---|---|---|
| agência do correio | post office | oficina de correos |
| água potável | water (drinking) | agua potable |
| amplitude, | tidal range, | repunte |
| águas paradas | stand, slack water | repute |
| alaranjado | orange | anaranjado |
| alfândega | customs | aduana |
| alga | weed | alga |
| alto/a | high | alto/a |
| altura | height, clearance | altura |
| alugar automóvel | car hire | aquilar coche |
| amarelo | yellow | amarillo |
| areia | sand | arena |
| atracar | berth | atracar |
| autocarro | bus | autobús |
| azul | blue | azul |
| baía, enseada | bay, inlet, cove | bahía, ensenada |
| baixa-mar, maré baixa | low tide | bajamar, marea baja |
| baixo | shoal, low | bajo |
| baliza | beacon | baliza |
| barco à vela | sailing boat, yacht | barca de vela |
| barlavento | windward | barlovento |
| bôca, entrada | entrance | boca, entrada |
| bóia | buoy | boya |
| bombordo | port (side) | babor |
| branco | white | blanco |
| burgau | gravel | cascajo |
| cabo | cape | cabo |
| calado | draught | calado |
| canal | channel | canal |
| capitania | port office | capitanía |
| cartas hidrográficas | charts | cartas náuticas |
| cilindro de gás, bilha de gás | bottled gas | carga de gas, cilindro de gas |
| clube náutico, | yacht club clube naval | club náutico |
| comprimento | length overall | eslora total |
| dique | dyke, pier | dique |
| diretor do porto | harbourmaster | capitán de puerto |
| do oeste | western | occidental |
| do sul | southern | meridional |
| doca | basin, dock | dársena |
| dragado | dredged | dragado |
| duches | showers (washing) | duchas |
| e pórtico, pórtico elevador, içar | travel-lift | grua giratoria, pórtico elevador |
| electricidade | electricity | electricidad |
| endereço para correio | mailing address | dirección de correio |
| enfiamento | leading line, transit | enfilación |
| engenheiro, técnico | engineer, mechanic | ingeniero, mecánico |
| esclusa | lock | esclusa |
| estaleiro | boatbuilder | astillero |
| este | east | este |
| esteiro | creek | estero |
| estibordo | starboard | estribor |
| estreito | narrows, strait | estrecho |
| fábrica | factory | fábrica |
| farol | lighthouse | faro |
| fechar | seal, to | precintar |
| fornecedor de barcos, aprestos | chandlery (shop) | apetrachamento, efectos navales |
| fundeadouro, ancoradouro | anchorage | fondeadero, ancladero |
| fundear | anchor, to | fondear |
| gasoleo | diesel | gasoil |
| gasolina | petrol | gasolina |
| gelo | ice | hielo |
| guindaste | crane | grua |
| igreja | church | iglesia |
| ilha, ilhéu | island | isla |
| ilhota | islet, skerry | islote |
| istmo | isthmus | istmo |
| lago | lake | lago |
| laje | slab, flat rock | laja |
| largura, boca | beam | manga |
| lavanderia, l. automática | laundry, launderette | lavandería, l. automática |
| laxe | rock | roca |
| levante, do este | eastern | levante, oriental |
| lôdo | mud | fango |
| lojas | shops | almacéns, tiendas |
| mar | sea | mar |
| margem | shore, edge | orilla |
| norte | north | norte |
| nós | knots | nudos |
| número registo | registration number | matricula |
| obras | works (building) | obras |
| oeste | west | oeste |
| pedra | rock, stone | piedra |
| pequeno | small | pequeño |
| pêso | weight | peso |
| petróleo para iluminãçao | paraffin | parafina |
| ponta | point | punta |
| pontão | pontoon | pantalán |
| Porto de Registo | Port of Registry | Puerto de Matrícula |
| porto desportivo, doca de recreio | marina, yacht harbour | puerto deportivo, dársena de yates |
| praia | beach | playa |
| preia-mar, maré alta | high tide | pleamar, marea alta |
| preto | black | negro |
| previsão de tempo, boletim meteorológico | weather forecast | previsión/boletin metereológico |
| profundidade | depth | profundidad, sonda |
| profundo | deep | profundo |
| propietário | owner | propietario |
| quebra-mar | jetty, pier | malecón |
| quebra-mar, molhe, cais | breakwater, pier, quay, dock | muelle, rompeolas |
| raiz | root (e.g. of mole) | raíz |
| rampa | ramp, slipway | rampa, varadero |
| recife | reef | arrecife |
| reparações | repairs | reparacións |
| restinga | reef, spit | restinga |
| salinas | saltpans | salinas |
| serviços médicas | medical services | servicios médicos |
| sotavento | leeward | sotavento |
| sujo | foul, dirty | sucio |
| sul | south | sur |
| supermercado | supermarket | supermercado |
| tôrre | tower | torre |

APPENDIX

| Portuguese | English | Spanish |
|---|---|---|
| veleiro, reparações velas | sailmaker, sail repairs | velero, reparacións velas |
| verde | green | verde |
| vermelho | red | rojo |
| viveiros | mussel rafts | viveros |

### Meteorology and sea state

| Portuguese | English | Spanish |
|---|---|---|
| calma | calm (Force 0, 0–1kns) | calma |
| aragem | light airs (Force 1, 1–3kns) | ventolina |
| vento fraco, brisa | light breeze (Force 2, 4–6kns) | flojito |
| vento bonançoso, brisa suave | gentle breeze (Force 3, 7–10kns) | flojo |
| vento moderado, brisa moderado | moderate breeze (Force 4, 11–16kns) | bonancible |
| vento fresco, brisa fresca | fresh breeze (Force 5, 17–21kns) | fresquito |
| vento muito fresco, brisa forte | strong breeze (Force 6, 22–27kns) | fresco |
| vento forte, ventania moderada | near gale (Force 7, 28–33kns) | frescachón |
| vento muito forte, ventania fresca | gale (Force 8, 34–40kns) | duro |
| vento tempestuoso, ventania forte | severe gale (Force 9, 41–47kns) | muy duro |
| temporal, ventania total | storm (Force 10, 48–55kns) | temporal |
| temporal desfieto, tempestade | violent storm (Force 11, 56–63kns) | borrasca, tempestad |
| furacão, ciclone | hurricane (Force 12, 64+kns) | huracán |
| aguaceiro | shower | aguacero |
| arrebentação | breakers | rompientes |
| bailadeiras | overfalls, tide race | escarceos |
| borrasca | squall | turbonada |
| chuva | rain | lluvia |
| crista | ridge (high) | dorsal |
| depressão | depression (low) | depresión |
| mar bravo | rough sea | mar gruesa |
| mar cavado | short, steep sea | mar corta |
| mar chão | slight sea | marejadilla |
| neblina | mist | neblina |
| nevoeiro | fog | niebla |
| nublado | cloudy | nubloso |
| ondulação | swell | mar de leva |
| rajada | gust | racha |
| saraiva | hail | granizada |
| trovoada | thunderstorm | tempestad |

## V. Abbreviations used on charts

| Spanish | Portuguese | Meaning |
|---|---|---|
| **Lights** | | |
| F. | F. | Fixed |
| D. | Rl. | Flashing |
| Gp.D. | Rl.Agr. | Group flashing |
| F.D. | F.Rl. | Fixed and flashing |
| F.Gp.D. | F.Rl.Agr. | Fixed and group flashing |
| Ct. | Ct. | Quick flashing |
| Gp.Ct. | Ct int. | Interrupted quick flashing |
| Oc. | Oc. | Occulting |
| Gp.Oc. | Oc.Agr. | Group occulting |
| Iso. | Is. | Isophase |
| Mo. | Morse | Morse |
| **Colours** | | |
| am. | am. | Yellow |
| az. | azul. | Blue |
| b. | br. | White |
| n. | pr. | Black |
| r. | vm. | Red |
| v. | vd. | Green |
| **Seabed** | | |
| A. | A. | Sand |
| Al. | Alg. | Weed |
| R. | R. | Rock |
| F. | L. | Mud |
| Co. | B. | Gravel |

## VI. Conversion tables

1 inch = 2·54 centimetres (roughly 4in = 10cm)

1 centimetre = 0·394 inches

1 foot = 0·305 metres (roughly 3ft = 1m)

1 metre = 3·281 feet

1 pound = 0·454 kilograms (roughly 10lbs = 4·5kg)

1 kilogram = 2·205 pounds

1 mile = 1·609 kilometres (roughly 10 miles = 16km)

1 kilometre = 0·621 miles

1 nautical mile = 1·1515 miles

1 mile = 0·8684 nautical miles

1 acre = 0·405 hectares (roughly 10 acres = 4 hectares)

1 hectare = 2·471 acres

1 gallon = 4·546 litres (roughly 1 gallon = 4·5 litres)

1 litre = 0·220 gallons

### Temperature scale

$$t°F \text{ to } t°C = \frac{t°F - 32 \times 5}{9}$$

$$t°C \text{ to } t°F = \frac{t°C \times 9}{5} + 32$$

So:

| | |
|---|---|
| 70°F = 21·1°C | 20°C = 68°F |
| 80°F = 26·7°C | 30°C = 86°F |
| 90°F = 32·2°C | 40°C = 104°F |

# Index